ENGLISH G

LIGHTHOUSE

Lehrerfassung Plus

1

Vokabel Trainer

Cornelsen

Vokabeltrainer-App

Verfügbar für: iOS, Android und Windows Phone

Cornelsen

English G · Lighthouse · Band 1

Lehrerfassung Plus

Erarbeitung und Redaktion
Klaus Unger (Projektleitung),
Annegret Hauser-Teubner (koordinierende Redakteurin),
Cornelia Frisse *sowie* Bernd Freiling und Anette Mertens

Schülerbuch (978-3-06-032373-9)
Konzepterarbeitung von
Susan Abbey, Nenagh, Ireland
Wolfgang Biederstädt, Köln
Frank Donoghue, Nenagh, Ireland

Erarbeitet von
Susan Abbey, Nenagh, Ireland
Frank Donoghue, Nenagh, Ireland

unter Mitarbeit von
Joachim Blombach, Herford
Joachim Sauer, Rerik
Jennifer Seidl, München
Udo Wagner, Voerde

Beratende Mitwirkung
Inga Bensmann, Bremen; Annette Bondzio-Abbit, Bielefeld; Hartmut Bondzio, Bielefeld; Prof. Dr. Heiner Böttger, Nürnberg; Verena Flocke, Düren; Uta Franke, Leipzig; Dagmar Höffner, Ingelheim am Rhein; Jürgen Lohmann, Dinslaken; Prof. Dr. Markus Ritter, Münster; Andrea Rohoff, Hannover; Dr. Daniela Schirmer, Kiel; Berit Schaarschmidt, Aschaffenburg; Nathalie Schlosser, Berlin; Prof. Dr. Norbert Schlüter, Leipzig; Martina Schroeder, Stedtlingen; Konstanze Stöckermann-Borst, Leimen; Herbert Willms, Herford sowie Ulrike Rath, Aachen

Die Handreichungen (978-3-06-032376-0) zum Schülerbuch wurden erarbeitet von
Annette Bondzio-Abbit, Bielefeld; Hartmut Bondzio, Bielefeld; Peer Brändel, Gütersloh; Uwe Chormann, Einselthum; Irene Rother, Karlsruhe; Martina Schroeder, Stedtlingen; Udo Wagner, Voerde

Illustrationen
Steffen Wolff, Brohl-Lützing sowie
Christian Görke, Berlin; Jeongsook Lee, Heidelberg; David Norman, Meerbusch; Elwood H. Smith, Rhinebeck, USA

Auftragsfotos
Trevor Burrows Photography, Plymouth

Layoutkonzept und technische Umsetzung
Klein & Halm Grafikdesign, Berlin *(Schülerbuch)*
zweiband.media, Berlin *(Lehrerfassung Plus)*

Umschlaggestaltung
Cornelsen Verlag Design unter Verwendung der Entwürfe von Klein & Halm Grafikdesign, Berlin und kleiner & bold, Berlin

Für die freundliche Unterstützung danken wir dem Eggbuckland Community College, Plymouth.

www.cornelsen.de

1. Auflage, 1. Druck 2018

Alle Drucke dieser Auflage sind inhaltlich unverändert und können im Unterricht nebeneinander verwendet werden.

Druck: H. Heenemann, Berlin

ISBN 978-3-06-036360-5

PEFC
PEFC/12-31-006
PEFC zertifiziert
Dieses Produkt stammt aus nachhaltig bewirtschafteten Wäldern und kontrollierten Quellen.
www.pefc.de

Dein Englischbuch enthält folgende Teile:

Unit 1 bis 5	Die fünf Kapitel des Buches
Unit 6	Ein zusätzliches Kapitel
Diff-Bank	Weitere Aufgaben – unterschiedlich schwer
Wordbank	Zusätzliche Wörter zu bestimmten Themen
Text file TF	Interessante Texte, passend zu den Units
Skills file SF	Beschreibung wichtiger Lern- und Arbeitstechniken
Language file LF	Zusammenfassung wichtiger Sprachregeln
Vocabulary	Wörterverzeichnis zum Lernen der neuen Wörter
Dictionary	Alphabetisches Wörterverzeichnis zum Nachschlagen (*English-German* und *German-English*)

Die Units bestehen aus diesen Teilen:

Lead-in	Einstieg in die neue Unit
Theme 1 / Theme 2	Neue Themen mit vielen Aktivitäten und Übungen
Focus on language	Texte und Aufgaben zum Entdecken von Regeln und Üben wichtiger Strukturen
Story	Eine Geschichte zum Lesen
Skills training	Hören: *Listening* – Lesen: *Reading* – Sprechen: *Speaking* – Schreiben: *Writing* – Sprachmittlung: *Mediation* – Hör-/Sehverstehen: *Viewing*
STOP! CHECK! GO!	Üben, Vertiefen, Lernfortschritt feststellen

In den Units findest du diese Symbole:

	Partnerarbeit / Gruppenarbeit
	nur auf CD / auf CD und im Schülerbuch
	Filme auf der DVD
○	leichtere Übungen
●	schwierigere Übungen
○ //●	Parallelaufgaben: die leichtere in der Unit – die schwierigere in der Diff-Bank
More help p. 125	Hilfen zu einer Aufgabe in der Diff-Bank
More practice 1 p. 123	Weitere Übungen in der Diff-Bank

INHALT

Nice to meet you!

	Thema	Kompetenzen	Sprachliche Mittel/Inhalte
8	**Meet Cyril**	S Sich begrüßen und vorstellen S Sagen, was man auf einem Bild sieht	*Hi, I'm … What's your names?* *I can see Cyril, a beach and …*
10	**My favourite colours**	S/W Über Farben sprechen	
11	**My favourite sports and hobbies**	S Sagen, welche Sportarten und Hobbys man mag und nicht mag	*I like/I don't like watching TV.*
12	**My favourite animals**	S Über Lieblingstiere sprechen	
13	**My favourite thing**	S/W Seinen liebsten Gegenstand beschreiben	*My favourite thing is my bike.* *It's new and it's big.*
14	**The last day of the holidays**	L Eine Geschichte verstehen	

Unit 1 · Welcome to our school

16	LEAD-IN **The first morning**	L Gehörtes verstehen und Bilder zuordnen S Sich begrüßen und verabschieden	*Hello, I'm Tim. How are you?* *Goodbye. See you later.*
18	THEME 1 **Me and my class**	S Sich und andere vorstellen ST/W Notizen anfertigen S/W Von sich, der Schule und der Klasse berichten	*I'm … I have … She's …* *She has … They're …* *I'm not twelve, I'm eleven.*
20	THEME 2 **The first day at school**	L Gehörtes verstehen und Aussagen zuordnen S Über Stundenpläne sprechen I Den englischen Schulalltag kennenlernen	*rooms at school, lessons, days of the week, timetable*
22	FOCUS ON LANGUAGE	ST Sprachliche Regelmäßigkeiten entdecken	*I'm – he's – they're* *I'm not – she isn't – we aren't*
24	STORY **The uniform is important**	R Eine Schulgeschichte verstehen ST Wörter gruppieren	*Uniforms: Good or bad?*
26	READING **A brochure**	R/M Einer Broschüre Informationen entnehmen und auf Deutsch wiedergeben	*School things*
27	LEARNING WORDS	ST Unterschiedliche Formen der Wortschatzarbeit kennenlernen und anwenden	*Networks* *Words and phrase cards*
28	SPEAKING **Talking to friends at school**	S Über den Schulalltag sprechen ST/W Ein Interview durchführen und die Ergebnisse schriftlich festhalten	*What's the next lesson?* *Who's your favourite teacher?*
29	VIEWING	V Filmszenen verstehen I Den englischen Schulalltag kennenlernen	*Meet the kids from Harbour Road* *Eggbuckland Community College*
30	*STOP! CHECK! GO!	S/W/L/R/M Üben; ST Lernfortschritte erkennen	*My learner log*

Unit 2 · At home with Ellie

34	LEAD-IN **Homes**	S/L Wohnungen und Häuser beschreiben	*My flat is big. It has …*
36	THEME 1 **Ellie's family**	W/S Über die Familie erzählen ST Wörter gruppieren	*Parents with new partners*
38	THEME 2 **Problems at home**	S Darüber reden, wem etwas gehört S Ein Zimmer beschreiben	*There's … / There are …*
40	FOCUS ON LANGUAGE	S Fragen stellen und kurz beantworten ST Sprachliche Regelmäßigkeiten entdecken	*Are your friends fun? – Yes, they are. / No, they aren't.*
42	STORY **The best of both worlds**	R/W Tagebucheinträge verstehen W Einen Tagebucheintrag verfassen	*At mum's house and dad's flat*
44	MINDMAPS/ WRITING	ST/W Eine Mindmap erstellen und einen Text schreiben	
45	CLASSROOM ENGLISH	S Englisch als Unterrichtssprache verwenden	*What's that in English?* *Can you spell that, please?*
46	LISTENING/SPEAKING **Addresses and phone numbers**	L/S Adressen und Telefonnummern weitergeben, buchstabieren und verstehen ST Nachfragen und Notizen machen	*The alphabet* *What's your address?* *Can you say that again, please?*
47	VIEWING	V Filmszenen verstehen I Ein englisches Haus kennenlernen	*Homework time* *A tour of my room*
48	*STOP! CHECK! GO!	S/W/L/R Üben; ST Lernfortschritte erkennen	*My learner log*

Unit 3 · My Plymouth

52	LEAD-IN **This is my town**	L/S Fotobeschreibungen verstehen S Seinen Wohnort beschreiben	*I live in … In my town we have …* *My favourite places are …*
54	THEME 1 **Weekends in Plymouth**	S Sagen, was man manchmal oder oft tut S Sagen, welche Kleidung man mag/nicht mag	*I sometimes go to the market.* *I love/hate the blue shoes.*
56	THEME 2 **Birthdays**	S Sich über Geburtstage austauschen S/W Das Datum auf Englisch nennen/schreiben	*When's your birthday?*
58	FOCUS ON LANGUAGE	S Sagen, was immer/manchmal/nie passiert ST Sprachliche Regelmäßigkeiten entdecken	*My dad always gets up early.* *I never make breakfast.*
60	STORY **Happy birthday, Luca!**	R/W Eine Fotogeschichte verstehen und nacherzählen	*Something different for Luca's birthday*
62	LISTENING **Luca's garage sale**	L Einkaufsdialoge und Preise verstehen S Sagen, was etwas kostet	*The crab is 50p. The footballs are £2.*
63	SPEAKING **In a bike shop**	S Einen Einkaufsdialog gestalten	*How much is the CD player?* *OK. I'll take it.*
64	READING **Plymouth adverts**	R Authentische Poster verstehen ST Unbekannte Wörter erschließen	
65	VIEWING	V Filmszenen verstehen I Mehr über Plymouth erfahren	*Sarah isn't happy* *Plymouth, England*
66	*STOP! CHECK! GO!	S/W/L/R Üben; ST Lernfortschritte erkennen	*My learner log*

INHALT

Unit 4 · Berry's world

70	LEAD-IN **On Merryweather Farm**	S Tiere auf einem Bauernhof benennen S Diskutieren, was man tun möchte	*I want to go to the picnic area.*
72	THEME 1 **Life on the farm**	W Den Tagesablauf beschreiben L/S Uhrzeit erfragen; sagen, wie spät es ist	*My mum wakes me. I go to …* *What's the time, please?*
74	THEME 2 **Feelings**	S/W Beschreiben, wie man sich fühlt R Einen Schulaufsatz verstehen ST/W Eine Vorlage für eigene Texte nutzen	*I feel great when I do sports. / I feel fed up when my sister is bossy.* *A girl in a wheelchair*
76	FOCUS ON LANGUAGE	S Gespräche über Lieblingstiere führen ST Sprachliche Regelmäßigkeiten entdecken	*Mum doesn't like cats. Do you have a pet? Where does your pet live?*
80	STORY **Adventures in the country**	R Eine szenische Geschichte verstehen	*A sleepover at Berry's farm*
82	READING/ MEDIATION **Signs in Plymouth**	R/M Englische Schilder verstehen und auf Deutsch erklären	
83	WRITING **Invitations**	W Eine Einladung schreiben und beantworten	
84	USING A DICTIONARY	ST Unbekannte Wörter erschließen ST Im Wörterbuch nachschlagen	
85	VIEWING	V Filmszenen verstehen; den Alltag eines Mädchens im Rollstuhl sehen	*A class project* *A normal day at school*
86	*STOP! CHECK! GO!	S/W/L/R Üben; ST Lernfortschritte erkennen	*My learner log*

Unit 5 · All about Adam

90	LEAD-IN **Plymouth harbour**	S Bilder beschreiben	*On the left / On the right there's …*
92	THEME 1 **In the cafe**	S Essen und Trinken bestellen S Sagen, was im Moment gerade passiert	*A sandwich, please. Anything else? That's £5. Here you are.*
94	THEME 2 **It's boring at home!**	R Eine Bildergeschichte verstehen R/ST Einer Broschüre Informationen entnehmen S Über Musik sprechen	*Who's your favourite singer?* *Can you play an instrument?*
96	FOCUS ON LANGUAGE	S Sagen, was andere gerade machen ST Sprachliche Regelmäßigkeiten entdecken	*Mum is making sandwiches.*
98	STORY **Music makes a difference**	R Eine Geschichte verstehen	*Adam's rap battle at PMZ*
100	DESCRIBING PICTURES	L/S Eine Bildbeschreibung richtigstellen	*There's a bike behind a tree.*
101	MEDIATION/ WRITING	R/W/M Englische Kurznachrichten verstehen, verfassen und auf Deutsch wiedergeben	*Hi U 2. Where R U?*
102	READING	R/I Ein englisches Rezept verstehen	
103	VIEWING	V Filmszenen verstehen I Einen englischen Musikclub sehen	*What's your talent?* *A visit to PMZ*
104	*STOP! CHECK! GO!	S/W/L/R Üben; ST Lernfortschritte erkennen	*My learner log*

*Unit 6 · School is out – for summer

108	LEAD-IN **Four trips**	**L** Dialoge verstehen **R/S** Broschüreninhalte erschließen und sich auf ein Ausflugsziel einigen	*What about a trip to Plymouth?* *I think that's a great idea. /* *Oh no! I'd prefer a canoe trip.*
110	THEME **A trip to the beach**	**ST** Wörter in einem *network* sammeln **ST** Sich auf eine Einkaufsliste einigen	
112	STORY **All aboard!**	**L** Eine Fantasiereise machen **R/L** Eine szenische Geschichte verstehen	*An exciting trip to Cawsand* *Berry's news*
116	LISTENING/SPEAKING **Summer plans**	**L** Gehörtes verstehen und Aussagen zuordnen **S** Über Pläne für die Ferien sprechen	*What are your summer plans?* *I'm staying at home.*
117	VIEWING	**V** Filmszenen verstehen **I** Mehr von Plymouths Umgebung sehen	*Summer holidays* *A ferry trip to Cawsand*

Anhang

118	PARTNER B-Seiten
121	DIFF-BANK
	* TEXT FILE
148	**Puppets for your classroom (Nice to meet you!)**
150	**You stupid boy! (Unit 1)**
152	**The best Christmas present (Christmas time)**
155	**What's bicycle motocross? (Unit 3)**
156	**The greatest show on earth (Unit 4)**
159	**Hip-hop workout (Unit 5)**
	SKILLS FILE
160	**Learning words – Vokabellernen leicht gemacht**
162	**Mindmaps**
163	**Unbekannte Wörter verstehen? – Kein Problem!**
164	**Im Wörterbuch nachschlagen**
165	**Über Bilder und Fotos sprechen**
	LANGUAGE FILE
166	**Personalpronomen · *be* („sein") in Aussagen, Fragen und Kurzantworten**
168	***There's … / There are …* · Der Plural der Nomen**
169	**Die einfache Form der Gegenwart (The simple present)**
171	**Die Verlaufsform der Gegenwart (The present progressive)**
172	**Grammatische Fachbegriffe**
	* WORDBANK
173	**Sports and hobbies**
174	**My favourite thing · Timetable**
175	**My family · My house**
176	**My town**
177	**Talking about pets · Instruments**
178	SOUNDS · ALPHABET
179	VOCABULARY
208	DICTIONARY (English – German)
219	DICTIONARY (German – English)
228	LIST OF NAMES
229	NUMBERS
230	CLASSROOM ENGLISH
232	QUELLEN

L *Listening*
R *Reading*
S *Speaking*
W *Writing*
M *Mediation*
V *Viewing*
I *Intercultural competence*
ST *Study skill*
* Fakultativ

Die Angebote des Schülerbuches sind nicht obligatorisch abzuarbeiten. Die Auswahl der Übungen und Übungsteile richtet sich nach den Schwerpunkten des schulinternen Curriculums.

NICE TO MEET YOU Navigator | Inhalt

Lernschwerpunkt: **Sich begrüßen und vorstellen**

Storyline: Die Strandszene vermittelt erste Einblicke in den Handlungsort (die Hafenstadt Plymouth im Südwesten Englands). Die S lernen den Krebs Cyril kennen, eines der Lehrwerksmaskottchen. Cyril stellt sich vor und stellt den S Fragen, so dass auch sie sich vorstellen.

Kompetenzen: **Listening** Kurzsequenzen aus Vorstellungsdialogen erfassen, nachsprechen und darauf reagieren | **Speaking** Sich begrüßen und vorstellen; sagen, was man auf einem Bild sieht | **Lern- und Arbeitstechniken** Sprachmuster hören und nachahmen; Vorkenntnisse aus der Grundschule reaktivieren und einbringen

Redemittel: Begrüßung, Vorstellung, Fragen zur Person des Partners; *I can see …* (erste Bildbeschreibungen)

Einstieg Ex 1 L: *My name is Mr/Ms … I'm from … in … – What's your name? (…)*
Überleitung L: *Now let's meet Cyril the crab. He goes with us through our English book.* (ggf. mit Bild oder Handpuppe) Hören gemäß SB.
Erarb. Ex 1b (SB geschl.) Hören u. Nachsprechen im Chor zur Lautschulung (Glossar, S. 279 ff.), Vorbereitung auf 2.
O Lernschwächere können beim Nachsprechen auch im SB Cyrils Sprechblasen mitlesen.
Erarb. Ex 1c (SB offen) S hören u. beantworten Cyrils Fragen mithilfe der Sprechblasen-Muster.

Erarb. Ex 2 (SB offen) Arbeitsanweisung klären: Walk around ist eine Milling-around activity. Ggf. mit Lernstärkeren demonstrieren. Mindestanzahl an zu befragenden Partnern festlegen (ca. 5). KV 0.1 (Part 1) für Notizen verwenden.
Ausw. Ex 2 (SB geschl.) Einzelne S-Paare präsentieren (freiwillig) ihre Mini-Dialoge. Zusätzlich: KV 0.1 (Part 1), Ex c lösen lassen.

Nice to meet you!

▸ Folie 2 ▸ IAT 0.1 ▸ KV 0.1 ▸ DFF N1 ▸ DFF N7 ▸ INKL 0.1 ▸ INKL 0.2

1 Meet Cyril[2)]

a) Listen. 1.02

b) Repeat. 1.03

c) Listen and answer Cyril's questions. 1.04

2 Meet your class

Walk around: Talk to different partners.

Hi, I'm …
What's your name?

I'm ten / eleven / twelve / …
What about you?

I'm from …
What about you?

1 ['plɪməθ] 2 ['sɪrɪl]

▸ Workbook 1, p. 2

Zeitbedarf: ca. zwei Stunden
Minimalversion: Ex **1**; **2**; **3**
Kooperative Lernformen: Milling-around activity (Ex **2**)
Materialbedarf: Ex **1** und **4**: Audio-CD + Player oder MP3 + PC/Lautsprecher | Ex **3**: Wandkarte GB bzw. Karte im SB, Umschlagseite 2
Einsatz von Begleitmedien: KV 0.1 | IAT 0.1 | DFF N1, N2, N7 | INKL 0.1–0.2 | Folien 1–2 | Workbook S. 4–5

▸ Folie 1 ▸ DFF N2 ▸ KV 0.1

3 GAME I can see ...

a) What can you see? Find five things in the picture.

Lösungsbsp. S. 232

b) Play the game.

4 Cyril's song

1.05

Listen to Cyril's song and sing the chorus.

Box: Voc., p. 180

CYRIL'S SONG

I'm Cyril the crab
°And I °like the °sea.
I °love °water
°All around me.

°Chorus:
I °run and I °hide,
I °dive in the °sand.
°Don't pick me up
°Or °I'll pinch your °hand.

Einstieg Ex 3 L: *Cyril is from Plymouth. Look at the map. Where is Plymouth?* Auf der Karte zeigen (lassen). L: *Plymouth is by the sea. There's a beach (sand, water, ...) and in the summer there are lots of people ...*
Überleitung L: *Open your books at p. 8 and look at the picture. Where is Cyril? (on the beach, by the sea)*
Erarb. Ex 3a
(SB offen) Bildbetrachtung, kurze Bedenkzeit, dann frontal sammeln. Vor-/Nachsprechen zur Lautschulung.
Erarb. Ex 3b
(SB offen) in Gruppen von 3–6 S. L demonstriert mit einer Gruppe das Spiel (analog „Koffer packen"). S spielen in ihrer Gruppe so lang wie möglich; kein Nomen wiederholen, nur kurze Pausen. Ein S pro Gruppe notiert die Nomen: Es gewinnt die Gruppe mit dem längsten Satz.

Einstieg Ex 4 L: *Cyril has a song. He sings about what he likes. What do you think: What things do crabs like?* – Ideen an Tafel notieren: *water, the sea, the beach ...*
Überleitung L: *Let's listen and find out.* Beim **1. Hören** (Str. 1, Refrain) Ideen überprüfen.
Erarb. Ex 4
(SB offen) L: *Let's sing along with Cyril. Look at the chorus* (zeigen). **2. Hören** und Mitsingen des Refrains, dann von Str. 1. Ggf. Str. 2–4 auf KV 0.1 (Part 2) mitsingen.

MY FAVOURITE COLOURS

Lernschwerpunkt: **Über (Lieblings-)Farben sprechen**
Storyline: Die S lernen Ellie kennen. Sie beschreibt ihre Lieblingsorte in Plymouth und spricht darüber, welche Farben sie mag / nicht mag.
Kompetenzen: **Listening** Kurze Sequenzen erfassen | **Speaking** Über (Lieblings-)Farben sprechen | **Writing** Farbkarten beschriften; Lieblingsfarben von Mit-S in einer Tabelle notieren | **Lern- und Arbeitstechniken** Notizen in Tabelle anfertigen
Redemittel: Wortfeld *colours*; Vorlieben/Abneigungen äußern

Zeitbedarf: ca. eine Stunde
Minimalversion: Ex **1b+c**; Ex **2a+b**
Kooperative Lernformen: Milling-around activity Ex **2a**
Materialbedarf: Ex **1a**: weiße (oder farbige) (Kartei-)Karten oder farbiger Zeichenkarton zum Basteln, Farbstifte (in allen genannten Farben bereithalten!); Ex **1b+c**: Audio-CD + Player oder MP3 + PC/Lautsprecher; Ex **2b**: Namensliste vorbereiten (Tafel/Folie)
Einsatz von Begleitmedien: KV 0.2 | DFF N3 | Folie 3 | INKL 0.3–0.4 | Workbook S. 3

Einstieg Ex 1 (SB offen) Bildbeschreibung. L: *Look at the photos. You can see a girl. What's her name? (Ellie Cole) Where is Ellie from? (from Plymouth) What colours can you see in the photos? (blue, green, red, white, …)* S zeigen Farben in den Bildern.
Erarb. Ex 1a (SB offen) Vorbereitung auf Hören in **1b**: S gestalten *colour cards* analog Foto.
Erarb. Ex 1b (SB offen) **1. Hören**: S zeigen zu jeder verstandenen Farbe ihre passende *colour card* hoch.
Erarb. Ex 1c (SB offen) Vor dem **2. Hören**: Übertragen der Satzanfänge ins Heft. Beim **2. Hören** (Detailverstehen): Vervollständigen mit Farbwörtern. **HA:** KV 0.2

Erarb. Ex 2a (SB offen) AA klären: *Walk around* ist eine Milling-around activity. Ggf. mit Lernstärkeren demonstrieren. Mindestanzahl an Partnern festlegen. Parallel mit **2b** bearbeiten.
Erarb. Ex 2b (SB offen) An Tafel / auf Folie eine Namensliste vorbereiten; in größeren Klassen Gruppen à 5–6 S bilden.
Erarb. Ex 2c (SB offen) Mithilfe der Sprechblasen. Auf Freiwilligkeit achten.

▸ *KV 0.2* ▸ *DFF N3* ▸ *Folie 3* ▸ *INKL 0.3* ▸ *INKL 0.4*

My favourite colours

I'm Ellie Cole. Welcome to Plymouth.

1

2

3

4

1 Colours

Box: Voc., p. 181

a) Make colour cards.

green red yellow brown
black blue purple grey
white pink orange

1.07 **b)** Listen to Ellie.
What colours can you hear?

c) Listen again. Ellie says:
– I like …
– I don't like …
– My favourite colour is …

Ex 1b) (1) red • pink (2) black • green • red • pink (3) orange • red • white (4) orange • white • yellow • purple • blue • red
Ex 1c) I like **red.** • I don't like **pink.** • My favourite colour is **red.**

2 Your favourite colour

a) Walk around:
Talk to different partners.

Hi, Anna. What's your favourite colour?
Blue!

b) Write the answers on the board.

Name	Favourite colour
Anna	blue
Ilja	…

c) Talk about favourite colours in your class.

Three students like blue.
Two students like red.

Box: Voc., p. 181

▸ Workbook 2, p. 3

MY FAVOURITE SPORTS AND HOBBIES

Lernschwerpunkt: **Über Sportarten/Hobbys sprechen**
Storyline: Adams Hobbys und Lieblingssportarten
Kompetenzen: Speaking Sagen, welche Sportarten und Hobbys man mag / nicht mag | **Writing** Bilder beschriften | **Lern- und Arbeitstechniken** kurze Musterdialoge ausgestalten; ein Plakat anfertigen; lexikalische Vorkenntnisse sammeln
Redemittel: Wortfelder *sports, hobbies*; Vorlieben/ Abneigungen

Zeitbedarf: ca. eine Stunde
Kooperative Lernformen: Partner talk Ex **2b**
Materialbedarf: Ex **3**: großes leeres Blatt Papier oder Zeichenkarton (mindestens DIN-A2) für Poster; Papierstreifen für Labels zum Beschriften, Fotos/ Abbildungen verschiedener Hobbys, Schere, Kleber
Einsatz von Begleitmedien: DFF N4 | Folie 4 | INKL 0.5 | Workbook S. 3–4

Einstieg Ex 1 (SB offen) L: *Look at picture 1 and find out: What's the boy's name? (Adam) What are his hobbies? (football, music, watching TV)*
Erarb. Ex 1 (SB offen) Bildbetrachtung, Notieren der Aktivitäten in einer Liste. Aussprachesicherung über mdl. Zuordnen und Nachsprechen.
Ausw. Ex 1 Vergleichen im Partner check, dann im Plenum.

Erarb. Ex 2a (SB offen) Vorbereitung auf **2b**: S notieren englische Begriffe für eigene Lieblingsaktivitäten, Hilfen in *Wordbank 1* (S. 173).
Erarb. Ex 2b (SB offen) Klären der AA. Befragung kann erfolgen als Milling-around activity oder im Double circle. L demonstriert Minidialog mit einem S. Mindestanzahl an Partnern festlegen.
● Lernstärkere notieren in Tabelle:

Name		
favourite sport		

Erarb. Ex 3 (SB offen) HA vorab: S bringen eigenes Foto/Abb. ihres Lieblingshobbys mit. Im Unterricht Verfassen von Bildunterschriften.
Ausw. Ex 3 Auf (vom L) vorbereitetes Poster heften S ihre Bilder und Bildunterschriften. In großen Klassen Gruppenposter (von je ca. 6 S) erstellen lassen.

► *DFF N4* ► *Folie 4* ► *INKL 0.5*

My favourite sports and hobbies

1

2

3

dancing • football • playing games • reading books • riding • skateboarding • swimming • watching TV

4

5

6

7

8

1 football • **2** swimming • **3** watching TV • **4** dancing • **5** reading books • **6** riding • **7** skateboarding • **8** playing games

1 What are the sports and hobbies?

Find the names of the eight sports and hobbies: *1 football, 2 ..., ...* Box: Voc., p. 181

2 What about you?

a) Find the names of your favourite sports and hobbies. ► *Wordbank 1, p. 173*

b) Talk to different partners.

I like ... What about you?
I like ... too.
I don't like ...
My favourite hobby is ...
My favourite sport is ...

3 A sports and hobbies poster

Make a big class poster. Write labels.

► *Workbook 3–4, pp. 3–4*

1 [ɒz'mænəvɪtʃ]

MY FAVOURITE ANIMALS

Lernschwerpunkt: **Über Tiere sprechen**

Storyline: Die S lernen Berry kennen. Sie ist Tierfreundin und wird mit ihrem Pony Harry vorgestellt.

Kompetenzen: Speaking Über Tiere sprechen | **Writing** Bildkarten zu Tieren beschriften | **Lern- und Arbeitstechniken** Mnemotechniken (Zuordnung von Bildern – Begriffen memorieren); eine Tabelle anfertigen

Redemittel: Wortfeld *animals*: *wild animals, pets*

Zeitbedarf: ca. eine Stunde

Minimalversion: Ex **1a+b**

Kooperative Lernformen: Partner talk Ex **1a** | Milling-around activity Ex **2**

Materialbedarf: Ex **2**: (Kartei-)Karten, Tierbilder (als HA sammeln lassen bzw. zur Verfügung stellen), Schere, Klebstoff

Einsatz von Begleitmedien: DFF N5 | Folie 5 | INKL 0.6 | Workbook S. 4

Einstieg Ex 1 (SB offen) L: *Look at the photo and the speech bubble on the top left* (hochhalten, zeigen). *You can see a girl. What's her name? (Berry) Where is Berry? (on a horse/pony) What's the name of the pony? (Harry)* L liest Sprechblase vor, S antworten.
Erarb. Ex 1a (SB offen) S prägen sich Bilder und Begriffe ein (Mnemotechniken). L lässt SB schließen. Im Partner talk nennen S möglichst viele Tiere, ergänzen einander und zählen mit.
Ausw. Ex 1a Nennen der Tierbezeichnungen, L sammelt an Tafel, dann Abgleich.
Erarb. Ex 1b (SB offen) Einige passen in beide Kategorien (z. B. *rat, fish* ...).
Ausw. Ex 1b Im Plenum, wobei L/S die Tabelle an der Tafel ergänzt.

Erarb. Ex 2 (SB offen) S basteln selbst ihr Memo-Spiel: Gruppen à 3–4 S bilden; Tierbilder und Materialien zur Verfügung stellen (bzw. das vorab als HA gesammelte Bildmaterial nutzen). Bilder ausschneiden, auf (Kartei-)Karten kleben und die zugehörigen Tiernamen auf andere Karten gleichen Formats schreiben. Anschließend nach den bekannten Memo-Regeln spielen.

▸ DFF N5 ▸ Folie 5 ▸ INKL 0.6

My favourite animals

Box: Voc., p. 182

1 Can you remember?

a) Look at the animals for one minute. Then close your book. How many animals can you and your partner remember?

b) Pets or wild animals? Make a table. Add more animals.

Pets	*Wild animals*
pony	...

Lösungsbsp. S. 232

2 GAME Animal pairs

Make your own animal cards or ask your teacher for animal cards.
Then play the *Animal pairs* game.

1 ['dɒnəvən] 2 ['pəʊni]

▸ Workbook 5, p. 4

MY FAVOURITE THING

Lernschwerpunkt: **Lieblingsgegenstände**
Storyline: Luca stellt sich mit seinem Fahrrad vor.
Kompetenzen: **Listening** Einen Text erfassen, Aussagen korrekt ordnen | **Speaking** Sätze nachsprechen, den Lieblingsgegenstand beschreiben
Writing Einen Text verfassen
Lern- und Arbeitstechniken Gemäß Hörtext-Muster eine Mini-Präsentation vorbereiten und halten
Redemittel: Gegenstände beschreiben

Zeitbedarf: ca. eine Stunde
Minimalversion: Ex **1a**; Ex **2a+b**
Materialbedarf: Ex **1a+b**: Audio-CD + Player oder MP3 + PC/Lautsprecher
Einsatz von Begleitmedien: Folie 6 | INKL 0.7
Workbook S. 6–7

► *Folie 6* ► *INKL 0.7*

My favourite thing

1 Luca's favourite thing

1.08 **a)** Listen to Luca. Put the sentences (A–G) in the right order: *C, ...*

C
F
A
E
B
D
G

I'm Luca Boateng[3].
A It's blue and black.
B I can go to the park on it.
C My favourite thing is my bike.
D It's great and it's fun!
E And it's small.
F It's old.
G I like my bike.

1.09 **b)** Now listen and repeat.

2 Your favourite thing

a) What's your favourite thing?

► *Wordbank 2, p. 174*

b) Write about your favourite thing.

My favourite thing is my ...
It's old / new / ...
It's red / green / black / ...
It's big / small / ...
I can go to ... / play / ... on it.
It's great / cool / nice / fun / ...
I like my ...

c) Talk to the class about your favourite thing.

Erarb. Ex 1a (SB offen) Ggf. Klären der AA: *Look at the example: C is sentence one, so please write down C in your exercise book. What is sentence two/three/...? Let's listen to Luca.* **1. Hören**; Ordnen der Sätze. **O** Lernschwächere erhalten Buchstabenkarten zum Ordnen. **Ausw. Ex 1a** Vergleichen im Plenum, ggf. **2. Hören**. **Erarb. Ex 1b** Lautschulung durch Chorsprechen in den Hörtextpausen. Vorbereitung auf **2c**.

Einstieg Ex 2 (SB offen) L: *Look at the pictures. What things can you see?* Benennen mithilfe der *Wordbank* 2, S. 174; Aussprache durch Nachsprechen im Plenum sichern. Überleitung L: *Luca's favourite thing is his bike. What's your favourite thing?* **Erarb. Ex 2a+b** (SB offen) S wählen ihr *favourite thing*, schreiben mit den angebotenen Redemitteln einen Text darüber. **Ausw.** in **Ex 2c** (SB geschl.) S tragen ihre Texte im Plenum vor (Read-and-look-up technique). Auch als Rätsel möglich: Gegenstand nicht benennen. Vortragender S fragt am Ende *What is it?* Mit-S erraten den beschriebenen Gegenstand.

3 ['bwɑːteŋ]

Lernschwerpunkt: **Eine Strandgeschichte hören und verstehen**

Storyline: Die Strandgeschichte zeigt Ellie, Berry, Adam und Luca an ihrem letzten Ferientag. Dabei sind auch die Maskottchen: Krebs Cyril mag die Menschenmassen am Strand überhaupt nicht und muss ständig flüchten. Möwe Sandy beobachtet das Geschehen aus der Luft.

Kompetenzen: **Listening** Eine Hörgeschichte bildgestützt verstehen; Bilder zum Handlungsverlauf ordnen; einen Chant hören | **Speaking** Einen Chant rhythmisch nachsprechen | **Lern- und Arbeitstechniken** Einem Hörtext wesentliche Handlungsstrukturen entnehmen

Redemittel: Wortfelder *holidays, beach*

Einstieg Ex 1 (SB geschl.) L: *What can you do in your holidays? (go swimming, play football, watch TV, read books, go skateboarding, go riding, …)*
Überleitung L: *Let's see what the kids in Plymouth do.*
Erarb. Ex 1a (SB offen) S betrachten Bilder und erkennen die LW-Kinder. Ggf. Redemittel bereitstellen: *I can see … in picture …*
● Lernstärkere sagen zusätzlich, wo sich die Kinder befinden.
Erarb. Ex 1b (SB offen) **1. Hören** (Globalverstehen); S notieren die Bild-Buchstaben in der richtigen Reihenfolge.
Alternative S erhalten vor dem Hören KV 0.3A, schneiden die Bilder aus und ordnen sie während des Hörens gemäß Text.
Ausw. Ex 1b Beim **2. Hören** durch Partner check; abschließend Vergleich im Plenum.

► *KV 0.3 A*

The last day of the holidays

Box: Voc., p. 183

A: Cyril, Sandy (in the water / on the beach) • B: Ellie, her friends (in the street) • C: Adam, woman, little boy (on a bike) • D: Berry, man (in a car) • E: Luca, his family (in the street / near the beach) • F: Sandy, Cyril (on the beach)

1 A story

a) Look at the pictures on this page. Who can you see?

1.10 b) Listen to part one of the story. Put the pictures (A–F) in the right order. A • E • B • C • D • F

A

B

C

D

E

F

Zeitbedarf: ca. zwei Stunden
Minimalversion: Ex **1b+c**
Kooperative Lernformen: Partner check Ex **1b+c**
Materialbedarf: Ex **1b+c**: Audio-CD + Player oder MP3 + PC/Lautsprecher; Schere, Klebstoff
Einsatz von Begleitmedien: KV 0.3A/B | DFF N6 | INKL 0.8 | Workbook S. 6

▸ KV 0.3B ▸ DFF N6 ▸ INKL 0.8

1.11 **c)** Listen to part two of the story. Put the pictures (A–E) in the right order. A • D • B • C • E

A

B

C

D

E

2 Chant[1)]
Listen and repeat.

Holidays are great,
Holidays are fun!
°No more work °or °school °for me,
°Just °sitting in the °sun.

The holidays °are over,
The holidays °are done.
No more sitting on the °beach,
No more °summer fun!

Erarb. Ex 1c (SB offen) **1. Hören** (Globalverstehen); S notieren die Bild-Buchstaben in der richtigen Reihenfolge.
Alternative S erhalten vor dem Hören KV 0.3B, schneiden die Bilder aus und ordnen sie beim Hören gemäß Text.
Ausw. Ex 1c Beim **2. Hören** durch Partner check; abschließend Vergleich im Plenum.
Zusatz S ordnen diese Aussagen (von Tafel/Folie) nach Lesen und nochmaligem Ansehen der Bilder den Sprechern zu: *Who says it?*
- *... a crab in my sandcastle. (Ellie)*
- *Stupid crab. (Sandy)*
- *I like music. (Sandy)*
- *It's a goal. (Adam)*
- *It's better here. (Cyril)*

Einstieg Ex 2 (SB offen) Bildbetrachtung im Unt.-Gespräch.
L: *Look at Cyril the crab in the pictures. In what picture is Cyril happy?* (E) *Why is he happy? (Because it's the last day of the holidays.)*
Überleitung L: *What about you? Are you happy on the last day of the holidays?* S stimmen ab.
Erarb. Ex 2 **1. Hören** (SB geschl.; Rhythmus erfassen, Globalverstehen), dann **2. Hören** (SB offen; Mitlesen und -sprechen zur Lautschulung).

1 [tʃɑːnt]

Lernschwerpunkt: Kennenlernen einer englischen Schule und der Lehrwerksprotagonisten
Storyline: Beginn des neuen Schuljahrs am *Eggbuckland Community College* in Plymouth (genannt *Eggy*; Fakten s. www.eggbuckland.com) für Berry, Ellie, Luca und Adam
Kompetenzen: Listening Kurzdialoge und Geräusche verstehen, Bilder zuordnen | **Speaking** Sich begrüßen und vorstellen
Redemittel: Dinge benennen, erste Bildbeschreibungen, Begrüßung und Kurzkonversation

Einstieg Ex 1 (SB geschl.) Vorentlastung des neuen WS über Flashcards, Lautschulung durch Nachsprechen, L: *Sandy the seagull can see lots of things at a school in Plymouth. Look!*
Erarb. Ex 1 (SB offen) Klären der AA; Vorgehen demonstrieren (*point at*); **1. Hören** (Globalverstehen): S zeigen auf passendes Bild.
Ausw. Ex 1 KV 1.1 (Part 1) einsetzen: Bilder ausschneiden (ggf. vorbereitet verteilen), S legen die Bilder während des **2. Hörens** in der richtigen Reihenfolge vor sich ab (optional: L oder ein S ordnet die Flashcards am OH-Projektor sichtbar für alle).

Unit 1 Welcome to our school

▸ *KV 1.1* ▸ *IAT 1.1*

1 School sounds

1.14

Listen. What can you hear? Point at the right pictures.

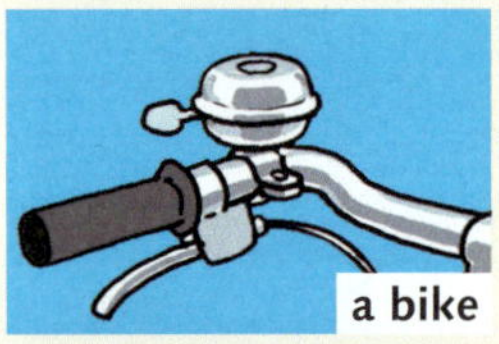

a bird | a dog | a car | boys and girls | a football | a teacher | a mobile phone | a bike

LEAD-IN Navigator | Vorbereitung

Zeitbedarf: ca. zwei Stunden
Kooperative Lernformen: Milling-around activity Ex **2c**
Materialbedarf: Ex **1–2**: Audio-CD + Player oder MP3 + PC/Lautsprecher | Ex **1**: Flashcards und OH-Projektor (Kopie der SB-Bilder auf Folie bzw. Ausschnitt per Smartboard); Bilder von KV 1.1 (Part 1) ggf. schon ausschneiden | Ex **2**: Namensschilder
Einsatz von Begleitmedien: KV 1.1 (Part 1) | IAT 1.1 | Workbook S. 7

1

▸ *INKL 1.1*

2 The first morning

1.15 **a)** Listen. Put the pictures (A–D) in the right order. A (Berry) | C (Ellie) | D (Luca) | B (Adam)

1.16 **b)** Listen to the people and repeat.

c) Pick a card. Practise with a partner. Find a new partner, pick a new card and practise.

①
A: Hello, I'm ...
What's your name?
B: Hi, I'm ...
A: Nice to meet you, ...
B: Nice to meet you too.

②
A: Hi, ...
B: Hi, ... How are you?
A: I'm fine, thanks.
How are you?
B: I'm OK, thanks.

③
A: Goodbye, ...
B: Bye, ...
A: Have a good day.
B: You too. See you later.
A: OK, see you.

Einstieg Ex 2
(SB offen) L: *For Ellie, Berry, Luca and Adam it's the first morning at a new school. It´s day one at Eggy. Who´s in picture A / B / C / D?* Redemittel vorgeben, ggf. Tafelnotiz: *In picture A / ... I can see Berry / ...*
S nennen im Partner talk die Protagonisten auf den Bildern.
Einstieg Ex 2a
Beim **1. Hören** notieren S die Buchstaben A–D in der richtigen Reihenfolge.
Ausw. Ex 2a Kontrolle beim **2. Hören**.
Einstieg Ex 2b
(SB geschl.) Lautschulung durch Nachsprechen in Vorbereitung auf 2c; Dialogteile ggf. mehrfach wiederholen lassen (Audio stoppen).
Einstieg Ex 2c AA klären: Milling-around activity, ggf. demonstrieren mit lernstärkerem S (*new partner – new card*). Danach mehrere Übungsrunden: S führen mit verschiedenen Partnern nacheinander Dialoge anhand der abgedruckten Karten (SB dabei mitnehmen).
Ausw. Ex 2c Einzelne S-Paare demonstrieren Minidialoge vor der Klasse (möglichst freiwillig).

▸ *Workbook 1–2, p. 7*

Lernschwerpunkt: Sich in der Klasse vorstellen

Storyline: Ms Lee, die neue Englischlehrerin, begrüßt Berry, Ellie, Luca und Adam in der Klasse 7Y. Die vier Kinder stellen sich vor und geben Informationen über sich und ihre Familien.

Kompetenzen: **Listening** Hörausschnitte erfassen: global und im Detail | **Speaking** Sich vorstellen; von sich und anderen berichten
Reading Texten gezielt Informationen entnehmen | **Writing** Mit Notizen einen kurzen Text über sich selbst schreiben
Lern- und Arbeitstechniken Notizen in einer Tabelle anfertigen

Grammatik: Vorbewusste Verwendung der Personalpronomen und der Formen von *be* (mit Kurzformen und Verneinung)

Redemittel: Begrüßung, Familienmitglieder

Einstieg Ex 1
L: *For the kids at Eggy it's the first day in their new class. Let's see how they're doing.*
Erarb. Ex 1a
(SB offen)
1. Lesen / Hören, ggf. im Mitleseverfahren; S beantworten Fragen mit Unterstützung durch Foto.
Ausw. Ex 1a
S nennen die gesuchten Namen im Plenum.
Erarb. Ex 1b
(SB offen) S schreiben Tabelle ab (oder erhalten KV 1.1), danach
2. Lesen / Hören (Detailverstehen); S tragen Informationen in Tabelle ein.
Ausw. Ex 1b
Lösungsvergleich im Partner check. Ergebnissicherung: L lässt Lösungen im Plenum nennen und eintragen in Tabelle (Tafel oder KV-Folie).
Erarb. Ex 1c
1. Hören (Globalverstehen) beim Betrachten beider Bilder Identifizieren des richtigen (im Plenum.)
Erarb. Ex 1d
2. Hören (Detailverstehen), S tragen Informationen in Tabelle (Adam ergänzen) oder auf KV 1.1 ein.
Ausw. Ex 1d Partner check, dann Lösungen im Plenum nennen und eintragen in Tabelle (Tafel / KV-Folie).

1 THEME 1

▸ KV 1.1 ▸ Folie 7 ▸ INKL 1.2

Me and my class

Berry, Ellie, Luca (Text + Foto); Adam (Foto)

1 Good morning, class 7Y

1.17

a) Who's in class 7Y? Who's the English teacher?

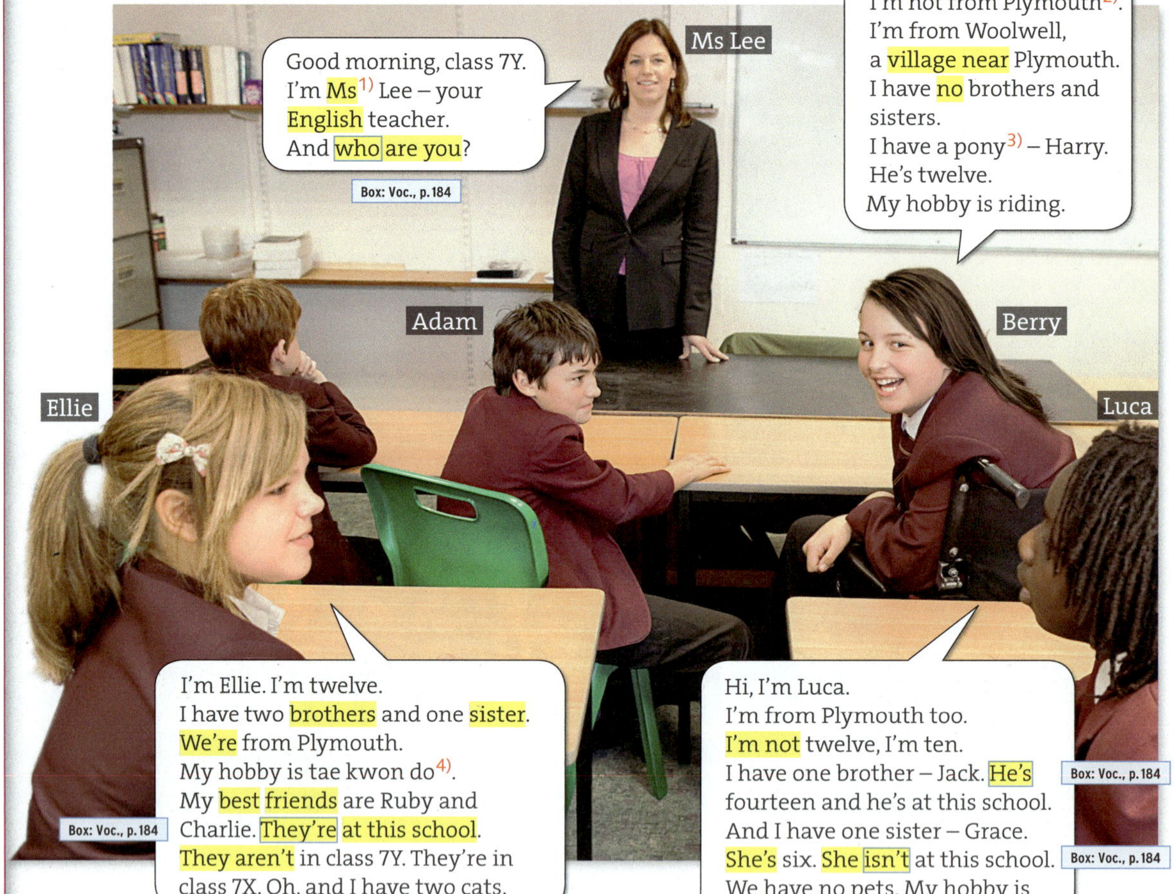

b) Copy and complete the table.

Name	Age	From	Brothers	Sisters	Hobbies	Pets
Berry						
Luca						
Ellie						

Berry: 11, Woolwell, no brothers, no sisters, riding, pony | **Luca:** 10, Plymouth, 1 brother (Jack), 1 sister (Grace), riding a BMX, no pets | **Ellie:** 12, Plymouth, 2 brothers, 1 sister, tae kwon do, 2 cats

1.18

c) Listen to Adam.
Which is the right picture?

d) Listen again.
Complete the table for Adam.

1

2

2 is the right picture.

Adam: 11, Plymouth, one brother, no sisters, no pet

1 [mɪz, məz] 2 [ˈplɪməθ] 3 [ˈpəʊni] 4 [taɪ kwɒn ˈdəʊ] 5 [biː em ˈeks]

▸ Workbook 3, p. 8

Zeitbedarf: ca. zwei Stunden
Minimalversion: Ex **1a–b**; **2a–b**; **3** ○
Kooperative Lernformen: Partner check (optional in Ex **1b** und **d**)
Gruppenarbeit (optional in Ex **2b** Austausch in Kleingruppen mit verschiedenen Partnern)
Materialbedarf: Ex **1**: Audio-CD + Player oder MP3 + PC/Lautsprecher | Ex **3**: Familienfotos
Einsatz von Begleitmedien: KV 1.1 (Part 2) | INKL 1.2–1.3 | Folie 7 | Workbook S. 8

1

▸ KV 1.1 ▸ INKL 1.3 ▸ Folie 7

2 NOW YOU

a) Copy the table and make notes about yourself.

Name:	Brothers:
Age:	Sisters:
From:	Pet:
School:	Best friends:
Class:	Hobby/Sport:
Class teacher:	Favourite colour:

b) Use your notes. Talk to your group.

○ Start like this:

I'm ... (name)
I'm ... (age)
I'm from ...
I'm at ... school.
I'm in class ...
My class teacher is ...

● Say more:

I have one brother. He's ...
I have one sister. She's ...
I have no pets / a pet / ...
My best friends are ...
My favourite hobby / sport is ...
My favourite colour is ...

c) ● Who's like you?
– Anna is eleven. I'm eleven too.
– Hendrik has one sister. I have one sister too.

Box: Voc., p. 184

3 About me and my class

Box: Voc., p. 185

Write a short text about you for your class.
You can put your text in your DOSSIER[6].

Das Dossier ist eine Mappe, in der du deine wichtigen und schönen Arbeiten sammeln kannst. Es gehört zum Portfolio.

Me and my class

○
I'm Vanessa.
I'm eleven.
I'm at Erich-Kästner-School.
I'm in class 5a.
My class teacher is Mrs Schmidt.

●
Hello, I'm Tim. I'm from Düsseldorf in Germany.
I'm at Erich-Kästner-School.
My favourite teacher is Mr Jahn. He's great!

I have two sisters and one dog.

My best friends are Samir and Patrick. They're cool.

My favourite sport is football and my favourite colours are red and white.

Einstieg Ex 2a
(SB offen) Arbeitsanweisung klären; L zeigt als Muster eine für sich selbst ausgefüllte Tabelle.
Überleitung L: *What can you tell the others about you? Copy and complete the table.* (Raster auf KV 1.1)
Erarb. Ex 2b
L erläutert Vorgehen (ggf. Beispielvortrag); gibt differenzierten Erwartungshorizont vor:
○ *You can talk about the points on the left.*
● *Look at the ideas on the right to say more.*
Ausw. Ex 2b
Austausch in Kleingruppen **oder** Präsentation einzelner S im Plenum. Zusammenhängend sprechen!
Erarb. Ex 2c S äußern Gemeinsamkeiten zu ihren Mit-S.
Einstieg Ex 3 Lesen der Muster (im Plenum oder still).
L: *Before you start to write about yourself, let's read the texts here.*
Erarb. Ex 3 S schreiben anhand der Mustertexte und ihrer Tabellen aus Ex 2a einen kurzen Text über sich selbst.
Ausw. Ex 3 Einzelne S lesen Texte vor, die anderen hören zu, ggf. Verbesserungsvorschläge. Anschließend Abheften der korrigierten Texte im Dossier oder Ausstellung in der Klasse.
Alternative: Namen weglassen, anschließend Erraten des Verfassers.

▸ Workbook 4–5, p. 8

6 ['dɒsieɪ]

THEME 2 Navigator | Inhalt

Lernschwerpunkt: Sich über Schulfächer, -räume und Stundenpläne informieren

Storyline: Berry, Ellie, Luca und Adam lernen bei einem Rundgang ihre neue Schule kennen und erhalten ihren Stundenplan. Der *School rap* bietet die Schulfächer in musikalischer Form.

Kompetenzen: Listening Gehörtes (kurze Dialoge) verstehen und Aussagen zuordnen; einen Rap Song hören | **Speaking** Einen Rap Song mitsingen | **Lern- und Arbeitstechniken** Aussagen zu Lese- und Hörtexten als richtig oder falsch einstufen

Grammatik: Vorbewusste Verwendung der Personalpronomen und der Formen von *be* (mit Kurzformen und Verneinung)

Redemittel: Schulfächer, -räume und -aktivitäten; Stundenplan, Wochentage

Einstieg Ex. 1
(SB geschl.)
L: *The students in class 7 Y have music on Tuesday, but where's the music room? They go on a tour of the school with Ms Lee. Let's go on the tour too.*

Erarb. Ex 1a
(SB offen) Klären der AA, Semantisieren der Bildunterschriften, Lautschulung; S zeigen beim **1. Hören** (Globalverstehen) gemäß Tourverlauf auf passende Bilder.

Ausw. Ex 1a Je zwei Sitznachbarn vergleichen im Partner check, auf welche Bilder sie zeigen.

Erarb. Ex 1b
(Vorentlastung) L liest Sprechblasentexte vor, S wiederholen.
Dann **2. Hören** und Zuordnen der Sprechblasen (Detailverstehen).

Ausw. Ex 1b Nach Vergleich im Plenum notieren S die Ergebnisse im Heft.

Differenzierung
○ Lernschwächeren teilt L die Sprechblasentexte als Satzkärtchen aus. S legen sie beim Hören auf die jeweiligen Bilder.
● Lernstärkere finden zusätzlich die Namen der Sprecher heraus (vgl. Lösungsteile in Blau).

1 THEME 2

► *INKL 1.4*

The first day at school

1 A tour of the school

1.19

a) Class 7Y is on a tour of the school with Ms Lee.
Listen and point at the pictures in the right order.

in the computer room

in the canteen

in the science lab | in the art room | in the sports hall | in the computer room | in the canteen

in the art room

in the science lab

in the sports hall

b) Listen again. Match the speech bubbles 1–5 with the rooms.

1 in the sports hall, 2 ..., 3 ...

1 We aren't in a PE lesson[1] now.

2 Welcome to Eggy!

3 Where's Ellie? She isn't here.

Box: Voc., p.185

4 I'm your ICT[2] teacher.

5 I'm not lost. I'm here.

1 [piː ˈiː] 2 [aɪ siː ˈtiː]

1 in the sports hall (Ms Lee) 2 in the art room (Mrs Ford / art teacher)
3 in the science lab (Ms Lee) 4 in the computer room (Mr Brown / ICT teacher)
5 in the canteen (Adam)

Zeitbedarf: ca. zwei Stunden
Minimalversion: Ex **1a–b**; **2b**; **3a**
Kooperative Lernformen: Partner check Ex **1a**
Materialbedarf: Ex **1a–b**; **2a**; **3b**: Audio-CD + Player oder MP3 + PC/Lautsprecher; Ex **1**: Satzkärtchen (Sprechblasentexte); Ex **3**: Stundenplan der S, leeres Blatt (mindestens Format DIN A2) für Plakat
Einsatz von Begleitmedien: INKL 1.4–1.5 | Folie 8 | Workbook S. 9–10

1

▸ *Folie 8* ▸ *INKL 1.5*

2 School rap

1.20 1.21

a) Listen to the rap. Then sing it.

b) What lessons in the rap do you know?

Chorus °All my teachers °say,
°Work °hard °every day!

Every day I go to class,
I have English, I have maths,
I have French, I have German,
I °do lots and °lots of °learnin'.

Chorus All my teachers say, ...

Science, French and ICT,
Art, history and PE,
Drama and technology,
Music and geography.

Chorus All my teachers say, ...

3 The new timetable

Eggbuckland Community College[1)]
Class 7Y timetable

Box: Voc., p. 185

Lesson	Time	Monday	Tuesday	Wednesday	Thursday	Friday
	8.40–9.00	ASSEMBLY / °REGISTRATION				
1	9.00–10.00	English	music	technology	geography	PE
2	10.00–11.00	maths	English	history	French	PE
	11.00–11.25	BREAK				
3	11.25–12.25	art	history	English	science	geography
4	12.25–1.25	art	science	maths	science	English
	1.25–2.05	LUNCH				
5	2.05–3.05	French	drama	science	ICT	technology

a) Look at the Eggy timetable.
What's right? What's wrong?
1 Class 7Y has lunch at school every day.
2 Class 7Y has six lessons every day.
3 Lesson one on Monday is French.
4 Lesson two on Tuesday is music.
5 Lesson three on Wednesday is English.
6 Lesson four on Thursday is science.

1 Right. | **2** Wrong. (Class 7 Y has five lessons every day.) | **3** Wrong. (It's English.) | **4** Wrong. (Lesson one on Tuesday is music. / Lesson two on Tuesday is English.) | **5** Right. | **6** Right.

1.22

b) Listen to Ellie and Adam.
What's right? What's wrong?

More practice 1 p. 121

Monday: Lesson 1: Right! | Lesson 2: Wrong! (It's maths!) | Lesson 3: Right! | Lesson 4: Right! | Lesson 5: Wrong! (It's French!) **Tuesday:** Lesson 1: Wrong! (It's music!) | Lesson 2: Wrong! (It's English!) | Lesson 3: Wrong! (It's history!) | Lesson 4: Wrong! (It's maths!) | Lesson 5: Right!

Einstieg Ex 2
(SB geschl.) L stellt Hörauftrag: *Let's listen to a rap song. It's a school rap. Listen and find out:* (**Multiple choice** an Tafel oder per Folie vorgeben)
It's a song about ...
(a) school rooms
(b) lessons at school
(c) teachers
Erarb. Ex 2a
(SB offen) **1. Hören** (Globalverstehen), Lösung des Hörauftrags: *(b) is correct.* S lesen Text leise murmelnd mit: Buzz reading.
2. Hören: S singen laut mit (zusätzlich möglich: Singen zur Instrumentalversion, Track 1.21).
Erarb. Ex 2b S nennen (auf D) die Schulfächer aus dem Rap, die sie kennen.

Vorentlastung Ex 3
Semantisieren unbekannter Wörter, z. B. durch Flashcards.
Einstieg Ex 3
(SB geschl.) L zeigt auf Stundenplan im Klassenzimmer: *This is your timetable. Lesson one on Monday is German / ... What's lesson two on Monday / Tuesday / ...?* Reaktivierung der *days of the week* (aus Grundschule).
Erarb. Ex 3a
(SB offen) Klären der AA, Semantisieren von *right / wrong* an einem Bsp. Dann Vorlesen je einer Aussage, S lesen mit, melden sich und ordnen *right/wrong* zu.
Erarb. Ex 3b Beim **1. Hören** rufen S die Lösung in die Sprechpausen.
Ausw. Ex 3b 2. Hören im Zusammenhang; Kontrolle anhand des Audios.

1 [egˈbʌklənd kəˈmjuːnəti kɒlɪdʒ]

Lernschwerpunkt: Formen von *be* mit Personalpronomen verwenden

Storyline: Mit einem Quiz über das *Eggbuckland Community College* erarbeiten die S die Personalpronomen sowie die positiven und negativen Formen von *be*.

Kompetenzen: Reading Quizfragen verstehen und beantworten | **Writing** Quizfragen verfassen; Schreiben über Freunde oder Haustiere | **Lern- und Arbeitstechniken** Sprachliche Regelmäßigkeiten entdecken

Grammatik: Personalpronomen und Formen von *be* (mit Kurzformen und Verneinung)

Redemittel: Auskunft geben über sich und andere

Einstieg Ex 1 (SB geschl.) L stellt zwei Quizfragen, S antworten: *He's from Plymouth. He's a crab. Who is he? (Cyril) – She's a seagull. She's Cyril's friend. Who is she? (Sandy)* Ggf. Vorentlastung neuen Wortschatzes (über Semantisierungstechniken).
Erarb. Ex 1 (SB offen) Klären der AA, Bearbeitung in EA/PA, Notieren der Lösungen, selbstständige Überprüfung auf SB S. 147 oder im Partner check.
Ausw. Ex 1 im Plenum, L erfragt und lobt Anzahl richtiger Lösungen.

Einstieg Ex 2 (SB offen) Ggf. vorab Bearbeitung eines Beispiels im Plenum: L schreibt Satz 1 an Tafel, S ermitteln Lösung mit Quizkarte 6; L (oder ein S) notiert sie farbig.
Erarb. Ex 2a Abschreiben der Sätze 2–7, Einsetzen fehlender Formen mithilfe der Quizkarten. Differenzierung ○/● möglich über Lerntempoduett.
Ausw. Ex 2a Vergleichen im Plenum über Tafel- oder Folienaufschrieb der fehlenden Formen; S korrigieren ggf. eigene Lösungen.
Erarb. Ex 2b (SB offen) Induktive Regelfindung ausgehend von Lösungen in a) – für positive Aussagen.
Ausw. Ex 2b Einzelne S tragen selbst formulierte Regeln vor. Ergänzend gemeinsames Lesen des Parts im *Language file* (SB S. 166/167).

1 FOCUS ON LANGUAGE

▸ *KV 1.2* ▸ *INKL 1.6* ▸ *INKL 1.7*

1 The unit quiz

How many questions can you answer?
You can work with a partner. Write your answers.
Check your answers on page 147.

1. It's in England. It's a city. It starts with 'P'. What is it?
2. We're two girls in class 7Y. We aren't sisters. Who are we?
3. He's a student at Eggy. He's ten. Who is he?
4. They're brothers. They aren't Adam and Zack[1]. Who are they?
5. He isn't a student. He's a pony. Who is he?
6. I'm at Eggy too. I'm not a student, I'm an English teacher. Who am I?
7. She isn't from Plymouth. She's from Woolwell. Who is she?
8. They're four new students in class 7Y. Who are they?
9. She's a girl. She's six. She isn't at Eggy. Who is she?
10. I'm a girl. I'm not eleven – I'm twelve. Who am I?
11. It's a lesson. It isn't in a classroom. It's in the sports hall. What is it?
12. You're a student. You aren't at Eggy. What's your name?

1 Plymouth | 2 Ellie and Berry | 3 Luca | 4 Luca and Jack | 5 Harry (Berry's pet) | 6 Ms Lee | 7 Berry | 8 Ellie, Berry, Luca, Adam | 9 Grace (Luca's sister) | 10 Ellie | 11 PE | 12 (student's name)

2 'm 's 're = Yes

a) Complete the sentences.

1 I... at Eggy too. (Card 6)
2 You... a student. (12)
3 He... ten. (3)
4 She... from Woolwell. (7)
5 It... in England. (1)
6 We... two girls in Class 7Y. (2)
7 They... brothers. (4)

1 I'm | 2 You're | 3 He's | 4 She's | 5 It's | 6 We're | 7 They're

b) Make the rule with: *'m • 's • 're*

FOCUS Yes
I + ...
he / she / it + ...
we / you / they + ...

I + 'm
he / she / it + 's
we / you / they + 're

3 'm not isn't aren't = No

a) Complete the sentences.

1 I... eleven – I'm twelve. (Card 10)
2 You ... at Eggy. (12)
3 He ... a student. (5)
4 She ... from Plymouth. (7)
5 It ... in a classroom. (11)
6 We ... sisters. (2)
7 They ... Adam and Zack. (4)

1 I'm not | 2 You aren't | 3 He isn't | 4 She isn't | 5 It isn't | 6 We aren't | 7 They aren't

b) Make the rule with: *'m not • isn't • aren't*

FOCUS No
I + ...
he / she / it + ...
we / you / they + ...

I + am not
he / she / it + isn't
we / you / they + aren't

▸ *Language file 2, pp. 166–167*

Erarb. und **Ausw. Ex 3a+b** analog **Ex 2a+b**. Abschließend Einsatz von KV1.2 zur Festigung möglich (ggf. als HA).

[1] [zæk]

▸ *Workbook 8, p. 11*

Zeitbedarf: ca. drei Stunden
Minimalversion: Ex **1–5**, **6a**
Kooperative Lernformen: Partner check optional in Ex **1** und **4**
Materialbedarf: Ex **2**: (optional) leere Folie, Farbstifte, OH-Projektor | Ex **7**: Karteikarten
Einsatz von Begleitmedien: KV 1.2 | INKL 1.6–1.7 | Folie 9 | Workbook S. 11–12

Ex 4 ist eine Parallelübung auf zwei Niveaus: ○ hier und ● auf S. 121.
Ausw. Ex 4 Lösungsvergleich im Partner check, anschließend Vorlesen der komplettierten Sätze im Plenum.

1

▸ Folie 9

4 ○ At Eggy //● p. 121

Put in: *He* • *She* • *It* • *They*

1 Eggy is my new school. ...'s big.
2 Ellie is a new student at Eggy. ...'s cool.
3 Mr Brown is at Eggy too. ...'s our ICT teacher.
4 Mrs Ford isn't our English teacher. ...'s our art teacher.
5 Adam and Berry aren't in the classroom. ...'re in the sports hall.
6 Look at our new books. ...'re nice. More practice 2 p. 121

Lösungen: 1 It, 2 She, 3 He, 4 She, 5 They, 6 They

▸ Language file 1, p. 166

5 Pets and friends

a) Put in: *'m* • *'s* • *'re* Box: Voc., p. 186

Hi, I... (1) Berry. Remember Harry? He... (2) my pony. Connie and William are our ponies too. They... (3) fun. Connie is old. She... (4) seventeen. William is five. He... (5) small. Harry is twelve. He... (6) big. He... (7) my favourite pony. But we... (8) all friends.

Lösungen: 1 'm, 2 's, 3 're, 4 's, 5 's, 6 's, 7 's, 8 're

b) ● Write about your friend or pet. More help p. 122

Bei Tieren, zu denen man eine persönliche Beziehung hat (z.B. Haustiere), sagt man *he* oder *she*, also merke:
dog → it
Charlie → he

6 People and places in Plymouth

a) Write about the people and places in Plymouth – as many sentences as you can.

Plymouth Eggy Cyril Sandy Mr Brown Ellie and Berry Luca and Adam Ms Lee and Mr Brown	isn't aren't	students. a seagull. teachers. in Germany. girls. a crab. a maths teacher. in London.

Lösungsbsp. S. 232

b) ● Write more sentences: *Plymouth isn't in Germany. It's in England.* More help p. 122

7 Make a quiz for the class

a) ● Write quiz cards – as many as you can. More help p. 122

It's a lesson.
It isn't English.
It's lesson one on Friday. What is it?

She's in our class.
She isn't from Halle.
She's from Berlin.
Who is she?

They're best friends.
They're in our class.
They aren't girls.
Who are they?

Maths.
Paul and Leo.
Sandra.

b) Read a card for the class. Who/What is it?

Erarb. Ex 5a Stilles Lesen des Texts im Zusammenhang, dann Abschreiben der Sätze und Einfügen der Kurzformen von *be* (auch mündlich möglich).
Ausw. Ex 5a Partner check der schriftl. Lösungen, anschließend Vorlesen der komplettierten Sätze im Plenum.
Überleitung zu **Ex 5b** L: *Who has a pet at home? What is it?* L spricht über (fiktives) Haustier (Art, Alter, ...) → weiteres Muster für Ex 5b.

Erarb. Ex 6a Klären der AA, L/S gibt mündlich Beispiele für die Satzbildung mit der *substitution table*. S notieren still so viele negative Aussagesätze wie möglich.
Ausw. Ex 6a Vorlesen und Vergleichen im Plenum.
Erarb. Ex 6b Erst mündl. Bilden von Satzpaaren: je Positiv- und (als Korrektur) Negativaussage, dann Schreiben eigener Paare.

Einstieg Ex 7a L gibt Bsp. vor *(a mouse)*: *It's an animal. It's grey. It isn't big. What is it?*
Erarb. Ex 7a Lesen der Muster im Plenum, dann Verfassen eigener Karten.
Ausw. in **Ex 7b** Abwechselnd: Wer eine Karte errät, trägt die nächste vor.

STORY Navigator | Inhalt

Lernschwerpunkt: Über englische Schuluniformen und ihre Teile sprechen

Storyline: Ellie hat ihre Krawatte vergessen, worauf sie mehrmals hingewiesen wird. Das Tragen der kompletten Schuluniform ist in *Eggy* Pflicht, wie fast überall in Großbritannien. Lucas Idee: Basteln einer Tageskrawatte für Ellie im Kunstunterricht.

Kompetenzen: Speaking Kleidungsstücke benennen; die eigene Meinung zu Schuluniformen äußern; *scenic play* | **Reading** (Bildgestütztes) Verstehen einer Geschichte und Beantworten von Fragen dazu | **Lern- und Arbeitstechniken** Eine Wortschatzliste anlegen

Redemittel: Wortfeld *clothes*, Schuluniformen und ihre Bestandteile; Bilder beschreiben; Meinungen äußern

Einstieg Ex 1 (SB geschl.) Bei geringen Vorkenntnissen das Wortfeld *clothes* semantisieren (mit realen Gegenständen oder Flashcards); Lautschulung durch Chorsprechen.
Erarb. Ex 1 (SB offen) L: *Look at the shop window. What (clothes:* ggf. als Oberbegriff einführen) *can you see?* Versprachlichung der Abb. in PA gemäß Muster (auch schriftlich möglich).
Ausw. Ex 1 Meldekette im Plenum (ein Satz pro S).
Überleitung zur **STORY** (SB geschl.) L: *Students at English schools have school uniforms. The uniform is important – the students must wear it at school all day. Every school has a special uniform – in special colours. What colour is the uniform at Eggy?* S: *It's red and black.*
Einstieg STORY (SB offen): S beschreiben Bilder; unbekannten WS über Semantisierungstechniken erschließen. Hilfen (evtl. an der Tafel): *In photo 1/2/... I can see ... They're ...*
Erarb. STORY (SB offen) L: *Ellie has a problem. Read the text and find out: What is her problem?*
1. Lesen (ggf. Hören und Mitlesen) und Beantworten, z. B.: *Ellie has no tie, but she needs a tie. / Ellie's tie is at home. The uniform is important.* Dann **2. Lesen** mit verteilten Rollen.

1 STORY

▸ *INKL 1.8*

1 Before you read

What can you see?

I can see a green ... / black ...

blazer • pullover[1] • shirt • shoes • skirt • socks • sweatshirt • tie • tights • trousers

Lösungsbsp. S. 232

Box: Voc., p. 187

The uniform[2] is important!

1.23

1

It's assembly at Eggy.

Miss Borowski[3] — Good morning, boys and girls. I'm Miss Borowski, the school principal[4]. I hope you're happy at this school. Please remember – the uniform is important!

Ellie — Oh no! My tie!

2

Assembly is over.

Miss B — Hello. What's your name?

Ellie — Hello, Miss Borowski. I'm Ellie Cole.

Miss B — Where's your tie, Ellie?

Ellie — Sorry. It's at home.

Miss B — That isn't good, Ellie. Remember – the uniform is important!

Box: Voc., p. 187

3

In the English lesson ...

Luca — Where's your tie, Ellie?

Ellie — It's at home.

Luca — The uniform is important!

Ellie — I know, I know.

4

In the science lesson ...

Berry — Where's your tie, Ellie?

Ellie — It's at home.

Berry — Oh, but the uniform is ...

Ellie — ... important! I know, I know.

1 [ˈpʊləʊvə] 2 [ˈjuːnɪfɔːm] 3 [bəˈrɒvski] 4 [ˈprɪnsəpl]

STORY Navigator | Vorbereitung

Zeitbedarf: ca. zwei Stunden
Minimalversion: Ex **1–3**
Kooperative Lernformen: Scenic play Ex **5**
Materialbedarf: **Story**: (optional) Audio-CD + Player oder MP3 + PC/Lautsprecher; Ex **5**: Requisiten, Poster, Klebepunkte
Einsatz von Begleitmedien: KV 1.3 | INKL 1.8 | Folie 10 | Workbook S. 13

► KV 1.3 ► Folie 10 ► INKL 1.8

5

In the art lesson ...

Ellie — Look, Adam – no tie. It's at home.
Adam — That's bad, Ellie.
Ellie — I know, I know. The uniform is important!
Luca — Hey, I have an idea.
Berry — What's your idea, Luca?
Luca — We need paper, scissors[5], colours, ...

Box: Voc., p. 187

6

In the canteen ...

Berry — I like your tie, Ellie.
Adam — Yes, it's a cool tie.
Luca — Nice colours.
Ellie — Thanks, guys.
Miss B — A very nice tie, Ellie.
Ellie — Thanks, Miss Borowski.
Miss B — But it isn't the school tie.
All — The uniform is important!
Miss B — Yes, that's right.

2 People in the story

1 Who has no tie?
2 Who has a good idea?
3 Who has a cool tie?
4 Who says, "Where's your tie?"?
5 Who says, "The uniform is important!"?

More practice 3 p. 123

1 Ellie | 2 Luca | 3 Ellie | 4 Miss Borowski, Luca, Berry | 5 Miss Borowski (scene 1 + 2), Luca (3), Berry and Ellie (4), all students (6)

3 Uniforms: What do you think?

1 I think uniforms are a good / bad idea.
2 I like / don't like the Eggy uniform.
3 Our school has no uniform. That's good / bad.
4 I think ties are / aren't cool.
5 I like / don't like Ellie's tie.

4 Eggy uniform words

Finish the lists in your exercise book.

Uniforms

for boys and girls	for girls
pullover	...

Lösungsbsp. S. 232

5 THEATRE[6] TIME

a) Make groups of six students: Ellie, Luca, Adam, Berry, Miss Borowski and a narrator. Read the scenes.

b) Act the scenes for the class. What's the best group?

More practice 4 p. 123

Erarb. Ex 2 (SB offen) schriftlich in EA oder mündlich in PA.
Ausw. Ex 2 Meldekette: S1 stellt erste Frage, S2 antwortet und stellt nächste Frage etc.

Einstieg Ex 3 L: *The uniform is important at Eggy. What do **you** think about school uniforms?*
Erarb. Ex 3 Stilles Lesen der 5 *statements*, dann Vervollständigen gemäß eigener Meinung. Auch als schriftliche **HA** möglich.
Ausw. Ex 3 Meldekette: Zu jedem *statement* äußern sich nacheinander 2–3 S (ggf. an der Tafel notieren) → Meinungsbild der Klasse.

Erarb. Ex 4 Ggf. Hinweis auf Hilfe in der Box von S. 24 oben. Auch als schriftl. **HA** möglich.

Einstieg Ex 5 L: *It's theatre time: Let's act the scenes of the story for the class.* Dann Mustervortrag einer Szene mit betonter Mimik/Gestik.
Erarb. Ex 5 L: *What's important when you act a scene?* (Kriterien auf KV 1.3) Arbeit in Sechser-Gruppen: in verteilten Rollen lesen und einüben, dann Aufführung vor Klasse (scenic play).
Ausw. Ex 5 S nutzen KV 1.3 zur Einschätzung der je anderen Gruppen, ermitteln so die *best group*.

► Workbook 14–16, p. 13

5 ['sɪzəz] 6 ['θɪətə]

Lernschwerpunkt: **Einer Broschüre Informationen entnehmen**
Kompetenzen: Reading Skimming (Globalverstehen); Texten gezielt Informationen entnehmen (Detailverstehen)
Lern- und Arbeitstechniken Kurznotizen (Liste) anfertigen
Mediation (E>D) Fragen mit Hilfe des Texts beantworten
Redemittel: Werbung, *school things*

Zeitbedarf: ca. eine Stunde
Minimalversion: Ex **1–3**
Kooperative Lernformen: Partner talk (optional in **3a**)
Materialbedarf: Ex **1**: (optional) deutschsprachige Werbeprospekte
Ex **3a**: eigenes Federmäppchen der S
Einsatz von Begleitmedien: DFF 1.1, 1.7 | Folie 11

Einstieg Ex 1 (SB geschl.) *brochure* über die Ähnlichkeit zum D semantisieren.
Alternative Zeigen deutschsprachiger Prospekte: *Look at this brochure. What is it for? What can you buy in this shop?*
Überleitung *Let's read an English brochure.*
Erarb. Ex 1 (SB offen) Broschüre betrachten, Auswahl der Lösung (Globalverstehen).
Ausw. Ex 1 Lösung im Plenum nennen, ggf. auch Hinweise auf *shop* (Bilder, Überschriften).

Erarb. Ex 2 (SB offen) **1. Lesen** (selektives Verstehen) S notieren, was sie für den Mathe-Unterricht bzw. zu bestimmten Preisen kaufen würden.
Ausw. Ex 2 L erfragt Antworten im Plenum, lässt S erklären, wie sie auf die Lösung kommen.

Einstieg Ex 3 (SB geschl.) L lässt raten: *What's in my pencil case?* → Liste mit Nennungen der S an Tafel; dann Zeigen, Benennen, ggf. Abhaken der Inhalte.
Erarb. Ex 3a S schreiben Liste zur eigenen *pencil case.*
Ausw. Ex 3a Liste im Plenum vorlesen.
Alternative Partner talk: *I have ... – I have ... too / I don't have (a) ...*

1 SKILLS TRAINING Reading

► *DFF 1.1* ► *DFF 1.7* ► *Folie 11*

1 A brochure[1]

Lösung: C

Before you read: What's Martins? (A) a book? (B) a school? (C) a shop?

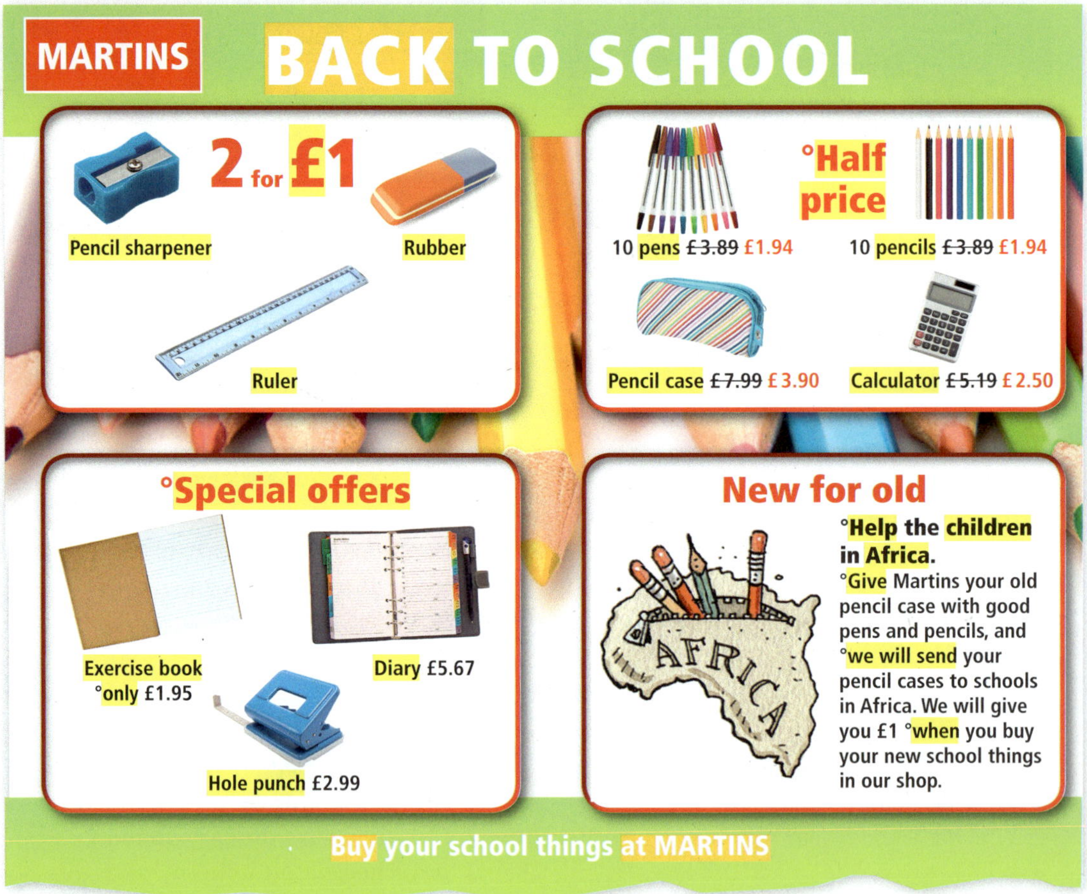

2 School things at Martins

Lösungsbsp. S. 232

Look at the brochure.
What can you buy for ...
1 maths lessons? → *a pencil, ...*
2 half price?

Erarb. Ex 4 (SB offen) Information auffinden, Lösung nennen.
Ausw. Ex 4 Lösungshinweise nennen (Abb., Signalwörter).

3 Your school things

a) Make a list of the things in your pencil case: *a ruler, ...*

b) You can buy some things at Martins. You have £10. Write a shopping list.

4 MEDIATION Help children in Africa

Wie kannst du Mädchen und Jungen aus Afrika mit der Aktion *New for old* helfen? Wähle (A), (B) oder (C).

(A) Schicke dein Federmäppchen an eine Schule in Afrika.
(B) Kaufe bei Martins so viele neue Dinge wie möglich.
(C) Martins schickt dein altes Federmäppchen an eine Schule in Afrika.

1 ['brəʊʃə]

► *Text file 2, pp. 150–151*

Lernschwerpunkt: Systematische Wortschatzarbeit lernen und üben

Kompetenzen: Lern- und Arbeitstechniken
Formen der Wortschatzarbeit kennenlernen und anwenden: *networks*, Vokabelkarten, gegenseitiges Abfragen

Redemittel: Wortfelder *days* und *school*

Zeitbedarf: ca. eine Stunde

Kooperative Lernformen: Partner check Ex **1b**
Partnerarbeit (optional) Ex **2a/b**, Ex **2d**

Materialbedarf: Ex **2:** Musterkasten mit Vokabelkarten
Ex **2a**: (optional) leere Vokabelkarte zum Vorführen der Beschriftung | Ex **2c**: Schuhkarton o. Ä.

Einsatz von Begleitmedien: KV 1.4 | Workbook S. 14 | DFF 1.8 | INKL 1.10

SKILLS TRAINING Learning words

1

▸ KV 1.4 ▸ DFF 1.8 ▸ INKL 1.9 ▸ INKL 1.10

1 Make networks

a) ○ Copy the network.
Complete it with words from the box.

Friday • Monday • school days • Thursday • Tuesday • weekend

Besonders gut behält man Vokabeln, wenn man sie aufschreibt, zum Beispiel in einem *network* (Aufgabe 1) oder auf kleinen Kärtchen (Aufgabe 2).

b) ● Now copy this school network. Find words for every group – as many as you can.
Then compare networks with your partner. More help p. 124

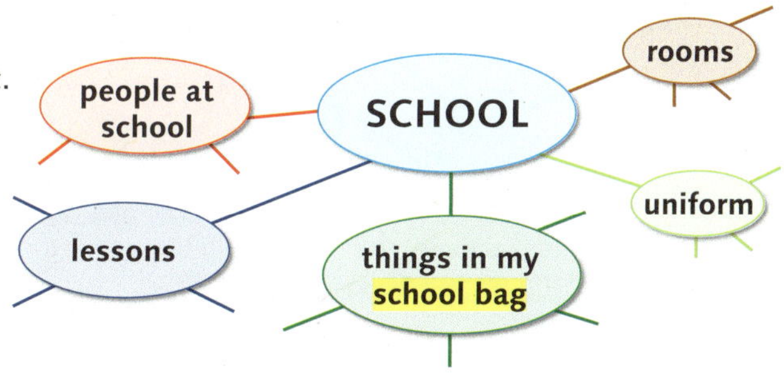

2 Make word and phrase cards

a) Pick words and phrases from the green box and make cards.

Nice to meet you.
Have a good day.
How are you?
Fine, thanks.
See you later.
Good morning.
Hello.
I'm in class 5.
Sorry.
Welcome to our school.
Thanks.
I'm from Germany.
We're best friends.
What's your name?
That's right.
I have an idea.
I know.
It's at home.

b) Write the German phrase on the back of the card.

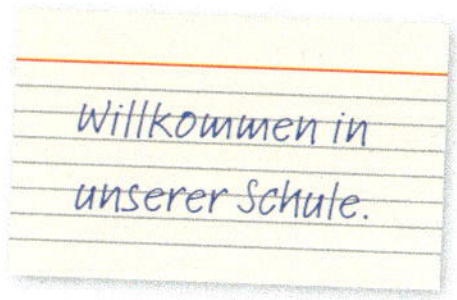

c) Put the cards in a box.

d) Swap cards with your partner. Ask your partner to check you. Then check your partner.

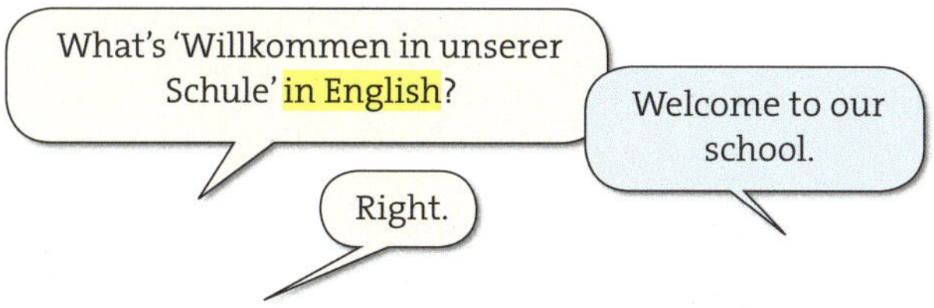

Lerne Vokabeln regelmäßig – lieber jeden Tag 5–10 Minuten als einmal die Woche zwei Stunden.
Mehr Tipps zum Wörterlernen findest du im *Skills file*.

▸ Skills file 1, pp. 160–161

▸ Workbook 17–18, p. 14

Einstieg Ex 1 (SB geschl.) S beschreiben, wie sie bisher Vokabeln lernen (D).
Überleitung: *You can collect new words in a network.*
Erarb. Ex 1a (SB offen) S notieren *DAYS-network* im Heft und ergänzen es aus der grünen Box.
Ausw. Ex 1a *DAYS-network* an Tafel oder auf Folie im Plenum ergänzen (ggf. im ganzen Satz, z. B. *I think … goes with …*).

Erarb. Ex 1b (SB offen) *SCHOOL-network* im Heft notieren und vervollständigen (alternativ auf KV 1.4, auch als HA möglich); More help p. 124 bietet Schwächeren Vokabeln zum Einsetzen.
Ausw. Ex 1b im Partner check: dabei nicht abschreiben, sondern gegenseitig vorlesen → Lautschulung.

Einstieg Ex 2 L zeigt an Musterkasten mit vorbereiteten Vokabelkarten die Verwendung und erklärt Vorteile (D).
Erarb. Ex 2a/b/c S: Arbeitsanweisung lesen, Abb. betrachten; L zeigt ggf. einzelne Beschriftungsschritte (vorn/hinten). S verfahren analog (ggf. in PA).
Ausw. Ex 2d Zwei S fragen sich im Plenum ab (Rechtschreibung trainieren: Jeder Begriff kann nach Nennung auch aufgeschrieben werden).

SKILLS TRAINING Speaking

Lernschwerpunkt: Alltagsdialoge in der Schule
Kompetenzen: **Listening** Inhaltliches Erfassen eines Dialogs; Dialogteile ordnen | **Speaking** Dialoge über den Schulalltag; Interviews führen | **Writing** Verfassen von Dialogen (mit Hilfen)
Lern- und Arbeitstechniken Notizen in Tabelle anfertigen
Redemittel: Sich begrüßen; etwas leihen; Schulalltag

Zeitbedarf: ca. eine Stunde
Minimalversion: Ex **1a+b** (nur *check*); Ex **2**; Ex **3a+c** (nur über sich selbst Notizen machen und sprechen)
Kooperative Lernformen: Milling-around activity Ex **2**
Materialbedarf: Ex **1**: Audio-CD + Player oder MP3 + PC/ Lautsprecher
Einsatz von Begleitmedien: KV 1.5 | INKL 1.11 | IAT 1.2 Workbook S. 15–16

Einstieg Ex 1 (SB geschl.) L: *Ellie talks to Berry at school. It's their break. What can they talk about?* → Sammeln an Tafel, z. B. *friends, teachers, lessons, ...* WS per Demonstration vorentlasten: *borrow; Here you are*
Erarb. Ex 1a Globalverstehen: Nennen und Abhaken der im Dialog vorkommenden Aspekte; Detailverstehen: Ordnen und Notieren der Antworten.
Erarb. Ex 1b Überprüfen, dann ggf. Aufschreiben des Dialogs.
Erarb. Ex 1c In PA Einüben des Dialogs (Read-and-look-up technique), dann Vortrag.

Erarb. Ex 2 (SB offen) S ergänzen das Dialoggerüst schriftlich in PA. // ● p. 124 Vorgaben auf D für Lernstärkere.
Ausw. Ex 2 2–3 S-Paare spielen ihren Dialog vor. Redemittel zur Kommentierung vorgeben: *I think the dialogue was great / good / OK / not so (very) good / ...*

Einstieg Ex 3 (SB geschl.) L: *Now talk to the students in your class. Here are some ideas for questions.* → Sammeln in Tabelle an Tafel.
Erarb. Ex 3a Abschreiben der Tabelle (oder Einsatz von KV 1.5), Ausfüllen der 1. Spalte.
Erarb. Ex 3b Milling-around activity: Befragen verschiedener Mit-S: ○ nur 2, ● 3–4 Mit-S → Notizen in Tabelle.
Ausw. Ex 3 Meldekette: 1–3 Sätze pro S; **HA:** *Write six sentences about you and your classmates.*

1 SKILLS TRAINING Speaking

▸ KV 1.5 ▸ INKL 1.11

1 Talking to friends at school

1 B • 2 D • 3 E • 4 C • 5 A

1.24

a) First listen. Then put Berry's answers (A–E) in the right order.

1 Hi, Berry. How are you?
2 I'm fine too, thanks. Can I borrow a pen, please?
3 Thanks. What's the next lesson? Box: Voc., p. 189
4 It's science. And who's your favourite teacher?
5 I like Luca.

A I like Luca too.
B Hi, Ellie. I'm fine, thanks. What about you?
C Mr Brown. He's nice. And who's your favourite boy in our class?
D Sure, here you are.
E It's PE. I like PE. What's your favourite lesson?

b) Listen again and check. Then write the dialogue.

c) Practise the dialogue with a partner. Then swap partners.

2 ○ NOW YOU // ● p. 124

Write the dialogue with a partner. Then practise with your partner.

Your names

A: Hi, ... How ... you?
B: Hello, ... I'm OK. What about ...?
A: ... fine, thanks. Can I borrow a ...?
B: Sure, here ...
A: Thanks. ...'s the next lesson?
B: It's ...
A: Oh, good. I like ...

hole punch • pen • pencil • rubber • ruler • ...

English • science • maths • German • history • geography • ...

Lösungsbsp. S. 233

3 Interviews

a) Copy the table and answer the four questions for you.

	ME	NAME: ...	NAME: ...	NAME: ...
1 Who's your favourite teacher?				
2 Who's your best friend in our class?				
3 What's your favourite hobby?				
4 What's your favourite animal?				

Who's ...? = *Wer ist ...?*
What's ...? = *Was ist ...?*

b) Walk around: Ask different partners. Write the names and the answers in the table.

c) Tell the class: My favourite ... Tina's best ... Karim's favourite ...

▸ Workbook 19–23, pp. 15–16

SKILLS TRAINING Viewing

Lernschwerpunkt: **Fiktionale und dokumentarische Filmszenen verstehen**
Kompetenzen: **Viewing** Filmische Szenen und Handlungsfolgen verstehen; dokumentarischen Formaten Informationen entnehmen, thematisch ordnen | **Speaking** Meinungen zum Film äußern
Redemittel: Englischer Schulalltag *(assembly, school uniforms, maths and PE lessons, lunch break)*

Zeitbedarf: ca. eine Stunde
Minimalversion: Ex **1a+b**, Ex **2a**
Kooperative Lernformen: Partner talk Ex **1c, 2a** Partner check Ex **1a** | Gruppenarbeit Ex **2b**
Materialbedarf: DVD + Player oder PC/Lautsprecher
Einsatz von Begleitmedien: KV 1.6 | IAT 1.2

Einstieg Ex 1 (SB geschl.) L zeigt Vorspann als *teaser* (DVD-Menüpunkt: *Play all parts*). Aufgabe: *Watch the film clip and find out: Who are the kids from Harbour Road? Where are they?* → Tafel-Stichpunkte; S beginnen Einträge auf KV 1.6 und ergänzen über die Folgeunits.
Erarb. Ex 1a (SB offen) S notieren vorab die 5 Ortsangaben der Filmstills untereinander; beim **1. Sehen** Ergänzen der Reihenfolge (Ziffern 1–5).
Ausw. Ex 1a Partner check der Ziffern; dann Formulieren ganzer Sätze im Plenum.
Erarb. Ex 1b S ordnen aus der Erinnerung (bzw. spekulativ) zu; Überprüfung beim **2. Sehen.** ◯ Vorentlasten durch gemeinsames Lesen der Sprechblasen. Ggf. **3. Sehen**.
Ausw. Ex 1b Erst Vergleichen der Ziffern, dann Notieren der vollständigen Aussagen.
Erarb. Ex 1c Sammeln bekannter Adjektive an Tafel *(small, old, stupid, happy ...)*, dann Partner talk zu persönlichen Eindrücken.
Ausw. Ex 1c im Plenum, ggf. Abstimmen.

SKILLS TRAINING Viewing

1

▸ *KV 1.6* ▸ *IAT 1.2*

First they're in Harbour Road. • And then they're in Assembly. • Then they're in a maths lesson. • Then they're in the canteen. • And then they're in the sports hall.

1 The kids from Harbour Road[1]: Meet the kids!

a) Watch the film. Where are the kids first? And then?
First they're in ... And then[2] they're in ...

2

assembly

3

the canteen

1

Harbour Road

3

a maths lesson

4

the sports hall

b) Who says what? Match the sentences (1–5) with the kids.

2 • 5 Anna says ...
1 • 3 Paul says ...
4 Sarah says ...

1 It's assembly now.
2 The uniform is important!
3 Maths is my favourite lesson.
4 I like lunch.
5 I love sport.

Then watch again and check.

c) What do you think about the kids? Tell your partner.
Example: Anna is nice / fun / great / cool / ... Sarah is ... I like Sarah. Paul is ....

2 People and places: Eggbuckland Community College

a) Watch the film. What do you think? Talk to a partner.
– I think the school is big / new / nice / terrible[3] / ...
– I think the film is cool / great / OK / boring[4] /...
– I like / don't like the music.

Lösungsbsp. S. 233

b) Watch the film again. Then work in groups. Write a list of things, people, places, lessons, sports that you see in the film – as many as you can. Which group has the best list?

Erarb. Ex 2a (SB offen) **1. Sehen**, dann Partner talk mithilfe vorgegebener Redemittel.
Ausw. Ex 2a Im Plenum
Erarb. Ex 2b In 5 Gruppen (à ca. 5 S) beim **2. Sehen** gemäß AA schriftl. Sammeln (zuerst ungeordnet) → Motivation durch Wettbewerb und Tempo. Anschließend in den Gruppen erstes Ordnen unter die Oberbegriffe *things, people, places, lessons, sports*.
Ausw. Ex 2b Im Plenum: Sammeln der Ergebnisse (Tabelle/Tafel).

[1] Harbour Road [hɑːbə ˈrəʊd] *Hafenstraße* [2] then [ðen] *dann, danach* [3] terrible [ˈterəbl] *schrecklich*
[4] boring [ˈbɔːrɪŋ] *langweilig*

Lernschwerpunkt: **Wiederholen und Üben, Lernfortschritte erkennen (Fokus: Unit 1)**

Kompetenzen: Reading Bilder zu einem Lesetext ordnen; Leseverstehen anhand von *right/wrong statements* überprüfen

Lern- und Arbeitstechniken Eigene Lernfortschritte erkennen

Grammatik: Sätze mit den korrekten Formen von *be* ergänzen

Redemittel: Wortfelder *school; school things; clothes*

Erarb. Ex 1 (SB offen) Ⓐ S notieren untereinander die Ziffern 1–8 und ergänzen die passenden Begriffe für die Teile der Schuluniform. Analoges Verfahren für die Schulgegenstände.

Erarb. Ex 2a (SB offen) S prüfen die vorgegebenen Wortreihen und notieren die „falschen" Wörter in ihrem Heft.
Erarb. Ex 2b (SB offen) S finden für jede Wortreihe mindestens einen weiteren passenden Begriff aus dem Wortfeld Schule und schreiben diesen in ihr Heft.
Erarb. Ex 2c (SB offen) S vervollständigen die Sätze, indem sie individuell auf ihre Situation passende Begriffe hinzufügen.

Erarb. Ex 3a (SB offen) S lesen den Text im rosa Kasten und ordnen zur Sicherung des Globalverstehens die Bilder A–D entsprechend der Themenabfolge.
Erarb. Ex 3b (SB offen) S überprüfen Aussagen zum Lesetext und notieren ihre Einschätzung: *right* (R) bzw. *wrong* (W).

°STOP! °CHECK! GO!

▸ KV 1.8 ▸ DFF 1.1 ▸ DFF 1.2 ▸ INKL 1.12

Ein Lösungsblatt für die Aufgaben 1 bis 9 kannst du von deiner Lehrerin / deinem Lehrer erhalten.
Du findest die Audiodatei (zu S. 32) online, zusammen mit den Workbook-Audiodateien.

1 WORDS School things

°Example: *1 blazer, 2 …, 3 …*

Ⓐ

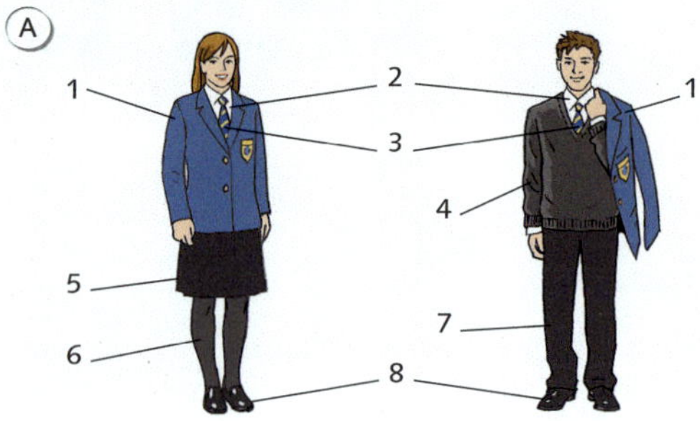

Ⓑ

2 WORDS °More school things

a) What's the wrong word?

1 pen, pencil, shirt, rubber → *shirt*
2 maths, Monday, French, science → …
3 lunch, °badminton, football, tae kwon do[1]
4 science lab, school, classroom, art room
5 assembly, break, lesson, calculator
6 brother, student, teacher, principal

b) Look at a) again. Find more words for 1–6. Example: *1 ruler, …*

c) Finish the sentences.

1 My favourite school day is …
2 My favourite lesson is …
3 I have … in my school bag.

3 READING Remember Cyril[2]?

a) Read the text. Put the pictures (A–D) in the right order.

Hi, I'm Cyril. I'm from Kingsand beach. It's nice. It's near Plymouth. Benny and Babe are my friends. They're from Kingsand too. We're crabs! Oh, look. This is Sandy. She isn't a crab. She's a seagull. Oh no! Mr Johnson is here. He isn't nice. °He likes crabs!

b) Right or wrong?

1 Cyril isn't from London.
2 Kingsand is near Plymouth.
3 Benny and Babe are students.
4 They're crabs.
5 Sandy is a crab too.
6 Mr Johnson is OK.
7 Mr Johnson and Cyril aren't friends.

1 [taɪ kwɒn 'dəʊ] 2 ['sɪrɪl]

Zeitbedarf: ca. zwei Stunden

Einsatz von Begleitmedien: KV 1.8 (**Lösungsschlüssel**, auch für die Hand der S zur selbstständigen Lösungsüberprüfung, ggf. im Partner check) | DFF 1.1–1.3 | INKL 1.12

► *KV 1.8* ► *DFF 1.3* ► *INKL 1.12*

4 LANGUAGE **Remember Sandy?**

Put in: *'m • 's • 're • is • are*

5 LANGUAGE **Remember Ellie?** //● p. 124

Ellie is with her dad. She has some pictures on her mobile. What's the right word?

1 Look, this is / am my new school.
2 It's / 're very big.
3 The students in my class is / are OK.
4 The teachers is / are OK too.
5 This are / is my new friend, Berry.
6 She's / 're great.
7 My friends Ruby and Charlie am / are at my school too.
8 But they aren't / isn't in my class.
9 This is / are my new uniform.
10 It aren't / isn't very nice.

6 LANGUAGE **That's wrong, Sandy!**

Sandy is wrong. Cyril is right. Finish Cyril's sentences.

1 Plymouth is in Germany.
2 Eggy is in London.
3 Cyril, you're a seagull.
4 I'm a crab.
5 Berry and Ellie are teachers.
6 Ms Lee and Mr Brown are students.
7 We're students at Eggy.

1 Plymouth isn't in Germany. – It's in ...
2 Eggy isn't ... – It's in ...
3 I'm ... – I'm ...
4 You ... – You're ...
5 They ... – They're ...
6 They ... – They're ...
7 We ... – ... animals.

Erarb. Ex 4 (SB offen)
S vervollständigen die Lückensätze, indem sie die passenden Formen von *be* auswählen.

Erarb. Ex 5 (SB offen)
S wählen zur Satzvervollständigung aus jeweils zwei angebotenen Formen von *be* die passende aus.
//● p. 124 Lernstärkere bilden selbstständig die passende (positive / negative) Form von *be* und fügen sie in den Lückentext ein.

Erarb. Ex 6 (SB offen)
S berichtigen Sandys Aussagen, indem sie Cyrils Satzanfänge unter Verwendung positiver und negativer Formen von *be* vervollständigen.

Lernschwerpunkt: **Wiederholen und Üben, Lernfortschritte erkennen (Fokus: Unit 1)**
Kompetenzen: Listening Einen Hörtext global erfassen und passende Bilder auswählen; Fragen und Antworten zuordnen
Speaking Im Dialog fehlende Informationen erfragen und notieren | **Writing** Einen unvollständigen Vorstellungsdialog ergänzen
Lern- und Arbeitstechniken Eigene Lernfortschitte erkennen
Redemittel: Mini-Konversationen (sich vorstellen, über Schulisches sprechen)

Eintieg Ex 7 (SB offen) S benennen vor dem **1. Hören** zunächst im Plenum die abgebildeten Gegenstände. L gibt Bsp. und Redemittel vor: *Number 1/2/ … is a …*
Erarb. Ex 7a **1. Hören** des Textes. S notieren die Nummern der Dinge, über die sich Adam und Luca unterhalten.
Erarb. Ex 7b S ordnen den Fragen 1–6 (links) die passende Antwort A–F (rechts) zu und notieren die Frage-Antwort-Paare (alternativ in Kurzform: Zahl + Buchstabe). Überprüfung durch **2. Hören**. (Ggf. erst danach Notieren der kompletten Sätze; als HA möglich.)

Erarb. Ex 8 (SB offen) S schreiben vervollständigte Lückensätze ins Heft. Überprüfung im Partner check möglich.

Erarb. Ex 9 (SB offen) Variante in **PA**: Beide Partner notieren den kompletten Dialog; alternativ in **EA**, ggf. als HA. Optional: anschließender Vortrag des Dialogs durch einzelne S-Paare.

STOP! CHECK! GO!

▸ KV 1.8 ▸ DFF 1.4 ▸ DFF 1.5 ▸ INKL 1.12

7 °LISTENING Adam and Luca

1.25

a) Listen. What things are Adam and Luca talking about? Write 1–10.

1

2

3

4

5

6

7

8

9

10

b) Match Adam's and Luca's questions and answers. Then listen and check.

1 How are you?
2 I like the Kaiser Chiefs. What about you?
3 What's your hobby?
4 Who's your favourite teacher?
5 What's the next lesson?
6 Can I borrow your calculator, please?

A I like football.
B Sorry, it's at home.
C French.
D I'm fine, thanks.
E They're OK.
F Ms Lee. She's great.

8 WORDS Talking to friends

Complete the mini-dialogues.

1 Hi. How are …? – I'm fine, thanks.
2 Welcome … our school. – Thanks.
3 I'm in … 7B. – Me too.
4 See … later. – OK, see you.
5 I like … sweatshirt. – Oh, thanks.
6 I'm Emma. – … to meet you, Emma.
7 What's the next …? – It's maths.
8 Have a … day. – You too.

9 °WRITING A °dialogue[1] with a new student

Write a dialogue. What can Berry say? What can Tamara say?

Berry	Tamara
– Hi – I – Berry What – name?	– Tamara I – from London What – you?
– I – from Woolwell I – class 7Y What – you?	– class 7D favourite lesson?
– I – science … you?	– history
– See – later – Tamara	– OK – you

More help p. 125

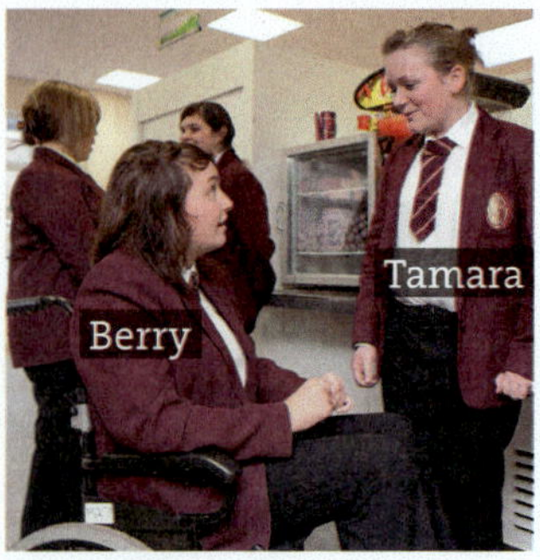

1 ['daɪəlɒg]

Zeitbedarf: ca. zwei Stunden
Kooperative Lernformen: Partner check (optional) Ex **8** | Info-gap activity Ex **10**
Materialbedarf: Ex **7**: Audio-CD + Player oder MP3 + PC/Lautsprecher
Einsatz von Begleitmedien: KV 1.8 (Lösungsschlüssel, auch für die Hand der S zur selbstständigen Lösungsüberprüfung, ggf. im Partner check), KV 1.7 | DFF 1.4–1.6 | INKL 1.12 | Workbook S. 17–20

► KV 1.7 ► DFF 1.6 ► INKL 1.12

10 °SPEAKING A timetable

a) Partner B: Look at page 118.

Partner A: Copy this timetable into your exercise book. Some lessons are missing. Ask partner B. Complete the timetable. And answer partner B's questions.

Lesson	Monday	Tuesday	Wednesday	Thursday	Friday
1	English	....	technology	geography	....
2	....	English	history	....	PE
3	science	history	....	music	....
4	....	....	maths	....	German
5	German	German	maths	science	technology

Check your answers with your partner's timetable.

b) Write your timetable in English.

► Wordbank 3, p. 174

11 My °learner log

Write your learner log. You can put it in your DOSSIER.

Im *learner log* schreibst du auf, was du gelernt hast, was du jetzt gut kannst und was noch nicht so gut geht. Führe dein *learner log* regelmäßig. Wichtig: Versuche immer ehrlich zu antworten!

My learner log

I THINK ENGLISH IS:
– OK.

MY FAVOURITE °CHARACTER[2]:
– Berry

MY FAVOURITE PHRASES:
– That's cool!
– See you later.
– Have a good day!
– How are you?

MY FAVOURITE WORDS:
– timetable
– lunch
– Eggy
– pony

DIFFICULT WORDS:
– scissors
– trousers
– remember
– science

I REMEMBER:
Lessons: French, German, English, history, ...
School things: pens, pencils, books, ...
Uniform words: pullover, shirt, shoes, ...
Animals: dog, cat, snake, ...
Colours: red, black, green, ...

°I'M GOOD AT:
– Listening, reading

I'M NOT GOOD AT:
– Speaking, writing

°I'M OK AT:
– Words, language

Erarb. Ex 10a (SB offen) Info-gap activity: Partner B arbeitet auf S. 118) und beantwortet mit dortigem Stundenplan die Fragen von Partner A. Dann übernimmt Partner B die Rolle des Fragenden zur Vervollständigung der Lücken im eigenen Stundenplan. **Alternative** S arbeiten mit KV 1.7 (Vorlage der Stundenpläne für A/B zum Eintragen). **Erarb. Ex 10b** (SB offen) S erstellen – ggf. mithilfe der *Wordbank* 3, S. 174 – schriftlich ihren eigenen Stundenplan.

Erarb. Ex 11 (SB offen) **My learner log** steht am Ende jeder Unit und dient der Dokumentation des individuellen Lernfortschritts. Hier finden die S ein ausgefülltes Muster und Tipps zum Führen des **learner logs**.

► Workbook pp. 17–20

2 ['kærəktə]

LEAD-IN Navigator | **Inhalt**

Lernschwerpunkt: Familie und Wohnen in Großbritannien am Beispiel von Ellie

Storyline: Ellie lebt mit ihrer Mutter in einer Patchwork-Familie und ist unglücklich über ihre beengte Wohnsituation. Ihr Vater bietet ihr eine Alternative an.

Kompetenzen: Listening Dialogen wesentliche Informationen entnehmen, Bilder zuordnen | **Speaking** Wohnungen und Häuser beschreiben, ein eigenes Traumhaus vorstellen

Redemittel: Wohnen, Räume benennen, Bilder beschreiben

Einstieg Ex 1 (SB geschl.) Vorentlastung neuen WS im Unterrichtsgespräch zur Wohnsituation der S. L: *Where do you live? In a house or in a flat? What is your bedroom like? ...* Lautschulung durch Nachsprechen.
Alternative: Vorentlastung anhand von KV 2.1 (als Folie). L: *Look at this house. How many rooms can you see? ...*
Überleitung: L: *Let's find out where Ellie lives.*
Erarb. Ex 1a (SB offen) Partner talk.
Ausw. Ex 1a Einige S-Paare stellen ihre Ergebnisse im Plenum vor.
Erarb. Ex 1b **1. Hören** (Globalverstehen): S notieren die Nummern der Bilder. Abgleich im Plenum.
Erarb. Ex 1c (SB offen) S schreiben die Satznummern ins Heft. Dann **2. Hören** (Detailverstehen): S notieren R für *right* und W für *wrong* hinter die Satznummern.
Ausw. Ex 1c Erstkontrolle durch Partner check. Anschließend Abgleich im Plenum, z. B. mithilfe von Right/wrong cards.
● Lernstärkere korrigieren die falschen Sätze.

Unit 2

At home with Ellie

▸ IAT 2.1 ▸ KV 2.1

1

2

Box: Voc., p.189

5

6

1 Homes

a) Talk to a partner about the eight photos on pages 34–35. Lösungsbsp. S. 233

– What can you see? – What do you like?	– In photo 1/... I can see a – I like/don't like the	big small ...	house/flat/ kitchen/bedroom/ garden/living room

1.26 **b)** **Listen. Ellie is with Berry. What photos (1–8) show Ellie's house? Write the numbers.**

1, 4, 5, 7, 8

c) **Listen again. What's right? What's wrong?**

1 Ellie's mum has a house.
2 The house is in Greatfield Street.
3 Ellie lives in Hill Road.
4 Ellie lives with her dad.
5 Ellie's bedroom is small.
6 Ellie is happy with her bedroom.

1 Right. • **2** Wrong. (Hill Road.) • **3** Right. • **4** Wrong. (with her mum, her partner and her brother and sister) • **5** Right. • **6** Wrong. (Ellie is not happy. / The bedroom is too small. / Ellie wants her own bedroom.)

LEAD-IN Navigator | Vorbereitung

Zeitbedarf: ca. zwei Stunden

Kooperative Lernformen: Partner talk Ex **1a** | Milling-around activity Ex **3b**

Materialbedarf: Ex **1–2**: Audio-CD + Player oder MP3 + PC/Lautsprecher | Ex **2**: (optional) OH-Projektor (Kopie der SB-Bilder auf Folie bzw. Ausschnitt per Smartboard) | Ex **3**: Zeichenpapier, Buntstifte, (optional) Prospekte, Zeitschriften

Einsatz von Begleitmedien: KV 2.1 | IAT 2.1| DFF 2.2| INKL 2.1 | Workbook S. 21

2

► *KV 2.1* ► *DFF 2.2* ► *INKL 2.1*

3

4

7

8

2 A new flat

1.27

a) Listen to Ellie and her dad. Point at the right photos (1–8). 2, 3, 6

b) Listen again. Find words in the box for the pictures (A–C):

A

B

C

a hall • a °balcony[1] • a toilet • a bathroom • a garage[2]

A a toilet. • B a balcony • C a bathroom

3 ACTIVITY My dream house

a) Draw your dream house. Make room labels.

More help p. 125

b) Walk around: Talk to different partners about your picture.

My dream house is big. It has three bedrooms, two bathrooms and a garden. The garden is ...

It's nice / big / cool.

► *Workbook 1–3, p. 21*

1 ['bælkəni] 2 ['gærɑːʒ]

Einstieg Ex 2 (SB geschl.) Unterrichtsgespräch zu Ellies Wohnsituation. L: *Can you remember where Ellie lives? Who does she live with? Is she happy? Why (not)? Ellie's dad doesn't live there. Let's find out where he lives.*
Erarb. Ex 2a (SB offen) Klären der AA; Vorgehen demonstrieren (*point at*); **1. Hören** (Globalverstehen): S zeigen auf die passenden Bilder (z. B. Folien-Kopie der SB-Bilder) oder notieren die Ziffern der genannten Bilder.
Erarb. Ex 2b Gemeinsames Lesen der Wörter im Kasten und Lautschulung durch Nachsprechen; **2. Hören** (Detailverstehen): S notieren die passenden Wörter.

Einstieg Ex 3 (SB geschl.)
L: *Let's see what your dream house looks like.*
Erarb. Ex 3a (SB offen) S gestalten und beschriften ihr Traumhaus. Sie können auch Möbel aus Prospekten ausschneiden. Alternative: Zeitersparnis durch KV 2.1.
Ausw. in **Ex 3b** (SB geschlossen) Milling-around activity. Freiwillige S stellen ihr Traumhaus im Plenum vor.

THEME 1 Navigator | Inhalt

Lernschwerpunkt: Über die Familie erzählen

Storyline: Ellies Familie wird vorgestellt: Sie wohnt mit ihrer Mutter Jackie, ihrem Stiefvater Pete und zwei Stiefgeschwistern (Zoe, Conor) in einem Haus zusammen. Ihr Vater Steve lebt getrennt mit neuer Partnerin (Alisha) und Baby Finn.

Kompetenzen: Speaking Über die Familie erzählen | **Reading** Texten und Grafiken (Stammbaum) gezielt Informationen entnehmen

Writing Einen eigenen Stammbaum erstellen und über die Familie schreiben

Lern- und Arbeitstechniken Wörter gruppieren und in Listen schreiben

Grammatik: Vorbewusste Verwendung der Possessivpronomen

Redemittel: Verwandtschaftsbezeichnungen, *there's / there are*, Possessivpronomen

Einstieg Ex 1 (SB offen) L: *Let's find out more about Ellie's family.*
Erarb. Ex 1a Anhand der *Pre-reading*-Fragen äußern S ihre Vermutungen im Plenum und überprüfen sie beim **1. Lesen**/Hören (Globalverstehen), ggf. im Mitleseverfahren.
● Lernstärkere S benennen alle weiteren Personen auf den Bildern.
Erarb. Ex 1b **2. Lesen** (Detailverstehen): S verbinden die Satzhälften.
Ausw. Ex 1b Durch Partner check und/oder im Plenum. Zusätzlich szenisches Lesen der beiden Dialoge möglich.
Überleitung Ausgehend von *But I miss my real dad.* kann L mithilfe der Box im *Vocabulary* (S. 190) weitere Possessivpronomen einführen und damit für Ex. 2 und 3 vorentlasten.

► IAT 2.1 ► Folie 12

Ellie's family

Ellie's mum is in the kitchen, near Berry.
Ellies's dad is in the photo on the mobile phone.

1 Meet the family

1.28

a) Look at the pictures: Who's Ellie's mum? Who's Ellie's dad? Guess and point. Then read and check.

Ellie — Hi, Mum, this is Berry.
Mum — Hi, Berry. Nice to meet you. I'm Jackie.
Berry — Hello.
Ellie — Is Zoe[1] upstairs?
Mum — Yes, she is. And Conor[2] is in the living room.
Ellie — Oh no! He's always in the living room. There's no space for Berry and me!
Mum — Oh, here's Conor. This is Berry, Ellie's new friend.
Conor — Hi, Berry. Are you at Eggbuckland?
Berry — Yes, I am. What about you?
Conor — I'm at Plymouth High School.
Mum — And here's Zoe, Ellie's big sister.
Zoe — Hi, welcome to the °madhouse!
Mum — Conor, can the girls go into the living room? Is that OK?
Conor — Oh, OK.

Berry and Ellie are in the living room.
Berry — Your family is fun. They're all nice.
Ellie — They're OK.
Berry — What about your stepdad? Box: Voc., p. 190 Is he nice?
Ellie — He's OK. But I miss my real dad. Box: Voc., p. 190 He lives with his new partner and his baby boy. Look, I have a photo on my mobile.
Berry — The baby is cute. You're lucky. You have a baby brother, a sister and a big brother.
Ellie — You're lucky. You live with your mum and your dad. That's cool.

b) Finish the sentences.

1 Berry is ...
2 Jackie is ...
3 Conor is ...
4 Ellie's dad has ...
5 Ellie lives with ...
6 Berry lives with ...

... her mum and stepdad. • ... at Ellie's house. • ... a new family. • ... Ellie's mum. • ... her mum and dad. • ... Ellie's big brother.

1 Berry is at Ellie's house. • **2** Jackie is Ellie's mum. • **3** Conor is Ellie's big brother. • **4** Ellie's dad has a new family. • **5** Ellie lives with her mum and stepdad. • **6** Berry lives with her mum and dad.

1 ['zəʊi] 2 ['kɒnə]

Zeitbedarf: ca. zwei Stunden
Minimalversion: Ex **1a–b**; **2a–b**; **3b** (**a** als vorbereitende und **c** als festigende HA)
Kooperative Lernformen: Partner talk Ex **3b**
Materialbedarf: Ex **1**: (optional) Audio-CD + Player oder MP3 + PC/Lautsprecher | Ex **3**: (optional) Zeichenpapier
Einsatz von Begleitmedien: KV 2.2 | IAT 2.1 | Folie 12 |DFF 2.1 | INKL 2.2 | Workbook S. 22

Einstieg Ex 2 (SB geschl.) Unterrichtsgespräch zum Sammeln von Worzschatz-Kenntnissen aus der Grundschule (Tafel). L: *Who belongs to your family? Do you know other family words? Let's look at Ellie's family tree.*
Ex 2 (SB offen) ist eine Parallelübung auf zwei Niveaus: ○ hier und ● auf S. 126.
Ausw. Ex 2 Lösungsvergleich im Partner check, anschließend Vorlesen der komplettierten Sätze im Plenum.
Erarb. Ex 2b Zur Festigung von Wortschatz und Schriftbild. Auch als **HA** geeignet.

▸ KV 2.2 ▸ Folie 12 ▸ DFF 2.1 ▸ INKL 2.2

2 Ellie's family tree

a) ○ Choose the right words for Ellie. //● p.126

1 My mum and dad are / aren't together.
2 I live with my mum / dad.
3 This is Pete. He's my stepdad / real dad.
4 Pete has two / three children.
5 Zoe is my stepmother / stepsister.
6 Conor is my baby brother / stepbrother.
7 My dad has a new partner. Her name is Alisha / Jackie.
8 This is Finn, my baby brother / big brother.

1 aren't • 2 mum • 3 stepdad • 4 two • 5 stepsister • 6 stepbrother • 7 Alisha • 8 baby brother

b) Put the family words into three lists.

♀	♂	♀♂
mum	dad	cousin
...	...	...

aunt[4] • baby • brother • children • cousin[5] • dad • father • grandfather • grandmother • grandparents • mother • mum • parents • partner • sister • stepbrother • uncle

Box: Voc., p. 190

♀: mum, aunt, grandmother, mother, sister
♂: brother, dad, father, grandfather, stepbrother, uncle
♀♂: cousin, baby, children, grandparents, parents, partner

3 ACTIVITY Your family tree

a) Draw your family tree or your dream family tree. You can put it in your DOSSIER. ▸ Wordbank 4, p. 175

b) Talk to a partner about your family tree.

I have a big / small family.
I have ... brothers / cousins / aunts / uncles / ...
I live with my ...
My mum's / dad's name is ...
My grandparents live in ...
...

c) ● Write sentences about your family – as many as you can.

Erarb. Ex 3a (SB offen) Unter Verwendung der *Wordbank 4* (S. 175) gestalten S einen Stammbaum, ggf. als vorbereitende **HA**.
Alternative: Zeitersparnis durch KV 2.2.
Ausw. in **Ex 3b** Partner talk. ● Lernstärkere notieren bei jedem Gespräch eine Gemeinsamkeit und einen Unterschied.
Erarb. Ex 3c Festigung, als **HA** geeignet. Nach Korrektur Ablage im Dossier.

▸ Workbook 4, p. 22

3 [əˈlɪʃə] 4 [ɑːnt] 5 [ˈkʌzn]

THEME 2 Navigator | Inhalt

Lernschwerpunkt: **Über Probleme reden, ein Zimmer beschreiben**
Storyline: Ellie und Zoe teilen sich ein Zimmer, haben aber unterschiedliche Vorstellungen über das Zusammenleben.
Kompetenzen: **Listening** Einen kurzen Dialog verstehen, Bilder zuordnen und Details heraushören | **Speaking** Darüber reden, wem etwas gehört, ein Zimmer beschreiben | **Reading** Texten gezielt Informationen entnehmen | **Writing** Ein Dialogskript für ein Streitgespräch vervollständigen | **Lern- und Arbeitstechniken** Wortschatz zu Einrichtungsgegenständen in Listen erfassen
Grammatik: *there's / there are*, vorbewusste Verwendung von Entscheidungsfragen und Kurzantworten
Redemittel: Einrichtungsgegenstände, Kleidungsstücke

Einstieg Ex 1 (SB offen) Erfassung von Vorkenntnissen aus der Grundschule und Semantisierung. L: *What can you see in the picture on the right/left? (...) It's Ellie's and Zoe's bedroom. They share a room. What can you see in the room? (...) Look, the shoes are everywhere on the floor. The room is messy.*
Erarb. Ex 1a/b **1. Lesen**/Hören und Überprüfung des Globalverstehens gemäß Leseauftrag. Anschließend ggf. szenisches Lesen. ● Lernstärkere S geben eine Begründung.

Erarb. Ex 2 (SB offen) S lesen vorab die Aufgabe. Dann **2. Lesen**/Hören (Detailverstehen). Abgleich im Plenum. Als **HA** geeignet.

Erarb. Ex 3a (SB offen) S notieren anhand der Vorgaben und des Satzmusters in den Sprechblasen Entscheidungsfragen und Kurzantworten.
Erarb. Ex 3b S üben das Gespräch mithilfe der Read-and-look-up technique ein. Nach drei Fragen Rollentausch.
Ausw. Ex 3b Einige S-Paare präsentieren Dialog im Plenum.
Zusatz S machen Unordnung auf ihrem Tisch und führen ähnliche Dialoge wie in **3b**.

2 THEME 2

▸ *Folie 13* ▸ *INKL 2.3*

Problems at home

1 What's your problem?

1.29 **a)** Read and find out: Is Zoe happy?
– Yes, she is. / No, she isn't. No, she isn't.

Ellie shares a bedroom with her stepsister, Zoe.

Zoe ___ Ellie, look at the room!
Ellie ___ What's your problem? It's OK!
Zoe ___ OK? What about the pullover? Is it yours?
Ellie ___ Yes, it is.
Zoe ___ And the shoes? Are they yours too?
Ellie ___ Yes, they are. What's your problem?
Zoe ___ The room is messy! That's my problem!
Ellie ___ Is it your room? No, it isn't. It's my room too!

1.30 **b)** Now Ellie is in the kitchen. Is she happy?
– Yes, she is. / No, she isn't. No, she isn't.

Mum ___ Are you OK, Ellie?
Ellie ___ No, I'm not. Zoe is bossy, Mum.
Mum ___ Oh, Ellie!
Ellie ___ And there's no space in our room. I can't do my homework. Box: Voc., p. 190
Mum ___ What about the kitchen?
Ellie ___ It's too busy!
Mum ___ What about the living room?
Ellie ___ It's too noisy!
Mum ___ Oh, Ellie!

2 ○ Ellie's problems

Look at the dialogues in 1 again. Pick A, B or C. 1 C • 2 B • 3 A • 4 A • 5 C

	A	B	C
1 It's ...	Ellie's room.	Zoe's room.	Ellie and Zoe's room.
2 The room is ...	OK.	messy.	big.
3 Ellie has no ...	space.	bedroom.	shoes.
4 The kitchen is too ...	busy.	new.	small.
5 The living room is too ...	big.	pink.	noisy.

3 Zoe is bossy!

a) Write Zoe's questions and Ellie's answers.

tie | books | T-shirts | football | shoes | pullover

b) Act the dialogue.

What about the ...? Is it yours?
What about the ...? Are they yours?

– Yes, it is.
– Yes, they are.

What about the tie/football/pullover? Is it yours? – Yes, it is.
What about the T-shirts/shoes/books? Are they yours? – Yes, they are.

Zeitbedarf: ca. zwei Stunden
Minimalversion: Ex **1a–b**; **3**; **4a–b**; **5**
Kooperative Lernformen: Information-gap activity Ex **5**
Materialbedarf: Ex **1a–b** (optional), Ex **4a–b**: Audio-CD + Player oder MP3 + PC/Lautsprecher
Einsatz von Begleitmedien: Folie 13 | INKL 2.3 | DFF 2.3 | Workbook S. 23–24

▸ Folie 13 ▸ DFF 2.3

4 Ellie's dream room

1.31 **a)** Ellie is talking to her friends. Listen. What's her dream room – 1 or 2?

Room 2 is Ellie's dream room.

1 rug • 2 desk • 3 chair • 4 lamp • 7 bed • 8 cushions • 9 mirror • 10 wardrobe • 11 posters • 12 shelves

b) Listen again. What's in Ellie's dream room? Write the numbers.

c) Things in Ellie's dream room: Make two lists.

There's ...	There are ...
a rug	shelves
...	...

More practice 1 p. 126

▸ Language file 4, p. 168

There's ...: a rug, a desk, a chair, a lamp, a table, a bed, a mirror, a wardrobe
There are ...: books, cushions, posters, shelves

5 What's different?

Partner B: Go to page 118.

Partner A: Look at room A. Talk about your room to your partner. Partner B starts. Find four different things or more. Make notes about the different things.

Partner B __ There's a bed in room B.
Partner A __ There's a bed in room A too.
Partner B __ OK. There are three cushions in room B.
Partner A __ There are no cushions in room A. That's different!

Room A	Room B
no cushions	3 cushions
...	...

Room A: no cushions, 3 posters, 1 wardrobe, 2 lamps, 1 rug, no mirror, no TV, 2 chairs, no table

Room B: 3 cushions, 2 posters, no wardrobe, 1 lamp, 2 rugs, 1 mirror, 1 TV, 1 chair, 1 table

▸ Workbook 5–8, pp. 23–24

Erarb. Ex 4a (SB offen) L: *Ellie is dreaming of her own bedroom.* **1. Hören** (Globalverstehen): S identifizieren das richtige Bild. Lernstärkere begründen ihre Wahl, indem sie spezifische Einrichtungsdetails aus dem Hörtext nennen.
Erarb. Ex 4b **2. Hören** (Detailverstehen).
Erarb. Ex 4c Zur Festigung von *there's / there are* in Verbindung mit Einzahl und Mehrzahl von Substantiven und zur Sicherung des Schriftbildes. Als **HA** geeignet. Sicherung im Plenum und ggf. Bewusstmachung anhand von LF4, S. 168.

Einstieg Ex 5 (SB offen) S einigen sich über Rollenverteilung und vereinbaren, wer Liste mit Unterschieden führt.
Achtung! Partnerübung auf unterschiedlichen Niveaus:
Partner B steuert den Dialog.
Partner A reagiert auf die Vorgaben von Partner B.
Erarb. Ex 5 Klären der Arbeitsanweisung: Partner B beginnt und beschreibt mithilfe der Wörter im grünen Kasten Raum B. Partner A betrachtet Raum A, hört zu und gleicht die genannten Gegenstände mit seinem Bild ab und weist auf Unterschiede hin.

FOCUS ON LANGUAGE Navigator | Inhalt

Lernschwerpunkt: Fragen stellen und kurz beantworten
Storyline: Ellie berichtet ihrem Vater vom schwierigen Zusammenleben in dem kleinen Haus.
Kompetenzen: Speaking Fragen stellen und kurz beantworten | **Reading** Einem Dialog gezielt Informationen entnehmen
Lern- und Arbeitstechniken Sprachliche Regelmäßigkeiten entdecken
Grammatik: Entscheidungsfragen und Kurzantworten (bejaht und verneint)
Redemittel: Sich nach dem Befinden, den Eigenschaften und Meinungen von Personen erkundigen und Fragen kurz beantworten

Einstieg Ex 1 (SB offen) Gemeinsame Bildbeschreibung im Plenum. L: *Who or what can you see? What are they talking about? Guess.*
Erarb. Ex 1 1. Lesen/Hören, ggf. im Mitleseverfahren. Sicherung des Globalverstehens anhand der *right/wrong statements.*
● Lernstärkere belegen ihre Einschätzung anhand des Textes.

Erarb. Ex 1 (SB offen) S lesen die Fragen und vervollständigen die Kurzantworten schriftlich im Heft. Den Text zu Ex. 1 decken sie dabei zunächst ab und nutzen ihn nur zur Überprüfung.
○ Lernschwächere suchen die Sätze direkt im Text.
Erarb. Ex 2b Je nach Leistungsstärke der Lerngruppe zunächst in EA oder gleich im Plenum. L legt zweispaltige Tabelle (Tafel/Folie) an und hält komplettierte Fragen in der linken Spalte fest.
Erarb. Ex 2c L oder ein lernstärkerer S notiert die Kurzantworten in der rechten Spalte. Die Formen von *be* werden unterstrichen. Anschließend Regelformulierung anhand von *Language file* 3b, S. 167.

2 FOCUS ON LANGUAGE

▸ *Folie 14*

1 Are you OK?

1.32

Right or wrong? Read and check.
1 Ellie's dad is happy in the new flat.
2 Ellie is happy in her mum's house.

1 Right.
2 Wrong.

Dad — Hi, Ellie. This is a nice surprise.
Ellie — Hi, Dad. Is Finn OK?
Dad — Yes, he is. He's fine.
Ellie — And Alisha? Is she OK?
Dad — Yes, she is. She's fine too, but she's tired.
Ellie — And the new flat? Is it OK?
Dad — Yes, it is. It's really nice.
Ellie — Are you and Alisha happy in the flat?
Dad — Yes, we are. We love it ... Ellie, are you OK?

Ellie

Steve

Ellie — Yes, I am. I'm fine.
Dad — Are you sure? Are you really OK?
Ellie — ... No, I'm not. I'm not happy.
Dad — Oh! What's the problem? Is your stepdad too strict?
Ellie — No, he isn't. Pete is OK.
Dad — And what about Zoe and Conor? Are they mean to you?
Ellie — No, they aren't. They're OK. But I share a room with Zoe and she's really bossy. And Conor is really noisy. There's no space for me. Dad, I'm not happy in this house.
Dad — Oh, Ellie. Listen. I have an idea.

Box: Voc., p. 191

2 Questions and answers

a) Complete the answers. Then find the sentences in 1 and check.
1 Is Finn OK? – Yes, he ...
2 And the new flat? Is it OK? – Yes, ...
3 Are you and Alisha happy in the flat? – Yes, we ...
4 Ellie, are you OK? – Yes, I ...
5 Are you really OK? – No, ...
6 Is your stepdad too strict? – No, ...
7 Are Zoe and Conor mean to you? – No, ...

Im Englischen antwortet man auf eine Frage oft nicht nur mit *Yes* oder *No*, sondern mit Kurzantworten. Das ist höflicher.

1 Yes, he is. • 2 Yes, it is. • 3 Yes, we are. • 4 Yes, I am. • 5 No, I'm not. • 6 No, he isn't. • 7 No, they aren't.

b) Questions
Complete the examples with:
Am • *Is* • *Are*

FOCUS
... I OK?
... he/she/it OK?
... you/we/they OK?

c) Answers
Complete the examples with:
am • *is* • *are* • *'m not* • *isn't* • *aren't*

FOCUS
Yes, I ... – No, I ...
Yes, he/she/it ... – No, he/she/it ...
Yes, you/we/they ... – No, you/we/they ...

Questions	Answers	
Am I OK?	Yes, I am.	No, I'm not.
Is he/she/it OK?	Yes, he/she/it is.	No, he/she/it isn't.
Are you/we/they OK?	Yes, you/we/they are.	No, you/we /they aren't.

▸ *Language file 3, p. 167*

Zeitbedarf: ca. drei Stunden
Minimalversion: Ex **1–3**, **6** (Ex **5** als HA)
Kooperative Lernformen: Partner talk Ex **3b** und **4** | Milling-around activity Ex **6**
Materialbedarf: Ex **2**: (optional) leere Folie, Farbstifte, OH-Projektor
Einsatz von Begleitmedien: KV 2.3 | Folie 14 | DFF 2.4 | INKL 2.4–2.5 | Workbook S. 25

2

▸ KV 2.3 ▸ DFF 2.4 ▸ Folie 14 ▸ INKL 2.4 ▸ INKL 2.5

3 ○ NOW YOU //● p.127

a) Write the answers for you.

1 Are you noisy? – Yes, I am. / No, I'm not.
2 Are your friends fun? – Yes, they are. / No, they aren't.
3 Is your grandmother from Germany? – Yes, she is. / No, she isn't.
4 Is your dad strict? – Yes, he is. / No, he isn't.
5 Is your mum bossy? – Yes, she is. / No, she isn't.
6 Is your room messy? – Yes, it is. / No, it isn't.

b) Ask your partner the same questions.

4 ○ Who am I?

Play this game with a partner. You're one of the people in the house. Can your partner guess who you are?

Are you a girl / boy?
Are you upstairs / downstairs?
Are you in the kitchen / ...?
Are you big / small?
Are you Ben / Liz / ...?

Yes, I am.

No, I'm not.

5 Quiz questions

Answer the questions.

1 Is Finn cute? – Yes, he ... / No, he ...
2 Is Berry Ellie's friend? – ...
3 Is Ellie's house big? – ...
4 Are Zoe and Conor mean? – ...
5 Are Pete and Jackie together? – ...

1 Yes, he is. / No, he isn't.
2 Yes, she is.
3 No, it isn't.
4 No, they aren't.
5 Yes, they are.

6 Is Alisha Ellie's sister?
7 Is Jackie Ellie's mum?
8 Is Steve Ellie's real dad?
9 Is Berry's family big?
10 Are you and your family from Plymouth?

6 No, she isn't. • 7 Yes, she is. • 8 Yes, he is. • 9 No, it isn't. • 10 No, we aren't. / Yes, we are.

More practice 2 p.127

6 An interview: What do you think?

a) Copy the table and answer the questions.

b) Walk around: Ask as many partners as you can.

c) ● Pick one interesting answer. Tell the class.

Meike says she isn't bossy!

Jan says school is fun!

	Me	Partner 1	Partner 2	...
1 Is English easy?	✓			
2 Is school fun?	✗			
3 Is the principal strict?				
4 Are your teachers nice?				
5 Are you bossy?				

Ex 3a (SB offen) ist eine Parallelübung auf zwei Niveaus: ○ hier und ● auf S. 127. S legen dreispaltige Tabelle an (Frage, eigene Antwort, Partner-Antwort) und notieren die für sie passende Antwort.
Alternative: S verwenden den Tabellenvordruck auf KV 2.3.
Ex 3b Partner befragen sich gegenseitig und notieren Antworten.
Ausw. Ex 3 ● Lernstärkere berichten im Plenum über Gemeinsamkeiten und Unterscheide (auch als schriftliche **HA** möglich).

Einstieg Ex 4 (SB offen) Bildbeschreibung und Klären der Arbeitsanweisung im Plenum.
Erarb. Ex 4 Partner talk ● / ○ Lernstärkere S beginnen in der Rolle des Fragenden. Rollenwechsel, wenn Name erraten wurde.

Erarb. Ex 5 Mündlich als Meldekette oder schriftlich als **HA**.

Erarb. Ex 6a S übertragen Tabelle in ihr Heft oder verwenden Vordruck von KV 2.3.
● Lernstärkere ergänzen weitere Fragen.
Erarb. Ex 6b Milling-around activity. L-Signal zum Partnerwechsel.
Ausw. in **Ex 6c** Anhand der Satzmuster in den Sprechblasen berichten S im Plenum.

▸ Workbook 9–11, p: 25

STORY Navigator | Inhalt

Lernschwerpunkt: Tagebucheinträge verstehen

Storyline: Ellie zieht zu ihrem Vater. Im Laufe der Woche erkennt sie die Nachteile dieser Entscheidung und findet einen Kompromiss.

Kompetenzen: Speaking Bilder beschreiben | **Reading** Tagebucheinträgen Informationen entnehmen (bildgestützt)
Writing Einen Tagebucheintrag verfassen

Redemittel: Bilder beschreiben; Gefühle beschreiben

Einstieg Ex 1 (SB geschl.) Reaktivierung von Vorwissen zur Storyline. L: *Ellie has some problems at home. What are they? (...) Ellie's dad has an idea. What could it be?*
Erarb. Ex 1 (SB offen) Vorentlastung der Story durch Beschreibung der Bilder gemäß Sprachmuster. ○ Lernschwächere nutzen KV 2.4. Sie ordnen den Bildern passende Stichworte zu. ● Lernstärkere beschreiben einander abwechselnd alle Bilder im Partner talk und benennen weitere Details im Bild.
Ausw. Ex 1 Versprachlichung der Bilder im Plenum, z. B. durch eine Meldekette. Abschließend greift L Eingangsfrage wieder auf: *What is Ellie's dad's idea? Why do you think so?*
Einstieg STORY (SB offen): L formuliert Leseaufträge (Tafel, Folie): *Let's read Ellie's diary and find out: Why is Ellie unhappy in her dad's flat? What is 'the best of both worlds' for Ellie?*
Erarb. STORY
1. Lesen/Hören (ggf. im Mitleseverfahren) Überprüfung des Globalverstehens über die Leseaufträge: *Ellie is unhappy because her dad has no time for her. She's lonely. Ellie can live with her mum from Monday to Friday and with her dad on Saturday and Sunday.*

2 STORY

▸ KV 2.4 ▸ Folie 15 ▸ INKL 2.6 ▸ INKL 2.8

1 Before you read Ellie's diary

Choose a picture (1–7). Answer the questions about your picture. Then tell the class.

1 Where is Ellie? (at her mum's house / at her dad's flat / in the kitchen / in the ...)
2 Is Ellie happy?

Example:
In picture 1 Ellie is at her mum's house. She's in the kitchen. She's happy.

The best of both worlds

1.33

1

MONDAY
Dear Diary
Great news! I can live with dad, Alisha and the baby, Finn.
Tuesday is the big day!
Zoe is happy. But mum isn't happy.

2

TUESDAY
Dear Diary
I'm in my new home. I'm in my new bedroom.
I have a desk and a lamp and a red rug.
I can do my homework here.
No bossy Zoe. This is my dream room.
It's pink, but it's great!

3
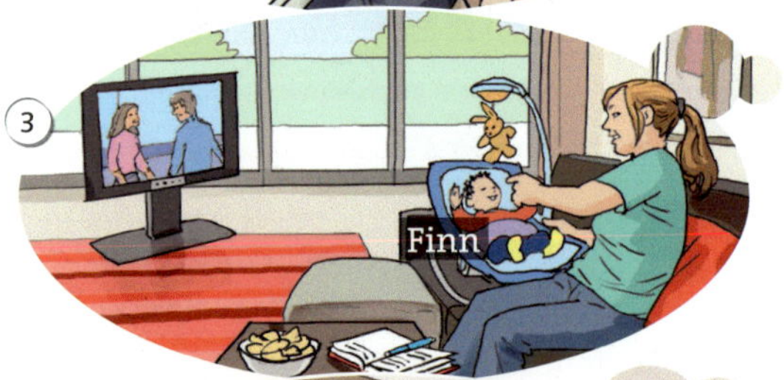

WEDNESDAY
Dear Diary
Finn is very cute. And Alisha is really nice.
Dad and Alisha are at the cinema now.
Finn is with me.
No Conor! Now I can watch all my favourite TV programmes.

Box: Voc., p. 192

4

THURSDAY
Dear Diary
Dad is at work. Alisha is tired.
She's in the bedroom.
Finn is with me. He isn't very happy.
I hope dad is home soon!

5

FRIDAY
Dear Diary
Dad and Alisha are at a restaurant.
It's Alisha's birthday. Finn is with me – again!
And he isn't very happy – again!
Be quiet, Finn!

Box: Voc., p. 192

2 In picture 2 Ellie is at her dad's flat. She's in her room. She's happy. • **3** In picture 3 Ellie is in the living room of her dad's flat (with baby Finn). She's happy. • **4** In picture 4 Ellie is at her dad's flat. She's in the kitchen (with baby Finn). She isn't happy. • **5** In picture 5 Ellie is in her pink room (with baby Finn). She isn't happy. • **6** In picture 6 Ellie is at her dad's house. She's in the living room (with baby Finn). She isn't happy. • **7** In the picture on the left Ellie is in her room at her dad's flat. She's happy. In the picture on the right Ellie is in the kitchen a her mum's house. She's happy.

STORY Navigator | **Vorbereitung**

Zeitbedarf: ca. zwei Stunden
Minimalversion: Ex **1–2**, **4** (Ex **3** als HA)
Kooperative Lernformen: Partner talk Ex **1**
Materialbedarf: Ex **1**: (optional) Audio-CD + Player oder MP3 + PC/Lautsprecher
Einsatz von Begleitmedien: KV 2.4 | Folie 15 | INKL 2.6–2.8 | DFF 2.6 | Workbook S. 26–27

▸ DFF 2.6 ▸ Folie 15 ▸ INKL 2.6 ▸ INKL 2.7 ▸ INKL 2.8

SATURDAY
Dear Diary
Dad and Alisha are in town.
And Finn? Yes, he's with me – again!
Dad has no time for me. He's °in love!
I miss mum. And I miss Conor and Pete
and my cats and I miss Zoe! I'm lonely.
Oh, a text. Is it from mum?

SUNDAY
Dear Diary
I have a new idea!
From Monday to Friday I'm with mum.
On Saturday and Sunday I'm with dad.
The best of both worlds! I'm happy again.

Erarb. Ex 2 (SB offen) **2. Lesen** und Zuordnung der Überschriften.
Ausw. Ex 2 Meldekette im Plenum: S1 stellt die erste Frage (*What is the heading for Monday?*), S2 antwortet und stellt die nächste Frage.

2 Ellie's week

Read the text. Match the headings with the days (Monday–Sunday) in Ellie's diary:
Example: Monday: Good news for Ellie   Tuesday: ...

Lots of TV now · A new idea · Good news for Ellie · Alisha's birthday · Day one in a new home · Dad at work · Ellie misses her mum

Monday: Good news for Ellie • **Tuesday:** Day one in a new home • **Wednesday:** Lots of TV now • **Thursday:** Dad at work • **Friday:** Alisha's birthday • **Saturday:** Ellie misses her mum • **Sunday:** A new idea

Erarb. Ex 3 (SB offen) Parallelübung auf zwei Niveaus: ○ hier und ● auf S. 127. Lernstärkere formulieren die Satzenden selbstständig. Ggf. **3. Lesen**. Als **HA** geeignet.
Ausw. Ex 3 Im Plenum oder als Lerntempoduett.

3 //○ Is Ellie happy? //● p.127

Pick the right endings. Write the sentences.

1 On Monday Ellie is happy because ...	she can watch her favourite TV programmes. 3
2 On Tuesday Ellie is happy because ...	she's lonely. 6
3 On Wednesday Ellie is happy because ...	Finn isn't happy. 4
4 On Thursday Ellie isn't happy because ...	she has a new idea. 7
5 On Friday Ellie isn't happy because ...	she can live with her dad. 1
6 On Saturday Ellie isn't happy because ...	dad and Alisha are at a restaurant. 5
7 On Sunday Ellie is happy again because ...	she has a nice room. 2

Einstieg Ex 4 (SB offen) Kurze Bildbeschreibung im Plenum. L: *Where is Ellie? Is she happy? Why (not)? Who is with her?*
Erarb. Ex 4 Klären der Arbeitsanweisung. Dann Bearbeitung in EA. Auch als **HA** geeignet.
Ausw. Ex 4 Partner check ● Lernstärkere oder *fast finishers* schreiben einen Tagebucheintrag aus der Sicht von Ellies Mutter, Ellies Vater, Zoe etc.

4 ● A week later

Write Ellie's diary for this picture.
Dear Diary
happy again / mum's house / in – bedroom – Zoe / cats – happy / mum – happy / Zoe – happy too / Conor – here / Finn – ~~here~~ / OK

More help p.127

More practice 3 p.128

Lösungsbsp. S. 233

SKILLS TRAINING Mind maps and writing

Lernschwerpunkt: **Mithilfe von Mindmaps Texte verfassen**
Kompetenzen: **Reading** Einer Mindmap Informationen entnehmen | **Writing** Auf Basis einer Mindmap einen eigenen Text verfassen | **Lern- und Arbeitstechniken** Eine Mindmap regelgeleitet erstellen und für die Textproduktion nutzen
Redemittel: Wohnen, Räume, Einrichtungsgegenstände

Zeitbedarf: ca. eine Stunde
Minimalversion: Ex **1, 2a** (**2b** als **HA**)
Kooperative Lernformen: Double circle (optional in Ex **2a**)
Materialbedarf: Ex **2c** (optional) Klebepunkte
Einsatz von Begleitmedien: DFF 2.7 | INKL 2.9 A/B

Einstieg Ex 1 (SB geschl.) L: *What do you think of when you hear the word 'house'? Write down as many ideas as you can in 2/3/... minutes.* Sammlung im Plenum in Form einer Mindmap.
Überleitung L: *This is our mindmap. Let's look at Cyril's mindmap.*
Erarb. Ex 1 (SB offen) Unterrichtsgespräch über Cyrils Mindmap. Lesen des Lückentexts (EA oder Plenum). S entnehmen der Mindmap die benötigten Informationen, schreiben den Text vollständig ins Heft.
Ausw. Ex 1 Partner check, Lösungen zur Selbstkontrolle an der Rückseite der Tafel.

Einstieg Ex 2 (SB offen) Erarbeitung grundlegender Mindmap-Regeln anhand von *Skills file 2* (Plenum). S beschreiben Aufbau von Cyrils Mindmap (auf Deutsch).
Überleitung L: *Cyril's house is near the sea. Where is your (dream) house?*
Erarb. Ex 1 in EA
Ausw. Ex 1 Correcting circle anhand der Kriterien im *Skills file* (Thema in der Mitte, Hauptäste, Nebenäste, Symbole etc.), freiwillige S präsentieren im Plenum.
Erarb. Ex 2b in EA (auch als **HA**), ggf. mit Zeichnung.
Ausw. Ex 2b Partner check oder L-Korrektur, abschließend Gallery walk, ggf. mit Klebepunkt-Vergabe.

2 SKILLS TRAINING °Mind maps and writing

▸ *DFF 2.7* ▸ *INKL 2.9 A/B*

1 ○ Cyril's house

Look at Cyril's mind map and finish the text in your exercise book.

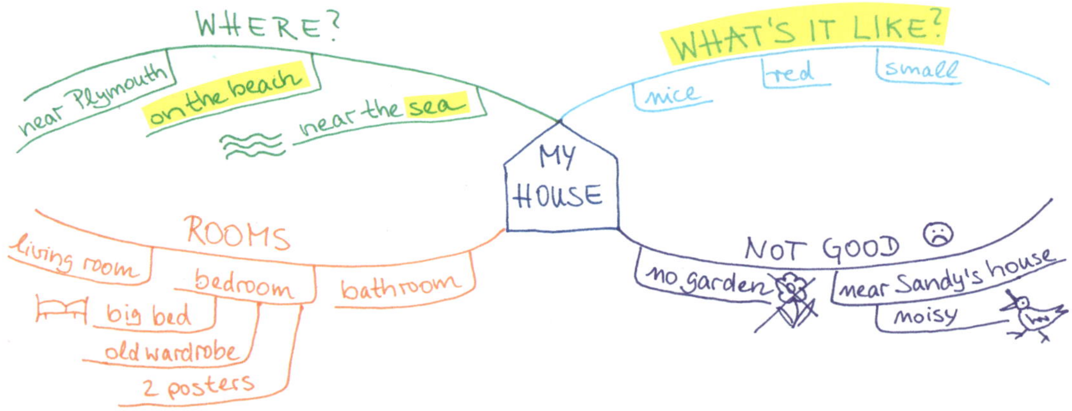

My house

Hi. This is my ... It's near Plymouth. It's on the ..., near the ...
It's nice. It's ... and it's ...
There are three rooms in my house. There's a ..., a ... and a ...
My favourite room is my bedroom. There's a big ... and an old ... in my bedroom.
There are two ... too.
What isn't good about my house? – There's ... garden and it's near Sandy's ...
She's very noisy!

house • beach • sea • small • red • bedroom • bathroom • living room • bed • wardrobe • posters • no • house

2 NOW YOU

a) Make a mind map for your house or flat, or for your dream house. Use ideas from Cyril's mind map. ▸ *Wordbank 5, p. 175*

Bewertungsraster für Mindmaps: S 233

b) ● Write about your dream house or flat with the words from your mind map. Cyril's text can help you. You can put your text in your DOSSIER. More help p. 128

Mind maps
Bevor du einen Text schreibst, ist es immer gut, deine Ideen zu sammeln und zu ordnen. Eine *mind map* kann dir dabei helfen.

▸ *Skills file 2, p. 162*

SKILLS TRAINING Classroom English

Lernschwerpunkt: **Englisch als Unterrichtssprache verwenden**
Kompetenzen: **Listening** Redewendungen des *classroom discourse* verstehen und zuordnen
Lern- und Arbeitstechniken Englisch als Unterrichtssprache verwenden
Redemittel: Redewendungen für den Unterrichtsgebrauch (rezeptiv und produktiv)

Zeitbedarf: ca. eine Stunde
Minimalversion: Ex **1a–b**
Materialbedarf: Ex **1b**: Audio-CD + Player oder MP3 + PC/Lautsprecher | Ex **2**: ein Würfel pro Gruppe, Spielsteine
Einsatz von Begleitmedien: KV 2.5 | IAT 2.2 | DFF 2.8 | Folie 16 | Workbook S. 28

SKILLS TRAINING Classroom English 2

▸ *IAT 2.2* ▸ *KV 2.5* ▸ *DFF 2.8* ▸ *Folie 16*

1 Classroom phrases

A 7 • B 10 • C 9 • D 4 • E 11 • F 1 • G 3 • H 8 • I 2 • J 6 • K 5 • L 12

a) Match the phrases (A–L) with the pictures (1–12) in the game.
Example: 'What's that in English?' goes with picture 7.

A What's that in English?	E Quiet, please!	I Listen, please!
B It's your turn.	F Can I go to the toilet, please?	J What page is it, please?
C Work with a partner.	G What's for homework?	K Please look at the board.
D Close the door, please.	H Can you say that again, please?	L Sorry, I forgot my homework.

1: 5 • 2: 4 • 3: 12 • 4: 2 • 5: 8 • 6: 1 • 7: 11 • 8: 6 • 9: 7 • 10: 10 • 11: 9 • 12: 3

1.34 **b)** Listen. When you hear the classroom phrases from 1a, point at the pictures in the game.

More practice 4 p. 128

2 GAME The °banana skin game

Play this game in groups of three or four.

WAS? 1 Würfel und 3 oder 4 Spielsteine.
WIE? Landest du auf einem Nummernfeld, nenne die *classroom phrase*. War sie korrekt, bleibe auf dem Feld. Hast du einen Fehler gemacht, gehe zwei Felder zurück. Dann ist der/die Nächste an der Reihe.

Erarb. Ex 1a (SB offen) S lesen zunächst alle *classroom phrases* still durch und ordnen sie anschließend dem jeweiligen Bild des Spielfelds zu. Sie notieren die Lösungen in Kurzform (Buchstabe-Zahl) im Heft und vergleichen sie ggf. im Partner check. Anschließend ggf. Semantisierung mithilfe der Bilder.
Ausw. Ex 1a Meldekette: S1 liest die erste Redewendung und ruft S2 auf. S2 nennt die Bildnummer gemäß Satzmuster in der Aufgabe und liest die nächste Wendung vor.
Erarb. Ex 1b Beim **1. Hören** der Dialoge zeigen S auf das entsprechende Bild.
Ausw. Ex 1b Im Plenum beim **2. Hören**: L stoppt Tonaufnahme nach jedem Dialog, S nennen Nummer.

Einstieg Ex 2 (SB offen) Klärung der Spielregeln und ggf. Probelauf gemeinsam im Plenum.
Erarb. Ex 2 S spielen das Spiel in 3er- oder 4er-Gruppen gemäß Anleitung. Ein S sollte die Rolle des Spielleiters übernehmen.
Alternative Um eine glatte und größere Spielfläche zu erhalten, kopiert L für jede Gruppe KV 2.5 auf DIN-A3.
Zusatz Für ein Memo-Spiel übertragen S die *classroom phrases* und ihre deutschen Entsprechungen auf Karten. Vorlage: Part 2 von KV 2.5

▸ Workbook 17–19, p. 28

SKILLS TRAINING Listening and speaking

Lernschwerpunkt: **Adressen und Telefonnummern**
Kompetenzen: **Listening** Adressen, Telefonnummern verstehen
Speaking Adressen und Telefonnummern erfragen, weitergeben und buchstabieren
Lern- und Arbeitstechniken Nachfragen, sich Notizen machen
Redemittel: Buchstaben und Zahlen, Adressen und Telefonnummern

Zeitbedarf: ca. eine Stunde
Minimalversion: Ex **2a–c**, **3b** (**3a** als **HA**)
Kooperative Lernformen: Double circle Ex **3b**
Materialbedarf: Ex **1**, Ex **2**: Audio-CD + Player oder MP3 + PC/Lautsprecher
Einsatz von Begleitmedien: DFF 2.5 | INKL 2.10–2.11 | Workbook S. 29–30

Erarb. Ex 1 (SB offen) Beim **1. Hören** lesen S das Lied leise mit. Beim **2. Hören** sprechen sie den Text mit. Als **HA** lernen S ihn auswendig. **Zusatz** S singen Song zur Instrumentalversion (Track 1.36).

Einstieg Ex 2 (SB offen) L: *Look at the picture and the speech bubbles. What do Ellie's friends want to know? (Ellie's address and phone number)* L verweist auf die Tipp-Box. Freiwillige S nennen ihre Nummer im Plenum.
Überleitung L: *Do you remember Ellie's address at her mum's house? (Hill Road) Let's find out what her new address is.*
Erarb. Ex 2 Vorab lesen S die Aufgaben 1–3. **1. Hören** und Notieren der Lösungen. **2. Hören** zur Überprüfung.
Erarb. Ex 2b Lautschulung durch Nachsprechen.
Erarb. Ex 2c Detailverstehen. **2. Hören** zur Überprüfung.

Erarb. Ex 3a (SB offen) Tipp-Box wird anhand einiger Beispiele im Plenum erläutert. Anschließend EA.
Erarb. Ex 3b Double circle unter Verwendung der Redemittel aus Ex 2. S notieren Adresse und Telefonnummer des Partners und lassen die Notizen überprüfen. Dann Rollentausch.

2 SKILLS TRAINING °Listening and speakin[g]

▸ DFF 2.5 ▸ INKL 2.10 ▸ INKL 2.11

1 The alphabet chant

Box: Voc., p. 193

1.35 / 1.36 Listen to Cyril and repeat.

AB–CDE	We're a happy family.
FG–HIJ	°Come and °visit °us °today.
KL–MNO	Plymouth is the place to go.
PQ–RST	Lots of fun for you and me.
UVW–XYZ	Now we're tired and °off to bed!

2 Addresses and phone numbers

More practice 5 p. 129

1.37 **a)** Listen. What are the right answers? 1 B

1 Ellie talks to her friends about …
A her mum's house. B her dad's flat. C her new room.

2 What's the right address?
A 11 Great Field Road. B 10 Gratefeld Street. C 11 Greatfield Street. 2 C

3 Two numbers are wrong in Ellie's phone number.
What's her phone number? 01752 804 3637

01752 803 3647

Bei Telefonnummern sagt man *oh* oder *zero* für die 0.

1.38 **b)** Listen and repeat the questions.

1.39 **c)** Listen and write Berry's address. More help p. 129

MERRYWEATHER FARM, WOOLWELL

3 What's your address?

a) How can you say your address and phone number in English? Think about it.

b) Double circle:
Talk to different partners.
Find out their address or their phone number.

What's your address?
What's your phone number?

Im Englischen gibt es kein **ä**, **ö**, **ü** und **ß**.
Du kannst sie ersetzen durch:
ä → ae **ö → oe**
ü → ue **ß → ss**

▸ Workbook 20–23, pp. 29–30

SKILLS TRAINING Viewing

Lernschwerpunkt: Fiktionale und dokumentarische Filmszenen verstehen
Kompetenzen: Viewing Filmszenen verstehen
Speaking Sich über Lieblingsdinge austauschen-
Lern- und Arbeitstechniken Strategien zum Hör-Sehverstehen anwenden: nonverbale Hinweise (Gestik, Mimik) nutzen
Redemittel: Englischer Schulalltag (Hausaufgaben, Fächer), Einrichtungsgegenstände, Lieblingsdinge

Zeitbedarf: ca. eine Stunde
Minimalversion: Ex **1a–b**, **2a–b** (**2d** als HA)
Kooperative Lernformen: Partner talk Ex **2a** | Partner check Ex **2b**
Materialbedarf: DVD + Player oder PC/Lautsprecher

SKILLS TRAINING Viewing

2

1 The kids from Harbour Road: Homework time

a) Watch the film. Then put the photos (A–F) in the right order.
First we see ... Then we see ... D • F • C • A • B • E

A

B

C

D

E

F

b) Before you watch again: What's the right answer? Then watch and check.

1 The three friends are at Sarah's / Anna's house.
2 They have lots of / no homework.
3 They talk about shopping / football.
4 Then they go upstairs into Sarah's / Tom's room.
5 Tom is Sarah's big brother / cousin.
6 Tom is / isn't happy because Sarah, Paul and Anna are in his room.
7 Anna and Paul say Tom is mean / OK.
8 Later Tom and Sarah are / aren't friends again.

1 Sarah's • 2 lots of • 3 football • 4 Tom's • 5 big brother • 6 isn't • 7 OK • 8 are

2 People and places: A tour of my room

a) Before you watch: What are your five favourite things in your room? Write a list.
Then tell a partner.

b) Now watch Joe's film. Name his favourite things – as many as you can. Make a list.
Compare your list with a partner.

poster, (lamp), history school book, T-shirt, (socks), dog, (photo of) Joe's baby sister, medals, guitar, MP3-player, phone, computer, computer games, football

c) Watch the film again. Pick the right words:

1 Joe's favourite lesson is English / history.
2 Joe's pet is a dog / cat.
3 Joe's tie / guitar isn't his favourite thing.
4 Joe has a baby brother / sister.
5 Joe is good at music / sport.
6 Joe's most favourite thing is his computer / football.

1 history • 2 dog • 3 tie • 4 sister • 5 sport • 6 football

d) Copy and complete this diagram:

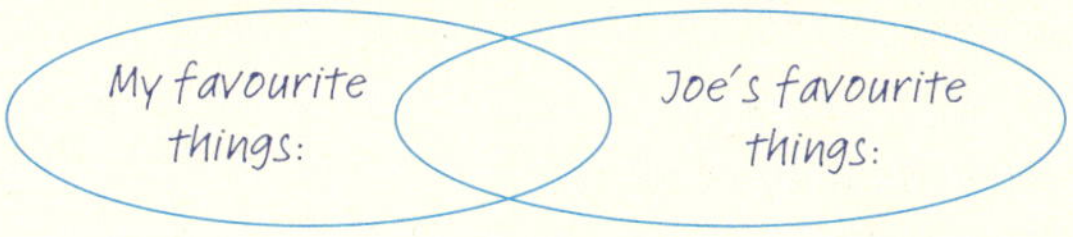

Einstieg Ex 1 (SB geschl.) Unterrichtsgespräch über Thematik des Films. L: *Where/When do you do your homework? Do you do it alone? Who can help you?*
Erarb. Ex 1a (SB offen) **1. Sehen:** S notieren die Buchstaben.
Ausw. Ex 1a S nennen die Satzanfänge mit den richtigen Buchstaben.
Erarb. Ex 1b S notieren die Nummern (1–8) und die Auswahlwörter im Heft und unterstreichen die Antwort, die ihrer Erinnerung nach richtig ist. Anschließend **2. Sehen** zur Überprüfung.
Ausw. Ex 1b S lesen die vervollständigten Sätze vor.

Erarb. Ex 1 (SB offen) EA (ggf. als Ranking), dann Partner talk. S markieren Gemeinsamkeiten.
Ausw. Ex 1 Freiwillige S berichten über Gemeinsamkeiten und Unterschiede.
Erarb. Ex 2b **1. Sehen:** S notieren die Gegenstände, dann Partner check.
Ausw. Ex 2b Bei einigen Dingen kann diskutiert werden, ob sie zu den *favourite things* gehören (*socks, lamp*). Hier kann Joes Gestik/Mimik helfen.
Erarb. Ex 2c Vertiefung durch **2. Sehen**. Vorgehen wie 2b.
Erarb. Ex 2d S zeichnen Venn-Diagramm ab (in Joes Seite müssen bis zu 14 Wörter passen!). Gemeinsame Gegenstände kommen in die Schnittmenge.

Lernschwerpunkt: **Wiederholen und Üben, Lernfortschritte erkennen (Fokus: Unit 2)**
Kompetenzen: **Listening** Telefonnummern und Adressen verstehen | **Lern- und Arbeitstechniken** Eigene Lernfortschritte erkennen
Grammatik: Sätze mit den korrekten Formen von *be* ergänzen, Kurzantworten
Redemittel: Wortfelder Familie und Wohnen/Räume

Erarb. Ex 1a (SB offen) S schreiben die Sätze 1–8 ins Heft und ergänzen anhand der Abbildung die entsprechenden Verwandtschaftsbezeichnungen.
Erarb. Ex 1b (SB offen) S ergänzen weitere Verwandtschaftsbezeichnungen.

Erarb. Ex 2a (SB offen) S schreiben die Zahlen 1–8 ins Heft und ordnen die entsprechenden Buchstaben bzw. Raumlabels zu.
Erarb. Ex 2b (SB offen) S übertragen den korrigierten Fehlertext in ihr Heft.
Erarb. Ex 2c (SB offen) S schreiben die passenden Räume in ihr Heft.

STOP! CHECK! GO!

► *DFF 2.1* ► *DFF 2.2* ► *DFF 2.3* ► *KV 2.6* ► *INKL 2.12 A/B*

Ein Lösungsblatt für die Aufgaben 1 bis 6 kannst du von deiner Lehrerin / deinem Lehrer erhalten. Du findest die Audiodatei (zu S. 32) online, zusammen mit den

1 WORDS Can you remember Ellie's family?

a) Find the right family word and write the sentences.

b) Do you know five more family words?

2 WORDS Sandy's house

a) Match the labels (A–H) with the places (1–8) in the picture.

A kitchen
B hall
C living room
D bedroom
E bathroom
F toilet
G garden
H garage

b) It's all wrong. But what's right? Correct the mistakes.

Hi! Welcome to my ~~madhouse~~ house.
The ~~hall~~ is yellow. And the ~~bathroom~~ is pink. This is my kitchen – it's very ~~small~~.
My ~~bedroom~~ is red – cool! Look at my living room – it's ~~red~~. Great! Now look at my garden.
It's ~~big~~, but it's my favourite place.

c) House quiz: Name the rooms.
1 It's a very small, white room!
2 I make lunch here.
3 My bed and wardrobe are here.
4 My bike is here.
5 I watch TV here.

STOP! – CHECK! – GO! Navigator | Vorbereitung

Zeitbedarf: ca. zwei Stunden
Materialbedarf: Ex **5**: Audio-CD + Player oder MP3 + PC/Lautsprecher
Einsatz von Begleitmedien: KV 2.6 (Lösungsschlüssel, auch für die Hand der S zur selbstständigen Lösungsüberprüfung, ggf. im Partner check) | DFF 2.1–2.5 | INKL 2.12 A/B

▸ *DFF 2.4* ▸ *DFF 2.5* ▸ *KV 2.6* ▸ *INKL 2.12 A/B*

3 REVISION Sandy's family

Complete the text for Sandy. Use: *'m • 's • is • are • 're*

My family ... (1) big. This ... (2) my father. Dad ... (3) very strict, but he ... (4) fun too. This ... (5) my mum. She... (6) cool, but she... (7) strict too.

My brothers and sisters ... (8) OK. But they... (9) very messy. We... (10) all very noisy. I... (11) happy because I... (12) in my new house. It... (13) great!

4 ○ Questions for Sandy //● p.129

Cyril has questions for Sandy. Choose the right answers.

1 Hey, Sandy. Are you happy?
2 Is your family small?
3 Are your parents strict?
4 Is your mum cool?
5 Are your brothers and sisters mean?
6 Are you and your family noisy?
7 Is your new house messy?

Yes, they are.
Yes, I am.
No, it isn't.
Yes, it is.
Yes, she is.
Yes, we are.
No, they aren't.

5 LISTENING Numbers and addresses

1.40 **a)** Numbers: The mobile numbers are wrong. Listen. Write the right numbers.

1.41 **b)** Addresses: Listen. Which address (1, 2 or 3) is Luca's address?

1 9 Windsor Road[1]
Plymouth PL3 1TE

2 9 Windsor Street[2]
Plymouth PL3 2ET

3 19 Winsbury Road[3]
Plymouth PL6 7NN

1.42 **c)** ● Listen. Write Adam's address.

1 [wɪnzə 'rəʊd] 2 ['wɪnzə striːt] 3 [wɪnzbəri 'rəʊd]

Erarb. Ex 3 (SB offen) S schreiben den Text ins Heft und setzen für die Zahlen die entsprechenden Formen von *be* ein.

Erarb. Ex 4 (SB offen) Es handelt sich um eine Parallelübung auf zwei Niveaus:
○ hier: S wählen zu Cyrils Fragen die passenden Kurzantworten aus dem Kasten.
● auf S. 129: S bilden die passenden Kurzantworten selbstständig.

Einstieg Ex 5 (SB offen) Zur Vorentlastung kann L die S im Plenum die Telefonnummern zunächst still lesen lassen, anschließend Chorsprechen.
Erarb. Ex 5a (SB offen) Nach dem **1. Hören** notieren S die korrigierten Telefonnummern. **2. Hören** zur Überprüfung.
Erarb. Ex 5b (SB offen) Beim **1. Hören** prüfen S die angebotenen Adressen und notieren ihre Lösung. **2. Hören** zur Überprüfung.
Erarb. Ex 5c (SB offen) S notieren beim **1. Hören** Adams Adresse. **2. Hören** zur Ergänzung/Überprüfung.

Lernschwerpunkt: **Wiederholen und üben, Lernfortschritte erkennen (Fokus: Unit 2)**

Kompetenzen: **Speaking** Adressen und Telefonnummern erfragen, weitergeben und buchstabieren | **Reading** Eine Bildergeschichte verstehen
Writing E-Mails schreiben | **Lern- und Arbeitstechniken** Eigene Lernfortschritte erkennen

Grammatik: Fragen und Kurzantworten

Redemittel: Buchstaben und Zahlen, Adressen und Telefonnummern; Sport und Hobbys

Einstieg Ex 6 (SB offen) Zur Vorentlastung kann L die S auffordern, sich zunächst Fragen zu überlegen, die sie selbst einem neuen E-Mail-Freund stellen würden.
Erarb. Ex 6a (SB offen) Stilles Lesen der E-Mail in EA. Anschließend fertigen S eine zweispaltige Tabelle an und schreiben Toms Fragen mit der passenden Form von *be* in die linke Spalte.
Erarb. Ex 6b (SB offen) S schreiben ihre persönliche Antwort (Kurzantwort) in die rechte Spalte.
Erarb. Ex 6c (SB offen) S orientieren sich beim Schreiben an Toms Mustertext und ihren Antworten aus b).

Erarb. Ex 7a/b (SB offen) Info-gap activity: Partner A beginnt, erfragt die gesuchten Informationen mithilfe der Sprechblasen und notiert Namen, Adresse und Telefonnummer des gesuchten Geschäfts. Partner B arbeitet auf S. 119 und beantwortet mithilfe des dort abgebildeten Werbeplakats die Fragen von Partner A. Anschließend Rollentausch.
Zusatz Freiwillige S-Paare tragen ihren Dialog im Plenum vor.

STOP! CHECK! GO!

▸ KV 2.6 ▸ INKL 2.12 A/B

6 WRITING An email to a new °e-pal[1]

Hi! I'm Tom, your new e-pal.
I live in England, but I'm from America. My family is small.
My parents aren't together. I live with my mum and my sister.
Our house is in Plymouth. Plymouth is nice. It's a big city in England.
My room is OK. I have a computer. I play games with my friends.
My school is in Plymouth too. It's very big. I have lots of friends.
They're very cool. My teachers are OK too. I have lots of questions for you.

a) ○ Read Tom's email.
Then write Tom's questions.
1 ... you from England?
2 ... your family small?
3 ... your house in a city?
4 ... your room nice?
5 ... your school big?
6 ... your friends cool?
7 ... your teachers OK?

b) Write your answers to Tom's questions.

Tom's questions	My answers
1 Are you from England? 2 Is ...	No, I'm not.

c) ● Write Tom an email about yourself.

7 SPEAKING Good shops

PARTNER B: Go to page 119.
a) PARTNER A:
Imagine you're in Plymouth.
You want to find a good mobile shop.
Ask partner B these questions.
Write: – the name of the shop
– the address
– the phone number.

b) Partner B doesn't know this sports shop. Answer partner B's questions.

1 ['i:pæl] 2 ['sɔ:ltæʃ]

Zeitbedarf: ca. zwei Stunden

Kooperative Lernformen: Info-gap activity Ex **7**

Einsatz von Begleitmedien: KV 2.6 (Lösungsschlüssel, auch für die Hand der S zur selbstständigen Lösungsüberprüfung, ggf. im Partner check) | INKL 2.12 A/B | Workbook S. 31–34

▸ *INKL 2.12 A/B*

8 READING A new hobby

a) Read the story.

Erarb. Ex 8a (SB offen) **1. Lesen** der Bildgeschichte in Stillarbeit.
Erarb. Ex 8b (SB offen) S beantworten Detailfragen zur Geschichte bildgestützt. **2. Lesen** zur Überprüfung der eigenen Antworten möglich. Optional: Die Geschichte kann im Plenum von freiwilligen S nachgespielt werden.

b) Answer the questions about the story.

1 Who's bored?
2 Who has an idea?
3 Who has no tae kwon do clothes?
4 Who's new at the club?
5 Who thinks tae kwon do is easy?
6 Who's tired?
7 Who has a new hobby?

9 My learner log

Write your learner log for Unit 2.
Put it in your DOSSIER.

My learner log

My favourite °pages in Unit 2 are: ...
My favourite text in Unit 2 is: ...
My favourite phrases in Unit 2 are: ...
Difficult words in Unit 2 are: ...
My °progress in English is: GREAT! / OK / NOT VERY GOOD

Erarb. Ex 9 (SB offen) Schriftlich gemäß Muster, siehe auch ausführlicheres Muster in Unit 1 (S. 33). Die S können ihr *learner log* mit entsprechenden Symbolen versehen.

Lernschwerpunkt: Die Heimatstadt vorstellen (am Beispiel von Plymouth)
Storyline: Luca Boateng, dessen Eltern aus Ghana kommen, stellt sich, seine Familie und seine Heimatstadt Plymouth vor.
Kompetenzen: Listening Fotobeschreibungen verstehen; einen Song global erfassen | **Speaking** Mithilfe einer Mindmap seinen Wohnort beschreiben; einen Song mitsingen | **Lern- und Arbeitstechniken** Mindmaps zur Ideensammlung nutzen
Redemittel: Wohnen, Räume benennen, Bilder beschreiben

Einstieg Ex 1 (SB geschl.) Aktivieren von WS-Vorkenntnissen der S zu Gebäuden/Plätzen in einer Stadt durch Bildimpulse (z. B. Bildkarten, Fotos) bzw. Einführen von unbekanntem Lern-WS. Aussprache und Schriftbild sichern (*often*).
Überleitung (SB offen) L: *Luca lives in Plymouth. He likes his town. What do you think are his favourite places in Plymouth? (his home, the park, the fire station, the shops, the swimming pool, the cinema)*
Erarb. Ex 1a *Pre-listening:* Zuordnung von Text und Bild in EA oder PA.
Erarb. Ex 1b 1. Hören (Globalverstehen): Überprüfen der Text-/Bild-Zuordnung.
Erarb. Ex 1c 2. Hören (Detailverstehen): nur Anfangsbuchstaben notieren, nach **Ausw.** in **Ex 1d** (im Plenum) komplette Lösung notieren.

Einstieg Ex 2 (SB geschl.) Mindmap-Struktur erarbeiten. L spricht beim Zeichnen: *In my town we have a ...*
Never (neuer WS) gestisch verdeutlichen.
Erarb. Ex 2a (SB offen) L weist S auf farbliche Gestaltungsmöglichkeiten sowie die *Wordbank* S. 176 hin.
● Lernstärkere ergänzen weitere Äste, z. B. *I often go to ...*

Unit 3 My Plymouth

► IAT 3.1 ► INKL 3.1 ► INKL 3.2 ► DFF 3.1 ► Folie 17

1 This is my town

a) Before you listen to Luca, match the sentences (A–F) with the photos (1–6).

A My favourite shop is a mobile shop.
B I often go to the cinema with my friends.
C I ride my BMX bike in the park. Box: Voc., p. 193
D We live in Windsor Street[1].
E We go to a swimming pool in the summer.
F My dad works at a fire station.

1

b) Listen and check. (2.02) A 4 • B 6 • C 2 • D 1 • E 5 • F 3

c) Listen again and pick the right notes.

Family name:	Boateng[2] / Windsor
House number:	1 / 9
Name of mobile shop:	Phones 4U / Mobiles 4U
Name of park:	Plymouth Park / Central Park
Name of fire station:	Greenbank / Charles
Name of swimming pool:	Big Pool / Tinside Lido[3]
Name of cinema:	Reel Cinema / Plymouth Cinema

d) Check your notes with a partner.

4

2 Your town

a) Make a mind map for your town or a town near you.

► Wordbank 6, p. 176

b) Compare your mind map with a partner. Can you find more ideas for your mind map?

c) Talk to your class about your town. Use your mind map.

6

1 ['wɪnzə stri:t] 2 [bwa:teŋ] 3 [tɪnsaid 'laidəu]

► Workbook 1–2, p. 37

Zeitbedarf: ca. zwei Stunden
Minimalversion: Ex **1a–c**; **2a–c**
Kooperative Lernformen: Partner check (optional) Ex **1b**; **2d**
Materialbedarf: Ex **1a**: Bildkarten oder Fotos zu folgenden Begriffen: *cinema, fire station, aquarium, shopping centre, market, supermarket, swimming pool* | Ex **1b**; **3**: Audio-CD + Player oder MP3 + PC/Lautsprecher
Einsatz von Begleitmedien: IAT 3.1 | INKL 3.1–3.2 | DFF 3.1 | Folie 17 | Workbook S. 37

3

2

3

5

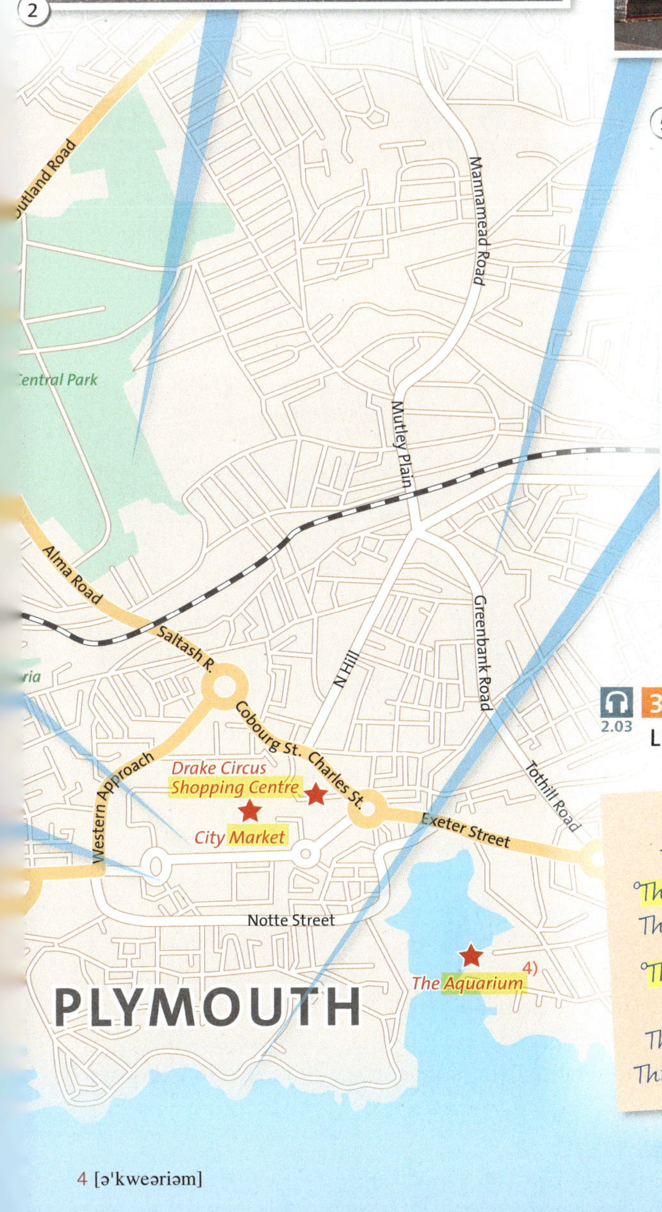

3 2.03 **SONG This is my city**
Listen to the song and sing along.

This is my city
This is my town, this is my city.
°Through my °eyes it °looks °so °pretty.
This is my town, this is my city now.
°These are my people, this is my song.
°Dirty streets, where I °belong.
This is my town, this is my city now.
This is my city now. Timothy Victor

Erarb. Ex 3 (SB offen)
1. Hören: S hören den Songauszug (Refrain) und lesen mit. Überprüfung des Globalverstehens (Tafel): *Does the singer love the city?* ☐ *Yes.* ☐ *No.*
2./3. Hören: S hören den Song mehrmals und singen mit. Im Song ist die amerikanische Aussprache von *city* und *pretty* für S ungewohnt.
Auf die korrekte Aussprache von *this* und *these* achten.
● Lernstärkere lernen einige Zeilen auswendig und präsentieren den Text allein oder paarweise.
Zusatz S suchen aus dem Kartenausschnitt im Hintergrund der SB-Seite unterschiedliche Bezeichnungen für Straßen heraus: *Road, Street (St.), Hill, Plain, Approach*

4 [ə'kweəriəm]

Lernschwerpunkt: **Tagesabläufe, Gewohnheiten und Vorlieben beschreiben**
Storyline: Luca beschreibt den Ablauf seiner Samstage. Heute sucht er mit seinem Vater ein Geburtstagsgeschenk aus.
Kompetenzen: **Speaking** Sagen, was man immer, manchmal oder nie tut; über Kleidungsvorlieben sprechen | **Reading** Texte global und im Detail verstehen | **Lern- und Arbeitstechniken** Eine Tabelle zur Strukturierung von Aktivitäten anfertigen
Grammatik: vorbewusste Verwendung des *simple present* für regelmäßige Ereignisse, Gewohnheiten
Redemittel: Gewohnheiten und Vorlieben beschreiben (u. a. mit Hilfe von Häufigkeitsadverbien); ein Geschenk auswählen

Einstieg Ex 1 (SB geschl.) Wdh der Wochentage: L zeigt Zahl zwischen 1 (= *Monday*) und 7 (= *Sunday*) und fragt: *Which day is it?* Bei Bedarf zusätzliche Hilfe an der Tafel, z. B. 5: *F _ i _ _ _ (Friday)*
Überleitung L: zeigt auf Zahl 6: *My favourite day is ... :*
S: *Saturday.*
L: *Let's see what Luca does on Saturdays.*
Erarb. Ex 1a (SB offen) *Pre-reading* gemäß Aufgabe
● Lernstärkere beschreiben die Abb. näher, z. B.: *In picture* **A** *I can see Luca, Luca's dad, Luca's brother, Luca's sister. They are in the living room.*
Erarb. Ex 1b **1. Lesen** (und optional Hören im Mitleseverfahren). S notieren unbekannten WS aus dem Text und erschließen ihn in PA (über Kontext, Bilder). L sammelt die neuen Wörter an Tafel; sichert Bedeutung und Aussprache (Vor- / Chorsprechen)
2. Lesen (Detailverstehen) und Zuordnen der Satzteile
Ausw. Ex 1b Kontrolle im Partner check, dann paarweise Präsentation im Plenum (Partner 1 liest ersten Satzteil, Partner 2 ergänzt passend den zweiten, dann Wechsel)
Mögliche HA: Die ganzen Sätze notieren.

3 THEME 1

► DFF 3.4 ► Folie 17

Weekends in Plymouth

2.04

1 Saturdays are great

a) **Before you read, look at the pictures: Where is Luca?**
In picture ... Luca is at the cinema / at the market / in the park / at home / ...

A

A Luca is at home.

Saturdays are great. I have no school. Mum always works on Saturdays. But dad always stays at home. I make a big breakfast for everybody. °Yummy!

B

B Luca is at the market.

In the morning we go shopping. First we go to the supermarket. Then we go to the market. Dad buys vegetables[1] – boring! We can buy nice things – like sweets.

C

C Luca is in the park.

In the afternoon dad and Grace usually[2] play games at home. Jack and I go to Central Park. We ride our BMX bikes there.

D

D Luca is at the cinema.

In the evening I sometimes go to the cinema. I meet my friends there. Jack often comes too. But Grace never comes.

Box: Voc., p.194
Box: Voc., p.194

b) **Match the sentence parts.**
1 On Saturdays Luca has no school.
2 Luca always makes ...

1 On Saturdays Luca has ...	shopping.	3
2 Luca always makes ...	to the cinema.	6
3 Then they all go ...	to Central Park.	5
4 Dad and Grace usually play ...	a big breakfast.	2
5 Jack and Luca go ...	no school.	1
6 In the evening they sometimes go ...	games at home.	4

1 ['vedʒtəblz] 2 ['ju:ʒuəli]

► Text file 4, p. 155

Zeitbedarf: ca. zwei Stunden
Minimalversion: Ex **1a+b**; **2a+b**; **3a**; **4a**
Kooperative Lernformen: Partner check Ex **1b** | Milling-around activity Ex **4a**
Materialbedarf: Ex **1a**; **3a** (optional): Audio-CD + Player oder MP3 + PC/Lautsprecher | Ex **2b**: Ball/Wollknäuel o. Ä.
Einsatz von Begleitmedien: KV 3.1 (optional) | INKL 3.3 | DFF 3.4; 3.6 | Folie 17–18 | Workbook S. 38–39

3

▸ Folie 18 ▸ INKL 3.3 ▸ KV 3.1 ▸ DFF 3.4 ▸ DFF 3.6

2 NOW YOU

a) Make a table about your Saturdays. Use ideas from the box. p. 130

I always	*I sometimes*	*I never*
go shopping	...	...

buy sweets • go shopping • go to the park • have a big breakfast • have lunch at a restaurant • meet friends • play football • play games • play music • ride my bike • stay at home • watch TV • ...

b) Tell the class. Throw a ball to the next student.

I always go shopping on Saturdays. What about you?

3 Shopping for a birthday present

2.05

a) Does Luca like shopping with his dad? Read and find out.

It's Luca's birthday soon. He's in a sports shop with his dad. They want to buy Luca's birthday present today.

Dad — Look, Luca. What about the black trainers?
Luca — Oh no, Dad! I don't like black trainers. What about the red trainers? They're cool. Box: Voc., p. 195
Dad — Red? Oh no! And they're too expensive – £99!
Luca — What about a hoodie then? I love the green hoodie!
Dad — It's OK. But what about the brown hoodie? It's nice.
Luca — A brown hoodie? Oh, Dad! I hate brown. It's boring. Shopping with you is terrible!

b) Finish the sentences.

A 
B 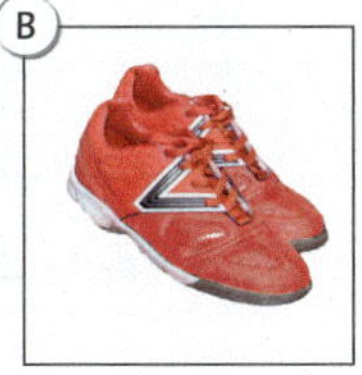
C 
D 

1 black; brown • 2 red; green • 3 brown

1 Dad likes the ... trainers and the ... hoodie.
2 Luca likes the ... and the ...
3 Luca hates the ...

4 I love the hoodie!

a) What do you love? What do you hate? Talk to different partners – as many as you can.

I love the hoodie! What about you?

Yes, I love the hoodie too.

Really? I hate the hoodie!

b) Tell the class.

- Everybody loves / hates the ...
- Lots of boys love ...
- Lots of girls hate the ...

Einstieg Ex 2 (SB geschl.) L verdeutlicht die Abstufung der Häufigkeitsadverbien anhand der Grafik im *Vocabulary* (S. 194).
Erarb. Ex 2 (SB offen) Parallelaufgabe: Lernstärkere finden auf S. 130 lediglich eine Auswahl an Verben als Hilfe vor.
Erarb. Ex 2b (SB geschl.) S stellen sich im Kreis auf und nutzen ihre Tabellen-Notizen als Formulierungshilfe

Einstieg Ex 3 (SB offen) Bildbeschreibung, Semantisierung. L: *Who's in the picture? (Luca, Luca's dad) Where are they? (in a sports shop) What can you see in the shop? (clothes, T-shirts, sweatshirts/hoodies, sports shoes/trainers, a football, a basketball)* ...
Erarb. Ex 3a **1. Lesen**/Hören (Globalverstehen). Für AA ggf. Hilfen an Tafel: ☺ *likes* ☹ *hates*
Erarb. Ex 3b S lesen Lückensätze, ergänzen nach dem **2. Lesen**

Einstieg Ex 4a (SB offen) S beschreiben Kleidungsstücke: *trainers, brown shoes, socks, mini skirt,* ...
Erarb. Ex 4a in Milling-around activity (optional mit KV 3.1)
Erarb. Ex 4b im Plenum

Lernschwerpunkt: **Über Geburtstage sprechen und Datumsangaben üben**
Storyline: Ellie, Luca, Adam und Berry unterhalten sich über ihre Geburtstage.
Kompetenzen: **Listening** Dialoge mit Datumsangaben global und im Detail verstehen | **Speaking** Sich über Geburtstage austauschen; das Datum (E) nennen | **Writing** Schreiben, was man am Geburtstag macht; das Datum (E) schreiben
Lern- und Arbeitstechniken Geburtsdaten in einer Tabelle erfassen
Redemittel: Geburtstagsgewohnheiten beschreiben (u. a. mit Hilfe von Häufigkeitsadverbien); Datumsangaben

Einstieg Ex 1 (SB geschl.) L notiert Monatsnamen im Jahreskreis an Tafel; Aussprache sichern. Dann Meldekette: L: *My birthday is in January / ... What about you?* S 1: *My birthday is in March / ... What about you?* S 2: *My birthday ...*
Überleitung L: *Let's find out more about Luca's and his friends' birthdays.*
Erarb. Ex 1a (SB offen)
1. Hören (Globalverstehen)
Ausw. Ex 1a Mdl. in PA, dann im Plenum
Erarb. Ex 1b (SB offen) L gibt Versprachlichungsmuster vor: *I think activity ... goes with picture ...*
Erarb. Ex 1c (SB offen)
2. Hören (Detailverstehen): S notieren die vier Daten, hören den Text und schreiben die passenden Namen dazu
Ausw. Ex 1c Kontrolle an Tafel, dann wiederholtes Sprechen (Chor, Gruppe, einzeln)

Erarb. Ex 2a (SB offen): *visit* einführen: L: *It's your birthday. Your friends come and* ***visit*** *you.* Zeit vorgeben, z. B.: *Write as many sentences as you can in five minutes.* (S benutzen jedes Adverb mindestens 1x)
Erarb. Ex 2b (SB geschl.) S stellen sich im Double circle auf, führen Kurzdialoge nach Muster (L: *On my birthday I always ... What about you?* S: *Me too / I never ...*); L gibt ca. alle 3 Min. Zeichen zum Wechsel im Uhrzeigersinn

3 THEME 2

► DFF 3.4 ► INKL 3.4 ► Folie 19

Birthdays

1 Birthday ideas

2.06

a) Listen. Which picture (1–4) is Luca's birthday, Ellie's birthday, Adam's birthday or Berry's birthday? Example: Picture ... is Luca's birthday.

1

Picture 1 is Ellie's birthday.

2

Picture 2 is Berry's birthday.

3

Picture 3 is Adam's birthday.

4

Picture 4 is Luca's birthday.

b) Match the activities with the pictures (1–4).

A I usually go to a nice place with my family – like the aquarium. 4
B We always stay at home on my birthday. 1
C I usually have a party with my friends. 3
D I sometimes go to the beach with my parents. 2

Box: Voc., p. 195

c) Listen again. Match the names with the birthdays.

Box: Voc., p. 195

B Luca
D Ellie
C Berry
A Adam

A 9th September
B 14th February[1]
C 1st August[2]
D 25th December

2 You and your birthday

a) What about your birthday? Write sentences.

On my birthday I	always usually sometimes never	go swimming. stay at home. get presents. go shopping. visit my aunt. have a party. go to a restaurant. go to the cinema. ...

b) Double circle: Talk to different partners about your birthday.

On my birthday I always / sometimes ... What about you?
Me too.
I usually ...

1 ['februəri] 2 ['ɔːgəst]

► Workbook 6, p. 39

Zeitbedarf: ca. zwei Stunden
Minimalversion: Ex **1a–c**; **2a**; **3b+c**; **4a+b**
Kooperative Lernformen: Double circle Ex **2b** | Partner check Ex **3+c** | Appointments Ex **5b**
Materialbedarf: Ex **1a+c**; **3b+d**: Audio-CD + Player oder MP3 + PC/Lautsprecher | Ex **4b**: Ball/Wollknäuel o. Ä.
Mp1, S. 130: 12 Blätter/Fotokarton (A4), Befestigungsmaterial (z. B. Wäscheleine, -klammern)
Einsatz von Begleitmedien: KV 3.2–3.3 | INKL 3.4–3.5 | DFF 3.3–3.4 | Folie 19 | Workbook S. 39–40

3

▸ Folie 19 ▸ KV 3.2 ▸ KV 3.3 ▸ INKL 3.5 ▸ DFF 3.3

3 Months[3] and dates

a) Write the months in the right order in your exercise book.

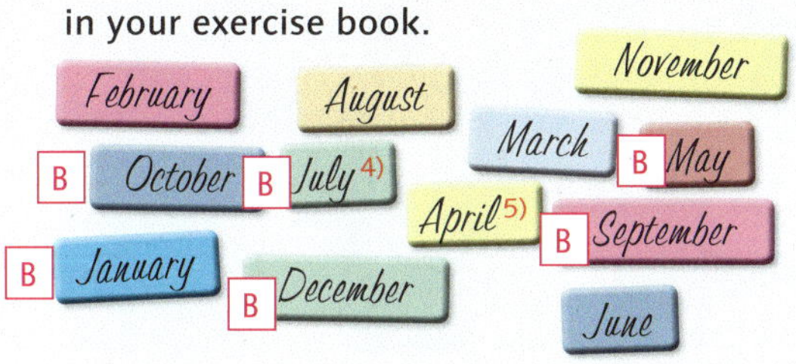

b) Listen. What months do you hear? (2.07)

c) Listen again. What dates do you hear, A or B?

1 A 15th January B 30th January
2 A 1st May B 5th May
3 A 2nd December B 22nd December
4 A 7th October B 11th October
5 A 16th July – 3rd September
B 17th July – 23rd September

d) Listen and repeat the dates. (2.08)

Box: Voc., p. 195

4 When's your birthday?

a) Write your birthday. How do you say it?
My birthday is on ...

You write:	You say:
1st March	the first of March
2nd July	the second of July
3rd September	the third of September
4th November	the fourth of November
5th December	the fifth of December

Box: Voc., p. 195

▸ More dates, p. 229

b) Birthday game: Throw the ball. Ask the question.

5 Talking about birthdays

a) Copy the table. Complete the 'Me' column for you.

Questions	Me	1 o'clock	2 o'clock	3 o'clock
		Tina	...	...
When's your birthday?	6th March	...	...	
When's your best friend's birthday?	10th July	...		
When's your mum's / dad's birthday?	mum 29th April			
When's your brother's / sister's birthday?	...			

b) Appointments: Make appointments for 1, 2 and 3 o'clock with three students. Write the names in the table.

c) Go to your appointments. Your teacher will tell you when it is 1, 2 or 3 o'clock. Talk to your partners. Ask two questions, or more. Write the birthdays on your table. More practice 1 p. 130

Ausw. Ex 3a im Partner check (korrekte Schreibung, Reihenfolge!)
Erarb. Ex 3b (SB geschl.) S verwenden die Liste aus **a)** und haken während des **1. Hörens** die gehörten Monate ab. Ein S arbeitet verdeckt an der Tafel; damit dann
Ausw. Ex 3b
Erarb. Ex 3c (SB offen) S übertragen Daten ins Heft, markieren beim **2. Hören** das korrekte
Ausw. Ex 3c im Partner check
Erarb. Ex 3d (SB geschl.) Hören und Nachsprechen

Einstieg Ex 4a (SB offen) Nachsprechen der Daten
Erarb. Ex 4a S notieren eigenes Geburtsdatum; Aussprache in PA üben
Erarb. Ex 4b gemäß Aufgabe
Zusatz Basteln eines Kalenders mit KV 3.2; diesen in den Folgewochen wiederholt zur Übung einsetzen

Einstieg Ex 5 (SB offen) L erklärt Appointments (Schritte a–c), Vorführen mit einem S; auch Wechselsignal einführen (z. B. L: *It's 1/2/3 o'clock now.*)
Erarb. Ex 5a–c mit Tabelle auf KV 3.3; dort zuerst Namen notieren
Ausw. Ex 5c zur Spalte Me mit Meldekette. Ggf. Muster vorgeben: *My mum's/ friend's/ ... birthday is on the ...*

FOCUS ON LANGUAGE Navigator | Inhalt

Lernschwerpunkt: Sich mit Hilfe des *simple present* über Tagesabläufe verständigen
Storyline: Ein typischer Wochentag in Lucas Familie
Kompetenzen: Listening Ein Gedicht hören und global verstehen | **Speaking** Ein Gedicht vortragen | **Reading** Eine bildgestützte Tagesverlaufsbeschreibung verstehen | **Writing** Den eigenen Tagesverlauf beschreiben | **Lern- und Arbeitstechniken** Verbformen in einer Liste erfassen; sprachliche Regelmäßigkeiten entdecken; Mindmap und Notizen zum eigenen Tagesverlauf erstellen
Grammatik: Bewusstmachen und Üben des *simple present* (Gebrauch, Bildung der 3. Person Singular)
Redemittel: Typische Tagesverläufe beschreiben

Erarb. Ex 1 (SB offen) Neuer WS kann mit Kontext/Bildern erschlossen werden. Nach der Auswertung sichern! Dazu liest L die Sätze in der richtigen Reihenfolge vor, notiert neuen WS an Tafel; S sprechen nach
○ Lernschwächere verwenden auf KV 3.4 Ex 1; die korrekte Zuordnung ergibt das Lösungswort GREENBANK
Ausw. Ex 1 Lösungsabgleich über Meldekette

3 FOCUS ON LANGUAGE

▸ *KV 3.4* ▸ *Folie 20* ▸ *INKL 3.6*

1 Luca's day

Match the sentences (A–I) with the pictures (1–9). Example: *1D, 2 ...*

A I get up early. I make breakfast for Grace. [2]
B I usually have lunch at school. [5]
C Lazy Jack! He gets up late. He never has breakfast! [3]
D Dad often works at night. He comes home in the morning. Box: Voc., p. 196 [1]
E After dinner we watch TV. Mum sometimes watches TV with us. Dad goes to work. [9]
F Mum often comes home late. We always have dinner together and we talk about the day. [8]
G In the afternoon dad stays in bed. We do our homework. [6]
H Jack and I go to school together. We usually go by bus. But I sometimes walk. Jack never walks. Lazy Jack! [4]
I In the evening dad usually makes dinner. [7]

Erarb. Ex 2a (SB offen) S notieren die Tabelle ins Heft und tragen die Verben im Satzzusammenhang ein: ggf. gekürzt, z. B. *Dad (usually) makes dinner.*
○ Lernschwächere markieren vorab auf KV 3.4 (Ex 2) die gesuchten Verben
Erarb. Ex 2b (SB offen) Anhand der Vorgaben und der Tabelle aus a) vervollständigen S die Regeln zu Gebrauch und Bildung des *simple present*. L erinnert S an den Merksatz „*He, she, it*: Das -s muss mit."

2 The simple present

a) There are lots of verbs in Luca's text, for example *get* and *gets*. Make two lists:

Verb ohne s	*Verb mit s*
I get up early.	*He gets up late.*

Lösung S. 234

b) Pick the right answers and make the rules.

FOCUS

Mit dem *simple present* sprichst du darüber, …	
(A) was jeden Tag, oft, manchmal oder nie passiert.	*I, you, we, they* → mit oder ohne 's' am Verb?
(B) was schon passiert ist.	*he, she, it* → mit oder ohne 's' am Verb?

▸ *Language file 6, p. 169*

Zeitbedarf: ca. zwei Stunden
Minimalversion: Ex **1**; **2a+b**; **3**; **5**
Kooperative Lernformen: Partner check Ex **6b**
Materialbedarf: Ex **4**: Audio-CD + Player oder MP3 + PC/Lautsprecher
Einsatz von Begleitmedien: KV 3.4 | INKL 3.6 | Folie 20–21 | Workbook S. 41–43

3

▸ *Folie 21*

3 Dad's day

Complete the sentences about Luca's dad.

1 Luca's dad ... (get up) late in the afternoon.
2 Then he usually ... (make) dinner.
3 In the evening he often ... (go) to work. He ... (work) at a fire station.
4 He usually ... (go) to work by car, but he sometimes ... (ride) his bike.
5 Sometimes it's quiet at the fire station and Luca's dad ... (watch) TV.
6 But usually it's busy and he ... (have) no time.
7 In the morning he ... (go) home.
8 He sometimes ... (have) breakfast with the kids.
9 Then he ... (go) to bed.

1 gets up • **2** makes • **3** goes, works • **4** goes, rides • **5** watches • **6** has • **7** goes • **8** has • **9** has

Vorsicht bei diesen Verben:
watch – watches
go – goes
have – has

Erarb. Ex 3 (SB offen) S notieren Text im Heft, unterstreichen Subjekt und Prädikat
Ausw. Ex 3 im Plenum; Aussprache (Kasten) sichern

4 Who is he?

2.09

Listen to the poem. Then repeat it. Who is 'he'?

He lives on the beach.
He walks on the °sand.
He swims in the sea.
He °pinches my hand.

He °chats and he °sings.
He °sits in the °sun.
He watches the °fishermen.
Then he °jumps up and °runs!

"He" is Cyril the crab.

Erarb. Ex 4 (SB offen)
1. Hören/Mitlesen (Globalverstehen);
2. Hören/Mitlesen: S Vermutungen äußern lassen, was Cyril tut (Zeile für Zeile, einzelne S flüstern Vermutetes auf D ins Ohr des L). Korrekte Vermutungen dürfen S pantomimisch darstellen.
3. Hören/Mitlesen: Zeile für Zeile, mehrmals mitsprechen und memorieren, in PA üben, dann präsentieren

5 ○ Cyril and Sandy's day

//● p. 130

Write about Cyril and Sandy. Pick the right form of the verbs.

1 In the morning I ... up early.

2 Sandy is lazy. She ... up late.

3 I usually ... breakfast on the beach.

4 I often ... my friends.

5 We ... swimming together.

6 Sandy often ... to Plymouth with her friends.

More practice 2 p. 131

Erarb. Ex 5 (SB offen) S notieren Sätze im Heft, setzen korrekte Verbform ein
//● Lernstärkeren wird auf S. 130 nur das Verb vorgegeben → 3. Person muss selbstständig gebildet werden.
Ausw. Ex 5 im Plenum

6 ● NOW YOU

a) Make notes about your day. You can use a mind map.

More help p. 131

b) Use your notes and write a text about your day. You can put it in your DOSSIER[1].

More help p. 131

Einstieg Ex 6 (SB offen) Ggf. Hilfe: abgestufte Häufigkeitsadverbien von S. 194. S nennen ihre Aktivitäten in Meldekette.
Erarb. Ex 6a Ggf. Unterstützung für Mindmap durch Bilder geben.
○ Lernschwächere nutzen More help auf S. 131, auch für die **Erarb. Ex 6b**
Ausw. Ex 6b im Partner check

▸ *Workbook 9–13, pp. 41–43*

1 ['dɒsieɪ]

STORY Navigator | Inhalt

Lernschwerpunkt: **Eine Fotogeschichte verstehen und nacherzählen**

Storyline: Lucas Geburtstag verläuft anders als geplant: Wegen seines Radunfalls kein Konzertbesuch bei *Francis and the Drakes* (http://www.francisandthedrakes.co.uk/), aber seine Freunde organisieren doch noch eine gelungene Party für ihn.

Kompetenzen: Listening Einen Dialog global und im Detail verstehen | **Speaking** Anhand von Fotos Hypothesen formulieren
Reading Eine Fotogeschichte global und im Detail verstehen | **Writing** Eine Fotogeschichte gestützt nacherzählen
Redemittel: Geburtstagspläne machen (und ändern)

3 STORY

▸ INKL 3.7 ▸ DFF 3.7 ▸ DFF 3.8

Erarb. Ex 1 (SB offen) Hypothesenbildung und Austausch im Partner talk
Ausw. Ex 1 im Plenum
Erarb. STORY (SB offen)
1. Lesen/Hören (Globalverstehen): S überprüfen Vermutung aus 1: *First Luca's birthday is fun. But then he falls and he's unhappy.*
Neuer WS kann von S selbstständig erschlossen werden (Bilder, Kontext, Ähnlichkeit zum Deutschen). Anschließend sichern. L klärt die Aussprache von *concert* (S. 210) und *zoo* (S. 218).
Hinweis: Jack deutet in Szene 2 eine scherzhafte Version des berühmten amerikanischen Geburtstagsliedes an.

1 Before you read

Look at the photos. Is Luca's birthday fun?
Talk to a partner.

– I think Luca's birthday is / isn't fun.
– Look at photo ... He's happy / unhappy.

Happy birthday, Luca!

2.10

1 It's Thursday. Luca's birthday is on Saturday. He wants to do something different for his birthday. But what? He has no ideas.

2 It's Saturday morning. Luca is excited. It's his birthday. He likes his presents.

3 Mum is at work. Grace and dad are at the shops. Luca and Jack are on their bikes.

Box: Voc., p. 196

1 [plɪməθ pə'vɪliənz] 2 ['kɒnsət] 3 [həʊ]

STORY Navigator | Vorbereitung

Zeitbedarf: ca. zwei Stunden
Minimalversion: Ex **1**; **3**; **4a**
Kooperative Lernformen: Partner talk Ex **1**
Materialbedarf: Ex **1** (optional); Ex **4**: Audio-CD + Player oder MP3 + PC/Lautsprecher
Einsatz von Begleitmedien: INKL 3.7 | Diff 3.7–3.8 | Workbook S. 43

▸ *DFF 3.7* ▸ *DFF 3.8*

4 Jack and Luca go to the Hoe. Jack meets his friends. They have great BMX bikes and they go down the hill fast.

5 Jack goes down the hill first. He's OK. Now it's Luca's turn.

6 Luca goes down the hill. But he falls.

7 Luca and Jack are back from the hospital. Luca has a sore leg. His mum is not happy!

Erarb. Ex 2 (SB offen) **2. Lesen**/Hören (Detailverstehen)
Zusatz S lesen die Geschichte mit verteilten Rollen (Erzähler, Luca, Lucas Mutter, Lucas Vater, Jack).

Erarb. Ex 3 (SB offen) S erzählen die Geschichte mithilfe der Satzanfänge nach.
○ Lernschwächere finden in More help (S. 132) zu den Satzanfängen passende Satzenden zum Zuordnen.
Ausw. Ex 3 in PA/GA, wobei immer mindestens ein S, der More help benutzt hat, beteiligt sein sollte

Erarb. Ex 4a (SB offen) Gemeinsames Lesen des Hörauftrags. Ggf. beide Fragen als Tafelnotiz/Gedächtnisstütze. Dann **1. Hören** und Fragenbeantwortung (Überprüfung des Globalverstehens).
Erarb. Ex 4b **2. Hören** (Detailverstehen): Informationen zu Lucas Geschenken
Zusatz L spielt einen Beispiel-Song von *Francis and the Drakes* vor (eine Folk-Akustik-Pop-Band aus Plymouth); S recherchieren Weiteres über die Band

2 ○ Right or wrong?

1	Luca wants a party.	Wrong
2	Luca likes mum's idea.	Right
3	Luca and Jack go shopping with dad on Saturday.	Wrong
4	Jack meets his friends at the Hoe.	Right
5	Luca goes down the hill first.	Wrong
6	Luca falls.	Right
7	Luca stays in the hospital.	Wrong
8	Luca is happy at home.	Wrong

3 ● Luca's birthday

Write the story.

Lösung S. 234

On Thursday Luca has no ideas for ...
But his mum has a great ...
On Saturday morning Luca gets ...
Later the boys meet Jack's friends at ...
Jack goes down ...
Then Luca goes ..., but ...
Jack and Luca go ...
Luca has ...

More help p. 132

4 The end of the story

2.11

Adam, Ellie and Berry come to Luca's house. Luca is happy in the end.

a) Listen to the end of the story. Who comes to Luca's house? Is Luca happy in the end?

b) Listen again. What presents does Luca get from his friends?

Luca gets a cake, chocolate and a CD of Francis and the Drakes from Adam, Ellie and Berry.

▸ *Workbook 14–16, p. 43*

SKILLS TRAINING Listening

Lernschwerpunkt: Preise und Geld in Großbritannien
Kompetenzen: **Listening** Einkaufsdialoge und Preise verstehen
Speaking Preise sprechen | **Writing** Preise ausschreiben
Lern- und Arbeitstechniken Dinge in Listen erfassen
Redemittel: Dinge beschreiben, Preise nennen und schreiben

Zeitbedarf: ca. eine Stunde
Kooperative Lernformen: Partner talk Ex **2b**
Materialbedarf: Ex **1** (optional): reales englisches Geld
Ex **1b**; **Mp3**: Audio-CD + Player oder MP3 + PC/Lautsprecher
Einsatz von Begleitmedien: DFF 3.9 | INKL 3.8–3.9 Workbook S. 44

Einstieg Ex 1 (SB offen) L: *Look at the picture. What can you see?* S äußern sich in Meldekette (unkommentiert). L sammelt in Tabelle (analog Ex **1**), ergänzt *There's* | *There are* im Laufe der Antworten.
Erarb. Ex 1a S vervollständigen die Tabelle in EA/PA; ○ Lernschwächere nutzen More help
Erarb. Ex 1b **1. Hören** ○ zuerst nur Spalte *There's* abhaken, danach *There are*
Überleitung L: *So Luca needs money. In Britain they don't have Euros (€). What money do they have?* S: *They have pounds and pence.*
Erarb. Ex 1c Vor **2. Hören** notieren S Satzanfänge, ergänzen beim Hören nur den Preis. //● Lernstärkere arbeiten mit S. 133. Auf unterschiedliche Schreib-/Sprechweise hinweisen (Box)!
Ausw. Ex 1c abwechselnd in PA

Einstieg Ex 2 (SB geschl.) L zeigt und benennt kleine Dinge (Stifte, Telefon ...) für fiktiven *garage sale*. S notieren die Preise (Ziffern). £-Schreibweise mehrmals üben!
Erarb. Ex 2a (SB offen) S notieren die Preise (Ziffernschreibung)
Erarb. Ex 2b S sprechen die Preise (in Langform).

3 SKILLS TRAINING Listening

▸ INKL 3.8 ▸ INKL 3.9 ▸ DFF 3.9

1 Luca's garage[1] sale

▸ Language file 5, p. 168

More help p. 132

a) Luca needs money for a new bike. Look at the picture. What's in Luca's garage sale? Make two lists:

There's ...	There are
a bike	2 footballs
a ...	3 ...

Lösung S. 235

2.12 b) Look at your lists. Listen and tick (✓) in your list what you hear.

c) ○ Listen again. How much are the things in the garage sale? //● p. 133

1 The calculator is ... £1
2 The mobile is ... £9.50
3 The crab is ... 50 p.
4 The posters are ... £5
5 The computer is ... £20
6 The school bag is ... £5.50
7 The blazer is ... £10
8 The footballs are ... £4

£5 £20 £9.50 £10 £4 £1 £5.50 50p

You write:	You say:
£1.50	One pound fifty
50 p	Fifty p

2 British money

a) Write labels for a sale: *A: £1.50, B: ...*

£1.50	A: One pound fifty
99 p	B: Ninety-nine p
£17	C: Seventeen pounds
£4.25	D: Four pounds twenty-five
£5.30	E: Five pounds thirty

b) What do you say? Practise with a partner.

1 £3.99 2 20p 3 £8.50 4 £11.25 5 £24.90 6 £15

1 three pounds ninety-nine (p)
2 twenty p
3 eight pounds fifty (p)
4 eleven pounds twenty-fi ve (p)
5 twenty-four pounds ninety (p)
6 fifteen pounds

More practice 3 p. 133 2.13

1 [gæra:ʒ]

▸ Workbook 17–18, p. 44

SKILLS TRAINING Speaking

Lernschwerpunkt: Verkaufsgespräche führen
Kompetenzen: **Listening** Ein Verkaufsgespräch verstehen | **Speaking** Verkaufsgespräche gestalten
Reading Einen Verkaufsdialog global verstehen
Lern- und Arbeitstechniken Einem Dialog Redemittel entnehmen
Redemittel: Dinge auswählen, Kaufentscheidungen treffen
Zeitbedarf: ca. eine Stunde

Minimalversion: Ex **1**, **2a+b**
Kooperative Lernformen: Role-play Ex **3**
Materialbedarf: Ex **1** (optional); Ex **2b**: Audio-CD + Player oder MP3 + PC/Lautsprecher | Ex **3**: Karteikarten, Spielgeld
Einsatz von Begleitmedien: DFF 3.2, 3.9 | INKL 3.10 Folie 22 | Workbook S. 45

SKILLS TRAINING Speaking 3

▸ DFF 3.2 ▸ DFF 3.9 ▸ Folie 22 ▸ INKL 3.10

1 In a bike shop
2.14

No, he can't buy his dream bike. It's too expensive.

Can Luca buy his dream bike? Read and find out.

Luca — Mum, it's the Montana. It's my dream bike.
Mum — It looks nice. Is it expensive? (Box: Voc., p. 197)
Luca — Excuse me, please. How much is this bike?
Man — It's £ 279.
Luca — That's too expensive. How much is the 5 Star?
Man — It's £ 159. It's a special offer.
Mum — That's OK. It looks nice too.
Luca — Yeah, and it's good value[2]. Jack has the same bike. Can I buy it, Mum?
Mum — It's your money.
Luca — Can I try it?
Man — Sure.
Luca — ... Wow, it's really great. I'll take it.
Man — Good. That's £ 159, please.

2 A new helmet

a) Copy and complete the dialogue. Look at 1 for help.

Luca — This helmet looks ... (1). I like it. Excuse me, ... (2). How ... (3) is the red helmet?
Man — ... (4) £ 24.99.
Luca — That's too ... (5)! ... (6) much is the white helmet?
Man — It's a ... (7) offer. It's £ 16.99.
Luca — That's OK. I'll ... (8) it. (More help p. 133)

b) Listen to the dialogue and check.
2.15

1 nice • 2 please • 3 much • 4 It's • 5 expensive • 6 How • 7 special • 8 take

3 ROLE-PLAY
A garage sale

Partner B: Go to page 119.
Partner A: You're at a garage sale in Plymouth. You have £ 15. Buy some things.

Excuse me, please.
How much is the ...?
That's too expensive / OK!
I'll take it.
Here you are.

Swap roles.

Einstieg Ex 1 (SB geschl.) Wdh/Sichern der Zahlen: Preise (auch > £100) von Tafel vorlesen lassen. S auf Hilfen S. 229 verweisen.
Erarb. Ex 1 (SB offen) **1. Lesen**/Hören des Dialogs (Mitleseverfahren); Fragebeantwortung: Globalverstehen sichern. Unbekannten WS sichern, dann **2./3. Lesen** mit verteilten Rollen

Einstieg Ex 2 (SB offen) L: *Luca needs a new helmet. Look at the photo. How much are the helmets?* S: *The red helmet is twenty-four pounds (and) ninetynine (p). The white helmet is sixteen pounds (and) ninety-nine (p).*
Erarb. Ex 2a Lernschwächere nutzen More help
Ausw. in **Ex 2b Hören** (ggf. mehrmals), Lösungskontrolle in EA/PA

Einstieg Ex 3 (SB offen) L: *What can you see on the table?* S betrachten die Abb., benennen angebotene Gegenstände; L notiert an Tafel mit (*red hoodie, yellow T-shirt, yellow sweatshirt, ...*)
Erarb. Ex 3 ist eine Info-gap activity: Partner B (= Verkäufer) arbeitet auf S. 119, nennt Preise. Partner A notiert Preise, errechnet Summe. Rollenwechsel je bei Erreichen von £15

▸ Workbook 19–20, p. 45
2 ['vælju:]

SKILLS TRAINING Reading

Lernschwerpunkt: **Veranstaltungsposter verstehen**
Kompetenzen: Reading Authentische Werbeposter verstehen (schlussfolgerndes Lesen)
Lern- und Arbeitstechniken Unbekannte Wörter erschließen
Redemittel: Veranstaltungsorte, -zeiten und Aktivitäten

Zeitbedarf: ca. eine Stunde
Einsatz von Begleitmedien: DFF 3.5 | INKL 3.11 Workbook S. 46

3 SKILLS TRAINING Reading

▸ INKL 3.11 ▸ DFF 3.5

Erarb. Ex 1 (SB offen)
1. Lesen (Globalverstehen). L: *Look at the posters. They are* ***adverts****. What do you think is the German word for advert?* (Anzeige, Werbung) *What are the adverts for? (A: a musical, B: a summer festival, C: an aquarium)*
2. Lesen (Detailverstehen): Zuordnung Poster-Aussagen in EA.

1 Plymouth adverts[1]

Match the sentences with the adverts: A, B or C. Sometimes there are two answers.

1 You can go there in February. – *Adverts A, C.*
2 You like music. A
3 You like fish and the sea. A
4 It's summer in Plymouth. B, C
5 You can go there in July. B, C
6 You can go there in March. C
7 You don't need money. B
8 You can watch a film here. C

A

B

C

Erarb. Ex 2 (SB offen) Mithilfe der deutschen Tipps zur Worterschließung in der Box äußern S Vermutungen zu deutschen Übersetzungen der ausgewählten Begriffe. ◯ Lernschwächere nutzen More help
Ausw. Ex 2 im Plenum (Alternative: S kontrollieren durch Nachschlagen in einem Wörterbuch)

2 Guessing new words

What are these words in German?

1 on stage (advert A), fireworks (advert B)
2 theatre (advert A), festival (advert B)
3 opening times (advert C), adults (advert C)

So kannst du manche neue Wörter verstehen:
1. Schau auf die Bilder.
2. Gibt es ein ähnliches Wort im Deutschen?
3. Schau auf die Wörter vor oder nach dem Wort.

More help p. 133 More practice 4 p. 134

▸ Skills file 3, p. 163

1 auf der Bühne, Feuerwerk • 2 Theater, Festival • 3 Öffnungszeiten, Erwachsene

1 ['ædvɜːts]

▸ Workbook 21, p. 46

SKILLS TRAINING Viewing

Lernschwerpunkt: **Fiktionale und dokumentarische Filmszenen verstehen**
Kompetenzen: **Viewing** Filmszenen verstehen; Beweggründe Handelnder herausfinden
Speaking Sich zur Attraktivität von *sights* in einer Dokumentation äußern | **Lern- und Arbeitstechniken** Gefühle von Figuren erfassen
Redemittel: Gefühle beschreiben, Wünsche äußern

Zeitbedarf: ca. eine Stunde
Kooperative Lernformen: Partner talk Ex **2b**
Materialbedarf: DVD + Player oder PC/Lautsprecher
Einsatz von Begleitmedien: KV 3.5 | IAT 3.2

SKILLS TRAINING Viewing 3

► *IAT 3.2* ► *KV 3.5*

1 The kids from Harbour Road: Sarah isn't happy!

a) Watch part 1 of the film. Why isn't Sarah with Anna and Paul at the shops?
1 Because Paul and Anna don't like Sarah.
2 Because Sarah hates shopping.
3 Because they want to buy Sarah a present.

b) Watch part 2 of the film. Then match the photos (1–4) with the sentences (A–D).

1 

2 

3 

4 

A It's £5.99. 3
B I'll take this hat[1], please. 4
C This is Sarah's favourite shop. 1
D What about this one[2]? 2

c) Watch part 3. Describe Sarah's feelings.
First she's ... Then she's ... Then ... In the end she's ...

angry[3] • happy • surprised[4] • unhappy

First she's surprised. Then she's unhappy. Then she's angry. In the end she's happy.

2 People and places: Plymouth, England

a) Watch the film about Plymouth. Which places can you see in the film? Lösungsbsp. ● S. 235

The Reel Cinema

The Hoe[5)]

The Lido[6)]

The aquarium

The shopping centre

The market

b) What do you think about Plymouth? What place do you want to visit?

Plymouth looks big / nice / great / boring / ...

I want to visit / see the ... What about you?

[1] hat [hæt] *Hut* [2] this one *der/die/das da* [3] angry ['æŋgri] *wütend* [4] surprised [sə'praɪzd] *überrascht*

5 [həʊ] 6 ['laɪdəʊ]

Einstieg 1 (SB offen) L bereitet die S auf abschnittsweises Sehen vor. **Vor** jedem der drei Abschnitte lesen S die AA (still / im Plenum), damit sie wissen, worauf sie beim Film später achten sollen.
Erarb. Ex 1a (SB offen) **1. Sehen** (Globalverstehen) von **Part 1**; Nummer der korrekten Begründung notieren
Ausw. Ex 1a im Plenum, ggf. **2. Sehen**
Erarb. Ex 1b (SB offen) **1. Sehen** von **Part 2**
Erarb. Ex 1c (SB offen) **1. Sehen** von **Part 3**, Beschreibung von Sarahs Gefühlslagen. Smileys stützen Verständnis von *angry* und *surprised* (unbekannt).
Zusatz KV3.5 Nach Sehen aller *parts* im Zusammenhang

Erarb. Ex 2a (SB offen) Vorab Durchlesen der Namen der 6 *sights*. Nach dem **1. Sehen** Nennen der entdeckten Attraktionen.
Ausw. Ex 2a im Plenum
● Lernstärkere notieren noch Zusatzinformationen, s. Lösungsbsp. S. 235.
Erarb. Ex 2b (SB offen) S äußern eigene Meinung im Partner talk: Gesamtbewertung abgeben und persönlich interessante Orte nennen; ggf. **2. Sehen**
Ausw. Ex 2b im Plenum

STOP! – CHECK! – GO! Navigator | Inhalt

Lernschwerpunkt: **Wiederholen und Üben, Lernfortschritte erkennen (Fokus: Unit 3)**
Kompetenzen: Listening Überprüfung des Detailverstehens (Multiple Choice) | **Lern- und Arbeitstechniken** Eigene Lernfortschritte erkennen
Grammatik: Sätze mit den korrekten Formen des *simple present* ergänzen
Redemittel: Wortfelder *town; shopping; dates; birthdays*

STOP! CHECK! GO!

▸ INKL 3.12 ▸ KV 3.6 ▸ DFF 3.1 ▸ DFF 3.2 ▸ DFF 3.3

Ein Lösungsblatt für die Aufgaben 1 bis 5 kannst du von deiner Lehrerin / deinem Lehrer erhalten.
Du findest die Audiodatei (zu S. 86) online, zusammen mit den Workbook-Audiodateien.

Erarb. Ex 1a (SB offen) S notieren die Zahlen 1–8, ergänzen den dargestellten Ort
Erarb. Ex 1b S notieren Satzanfänge (1–3), fügen passende Begriffe hinzu
Erarb. Ex 1c S vervollständigen vorgegebene Satzbausteine
○ Lernschwächere nutzen More help

1 WORDS In a town

a) ○ What are the places? Write the names in your exercise book.

b) Finish the sentences.

1 You can watch a film in a ... 2 You can buy vegetables in a ... or a ...
3 You can buy trainers in a ...

c) ● Make sentences.

1 ... in a park. → *You can play games in a park.*
2 ... in a restaurant. → *You can ...*
3 ... in a shopping centre.
4 ... in a swimming pool.
5 ... in a mobile phone shop.
6 ... in a bike shop.

More help p. 134

Erarb. Ex 2 (SB offen) **1. Hören**: S notieren die korrekten Buchstaben, **2. Hören** zur Überprüfung

2 LISTENING In a sports shop

2.16

Listen to Ellie. She's in a sports shop. Pick the right answer – A, B or C.

		A	B	C
1	Ellie wants ...	a T-shirt.	a hoodie.	a sweatshirt.
2	The hoodie is ...	£14.99.	£40.19.	£40.99.
3	The T-shirts are ...	good value.	expensive.	a special offer.
4	The red trainers are ...	£58.	£85.	£18.50.
5	The white trainers are ...	expensive.	boring.	good value.
6	Ellie buys ...	a T-shirt.	trainers.	a hoodie.

Erarb. Ex 3a (SB offen) ○ Ggf. Hinweis für lernschwächere S: *Start your question with the question word (when/what)*
Erarb. Ex 3b S schreiben Daten ins Heft.
Erarb. Ex 3c **1. Hören**: S schreiben die gehörten Daten ausführlich, dann **2. Hören** zur Überprüfung.

3 WORDS Days, months and dates

a) ○ Write correct questions.

1 month / what / it / is ?
2 your / when's / birthday ?
3 date / it / what / is / today ?
4 best friend's / when's / your / birthday ?
5 day / what / today / is / it ?

b) What do you write?

1 3. 1. – *3rd January*
2 9. 3. – ...
3 12. 5. – ...
4 18. 7. – ...
5 20. 10. – ...
6 25. 12. – ...

2.17 **c)** ● Listen. Write the six dates.

Zeitbedarf: ca. zwei Stunden

Materialbedarf: Ex **2**: Audio-CD + Player oder MP3 + PC/Lautsprecher

Einsatz von Begleitmedien: KV 3.6 (Lösungsschlüssel, auch für die Hand der S zur selbstständigen Lösungsüberprüfung, ggf. im Partner check) | DFF 3.1–3.4 | INKL 3.12

▸ *KV 3.6* ▸ *DFF 3.4*

4 REVISION Stupid Cyril!

a) ○ Cyril has lots of questions for Sandy. Write the questions with *Is* or *Are*.

1 ... Eggbuckland school busy?
Is Eggbuckland school busy?
2 ... the students at school ?
3 ... Luca on his bike ?
4 ... the town quiet?
5 ... Grace and Mr Boateng at the market?
6 ... Mrs Boateng at work?

b) Write Sandy's answers.

1 No, ...
No, it isn't.
2 No, ...
3 Yes, ...
4 Yes, ...
5 No, ...
6 No, ... It's Sunday, Cyril! You stupid crab!

Erarb. Ex 4a (SB offen) S setzen passende Formen von *be* ein. L empfiehlt S, nach jeder Frage aus
a) Platz zu lassen, um die Antworten aus
b) im zweiten Schritt dahinterzuschreiben
Erarb. Ex 4b S setzen passende Kurzantworten ein.

5 LANGUAGE Cyril's birthdays

a) ○ Complete the text with the words in the box.

get up • go • have • love • meet • play • talk

On Cyril's birthdays Cyril and Sandy usually ... (1) early. They ... (2) to the beach. They ... (3) about the day.

Cyril — It's my birthday today. I always ... (4) a party. I ... (5) all my friends.

Sandy — Great! I ... (6) your parties. We always ... (7) lots of games.

b) Complete this text. Use the *simple present*.

come • go • help • make • plan • stay • work

Sandy always ... (1) to the market. She usually ... (2) home with lots of nice things: vegetables and pizza. Cyril always ... (3) at home. He ... (4) in the kitchen. He ... (5) a big birthday lunch for his friends. Cyril always ... (6) lots of good games. Sandy ... (7) Cyril with the games too.

c) ● Complete the sentences about Cyril's parties with the verbs in brackets. Use the simple present.

1 All Cyril's friends ... (come) to the party.
2 Cyril always ... (get) lots of presents.
3 Sandy ... (meet) Cyril's friends.
4 They usually ... (play) games.
5 They often ... (go) swimming in the sea.
6 Cyril ... (have) a great day.

Erarb. Ex 5a (SB offen) Gemäß Aufgabe (Formen ohne *-s*)
Erarb. Ex 5b (SB offen) Gemäß Aufgabe (Formen mit *-s*)
Erarb. Ex 5c (SB offen) Gemäß Aufgabe (Formen mit und ohne *-s*)

Lernschwerpunkt: Wiederholen und Üben, Lernfortschritte erkennen (Fokus: Unit 3)

Kompetenzen: Speaking Partner über ihre Aktivitäten befragen, dazu Notizen machen, anhand dieser berichten

Reading Textsorten erschließen; fehlende Begriffe in Zusammenhang einsetzen

Writing mit Textbausteinen über den Lieblingstag schreiben | **Lern- und Arbeitstechniken** Eigene Lernfortschritte erkennen

Redemittel: Wortfelder *weekend; my favourite day;* Gewohnheiten

Erarb. Ex 6a (SB offen) S tragen das passende Häufigkeitsadverb in die Spalte *Me* ein.
Erarb. Ex 6b (SB geschl.)S befragen nach der Methode Appointments 2 Partner; tragen das genannte Häufigkeitsadverb in die jeweilige Partner-Spalte ein. L sollte Redemittel aus den Sprechblasen an Tafel übertragen, damit S bei der Befragung nur Tabelle und Stift in der Hand haben müssen.
Erarb. Ex 6c (SB offen) S bilden mit ihrer Tabelle Sätze über ihre Gesprächspartner (wobei sie das Verb in die 3. Person Singular setzen müssen) und lassen die Klasse raten, um wen es sich handelt.

Erarb. Ex 7 (SB offen) S schreiben ihren Text mit vorgegebenen Textbausteinen und Tipps. Partner check nach diesen Kriterien:
- korrekte Schreibweise (z. B. Wochentage)
- richtige Satzstellung der Häufigkeitsadverbien (*always, usually, often, sometimes, never*)

STOP! CHECK! GO!

▸ *DFF 3.4*

6 SPEAKING At the weekend

a) What about your weekends? Copy the table. Fill in the table for you. Write: always, usually, often, sometimes, never.

At the weekend	Me	Partner 1	Partner 2
I ... go shopping.	often	...	...
I ... play football.	...		
I ... watch TV			
I ... go to the cinema.			
I ... meet friends.			
I ...			

b) Appointments: Talk to two partners and fill in the table.

I **sometimes** go shopping at the weekend. What about you?

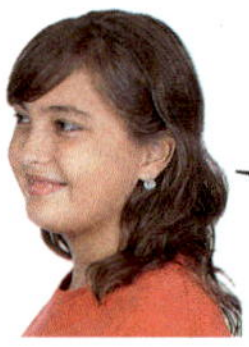

I **usually** go shopping at the weekend. And I ...

c) Use your table. Tell the class about one of your partners. Don't say the name. Can the class guess?

This girl **usually** goes shopping at the weekend.
She **never** plays football.
She **sometimes** watches TV.
...

Is it Lisa?

Is it Abida?

7 WRITING My favourite day

Write about your favourite day.

My favourite day is
- Friday.
- Saturday.
- ...

I get up
- early.
- late.
- ...

Then I have breakfast
- in the kitchen.
- with ...
- ...

After breakfast I
- play ...
- meet friends ...
- go to ...
- ...

I have lunch
- at home with ...
- in town with ...
- ...

In the afternoon I
- go shopping.
- ride my bike ...
- ...

In the evening I
- visit ...
- watch ...
- ...

I love	Friday Saturday ...	because	– I go to school. – I stay at home. – I do something different. – I meet my friends. – ...

Use **always** • **usually** • **often** • **sometimes** • **never**:
– I often get up late.
– Then I always have breakfast ...
– I never go shopping.

Zeitbedarf: ca. zwei Stunden
Kooperative Lernformen: Appointments Ex **6b** | Partner check Ex **7**; **8c**
Einsatz von Begleitmedien: DFF 3.4–3.5 | INKL 3.12

► *DFF 3.5* ► *INKL 3.12*

8 READING Casper[1] the cat

a) ○ Look at the text. Is it from a book, a comic or a newspaper? What do you think?

THE PLYMOUTH NEWS — Saturday, 16th January 2010

A cat story from Plymouth

Casper is a cat. He's twelve. He lives in Plymouth with Susan Finden.

Every morning Casper leaves the house at the same time. He walks to the bus stop and he waits there for the number 3 bus. When it comes, Casper gets on the bus. He sits on a seat and looks out of the window. The bus goes to the centre. Then it goes to the harbour. Casper watches everything. He watches the people, the cars, the buses, the houses. The bus travels 11 miles. When the bus comes to Casper's house again, the bus driver opens the doors and Casper gets out.

Everybody on the bus knows Casper. Everybody loves Casper. And Casper loves the number 3 bus. But he never buys a ticket.

b) Read the text. Finish the sentences and tell Casper's story.

Casper is a ... (1). He's from ... (2). Every day he travels on the number 3 ... (3). He watches ... (4). Everybody loves ... (5). Casper never ... (6).

c) ● Find these words in the text. Guess what they mean in German.

1 leaves (line 3)	4 sits (l. 5)	7 bus driver (l. 9)
2 bus stop (l. 4)	5 window (l. 6)	8 gets out (l. 9)
3 waits (l. 4)	6 travels (l. 8)	

More help p. 134

Was hat dir geholfen, unbekannte Wörter zu verstehen?
– Das Bild zum Text?
– Ein ähnliches deutsches Wort?
– Andere Wörter im Text?

9 My learner log

Copy and complete your learner log.

You can put it in your DOSSIER.

My learner log

I can ...	Examples	😊	😐	☹
– say the names of places in a town:	cinema	...	...	...
– say what I do at the weekend:	I often go shopping.	...	...	...
– say what I do every day:		...	...	...
– say what I like and don't like:		...	...	...
– say the numbers 1–100:		...	...	...
– say the months:		...	...	...
– say today's date:		...	...	...
– say what I do on my birthday:		...	...	...
– buy things in a shop:		...	...	...

My progress in English is: GREAT! / OK / NOT VERY GOOD

Erarb. Ex 8a (SB offen) S nennen (auf D) die Elemente des Textes (Überschrift, Foto, Datumsangabe) und folgern daraus die Textsorte (Zeitungsartikel).
Erarb. Ex 8b Zur Überprüfung des Leseverstehens ergänzen S eine lückenhafte Zusammenfassung.
Erarb. Ex 8c Abgleich im Partner check
○ Lernschwächere nutzen More help

Erarb. Ex 9 (SB offen) S bearbeiten ihr **My learner log** gemäß Muster. Sie können es mit entsprechenden Symbolen versehen.

► Workbook pp. 48–50

1 ['kæspə]

LEAD-IN Navigator | **Inhalt**

Lernschwerpunkt: **Eine englische Farm kennenlernen**

Storyline: Die *Merryweather Farm*, auf der Berry wohnt, ist ein beliebtes Ausflugsziel: Es gibt z. B. einen Streichelzoo, verschiedene Spielgeräte und einen Souvenirshop sowie die Möglichkeit, Ponys zu reiten.

Kompetenzen: Listening Einen Dialog selektiv erfassen; Bilder zuordnen; Detailinformationen entnehmen | **Speaking** Tiere auf einem Bauernhof benennen; diskutieren, was man tun möchte; sich mit dem Partner einigen

Redemittel: Wortfeld *farm animals*; sich abstimmen

Einstieg Ex 1 (SB geschl.) L: *Think of as many animal words as you can in two minutes.* S antworten in Meldekette, dabei jedes Tier nur einmal nennen. L notiert verdeckt an Tafel. Anschließend übernehmen S Tafelbild ins Heft.
Überleitung L: *Do you like farm holidays?* (Meinungsbild im Plenum durch Melden für *Yes/No* einholen) L: *What can you see or do on a farm?* – S: *You can see pigs/... / You can play with the cats/...*
Erarb. Ex 1 (SB offen) Bildbetrachtung, Tiersuche in EA; dann im Partner talk ggs. Nennen der Tiere
Ausw. Ex 1 S nennen die abgebildeten Tiere im Plenum (ggf. am Whiteboard zeigen). Einzelne S kreisen den betreffenden Tiernamen an Tafel (im Tafelbild aus dem Einstieg) ein. Tiere, die noch nicht an der Tafel stehen, dort und im Heft ergänzen

Unit 4 Berry's world

▸ IAT 4.1 ▸ INKL 4.1

1 On Merryweather Farm

How many different animals can you find in the brochure[1]?
Check with a partner.

Lots of visitors come to Merryweather Farm.

a rabbit

ducks

Watch the ducks on the pond!

ponies

Children can ride the ponies in the fields.

a duck

Welcome to Merryweather Farm

cows • sheep • donkeys • pigs • chickens • rabbits • a hamster • a rat • a chipmunk

a guinea pig

You can meet the animals in Pets Corner.

a horse

1 ['brəʊʃə]

LEAD-IN Navigator | Vorbereitung

Zeitbedarf: ca. zwei Stunden
Kooperative Lernformen: Partner talk Ex **1**; Think-Pair-Share Ex **3**
Materialbedarf: Ex **2**: Audio-CD + Player oder MP3 + PC/Lautsprecher
Einsatz von Begleitmedien: KV 4.1 | IAT 4.1 | INKL 4.1 | DFF 4.1 | Workbook S. 51

4

► IAT 4.1 ► KV 4.1 ► DFF 4.1

a donkey

a fox

You can go into the **barn** and **stroke** the **donkeys**.

Everybody loves the °**trampolines**[2] and the °**zip wire**.

a goat

There are lots of nice things in the shop.

2 Welcome to the farm

2.18

a) Which animals are on Berry's farm? Listen. Write the numbers or point at the pictures (1–12). 1 • 2 • 4 • 5 • 6 • 7 • 9 • 10 • 11

b) Listen again. Pick the right answer.

1 Berry is ... A in the field. B in the shop. C in the barn.
2 The tickets are ... A £15.50. B £60.00. C £59.50.
3 They don't have ... A cows. B sheep. C pigs.
4 The kids don't like ... A pets. B rats. C cats.
5 The toilets are near the ... A shop. B field. C barn.

More practice 1 p. 135

3 NOW YOU

a) Think: You're at Merryweather Farm. Where do you want to go? Pick two places.

b) Pair: Talk to a partner. Agree on two places.

- I want to go to the zip wire / ...
- I like donkeys / ...
- I don't like ...
- ... are boring / great / nice.
- OK. Let's go to ... and ...

c) Share: Tell the class.

Einstieg Ex 2 (SB offen) L liest vor dem Hören des Textes Hörauftrag vor und demonstriert ggf. Vorgehensweise (*point at*). Ggf. Lautschulung durch Nachsprechen
Erarb. Ex 2a Während des **1. Hören**s zeigen S auf das jeweilige Bild (zur Kontrolle Bildnummern im Heft notieren).
Ausw. Ex 2a **2. Hören** zur Kontrolle im Plenum. L/S notiert die genannten Tiere an Tafel/auf Folie.
Erarb. Ex 1b Ggf. vorab Vorgehen an Bsp. demonstrieren.
2. Hören, richtige Antwort auswählen und halten in Kurzform notieren (z. B. *1B*).

Erarb. 3a (SB offen) AA klären: Aufgabe ist ein Think-Pair-Share: Schritte erklären und eng steuern.
O Lernschwächere erhalten als Formulierungshilfe KV 4.1 (Ex 1+2)
Erarb. 3b S tragen sich gegenseitig ihre Präferenzen vor und einigen sich auf zwei Aktivitäten.
O Lernschwächere ordnen auf KV 4.1 (Ex 3) den Musterdialog, lesen ihn dann mit verteilten Rollen vor. Danach passen sie die grau hinterlegten Angebote für sich an.
Erarb. 3c gemäß Aufgabe

► Workbook 1–2, p. 51

2 ['træmpəliːn]

Lernschwerpunkt: Tagesabläufe auf einer Farm (inklusive Uhrzeitangaben)
Storyline: Berrys Tagesablauf auf der Farm sowie ein Tagesprogramm für Besucher der *Merryweather Farm*
Kompetenzen: **Listening** Kurzdialoge global erfassen, Bilder zuordnen; Zeitangaben verstehen | **Speaking** Über den eigenen Tagesablauf sprechen; die Uhrzeit erfragen und angeben | **Reading** Einem Text gezielt Informationen entnehmen; Sätze über Berrys Tagesablauf ergänzen
Redemittel: Gewohnheiten und Aktivitäten mit Uhrzeitangaben beschreiben

Einstieg Ex 1 (SB offen) Vorentlastung Textinhalt:
L: *Look at picture A/B/C/D: Who can you see? (**A**: Berry and her dog. **B**: Berry and her pony, Harry. **C**: Berry and her dad. **D**: Berry and two ponies, Harry and William.)*
*Where is Berry? (**A**: In bed. **B**: Near the barn. **C**: In the car. **D**: In the barn.)*
Zentralen neuen WS einführen mit dargestellten Situationen oder einfachen Tafelskizzen (*alarm clock, eat, do sport, …*)
Überleitung L: *Let's find out more about Berry's day.*
Erarb. Ex 1 (SB offen) **1. Lesen**/Hören (Globalverstehen). Dabei Sätze ergänzen, anschließend Partner check (ggs. Vorlesen).
Alternative KV 4.2 (Part 1), dann auch als reine HV-Aufgabe möglich oder als **HA**.
Ausw. Ex 1 im Plenum durch **2. Lesen**/Hören

Überleitung (SB geschl.) L: *What about you? Talk about your day. Each of you say one sentence, then pick the next student.* → Meldekette; L notiert dabei Beispielsätze als Sprachmuster an Tafel
Erarb. Ex 2a gemäß Aufgabe
Erarb. Ex 2b Partner talk, anschließend Präsentation im Plenum (einige freiwillige Paare)

4 THEME 1

▸ KV 4.2 ▸ INKL 4.2

Life on the farm

1 From Monday to Friday

2.19

Box: Voc., p. 198

Berry doesn't have an alarm clock. She has Sam. Sam is Berry's dog. Every morning Sam wakes Berry at 6 o'clock. He lives in the house with the family. The other animals don't live in the house. They live outside on the farm.

Berry goes outside before breakfast. She feeds her pony, Harry.

After breakfast Berry gets ready for school. She doesn't go to school by bus. She goes by car with her dad.
Berry stays at school all day. She usually comes home before 4 o'clock. Then she eats something and does her homework.

At about 5.30 she goes outside again. Sam comes too. First she looks after Harry. Then she helps with the other animals. She sometimes does sport in the evening. She doesn't watch TV. She doesn't have time!

Read the text. Then finish the sentences.

1 Every morning … (mum / the alarm clock / the dog) wakes Berry.
2 Before breakfast she … (watches TV / does nothing / feeds Harry).
3 She goes to school by … (car / bike / bus).
4 She comes home … (at 4 o'clock / before 4 o'clock / after 4 o'clock).
5 In the evening she sometimes … (does nothing / watches TV / does sport).

2 NOW YOU

a) Write sentences.

1 Every morning my … wakes me.
2 Before breakfast I …
3 I go to school by … / I walk to school with …
4 I come home at / before / after … o'clock.
5 In the evening I …

More help p. 135

b) Tell a partner about your day.

▸ Workbook 3–5, p. 52

Zeitbedarf: ca. zwei Stunden
Minimalversion: Ex **1**; **3a–c**; **4b+c**; **5a–c**
Kooperative Lernformen: Partner check Ex **1**; **3+b** | Partner talk Ex **2b** | Milling-around activity Ex **5c**
Materialbedarf: Ex **1** (optional); **3b**; **4a+b**: Audio-CD + Player oder MP3 + PC/Lautsprecher Ex **4**: didaktisierte Uhr, z. B. von Folie 23
Einsatz von Begleitmedien: KV 4.2 | INKL 4.2 | DFF 4.6 | Folie 23 | INKL 4.3 | Workbook S. 52–53

4

► Folie 23 ► DFF 4.6 ► INKL 4.3 ► INKL 4.4

3 At the weekend

a) Look at the board. Then put the photos (A–F) in the right order. F • A • D • C • E • B

2.20 b) Listen to the four dialogues. What activities (A–F) do the visitors want to do?
Dialogue[2] 1 is photo ..., ... 1 – F • 2 – A • 3 – D • 4 – B

c) Listen again. What's the right time?
Dialogue 1: 10.40 / 10.45
Dialogue 2: 10.55 / 11.15
Dialogue 3: 12.00 / 12.45
Dialogue 4: 4.30 / 4.45

4 The time

2.21 a) Listen and repeat.
1.00 10.00 12.05 4.05 5.10 9.15 7.20
8.25 3.30 12.30 11.35 2.45 6.50 1.55

You write:	You say:
2.00	two o'clock
2.05	two oh five
2.15	two fifteen
2.30	two thirty
2.45	two forty-five

2.22 b) Say one of the times in a). Your partner points at it.

c) Listen and write the times. 1 – 1.15 2 – 3.30 3 – 4.45

Sometimes people say:
– quarter past two (2.15)
– half past two (2.30)
– quarter to three (2.45)

More practice 2 p. 135

5 What's the time, please?

a) Draw a digital clock and write a time on it.

b) Talk to a partner like this:
A: What's the time please? B: It's ... Box: Voc., p. 199
A: Thanks. B: You're welcome.
Write your partner's name and time.
Then swap clocks.

Name	Time
Paul	6.15
...	...

c) Walk around: Find a new partner. Write your new partner's time.
Then swap clocks again. Talk to as many partners as you can.

► Workbook 6–8, p. 53 1 ['gru:mɪŋ] 2 ['daɪəlɒg]

Einstieg (SB geschl.) Tiere vom *Lead-In* wiederholen. An Tafel: *On Merryweather Farm there are ...*
Erarb. Ex 3a (SB offen) AA klären. Schild lesen, in EA Bilder nach Ablauf ordnen. Dann Partner check.
Erarb. Ex 3b **1. Hören** (Globalverstehen). Vorab Zahlen 1–4 notieren, beim Hören Buchstaben zuordnen
Ausw. Ex 3b im Partner check, dann im Plenum
Erarb. Ex 3c **2. Hören** und Notieren der Zeiten. Lautschulung (Uhrzeiten) durch Vor-/Nachsprechen

Einstieg Ex 4 (SB geschl.) Wdh. volle Stundenangabe): Zeit einstellen und abfragen *What's the time?* durch L/S → *It's one/two ... o'clock.*
Erarb. Ex 4a (SB offen) **1. Hören**, Chorsprechen (in Pausen der Aufnahme)
Erarb. Ex 4b+c gemäß Aufgabe
Ausw. im Partner check

Erarb. Ex 5a auch als vorbereitende **HA** geeignet
Erarb. Ex 5b (SB offen) Partner talks anhand der Uhrzeiten; Notieren der Zeit des Partners, dann tauschen. Für Lernschwächere vorab demonstrieren
Erarb. Ex 5c Milling-around activity; Zeiten der Partner in Tabelle notieren

Lernschwerpunkt: **Sich über Gefühle austauschen**

Storyline: Schüler*innen der Klasse 7 Y sprechen darüber, in welchen Situationen sie sich gut bzw. genervt fühlen. Berry erzählt über ihren Alltag, der aufgrund der Tatsache, dass sie im Rollstuhl sitzt, anders ist als bei vielen anderen Kindern.

Kompetenzen: Listening Einer Diskussion Detailangaben entnehmen | **Speaking** Sich mit Partnern über Gefühle austauschen
Reading Gefühlsbeschreibungen verstehen | **Writing** Beschreiben, wie man sich fühlt
Lern- und Arbeitstechniken Notizen in einer Tabelle festhalten; eine Vorlage für eigene Texte nutzen

Redemittel: Wortfeld *feelings*

Einstieg (SB geschl.) 3 Poster mit ☹☺☹ aufhängen; je passende Adjektive dazu notieren. Anschließend stellen sich S zu dem für ihre Stimmung passenden Smiley. L steuert: *When you feel* ***happy or great****, please go to this smiley* (zeigen). ... ***OK****, please go to ...* ...***sad or fed up****, please...*
Überleitung L: *Now listen and find out when Ellie, Berry, Luca and Adam feel great or fed up.*
Erarb. Ex 1a (SB offen) Arbeitsteilige PA: vor Hören klären S, wer A/B ist. Übertragen der jeweiligen Tabelle ins Heft (oder Nutzung von KV 4.3 Part 1) **1. Hören** und Eintragen der Namen (Notetaking)
Ausw. in **1b** **2. Hören**, Partner check, danach Kontrolle im Plenum (mit Folienkopie der KV)

Erarb. Ex 2a (SB offen) Übertragen der Tabelle ins Heft (oder Nutzung von KV 4.3 Part 2) zum Note making
○ Lernschwächere wählen Redemittel aus More help aus
Erarb. Ex 2b Beispielvortrag eines Dialogs mit den Sprechblasen durch L+S, danach Partner talk der S
Erarb. Ex 2c AA klären (mit Foto). In EA je eine Situation für *really great / really fed up* formulieren und hinlegen/aufhängen
Ausw. in **Ex 2d** im Reading circle (still!)

4 **THEME 2**

▸ *KV 4.3* ▸ *INKL 4.5*

Feelings

2.23 **1** **A class discussion**

a) Ms Lee, the English teacher, has two questions for the students in her class.

Partner A: Copy table A. Listen and write the names: Adam, Luca, Berry or Ellie.

(A)

☺ *I feel great when ...*	
... I do sport.	*Luca, ...*
... I'm with my animals.	Ellie
... I'm with my friends.	Berry Berry
... I listen to music.	Adam
... I don't have homework.	Adam

Partner B: Copy table B. Listen and write the names: Adam, Luca, Berry or Ellie.

(B)

☹ *I feel fed up when ...*	
... my sister is bossy.	*Ellie*
... my mobile doesn't work.	Ellie
... my friends don't text me.	Luca Luca
... people don't talk to me.	Berry
... I have lots of homework.	Adam

b) Swap[1] tables with your partner. Listen again and check your partner's answers.

2 **NOW YOU**

a) When do you feel great? When do you feel fed up? Make notes like this:

More help p. 135

☺ *I feel great ...*	☹ *I feel fed up ...*
when I play football.	*when my dad is bossy.*
when I ...	...
...	

b) Talk to your partner. Ask and answer the questions:

When do you feel great? – When ...

When do you feel fed up? – When ...

c) Write two sentences on a piece of paper. Then put it on the wall.

I feel really great when ...	*I feel really fed up when ...*

d) **Reading circle:** Walk round and read other people's sentences. You can write your name and a comment:
Me too! or *Not me!*

1 [swɒp]

Zeitbedarf: ca. zwei Stunden
Minimalversion: Ex **1a**; **2+b**; **3a–c**
Kooperative Lernformen: Partner talk Ex **2b** | Reading circle Ex **2d** | Partner check Ex **1b**; **3b**
Materialbedarf: Ex **1a+b**; **3a** (optional): Audio-CD + Player oder MP3 + PC/Lautsprecher | Ex **2**: leere DIN-A4-Blätter
Einsatz von Begleitmedien: KV 4.3 | INKL 4.5–4.6 | DFF 4.7 | Folie 24 | Workbook S. 54

4

▸ KV 4.3 ▸ DFF 4.7 ▸ Folie 24 ▸ INKL 4.6

2.24

3 Berry's homework

E • C • A • B • D

a) ○ Read Berry's homework. Put the photos in the right order.

Feelings by Berry Donovan

I feel great when I'm with the animals at home. I really love animals.

I sometimes feel a bit fed up because I'm the only student at school in a wheelchair. I'm always different.

But I feel great when I'm with my friends. With my friends I'm not 'the girl in the wheelchair'. I'm a normal teenager!

I feel great when I do sport. My favourite sport is wheelchair basketball. When I'm in my wheelchair I can go really fast. And I feel really great when my team wins.

I feel really fed up when people don't talk to me. They do that because I'm in a wheelchair. They ask my mum: 'Does she want a drink?' They don't ask ME: 'Do YOU want a drink?' At school people ask my friends: 'Does she understand?' But I can speak for myself. My legs don't work well. But my mouth works fine.

A

B

C

D

E

b) Read the text again. Find sentences in the text for the photos.
Example: Photo A – I feel great when I'm with my friends. Lösungen zu **b)** Seite 235 und **c)** S. 236

c) Copy and complete Berry's notes.

I feel great	I feel fed up
when I'm with …	because I'm …
when …	when …

d) ● Write a short text about your feelings. Use your notes from exercise 2 on page 74. Write more than one sentence for each feeling. You can put your text in your DOSSIER[2].

More help p. 136

Einstieg Ex 3 (SB offen) Benennen von Personen und Orten auf den Fotos (Vorentlastung für **3a**):
L: *Look at the photos. Where's Berry? (A, C, D: at school; B: in the sports hall; E: on the farm) Who's she with? (A: Ellie and Adam; B: she's alone; C, D: other students; E: her animals: a dog (Sam) and a pony (William)) Look at Berry's face* (zeigen). *What do you think: In which photos does Berry feel great? (A, B, E) In which photos does she feel fed up? (C, D)*
Erarb. Ex 3a **1. Lesen**/Hören (Globalverstehen) S ordnen die Abbildungen.
Ausw. Ex 3a im Plenum
Erarb. Ex 3b in EA, S notieren Bildunterschriften ins Heft, dann Partner check
Ausw. Ex 3b im Plenum
Erarb. Ex 3c Gemeinsame mdl. Vervollständigung der ersten Zeile im Plenum. Dabei ggf. auf *because* als Begründungsalternative zu *when* verweisen. S arbeiten auf KV 4.3 Part 3.
Ausw. Ex 3c im Plenum
Erarb. Ex 3d auch als schriftl. **HA** (auf Einfügen einer passenden Überschrift hinweisen) ○ Lernschwächere nutzen Redemittel aus More help
Ausw. Ex 3d Vorlesen der Texte im Plenum; alternativ Aushängen, anschließend Gallery walk. Danach sagen und begründen S, welcher Text je am besten gefällt.

2 ['dɒsier]

FOCUS ON LANGUAGE Navigator | Inhalt

Lernschwerpunkt: Entscheidungsfragen und bejahte/verneinte Aussagen *(simple present)* zum Sprechen über *pets* nutzen
Storyline: Ellie und Berry sprechen über ihre Haustiere; Luca und Adam darüber, warum sie keine haben.
Kompetenzen: Speaking Gespräche über Lieblingstiere führen | **Reading** Einem Dialog gezielt Informationen entnehmen
Writing Einen Text über ein Haustier verfassen | **Lern- und Arbeitstechniken** Sprachliche Regelmäßigkeiten entdecken
Grammatik: Bewusstmachen und Üben des *simple present* (verneinte Aussagen, Entscheidungsfragen)
Redemittel: Wortfeld *pets*; Sprechen über Gewohnheiten

4 FOCUS ON LANGUAGE

▸ DFF 4.2 ▸ Folie 25 ▸ INKL 4.7

Einstieg Ex 1 (SB geschl.) Unterrichtsgespräch anhand der *Pre-reading*-Frage; L notiert dabei an Tafel mit.
Überleitung L: *Let's see if you are right.*
Erarb. Ex 1 (SB offen)
1. Lesen/Hören (Globalverstehen), Annahmen prüfen → Abhaken an Tafel:
The kids' pets
Berry: dog ✓ pony ✓
Luca: no pets ✓
Adam: no pets ✓
Ellie: two cats ✓

1 A pet or a wild animal?

2.25

Berry has lots of pets. But do Ellie, Luca or Adam have pets? Can you remember? Read and check.

Luca — Do you have a cat or a dog, Adam?
Adam — No, we don't have a pet.
Luca — What about you, Ellie? Do you have a pet?
Ellie — Yes, I do. I have two cats at mum's house.
Luca — What about your dad? Does he have a pet?
Ellie — No. Dad and Alisha don't have a pet. They don't have time.
Berry — And what about you, Luca?
Luca — No, we don't have a pet. Dad is the problem. He doesn't like dogs.
Adam — And what about your mum? Does she like animals?
Luca — She likes dogs, but she doesn't like cats. But I want a pet!
Ellie — I have an idea. What about a °chipmunk[1]?
Luca — A chipmunk? Does it look like a monkey?

A chipmunk

Ellie — No, it doesn't look like a monkey – you °idiot[2].
Berry — We have chipmunks on the farm. They're small and furry[3]. They're really cute.
Ellie — Do they like cats?
Berry — No, they don't like other animals. And they hate cats!
Luca — I want a chipmunk.
Berry — I don't know. A chipmunk is a wild animal. It isn't really a good pet for a house.
Luca — Oh!

Erarb. Ex 2a (SB offen) S ergänzen Sätze schriftlich anhand der Textvorlage in **1**. Danach Kontrolle im Plenum
Erarb. Ex 2b S ergänzen die Regel im Heft.
Auswertung Ex 2b S tragen ihre Regeln vor. Ergänzend gemeinsames Lesen von *Language file* 7, S. 169

2 The simple present – negative sentences

a) Put in *doesn't* or *don't*.

1 We ... have a pet. (line 2) — don't
2 They ... have time. (l. 10) — don't
3 He ... like dogs. (l. 13) — doesn't
4 She ... like cats. (l. 16–17) — doesn't
5 It ... look like a monkey. (l. 22) — doesn't
6 I ... know. (l. 31) — don't

b) Complete the rules with *doesn't* or *don't*.

FOCUS — No

I, you, we, they	+	...	+ verb	don't
he, she, it	+	...	+ verb	doesn't

▸ *Language file 7, p. 169*

Erarb. 3 (SB offen) individualisierte Übung; schriftl. in EA
Ausw. Ex 3 Partner check: ggs. Vorlesen der komplettierten Sätze, anschließend ggf. Vergleich im Plenum

3 NOW YOU

Write sentences about you.

1 I have / don't have a pet.
2 My mum /dad likes / doesn't like animals.
3 We have / don't have a big garden.
4 I like / don't like cats / dogs / chipmunks / ...
5 My best friend has / doesn't have a pet.
6 He / She wants / doesn't want a dog / cat / ...

1 ['tʃɪpmʌŋk] 2 ['ɪdiət] 3 ['fɜːri]

Zeitbedarf: ca. 1–2 Stunden
Minimalversion: Ex **1**; **2a+b**; **4**; **5**; **6**
Kooperative Lernformen: Partner check Ex **3**; **5** | Lerntempoduett Ex **4a**
Materialbedarf: Ex **1** (optional); **7b**: Audio-CD + Player oder MP3 + PC/Lautsprecher
Einsatz von Begleitmedien: DFF 4.2 | INKL 4.7–4.8 | Folie 25–26 | Workbook S. 55

▸ *DFF 4.3* ▸ *Folie 26* ▸ *INKL 4.8*

4 That's wrong! Lösungen S. 236

a) Complete the sentences. Use *doesn't* or *don't*. // p. 136

1 Berry lives in the city. – That's wrong! She doesn't live in ...
2 Berry's parents have a pet shop. – That's wrong! They don't ...
3 Berry rides a donkey. – That's wrong! She ...
4 Berry has a cat. – That's wrong! She ...
5 Berry's mum and dad have cows on the farm. – That's wrong! They ...
6 Sam the dog lives in the field. – That's wrong! He ...
7 Berry goes to school in Woolwell. – That's wrong! She ...
8 Luca and Adam have dogs. – That's wrong! They ...
9 Ellie has two ponies. – That's wrong! She ...
10 Chipmunks like cats. – That's wrong! They ...

b) Work with a partner. Write five wrong sentences about Ellie, Luca and Adam. Swap your sentences with other students. Can you correct all the sentences?

5 My interesting pets // p. 136

Complete the text. Put in *don't* or *doesn't*.

on't / oesn't / on't / oesn't / oesn't / on't / on't / on't

1 I live in a small flat and we ... have a garden.
2 My mum likes small pets. She ... want a big pet.
3 I ... have a 'normal' pet, like a dog. I have three °degus.
4 A degu ... come from England. It comes from Chile.
5 A degu needs a friend. It ... like to be lonely. Box: Voc., p. 200
6 Degus need lots of space. They ... like small cages.
7 And degus ... like other animals. They hate dogs and cats.
8 I often play with Pip, my favourite degu. But we ... go outside.

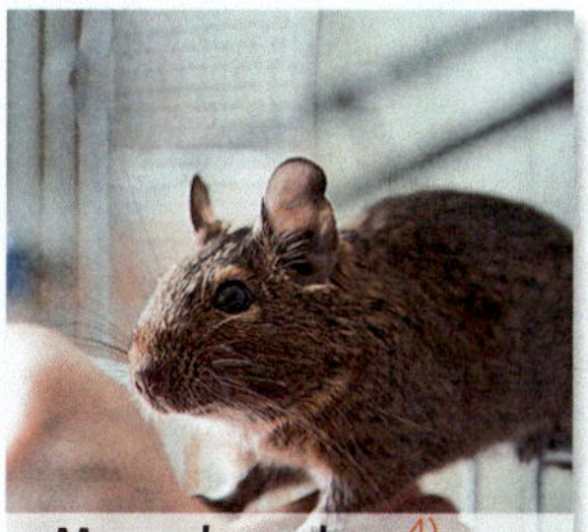
Me and my degu[4]

6 The simple present – questions

a) Put *do* or *does* in the questions.
You can look at text 1 on p. 76 again.

o / oes / oes / oes / o

1 ... you have a pet? (line 4)
2 ... he have a pet? (l. 8)
3 ... she like animals? (l. 15)
4 ... it look like a monkey? (l. 20)
5 ... they like cats? (l. 27)

b) Complete the rules with *do* or *does*.

FOCUS
... + I, you, we, they + verb ?
... + he, she, it + verb ?

Do
Does

▸ *Language file 8, p. 170*

7 NOW YOU

a) Complete the questions with *do* or *does*.

o / o / oes / oes

1 What about you? ... you like animals?
2 What about your parents? ... they like animals?
3 And your best friend? ... he / she have a pet?
4 And your teacher? ... he / she have a pet?

2.26 b) Listen. Answer the questions about you.

Yes, I do.
No, I don't.

▸ *Workbook 11–13, p. 55*

4 ['deɪɡuː, 'deɡuː]

Einstieg Ex 4 (SB offen) L: *Look at the picture. What's wrong?* S: *Berry doesn't have a cat. (She has a dog.)*
Erarb. Ex 4a // Lernstärkere ergänzen die Berichtigungen. Früher fertige S vergleichen im Lerntempoduett ihre Lösungen.
Erarb. Ex 4b gemäß Aufgabe

Einstieg Ex 5 (SB offen) L: *In the photo you can see a degu* (zeigen) *and a cage* (zeigen). *Let's find out more about degus. Are they good pets?*
Erarb. Ex 5 auch als schriftl. **HA** möglich
// Lernstärkere bilden alle Verbformen (bejaht/verneint).

Einstieg Ex 6 (SB geschl.) L stellt Frage und gibt Antwortmöglichkeiten vor: *Do you have a pet? – Yes I do. I have a ... / No, I don't.* Dann Übung in Meldekette
Erarb. Ex 6a (SB offen) in EA
Ausw. Ex 6a im Plenum; an Tafel notieren
Erarb. Ex 6b Regel ergänzen
Ausw. Ex 6b im Plenum; Lesen von *Language file* 8, S. 170

Erarb. Ex 7a (SB offen) schriftl. in EA
Erarb. Ex 7b 1. Hören und murmelndes Beantworten der Fragen in Pausen
Ausw. Ex 7b 2. Hören/Kontrolle: L stoppt jeweils, einzelne S antworten

Lernschwerpunkt: **Fragen mit Fragewörtern und bejahte/verneinte Aussagen *(simple present)* zum Sprechen über *pets* nutzen**
Storyline: Ellie und Berry sprechen über ihre Haustiere; Luca und Adam darüber, warum sie keine haben
Kompetenzen: **Speaking** Gespräche über Lieblingstiere führen | **Reading** Einem Dialog gezielt Informationen entnehmen
Writing Einen Text über ein Haustier verfassen **Lern- und Arbeitstechniken** sprachliche Regelmäßigkeiten entdecken
Grammatik: Bewusstmachen und Üben des *simple present* (verneinte Aussagen, Entscheidungsfragen)
Redemittel: Wortfeld *pets*; Sprechen über Gewohnheiten

Einstieg Ex 8 (SB geschl.) Umfrage: L: *Do you have a rat?* S: *Yes, I do. / No, I don't.* Einführen neuen WS: L: *What do you think: Do rats eat **fruit** like apples or bananas? (Yes, they do.) Do they eat **nuts**? (Yes, they do.) Do they **sleep** in a bed? (No, they don't.) ...*
Erarb. Ex 8 (SB offen) **1. Lesen**/Hören, Beantworten der Frage

Erarb. Ex 9a (SB offen) **2. Hören**/Lesen: S notieren die 5 Fragen.
Erarb. Ex 9b S ordnen engl. und dt. Fragewörter zu.
Ausw. Ex 9b im Plenum; *Language file 9*, S. 170 lesen

Erarb. Ex 10 (SB offen) schriftl. in EA, auch als HA geeignet
Ausw. Ex 10 in Meldekette: S1: Frage – S2: Antwort usw.
L notiert vervollständigte Fragen an Tafel

Einstieg Ex 11 (SB offen) L: *Today I want you to talk about pets with your partner like this: ...* (ggf. demonstrieren)
Erarb. Ex 11a mit *Wordbank* 7, S. 177; Partner verfassen Dialogskript, üben es dann ein → Partner talk
Ausw. Ex 11a freiwillige Paare tragen im Plenum vor
Erarb. Ex 11b schriftl. in EA; L korrigiert und lässt Reinschrift anfertigen (ggf. als HA)

4 FOCUS ON LANGUAGE

▸ DFF 4.5 ▸ INKL 4.9

8 A good pet?

2.27

Are rats good pets? Read and find out. Yes, they are.

Luca — What pets do you have, Berry?
Berry — I have a dog – Sam. And we have hamsters, rabbits, chipmunks and rats.
Luca — Rats? Are they good pets?
Berry — Yes. I love our rats.
Ellie — Why do you love rats? Box: Voc., p. 200
Berry — Because they're friendly. They play. They sit on my shoulder. They're very cute.
Luca — Where do they live?
Berry — They live in a cage in Pets Corner.
Adam — What do they eat?
Berry — Lots of things like fruit and nuts and ...
Ellie — When do they sleep?
Berry — At night. I have an idea. Come to the farm and see our pets.

9 Question words s. Unterstreichungen

a) Find five questions in the dialogue with question words: what, when, where, why.

b) Match the English and the German question words.

FOCUS

English:	German:	
What?	Was? Welche?	Warum?
When?		
Where?	Wo? Wohin?	Wann?
Why?		

▸ Language file 9, p. 170

10 What pet do you have?

Find the right question words for the interview.

1 What
2 Why
3 Where
4 What
5 When
6 What

1 ... pet do you have?
2 ... do you like rabbits?
3 ... does your rabbit live?
4 ... does your rabbit eat?
5 ... do you feed your rabbit?
6 ... other pets do you have?

– I have a rabbit. His name is Bunny.
– Because they're fun and friendly.
– He lives in a big cage in my room.
– He eats lots of things. He loves vegetables.
– In the morning and in the evening.
– A snake, a monkey, a fish, a duck, a ...

The orange words can help you.

11 Talking about pets

a) Make a dialogue with a partner.

▸ Wordbank 7, p. 177

A: Do you have a pet?
- B: Yes, I do.
  - A: What pet do you have?
  - B: I have a ...
  - A: Where does your pet live?
  - B: It lives inside / outside / ...
- B: No, I don't.
  - A: Do you want a pet?
    - B: Yes, I do.
      - A: What pet do you want?
      - B: I want a ...
    - B: No, I don't.
      - A: Why not?
      - B: Because ...

More practice 3 p. 137

b) Write about your favourite pet or a friend's pet. You can put your text in your DOSSIER. More help p. 137

▸ Workbook 14–16, p. 56

FOCUS ON LANGUAGE Navigator | **Vorbereitung**

Zeitbedarf: ca. 1–2 Stunden
Minimalversion: Ex **8**; **9a**; **3**; **10**; **11a**; **12a+b**
Kooperative Lernformen: Partner talk Ex **11a** | Partner check Ex **12a** | Milling-around activity Ex **13c**
Materialbedarf: Ex **8** (optional): Audio-CD + Player oder MP3 + PC/Lautsprecher
Einsatz von Begleitmedien: KV 4.4 | DFF 4.4–4.5 | INKL 4.9 | Folie 27 | Workbook S. 56

► *KV 4.4* ► *DFF 4.4* ► *Folie 27*

12 Who is it?

a) ○ Match the answers (A–F) with the questions (1–6). Who is it? It's Berry

1 When do you get up? D
2 What do you like? B
3 Where do you go to school? A
4 When do you come home? C
5 What do you do after school? E
6 Where do you live? F

A Eggy.
B Before 4 o'clock.
C I like my animals.
D Very early - at 6 o'clock.
E In Woolwell.
F My homework.

b) Make the questions for the answers. Who is it?

1 Where / you / live / do / ?	– In Plymouth.	Where do you live?
2 What / like / do / you / ?	– My bike!	What do you like?
3 Where / to school / do / you / go / ?	– In Plymouth too.	Where do you go to school?
4 When / to the cinema / you / go / do / ?	– At the weekend.	When do you go to the cinema?
5 What / do / on Saturdays / you / do / ?	– I ride my bike.	What do you do on Saturdays?
6 Where / bike / do / ride / you / your / ?	– In Central Park.	Where do you ride your bike?

c) ● Now make questions for these answers. Who is it?

1 On the beach in Kingsand.
2 I don't go to school!
3 On Saturdays I play with Sandy.
4 I like swimming and games.
5 I don't go to the cinema!
6 I get up late, at 10 o'clock.

1 Where do you live? • **2** Where do you go to school? • **3** What do you do on Saturdays? • **4** What do you like? • **5** When do you go to the cinema? • **6** When do you get up? **It's Cyril.**

13 ● Find a person who …

a) You want to find interesting people in your class. Pick three things in this box – or more.

b) What questions can you ask? More help p. 137

Find a person who …
– has an interesting pet.
– has an interesting hobby.
– gets up very early.
– goes to a nice place in the holidays.
– likes an English football team.
– likes homework.

Do you have a pet?
What pet do you have?
Do you go to a nice place in the holidays?
Where …?

c) Walk around: Talk to different people. Ask your questions. Take notes.

d) Write about the interesting people in your class.

Dana has an interesting pet – a snake!
Jakob gets up very early – at about 6 o'clock.
Hanna loves homework. She loves maths!
Kenan …

Einstieg Ex 12 L: *Let's do a quiz, shall we? Who is it?*
Erarb. Ex 12a (SB offen) schriftl. in EA, danach **Ausw. Ex 12a** durch Partner check und Vorlesen im Plenum
Erarb. Ex 12b gemäß Aufgabe
Ausw. Ex 12b in Meldekette: S1: Frage – S2: Antwort usw.
Erarb. Ex 12c S bilden eigenständig Fragen zu den vorgegebenen Antworten.
Ausw. Ex 12c in Meldekette

Einstieg Ex 13
L: *I have an interesting pet. It's a snake. Find a person who has an interesting pet, too. Ask questions like this: Do you have an interesting pet?* Ggs. Befragen/(Kurz)Antworten in Meldekette
Erarb. Ex 13a (SB offen) AA klären, Lesen der lila Box im Plenum
Erarb. Ex 13b S formulieren mdl. zu jeder Idee passende Fragen (mit den Sprechblasen). Dann in EA auf KV 4.4 Fragen für Mit-S ● notieren bzw. ○ auswählen
Erarb. Ex 13c S führen Milling-around activity mit KV 4.4 durch, differenziert nach ●/○
Erarb. Ex 13d Notieren interessanter Ergebnisse, ggf. als **HA**

STORY Navigator | Inhalt

Lernschwerpunkt: **Eine szenische Geschichte verstehen**

Storyline: Berry lädt Luca, Ellie und Adam zu einem Wochenende mit Übernachtung (*sleepover*) auf die Farm ein. Dort erleben sie allerlei Abenteuer mit kleinen und großen Tieren.

Kompetenzen: **Reading** Eine szenische Geschichte verstehen; Fragen zum Text beantworten; Überschriften zu Szenen ordnen

Speaking Einzelne Szenen mit verteilten Rollen gestaltend vortragen

Redemittel: Wortfeld *farm life*

Erarb. Ex 1 (SB offen) Bildbetrachtung und Bearbeitung der *Pre-reading* activity
Ausw. Ex 1 S tragen vollständige Sätze vor
Zusatz S beschreiben die Abb. (weitere Personen/Orte/Dinge). L-Impulse: *Where are the Eggy kids in the picture for scene 2/ 3/ ...? What else can you see in the picture?*
Einstieg STORY (SB geschl.) L: *Today we're going to read the story 'Adventures in the country'* (neuen WS semantisieren) L: *In the story, Ellie, Luca and Adam visit Berry in the country. What adventures do they have? Any ideas?*
S1/2: *I think they ride the ponies / go to Pets' Corner / see lots of animals / sleep in the barn / go to bed late / ...*
S3/4: *They can't sleep / have problems with animals /...*
→ Ideen an Tafel notieren
Erarb. STORY (SB offen) **1. Lesen**/Hören der Geschichte (still). Anschließend Überprüfen der Vermutungen aus Einstieg, welche Abenteuer die Kinder auf der Farm erleben; Ergänzen bisher nicht genannter Abenteuer
Alternative (SB geschl.) reines HV mit KV 4.5 (Ex 1): Abb. ausschneiden, während des **1. Hörens** korrekt ordnen; Kontrolle beim **2. Hören** oder im Mitleseverfahren

4 STORY

▸ *KV 4.5* ▸ *INKL 4.10 A/B*

1 Before you read

Look at the pictures. Who is it – Adam, Berry, Ellie or Luca?

1 Ellie and ... are on the bus.
2 ... doesn't have his sweets.
3 ... has a problem with a chipmunk.
4 ... doesn't like cows.
5 Luca and ... are in the barn.
6 ... isn't nervous.

1 Adam and Luca • 2 Luca • 3 Luca • 4 Luca • 5 Ellie, Berry and Adam • 6 Berry

Adventures[1] in the country

2.28

Scene 1 Berry wants to invite her friends to the farm. This is her email.

> Hi guys
>
> Do you want to see our chipmunks? Do you want to come to the farm for a sleepover[2]? What about next Saturday? There's a bus at 3 o'clock. Bring your sleeping bags.
> Berry

Scene 2 It's 3 o'clock on Saturday. Luca, Ellie and Adam are excited. They all have their sleeping bags. Ellie has a bag with fruit. Adam has a bag with sandwiches.
"OK. Let's go!" Ellie says.
"Yeah, let's go to the country!" Adam says.
"Yeah, for lots of adventures!" Luca says.

Scene 3 It's 3.45. The three friends are in Woolwell. They are excited. But Luca is unhappy.
"Oh no!" Luca says. "I don't have my sweets."
"Don't worry, Luca," his friends say.
"We have lots of nice things." Box: Voc., p. 201

Scene 4 It's 4.30. The friends do a tour of the farm. They visit the donkeys, ponies and sheep in the fields. Then they go to Pets Corner.
"I want to stroke a chipmunk," Luca says.
"This is Lulu. Do you want her on your shoulder?" Berry asks. Box: Voc., p. 201
"Oh, she's very cute!" Ellie says.
"Look!" Adam says.
"Oh no! My shoulder is wet!" Luca says.
Everybody laughs.

1 [əd'ventʃə] 2 ['sli:pəʊvə]

STORY Navigator | Vorbereitung

Zeitbedarf: ca. zwei Stunden
Minimalversion: Ex **1**; **2a**+**b**; **3**
Kooperative Lernformen: Partner check Ex **2b**; Scenic play Ex **4**
Materialbedarf: **STORY** (optional): Audio-CD + Player oder MP3 + PC/Lautsprecher
Einsatz von Begleitmedien: KV 4.5 und 1.3| INKL 4.10A/B | Workbook S. 57

▸ KV 4.5, 1.3 ▸ INKL 4.10 A/B

Scene 5 It's 5.30.
"Let's eat," Ellie says.
"But we don't have nice things," Luca says.
"We have lots of nice things," Adam says.
"I want to buy sweets," Luca says. "Where's the village?" Box: Voc., p. 201
"OK, Luca. Go through that field," Berry says.

Scene 6 It's 6.15. Adam, Berry and Ellie are hungry.
"Where's Luca?" Adam asks.
"I want to eat," Ellie says.
Adam gets a text from Luca:

They go to the field.
"Help! It's a bull!" Luca says.
"It isn't a °bull. It's a cow," Berry says. "Cows aren't dangerous[3)]!"
Everybody laughs. But Luca doesn't laugh.

Scene 7 It's 11 o'clock. The four friends are in sleeping bags in the barn.
"What's that noise?" Adam asks. He's nervous.
"It's a donkey," Berry says.
"What's that noise?" Ellie asks.
"It's a sheep," Berry says.
"Oh no! What's that noise?" Luca asks.
"Oh, Luca! It's only a chicken," Berry says.
"Go to sleep!"
"Good night," everybody says.

Scene 8 On Sunday the friends have lots of fun. They play on the trampolines. They ride Harry, Berry's pony. They feed the animals. In the afternoon Ellie, Adam and Luca go back to Plymouth by bus.
"Thanks Berry. It's great here," Ellie says.
"Yeah, I love the country," Adam says.
"It's nice, but I'm a city boy," Luca says.
"And I'm a country girl," Berry says.

2 The scenes

a) Match the headings with the scenes (1–8) in the story.

- A cute chipmunk 4
- Time to go home 8
- Time to eat 5
- Let's go to the country 2
- Noises at night 7
- Come to a sleepover 1
- A dangerous animal? 6
- No sweets! 3

b) Check with a partner.

3 Questions on the story

Answer the questions in 1–5 words.

1 How do the three friends go to Woolwell?
– By …
2 What's in Adam's bag?
3 What animals do they see on the farm?
4 What animal does Luca meet in the field?
5 Who's nervous at night?
6 Who's a country girl? More practice 4 p. 138

1 By bus • 2 Sandwiches • 3 Donkeys, ponies, sheep and chipmunks • 4 A cow • 5 Adam, Ellie and Luca • 6 Berry

4 THEATRE TIME

Work in groups of five. Pick a scene from the story. Read and act the scene.
More help p. 138

Einstieg Ex 2 (SB offen) AA klären; S auf die Beachtung der Abb. hinweisen
Erarb. Ex 2a **2. Lesen**/Hören (Globalverstehen) und schriftl. Zuordnen der Überschriften zu den Szenen
O Lernschwächere arbeiten mit KV4.5 (Ex 2): Ausschneiden und Zuordnen der Überschriften
Ausw. in **Ex 2b** durch Partner check, dann im Plenum. L notiert an Tafel.
Erarb. Ex 3 (SB offen) Beantwortung der Fragen in EA, ggf. als HA
Ausw. Ex 3 im Plenum. L notiert an Tafel, S korrigieren ggf. ihre Fehler im Heft.

Erarb. Ex 4 (SB offen) S-Gruppen bilden, Auswahl der Szene(n) pro Gruppe bzw. Zuteilung durch L. Zum Einstudieren evtl. auf andere Räume ausweichen.
O Lernschwächere erhalten in More help Tipps zum szenischen Lesen.
Ausw. Ex 4 Gruppenweises Vortragen; Mit-S geben Feedback (mit Kriterien von KV 1.3)

3 ['deɪndʒərəs]

SKILLS TRAINING Reading and mediation

Lernschwerpunkt: **Hinweisschilder verstehen**
Kompetenzen: Reading Englische Schilder verstehen
Mediation (E>D) Einem Partner englische Schilder erklären
Lern- und Arbeitstechniken Wortschatzerschließung; Sprachmittlung
Redemittel: Über Hinweisschilder sprechen

Zeitbedarf: ca. eine Stunde
Minimalversion: Ex **1**; **2a**
Kooperative Lernformen: Partner check Ex **1** | Partner talk Ex **2a+b**
Einsatz von Begleitmedien: IAT 4.2 | Workbook S. 58

Einstieg Ex 1 L: *When you are in a town, you often see lots of signs. Today we are going to learn how to read signs in a town.*
Erarb. Ex 1 (SB offen) S betrachten die Schilder und ordnen passende Beschreibungen zu.
Ausw. Ex 1 im Partner check, danach im Plenum
Zusatz L/S bringen weitere Bilder von Schildern mit, S bereiten Beschreibungen (E) vor und stellen diese der Klasse vor.

Erarb. Ex 2a (SB offen) mdl. gemäß Aufgabe
Erarb. Ex 2b L liest mit S gemeinsam den gelben Hinweiskasten und lässt ggf. einige Satzanfänge (z. B. für Schild A) im Plenum vervollständigen, dann Partner talk
Ausw. Ex 2b Einzelne S-Paare präsentieren ihr Ergebnis vor der Klasse; die Mit-S ergänzen entsprechend.

4 SKILLS TRAINING Reading and mediation

▸ *IAT 4.2*

1 READING Signs in Plymouth

Look at the signs. Then match the sentences (1–5) with the signs (A–E).

1 You can get the bus here. → Sign ...
2 You can find this sign at a restaurant.
3 This sign is on Berry's farm.
4 This sign is in a park in Plymouth.
5 People in wheelchairs, please go left.

A

B

C

D

E

Du kannst die Schilder verstehen, auch wenn du nicht jedes Wort kennst.

1 E • 2 B • 3 C • 4 A • 5 D

2 MEDIATION Understanding the signs

a) Partner A: Imagine you're in Plymouth. Answer partner B's questions – in German.
Partner B: You can't understand the signs in Plymouth. Ask partner A three questions. Then swap roles.

1 Schild A: Warum steht der Hund hinter Gittern? Ist er im Gefängnis?
2 Schild A: Was bedeutet „No smoking"?
3 Schild B: Ich habe Hunger. Können wir hier gleich frühstücken?
4 Schild C: Es geht um *animals*, also Tiere. Was dürfen wir nicht tun?
5 Schild D: Können wir hier hineingehen?
6 Schild E: Wie können wir herausfinden, wann der nächste Bus kommt?

Lösungsbeispiele für **a)** und **b)** S. 236

b) Pick a sign and talk about it with your partner – in German.

Ich denke, man findet so ein Schild ...

Ja, und ...

So kannst du über Schilder sprechen:
– Man findet so ein Schild an einer Bushaltestelle / in der Stadt / ...
– Das Schild ist für Leute mit Hunden / Leute, die ...
– Du darfst / kannst / darfst hier nicht ...

▸ Workbook 21–22, p. 58

SKILLS TRAINING Writing invitations

Lernschwerpunkt: Einladungen verfassen
Kompetenzen: Writing Eine Einladung schreiben und beantworten | Lern- und Arbeitstechniken Eine Vorlage für eigene Texte nutzen
Redemittel: *inviting people*

Zeitbedarf: ca. eine Stunde
Minimalversion: Ex **1**, **2a–c**
Kooperative Lernformen: Gallery walk Ex **1b**
Reading circle Ex **3b**
Materialbedarf: Ex **2**; **3** bunte Papierbögen, bunte Stifte, evtl. Bilder von S mitbringen lassen
Einsatz von Begleitmedien: DFF 4.8 | INKL 4.11
Workbook S. 59

SKILLS TRAINING Writing invitations 4

▸ *DFF 4.8* ▸ *INKL 4.11*

1 An English evening

Match the headings with the boxes (A-E):
Invitation – C, Date – ...

A: 5b classroom, Eugen Bolz School, Baumweg 57-59

E: From 5.30 pm to 8.30 pm

B: On Friday, 27th May

D: Something to eat and drink for a picnic in the classroom

C: Please come to our class 5b English evening

Dear parents
Invitation: ... C
Date: ... B
Time: ... E
Address: ... A
Please bring: ... D

2 An invitation to a sleepover

a) Write an invitation for your partner like this. You can use colours and pictures on your invitation.

INVITATION TO
a sleepover at ...'s house
Dear ...
Please come to my party.
It's on ...
It's at my house: ...
It's from ... to ...
We can ...
Please bring ...
I hope you can come.
...

Write your name here.

Write your partner's name.

Write the day and the date of your party here. Example: *Saturday, 21st May*

Write the times here. Example: *From Saturday evening 6.00 pm to Sunday morning*

Write your address here.

What can you do together? Examples: *go swimming, watch a film, listen to music, ...*

What can people bring? Examples: *a sleeping bag, °pyjamas, swimming things, DVDs, CDs, something to eat, ...*

b) Give your invitation to your partner.

c) Write an answer to your partner.

Dear ...
Thank you for the invitation.
I'd love to come! / Sorry I can't come.
Best wishes
... (your name)

3 Other invitations

a) Write an invitation. It can be for:
an English evening, a class party, a birthday party, a Halloween party, a picnic, a DVD evening, a computer game evening, ...
Put your invitation on the wall.
You can put it in your DOSSIER later.

b) Reading circle: Look at all the invitations. Which party do you want to go to? Write an answer and put it on the wall.

▸ *Workbook 23–25, p. 59*

Einstieg Ex 1 (SB geschl.) L: *Imagine it's your birthday. You want to have a party. Who can you invite to your party? (friends, family)*
Erarb. Ex 1a (SB offen) L: *Look at this invitation.*
An Tafel: *What kind of invitation is it?*
Auswahl vorgeben:
a) an English breakfast
b) an evening for parents and students at school ✓
c) a picnic in the park.
S ordnen Kategorien zu, notieren die vollständige Einladung ins Heft

Erarb. Ex 2a (SB offen) L: *What is a sleepover?* S: *Your friends come to your house and sleep there.*
L: *What do you need for a sleepover?*
S: *You need a sleeping bag, pyjamas, ...*
Danach schriftl. Verfassen (und Ausgestalten) einer Einladung für Partner mit Redemitteln aus den Boxen
Erarb. Ex 2b+c gemäß Aufgaben
Ausw. Ex 2 Einladungen aushängen, im Gallery walk die gelungenste auswählen; Sprachmittel dafür ggf. vorgeben:
I like ...'s invitation.
It looks nice. I'd like to go to ...'s party.
The invitation is great.

Erarb. Ex 3a (SB offen) S wählen ein Thema aus und erstellen mithilfe der Sprachmittel aus **2** eine eigene Einladung.
Ausw. in **Ex 3b** Reading circle S lesen Einladungen, verfassen auf eine selbst ausgewählte eine Antwort

SKILLS TRAINING Using a dictionary

Lernschwerpunkt: **Ein Gedicht mithilfe eines Wörterbuchs verstehen**
Kompetenzen: **Reading** Ein Gedicht lesen und verstehen (schlussfolgerndes Lesen) | **Lern- und Arbeitstechniken** Unbekannte Wörter erschließen und (alphabetisch) nachschlagen
Redemittel: Wortfeld *animals*

Zeitbedarf: ca. eine Stunde
Materialbedarf: Ex **1** (optional): Audio-CD + Player oder MP3+ PC/Lautsprecher | Ex **2b+c**: Blanko-Karteikarten; vorbereiteter Kartensatz mit Tierwörtern; Magnete/Klebestreifen
Einsatz von Begleitmedien: DFF 4.9

Einstieg Ex 1 (SB geschl.) L: *Let's read/listen to a* ***poem*** *today. Do you all know what a poem is?* – Semantisierung, ggf. mit Bsp. an Tafel (auf Reimwörter verweisen):
There's a mouse
That lives in my house.
Can you see it run?
Hey, that's fun!
Erarb. Ex 1 (SB offen) Gemeinsames Lesen der *Pre-reading*-Fragen, dann **1. Lesen**/Hören (ggf. im Mitleseverfahren), schriftl. Beantworten in EA
Ausw. Ex 1 im Plenum, L notiert an Tafel, S korrigieren ggf. im Heft.
Zusatz S lesen Gedicht laut vor (einzeln/im Chor, ggf. nochmals abspielen).

Erarb. Ex 2a (SB offen) S erschließen Wortbedeutungen, ordnen Abb. zu
Ausw. Ex 2a L präsentiert im Plenum die Abb. im hochgehaltenen SB. S nennen abgebildete Tiere und sagen (D), wie sie unbekannte Wörter erschlossen haben (vgl. Tipp-Box)
Erarb. Ex 2b+c gemäß Aufgabe ● Lernstärkere arbeiten im Heft, ggf. mit Bleistift.
Ausw. Ex 2b+c mit vorbereiteten Vokabelkarten: S heften diese in der richtigen Reihenfolge an Tafel
Erarb. Ex 2d unbekannte identifizieren; *Dictionaries* im SB erklären (alphabet. Ordnung); nachschlagen

4 SKILLS TRAINING Using a dictionary

▸ *DFF 4.9*

Box: Voc., p. 202

1 A poem[1]

2.29

Read or listen to the poem and find out:
1 What's the title of the poem? Can you say it?
2 What does the writer want?
3 Who's the writer? A mum, a dad or a child?

1 Muuuuuuummmmmmm • **2** The writer wants a pet. • **3** The writer is a child.

2 Do you need a dictionary[2]?

a) ○ Find the English words for these animals in the poem.

Du kennst schon viele Tierwörter, andere sind neu, aber du kannst sie erraten.

b) Write these animal words on small cards. Then put them in alphabetical order.

stoat 7 (12) | budgie 1 (1) | owl 5 (7) | guinea pig 2 (1) | parrot 6 (8) | kitten 4 (6) | horse 3 (5)

Einige Tierwörter musst du im Wörterbuch nachschlagen (ab S. 208). Bringe die Wörter zuerst in eine alphabetische Reihenfolge, dann findest du sie schneller.

c) Now write these animal words on cards too. Put all the words from 2b and 2c in alphabetical order.

goat 3 | peahen 9 | stick insect 11 | gibbon 2 | puppy 10

d) Which animal words do you need to look up? Find the words in the Dictionary (pp. 208–218). Write the German words under the English words or on the back of the cards. Lösung S. 236

Muuuuuuummmmmmm

Can we have a °kitten
Can we have a dog
Can we call her Frisky
Can we call him Bob?
I can take him out each day
I can brush his fur
I will buy the dog meat
And milk to make her purr
Mum!!

Oh … no … well –

Can we have a donkey
Or can we have a °horse
A monkey or a °parrot
Hamster or a snake?
Can we have a °guinea pig[3]
A °peahen[4]
Or a °stoat[5]
°Llama[6] or a °budgie[7]
A rabbit or a °goat?

Can we have a crocodile
°Gibbon or an °owl
All the zoos are closing
There's lots and lots around …
A °penguin[8] would be really good
Keep it in the bath
A °hyena[9] in the garden
To make the milkman laugh.

No, WE DON'T WANT °stick insects
And °goldfish aren't much fun …
Oh can we have a °puppy …
Mum, mum, muuuuuuummmmmmm.

Peter Dixon

▸ *Skills file 4, p. 164*

1 ['pəʊɪm] 2 ['dɪkʃənri] 3 ['gɪni pɪg] 4 [piːhen] 5 [stəʊt] 6 ['lɑːmə] 7 ['bʌdʒi] 8 ['peŋgwɪn] 9 [haɪ'iːnə]

▸ *Text file 5, pp. 156–158*

SKILLS TRAINING Viewing

Lernschwerpunkt: **Fiktionale und dokumentarische Filmszenen verstehen**
Kompetenzen: **Viewing** Filmszenen verstehen; Alltag eines Mädchens im Rollstuhl miterleben
Redemittel: Gefühle beschreiben, Handlungen einschätzen

Zeitbedarf: ca. eine Stunde
Minimalversion: Ex **1a+b**, **2a**
Materialbedarf: DVD + Player oder PC/Lautsprecher
Einsatz von Begleitmedien: KV 4.6

SKILLS TRAINING Viewing 4

▸ *KV 4.6*

1 The kids from Harbour Road: A class project

a) Watch the film.
Then complete the captions.

1 aquarium • 2 mobile phone • 3 fish/sharks • 4 questions • 5 mobile phone / camera • 6 mobile phone / recording.

1 The kids meet outside the ...

2 Paul is busy with his ...

3 First they look at the ...

4 Then they ask lots of ...

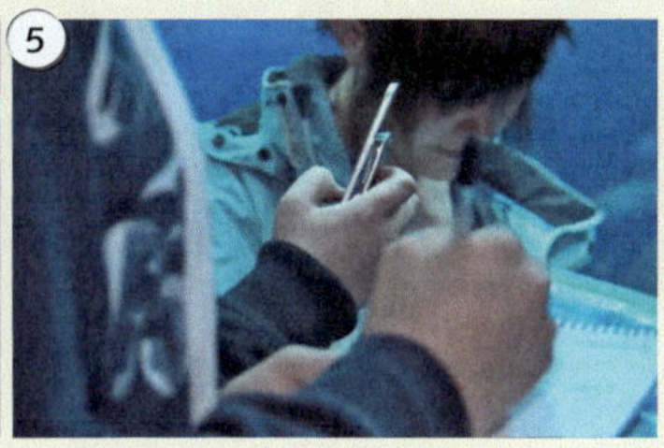
5 Sarah and Anna write notes, but Paul uses his ...

6 Paul has a big problem with his ...

b) Watch the film again. Try to remember: Who says it – Anna, Paul, or Sarah?

1 Let's do our project on sharks[1].
2 You're no help!
3 I love my new mobile.
4 Do sharks eat other fish in the tank[2]?
5 Do you think we have all the information?
6 Pens and paper are better than[3] mobile phones.

1 Anna • 2 Sarah • 3 Paul • 4 Paul • 5 Sarah • 6 Anna

2 People and places: A normal day at school

a) Watch the film. Then talk about how Emily feels in the scenes: In scene A / B / ...

A Emily feels ... when she can't do things alone. bad/unhappy

B Emily feels ... when her friends help her too much[4]. unhappy/fed-up

C Emily feels ... when people don't listen to her. fed-up

D Emily feels ... when Laura invites her. great/happy

b) Watch the film again. Is it a good or bad day for Emily? Emily's day has good and bad parts. It's a normal day for Emily.

[1]shark [ʃɑːk] *Haifisch* [2]tank [tæŋk] *Aquarium* [3]better than ['betə ðæn] *besser als* [4]too much *zu viel*

Einstieg Ex 1 (SB geschl.) L formuliert Sehaufträge:
- *Which animal do Paul, Anna and Sarah choose? (sharks)*
- *Where and how do they get information on their animal? (They go to the aquarium and ask questions.)*

Erarb. Ex 1a (SB offen) AA klären, dann **1. Sehen** (Globalverstehen), Bildunterschriften ergänzen (ggf. an Tafel → Kontrolle)
Erarb. Ex 1b AA und Aussagen lesen, Ziffern 1–6 untereinander notieren, beim **2. Sehen**, A(nna), P(aul), S(arah) dazuschreiben
Ausw. Ex 1b im Plenum

Einstieg Ex 2 (SB geschl.) L: *Let's collect some adjectives for feelings.* (als *warm-up*, an Tafel sortieren):

Feelings

☺	😐	☹
happy fine ...	OK surprised ...	fed-up lonely ...

Erarb. Ex 2a (SB offen) L: *The film is about a girl. Her name is Emily. This is her normal day at school.* **1. Sehen**, dann Austausch über Emilys Gefühle in den Situationen A–D
Ausw. Ex 2a im Plenum
Erarb. Ex 2b **2. Sehen**, Globaleinschätzung.
Zusatz Vertiefung mit KV 4.6

STOP! – CHECK! – GO! Navigator | Inhalt

Lernschwerpunkt: **Wiederholen und Üben, Lernfortschritte erkennen (Fokus: Unit 4)**
Kompetenzen: **Listening** Sprechende erkennen; Sätze verstehen und vervollständigen | **Speaking** Tiere benennen
Writing Tabelle anlegen; *note-making* | **Lern- und Arbeitstechniken** Eigene Lernfortschritte erkennen
Grammatik: Bejahte/verneinte Aussagen und Fragen mit den korrekten Formen des *simple present* ergänzen
Redemittel: Wortfelder *farm; animals*

Erarb. Ex 1a (SB offen) S notieren die Zahlen 1–9 und ordnen die Begriffe zu
Erarb. Ex 1b S notieren die Buchstaben A–L und ordnen entsprechende Tiernamen zu.
Erarb. Ex 1c S betrachten das Bild für 1 Minute, schließen dann SB. Danach notieren sie eine Liste der gemerkten Begriffe. Vergleich im Partner check

Erarb. Ex 2a (SB offen) **1. Hören**, gemäß Aufgabe
○ Lernschwächere notieren vorab *Berry* und *visitor* untereinander, ergänzen beim Hören je die passenden Ziffern
Erarb. Ex 2b (SB offen) S ergänzen beim **2. Hören** die Satzanfänge schriftlich
○ Lernschwächere übertragen die Satzanfänge vorab untereinander ins Heft. Nach jedem Satz Pause einlegen.
Erarb. Ex 2c Gemäß Aufgabe
Zusatz ● Lernstärkere üben Redemittel mit Read-and-look-up technique mdl. ein.

STOP! CHECK! GO!

▸ *KV 4.8* ▸ *DFF 4.1* ▸ *DFF 4.2* ▸ *INKL 4.12 A/B*

Ein Lösungsblatt für die Aufgaben 1 bis 5 kannst du von deiner Lehrerin / deinem Lehrer erhalten. Du findest die Audiodatei (zu S. 86) online, zusammen mit den Workbook-Audiodateien.

1 WORDS On Merryweather Farm

a) ○ Match the things (1–9) in the picture with the words in the green box.

barn • cage • farm • field • pond • toilet • shop • village • wheelchair

b) Name the animals (A-L) in the picture.

c) Close your book. What things and animals can you remember? Make a list – write as many as you can.
Compare with a partner.

2 WORDS Visitors at the farm

2.30

a) Listen to the phrases (1–8). Who's the speaker? Berry or a visitor? – *1 visitor, 2 ...*

b) Listen again. Finish the sentences.

1 Excuse me, please. We want to visit ...
2 When do you feed the ...?
3 We feed the ducks at ...
4 Excuse me, please. Where are the ... ?
5 What's that ...?
6 It's only a donkey. Don't ...
7 Look at the hamsters. They're really ...
8 Come on, Sam. Let's go ...

c) Listen again and repeat.

STOP! – CHECK! – GO! Navigator | Vorbereitung

Zeitbedarf: ca. zwei Stunden
Kooperative Lernformen: Partner check Ex **1c** | Partner talk Ex **3b**
Materialbedarf: Ex **2**: Audio-CD + Player oder MP3 + PC/Lautsprecher
Einsatz von Begleitmedien: KV 4.8 (Lösungsschlüssel, auch für die Hand der S zur selbstständigen Lösungsüberprüfung, ggf. im Partner check) | DFF 4.1, 4.3 | INKL 4.12A/B

▸ *KV 4.8* ▸ *DFF 4.3* ▸ *INKL 4.12 A/B*

3 REVISION A day with my family

a) Complete the text.

Every morning mum, dad and I ... (get up) at 6 o'clock.
After breakfast I ... (go) to school by car with my dad.
At about 9 o'clock the first visitors ... (come).
Mum and dad ... (have) lunch at 1 o'clock. After lunch dad usually ... (stay) in the shop and mum ... (work) with the ponies.
I ... (come) home from school with dad before 4 o'clock.
Dad ... (have) something to eat with me. Then we ... (go) outside. Sam ... (come) with me. We ... (look) after all the animals.
There's lots of work on a farm every day.

b) ● Make a table like this for a day with your family.
Then tell your partner.

When?	Who?	What?
every morning / before 6 o'clock	mum, dad and I	get up

More help p. 138

4 ○ LANGUAGE An interview with Cyril and Sandy

//● p. 139

a) Complete the reporter's questions with *do* or *does*.

1 ... you like Plymouth?
2 ... you have a best friend?
3 ... you and Sandy live on the beach?
4 ... Sandy like Plymouth too?
5 ... Sandy have a best friend?

– Yes, it's great.
– Yes, I do. Her name is Sandy.
– Yes, we live in Kingsand.
– Yes, she loves Plymouth.
– Yes, she does. I'm her best friend!

b) Complete Cyril's answers with *don't* or *doesn't*.

1 Do you like Mr Johnson?
2 Do you live in a big house?
3 Do you and Sandy go to school?
4 Does Sandy have a car?
5 Does Sandy eat crabs?

– No, I ... like Mr Johnson. He's terrible.
– No, I ... live in a big house. I like small houses.
– No, we ... go to school.
– No, she ... have a car. But she has a bike.
– No, she ... eat crabs. I'm a crab!

c) Match the questions with Sandy's answers.

1 Where do you live?
2 When do you get up?
3 Where do you have breakfast?
4 What do you do after breakfast?
5 Why do you like Cyril?

– Very late – after 10 o'clock.
– I always have breakfast on the beach.
– Because he's friendly and he's fun!
– In Kingsand.
– I often go to Plymouth.

Erarb. 3a (SB offen) S übertragen den Text ins Heft, ergänzen Verbformen. L erinnert zuvor an die Merkregel: "*He, she, it* – das *-s* muss mit!"
Erarb. 3b S legen entsprechende Tabelle im Heft an und machen Notizen zu eigenen Tagesaktivitäten (*note-making*), anschließend berichten sie einander im Partner talk mithilfe ihrer Notizen
○ Lernschwächere nutzen Redemittel aus More help

Erarb. Ex 4a (SB offen) S ergänzen die Entscheidungsfragen mit *Do/Does* schriftl. in EA.
//● Lernstärkere bilden vollständige Fragesätze.
Erarb. Ex 4b S ergänzen die Antworten schriftlich mit *don't/doesn't*.
//● Lernstärkere bilden verneinte Verbformen vollständig.
Erarb. Ex 4c S ordnen Fragen/Antworten zu, schreiben den Dialog ins Heft.
//● Lernstärkere ergänzen dabei die fehlenden Fragewörter

Lernschwerpunkt: **Wiederholen und Üben, Lernfortschritte erkennen (Fokus: Unit 4)**
Kompetenzen: Writing Interviewfragen im *simple present* beantworten; einen gelenkten Dialog schreiben
Lern- und Arbeitstechniken Eigene Lernfortschritte erkennen; ein Projekt durchführen
Redemittel: Wortfelder Gewohnheiten; *feelings; animals*

STOP! CHECK! GO!

▸ KV 4.8 ▸ DFF 4.4 ▸ INKL 4.12 A/B

Erarb. Ex 5a (SB offen) S wählen vorgegebene Präpositionen aus, setzen sie in die Sätze ein und notieren diese.
Erarb. Ex 5b S ordnen die in a) vervollständigten Sätze den Abbildungen zu.

5 WORDS °Useful phrases

at • by • in • through • to (3x) • with

a) Find the right word for these phrases from the box.

1 Help! I'm ... trouble!
2 I want to go ... the toilet!
3 I get up ... 6 o'clock.
4 I go to school ... bus.
5 I listen ... music every evening.
6 I feel great when I'm ... my friends.
7 Go ... that field.
8 Go ... sleep. Good night!

b) ○ Match the phrases in a) with the pictures (A–H).

Erarb. Ex 6a (SB offen) S schreiben Lucas Fragen und ihre Antworten darauf ins Heft
○ Lernschwächere nutzen Redemittel aus More help
Erarb. Ex 6b S schreiben analog zu a) Fragen an Luca auf und beantworten diese mit Hilfe ihres Wissens über Luca.

6 WRITING Luca and you

a) Write the dialogue with Luca in your exercise book. Write as many sentences as you can.

Luca	You
Hi, I'm Luca. What's your name?	– Hi, Luca. I'm ...
Do you live in England?	– No, I live in ...
Do you live in the country?	– ...
Do you like English?	– ...
Do you have a pet?	– ...
When do you feel fed up?	– ...
When do you feel great?	– ...
Do you want to come to Plymouth?	– ...

More help p.139

b) ● Write a dialogue between you and Luca.
Now you ask the questions – as many as you can.

Erarb. Ex 7a (SB offen) S überlegen gemäß den Beispielen 6 Interviewfragen und notieren sie auf Zettel.
○ Lernschwächere nutzen Redemittel aus More help
Erarb. Ex 7b S führen mit ihren Fragen in einer Milling-around activity mit möglichst vielen Mit-S kurze Interviews; nach jeder Befragung Fragezettel austauschen, um möglichst viele verschiedene Fragestrukturen zu üben

7 SPEAKING An interview with a student in your class

a) Think of good questions for your interview. Write your six best questions on a piece of paper.
Example: *What do you ...?*
Where do you ...?
When do you ...?

More help p.140

b) Walk around: Find a partner. Ask and answer your questions. Then swap questions and find a new partner.

Zeitbedarf: ca. zwei Stunden
Kooperative Lernformen: Milling-around activity Ex **7b** | Gallery walk Ex **8** (STEP 5b)
Einsatz von Begleitmedien: KV 4.8 (Lösungsschlüssel, auch für die Hand der S zur selbstständigen Lösungsüberprüfung, ggf. im Partner check), KV 4.7 A/B | DFF 4.1, 4.5 | INKL 4.12A/B | Workbook S. 61–64

▸ KV 4.7 A/B ▸ DFF 4.5 ▸ INKL 4.12 A/B

8 °PROJECT[1] Interesting animals

Find out about an interesting animal. You can work alone, with a partner or in a small group.

STEP 1: Pick an animal for your project.

budgie | elephant | guinea pig | tiger | polar bear

STEP 2: Pick five questions – or more – for your project.

Where do the animals come from? (what country) • What do they look like? (colour/furry) • Are they big or small? • How long[1] are they? • Where do they live? (cage/nest[2]) • Do they live inside/outside? • What do they eat? • What can they do? (run/swim/talk) • How long[1] do they live? (1 year/2 years) • Are they good pets?

STEP 3: Find the information on the internet. Go to www.cornelsen.de/lighthouse and put in the webcode LH-1-89.

STEP 4: Make a mind map like this:

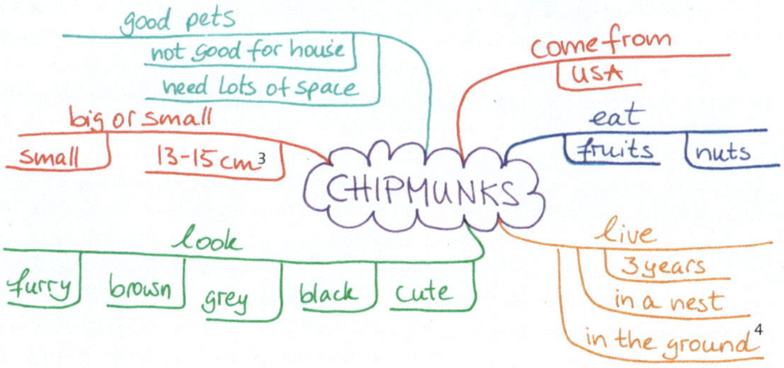

STEP 5: Pick a) OR b).

a) Talk about your animal for 1 minute.

b) Write a text about your animal. Find photos for your text. Then put the text on the wall. More help p. 140

Erarb. Ex 8 STEP 1–4 (SB offen) S wählen ein Tier aus, zu diesem mindestens 5 Fragen aus STEP 2. Von angegebener Website oder KV 4.7A/B notwendige Informationen entnehmen und in Mindmap strukturieren (auf der KV sind als Zwischenschritt Markierungen möglich). Durchführbar in EA/PA/GA
○ Mit Lernschwächeren ggf. *Mind maps* wiederholen (mit *Skills file*, S. 162)
STEP 5a S halten mit ihrer Mindmap Kurzvortrag über ihr Tier (in PA oder im Plenum).
STEP 5b S verfassen mit ihrer Mindmap einen Text über das ausgewählte Tier, gestalten diesen (mit Fotos, Zeichnungen ...) und stellen ihn im Klassenraum aus
Zusatz Gallery walk

9 My learner log

Copy and complete your learner log. You can put it in your DOSSIER.

My learner log

Now I can ...
– say the names of lots of animals: ...
– say the time: ...
– ask questions in an interview: ...
– say when I feel great or fed up: ...
– write an invitation: 😃 😐 😟
– use a dictionary: 😃 😐 😟

In Unit 4 ...
– my favourite text is on page ...
– my favourite words are ...
– my favourite phrases are ...
– my favourite people are ...
– difficult words are ...

My progress in English is: GREAT! 👍 / OK 👉 / NOT VERY GOOD 👎

Erarb. Ex 9 (SB offen) S bearbeiten ihr **My learner log** gemäß Muster. Sie können es mit entsprechenden Symbolen versehen.

[1] how long? [haʊ ˈlɒŋ] *wie lang? / wie lange?* [2] nest *Nest* [3] cm = centimetre [ˈsentɪmiːtə] *Zentimeter*
[4] ground [graʊnd] *Erde*

Lernschwerpunkt: **Leben und Arbeiten in Plymouth Harbour**

Storyline: Die Doppelseite stellt das lebendige Hafenviertel von Plymouth, *The Barbican*, als Lebensmittelpunkt von Adam Osmanovic und seiner Familie vor.

Kompetenzen: Listening Einem Text Detailinformationen entnehmen | **Speaking** Bilder beschreiben

Redemittel: Wortfelder *harbour life, work*

Einstieg Ex 1 (SB geschl.) L: *Plymouth is by the sea and has a really nice harbour. You can see big ferries* (ggf. Foto zeigen) *and many other interesting things. Let's look at the harbour.*
Erarb. Ex 1a (SB offen) gemäß Aufgabe.
○ Für Lernschwächere AA gemeinsam lesen und *who* wiederholen → keine Verwechslung mit dt. „wo"!
Erarb. Ex 1b gemäß Aufgabe in EA.
L gibt Zeitvorgabe (ca. 2 Minuten).
Ausw. Ex 1b S zeigen und benennen im Partner talk Dinge, die sie gefunden haben, und ergänzen/korrigieren entsprechend ihre Listen (ggf. SB-*Dictionary* nutzen lassen).
Einstieg Ex 1c (SB geschl.) L steht im hinteren Raumteil mit derselben Blickrichtung wie die S und führt *on the left, on the right* und *in the middle* ein: *Close your eyes and think of our classroom. On the* ***left*** *there's a window. On the* ***right*** *there's a door. In the* ***middle*** *there's my desk. What do you remember about our classroom? Where is the board/poster/… ? Is it on the left, on the right or in the middle of the room?*
S: The board/poster/… is …
Anschließend an Tafel schreiben, Aussprache/Bedeutung sichern
Erarb. Ex 1c (SB offen) gemäß Aufgabe.

Unit 5 All about Adam

▸ *Folie 1* ▸ *IAT 5.1*

C

1 The harbour[1] in Plymouth

1 ['hɑːbə]

a) Do you know the people in photos A-D? Who are they? Can you guess?
Example: I think the boy in photo C is …

b) What can you see on pages 90–91? Name ten things. Write a list. More help p. 140

c) Choose one of the photos and talk about it with your partner.

In the big photo / In photo A / … On the left / On the right / In the middle	there's a … I can see …

I think the man in photo A is Adam's father / Mr Osmanovic.
I think the boy in photo B is Adam.
I think the boy in photo C is Zack / Adam's brother.
I think the woman in photo C is Alisha / Ellie's stepmum / Zack's babysitter.
I think the woman in photo D is Adam's mother / Mrs Osmanovic.

LEAD-IN Navigator | **Vorbereitung**

Zeitbedarf: ca. zwei Stunden
Kooperative Lernformen: Partner talk Ex **1a–c**
Materialbedarf: Ex **2**: Audio-CD + Player oder MP3 + PC/Lautsprecher
Einsatz von Begleitmedien: IAT 5.1 | Folie 1 | Workbook S. 65

2 Adam's family

2.31

a) Adam is talking to Ellie. Listen and look at the small photos. Write the letters (A–D) in the right order.

D • A • B • C

b) Listen again. Answer the questions.

1 Where is Adam going?
A To school. B To the cafe. C Home.

2 Where is Adam's dad working now?
A In the cafe. B On the ferry.
C In France.

3 What does Adam want to do?
A Help in the cafe. B His homework.
C Nothing.

4 Where is Adam's brother in the afternoons?
A With his mum. B At school.
C With his babysitter.

Erarb. Ex 2a (SB offen) **1. Hören** (Globalverstehen).
Erarb. Ex 2b **2. Hören** (Detailverstehen).
Ausw. Ex 2b beim **3. Hören** mit abschnittsweisem Anhalten und Abgleich im Plenum.

▸ Workbook 1, p. 65

Lernschwerpunkt: **Der Alltag eines britischen Teenagers am Beispiel von Adam**

Storyline: Adam hilft seiner Mutter im Hafen-Café der Familie. Er hat Spaß daran, aber auf Dauer leidet seine schulische Arbeit. Ein Brief der Klassenlehrerin an seine Eltern zeigt seine gegenwärtigen schulischen Probleme.

Kompetenzen: **Listening** Einem Verkaufsdialog Detailinformationen entnehmen | **Speaking** Einen Verkaufsdialog führen; sagen, was gerade passiert | **Reading** Ein Telefonat und einen Brief verstehen | **Writing** Beschreiben, was gerade passiert

Grammatik: Vorbewusste Verwendung des *present progressive*

Redemittel: Wortfeld *food*; gerade stattfindende Aktivitäten beschreiben

Einstieg Ex 1 (SB geschl.) L: *Adam's family has a cafe. What can you get in a cafe?* S reaktivieren WS zum Thema *food*.
(SB offen) L: *What other things can you get?* L liest die Begriffe A–J vor, S wiederholen im Chor: Lautschulung bei *juice* und *cafe*.
Erarb. Ex 1a (SB offen) **1. Hören** (Globalverstehen). **Ausw. Ex 1a** im Plenum.
Erarb. Ex 1b S schreiben Sätze 1–8 ins Heft, dann **2. Hören** (Detailverstehen).
Ausw. Ex 1b im Plenum.
Erarb. Ex 1c (SB geschl.) **1./2. Hören**: S wiederholen satzweise im Chor.
Erarb. Ex 1d S entwickeln einen Dialog, notieren ihn und üben ihn ein.
Ausw. Ex 1d Präsentation einiger Dialoge im Plenum.

Einstieg Ex 2 (SB offen) Mit Fotos die Situation klären, z. B. L: *Where are Adam and his mother? (in the cafe, in the kitchen). Adam's phone is ringing* (Lautmalerei). *Who wants to talk to Adam? (his father) Look, Adam is really busy. He's washing up. But he answers the phone. ...*
Erarb. Ex 2a **1. Lesen**/Hören (Globalverstehen): S zitieren als Antwort die Textstelle.
Erarb. Ex 2b **2. Lesen** (Detailverstehen).
Ausw. Ex 2b Partner check, anschließend im Plenum.

5 THEME 1

▸ DFF 5.4 ▸ DFF 5.6 ▸ Folie 28 ▸ INKL 5.1 ▸ INKL 5.2

In the cafe

A a (chicken) sandwich
B omelette and chips
C fish and chips
E (vegetable) soup
F a bottle of water

1 Can I help you?

2.32
a) It's 4 pm in the cafe. Adam's mum is busy. Listen. Look at the photos. What things (A–J) do the customers want?

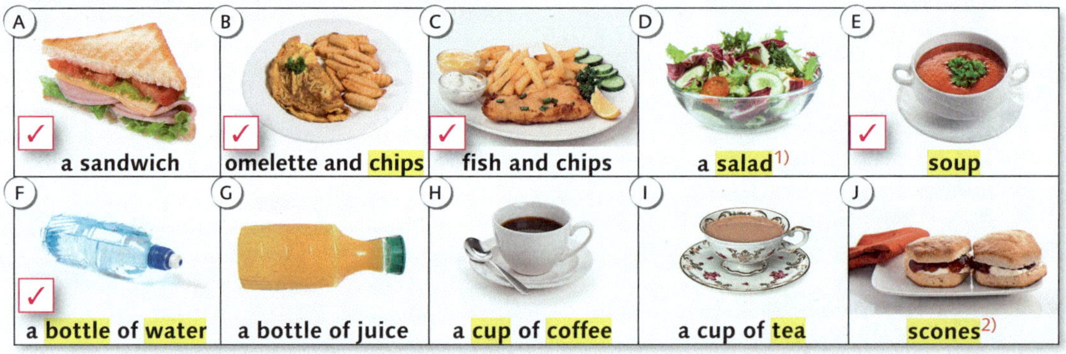

b) Listen again. Who says this – mum (write M) or a customer (write C)?

1 Can I help you? M
2 One fish and chips, please. C
3 Something to drink? M
4 A bottle of water, please. C
5 That's £10.50, please. M
6 Next please. M
7 Anything else? M
8 No thanks. That's all. C

2.33
c) Listen and repeat.

d) Make a dialogue in a cafe. Use words and phrases from a) and b). More help p. 141

2 How's it going?

2.34
Adam's dad likes his job.

a) Does Adam's dad like his new job? Read and find out.

Adam is helping in the cafe. His mobile is ringing.

Adam — Hey dad, how's it going?
Dad — Fine, thanks. How's it going at home?
Adam — Oh, OK. But I miss you! How's your new job on the ferry?
Dad — It's great. But I miss you all too. Is mum busy[3] now? Is she working?
Adam — She's cooking. She can't talk to you. The cafe is busy.
Dad — Oh, OK. Are you helping mum?
Adam — Yeah, I'm washing up.
Dad — That's great. But you must work hard at school too.
Adam — Yeah, dad. Sorry, I must go. We're very busy here.
Dad — OK. Say hi to everybody. Bye, Adam.
Adam — Bye, dad. See you at the weekend.

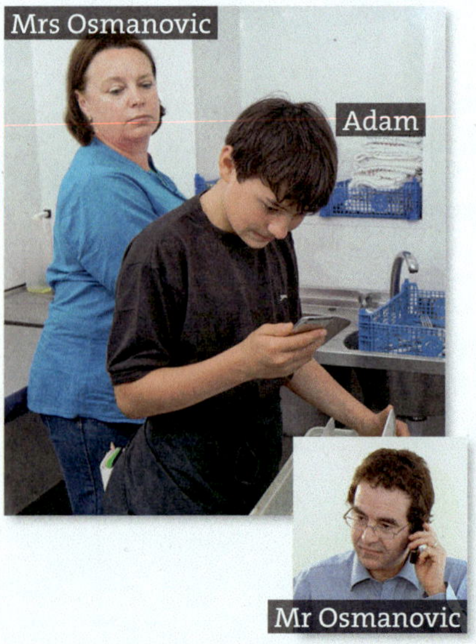

b) Who's doing what? Write five sentences.
1 Dad is ... 2 Mum is ... 3 Adam is ... 4 ...

cooking • talking to Adam • washing up • working on a ferry • helping in the cafe

Lösungsbsp. S. 237

1 ['sæləd] 2 [skɒnz] 3 ['bɪzi]

▸ Workbook 2–3, p. 66

THEME 1 Navigator | Vorbereitung

Zeitbedarf: ca. zwei Stunden
Minimalversion: Ex **1a**+**b**; **2a**; **3a**; **4a**
Kooperative Lernformen: Partner check Ex **2b** | Partner talk Ex **4a** | GA *(miming/guessing)* Ex **4b**
Materialbedarf: Ex **1a** und **2** (optional): Audio-CD + Player oder MP3 + PC/Lautsprecher | Ex **3** (optional): Briefumschlag
Einsatz von Begleitmedien: INKL 5.1–5.2 | DFF 5.4, 5.6 | Folie 28 | Workbook S. 66–67

5

3 A letter from school

a) Read the letter. Is it good news for Adam?

No, it's bad news for Adam.
- Adam isn't happy.
- Adam isn't working hard.
- Adam isn't doing his homework.
- Adam is often tired.

Eggbuckland Community College
A DCSF Designated Technology College • Principal : Katrina Borowski
LEARNING - CARING - ACHIEVING

Dear Mr and Mrs Osmanovic

I'm a bit **worried about** Adam. I don't think he's very happy **at the moment**. He isn't working very hard at school. He isn't doing his homework and he's often tired. Please **phone** me and we can talk about it.

Best wishes
R Lee
Class 7 teacher

b) What do you think Adam's mother says?

1 Ms Lee is ... about you, Adam.
2 Miss Lee thinks that you aren't very ... at the moment.
3 You aren't working very hard ...
4 You are ... tired at school.
5 I'm ... about this letter, Adam. More practice 1 p. 141

1 worried
2 happy
3 at school
4 often
5 worried

Einstieg Ex 3 (SB geschl.) L führt mit Briefumschlag/Tafelzeichnung *letter* sowie *be worried about* ein: *There's a **letter** from school. What do you think is in the letter? Good news or bad news? (bad news, problems, homework, ...). So you are **worried about** the letter – worried about what your parents will say.*
Erarb. Ex 3a (SB offen) **1. Lesen** (Globalverstehen).
● Lernstärkere benennen Adams Probleme.
Erarb. Ex 3b 2. Lesen (Detailverstehen): S setzen korrekte Satzteile ein und notieren die Sätze.
Ausw. Ex 3b im Partner check.

4 What's happening?

a) It's 7 pm. Look at Adam's family and friends. What are they doing? Look at the box and complete the sentences.

doing homework • eating • playing a game • reading a book • riding a bike • riding a pony • watching TV • working

b) One student mimes one of the activities in the green box. The other students guess. Then swap roles.

"You're doing homework." – "Wrong."
"You're reading a book." – "Right."

Erarb. Ex 4a (SB offen)
L klärt Bedeutung von *happen*. S ordnen den Abb. die Satzbausteine zu und notieren die kompletten Sätze.
Ausw. Ex 4a im Partner talk:
S 1 zeigt auf ein Bild / nennt eine Bildnummer (1–6), S 2 nennt entsprechenden Satz.
Erarb. Ex 4b (SB offen) L klärt Aufgabenstellung und *mime*. Nach Probedurchlauf im Plenum GA (3–4 S) gemäß Aufgabe.

► Workbook 4–5, p. 67
3 [ə'lɪʃə] 4 [ɑːnt] 5 ['kʌzn]

Lernschwerpunkt: **Sich über Möglichkeiten der Freizeitgestaltung austauschen**

Storyline: Adam langweilt sich. Alisha (die Tagesmutter seines Bruders) erwischt ihn beim (verbotenen) Tauchen am Hafen. Sie vermittelt Adam einen Kontakt zum Jugendmusikclub *Plymouth Music Zone* (PMZ, https://www.plymouthmusiczone.org.uk/).

Kompetenzen: **Listening** Ein Telefonat global und im Detail verstehen | **Speaking** Über Musik sprechen | **Reading** Eine Bildergeschichte und eine Broschüre verstehen | **Writing** Über Musikerfahrungen schreiben | **Lern- und Arbeitstechniken** Sich Notizen machen

Grammatik: Vorbewusste Verwendung des *present progressive*

Redemittel: Über Freizeitgestaltung sprechen; Wortfeld *music*

Einstieg Ex 1 (SB geschl.) L: *Do you like it when you're at home alone?* S1: *Yes, I can do what I want / …* S2: *No, I don't like it. I'm worried / I don't know what to do / it's boring / …* L: *Adam doesn't like to be at home alone. He thinks it's boring. But he has an idea. Let's find out what it is.*
Erarb. Ex 1a (SB offen) Pre-reading-Aufgabe, dann **1. Lesen**/Hören (Globalverstehen): S überprüfen ihre Antworten, L sichert neuen WS. *Dive* möglicherweise schon als „tauchen" bekannt, deshalb verdeutlicht L die Bedeutung hier: „einen Kopfsprung ins Wasser machen".
Alternative (SB offen) Präsentation der Geschichte als Hörtext. L lässt den Text unter den Bildern abdecken. S verfolgen beim Hören die Geschichte auf den Bildern. Anschließend Erarb. wie oben.
Erarb. Ex 1b (SB offen) **2. Lesen**/Hören gemäß Aufgabe.

5 THEME 2

It's boring at home!

Where's Adam?
1 in the cafe • **2** in town • **3–6** at the harbour
Who is with Adam?
1 his mum • **2** – (nobody) • **3** his friends • **4** Alisha, Alisha's baby Finn, his brother Zack • **5** his friends, Alisha, Zack • **6** Alisha

1 Trouble for Adam

2.35

a) Look at the pictures. Where's Adam? Who is with Adam?

1

It's Tuesday, after school. Adam is in his mum's cafe. He's helping.
"Go home, Adam. You can't stay here. You must do your homework," his mum says.

2

Adam thinks, "It's so boring at home! No mum, no dad, and Zack is with his new babysitter." But then he has an idea. Now he's phoning his friends. "Hey, come to the harbour."

3

Adam is diving. His friends are diving too. They're having lots of fun.
But diving in the harbour is dangerous.

4

Zack and Alisha are walking in the harbour.
"Oh no! It's my brother and Alisha. I must hide!" Adam says. But it's too late.

Box: Voc., p. 203

5

Alisha is talking to Adam.
"You can't dive here, Adam. It's very dangerous. Go home."
"It's boring at home," Adam says.
"You need a hobby, Adam."

6

Alisha has a good idea.
Her friend Josie works at the PMZ music club. And Adam likes music.
"Hi, Josie. Can you send me a brochure for PMZ, please?"

b) What's happening in the pictures? Read the text again and finish the sentences.

1 In picture 1 Adam is ...
2 In picture 2 Adam is ...
3 In picture 3 Adam and his friends are ...
4 In picture 4 Zack and Alisha are ...
5 In picture 5 Alisha is ...
6 In picture 6 Alisha is ...

- phoning his friends.
- helping in the cafe.
- talking to Adam.
- walking in the harbour.
- phoning Josie.
- diving in the harbour.

1 helping in the cafe • **2** phoning his friends **3** diving in the harbour **4** walking in the harbour • **5** talking to Adam • **6** phoning Josie

► Workbook 6, p. 68

Zeitbedarf: ca. zwei Stunden
Minimalversion: Ex **1a**+**b** (zusammengefasst); **2a**+**b**; **3a**–**c**
Kooperative Lernformen: Appointments Ex **3a**–**c**
Materialbedarf: Ex **1a** (optional); Ex **2b**: Audio-CD + Player oder MP3 + PC/Lautsprecher
Einsatz von Begleitmedien: INKL 5.3–5.4 | DFF 5.3 | Workbook S. 68

Einstieg Ex 2 (SB geschl.) Einführung von neuem WS, z. B. L: *Adam likes music. Do you like music? Do you play an instrument?*
Erarb. Ex 2a (SB offen)
1. Lesen (Globalverstehen); Aussprache von *music* und *zone* durch Vor-/Nachsprechen sichern.
2. Lesen (Detailverstehen). L: *What music can you make there?* S antworten (Meldekette): *You can learn to play the guitar. / You can play the drums in a group. / ...*
Erarb. Ex 2b S notieren Fragen 1–4 untereinander. Beim **1. Hören** ergänzen sie die Lösungsbuchstaben dahinter.
Ausw. Ex 2b Hefttausch mit Partner, Kontrolle beim **2. Hören**, danach im Plenum.
Erarb. Ex 2c S notieren Tabelle, ergänzen Informationen beim **3. Hören.**
Ausw. Ex 2c wie in **2b**.

Erarb. Ex 3a S erstellen Tabelle (+ 3 Spalten: *Me, Partner 1, Partner 2*), füllen *Me* aus, nutzen dabei *Wordbank* 8, S. 177.
Erarb. Ex 3b S befragen Partner, notieren Antworten; L signalisiert Wechsel.
Erarb. Ex 3c Ggf. Redemittel an Tafel vorgeben (*Mia's favourite band is ... / She can / can't play ...*).
Erarb. Ex 3d mit Informationen aus **3a**.
O Lernschwächere nutzen More help
Ausw. Ex 3d Gegenseitiges Vorlesen der Texte partner-/gruppenweise.

5

▸ INKL 5.3 ▸ DFF 5.3 ▸ INKL 5.4

2 Welcome to PMZ

It means *Plymouth Music Zone*. You can make music there (for free).

a) Look at the brochure. Find out: What does PMZ mean? What can you do there?

MAKE MUSIC °FOR FREE
EVERY NIGHT OF THE WEEK AT PLYMOUTH MUSIC °ZONE

www.plymouthmusiczone.org.uk

MON — **THE PMZ GUITAR CLUB**
4 pm – 6.15 pm ¦ Everybody welcome!
Learn to play the guitar.

TUE — **THE BIG BASH**
5 pm – 6 pm ¦ 8 – 18 yrs
Play the drums in a group.

WED — **JAM BAND**
4 pm – 5 pm ¦ 8 – 18 yrs
Bring your instrument. Play in a band.

THUR — **°BEATS PER MINUTE (BPM)**
4.30 pm – 5.30 pm ¦ 11 – 25 yrs
Instrument workshop for young °disabled musicians. Make some new music.

FRI — **STREETBEATZ**
4 pm – 6.15 pm ¦ 12 – 19 yrs
For all young rappers.
Make your music in the PMZ studio.

SAT — **THE ROOF RAISERS**
10 am – 12.30 pm ¦ 11 – 18 yrs
For young singers. Sing with a real band.

2.36 **b)** O Listen to Adam. Pick A, B, C or D.

1 Who is talking to Adam? — A His mum. B His dad. C Josie. D Alisha.
2 What does Adam like? — A The drums. B Rapping. C The guitar. D The piano.
3 Where is PMZ? — A At Eggy. B In London. C In a village. D Near the city centre.
4 What does Adam want to join? — A The guitar club. B Streetbeatz. C Jam Band. D The Big Bash.

c) ● Copy this table. Listen again and take notes. More help p. 141

PMZ address: ...	Times (Sat): ... ...
Bus number: ...	Price: ...
Times (Mon–Fri):	

PMZ address: Raglan Road • **Bus number:** 34 • **Times (Mon–Fri):** From 4 pm to 7 pm • **Times (Sat):** From 10 am to 12.30 pm • **Price:** Free

3 NOW YOU

a) Appointments: Write the questions in the green box in a table and write your answers. More help p. 142

▸ Wordbank 8, p. 177

b) Make appointments with two partners. Go to your appointments. Take notes.

c) Tell the class about one partner.

d) ● Write a text about you and music. You can put it in your DOSSIER. More help p. 142

- What's your favourite band?
- Who's your favourite singer?
- What's your favourite English song?
- Can you play an instrument? What instrument?
- Can you sing? Can you rap?
- Are you in a band?

▸ Workbook 7–8, p. 68

Lernschwerpunkt: **Das *present progressive* zum Sprechen darüber benutzen, was gerade passiert**
Storyline: Adam spricht über Fotos auf seinem Handy. Später tauschen sich Ellie und er darüber aus, was sie und ihre Familienmitglieder gerade tun.
Kompetenzen: Listening Geräusche in Verbindung mit Text verstehen | **Speaking** Sagen, was andere gerade machen | **Reading** Einen Dialog verstehen | **Writing** Schreiben, was andere gerade machen **Lern- und Arbeitstechniken** Sprachliche Regelmäßigkeiten erkennen
Grammatik: Bewusstmachen und Üben des *present progressive* (bejahte/verneinte Aussagen, Fragen)
Redemittel: Wortfelder Alltagstätigkeiten, Hobbys

Einstieg Ex 1 (SB geschl.) L notiert einige Aktivitäten (z. B. *diving, hiding, cooking, washing up*) verdeckt auf Tafel, wählt dann einige S aus, die die Aktivitäten darstellen. Die anderen S raten. Dafür Strukturhilfe geben: *He/She is ... -ing*.
Dann neue Verben pantomimisch einführen (*setting the table / cleaning the table*), an Tafel notieren und Aussprache üben.
Erarb. Ex 1a (SB offen) **1. Lesen**/Hören (Globalverstehen), S ordnen Buchstaben der Fotos in Vorbereitung auf **b)** korrekt untereinander im Heft an.
Erarb. Ex 1b **2. Lesen** (Detailverstehen): S suchen im Text passende Sätze und schreiben sie zum entsprechenden Buchstaben aus **a)**.
Ausw. Ex 1b Partner check, dann im Plenum.

Erarb. Ex 2a (SB offen) S erstellen beide Tabellen, suchen in PA aus Text alle mit *What* beginnenden Fragen sowie Antworten dazu heraus und tragen sie ein. (Ggf. erklären, dass man *is* nach Fragewort zu *'s* verkürzen kann, vgl. LF 10, S. 171).
Ausw. Ex 2a S1: Frage, S2: Antwort vortragen usw.
Erarb. Ex 2b S vervollständigen die Regel mündlich.
Ausw. Ex 2b Im Plenum (ggf. an Tafel), dann Übertragen ins Heft.

5 FOCUS ON LANGUAGE

► INKL 5.5 ► Folie 29

1 Photos on Adam's mobile

2.37

a) Read the dialogue. Put the photos in the right order. B • D • E • A • C

Ellie __ Let's see the photos on your mobile then. ... That's your mum. What's she doing?
Adam __ Good question. She's in the cafe. She's making sandwiches, I think. This is me.
Ellie __ Oh, yes. You're in the cafe too. What are you doing? Box: Voc., p. 203
Adam __ Let's see. I'm setting the tables. Or I'm cleaning the tables. I'm not sure.
Ellie __ This must be your little brother Zack. He's with my stepmum, Alisha. What are they doing?
Adam __ They're sitting in a park. I think it's near our house, or maybe it's the Hoe.
Ellie __ And this must be your dad. What's he doing?
Adam __ He's cooking. He's a great cook. And this is me with my group at PMZ.
Ellie __ Cool. Let's see. What are you doing?
Adam __ We're rapping.
Ellie __ You're rapping? Really? Can you rap?
Adam __ Well, I'm learning!

b) Find a sentence from the dialogue for each picture.

B She's making sandwiches. • **D** I'm setting the tables. / I'm cleaning the tables. **E** They're sitting in a park. • **A** He's cooking. **C** We're rapping. / Well, I'm learning.

2 Questions and answers with 'ing'

a) Copy and complete the tables with questions and answers from 1.

Question word	form of 'be'	Pronoun	verb + -ing
What	's	she	doing?
What	...		...

Lösung S. 237

Pronoun	form of 'be'	verb + -ing
She	's	making sandwiches.
I	'm	...

b) Look at the tables again. Complete the rule.

FOCUS

Das *present progressive* wird gebildet mit:

I + 'm	+	verb + ing
he / she / it + ...	+	verb + ing
you / we / they + ...	+	verb + ing

Man benutzt die Verlaufsform in der Gegenwart (*present progressive*),
a) um Bilder zu beschreiben und
b) um zu sagen, was gerade passiert.

► *Language file 10, p. 171*

FOCUS ON LANGUAGE Navigator | Vorbereitung

Zeitbedarf: ca. 1–2 Stunden
Minimalversion: Ex **1a**+**b**; **2a**+**b**; **3a**+**b**; **4a**+**b**
Kooperative Lernformen: Partner check Ex **1b**; **3b**; **4b** | **Gruppendiskussion** Ex **6a**
Materialbedarf: Ex **1a** (optional); **4**: Audio-CD + Player oder MP3 + PC/Lautsprecher | Ex **6a**: ca. 6–8 DIN-A4-Blätter
Einsatz von Begleitmedien: KV 5.1 | DFF 5.1 | INKL 5.5 | Folie 29–30 | Workbook S. 69–70

▸ KV 5.1 ▸ DFF 5.1 ▸ Folie 30

3 What are you doing?

a) It's Saturday. Ellie is talking to Adam on the phone. Complete the sentences with *'m • is • 's • are • 're.*

Ellie

1 What am I doing? I'm with my family. My stepdad is making breakfast. He... cooking omelettes. My favourite food! I... making toast.
2 My sister Zoe ... feeding the cats. They... making lots of noise. They're hungry!
3 Mum ... sitting at the table. She... writing an email.
4 My brother Conor ... watching TV. What ... you doing now, Adam?

Adam

1 He's, I'm • 2 Zoe is, They're
3 Mum is, She's • 4 Conor is, What are

More practice 2 p. 142

1 Mum is sitting, Zack is riding, Mum is looking
2 I'm looking, They're laughing
3 Dad and I are working, Dad is making, I'm setting
4 Dad is talking

b) Adam is talking to Ellie. Complete the sentences with the *present progressive*.

1 Today is a nice day because dad is home. Mum ... (sit) in the garden. Zack ... (ride) his bike there. Mum ... (look) after him.
Box: Voc., p. 204
2 I... (look) at them through the window. Can you hear that noise? That's Zack with mum. They... (laugh).
3 Dad and I ... (work) in the kitchen. Dad ... (make) something special because it's mum's birthday. I... (set) the table.
4 OK Ellie, Dad ... (talk) to me. I must go now. See you on Monday.

More practice 3 p. 143

4 What's Cyril doing?

2.38

a) What's Cyril doing now? p. 143
Write the numbers 1–5. Then listen and choose an answer from the box:
1 Cyril is swimming, 2 ...

playing football • playing tennis • rapping • reading a story • riding a bike • swimming • talking on the phone • washing up • watching TV • writing a text • writing an email

b) Listen again. Compare answers with a partner.

I think Cyril is swimming.

Me too. / No, I think Cyril is ...

1 Cyril is washing up • 2 Cyril is playing football • 3 Cyril is writing an email • 4 Cyril is talking on the phone • 5 Cyril is watching TV.

5 NOW YOU

What is your father/mother/sister/friend/... doing now?
Write sentences about your family and friends – as many as you can.

I think my	best friend mum dog ...	is working is doing homework is playing ...	now.

6 What are they doing?

a) Look at the photos. Discuss what you think the people are doing. Then write sentences.
A: I think the boy in photo 1 is ...
B: Really? I think he's ...
C: OK. Let's write: 1 He's ...

b) The groups tell the class.
In photo 1 we think she's ...

Check on page 120.

The boy in photo 1 is skateboarding. • The girl in photo 2 is riding a bike. • The girl in photo 3 is playing football. • The boy in photo 4 is playing the guitar. • The girl in photo 5 is washing up. • The boy in photo 6 is reading a book.

▸ Workbook 9–14, pp. 69–70

Erarb. Ex 3a (SB offen)
Schriftlich gemäß Aufgabe; Hinweisen darauf, dass nach Eigennamen/Nomen meist die Langform (*is, are*) verwendet wird.
Erarb. Ex 3b Ggf. zuerst mdl.; schriftl. Korrektheit durch **Mp2** vorbereiten (vgl. auch LF 10, S. 171).
Ausw. Ex 3b Partner check.
Zusatz KV 5.1: Übungen zur Festigung der Personalpronomen.

Erarb. Ex 4a **1. Hören** (Aufnahme: kleine Episoden mit Cyrils Geräuschen, die sich durch seine Kommentare erklären. **Achtung: 1. Lösungsangabe falsch**, soll kritisch überprüft werden!).
Erarb. Ex 4b **2. Hören**, Partner check.

Einstieg Ex 5 (SB geschl.) L: *It's 9/ ... o'clock. What is/are my partner/children/friends/... doing? I think he/she is / they are working/playing/... now.* ... Dann S befragen; Bsp-Sätze an Tafel, ggf. abschreiben.
Erarb. Ex 5 auch als schriftl. **HA** möglich.

Einstieg Ex 6 (SB geschl.) Gruppenbildung, dann Hinweis auf paralleles Arbeiten der Gruppen und Kontrolle am Ende (S. 120).
Erarb. Ex 6a (SB offen) erst mdl., dann schriftl. (ein DIN-A4-Blatt pro Gruppe).
Ausw. in **Ex 6b** Jeder pro Gruppe liest mindestens einen Satz, die anderen kontrollieren auf S. 120.

STORY Navigator | Inhalt

Lernschwerpunkt: Eine Geschichte und einen Rap verstehen

Storyline: Adam verarbeitet seine persönlichen Probleme in einem Rap und erkennt die Bedeutung seiner Musik für sich sowie für seine Freunde und Eltern. Bei einer *rap battle* im PMZ (*Plymouth Music Zone*) wird er Zweiter und gewinnt persönliche Anerkennung.

Kompetenzen: Listening Musikstile (emotional) erfassen | **Reading** Eine Geschichte global und im Detail verstehen

Speaking Sich über Songs austauschen; einen Rap vortragen

Redemittel: Wortfelder *problems, music*

Erarb. Ex 1 (SB geschl.) S notieren Ziffern 1–6 untereinander. Beim **1. Hören** bewerten sie die Stücke 1–6 mit 😐😊☹. (SB offen) **2. Hören** (Song für Song): S äußern sich mithilfe der Redemittel. Im Plenum beliebtestes Stück ermitteln. L: *Who likes song 1/ 2/ …?* (Auszählen) **Hinweis:** Musikbeispiele (alle ohne Text) angelehnt an diese Stilrichtungen: 1: *Rap*; 2: Klassische Musik; 3: *Alternative Rock*; 4: *Country*; 5: *Traditional bagpipe music*; 6: *Hard Rock*

Überleitung L: *Adam wants to make music too. Which song do you think he likes best? Why?* S: *I think he likes the rap song. There's a poster with the word 'rap' on it. / …* L: *Let's find out if you are right.*

Einstieg STORY (SB offen) L schreibt *Music makes a difference* an Tafel und lässt S über Titel spekulieren (*different* schon bekannt): *Adam likes different music. / Adam feels better with music. / …* Ideen an Tafel notieren

Erarb. STORY (SB offen) **1. Lesen**/Hören in 5 Abschnitten, für die S Überschriften finden, z. B.: **(1)** ll. 1–9: *Trouble on the bus* **(2)** ll. 10–16: *Josie and Adam* etc. Anschließend Hypothesen zum Titel prüfen: L: *Look at your ideas about the title again. Which is the best? How can you say it in German?*

5 STORY

▸ INKL 5.6

2.39 **1 Before you read**

Listen to the songs. Do you like them?

> I like / don't like song number …
> – It's great / OK / terrible!
> – I love it! / I don't like it. / I hate it!

Music makes a difference[1]

2.40

Box: Voc., p. 204

It was Friday afternoon. Adam was on the bus, on the way to PMZ. Some other kids were on the bus too.

Box: Voc., p. 205

"Hey you," one boy said to Adam. "You're sitting on my seat!" The other boys and girls laughed. "Hey babyface, how old are you? Five?" a girl asked. They all laughed again. Adam said nothing.

Adam was at PMZ with his rap teacher, Josie. "Are you feeling OK, Adam?" Josie asked. "I had a bit of trouble on the bus," Adam said. "Some kids were mean. I'm fed up." "That's terrible," Josie said. "But you can use that feeling in your rap."

In the lesson, Josie said, "When you rap, you must rap about your life." Josie asked, "What's important in your life?" "Friends ... my girlfriend ... TV ... my family ... music." Everybody had different ideas. "Cool," Josie said. "And you can rap about problems too. Any ideas?" "Trouble at school ... trouble with parents ... trouble with other kids ...," they said. "OK. We have a rap °battle here at PMZ next week. You can write a rap," Josie said.

On Monday morning Adam was at school. "How's it going at PMZ?" Luca asked. "It's great. I'm writing a rap. But it's hard," Adam said. "Can we listen to it?" Ellie asked. "Sure. You can all come to the rap battle on Friday," Adam said.

1 ['dɪfrəns]

Zeitbedarf: ca. zwei Stunden
Minimalversion: Ex **1**; **2**; **3**
Kooperative Lernformen: **Rap** Ex **4**
Materialbedarf: **STORY** (optional): Audio-CD + Player oder MP3 + PC/Lautsprecher; Ex **3**: Right/wrong cards
Einsatz von Begleitmedien: INKL 5.6–5.7 | DFF 5.7 | Workbook S. 71

▸ INKL 5.7 ▸ DFF 5.7

On Friday evening lots of people were at PMZ. And Adam was very happy because his dad was there.
"Welcome to PMZ everybody. And welcome to our rap battle," Josie said.
Adam was nervous. His friends were excited.
"Go, Adam, go!" ...

Adam's rap was great. He was second in the rap battle.
"Well done, Adam," his mum said.
"I'm very proud of you, Adam," his dad said.
"Thanks," Adam said. "Music really makes a difference for me."

Music makes a difference

°Chorus
Music makes a difference, a difference, a difference.
Yes, music makes a difference – for me.

Trouble at school, trouble on the bus,
Trouble at home, but °I don't make a fuss.
There's °one thing that I know
And now I'm °telling you,
I need music – and you need it too.
Chorus

Trouble with my mum, and trouble with my dad
°Nobody understands, when I'm feeling so bad.
But there's one thing that I know
And now I'm telling you,
I need music – and you need it too.
Chorus

I'm not like you, and you're not like me
Everybody's different – everybody's free.
There's one thing that I know
And now I'm telling you,
I need music – and you need it too.
Chorus

Adam Osmanovic

Erarb. Ex 2 (SB offen) **2. Lesen**/Hören (Detailverstehen) gemäß Aufgabe.

Erarb. Ex 3 (SB offen) Weitere Aufgabe zur Überprüfung des Detailverstehens. S belegen ihre Einschätzung durch Textstellenangabe.
● Lernstärkere korrigieren zusätzlich die falschen Aussagen (1, 5 und 6, siehe blaue Lösungen in Klammern).
Ausw. Ex 3 Abgleich mit Right/wrong cards im Plenum.

Erarb. Ex 4a (SB geschl.) **1. Hören** und spontane Äußerungen (ggf. Redemittel von S. 98 oben), dann **2. Hören**/Lesen im Mitleseverfahren; neuen Wortschatz klären.
Erarb. Ex 4b (SB geschl.) „Rapper" erhalten Startnummer oder geben sich selbst einen Namen. Aufführen nacheinander zur Instrumentalversion des Raps.
Ausw. Ex 4 Klasse ist Jury, vergibt Punkte. Nach Auszählen die drei Besten nennen: *Number 3/2/1 with ... points is rap number ... / by ...*

2 ○ Can you remember?

Who said this in the story?
1 "You're sitting on my seat!" (lines 4–5)
2 "Are you feeling OK, Adam?" (line 12)
3 "I'm fed up." (l. 14)
4 "How's it going at PMZ?" (l. 29)
5 "Go, Adam, go!" (l. 43)
6 "Music really makes a difference for me." (ll. 48–49)

Lösungen zu **Ex 2** und **3** S. 237

3 ● True, false[2] or not in the text?

1 The boys and girls on the bus were nice. F
2 Adam's rap teacher is Josie. T
3 Josie is from Plymouth. NiT
4 The rap battle was on Friday. T
5 Adam's dad wasn't there. F
6 Adam was first in the rap battle. F
7 Adam's mum listens to rap every day. NiT
8 Music is important for Adam. T

4 RAP Music makes a difference

2.41
2.42

a) Listen to Adam's rap. Do you like it?

b) Who wants to be a rapper? You can have a rap battle in your class. Pick one verse of Adam's rap. Learn it. Rap for the class. Who's the best rapper?

More practice 4 p. 144

Lernschwerpunkt: **Abbildungen beschreiben**
Kompetenzen: **Listening** Eine Bildbeschreibung verstehen und richtigstellen | **Speaking** Eine abgebildete Szene beschreiben
Lern- und Arbeitstechniken Abbildungen beschreiben
Grammatik/Redemittel: Eine abgebildete Szene unter Nutzung des *present progressive* sowie korrekter Präpositionen beschreiben

Zeitbedarf: ca. eine Stunde
Kooperative Lernformen: Partner talk Ex **2**
Materialbedarf: Ex **1c**: Audio-CD + Player oder MP3 + PC/ Lautsprecher
Einsatz von Begleitmedien: IAT 5.2 | INKL 5.8–5.9 | DFF 5.2 | Folie 31 | Workbook S. 72–73

Einstieg Ex 1 (SB offen) („Ich-sehe-was-was-du-nicht-siehst" in E) L: *Bumblebee, bumblebee / I see something you don't see / and the colour is red.*
S raten: *Is it the bike? (no) Is it the little ball on the right? (yes)* Wer richtig rät, stellt nächstes Rätsel. Weiterführung in Kleingruppen zur Wiederholung der dargestellten Begriffe (*bike, football, girl, boy, man, woman, seagull, dog, banana, …*), von Farben, Ortsangaben.
Erarb. Ex 1a S notieren zugeordnete Sätze, dann abwechselndes Vorlesen.
Ausw. Ex 1a Abgleich und Sicherung der Präpositionen im Plenum.
Erarb. Ex 1b S bilden Sätze unter Verwendung des *present progressive*.
Ausw. Ex 1b S liest Satz vor, Partner zeigt auf passende Bildstelle.
Erarb. Ex 1c *right / wrong* an Tafel; S antworten jeweils in Pause vor dem *chorus*.

Erarb. Ex 2 (SB offen) Tipp-Box lesen, dann Partner talk: **A** beschreibt Bild S. 147. Bemerkt **B** Unterschied zu Bild S. 120, *Stop!* rufen und Unterschied beschreiben (und *vice versa*).
○ Lernschwächere betrachten vorab Bild des Partners für ca. 30 Sekunden.
Ausw. Ex 2 S vergleichen ihre Bilder und Notizen, legen ihre SB geöffnet nebeneinander

5 SKILLS TRAINING Describing pictures

► IAT 5.2 ► INKL 5.8 ► INKL 5.9 ► DFF 5.2 ► Folie 31

1 In the park

On the left | On the right

next to | on | between | In the middle | behind | under | in front of

Box: Voc., p. 205

a) ○ What can you see? Match the sentences.

1 On the left I can see a bike. E
2 On the right there's a baby. C
3 There are apples. A
4 I can see a red ball. B
5 There are two dogs. F
6 There's a seagull. D

A They're **on** the table.
B It's **in front of** the baby.
C He's **between** the boys.
D It's **next to** the apples.
E It's **behind** the tree.
F They're **under** the table.

b) ● What are they doing? Make sentences – as many as you can. Lösungsbsp. S. 237

On the left In the middle On the right	two dogs … a boy … three girls … children … a girl … a baby … two men …

More help p. 144

2.43 **c)** Look at the picture and listen. Say what's right or what's wrong.

2 ● NOW YOU

Partner A: Go to page 147.
Partner B: Go to page 120.

Lösungsbsp. S. 237–238

Wenn du ein Bild beschreibst, nenne die Gegenstände und Personen auf dem Bild nicht einfach, sondern sage, **wo** sie sich befinden.
Wenn du sagen möchtest, was die Personen auf dem Bild machen bzw. was gerade auf dem Bild passiert, benutze das *present progressive*:
– *The kids **are playing** football. / The baby **is sleeping**.*

► Skills file 5, p. 165

► Workbook 19–21, pp. 72–73

SKILLS TRAINING Mediation and writing

Lernschwerpunkt: **Kurznachrichten verstehen und verfassen**

Kompetenzen: **Reading** Englische Kurznachrichten verstehen und laut lesen | **Mediation (E>D)** Zentrale Informationen einer Kurznachricht wiedergeben | **Writing** Kurznachrichten verfassen

Grammatik/Redemittel: Gegenwärtige Tätigkeiten mit dem *present progressive* kurz beschreiben

Zeitbedarf: ca. eine Stunde

Minimalversion: Ex **1a**, **2**, **3**

Kooperative Lernformen: Partner check Ex **1a**; Partner talk Ex **2**

Materialbedarf: Ex **3**: (optional) Karteikarten, Klebepunkte

Einsatz von Begleitmedien: DFF 5.8 | INKL 5.10 | Workbook S. 74

SKILLS TRAINING Mediation and writing 5

▸ *DFF 5.8* ▸ *INKL 5.10*

1 Four text messages

A Luca • B Josie • C Adam • D Adam's mum

a) Look at the four text messages. Are they from Adam, Adam's mum, Luca or Josie? Example: I think text message A is from ...

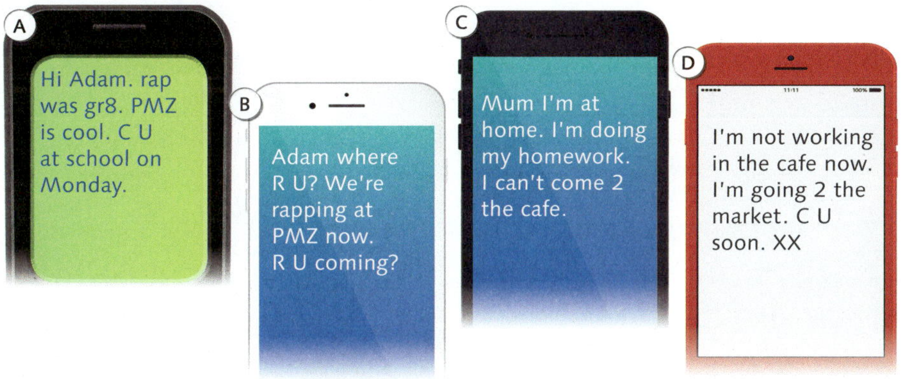

Text message language
+ = and
U = you
C = see
2 = to/too/two
gr8 = great
R U = are you
L8r = later
X = kiss

b) Read the text messages aloud. Lösung S. 238

2 MEDIATION What's that in German?

You and your partner get a text from an English friend, Amanda. She's in Germany at the moment. Work with your partner. How do you say it in German?

Amanda fragt, wo ...?

Ja, sie schreibt, dass sie ...

Lösungsbsp. S. 238

3 WRITING A text to Amanda

Write a text message to Amanda. More help p. 144

Einstieg Ex 1 (SB geschl.) L: *You know text messages. There's a special language for text messages. It's shorter. Do you know any special words or signs?* S nennen ihnen bekannte Abkürzungen und Symbole, L notiert einige an Tafel.

Erarb. Ex 1a (SB offen) **1. Lesen** (Globalverstehen) S notieren ihre Vermutungen ins Heft. Gelben Kasten beachten!

Ausw. Ex 1a Partner check: abwechselndes Erklären.

Erarb. Ex 1b **2. Lesen** per Meldekette.

Erarb. Ex 2 (SB offen) Lautes Lesen der Mitteilung zur Verständniserleichterung. Anschließend Wiedergabe des Inhalts der Nachricht auf D. L weist S darauf hin, dass Mediation keine wörtliche Übersetzung ist, sondern eine freie Wiedergabe der wichtigsten Informationen.

Erarb. Ex 3 (SB offen) gemäß Aufgabe.
O Ideen und Satzbausteine für Lernschwächere in More help.
Zusatz S schreiben ihre Antwort auf Karteikarte, ggf. noch Ausgestaltung mit Emoticons etc. → Im Klassenraum ausstellen; jeder S erhält drei Klebepunkte, die für die persönlichen Favoriten vergeben werden können.

▸ *Workbook 22, p. 74*

Lernschwerpunkt: Eine Anleitung (Rezept) verstehen
Kompetenzen: **Reading** Ein Rezept verstehen
Lern- und Arbeitstechniken Unbekannte Wörter erschließen
Redemittel: Wortfeld *preparing food*

Zeitbedarf: ca. eine Stunde
Materialbedarf: Ex **2** (optional): Rezept-Zutaten und Equipment
Kooperative Lernformen: Partner talk Ex **2a** | Gruppenarbeit (optional: *Scones* zubereiten) Zusatz nach Ex **2**
Einsatz von Begleitmedien: INKL 5.11 | DFF 5.4, 5.9 | Workbook. S. 74

Einstieg Ex 1 (SB geschl.) L: *I really love scones, but it's hard to find them in Germany. I'd like to make them at home. But how do I make them? Where can I find out? (internet, book) There's a recipe* (Aussprache!) *for scones in our book. It tells you what you need and how you make them.*
Erarb. Ex 1a (SB offen) Aufgabe zur Vorentlastung.
Erarb. Ex 1b **1. Lesen** (Detailverstehen): S notieren die Zahlen 1–8, setzen die Buchstaben der passenden Bilder dahinter. Ein Vorlesen bietet sich nach **2b)** an.
Ausw. Ex 1b im Plenum

Erarb. Ex 2a (SB offen) **2. Lesen** (Detailverstehen): S erarbeiten deutsche Bedeutung, indem sie Hilfen in der Box nutzen.
Ausw. in **Ex 2b** gemäß Aufgabe.
Zusatz (GA) S erproben das Rezept z. B. im Hauswirtschaftsunterricht. Ein S präsentiert das Rezept (ähnlich wie in einer TV-Koch-Show), 2–3 S führen die Anweisungen durch, zwei weitere S dokumentieren die Backaktion z. B. durch Fotos oder Videos (Vorab Zustimmung der Eltern einholen!). Alle S probieren die Scones mit *cream and jam* und bewerten sie, z. B. Vergabe von Emoticons.

5 SKILLS TRAINING Reading

▸ *INKL 5.11* ▸ *DFF 5.4* ▸ *DFF 5.9*

1 A recipe[1] for scones

cream: Sahne • **scone:** kleines, süßes Brötchen • **jam:** Marmelade

a) Look at the picture in the recipe. Try to explain these words in German: *scone*, *jam*, *cream*.

What are scones?

In England people often eat them in the afternoon with tea, coffee or °milk.

How do you make scones?

1. Put °butter (50g), °flour[2] (225g), °sugar[3] (50g), °baking powder (3 °teaspoons) and °salt[4] (half a teaspoon) in a °bowl.
2. Rub the butter into the flour with your fingers.
3. Add milk (75ml) and one °egg.
4. Mix everything together.
5. Make 12 scones with a °glass.
6. Put the scones in the °oven[5] (230°C) for 8–10 minutes.
7. Cut a scone.
8. Put cream and jam on it – and eat it!

b) Read the recipe for scones and put the pictures (A–H) in the right order (1–8).

1 D
2 B
3 H
4 F
5 A
6 E
7 C
8 G

2 New words in the recipe

a) Work with a partner. Find these eleven words in the recipe. What do you think they mean in German?

milk | flour | butter | sugar | teaspoon | egg | baking powder | bowl | oven | glass | salt

▸ *Skills file 3–4, pp. 163–164*

b) Check in the Dictionary (pages 208–218).

You can often guess the new words.
Remember:
Some words are like German words: *butter, milk, glass, oven, salt.*
Look at the pictures in 1b for help:
– *bowl (picture B)*
– *teaspoon, flour, baking powder (picture D)*
– *egg (picture H)*

1 [ˈresəpi] 2 [flauə] 3 [ˈʃugə] 4 [sɔːlt] 5 [ʌvn]

▸ *Workbook 23, p. 74*

SKILLS TRAINING Viewing

Lernschwerpunkt: **Fiktionale und dokumentarische Filmszenen verstehen**
Kompetenzen: Viewing Filmszenen verstehen; einen Filmabschnitt gelenkt zusammenfassen | **Speaking** Sich über eigene Talente austauschen; persönliche Eindrücke gewinnen und diskutieren
Redemittel: Wortfeld *talents*

Zeitbedarf: ca. eine Stunde
Minimalversion: Ex **1b–d, 2b**
Materialbedarf: DVD + Player oder PC/Lautsprecher
Einsatz von Begleitmedien: KV 5.2

SKILLS TRAINING Viewing

5

▸ *KV 5.2*

1 The kids from Harbour Road: What's your talent[1]?

a) What's your talent? – I can ...

Anna can dance. • Paul can play the guitar. • Sarah can sing.

Then watch the film and find out what Anna, Paul and Sarah can do.

b) Look at the picture. Put the sentences in the right order. Then watch part 1 again and check.

A That's four pounds for you, and four pounds for you, please.
B I'm hungry! Can I have a muffin, and ... a hot chocolate[2], please.
C Hi!
D Thanks. / Thank you!
E Chocolate or blueberry[3]?
F Hi, Anna!
G I'll have a chocolate muffin, please.
H And yourself[4]?
I A hot chocolate and a blueberry muffin, please.
J We're here!

F (Sarah)
J (Paul)
C (Anna)
B (Sarah)
E (waitress)
G (Sarah)
H (waitress)
I (Paul)
A (waitress)
D (Paul/ Sarah)

c) Match the sentence parts. Then watch part 2 and check.

1 In the cafe Anna	cool dance for Anna.
2 She has no idea	wants to sing.
3 Paul wants to	isn't happy.
4 And Sarah	play the guitar.
5 But then Sarah	for the class party.
6 She knows a	has an idea.

d) Watch part 3. Do Anna's dance.

▸ *Text file 6, p. 159*

2 People and places: A visit to PMZ

a) Watch the film. Talk about PMZ with a partner.
– I think PMZ looks interesting / boring / ... What about you?
– I think Jimmy is a good / great / terrible / ... rapper.
– I think the Jam Band's music is ...

Jimmy

Debbie

Simon

b) Answer these questions. Watch again and check.
1 Who works at PMZ?
2 How many people come to PMZ every week?
3 What instrument does Jimmy play?

1 Debbie and Simon • 2 1000 • 3 the drums

[1] talent ['tælənt] *Talent* [2] hot chocolate [hɒt 'tʃɒklət] *heiße Schokolade* [3] blueberry *Heidelbeere, Blaubeere*
[4] And yourself? *Und du?*

Einstieg Ex 1 (SB geschl.) L sammelt mit S Talente. *What's your talent?* – Mögliche Hilfen: *I can dance / sing a song / play the guitar ... / act a scene / read a poem / tell jokes / draw a picture (story) / ...*
Überleitung L: *Let's see what Anna's, Paul's and Sarah's talents are.*
Erarb. Ex 1a (SB offen) Namen untereinander notieren, beim **1. Sehen** (Globalverstehen) Talente ergänzen.
Ausw. Ex 1a im Plenum.
Erarb. Ex 1b S ordnen Dialogteile: entweder Buchstaben notieren oder Teile von KV 5.2 (Part 1) ausschneiden und sortieren.
Ausw. Ex 1b beim **2. Sehen** (Detailverstehen), danach Abgleich und Vorlesen mit verteilten Rollen.
Zusatz KV 5.2 (Part 2): Eigener Bestelldialog der S.
Erarb. Ex 1c+d gemäß Aufgaben.

Erarb. Ex 2a Nach dem **1. Sehen** (Globalverstehen) tauschen sich S mithilfe der Redemittel über das PMZ und die musikalischen Leistungen der Jugendlichen aus.
Erarb. Ex 2b S notieren vor **2. Sehen** ihre Antworten (Stichworte) aus dem Gedächtnis.
Ausw. Ex 2b Kontrolle beim **2. Sehen** (Detailverstehen).

Lernschwerpunkt: **Wiederholen und Üben, Lernfortschritte erkennen (Fokus: Unit 5)**
Kompetenzen: Listening Eine Bildbeschreibung verstehen | Reading Bildbeschreibung am Bild überprüfen (v. a. Ortsangaben)
Writing Tätigkeiten beschreiben | Lern- und Arbeitstechniken Eigene Lernfortschritte erkennen
Grammatik: Fragen und Kurzantworten mit *do/does*; Nutzen des *present progressive* für Tätigkeitsbeschreibungen
Redemittel: Wortfelder *on the beach; on the ferry*

Erarb. Ex 1a (SB offen) S notieren die Fragen 1–8 und setzen passende Kurzantworten dazu.
Erarb. Ex 1b S nutzen a) als Hilfe für die Fragebildung und lassen unter jeder Frage eine Zeile frei für c).
Erarb. Ex 1c S notieren Kurzantworten unter den in b) gebildeten Fragen.
Erarb. Ex 1d S schreiben mit „ja“ oder „nein“ beantwortbare Quiz-Fragen auf eine Karteikarte, dekorieren sie ggf. mit Foto/Zeichnung und hängen sie an die Tafel.
Ausw. Ex 1d Jeweils ein Verfasser einer Quiz-Karte kommt an die Tafel, stellt dem Plenum seine Quiz-Fragen und wählt nach Beantwortung der Fragen die nächste Quiz-Karte. Auch in GA möglich.

Erarb. Ex 2a (SB offen) S setzen die vorgegebenen Verben passend in den Lückentext ein und notieren die Sätze.
Erarb. Ex 2b S setzen die passende Kurzform von *be* in die Lücken ein und notieren die Sätze.
Erarb. Ex 2c S vervollständigen den Dialog mithilfe der Bilder in a) und b) und schreiben ihn ins Heft.

STOP! CHECK! GO!

▸ KV 5.3 ▸ DFF 5.1 ▸ DFF 5.2 ▸ INKL 5.12

Ein Lösungsblatt für die Aufgaben 1 bis 5 kannst du von deiner Lehrerin / deinem Lehrer erhalten. Du findest die Audiodatei (zu S. 105) online, zusammen mit den Workbook-Audiodateien.

1 REVISION Questions and answers

a) What do you know about crabs? Do this crab quiz. Write the answers: *1 No, they don't. 2 Yes, ...*

1 Do crabs live in towns?
2 Do crabs live on the beach?
3 Do crabs eat fish?
4 Do normal crabs sing?
5 Does Cyril live in a house?
6 Does Cyril talk?
7 Does Cyril walk fast?
8 Does Cyril like people?

b) Now make a seagull quiz. Write the questions.

1 seagulls / live near the sea?
2 seagulls / live in towns?
3 seagulls / eat crabs?
4 seagulls / sing or make a noise?
5 Sandy / live in a house?
6 Sandy / eat crabs?
7 Sandy / talk?
8 Sandy / like °pizza?

c) Now answer the questions about seagulls.

d) Make a quiz about another animal. Put it on the board. Who knows the answers?

More help p. 145

2 LANGUAGE Describing pictures

a) Say what Cyril is doing. Finish the sentences with the verbs in the box.

ringing • playing • sitting • watching • listening

Cyril is ... (1) on a chair, on the beach. He's ... (2) to music. He's ... (3) three kids. They're ... (4) football. His mobile is ... (5).

b) Say what Sandy is doing. Finish the sentences with *'s* or *'re*.

Sandy is on the beach too. She... (1) watching Mr Johnson. He... (2) walking on the beach. Mrs Johnson is there too. They... (3) looking at Cyril. They... (4) feeling hungry! Sandy has a mobile. She... (5) phoning Cyril.

c) Look at the pictures in 2a and 2b again. Finish the dialogue between Sandy and Cyril.

Sandy	Cyril
Hi, Cyril. Where are you sitting?	1 ... on my favourite chair.
What are you doing?	2 ... to music.
What are you watching?	3 ... kids.
What are the kids doing?	4 ...
Cyril, look! The Johnsons ... coming!	5 Help! I... going!

STOP! – CHECK! – GO! Navigator | Vorbereitung

Zeitbedarf: ca. zwei Stunden
Minimalversion: Ex **1a–c**, **2a** ○ oder **b** oder **c** ●; **3a+b**; **4a+b**
Materialbedarf: Ex **3a**: Audio-CD + Player oder MP3 + PC/Lautsprecher
Einsatz von Begleitmedien: KV 5.3 (Lösungsschlüssel, auch für die Hand der S zur selbstständigen Lösungsüberprüfung, ggf. im Partner check) | DFF 5.1–5.3 | INKL 5.12

▸ DFF 5.1 ▸ DFF 5.2 ▸ DFF 5.3 ▸ KV 5.3

3 LANGUAGE People on the ferry

2.44 **a)** Copy the table. Then look at the picture and listen to Adam and his dad. Match the people (A–I) in the picture with the names.

Sam	*D*	*Linda*	...	*David*	...
Anna	...	*Toby*	...	*Uma*	...
Rick	...	*Gemma*	...	*Adam's dad*	...

Mr Osmanovic

b) Look at the picture again. What are the people doing? Write sentences like this:
Sam is eating. Anna ...

clean the table • cook • do nothing • eat • laugh • play a game • talk • talk on the phone • wash up • watch TV

Erarb. Ex 3a (SB offen)
1. Hören gemäß Aufgabe. Überprüfung durch **2. Hören**.
Erarb. Ex 3b in EA anhand der Hilfen in der grünen Box.

4 READING A picture

a) Look at the picture. Read the text. Are the sentences true (T) or false (F)?

1 There are lots of people in the park.
2 On the left I can see a boy and a girl.
3 The boy is talking on the phone.
4 The girl is reading.
5 On the right I can see a family.
6 They're eating lunch.
7 There's a big dog in front of a yellow bag.
8 It's looking at the sandwiches.
9 In the middle I can see a red chair.
10 A boy is sitting on the chair.
11 There's a cat under the chair.
12 I can see a big red ball next to the chair.

b) Describe the picture. You can use the ideas in a).

Erarb. Ex 4a (SB offen)
S notieren hinter jeder Satznummer (1–12) ein T für *true* oder ein F für *false*.
Erarb. Ex 4b gemäß Aufgabe.
○ Lernschwächere beschreiben das Bild in zwölf Sätzen, indem sie die richtigen Sätze aus a) übernehmen und die falschen korrigieren.

STOP! – CHECK! – GO! Navigator | Inhalt

Lernschwerpunkt: Wiederholen und Üben, Lernfortschritte erkennen (Fokus: Unit 5)

Kompetenzen: Mediation Einem Freund in einem englischen Café das Angebot erklären | **Writing/Speaking** Mit Tipps und Redemitteln einen Bestelldialog verfassen und einüben | **Reading/Writing** Eine Bildergeschichte verstehen, Textbausteine passend zuordnen und erweitern
Lern- und Arbeitstechniken Eigene Lernfortschritte erkennen

Redemittel: Bestelldialoge in einem Restaurant/Café

Erarb. Ex 5a (SB offen)
S schreiben alle Begriffe ab und kreisen den jeweils nicht passenden farbig ein (Begriffe werden für **b)** benötigt).
Erarb. Ex 5b S vervollständigen die Sätze mit den *odd words out* aus **a)**.

Erarb. Ex 6 (SB offen)
S lesen abwechselnd die Fragen vor und geben dem Partner die entsprechende Antwort auf der Grundlage des Bildes.

Erarb. Ex 7a (SB offen)
S entwickeln gemeinsam ein Gespräch zwischen Kunden und Bedienung in einem Café mit den gegebenen Hilfen. Beide S schreiben das gesamte Gespräch auf. Dabei die Gesprächsanteile der beiden Personen mit unterschiedlichen Farben markieren.
○ Lernschwächere erhalten das Lösungsbeispiel von S. 238 als *scrambled dialogue* und ordnen diesen.
Erarb. Ex 7b Einüben des Dialogs im Partner talk.

STOP! CHECK! GO!

▸ KV 5.3 ▸ DFF 5.5 ▸ DFF 5.6

5 WORDS Food and drinks

a) ○ **Find the odd word out.**

1 sweets, tea, sandwich, cafe
2 breakfast, soup, lunch, dinner
3 tea, juice, water, chips
4 coffee, chicken, fish, omelette
5 fruit, salad, scones, vegetables

b) Complete the sentences with answers from a.

1 You can buy food and drinks in a ...
2 I often have vegetable ... for lunch.
3 My favourite food is fish and ...
4 Some people drink ... for breakfast.
5 We often have tea and ... in a cafe at the weekend.

6 MEDIATION I'm hungry!

Du bist in Plymouth mit einem Freund. Beantworte seine Fragen auf Deutsch.

1 Ich habe Hunger.
Was gibt es hier zu essen?
2 Ich habe auch Durst.
Was kann ich hier trinken?
3 Gibt es auch etwas Süßes?
4 Wir haben £10 für uns beide.
Was schlägst du vor?
5 Müssen wir alles hier essen oder können wir es auch mitnehmen?

Lösungsbsp. S. 238

7 WRITING and SPEAKING In the Harbour Cafe

a) ● **Write a dialogue in your exercise book. Here are some ideas.**

Lösungsbsp. S. 238

Frage, was der Kunde möchte.

You work in the cafe:
– Hello. Can I ... ?
– OK. Anything ...?
– ... to drink?
– ... else?
– That's £ ...
– Thanks. ...

Rufe den nächsten Kunden auf.

Schau auf die Speisekarte in Aufgabe 6 und bestelle etwas zu essen und zu trinken.

You are hungry:
– Hello. Yes, please – ..., please.
– Yes, ..., please.
– Oh, yes, ..., please. And ...
– No, thanks. ...
– OK. Here ...

Bestelle noch mehr, z.B. etwas Süßes.

Wenn du genug bestellt hast, sage, dass das alles ist.

Bezahle alles.

b) Practise your dialogue with a partner.

1 ['fleɪvə]

STOP! – CHECK! – GO! Navigator | Vorbereitung

Zeitbedarf: ca. zwei Stunden
Kooperative Lernformen: Partner talk Ex **6**; **7b**
Materialbedarf: Ex **8**: Zeichenpapier oder Blanko-Karteikarten
Einsatz von Begleitmedien: KV 5.3 (Lösungsschlüssel, auch für die Hand der S zur selbstständigen Lösungsüberprüfung, ggf. im Partner check) | DFF 5.5–5.7 | INKL 5.12 | Workbook S. 75–78

► DFF 5.7 ► KV 5.3 ► INKL 5.12

8 READING and WRITING On Saturday morning …

1 B • 2 E • 3 A • 4 F • 5 G • 6 C • 7 D

a) Read the story. Put the phrases (A–G) with the photos (1–7).

1 The cafe was very busy.

2 Ms Lee was in the cafe.

3 She was hungry.

4 Adam was very fast.

5 Oh no! Trouble?

6 It was Adam's rap!

7 Ms Lee was happy.

A Can I help you?
B I'm washing up.
C That's a great rap!
D You're welcome. Bye.
E Hello, Ms Lee. I'm fine, thanks.
F Here you are. One tea and a scone.
G Yes, Adam is working very hard at school now.

b) ● Draw another picture for the story and write speech bubbles for it. More help p. 145

9 My learner log

Copy and complete your learner log. You can put it in your DOSSIER.

My learner log

Now I can …
- use the present progressive and say what's happening. Example: …
- describe a picture
- buy something to eat and drink in a cafe:
- understand a text message:
- understand a recipe:

In Unit 5 …
- my favourite text is on page …
- my favourite words are …
- my favourite phrases are …
- my favourite food is …
- my favourite people are …

My progress in English is: GREAT! / OK / NOT VERY GOOD

Erarb. Ex 8a (SB offen) gemäß Aufgabe.
Erarb. Ex 8b S gestalten ihre Szene auf Zeichenpapier oder Blanko-Karteikarten.
○ Lernschwächere nutzen die Ideen aus More help.
● Lernstärkere fertigen zwei bis drei Szenen an.
Ausw. Ex 8b In Kleingruppen (3–4 S) betrachten S die Szenen ihrer Mit-S und einigen sich auf einen Favoriten. Sie stellen diesen im Plenum vor und begründen ihre Auswahl. Dafür ggf. Hilfen an Tafel, z. B.: *The picture is very nice. / The speech bubbles are funny. / It's like in real life. / …*
Die Gruppenfavoriten im Klassenzimmer ausstellen.
Zusatz Einige Gruppen spielen die gesamte Szene einschließlich der Erweiterungsszene im Plenum vor.

Erarb. Ex 9 (SB offen) S bearbeiten ihr **My learner log** gemäß Muster. Sie können es mit entsprechenden Symbolen versehen.

LEAD-IN Navigator | **Inhalt**

Lernschwerpunkt: Sommeraktivitäten in England

Storyline: Die Lehrwerkskinder planen anhand von vier Broschüren einen Tagesausflug.

Kompetenzen: Listening Kurze Hörtexte anhand von Geräuschen passenden Broschüren zuordnen, Dialogen gezielt Informationen entnehmen **Speaking** Sich auf ein Ausflugsziel einigen | **Reading** Broschüreninhalte erschließen | **Lern- und Arbeitstechniken** Sprachmuster für die eigene Sprachproduktion nutzen

Redemittel: Urlaubsaktivitäten, Vorlieben diskutieren und sich einigen

Einstieg Ex 1 (SB geschl.) L schreibt Thema der Unit an und fragt: *What are your plans for the summer holidays?*
Erarb. Ex 1 (SB offen) S beschreiben die Broschüren kurz im Plenum. Dann **1. Hören** und Sicherung des Globalverstehens durch Zuordnung der Broschüren. Semantisierung von *canoe* und *theme park*. **2. Hören** zur Überprüfung.
Zur Sicherung des Detailverstehens kann L Sätze präsentieren, die S den Broschüren zuordnen: *You …*
can bring your dog. (A, B)
have to sleep outside. (C)
cook your own food. (C)
have fun on the water. (B)
can buy a group ticket. (D)
learn about smugglers. (A)
can eat at a cafe. (A)
can make a fire. (C)
can go on a zip wire. (D)
can't always visit during the winter. (D)

Erarb. Ex 2a (SB offen) **1. Hören** (Globalverstehen) gemäß Aufgabe. Lernstärkere begründen ihre Lösung (*… because Berry likes the beach.*).
Erarb. Ex 2b Gemeinsames Lesen der Redemittel zum Diskutieren von Vorschlägen (Sprechblasen) und Semantisierung von *I'd prefer*. Anschließend **2. Hören** (Detailverstehen): S ordnen die Vorschläge 1–4 den Reaktionen A–D zu.

Unit 6 °School is out – for summer

▸ *DFF 6.1*

3.02 1 Summer sounds

Listen to the summer sounds (1–4) and match them with the brochures (A–D).

Summer sounds 1: Brochure …
Summer sounds 2: …
Summer sounds 3: …
Summer sounds 4: …

1: A • 2: D • 3: C • 4: B

A

The Cawsand Ferry Co.[2]

Visit the smuggler villages of Cawsand and Kingsand. Great beaches, walks, restaurants, shops and cafes.

Smuggler's cave in Cawsand

Ferry times:

Plymouth
10.30 am, 12.00 pm, 2.30 pm, 4.00 pm

Cawsand
9.30 am, 11.00 am, 12.30 pm, 3.00 pm, 4.30 pm

Tickets:
Adults £4 one way
Children £2 one way
Dogs free

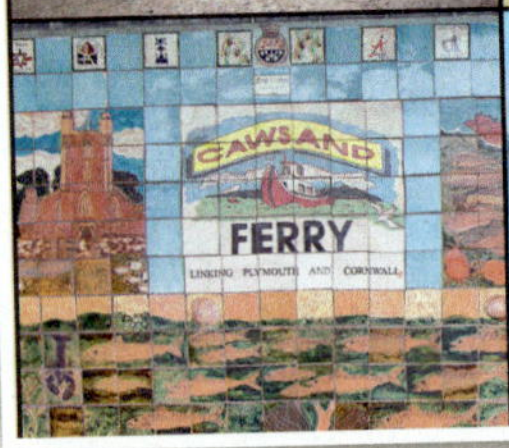

B

Canoe Tamar[1]

Experience …. discover …. enjoy ….

Canoe trips: 3–3½ hours with picnic stop

Trips cost: £22 per person

Everybody welcome – dogs too!

3.03 2 Four trips

a) Ellie, Luca, Adam and Berry are at school. Listen. Which trip do they pick – A, B, C or D? They pick trip A.

b) Listen again. Match the ideas (1–4) with the answers (A–D).

1 What about a trip to Dartmoor?
2 Well, °I'd prefer a °canoe trip.
3 I love °theme parks.
4 I really want to go to the beach!

A Yes, but they're expensive.
B Oh no! That's boring!
C I think that's a great idea!
D But I can't swim very well!

1: B • 2: D • 3: A • 4: C

1 [kəˈnuː ˈteɪmɑː] 2 [ˈkɔːsænd]

LEAD-IN Navigator | **Vorbereitung**

Zeitbedarf: ca. zwei Stunden
Kooperative Lernformen: Think–Pair–Share Ex **3**
Materialbedarf: Ex **1**–**2**: Audio-CD + Player oder MP3 + PC/Lautsprecher
Einsatz von Begleitmedien: DFF 6.1–6.2 | IAT 6.1

▸ IAT 6.1 ▸ DFF 6.2

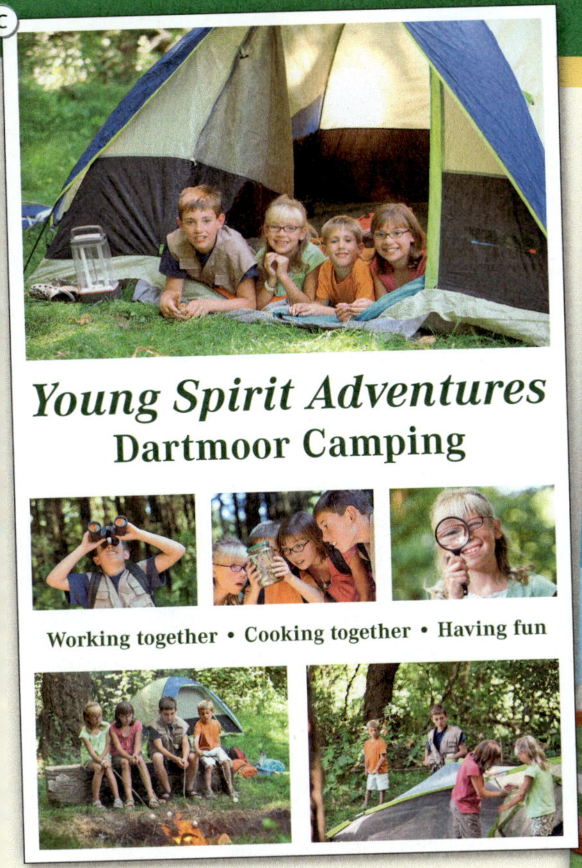

D

3 NOW YOU

a) Think: Look at the brochures.
Pick your favourite trip.
Example: My favourite trip is ...

> the canoe trip • the ferry trip • the camping trip • the trip to a theme park

b) Pair: Talk to a partner. Agree on one trip.

- What about a ...?
- I'd prefer a ...
- I really want to do a ...
- I love ...

- I think that's a great / terrible idea.
- Oh no! That's boring / expensive / ...
- Me too. I really like walking / ferry trips / the beach / ...

c) Share: Now work in groups of four. Agree on one trip in your group. Tell the class what your group wants to do.

We want to do a ...

Einstieg Ex 3 (SB offen) Einüben der Redemittel zum Diskutieren durch Chorsprechen und Meldekette: S1 schlägt etwas vor und ruft S2 auf. S2 reagiert und macht neuen Vorschlag.

Erarb. Ex 3a
L wiederholt Ablauf der kooperativen Lernform Think–Pair–Share. Anschließend Sichten und Auswahl der Unternehmung in EA.
● Lernstärkere überlegen sich eine Begründung, die sie in b) und c) nutzen können.

Erarb. Ex 3b
S tauschen sich aus, einigen sich und halten ihr Ergebnis (ggf. mit Begründung) auf einem Notizzettel fest.

Erarb. Ex 3c
Je zwei S-Paare tun sich zu einer Gruppe zusammen, diskutieren erneut, einigen sich und berichten im Plenum über ihre Entscheidung.

Ausw. Ex 3c
L: *What's the most popular trip in our class?* Ein S erfasst durch Auszählen die Ergebnisse der Gruppenarbeit und gibt sie anschließend bekannt: *The most popular trip in our class is trip A/B/C/D. ... students want to do trip A/...*

THEME Navigator | **Inhalt**

Lernschwerpunkt: Einen Strandausflug planen

Storyline: Die vier Lehrwerkskinder planen ihren Ausflug nach Kingsand und legen fest, wer was mitbringt.

Kompetenzen: Listening Einen Hörtext arbeitsteilig erfassen, einen Song verstehen und mitsingen | **Speaking** Diskutieren, wer welche Picknicksachen mitbringt | **Reading** Dialogen und Textnachrichten gezielt Informationen entnehmen | **Lern- und Arbeitstechniken** Wörter in einem Network sammeln

Redemittel: Strandutensilien, Picknicksachen

6 THEME

A trip to the beach

3.04

1 Planning a trip

a) What things do you need on the beach? Read the text for ideas. Then start a network.

More help p. 145

It's Friday, the last day of school. The four friends want to plan the trip to Kingsand.

Berry — OK, guys! When are we going to Kingsand?

Luca — What about next Monday – the first day of the summer holidays?

Ellie — That's a great idea. What can we bring?

Adam — Well, we need beach things, like °swimsuits[1] and °swimming trunks and °towels.

Box: Voc., p. 206

Ellie — And °sunglasses ... and °hats ...

Luca — Yeah, and we need things for a picnic – like sandwiches.

Ellie — And water – lots of water ...

beach things: swimsuits, swimming trunks, towels, sunglasses, hats • **picnic:** sandwiches, water

Berry — Yeah. My dad is coming in the car, he can bring our things. Mum is staying on the farm because she's busy.

Luca — Is Sam coming too?

Berry — No. He's staying with mum.

Ellie — Oh, °that's a pity.

Luca — Now let's talk about food!

b) True or false?

1 The friends are going to Kingsand on Friday.

2 Berry's parents are coming too.

3 Her dog Sam is staying at home on the farm.

1 False. (on Monday) **2** False. (Berry's dad) **3** True.

3.05

2 Shopping for the picnic

a) Listen and take notes.

Partner A: Make shopping lists for Adam and Luca.

Partner B: Make shopping lists for Ellie and Berry.

Adam: apples, sandwiches

Luca: crisps, chocolate

Ellie: cake, orange juice

Berry: water, biscuits

b) Swap lists with your partner. Listen again and check your partner's lists.

c) Look at the four lists. Agree on more things you can bring for the picnic.

What about ...?

Yes, good idea./ No, I don't like ...

d) Add more words to your network in 1a.

Lösungsbsp. S. 239

Einstieg Ex 1 (SB offen) Bildbetrachtung zur Vorentlastung. L: *Look at the picture. Who can you see? Where are they? What are they doing? What do you think they're talking about?*
Erarb. Ex 1a **1. Lesen**/ Hören: S erfassen den Text und erstellen ein Network. Unbekannte Wörter können sie nachschlagen. Dann Sicherung der Aussprache.
Erarb. Ex 1b **2. Lesen**/ Hören und Überprüfung des Detailverstehens.
Lernstärkere korrigieren die falschen Aussagen.

Einstieg Ex 2 (SB offen) L: *The kids from Eggy want to have a picnic at Kingsand. What can you take for a picnic at the beach?* Neuer Wortschatz wird anhand der Abbildung semantisiert.
Erarb. Ex 2a **1. Hören**: S notieren die Dinge für den Einkaufszettel arbeitsteilig.
Erarb. Ex 2b Beim **2. Hören** kontrollieren und ergänzen S die beiden Einkaufszettel des Partners.
Erarb. Ex 2c S besprechen und ergänzen die Listen mit Dingen aus der Abbildung oder weiteren bekannten Wörtern.
Erarb. Ex 2d Erweiterung des Networks als HA geeignet.

1 ['swɪmsuːts] 2 ['tʃɒklət] 3 ['bɪskɪts] 4 [ɒrɪndʒɪz] 5 ['sɒsɪdʒɪz]

Zeitbedarf: ca. zwei Stunden
Minimalversion: Ex **1**; **2a–c**; **3a–b** (**2d** und **3c** als festigende HA)
Kooperative Lernformen: Partner check Ex **2**
Materialbedarf: Ex **1** (optional), **2**, **5**: Audio-CD + Player oder MP3 + PC/Lautsprecher
Einsatz von Begleitmedien: KV 6.1 | Folie 32 | DFF 6.3 | Workbook S. 81

▸ Folie 32 ▸ KV 6.1 ▸ DFF 6.3

3 Things for the beach

a) It's Sunday – the day before the Kingsand trip. Look at the pictures and guess what the friends want to bring.

b) Then read the text messages and find out. What are the friends bringing?
Example: They're all bringing ... Ellie / Luca / ... is bringing ...

Hi everybody. Don't °forget suncream for the beach. **Berry**

Right! + don't forget swimming things + shorts. :) **Ellie**

OK. I'm bringing my bodyboard. **Luca**

Gr8! I'm bringing a football. Who has a tube? **Adam**

I have a big tube. I can bring it. :) **Berry**

Gr8. R U bringing ur frisbee, Ellie? **Luca**

Yes + speakers for my phone. C U. **Ellie**

OK. Don't forget towels. C U at the ferry! XXX **Berry**

They're all bringing: suncream, swimming things, shorts, towels
Luca is bringing: a bodyboard
Adam is bringing: a football
Berry is bringing: a tube
Ellie is bringing: a frisbee, speakers

c) Add more words for the trip to the beach to your network from 1a.

Lösungsbsp. S. 239

4 °Chain game

Imagine that you're going to the beach. What do you want to bring?

I want to bring a tube.

I want to bring a tube and sandwiches.

I want to bring a tube, sandwiches and a ...

5 A summer song

3.06

a) Listen to Adam's favourite summer song. Do you like it?

It's great! It's OK! It's ...

b) Listen and sing along.

Magic Summer Night

Come on happy people get on the floor,
Do you feel it so right?
So come on raise your hands up, hands in the air,
Magic summer night – shakalakaboom!

School is out, that's all what we need,
Stars are shining so bright.
So come on raise your hands up, hands in the air,
Magic summer night – shakalakaboom!

by Oliver Boehm & Thomas Schleh

Einstieg Ex 3 (SB geschl.) L: *The four friends have lots of food for their trip. What other things do they need for the beach? What do you think? (games, music, ...)*
Erarb. Ex 3a (SB offen) S spekulieren, L sammelt Wörter (Tafel, Folie) und sichert die Aussprache.
Erarb. Ex 3b **1. Lesen:** S vergleichen die genannten Dinge mit ihrer Liste (abhaken, ergänzen).
Ausw. Ex 3b S versprachlichen ihre Ergebnisse mithilfe der Redemittel.
Erarb. Ex 3c Erweiterung des Networks als HA geeignet. Festigung anhand von KV 6.1.

Einstieg Ex 4 (SB offen) L demonstriert mit einigen S das Vorgehen des Spiels („Kofferpacken").
Erarb. Ex 4 In Gruppen à 4–6 S. Es darf kein Nomen wiederholt werden, die Denkpause muss kurz sein. Ein S pro Gruppe kann die Durchführung beobachten und die Nomen zählen, sodass am Ende die Gruppe mit dem längsten Satz ermittelt werden kann.

Erarb. Ex 5a (SB offen) S hören das Lied und äußern ihre Meinung mithilfe der Redemittel.
Erarb. Ex 5b Vor dem Mitsingen Songtext mehrfach lesen lassen. Zur Abwechslung Strophen aufteilen (Geschlecht, Bankreihe ...).

▸ Workbook 1–3, p. 81

STORY Navigator | Inhalt

Lernschwerpunkt: Eine szenische Geschichte verstehen

Storyline: Die vier Freunde fahren mit der Fähre nach Cawsand. Dort sollten sie eigentlich Berrys Vater treffen. Stattdessen finden sie eine Flaschenpost, die den Auftakt zu einer Art Schnitzeljagd darstellt. Eine mysteriöse alte Frau scheint in das Verschwinden von Berrys Vater involviert zu sein.

Kompetenzen: Listening Eine Fantasiereise machen | **Speaking** Bilder beschreiben, über Eindrücke von einer Fantasiereise sprechen **Reading** Eine szenische Geschichte verstehen

6 STORY

▸ *DFF 6.4*

Erarb. Ex 1 (SB offen) Die Bootsfahrt nach Cawsand wird zunächst (in Ex 1) bildlich dargestellt und anschließend (in Ex 2) zum Gegenstand einer Fantasiereise. Zur Vorentlastung beschreiben S einander abwechselnd die Bilder anhand der Leitfragen im SB. ● Lernstärkere beschreiben zusätzlich, was auf den Bildern geschieht.

1 Before you read

Look at the pictures on this page. Talk to a partner. Who can you see? Where are they?

Lösungsbsp. S. 239

A

B

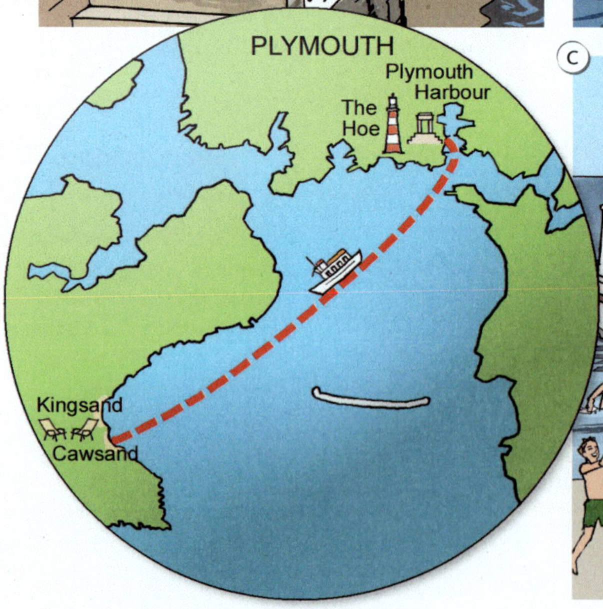

C

Einstieg Ex 2 (SB offen) L: *So Berry, Ellie, Luca and Adam are going on a ferry trip. Look at the map: Where are they going? Where does the ferry trip start? What else can you see on the map? Do you like ferry trips? Why (not)? Let's go on a ferry trip too.* Optional kann L die S auf die Versprachlichung der Eindrücke in b) vorbereiten: *Enjoy the ferry trip. What can you see, hear and feel?*
Erarb. Ex 2a **1. Hören.**
Erarb. Ex 2b S tauschen sich anhand der Fragen über ihre Sinneseindrücke aus.
Ausw. Ex 2b S geben abwechselnd oder reihum im Plenum in Form einer Meldekette ihre Eindrücke wieder.

2 You're going on a ferry trip!

3.07

a) Close your eyes. Listen.
Enjoy the ferry trip.

b) Talk to a partner.
What's the ferry trip like?
What do you see?
What do you hear?
What do you feel?

More help p.146

STORY Navigator | **Vorbereitung**

Zeitbedarf: ca. zwei Stunden
Kooperative Lernformen: Partner talk Ex **1**, Ex **2b**
Materialbedarf: Audio-CD + Player oder MP3 + PC/Lautsprecher
Einsatz von Begleitmedien: KV 6.2 | DFF 6.4

▸ KV 6.2

3.08

All °aboard!

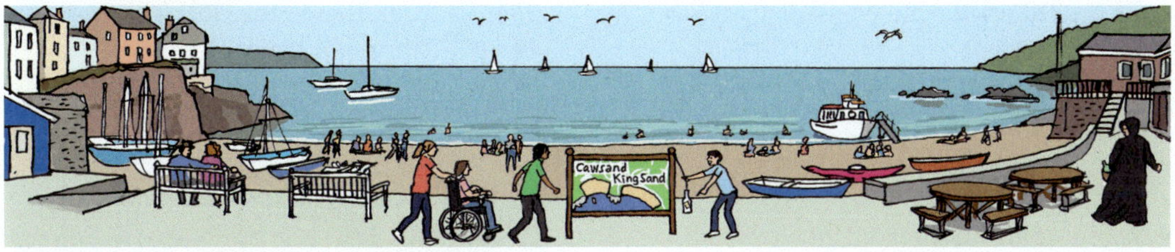

Scene 1 *A °message in a bottle*

Berry — Where's my dad? He's late.
Adam — Don't worry, Berry.
Berry — But he's never late.
Luca — And he has our picnic!
Ellie — Look at that old °woman. She looks like a °smuggler from an old story! What's she doing?
Adam — She's °putting something in a bottle. I think it's a message!
Luca — A message? Maybe it's for us!
Ellie — She's going away ... Let's go and look!
Luca — The message is for you, Berry.
Berry — For me? What? Oh!

To Berry and her friends!
Cawsand is great,
But Kingsand is °better.
Find the next bottle
And read the letter!
We have your dad,
°The sea's coming in.
You have 30 °minutes -
But °hurry! He can't swim!
Walk for two minutes
And then stop.
You're in a °square
Now find a shop.
From a Kingsand smuggler

Berry — We must find dad!
Ellie — But how?
Berry — First we must find a shop.
Luca — This is exciting!
Adam — Look at the big °map. There's a shop near here, THE SHOP IN THE SQUARE!
Ellie — That's it. Let's go.

Scene 2 *We only have 30 minutes!*

Luca — Here's the shop. Can we stop and buy some sweets? I'm hungry.
Adam — Don't be stupid, Luca. We only have 30 minutes.
Ellie — Where's the next message?
Berry — Maybe there's °another bottle?

Luca — I see one. Look, on that chair.
Ellie — I have it. And here's the message.
Adam — Oh, great!

Smugglers are hungry
They want to eat.
Find a cafe
Where smugglers meet.

Luca — We must find a cafe. But where?
Adam — Look, there's the old woman.
Ellie — Let's °follow her. Come on, Berry!
Berry — I'm coming!

Erarb. STORY
(SB offen)
1. Lesen/Hören aller Szenen im Zusammenhang im Mitleseverfahren.
Mögliche Leseaufträge:
What's the problem when Ellie, Adam, Luca and Berry arrive at Cawsand? (Berry's dad isn't there.)
What do they find instead? (a message in a bottle)
Do they find Berry's father in the end? (Yes, they do.)
Who's the Kingsand smuggler? (Berry's mum)
O Um sicherzustellen, dass auch Lernschwächere die Stationen der Schnitzeljagd nachvollziehen, verteilt L vorab KV 6.2. Dann wird das Stück komplett vorgespielt. S lesen mit und füllen anschließend die Tabelle mit *wh*-Fragen aus. Dazu kann ein szenenweises **2. Lesen**/Hören nötig sein. S beantworten die Fragen nach jeder Szene. Vergleich der Antworten im Plenum vor dem Vorspielen der nächsten Szene (Lösungsbeispiel S. 239).

STORY Navigator | **Inhalt**

Lernschwerpunkt: Eine szenische Geschichte verstehen und gestaltend vortragen

Storyline: Die vier Freunde folgen der alten Frau. Mithilfe weiterer Mitteilungen finden sie schließlich Berrys Vater, und es stellt sich heraus, dass die mysteriöse Frau Berrys Mutter ist. Am Ende erfahren die Kinder, dass Berry mit ihrer Familie für einige Zeit in die USA zieht.

Kompetenzen: Listening Einer Hörszene gezielt Informationen entnehmen | **Speaking** Szenen mit verteilten Rollen gestaltend vortragen
Reading Eine szenische Geschichte verstehen

6

Scene 3 *We only have 20 minutes!*

Luca — There's the old woman again.
Let's go!
Adam — Are you OK, Berry?
Berry — It's hard work!
Ellie — We can °push you.
Berry — Yes, please!
Ellie — Come on, guys. Push!
Berry — That's great! Thanks!
Adam — Look, a cafe!
Ellie — The *Smuggler's Rest*. That's it –
a cafe where smugglers meet!

Adam — Look, there's another bottle.

> **W**hat's the time?
> You don't know?
> Find a big °clock.
> Go, go, go!

Berry — What's the time? I can look at my
phone.
Luca — No, it says: Find a big clock.
Ellie — I can't see a clock. Can you see the
old woman?
Adam — No, she isn't here. What can we do?
Luca — °Quick. We're too °slow. We only
have twenty minutes. °Look for a
big clock.

Scene 4 *We only have 10 minutes!*

Ellie — Look, there's the clock!
Berry — Oh, yes! A really big clock!

Ellie — There's the bottle!
Adam — Quick. We only have ten minutes.
Luca — I have the bottle. And here's the
message.

> **F**eeling °hot?
> Want an °ice cream?
> Look for the cows
> And find your dream.

Berry — Well, I'm feeling very hot.
Luca — And I really want an ice cream.
Adam — But what are we looking for?
Ellie — Cows?
Adam — Cows on the beach?

Berry — Look. I can see cows.
Ellie — Me too.
Luca — And a bottle. Quick.

STORY Navigator | **Vorbereitung**

Zeitbedarf: ca. zwei Stunden
Kooperative Lernformen: Gruppenarbeit Ex **4** (THEATRE TIME)
Materialbedarf: Audio-CD + Player oder MP3 + PC/Lautsprecher, Ex **4**: ggf. Requisiten
Einsatz von Begleitmedien: Folie 33 | Workbook S. 82

► *Folie 33*

Scene 5 *We only have one minute!*

Luca — There's a message in the bottle.

> Only one minute,
> Look near the water.
> A dad is °waiting
> For his °daughter!

Adam — Let's look on the beach.
Ellie — I can see the old woman.
Luca — But where's Berry's dad?
Adam — Quick! We only have one minute!
Berry — There he is – in the sand! Hey Dad!
Dad — Help! I can't °get out!
Luca — We're coming! Don't worry!
Mum — Hello, everybody.
Berry — Mum! You are the Kingsand smuggler! – Dad, let's get you °out of there.
Ellie — That was a great game!
Adam — Yeah, it was really good.
Berry — But a bit °scary too.
Mum — Are you OK now? Are you hungry?
Luca — Yes!
Dad — Your picnic is °over there. Sam is looking after it.
Luca — I can see Sam.
Adam — He's eating something.
Berry — Oh no! He's eating our picnic! Sam! Stop!

Scene 6 *Berry's news*

1: She's going to America with her mum and dad.
2: No, she isn't happy.
3: She doesn't want to leave Plymouth, her friends, Eggy and the farm.

3.09 **3 The last scene**

Listen to Scene 6. Answer the questions:

1 Where is Berry going in August?
2 Is she happy?
3 Why? Why not?

4 THEATRE TIME

a) Pick a scene. Make groups of five to six students: Ellie, Berry, Luca, Adam, Berry's mum and Berry's dad. Read the scene together.

b) Act your scene for the class.

Erarb. Ex 3a 1. Hören und Sicherung des Globalverstehens anhand der Fragen 1–3. Optional **2. Hören**. Abschließend kann L fragen: *At the end Berry is feeling better. Why? (Her friends can email her and maybe visit her in America.)*

Erarb. Ex 4a+b Je nach Klassenstruktur bilden die S selbstständig Gruppen oder L steuert die Zusammensetzung (Gruppenbildung). Um sicherzustellen, dass alle Szenen ausgewählt werden, lässt L Karten mit den Zahlen 1–5 für die jeweilige Szene ziehen. S finden sich zusammen und ziehen dann Namenskarten für ihre Rolle. S, die innerhalb der Gruppen nicht untergekommen sind, können die Rolle des Souffleurs übernehmen.
Zum Training von Aussprache und Intonation hören die S ihre Szene mindestens ein weiteres Mal und konzentrieren sich dabei ausschließlich auf ihre Rolle. Anschließend lernen die S ihre Rolle auswendig (ggf. als HA).
Tipp: Die S erhalten ihre Szene als Kopie, sodass sie ihre Rolle markieren und Ausprachehinweise eintragen können.

► *Workbook 4, p. 82*

SKILLS TRAINING Listening and speaking

Lernschwerpunkt: Über Ferienpläne sprechen
Kompetenzen: Listening Ein Gespräch über Ferienpläne verstehen | **Speaking** Über Pläne für die Ferien sprechen
Lern- und Arbeitstechniken Ein *flow chart* für die Entwicklung eines eigenen Dialogs nutzen
Redemittel: Sommeraktivitäten, Reisen, Pläne

Zeitbedarf: ca. eine Stunde
Kooperative Lernformen: Partner talk Ex **2**
Materialbedarf: Ex **1**: Audio-CD + Player oder MP3 + PC/ Lautsprecher
Einsatz von Begleitmedien: Folie 34 | IAT 6.2 | DFF 6.5| Workbook S. 83–84

Einstieg Ex 1 (SB geschl.) L berichtet von den eigenen Ferienplänen und fragt die S: *What about you?*
Erarb. Ex 1a (SB offen) Lesen des Arbeitsauftrags und der Tickets (still oder Plenum). Beim **1. Hören** (Globalverstehen) ordnen S den Tickets 1–4 die entsprechenden Personen zu.
Erarb. Ex 1b 2. Hören (Detailverstehen): Die S schreiben zunächst die Namen in ihr Heft und ordnen dann die Zahlen zu.

Einstieg Ex 2 (SB offen) Es handelt sich um eine Parallelübung auf zwei Niveaus: ○ hier und ● auf S. 146. Lernstärkere S arbeiten nur mit *flow chart* und ohne Redemittel. Vor der Bearbeitung entscheiden L oder S, wer die leichtere oder schwierigere Aufgabe bearbeitet. Anschließend homogene Gruppenbildung.
Erarb. Ex 2 S führen Gespräche über ihre Ferienpläne.
Ausw. Ex 2 Partner üben ihren Dialog und führen ihn im Plenum vor.
○ Lernschwächere S können als Gedächtnisstütze auch ein schriftliches Dialogskript erarbeiten, das sie mithilfe der Read-and-look-up technique vortragen.

6 SKILLS TRAINING Listening and speaking

► *Folie 34* ► *IAT 6.2* ► *DFF 6.5*

1 Talking about summer plans

3.10

a) The four friends are talking about summer plans.
Listen. Match the names (Luca, Ellie, Adam and Berry) and the tickets (1–4).

1: Adam • 2: Berry • 3: Luca • 4: Ellie

b) Listen again. Who says what – Luca, Berry, Adam or Ellie?

1 We're °flying from London.
2 Nothing special. I'm staying at home all summer.
3 I'm staying at home in July.
4 I'm going to Spain for a week with dad.
5 Mum and dad are working.
6 My granny from Ghana[2] is visiting us.

Luca: 5, 6 • Berry: 1 • Adam: 2 • Ellie: 3, 4

2 ○ What are your summer plans? //● p. 146

Work with a partner. Talk about your summer plans. Use the ideas in the green boxes.

A: Begrüße deinen Partner / deine Partnerin. Frage, wie es ihm / ihr geht.
– Hi.
– Hello Anna / …
– How are you?
– Are you OK?

B: Grüße zurück. Sage, wie es dir geht.
– Hi …
– I'm fine, thanks.
– I'm OK.

A: Frage, was er / sie im Sommer vorhat.
– What are your summer plans?
– What are you doing in the summer?

B: Sage, was du vorhast. (2 oder 3 Ideen)
– Nothing special!
– I'm going to Turkey / …
– I'm staying at …
– I'm flying to …
– My uncle / cousin / friend / … is visiting us.

A: Sage, wie du die Pläne deines Partners / deiner Partnerin findest.
– That's interesting / nice / cool / …
– Really? Can I come too?
– Wow! Great!

B: Nun frage deinen Partner / deine Partnerin, was er / sie vorhat.

A: Sage, was du vorhast.

B: Sage, wie du die Pläne deines Partners / deiner Partnerin findest.

Lösungsbsp. S. 239

1 ['mæləgə] 2 ['gɑːnə]

► Workbook 5–6, pp. 83–84

Lernschwerpunkt: Fiktionale und dokumentarische Filmszenen verstehen, mehr über Cawsand erfahren
Kompetenzen: **Listening** Filmszenen verstehen
Speaking Sich über die Kinder von Harbour Road austauschen
Redemittel: Sommeraktivitäten, Reisen, Pläne

Zeitbedarf: ca. eine Stunde
Kooperative Lernformen: Partner talk Ex **1d**
Minimalversion: Ex **1a–b**, Ex **2b**
Materialbedarf: DVD + Player oder PC/Lautsprecher

SKILLS TRAINING Viewing 6

1 The kids from Harbour Road: Summer holidays

a) The kids are going on a camping trip. What do you think they take? Watch the film and find out. They take a tent (2), sausages (4) and a can of beans (5).

1 
ice cream

2 
a tent[1]

3 
sandwiches

4 
sausages

5 
a can of beans[2]

6 
a bike

7 
matches[3]

8 
a can opener[4]

b) Put the photos in the right order.

C • A • D • B

A 

B 

C 

D 

c) Are these sentences true or false? Watch the film again and check your answers.

1 First the three friends are in a park.
2 They want to sleep in a holiday flat.
3 They want to eat beans and sausages.
4 They need a can opener.
5 They can't find the can of beans.
6 Anna's father helps the kids.

1 True. • **2** False. (in a tent) • **3** True. • **4** True. • **5** False. (They can't open it.) • **6** False. (Anna's mother)

d) Talk to a partner about the kids from Harbour Road.

I like Paul because ...

Yes, Paul is nice. But I prefer ... because ...

I think ... is fun / cool / ...

2 People and places: A ferry trip to Cawsand

a) You're going on a ferry trip to Cawsand. What do you think you can see? Make a list.

More help p. 146

b) Watch the film. What things on your list do you see?

[1]tent [tent] *Zelt* [2]can of beans [kæn əv 'bi:nz] *Dose mit Bohnen* [3]matches ['mætʃɪz] *Streichhölzer*
[4]can opener ['kæn əʊpnə] *Dosenöffner*

Einstieg Ex 1 (SB geschl.) L: *It's the first day of the summer holidays. What do you do? (...) The kids from Harbour Road want to do something together in their holidays. What can they do? (...) Let's watch the film and find out.*
Erarb. Ex 1a (SB offen) Die S spekulieren und notieren die Nummern oder Wörter im Heft. Beim **1. Sehen** Überprüfen der Vermutungen.
Erarb. Ex 1b S notieren die Buchstabenfolge im Heft.
Erarb. Ex 1c S notieren die Nummern 1–6 im Heft und dahinter *true* bzw. *false*.
2. Sehen zum Überprüfen.
Ausw. Ex 1c anhand von Right/wrong cards.
● Lernstärkere korrigieren die falschen Aussagen.
Erarb. Ex 1d Partner talk mithilfe der Redemittel.

Erarb. Ex 2a (SB offen) S stellen Vermutungen an, was die Passagiere alles sehen können, und sammeln mögliche Nomen in einer Liste.
Erarb. Ex 2b S überprüfen beim **1. Sehen** ihre Vermutungen, haken ihre Liste ab und ergänzen weitere Nomen.
Ausw. Ex 2b Einzelne S tragen ihre Ergebnisse vor. Sammlung an der Tafel.

PARTNER B

▸ KV 17

Unit 1 Stop! Check! Go!

10 SPEAKING A timetable ▸ Unit 1, p. 33

a) Copy this timetable into your exercise book. Some lessons are missing. Answer partner A's questions. Then ask partner A. Complete the timetable.

Lesson	Monday	Tuesday	Wednesday	Thursday	Friday
1	………	music	technology	geography	PE
2	maths	English	history	German	………
3	science	………	PE	………	English
4	art	maths	………	science	German
5	………	German	maths	………	………

Unit 2

5 What's different? ▸ Unit 2, p. 39

● Look at room B. Your partner looks at room A.

You start. Describe your room to your partner.
Find four different things or more.
Make notes about the different things.

Partner B — There's a bed in room B.
Partner A — There's a bed in room A too.
Partner B — OK. There are three cushions in room B.
Partner A — There are no cushions in room A. That's different!

bed • chair • cushions • desk • lamp • mirror • posters • rugs • shelves • table • TV • wardrobe

Room A	Room B
no cushions	3 cushions
…	…

7 SPEAKING Good shops ▸ Unit 2, p. 50

a) Answer partner A's questions about this shop:

b) Imagine you're in Plymouth. You want to find a good sports shop. Ask partner A these questions. Write down:
- the name of the shop
- the address
- the phone number.

3 ROLE-PLAY A garage sale ▸ Unit 3, p. 63

You have a garage sale in Plymouth. Listen to your partner's questions. Pick the best answer.

It's £ ...
It's a special offer.
It isn't expensive.
It's good value.
Good. That's £..., please.
Thank you.

Swap roles.

PARTNER B

Unit 5

2 **NOW YOU** ▸ Unit 5, p. 100

Partner B

a) Listen to your partner. He/She is talking about *picture 1*. There are five differences in your picture. When you hear a difference, tell your partner.

In my picture the car is ...

In my picture the boy is ....

b) Now describe *picture 2* to your partner. Say what you can see, where the things and people are, and what they're doing.

On the left / In the middle / On the right I can see ...

There's a ... next to / in front of ...

He's / She's playing ...

Your partner listens and looks at his/her picture. Some things are different in your picture. He/She must find five differences.

1

2

Lösung:

Unit 5

6 **What are they doing?** ▸ Unit 5, p. 97

Look at the photos and check your answers.

Unit 1

More practice 1 The new timetable ▸ Unit 1, p. 21

a) Write right and wrong sentences about the timetable on page 21 – as many as you can.
Lesson one on Friday is …
Lesson … on Thursday is science.
Lesson three on … is …
Lesson … on … is …
…

Lösungsbsp. S. 232

b) Read your sentences to your partner. He/She says 'right' or 'wrong'.

Erarb. Mp1a S verfassen in EA mit vorgegebenen Redemitteln eigene Aussagen zum Stundenplan auf SB-Seite 21. Dafür ggf. Zeitrahmen vorgeben (z. B. 10 min): *Write as many sentences as you can in ten / … minutes.*
Auswertung in Mp1b Gemäß SB tragen die S einander ihre Aussagen zum Eggy-Stundenplan im Partner talk vor. Die jeweiligen Partner beurteilen, ob diese richtig oder falsch sind.

//● 4 At Eggy ▸ Unit 1, p. 23

Put in: *He's • She's • It's • They're*

1 Eggy is my new school. … big.
2 Ellie is a new student at Eggy. … cool.
3 Mr Brown is at Eggy too. … our ICT teacher.
4 Mrs Ford isn't our English teacher. … our art teacher.
5 Adam and Berry aren't in the classroom. … in the sports hall.
6 Look at our new books. … nice.

1 It's
2 She's
3 He's
4 She's
5 They're
6 They're

More practice 2 °Photos from Eggy ▸ Unit 1, p. 23

he • she • it • they

Match the words in the box with the photos: *1 it, 2 …, 3 …*

1 

2 

3 

4 

5 

6 

7 

8 

9 

10 

Unit 1

More help 5 Pets and friends ▸ Unit 1, p. 23

b) Write about your friend or pet. You can write:

(Name) is my pet.
He's / She's a dog / cat / ...
He's / She's four / six / ...
He's / She's big / small / ...
He's / She's brown / black / ...
He's / She's nice / fun / great / ...

(Name) is my friend.
He's / She's ten / ...
He's / She's from ...
He's / She's nice / fun / great / ...
My friend is / isn't at my school.
... is / isn't in my class.

More help 6 People and places in Plymouth ▸ Unit 1, p. 23

b) Match the sentences.

1 Plymouth isn't in Germany.
2 Eggy isn't in London.
3 Cyril isn't a seagull.
4 Sandy isn't a crab.
5 Mr Brown isn't a maths teacher.
6 The four friends aren't from Germany.
7 Ellie and Berry aren't teachers at Eggy.
8 Luca and Adam aren't girls.
9 Ms Lee and Mr Brown aren't students.

A He's a crab.
B They're teachers.
C It's in Plymouth.
D They're boys.
E They're from England.
F It's in England.
G She's a seagull.
H They're students at Eggy.
I He's an ICT teacher.

More help 7 Make a quiz for the class ▸ Unit 1, p. 23

a) Pick some quiz cards. Complete the cards with the ideas in the green boxes.

big • small • black • a pet • a wild animal • ... →
It's an animal.
It's ...
It isn't ...
What is it?

He's / She's a boy / girl.
He's / She isn't ...
He's / She's ...
Who is she?
← eleven • my best friend • my brother / sister • in my class • ...

big • small • black • great • cool • fun • new • ... →
It's a thing.
It's ...
It isn't ...
What is it?

They're students.
They're ...
They aren't ...
Who are they?
← twelve • my best friends • from ... • in my class • at my school • ...

fun • cool • my favourite sport / hobby • ... →
It's a sport / hobby.
It's ...
It isn't ...
What is it?

He's / She's a teacher.
He's / She isn't ...
He's / She's ...
Who is she?
← nice • cool • my class teacher • PE teacher • from ... • at my school • ...

More practice 3 **The story** ▸ Unit 1, p. 25

Put the sentences in the right order and tell the story.

°Part 1

1 Miss Borowski is in the assembly hall.
2 But Ellie has no tie.
3 It's assembly at Eggy.
4 The students are in the assembly hall too.
5 Miss Borowski says, "The uniform is important!"

It's assembly at Eggy.
...

Part 2

1 Now Ellie has a tie.
2 Class 7Y is in the art lesson.
3 They need paper, scissors and colours.
4 It's a very nice tie. But it isn't the school tie.
5 Luca has an idea.

Luca has an idea.
...

More practice 4 **ACTIVITY** **Make a school tie** ▸ Unit 1, p. 25

1 °Pick your colours.

2 Make the tie.

3 Pick the best tie.

Unit 1

More help 1 Make networks
▸ Unit 1, p. 27

b) Copy this school network and add the words from the box to your network.
Can you add more words?
Then compare networks with your partner.

art room • blazer • classroom • class teacher • computer room • diary • English • French • history • hole punch • maths • PE • pencil case • rubber • ruler • skirt • sports hall • student • sweatshirt • teacher • tie • trousers • …

//● 2 NOW YOU
▸ Unit 1, p. 28

Write the dialogue with a partner. Then practise with your partner.

A	B
Begrüße B. Frage, wie es ihm/ihr geht.	Grüße zurück. Sage, wie es dir geht und frage A, wie es ihm/ihr geht.
Sage, wie es dir geht. Frage B nach seinem/ihrem Lieblingsfach.	Nenne dein Lieblingsfach. Frage A, ob du etwas ausleihen darfst.
Stimme zu und gib es B.	Bedanke dich. Frage A nach dem besten Freund/der besten Freundin in der Klasse.
Sage, wer dein bester Freund/deine beste Freundin ist.	Sage, ob du ihn/sie auch magst oder nicht.

Unit 1 Stop! Check! Go!

//● 5 LANGUAGE Remember Ellie?
▸ Unit 1, p. 31

Ellie is with her dad. She has some pictures on her mobile. Complete the sentences.

1 Look, this ... my new school.
2 It... very big.
3 The students in my class ... OK.
4 The teachers ... OK too.
5 This ... my new friend, Berry.
6 She... great.
7 My friends Ruby and Charlie ... at my school too.
8 But they ... (No) in my class.
9 This ... my new uniform.
10 It ... (No) very nice.

More help **9** WRITING **A dialogue with a new student** ▸ *Unit 1, p. 32*

Put Tamara's sentences in the right order and write the dialogue.

Berry

- Hi, I'm Berry. What's your name?
- I'm from Woolwell. I'm in class 7Y. What about you?
- I like science. What about you?
- See you later Tamara.

Tamara

- I'm in class 7D. What's your favourite lesson?
- OK. See you.
- Hi, I'm Tamara. I'm from London. What about you?
- I like history.

Unit 2

More help **3** ACTIVITY **My dream house** ▸ *Unit 2, p. 35*

a) Draw your dream house.
Here's an example.

b) Walk around: Talk about your dream house. Use these phrases:

My dream house is …	new/old big/small
My dream house has …	two bedrooms/… one bathroom/… a nice garden a big garage
The living room is …	pink/red/…

1 Wrong. My mum and dad aren't together. • 2 Wrong. I live with my mum. • 3 Right. • 4 Wrong. Pete has two children. • 5 Right. • 6 Wrong. Conor is my (big) stepbrother. • 7 Wrong. Her name is Alisha. 8 Wrong. This is Finn, my baby brother.

Unit 2

//● 2 Ellie's family tree

▸ Unit 2, p. 37

a) Right or wrong? Correct the wrong sentences for Ellie.

1 My mum and dad are together.
2 I live with my dad.
3 This is Pete. He's my stepdad.
4 Pete has three children.
5 Zoe is my stepsister.
6 Conor is my baby brother.
7 My dad has a new partner. Her name is Jackie.
8 This is Finn, my big brother.

1 Wrong. My mum and dad aren't together.

Einstieg Mp1 S sammeln in EA Einrichtungsgegenstände in zwei Listen *(There's ... / There are ...)*. Anschließend Partner check und Sammeln an Tafel
Erarb. Mp1 S verfassen je nach Leistungsstärke in EA so viele Sätze wie möglich zu Katies Zimmer.

More practice 1 Katie's room

▸ Unit 2, p. 39

Describe Katie's room.
Write sentences – as many as you can:

Lösungsbsp. S. 233

– The room is ...
– There's a ...
– There are ...
– I like / don't like ...

//● 3 NOW YOU

▸ Unit 2, p. 41

a) Answer the questions. Choose answers from the box.

1 Are you noisy?
2 Are your friends fun?
3 Is your grandmother from Germany?
4 Is your dad strict?
5 Is your mum bossy?
6 Is your room messy?

Yes, I am. / No, I'm not.
Yes, he is. / No, he isn't.
Yes, she is. / No, she isn't.
Yes, it is. / No, it isn't.
Yes, they are. / No, they aren't.

b) Ask your partner the same questions.

More practice 2 More questions

▸ Unit 2, p. 41

Write the correct questions in your exercise book and answer them.

1 from – you – Are – Germany – ?
2 mum and dad – Germany – Are – from – your – ?
3 a – Is – father – teacher – your – ?
4 your – English – school bag – Is – book – your – in – ?
5 your best friend – class – Is – your – in – ?
6 strict – your – Are – teachers – ?

1 Are you from Germany? Yes, I am. / No, I'm not. • **2** Are your mum and dad from Germany? Yes, they are. / No, they aren't. • **3** Is your father a teacher? Yes, he is. / No, he isn't. • **4** Is your English book in your school bag? Yes, it is. / No, it isn't. • **5** Is your best friend in your class? Yes, he/she is. / No, he/she isn't.

Erarb. Mp2 Zur weiteren Festigung der Entscheidungsfragen und Kurzantworten bilden S aus den *jumbled sentences* Fragen, die sie für sich in EA beantworten. Auch als schriftliche **HA** geeignet.

//● 3 Is Ellie happy?

▸ Unit 2, p. 43

Complete the sentences.

1 On Monday Ellie is happy because she can live with ...
2 On Tuesday Ellie is happy because she has a nice ...
3 On Wednesday Ellie is happy because she can watch ...
4 On Thursday Ellie isn't happy because Finn ...
5 On Friday Ellie isn't happy because dad and Alisha ...
6 On Saturday Ellie ... because ...
7 On Sunday Ellie ... because ...

More help 4 A week later

▸ Unit 2, p. 43

Write Ellie's diary for this picture.

Dear Diary
I'm very ... ☺ again.
I'm at mum's ...
I'm in the ... with ...
The cats ... happy.
Mum ... happy.
And Zoe is ... too.
Conor ... here.
Finn isn't ...
That's ... (OK / ...)!

Unit 2

Erarb. Mp3 S legen eine zweispaltige Tabelle an und füllen sie mit positiven und negativen Äußerungen Ellies.
Ausw. Mp3 Partner check
Zusatz S wählen je eine Redewendung aus und formulieren einen passenden Satz dazu: *Great news! I can go to the cinema with you! / I'm lonely. My friends aren't here. / …*

More practice 3 WORDS Favourite phrases

▸ Unit 2, p. 43

a) Put the phrases from the story in two lists: 😃 ☹

b) Check your lists with a partner.

Great news! • I'm lonely. • He isn't very happy. • Finn is very cute! • Be quiet, Finn! • Tuesday is the big day. • I miss mum. • Dad has no time for me. • The best of both worlds!

☺: Great news! Finn is very cute! Tuesday is the big day. The best of both worlds!
☹: I'm lonely. He isn't very happy. Be quiet, Finn! I miss mum. Dad has no time for me.

More help 2 NOW YOU

▸ Unit 2, p. 44

b) Write about your dream house or flat. Use your mind map. You can use sentences like this. Write as much as you can.

My (dream) house / flat is in Hamburg / Dresden / …
It's near a village / city / …
The colour is nice. It's yellow / red / …
It's small / big / great / cool / …
There are three / four / … rooms in my house / flat.
There's a kitchen, a living room, a … / …
My favourite room is …
There's a table / … in the living room / …
There are lots of chairs / pictures / … too.
It's messy / noisy / …!
There's no TV / I share a room with my brother / sister / …

More practice 4 NOW YOU

▸ Unit 2, p. 45

Erarb. Mp4 S formulieren zu den deutschen Fragen die passenden englischen *classroom phrases*. Auch als schriftliche HA geeignet.

How do you say these things in English?

1 Wie fragst du nach einem englischen Wort?
2 Wie fragst du, ob du auf die Toilette gehen darfst?
3 Wie fragst du, was ihr als Hausaufgaben aufhabt?
4 Wie bittest du jemanden, etwas noch einmal zu wiederholen?
5 Wie fragst du, auf welcher Seite ihr gerade seid?
6 Wie sagst du, dass dir etwas leidtut?
7 Wie bedankst du dich?
8 Wie fragst du, ob du dir einen Radiergummi borgen kannst?
9 Wie fragst du, was ihr in der nächsten Stunde habt?

1 What's that in English? • 2 Can I go to the toilet, please? • 3 What's for homework? • 4 Can you say that again, please? • 5 What page is it, please? • 6 Sorry. / I'm sorry. • 7 Thank you. • 8 Can I borrow your eraser, please? • 9 What's the next lesson?

More practice 5 Can you spell that? ▸ Unit 2, p. 46

Partner A: Look at the pictures in box A. **Partner B:** Turn the page upside down.

A

a) Choose one of the words from your box. Spell it for partner B. Partner B listens and writes the word. Check the spelling.

b) Swap roles.

b) Choose one of the words from box B. Spell it for partner A. Partner A listens and writes the word. Check the spelling. Then swap roles again.

B

a) Partner B: Listen to partner A. Write the word. Then check the spelling.

More help 2 Addresses and phone numbers ▸ Unit 2, p. 46

c) Copy the notes. Listen to Berry. Add the missing letters.

M	E	R		Y	W		A		H	E	R					M

W	O		L		E		

Unit 2 Stop! Check! Go!

//● 4 Questions for Sandy ▸ Unit 2, p. 49

Answer Cyril's questions for Sandy.

1 Hey, Sandy. Are you happy? – *Yes, I am.*
2 Is your family small? – *No, ...*
3 Are your parents strict? – ...
4 Is your mum cool?
5 Are your brothers and sisters mean?
6 Are you and your family noisy?
7 Is your new house messy?

Einstieg Mp5 (SB offen) Klären der Arbeitsanweisung und ggf. Probelauf mit zwei Freiwilligen im Plenum. Partnerübung: Partner B dreht die Seite um, sodass Bilder, Begriffe und Arbeitsanweisung zu B richtig herum (und die Begriffe etc. zu A über Kopf) stehen.

Erarb. Mp5 Partner A beginnt. Rollentausch nach jedem Begriff.

Unit 3

Erarb. Mp1 gemäß Aufgabe; Step 2: Milling-around activity
Ausw. Mp1 Zur Auswertung zeigt L auf einen Monat; alle S, die in diesem Monat Geburtstag haben, stehen auf und sagen nacheinander ihr Geburtsdatum, z. B. *My birthday is on the 15 th of March.*

//● 2 NOW YOU ▸ Unit 3, p. 55

a) Make a table about *your* Saturdays.

buy … • go to … • have … • meet … • play … • ride … • stay … • watch … • …

I always	*I sometimes*	*I never*
go shopping	…	…

More practice 1 ACTIVITY A birthday °calendar[1] ▸ Unit 3, p. 57

You can make a birthday calendar for your family and friends too.

Step 1: Make 12 groups. Pick a month for your group. Write it on a piece of paper.

Step 2: Find out who has a birthday in your month – and the date. Write it on your month.

Step 3: Draw a picture for your month.

Step 4: Put the months together. Put the calendar on the wall of your classroom.

//● 5 Cyril and Sandy's day ▸ Unit 3, p. 59

Write about Cyril and Sandy's day. Put in the correct forms of the verbs: *get* • *go* • *have* • *meet*

1 get
2 gets
3 have
4 meet
5 go
6 goes

1 In the morning I … up early.

2 Sandy is lazy. She … up late.

3 I usually … breakfast on the beach.

4 I often … my friends.

5 We … swimming together.

6 Sandy often … to Plymouth with her friends.

1 ['kælɪndə]

More practice 2 **Ellie's weekend** ▸ Unit 3, p. 59

Complete the sentences about Ellie.

1 °At the weekend I ... (go) to my dad's flat.
2 He always ... (get up) first.
3 He ... (make) breakfast for me and Finn.
4 Alisha, my stepmum, ... (stay) in bed.
5 Dad, Finn and I sometimes ... (go) shopping at the supermarket.
6 After lunch I ... (meet) my friends in town.
7 In the evening dad ... (watch) TV with Alisha.
8 I sometimes ... (watch) too. I sometimes ... (play) with Finn.
9 °On Sunday evening I ... (go) to my mum's house.

More help **6** **NOW YOU** ▸ Unit 3, p. 59

a) Make notes about your day. You can use a mind map like this:

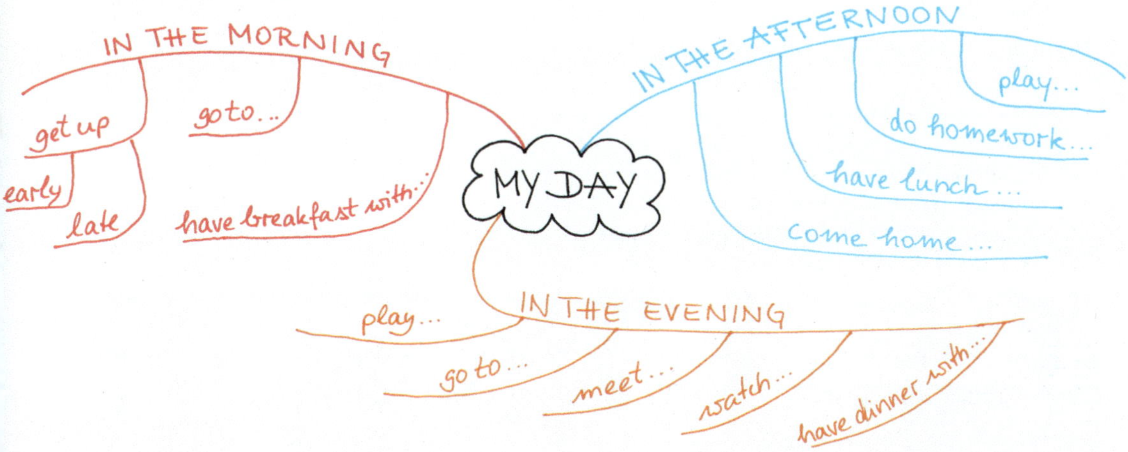

More help **6** **NOW YOU** ▸ Unit 3, p. 59

b) Use your notes and write a text about your day. Use phrases like this:

My day
In the morning I get up (early / late).
I (usually / always) have breakfast (with ...)
Then I (go to school / ...)
In the afternoon I (come home / ...)
I have lunch. Then I (sometimes) ...
In the evening I (make ... / play ... / watch ... / ...)
Then I (go to ... / ...)

Use **always • usually • often • sometimes • never**:
– I usually get up late.
– I always have lunch at school.

You can put your text in your DOSSIER.

3 DIFF BANK

Unit 3

More help **3** **Luca's birthday** ▸ *Unit 3, p. 61*

Write the story. The sentence parts in the green box can help you.

On Thursday Luca has no ideas for ...
But his mum has ...
On Saturday morning Luca gets ...
Later the boys meet Jack's friends ...
Jack goes ...
Then Luca goes down the hill ...
Jack and Luca go to ...
Luca has ...

... a great idea – a concert!
... down the hill first.
... his birthday.
... the hospital.
... a sore leg.
... at the Hoe.
... but he falls.
... great presents.

More help **1** **Luca's garage sale** ▸ *Unit 3, p. 62*

a) What's in Luca's garage sale? Make two lists.
The words in the box can help you.

bike • blazer • books • boxes • calculator • car • cat • computer • computer games • crab • cushion • footballs • hoodie • lamp • mobile phones • pencils • pencil case • pens • picture • posters • rulers • schoolbag • shirt • sweatshirts • ties • ...

There's ...	*There are*
a bike	*2 footballs*
a ...	*3 ...*

Lösung S. 235

1 The calculator is £1. • 2 The mobile is £9.50. • 3 The crab is 50 p. • 4 The posters are £5 (two pounds fifty each). 5 The computer is £20. • 6 The school bag is £5.50. • 7 The blazer is £10. • 8 The footballs are £4.

1 Luca's garage sale ▸ Unit 3, p. 62

2.12

c) Listen again. How much are the things in the garage sale? Write the prices.

1 The calculator is £...
2 The mobiles are £...
3 The crab is ...
4 The posters are ...
5 The computer is ...
6 The school bag is ...
7 The blazer is ...
8 The footballs are ...

You write:	You say:
£1.50	One pound fifty
50 p	Fifty p

More practice 3 Jack helps with the °prices ▸ Unit 3, p. 62

2.13

Listen and write the prices in your exercise book.

1 £5 • 2 50 p • 3 £1.50 • 4 90 p • 5 £3.20 • 6 30 p

Erarb. Mp3 **1/2. Hören** gemäß Aufgabe
Ausw. Mp3 Kontrolle durch Partner check und im Plenum

More help 2 A new helmet ▸ Unit 3, p. 63

a) Copy and complete the dialogue. Choose the right words.

Luca — This helmet looks big / nice (1). I like it. Excuse me, please / thank you (2). How much / What (3) is the red helmet?
Man — It's / They're (4) £24.99.
Luca — That's too expensive / big (5)! How much / Where (6) is the white helmet?
Man — It's a stupid / special (7) offer. It's £16.99.
Luca — That's OK. I'll do / take (8) it.

More help 2 Guessing new words ▸ Unit 3, p. 64

a) What are these words in German? Find the words in the adverts on p. 64. Then read the sentences in German here. They can help you.

1	on stage (advert A)	Wo befinden sich bei einer Show die Leute, die singen und tanzen? Schau dir das Bild an.
	fireworks (advert B)	Das Bild hilft dir. Gibt es ein ähnliches deutsches Wort?
2	theatre (advert A)	Das deutsche Wort ist sehr ähnlich, es wird nur etwas anders geschrieben.
	festival (advert B)	Das Wort gibt es auch im Deutschen. Schau auf das Wort davor. Gibt es auch ein *summer festival* bei euch?
3	opening times (advert C)	Was kommt nach diesem Wort im Text? Es sieht aus wie Uhrzeiten, oder? Du hörst oft im Unterricht: *Open your book*. Und dann öffnest du dein Buch. Was könnte *opening times* heißen?
	adult (advert C)	*Adults* müssen £11 Eintritt zahlen. *Children* zahlen nur £6.50. Sind *adults* älter oder jünger als Kinder? Was könnte das Wort heißen?

Unit 3

Erarb. Mp4a (SB offen) ein S öffnet S. 64, ein S öffnet S. 134. Gemäß Aufgabe.
Erarb. Mp4b Aufgabe zur Metakognition
Ausw. Mp4b im Plenum

More practice 4 More words from the adverts

▸ Unit 3, p. 64

a) Work with a partner. One of you open your book at p. 64.
Look together at the adverts and try to guess these words:

In advert A: live, price, book
In advert B: championships, free
In advert C: fantastic, dive show, tiger sharks, tickets

live, Preis, buchen
Meisterschaft, (Eintritt) frei/kostenlos
fantastisch, Tauch-Show, Tigerhaie, Eintrittskarten

b) What helps you to guess the words? Lösungsbsp. S. 235

Unit 3 Stop! Check! Go!

More help 1 WORDS In a town

▸ Unit 3, p. 66

c) Make sentences.
You can use ideas from the box.

1 ... in a park.
→ *You can play games in a park.*
2 ... in a restaurant.
→ *You can ...*
3 ... in a shopping centre.
4 ... in a swimming pool.
5 ... in a mobile phone shop.
6 ... in a bike shop.

- buy a bike / a helmet / a mobile / things
- go swimming / shopping
- have lunch / breakfast
- meet friends
- play football / games
- ride a bike

More help 8 READING Casper the cat

▸ Unit 3, p. 69

Find these words in the text. Guess what they mean in German.
The sentences in German can help you.

1 leaves (line 3)	Schau dir die Wörter davor und danach an. Was macht Casper jeden Morgen?
2 bus stop (l. 4)	Du kennst beide Wörter aus dem Deutschen. Das erste Wort ist klar, aber das zweite Wort musst du etwas anders übersetzen, dort stoppt der …
3 waits (l. 4)	Casper ist an der Bushaltestelle. Was macht er dort zunächst?
4 sits (l. 5)	Das Wort ist auch einem deutschen Wort sehr ähnlich.
5 window (l. 6)	Schau dir das Foto an. Wo sitzt Casper? Wohin schaut er?
6 travels (l. 8)	Es geht um den Bus. Was macht er? Achte auf die Zahl nach dem Wort.
7 bus driver (l. 9)	Schau dir die Wörter davor und danach an. Könnte das eine Person sein? Wer ist das?
8 gets out (l. 9)	Schau auf die Wörter davor. Casper ist wieder an seinem Haus. Was macht er?

Pets	Pets or farm animals	Farm animals
cat	donkey	cow
budgie	dog	pig
hamster	rabbit	sheep
rat	horse	chicken
chipmunk	pony	goat
guinea pig	…	duck
…		…

▸ KV 4.1

Unit 4

More practice 1 Animal words ▸ Unit 4, p. 71

Collect as many animal words as you can.
Copy this diagram and complete it.

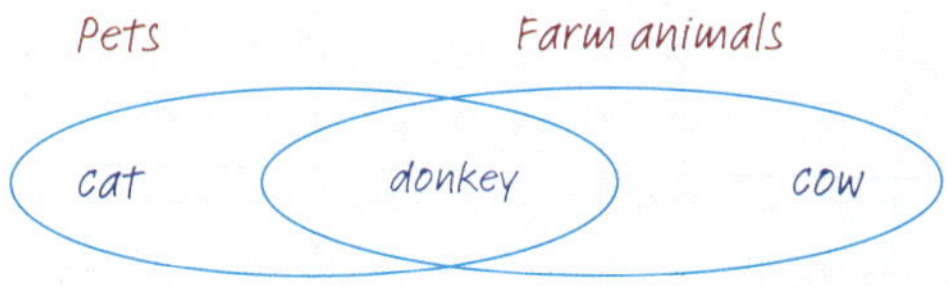

Or write two lists, like this:

Pets	Farm animals
…	…

More help 2 NOW YOU ▸ Unit 4, p. 72

a) Write sentences. You can use the ideas in the brackets.

1 Every morning … (my mum / my sister / my alarm clock / …) wakes me.
2 Before breakfast I … (go to the bathroom / get ready for school / …)
3 I go to school by … (bus / car / bike) / I walk to school with …
4 I come home before / at … (one o'clock / two o'clock / …)
5 In the evening I … (watch TV / do my homework / do sport / listen to music / …)

More practice 2 On school days ▸ Unit 4, p. 73

a) Copy and complete the table for you.

b) Appointments: Make appointments with two partners. Then talk to your partners like this:

> I get up at 6 o'clock. What about you?

Listen to their answers and complete the table.

	Me	1 o'clock …	2 o'clock …
get up	6.00	…	…
have breakfast	6.15	…	…
go to school	…		
come home			
have lunch			
do my homework			
have dinner			
go to bed			

More help 2 NOW YOU ▸ Unit 4, p. 74

a) Find more ideas when you feel great or when you feel fed up. Look at the box for help.
Make notes like this:

I feel great …	I feel fed up …
when I play football	when my dad is bossy.
when I …	…
…	

- when I'm with my family / …
- when I (don't) have school
- when my best friend / … doesn't text me
- when my parents / teachers are strict
- when my brother / … borrows my things
- when my mum / … doesn't have time for me

4 DIFF BANK

Unit 4

More help **3 Berry's homework** ▸ *Unit 4, p. 75*

d) Write a short text about your feelings. Use your notes from exercise 2 on p. 74. Write more than one sentence. Here are some ideas:

I feel great when I do sport.
My favourite sport is …
I often play with …

I feel great when I'm with my animals.
My (dog/cat/…) makes me happy.
We play every evening.

I feel fed up when my parents are strict.
They say: Do your homework!
Go to bed early!
You can't … (watch TV / go to the cinema with your friends/…)!

I feel fed up when my sister borrows my things.
She always borrows (my pullovers/…).
She never asks me.

//● **4 That's wrong!** ▸ *Unit 4, p. 77*

a) Correct the sentences. Use *doesn't* or *don't*. Then write the right sentences.

1 Berry lives in the city. – That's wrong! She doesn't live in the city. She lives in a village.
2 Berry's parents have a pet shop. – That's wrong! They don't … They have …
3 Berry rides a donkey. – That's wrong! … …
4 Berry has a cat. – That's wrong! … …
5 Berry's mum and dad have cows on the farm. – That's wrong! … …
6 Sam the dog lives in the field. – That's wrong! … …
7 Berry goes to school in Woolwell. – That's wrong! … …
8 Luca and Adam have dogs. – That's wrong! … …
9 Ellie has two ponies. – That's wrong! … …
10 Chipmunks like cats. – That's wrong! … …

Lösungen S. 236

//● **5 My interesting pets** ▸ *Unit 4, p. 77*

Complete the text. Put the verbs in brackets in the right form.

live • don't
likes • doesn't
don't have • have
doesn't come • comes
doesn't need • likes
don't need • like
don't like • hate
play • don't go

1 I … (live) in a small flat and we … (~~have~~) a garden.
2 My mum … (like) small pets. She … (~~want~~) a big pet.
3 I … (~~have~~) a 'normal' pet, like a dog. I … (have) three degus.
4 A degu … (~~come~~) from England. It … (come) from Chile.
5 A degu … (need) a friend. It … (~~like~~) to be lonely.
6 Degus … (need) lots of space. They … (~~like~~) small cages.
7 And degus … (~~like~~) other animals. They … (hate) dogs and cats.
8 I often … (play) with Pip, my favourite degu. But we … (~~go~~) outside.

Me and my degu

More practice 3 **More questions about pets** ▸ Unit 4, p. 78

With your partner think of three more questions for your dialogues on page 78. Use the ideas in the boxes or your own ideas.

Questions for partners with a pet:	Questions for partners with no pet:
Do you ... play with your pet? / talk to your pet? / go outside with your pet?	Does your mum / dad / ... like animals? / want a pet?
Where does your pet sleep?	Does your grandmother / your friend / ... have a pet?
Does your pet ... sleep in your room? / have a cage?	Do you play with the pet?

Erarb. Mp3 Lernstärkere bauen ihren Dialog weiter aus. Dazu können sie auf die Ideen und Fragemuster aus den beiden Boxen zurückgreifen.

More help **11** **Talking about pets** ▸ Unit 4, p. 78

b) Write about your favourite pet or a friend's pet. Use the ideas in the boxes.

My favourite pet	*Martin's pet*	*Pia's favourite pet*
I like / don't like	*Martin has a dog / cat / ....*	*Pia wants a pet.*
I have / don't have ...	*It lives in the house / a cage / ...*	*She doesn't want a cat / crocodile / ...*
My aunt / friend has a dog / ...	*It eats ...*	*She wants a degu / a hamster / ...*
It lives inside / in the garden /	*It likes games / ...*	*Hamsters / ... are cute / nice.*
It eats ...	*It doesn't like dogs / children / cars / ...*	*They eat ...*
		They live in a cage / outside / ...

▸ Wordbank 7, p. 177

More help **13** **Find someone who ...** ▸ Unit 4, p. 79

b) Ask questions like this:

Find someone who ...	Questions
... has an interesting pet.	Do you have an interesting pet? What pet do you have?
... has an interesting hobby.	Do you have an interesting hobby? What hobby do you have?
... gets up very early.	Do you get up very early? When do you get up?
... goes to a nice place in the holidays.	Do you go to a nice place in the holiday? Where do you go?
... likes an English football team.	Do you like an English football team? What team do you like?
... likes homework.	Do you like homework? What homework do you like?

Erarb. Mp4
● Lernstärkere formulieren gleich ganze Sätze → gelenkte *summary* der Geschichte. L gibt ggf. Bsp. vor: *The three friends are excited because they can go to the country.*
Ausw. Mp4 im Plenum: S tragen Antworten vor. L notiert richtige Lösungen an Tafel (für Abgleich und Korrektur).

Unit 4

More practice 4 ● More questions on the story ▸ Unit 4, p. 81

Answer the questions.

1 Why are the three friends excited? – Because ...
2 Why is Luca unhappy? – Because ...
3 Why does Luca go to the village? – Because ...
4 Is Luca really in trouble? Why / Why not? – ...
5 What do the friends do on Saturday evening? – ...
6 What do they do on Sunday? – ...

1 (The three friends are excited) Because they can go to the country / visit Berry on her farm. • **2** (Luca is unhappy) Because he hasn't got his sweets. • **3** (He goes to the village) Because he wants to buy sweets. • **4** No, (Luca isn't in trouble) because the bull is a cow. • **5** (On Saturday evening) They sleep in the barn. • **6** (On Sunday) They play on the trampolines. They ride Harry, the pony and feed the animals too.

More help 4 THEATRE TIME ▸ Unit 4, p. 81

Here are some ideas to help you to act the story:

1	Die Geschichte soll spannend klingen, deshalb solltet ihr die Sätze mit Betonung sprechen.	→ For ideas, listen to the story on the CD.
2	Lest nicht alles vor. Anweisungen und Beschreibungen wie "Ellie says" oder "Adam says" könnt ihr weglassen.	→ In your group read through your scene. Which words can you leave out?
3	Andere Dinge könnt ihr weglassen, weil ihr schauspielert. Im Text steht z.B. "Everybody laughs. But Luca doesn't laugh." Also hier lachen alle, außer Luca!	→ Are there more parts in your scene like this?

Unit 4 Stop! Check! Go!

More help 3 REVISION A day with my family ▸ Unit 4, p. 87

b) Make a table like this for a day with your family. You can use some ideas from the boxes.
Then tell your partner.

When?	*Who?*	*What?*
every morning / before 6 o'clock	*mum, dad and I*	*get up*

When?
– Every day / morning / afternoon / evening
– Before breakfast / lunch / dinner / school
– After breakfast / lunch / dinner / school
– In the morning / afternoon / evening
– At 10 o'clock / 11.15 / 12.30 / 1.45

Who?
– I
– my mum
– my dad
– my brother
– my sister
– my aunt
– ...

What?
– get up / have breakfast / feed my hamster / ...
– go to school / go to work
– stay at home / work at home
– go shopping / have lunch
– come home from work / from school
– do homework / do sport / play a game
– watch TV / meet friends / read a book
– make / have dinner with ...
– go to bed

//● 4 LANGUAGE An interview with Cyril and Sandy

▸ Unit 4, p. 87

Lösung s. KV 4.8

a) Make the questions for the reporter.

1 Plymouth / you / ... / like / ?
2 you / ... / a best friend / have / ?
3 you and Sandy / live / ... / on the beach / ?
4 like / ... / Sandy / Plymouth too / ?
5 Sandy/ have / a best friend / ... / ?

– Yes, it's great.
– Yes, I do. Her name is Sandy.
– Yes, we live in Kingsand.
– Yes, she loves Plymouth.
– Yes, she does. I'm her best friend!

b) Complete Cyril's answers.

1 Do you like Mr Johnson?
2 Do you live in a big house?
3 Do you and Sandy go to school?
4 Does Sandy have a car?
5 Does Sandy eat crabs?

– No, I ... (~~like~~) Mr Johnson. He's terrible.
– No, I ... (~~live~~) in a big house. I like small houses.
– No, we ... (~~go~~) to school.
– No, she ... (~~have~~) a car. But she has a bike.
– No, she ... (~~eat~~) crabs. I'm a crab!

c) Complete the questions for Sandy.

1 ... do you live?
2 ... do you get up?
3 ... do you have breakfast?
4 ... do you do after breakfast?
5 ... do you like Cyril?

– In Kingsand.
– Very late – after 10 o'clock.
– I always have breakfast on the beach.
– I often go to Plymouth.
– Because he's friendly and he's fun!

More help 6 WRITING Luca and you

▸ Unit 4, p. 88

a) Write the dialogue with Luca in your exercise book.
Write as much as you can.

Luca	You
Hi, I'm Luca. What's your name?	– Hi, Luca. I'm ...
Do you live in England?	– No, I live in ...
Do you live in the country?	– Yes / No, I live in a city / town / village.
Do you like English?	– Yes, it's great. / No, it isn't easy.
Do you have a pet?	– Yes, I have a ... / No, I don't. But I want a ...
When do you feel fed up?	– I feel fed up when my friend doesn't text me / when I have lots of homework / ...
When do you feel great?	– I feel great when I do sport / when I'm with my friends / when I have holidays / ...
Do you want to come to Plymouth?	– Yes, I do. Great! / No, thanks.

Unit 4 — Stop! Check! Go!

More help **7** **SPEAKING** **An interview with a student in your class** ▸ *Unit 4, p. 88*

a) Here are some more ideas for your interview questions:

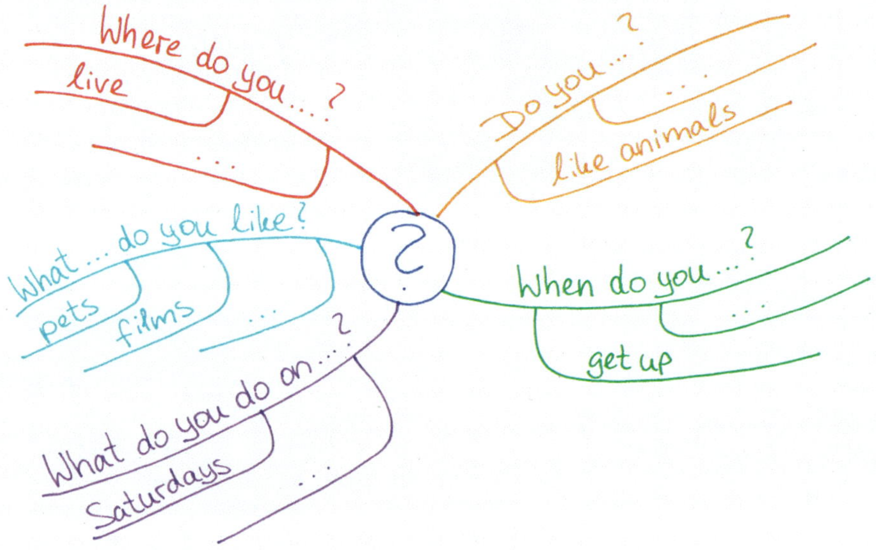

More help **8** **PROJECT** **Interesting animals** ▸ *Unit 4, p. 89*

b) You can write a text like this about your animal.

My project is about chipmunks.
Chipmunks come from the USA. They're brown, grey and black. They're furry and very cute.
They're small – 13 to 15 cm long.
They live in a nest, in the ground.
They eat fruit and nuts. They usually live for three years[1].
Chipmunks are fun, but they aren't good pets.

Unit 5

More help **1** **The harbour in Plymouth** ▸ *Unit 5, p. 90*

b) How many of the things in the box can you find on pages 90–91? Write a list.

baby • beach • bike • blazer • bus • car • chair • child/children • city • dog • garden • helmet • house • kid • man • park • people • phone • restaurant • road • sea • seagull • shop • sign • swimming pool • table • teenagers • tree • visitors • …

[1] for three years *drei Jahre lang*

More help **Can I help you?** ► Unit 5, p. 92

d) Make a dialogue in a cafe.

Here are some useful words and phrases.

What can you eat?
a sandwich • a chicken sandwich • omelette and chips • fish and chips • a salad • soup • scones • …

What can you drink?
- a bottle of water/juice
- a cup of coffee/tea
- a bottle of orange/ banana / … juice

Can I help you?
↓
…, please.
↓
Something to drink?
↓
…, please.
↓
Anything else?
↙ And …, please. | ↓ | ↘ No, thanks. That's all.
↓
That's £…, please.
↓
OK. £… – Here you are.
↓
Thanks. Next, please.

More practice 1 **Adam and his family** ► Unit 5, p. 93

Finish the sentences about Adam and his family. You can use the ideas in the box.

1 Adam's dad works on …
2 Adam's dad likes …
3 But Adam misses …
4 The cafe is often …
5 Adam's mum works …
6 Adam sometimes helps in …
7 At school Adam isn't very …
8 And he isn't doing … at the moment.

a ferry • happy • his dad • his homework • his new job • the cafe • very busy • very hard

1 a ferry
2 his new job
3 his dad
4 very busy
5 very hard
6 the cafe
7 happy
8 his homework

More help **2** **Welcome to PMZ** ► Unit 5, p. 95

c) Copy this table. Listen again and put in the notes from the box.

PMZ address: …	Times (Sat): … …
Bus number: …	Price: …
Times (Mon–Fri): … …	

- From 4 pm to 7 pm
- From 10 am to 12.30 pm.
- Raglan Road
- Free
- 34

Unit 5

More help 3 NOW YOU ▸ Unit 5, p. 95

a) Appointments: Copy this table and write your answers.

	Me	1 o'clock …	2 o'clock …
What's your favourite band?			
Who's your favourite singer?			
What's your favourite English song?			
Can you play an instrument? What instrument?			
Can you sing? Can you rap?			
Are you in a band?			

▸ Wordbank 8, p. 177

More help 3 NOW YOU ▸ Unit 5, p. 95

d) Write a text about you and music. Here are some ideas.
You can put your text in your DOSSIER.

I love pop / rap / … music
My favourite band / singer is …
My favourite English song is …
I (can't) play an instrument.
My favourite instrument is the guitar / drums / …
I play the guitar / piano / …
I can sing / rap / …
I'm in a band. / My friend is in a band.
The name of the band is …

Erarb. Mp2a–c
schriftl. Übung der Verbformen, bei denen im *present progressive* die Endung *-e* wegfällt oder der letzte Konsonant verdoppelt wird. S markieren diese Besonderheiten der Schreibung im Heft
Ausw. Mp2a–c Zunächst Partner check: abwechselnd Sätze vorlesen und Sichern der richtigen Schreibweise, durch Nachweisen im SB, z. B. *sitting* durch Belegstelle *They're sitting in a park* (S. 96) oder durch die Regel im *Language file* 10, S. 171. Anschließend Sicherung im Plenum.

More practice 2 What's the fourth word? ▸ Unit 5, p. 97

a) Just add 'ing'.
1 read – reading
clean – …
2 eat – eating
do – …

b) There's no 'e' with -ing!
1 ride – riding
make – …
2 come – coming
write – …

c) Look at the examples!
1 rap – rapping
get – …
2 swim – swimming
sit – …

a) 1 cleaning 2 doing • b) 1 making 2 writing • c) 1 getting 2 sitting

More practice 3 What are they saying?

▸ Unit 5, p. 97

Finish the sentences A–F. Use the *present progressive*.

A

Berry — It's 2 o'clock. We're late, Ellie!
Ellie — OK, I... (come)!

B

Adam — Is Luca at home?
Ms Boateng — Sorry, Luca ... (ride) his bike in the park.

C

Ms Lee — What are you doing, Ellie?
Ellie — Sorry, Miss. I... (eat) a sweet.

D

Ms Lee — Is Ellie OK?
Berry — She... (feel) tired.

E

Adam — Are they looking at me?
Luca — No, they... (look) at me!

F

Adam — Who... (sit) here?
Luca — Ellie. Look, she's there.

Erarb. Mp3 gemäß Aufgabe
Ausw. Mp3 Zunächst Partner check: abwechselnd Sätze vorlesen und Sichern der richtigen Schreibweise, durch Nachweisen im SB, z. B. *sitting* durch Belegstelle *They're sitting in a park* (S. 96) oder durch die Regel im *Language file* 10, S. 171. Anschließend Sicherung im Plenum.

A I 'm coming • **B** Luca's riding • **C** I'm eating • **D** She's feeling • **E** they're looking • **F** Who's sitting

4 What's Cyril doing?

▸ Unit 5, p. 97

a) What's Cyril doing now? Write the numbers 1–5. Then listen and write what you think.
Example: *1 Cyril is ..., 2 ...*

Unit 5

Erarb. Mp4 schriftl. in EA gemäß Aufgabe
Ausw. Mp4 S lesen die Texte ihrer Mit-S reihum in Kleingruppen (à 3–4 S)

More practice 4 An email to Adam

▸ Unit 5, p. 99

Write an email to Adam about the story. Here are some ideas.

I think	the girls and boys on the bus were ... you were ... Josie was ... your rap is ... PMZ is ... your parents are ...

bad • boring • bossy • cool • different • friendly • fun • great • good • happy • important • interesting • mean • nervous • nice • stupid • terrible • ...

Dear Adam

I think the story about you at PMZ is ...

Best wishes
(Your name)

You can also tell Adam something about you:
– Do you like rap?
– Who's your favourite rapper?
– Can you rap?
– ...

More help 1 In the park

▸ Unit 5, p. 100

b) What are they doing? Make sentences.

On the left In the middle On the right	two dogs a boy three girls children a girl a baby two men	are working. are eating. is riding a bike. is sleeping are playing football. are talking and laughing. is reading a book.

More help 3 WRITING A text to Amanda

▸ Unit 5, p. 101

Write a text message to Amanda. Here are some ideas for your text.

Amanda

- I'm sitting at home / ...
- I'm (not) working hard / ...
- I'm learning English / doing my homework / ...
- My friend / mum / brother / ... is here.
- He's / She's listening 2 music / ...
- I'm feeling gr8 / happy / terrible / ...
- How R U?
- Yes, I can come 2 the party.
- Sorry. I can't come 2 the party.

Unit 5 Stop! Check! Go!

More help 1 REVISION Questions and answers ► Unit 5, p. 104

d) Make a quiz about another animal. Use these ideas:

- Do ... live in Germany?
- Do ... live in fields / on farms / in the sea / ...?
- Do ... live in cages / in zoos / ...?
- Do ... eat fruit / nuts / special food / other animals / ...?
- Do ... like people?
- Do ... walk fast?

More help 8 READING and WRITING On Saturday morning ► Unit 5, p. 107

b) Here are some ideas for another picture for the story.

I'm hungry. • A big chicken sandwich, please. • Can I help you? • Anything else? • ...

Hi, Dad. • You're early. • That's great. • This is a surprise. • I'm really happy. • How's it going? • How are you? • ...

Unit 6

More help 1 Planning a trip ► Unit 6, p. 110

a) What things can you bring to the beach? Start a network like this. Then read the text for more ideas.

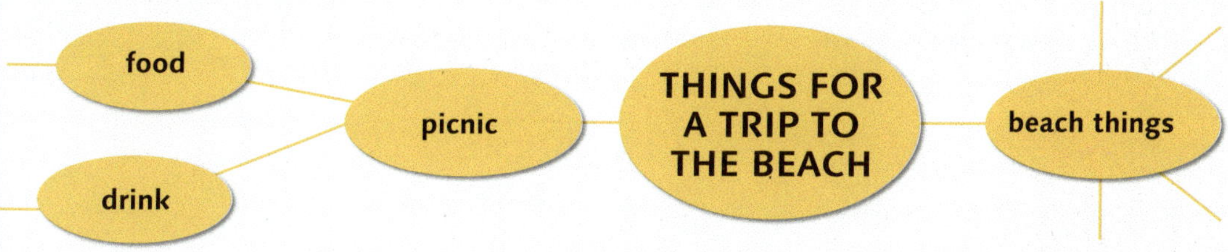

Unit 6

More help 2 You're going on a ferry trip! ▸ Unit 6, p. 112

b) Talk to a partner.

What's the ferry trip like? – It's fun / nice / ...
What do you see? – The harbour / ...
What do you hear? – The noisy ferry / ...
What do you feel? – The cool water / ...

the sea • seagulls • the harbour • buses • the cool water • the city • a beach • the noisy ferry • an old woman • a cafe • lots of kids • the swimming pool • cars • a village • nice houses • a man / ... • ...

//● 2 What are your summer plans? ▸ Unit 6, p. 116

Work with a partner. Talk about your summer plans.

A	B
Begrüße deinen Partner / deine Partnerin. Frage, wie es ihm / ihr geht.	
	Grüße zurück. Sage, wie es dir geht.
Frage, was er / sie im Sommer vorhat.	
	Sage, was du vorhast. (2 oder 3 Ideen)
	Nun frage deinen Partner / deine Partnerin, was er / sie vorhat.
Sage, wie du die Pläne deines Partners / deiner Partnerin findest.	
Sage, was <u>du</u> vorhast.	
	Sage, wie du die Pläne deines Partners / deiner Partnerin findest.

More help 2 People and places: A ferry trip to Cawsand ▸ Unit 6, p. 117

a) You're going on a ferry trip to Cawsand.
What do you think you can see?
Make a list.

buses • people • bags • food • shops • dogs • seagulls • bikes • cars • crabs • a ferry • boats • a harbour • houses • books • a beach • the sea • tents • picnics • smugglers • sunglasses • kids • tickets • a map • ...

Lösungsbeispiel:
Cyril: Thanks, Sandy!
Sandy: That's OK, Cyril. We're friends.
Cyril: Yes, we're good friends!
Sandy: Are you OK now?
Cyril: (Yes,) I'm OK. Toby is a stupid boy.
Sandy: The Johnsons are stupid.
Cyril: Is the picnic good?
Sandy: (Yes,) This is good!
Cyril: Oh, thanks, Johnsons!
Sandy: Yeah, thanks, Toby!

TF 2

More practice **You stupid boy!** ▸ *Text file 2, p. 151*

Use your Cyril and Sandy puppets. Act a scene. The ideas in the boxes can help you.

- Thanks Sandy!
- Yes, we're good friends!
- Toby is a stupid boy.
- I'm OK.
- Is the picnic good?
- Oh, thanks, Johnsons!
- ...

- That's OK, Cyril.
- Are you OK now?
- We're friends.
- The Johnsons are stupid.
- This is good!
- Yeah, thanks, Toby!
- ...

Erarb. Mp Zur weiteren Vertiefung und Fortsetzung der Geschichte ordnen die S die angebotenen Redemittel, sodass ein Dialog zwischen Sandy und Cyril entsteht. L kann darauf hinweisen, dass mehrere Ideen zu einem Redebeitrag zusammengefasst und ggf. Füllwörter hinzugefügt werden können.
S üben den Dialog ein und spielen Szene mithilfe der Stabpuppen aus TF 1.

2 NOW YOU ▸ *Unit 5, p. 100*

Partner A

a) Describe *picture 1* to your partner. Say what you can see, where the things and people are, and what they're doing:
On the left / In the middle / On the right I can see ...
There's a ... next to / in front of ...
He's / She's playing ...

Your partner listens and looks at his / her picture. Some things are different in your picture. He / She must find five differences.

b) Then listen to your partner. He/She is talking about *picture 2*. There are five differences in your picture. When you hear a difference, tell your partner.
In my picture there's a seagull on the ...
In my picture the boy is ...

1

2

Lösung:

Unit 1

1 The unit quiz ▸ *Unit 1, p. 22*

Check your anwers:

1 Plymouth
2 Ellie and Berry
3 Luca
4 Luca and Jack
5 Harry / Berry's pet
6 Ms Lee
7 Berry
8 Ellie, Berry, Luca, Adam
9 Grace / Luca's sister
10 Ellie
11 PE
12 (your name)

Lernschwerpunkt: Gespräche zum Kennenlernen führen
Storyline: Die Lehrwerksmaskottchen Cyril und Sandy führen Gespräche zum Kennenlernen
Kompetenzen: Speaking In der Rolle von Cyril und Sandy ein Gespräch zum Kennenlernen einüben und präsentieren | **Reading** Mithilfe von Bildern eine Bastelanleitung verstehen | **Lern- und Arbeitstechniken** Eine Bastelanleitung verstehen und umsetzen
Redemittel: Begrüßung und Kurzkonversation

Einstieg (SB geschl.)
L: *Do you remember Cyril and Sandy? What animals are they? (crab, seagull) Today we are going to make crab and seagull puppets.*
L zeigt Muster (empfohlen) oder verweist auf die Abbildung im SB.
Erarb. (SB offen) Anhand der Bilder und Bildunterschriften legen S Bastelutensilien bereit. Dann **1. Lesen** der Bastelanleitung im Zusammenhang (Plenum) und Klärung von Fragen.

TEXT FILE

▸ KV KV F.1

TF 1 Puppets[1] for your classroom[2]

Make crab and seagull puppets for your classroom.

[1] puppet ['pʌpɪt] *Handpuppe* [2] classroom ['klɑːsruːm] *Klassenzimmer*

TEXT FILE Navigator | Vorbereitung

Zeitbedarf: ca. zwei Stunden

Kooperative Lernformen: Partner talk STEP **4**

Materialbedarf: Tonpapier oder Zeichenkarton (orange und/oder weiß), Schere, Stifte, Strohhalme, durchsichtiges Klebeband, Gefäß (z. B. Blumenkasten) mit Sand oder Steckmasse

Einsatz von Begleitmedien: KV TF.1

You need[1] ...

two cards

scissors

felt tips or crayons[1)]

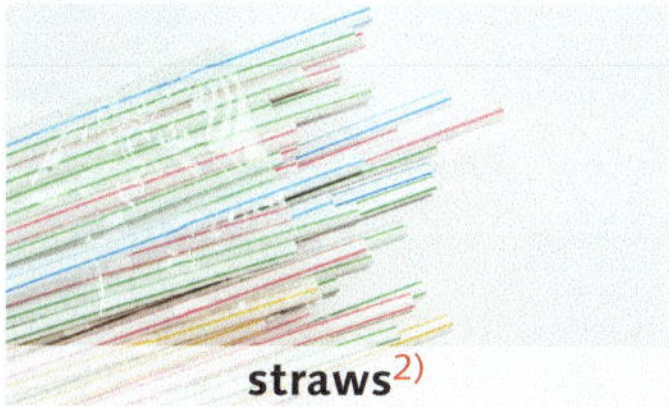

straws[2)]

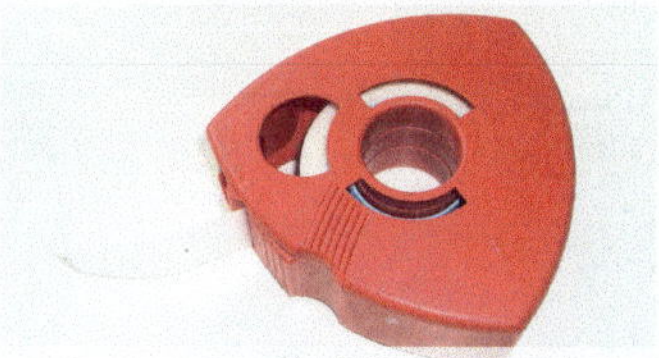

cellotape

STEP 1: Copy or draw a puppet on the card.

STEP 2: Cut out the puppet.
Put the straw on your puppet.

STEP 3: Make a 'beach' for your puppets.

STEP 4: Make dialogues with your puppets.

Erarb. STEP 1: S zeichnen oder kopieren mithilfe von Pergamentpapier die Umrisse auf Tonpapier.
Alternative Zeitersparnis durch KV TF.1 (auf A3 kopieren).
Erarb. STEP 2: S schneiden die Tiere aus, gestalten sie und befestigen den Strohhalm als Griff.
Erarb. STEP 3: L oder S bringen Material zur Gestaltung eines Strandes oder mehrerer Strände mit (Blumenkasten, Sand, Muscheln etc.). Die Stabpuppen werden auf dem „Strand" zusammengebracht und in einem Gallery walk gewürdigt.
Erarb. STEP 4: Je zwei S mit einer Cyril- und einer Sandy-Puppe erarbeiten ein Gespräch zum Kennenlernen, wobei sie die Fragemuster aus *Nice to meet you!* aufgreifen können.
O In lernschwächeren Klassen kann L vorab Redemittel sammeln lassen oder bereitstellen (Tafel, Folie).

[1] need [niːd] *brauchen*

1 ['kreɪənz] 2 [strɔːz]

TEXT FILE Navigator | Inhalt

Lernschwerpunkt: **Einen Comic verstehen**

Storyline: Cyril und Sandy setzen sich am Strand gegen die Familie Johnson zur Wehr.

Kompetenzen: **Reading** Einen Comic verstehen | **Writing** Eine Comicgeschichte fortsetzen (More practice) | **Lern- und Arbeitstechniken** Einen Comicdialog szenisch präsentieren (More practice)

Zeitbedarf: ca. eine Stunde

Materialbedarf: Stabpuppen aus TF 1 (More practice)

Einstieg (SB geschl.) Anknüpfen an Vorkenntnisse der S: L schreibt *A nice day on the beach* an und zeichnet darunter eine Strichmännchenfamilie. S sagen, was für sie einen schönen Strandtag mit der Familie ausmacht. Die S-Äußerungen werden notiert.
Überleitung L: *And what's a nice day on the beach for Cyril and Sandy? What do they like? Let's find out.*
Erarb. (SB offen) S betrachten die Bilder und benennen die Protagonisten der Geschichte (Cyril, Sandy, Mr und Mrs Johnson, Toby Johnson).
Hinweis: Da Mr Johnson erst im *Stop! Check! Go!* zu Unit 1 eingeführt wird, kann L ggf. vor Behandlung des TF 2 das Bild auf Seite 30 präsentieren und erklären: *Mr Johnson isn't nice. He likes crabs because he likes fishing.*
1. Lesen in Stillarbeit (nur Sprechblasen). Leseauftrag: *Look at the pictures and the speech bubbles and find out: Is it a nice day for the Johnsons? (No, it isn't.) ... and for Cyril and Sandy? (Yes, it is – in the end.)*
Anschließend **2. Lesen** des kompletten Comics laut im Plenum (oder in Gruppen à sechs S). S lesen Sprechblasen mit verteilten Rollen; L oder ein lernstärkerer S liest die Bildunterschriften.

TEXT FILE

TF 2 You stupid boy!

1

It's Sunday morning at Kingsand. Cyril is on the beach. No people. No children. Cyril is happy!

2

Sandy is near the beach. No people. No children. No lunch for Sandy! She isn't very happy!

3

Look! It's Mr Johnson, Mrs Johnson and Toby Johnson! They're very happy – a nice day on the beach!

4

Look! Sandy is on the beach now. She's with Cyril. Cyril isn't happy now.

5

6

Can Toby Johnson see Cyril? Can he see Benny and Babe?

7

Toby can see Cyril!

8

Go, Cyril, go!

9

Toby has Cyril!

Cyril isn't very happy. But Toby is happy!

Benny and Babe are Cyril's friends. They're next!

Toby isn't very happy now!

Where's Toby?

Cyril is OK now!

Mrs Johnson can't[1] see Toby.

Toby is wet[2]. He's cold. He isn't happy.

The nice day on the beach is over – for the Johnsons.

More practice p.147

[1] can't [kɑːnt] *kann nicht* [2] wet [wet] *nass*

Lernschwerpunkt: Eine längere Geschichte verstehen, Weihnachtsbräuche in Großbritannien kennenlernen
Storyline: Ellie feiert mit ihrer Familie Weihnachten.
Kompetenzen: Reading Eine längere Geschichte verstehen (bildgestützt), einer Geschichte Informationen über Weihnachtsbräuche in Großbritannien entnehmen
Redemittel: Weihnachtsbräuche
Zeitbedarf: ca. zwei Stunden
Materialbedarf: (optional) Audio-CD + Player oder MP3 + PC/Lautsprecher

Einstieg (SB geschl.)
L schreibt das Thema Christmas an und aktiviert Vorwissen zum britischen Weihnachtsfest. L: *What do you know about Christmas in Great Britain? When do British children get their Christmas presents? (on 25th December) Who brings the presents? (Father Christmas) What do English families eat for Christmas? (turkey) Do you know any English Christmas songs? (Rudolph, the Rednosed Reindeer, …)*
L sammelt Ideen der S an der Tafel.
Überleitung
L: *Let's see what Ellie and her family do at Christmas.*
Erarb. (SB offen)
L: *Look at the pictures and try to remember as many details as possible. You have two minutes.*
Anschließend stellt L Fragen zu den Bildern und kann auf diese Weise auch unbekannten Wortschatz einführen.
Mögliche Fragen zum Abschnitt *24th December:*
Where are Ellie and her mum?
What's the name of the toy shop?
Who's in the living room? Who can you see outside the window?
What can you read on the Christmas cards?

TEXT FILE

▸ KV 59

TF 3 The best Christmas present[1]

3.11–3.13

24th December: Christmas Eve[2]

It's Christmas Eve and there are lots of people in Plymouth. They all need things for Christmas. Ellie and her mum are in Plymouth too. First they go to the big supermarket. It's very busy. They need icing[3] for the Christmas cake[4]. Then they go to *Whoopee*, a nice toy[5] shop. Ellie buys a present for Finn – a small red crab.
Now Ellie and her mum are at home. Pete and Conor are there too. But Zoe isn't at home. She's with her boyfriend, Alan.

There are lots of jobs for Christmas Day[6]. Ellie helps her mum with the Christmas cake.

The living room is very nice. There are lots of Christmas cards and decorations. Conor and Ellie put[7] decorations on the Christmas tree.
"It's great!" Pete says.
"It's really nice!" mum says.

"Ding-dong." Carol singers are at the door.

"We wish you a Merry Christmas,
We wish you a Merry Christmas,
We wish you a Merry Christmas
And a Happy New Year."

"Ding-dong." Now Zoe is at the door too. But she isn't happy.
"Hi, Zoe," mum says. "What's the problem?"
"I think it's over with Alan and me," Zoe says and she goes to her room.

1 Christmas present ['krɪsməs preznt] *Weihnachtsgeschenk* 2 Christmas Eve [krɪsməs 'iːv] *Heiligabend* 3 icing ['aɪsɪŋ] *Zuckerguss* 4 cake [keɪk] *Kuchen* 5 toy [tɔɪ] *Spielzeug* 6 Christmas Day [krɪsməs 'deɪ] *1. Weihnachtsfeiertag* 7 put [pʊt] *hängen*

25th December: Christmas Day

It's Christmas morning – 6 o'clock. Ellie is in bed.
"Zoe! Zoe!" she says.
"What?" Zoe says.

"Our Christmas stockings[1] are here!" Ellie says.
She looks into her stocking.
"Oh, look Zoe. A computer game – *Let's Dance!* Great!"
"Ellie, please be quiet," Zoe says.
"And a book ... and a new hoodie ... and chocolate ... Thank you, Father Christmas," Ellie says and she laughs[2].
Ellie is happy. But Zoe isn't very happy.

Later the family has a big Christmas breakfast. Then they go to the living room. It's present time.
"Here's a present for you, Conor. It's from Pete," mum says.

"Thanks dad," Conor says. "Oh, speakers – great!"
"And here's a present for you Zoe – from Alan," mum says.
"I don't want it![3]" Zoe says and she goes to her room. She isn't very happy.

It's time for Christmas lunch. There are lots of nice things – a big turkey[4], potatoes[5], vegetables[6]. And then there's Christmas pudding. And they all have Christmas crackers.
"Conor, pull[7] a cracker with me," Ellie says.

BANG! In the cracker there's a small present – a pen. There's a paper hat[8] and a joke[9] too.
"Why[10] is it always cold at Christmas?" Ellie reads.
"Er ... no idea! What's the answer?" Pete says.
"Because it's Decemberrrrrrrrr!" Ellie says and they all laugh.
"Zoe, pull a cracker with me," Pete says.
"No, thanks," Zoe says.

Fragen zu den Bildern zum Abschnitt *25th December:*
When do Zoe and Ellie get up on Christmas morning? What's on the dinner table?

Christmas dinner

Christmas pudding

[1] stocking ['stɒkɪŋ] *(langer) Strumpf* [2] laugh [lɑːf] *lachen* [3] I don't want it! [dəʊnt 'wɒnt] *Ich will es nicht!*
[4] turkey ['tɜːki] *Truthahn* [5] potatoes [pə'teɪtəʊz] *Kartoffeln* [6] vegetable ['vedʒtəbl] *Gemüse* [7] pull [pʊl] *ziehen*
[8] hat [hæt] *Hut* [9] joke [dʒəʊk] *Witz* [10] why [waɪ] *warum*

Fragen zu den Bildern zum Abschnitt *Later on Christmas day: Who's watching TV? Who is on TV? Who are the two text messages from?* Anschließend **1. Lesen** der gesamten Geschichte im Plenum, z. B. im Mitleseverfahren.

TEXT FILE

Later on Christmas Day

The Queen's Christmas Message[2]

"Ellie, it's your dad," Conor says. "He's at the door."
"Happy Christmas, dad," Ellie says.
"Happy Christmas, Ellie. Let's go to our flat, to Finn and Alisha," her dad says.
It's Finn's first Christmas.
He's very happy.
And his present from Ellie is great.

Erarb. Ex 1 (SB offen) S ordnen den abgebildeten Gegenständen die passenden Begriffe zu.

At 3 o'clock the Queen[1] is on TV. She's always on TV on Christmas Day.
"At Christmas, family and friends are very important ...," the Queen says.
Ellie has an idea. She writes a text message on her mobile phone to Alan, Zoe's boyfriend:

Later Ellie is in the kitchen with her dad, Finn and Alisha. It's time for tea and Christmas cake. Ellie has a text message from Zoe:

Erarb. Ex 2 (SB offen) **2. Lesen**: S notieren R für *right* und W für *wrong* hinter die Satznummern.
Ausw. Ex 2 Erstkontrolle durch Partner check. Anschließend Abgleich im Plenum, z. B. mithilfe von Right/wrong cards.
Lernstärkere S korrigieren die falschen Aussagen.

1 Christmas in Britain

What are the Christmas things (1–5) in the photo?

a paper hat • a turkey • a Christmas cracker • a Christmas tree • a Christmas card

1 a Christmas card • 2 a Christmas tree) • 3 a turkey • 4 a paper hat • 5 a Christmas cracker

2 Be a Christmas detective: Right or wrong?

1 Right. • 2 Wrong. (Christmas Day) • 3 Right. • 4 Right. • 5 Wrong. (There are presents from the family under the tree.) • 6 Wrong. (There's turkey for lunch on Christmas Day.) • 7 Right. • 8 Wrong. (on Christmas Day)

1. On Christmas Eve lots of people go shopping.
2. In Britain people get presents on Christmas Eve.
3. Carol singers go from door to door and sing Christmas songs.
4. The presents in the Christmas stockings are from Father Christmas.
5. There are no presents under[3] the Christmas tree.
6. There's fish for lunch on Christmas Day.
7. There's a small present, a paper hat and a joke in a Christmas cracker.
8. The Queen is on TV on Christmas Eve.

[1] queen [kwiːn] *Königin* [2] Christmas Message [ˈkrɪsməs mesɪdʒ] *Weihnachtsansprache* [3] under [ˈʌndə] *unter*

Lernschwerpunkt: **Die Sportart BMX und eine englische BMX-Sportlerin kennenlernen**
Kompetenzen: **Reading** Eine Grafik, kurze Sachtexte und einen Zeitungsartikel verstehen
Lern- und Arbeitstechniken Die Bedeutung unbekannter Wörter mithilfe von Bildern erschließen
Redemittel: Sport, Fahrrad, BMX
Zeitbedarf: ca. eine Stunde
Materialbedarf: Tonpapier für Plakate

TF 4 What's bicycle[1] motocross?

Bicycle motocross (BMX) is a popular bicycle sport.

The equipment[2]

Where you can ride

On a track[5] – You can ride your bike on a special BMX track. BMX is a new Olympic sport. It's very fast[6].

In a special park – You can do tricks on your bike in BMX parks or skateboard parks. There are special jumps[7].

In the street – You can ride in the street or in a sports hall. You can do tricks there too. You don't need jumps.

THE PLYMOUTH NEWS

A world champion

This is Shanaze Reade. She's from England. Her dad is from Jamaica. Her mum is from Ireland.
Shanaze rides on BMX tracks all around the world for the British national team. She's the world champion of 2008.
She got[8] her first BMX bike when she was 10. It was £1!

Shanaze Reade

Find a picture of your bike or your dream bike. Make labels for the bike.

[1] bicycle [ˈbaɪsɪkl] *Fahrrad* [2] equipment [ɪˈkwɪpmənt] *Ausrüstung* [3] low [ləʊ] *niedrig* [4] gears (pl) [ɡɪəz] *Gänge; Gangschaltung* [5] track [træk] *Piste* [6] fast [fɑːst] *schnell* [7] jump [dʒʌmp] *Schanze, Rampe (zum Springen)* [8] got [ɡɒt] *bekam*

Einstieg (SB geschl.)
L knüpft an Vorwissen der S zu Luca an: *What's Luca's favourite thing? (his bike) It's a special bike: a BMX bike. Do you know what BMX means?*
L schreibt Langform an die Tafel:
BICYCLE MOTOCROSS
B M X

Überleitung L: *Let's find out more about this sport.*

Erarb. The equipment
(SB offen) S betrachten die beschriftete Abbildung und erschließen die deutsche Bedeutung der Begriffe. Die Annotationen und ggf. ein Wörterbuch können unterstützend hinzugezogen werden.
Überleitung L: *Do you ride a BMX bike? Do you know where you can ride BMX bikes (around here)? Look at the photos for ideas.*

Erarb. Where you can ride
1. Lesen der drei Beschreibungen laut im Plenum.

Erarb. A world champion
1. Lesen des Artikels je nach Lernstärke der Klasse in Stillarbeit oder gemeinsam im Plenum.
Fragen zum Globalverstehen: *Who is the BMX world champion of 2008? Where's she from?*
Zur Sicherung des Detailverstehens können S einen Steckbrief zu Shanaze Reade anfertigen.
Abschließend fertigen S in EA ein Poster bzw. beschriftetes Bild ihres Fahrrads an (**HA**).

Auswertung Gallery walk

TEXT FILE Navigator | Inhalt

Lernschwerpunkt: **Eine längere Geschichte verstehen**

Storyline: Ben, ein neuer Klassenkamerad von Ellie, Berry, Luca und Adam, gehört zu einem Wanderzirkus. Die Kinder besuchen ihn im Zirkus und erhalten die Chance, hinter die Kulissen zu blicken.

Kompetenzen: Reading Die Handlung und ausgewählte Details eines längeren Erzähltextes erfassen (bildgestützt)

Redemittel: Die Welt der Unterhaltung

Zeitbedarf: ca. zwei Stunden

Materialbedarf: (optional) Audio-CD + Player oder MP3 + PC/Lautsprecher

Einstieg (SB offen) Gespräch über die Bilder. L: *Who can you see in the pictures? (Ellie, Adam, Luca, Berry, a new boy with red hair) Where are they? (classroom, canteen, show/circus)*

Überleitung L: *Let's find out more about the new boy.*

Erarb. Es empfiehlt sich, den Text abschnittsweise zu erarbeiten (Mitleseverfahren) und am Ende jedes Abschnitts die Verständnisfragen 1–7 zu klären.
Vor der Präsentation des letzten Abschnitts spekulieren die S über Bens Gefühlslage zum Abschied.
L hält die Ideen an der Tafel fest. Nach der Präsentation vergleichen die S ihre Ideen mit den Eindrücken aus dem Text (Frage 7).

Hinweis: Die Tonaufnahme enthält jeweils zwei Abschnitte hintereinander, sodass L die Aufnahme ggf. nach jedem Abschnitt stoppen muss.

Auswertung Vertiefendes Unterrichtsgespräch. L: *Look at the title of the story again. What do you think: Is it the greatest show on earth? Why do you think so?*

TEXT FILE

▸ *KV 60*

TF 5 The greatest show on earth[1]

3.14–3.16

It's 9 o'clock on Friday morning. The classroom is noisy because the teacher isn't there. All the students are happy. They like Fridays. Then Ms Lee comes in – with a boy. "Good morning," she says. "We have a new student." All the students look at the new boy.
"This is Ben", Ms Lee says.
"Hello," Ben says. He's very quiet and doesn't look happy.
"Ben is from Russell's Circus," Ms Lee says.
"Wow – a circus!" Luca says.
"Do you live in Plymouth?" Ellie asks.
"No. We're here for two weeks," Ben says. "We go to different towns and I go to different schools."
"Cool," Berry says.

1 How does Ben feel at 9 o'clock?

1 Ben feels unhappy and alone.

It's 1 o'clock, time for lunch, Ellie, Adam, Luca and Berry are in the canteen. They see Ben.
"Hi, Ben. Do you want to sit with us?" Berry asks.
"Sure, thanks," Ben says.

"I bet[2] life in a circus is fun," Adam says.
"Yeah, it's OK," Ben says.
"Where do you live?" Ellie asks.
"In a caravan. We're in Central Park now," Ben says.
"Cool – it's like camping!" Luca says.
"And what animals do you have?" Adam asks.
"We don't have animals in our circus," Ben says.
Luca is surprised. "No animals? Why?"
"Because it isn't good for animals to live in a circus," Ben says.
"But a circus with no animals – that isn't a real circus," Adam says.
"You can visit our circus and see a real circus – with no animals," Ben says.
"Great. When can we come?" Berry asks.
"Tomorrow is Saturday. Come tomorrow morning," Ben says.
"OK. See you tomorrow morning."

2 He feels happy because he can talk to Berry, Ellie, Luca and Adam.
3 There are no animals.

2 How does Ben feel at lunch time?
3 What's special about[3] Ben's circus?

[1] The greatest show on earth [ˈɡreɪtɪst ʃəʊ ɒn ˈɜːθ] *Die großartigste Show der Welt* [2] bet [bet] *wetten*
[3] special about [ˈspeʃl əbaʊt] *besonders in*

1 Right. • 2 Wrong. (Hill Road.) • 3 Right. • 4 Wrong. (with her mum, her partner and her brother and sister) • 5 Right. • 6 Wrong. (Ellie is not happy. / The bedroom is too small. / Ellie wants her own bedroom.)

It's Saturday morning and Ellie, Luca, Adam and Berry are in Central Park, at Russell's Circus. Ben sees his new friends.
"Hi. Welcome to my home," he says.
Ben brings the four kids to his caravan first.
"This is cool," Ellie says. "And so big!"
"This isn't like camping!" Luca says. "It's like a normal house."
"Where do you sleep?" Adam asks.
The friends visit Ben's room. It's very nice. They meet Ben's mum. She works in the ticket office[1]. And they meet Ben's dad. He's a clown.

4 What is Ben's caravan like?

4 It's big. It's like a house.

It's time for a tour of the circus. There are lots of people in the big tent[2].
"This is Maria. And this is Darek. They're from Poland. And they're trapeze artists," Ben says.
"Do you like your work?" Berry asks.
"Yes, we love it," Maria says.
"Is it dangerous?" Luca asks.
"Yes, it is. But we're careful[3]," Darek answers.

Then they talk to Raymond. He's from France and he's a juggler[4].
"Do you want to try?" he asks Ellie.
"OK," she says. But she's terrible. The other kids laugh.

"Come here," Ben's dad says. He's with two other clowns. He's on their shoulders, but then they all fall down. The friends laugh.

5 two trapeze artists (Maria, Darek), a juggler (Raymond), three clowns (Ben's dad, two other clowns)

They have lunch in Ben's caravan.
"Do you want to see the show today?" Ben's mum asks. "It's at 3 o'clock."
"Wow. Yes please. That's great!" the kids say.
"Can we help you?" Berry asks.
"That's a good idea," Ben's father says. "You can see what life in the circus is really like."

5 What circus people do the kids meet?

[1] ticket office ['tɪkɪt ɒfɪs] *Schalter* [2] tent [tent] *Zelt* [3] careful ['keəfl] *vorsichtig* [4] juggler ['dʒʌglə] *Jongleur/in*

It's 2.30 on Saturday afternoon. Lots of people are at Russell's Circus. Berry is in the ticket office with Ben's mum.
"Do you want a circus brochure?" Berry asks. Then she sees her parents. They're at the circus too.
"Hi mum, hi dad! This is great fun," she says.

Luca is in the big tent. His job is to bring people to their seats[1].
"Hello, Mr and Mrs Donovan," he says. "Let me look at your tickets. Yes, here are your seats."

It's 3 o'clock, time for the circus. First there's music. Then the ringmaster[2] speaks to the people. "Welcome to Russell's Circus – the greatest show on earth! And here are my two helpers – Ben and Ellie!"

The first act is the clowns. It's Ben's dad and the two other clowns. Today there's a fourth clown – it's Adam!

6 Who has the best job at the circus – Adam, Berry, Ellie or Luca? What do you think?

6 Individuelle Lösungen.

Two weeks later the four friends are at Russell's Circus again. But today things are different. The big tent isn't there. The circus people are in their cars and trucks. The circus is over. It's time to go to the next town.
"Bye, Ben. Thanks for a great day at the circus. It really is the greatest show on earth!" Berry says.
"You're welcome. See you next year!" Ben says.

7 Is Ben happy or unhappy in the end? What do you think?

Lösungsbeispiel: I think Ben is happy because he has got new friends now. They can meet again next year. / Maybe Ben is a bit unhappy because it's time to go to the next town.

[1] seat [siːt] *Sitzplatz* [2] ringmaster ['rɪŋmɑːstə] *Zirkusdirektor/in*

TEXT FILE Navigator | Vorbereitung

Lernschwerpunkt: **Hip-Hop-Tanzschritte nach Anleitung vorführen**

Kompetenzen: **Reading** Anleitungen bildgestützt verstehen und umsetzen | **Listening** Anleitungen bildgestützt verstehen und umsetzen

Redemittel: Hip-Hop-Tanzschritte, Anweisungen

Zeitbedarf: ca. eine Stunde

Materialbedarf: Audio-CD + Player oder MP3 + PC/Lautsprecher

TF 6 Hip-hop workout[1]

3.17

1 Listen and look at the instructions

A Step[2]-touch[3]

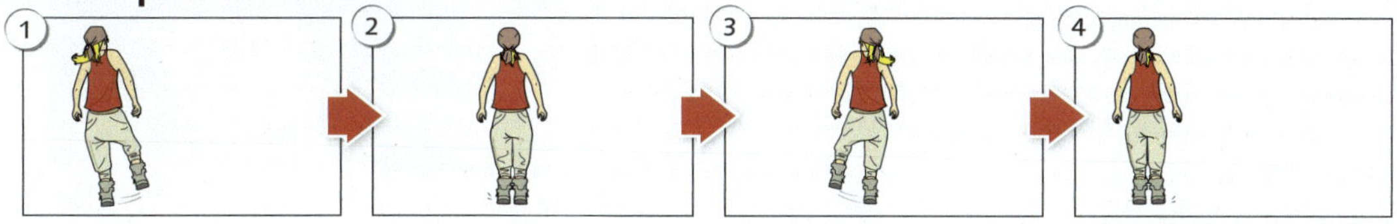

1 Step to the right[4]. 2 Left foot[5] – touch. 3 Step to the left. 4 Right foot – touch.

B Two step-touch

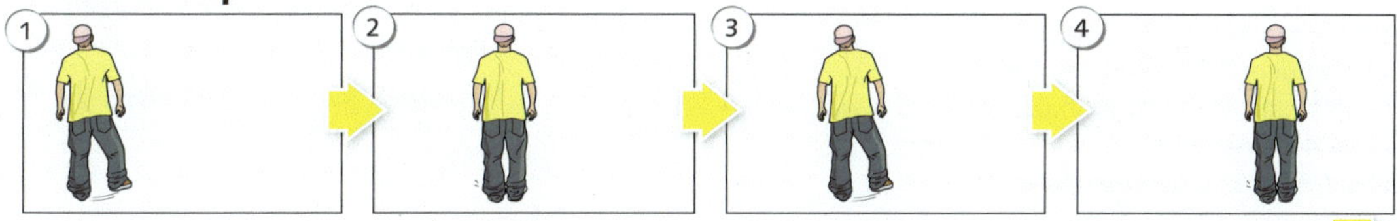

1 Step to the right. 2 Left foot – touch. 3 Step to the right again. 4 And left foot – touch.

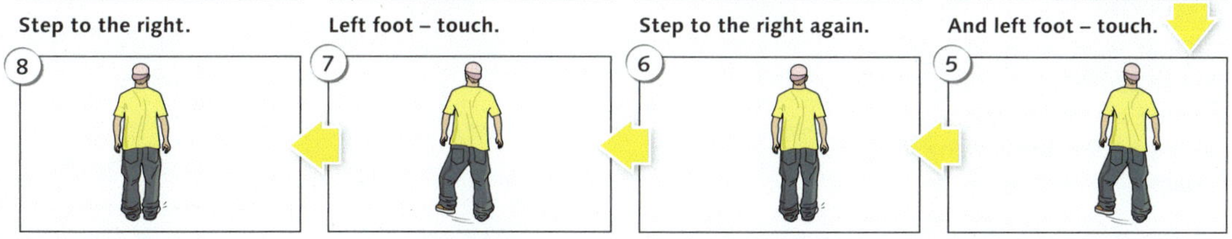

8 And right foot – touch. 7 Step to the left again. 6 Right foot – touch. 5 Step to the left.

C Grapevine[6]

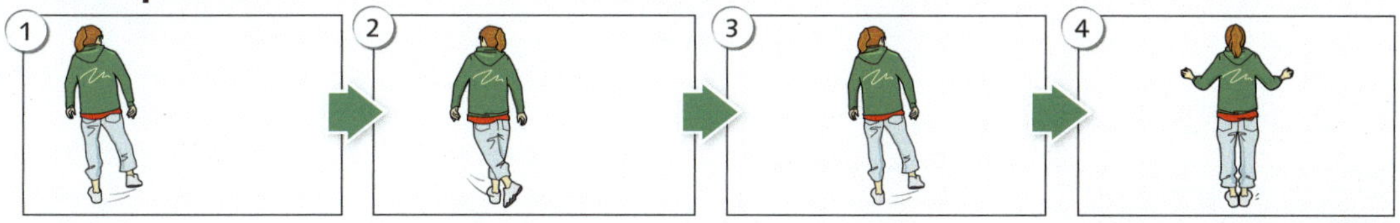

1 Step to the right. 2 Left foot behind[7] right foot. 3 Step to the right again. 4 Left foot – touch. Arms out[8].

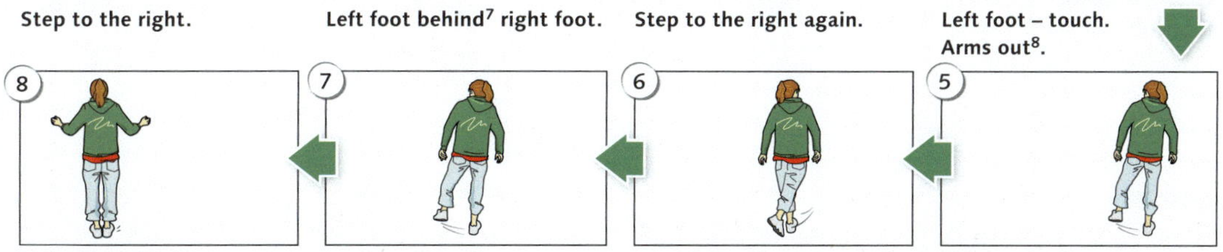

8 Right foot – touch. Arms out. 7 Step to the left again. 6 Right foot behind left foot. 5 Step to the left.

2 Practise the workouts with your class. One student can say the instructions. Play the CD and do the hip-hop workout. Have fun!

[1] workout ['wɜːkaʊt] *Fitnesstraining* [2] step [step] *einen Schritt machen* [3] touch [tʌtʃ] *berühren*
[4] to the right [raɪt] *nach rechts* [5] foot [fʊt] *Fuß* [6] grapevine ['greɪpvaɪn] *Kreuzschritt* [7] behind [bɪ'haɪnd] *hinter*
[8] arms out [ɑːmz 'aʊt] *Arme ausstrecken*

Einstieg Ex 1 (SB geschl.)
L präsentiert die ersten Takte der Musik von CD (bis 00.21), stoppt nach der Frage der Sprecherin *Do you like that music?* und fragt die S nach ihrer Meinung.
Überleitung L: *Let's do some hip-hop today. Listen to the instructions first.*
Erarb. Ex 1 (SB offen)
1. Hören/Lesen: S erschließen die deutsche Bedeutung der unbekannten Begriffe mithilfe der Bilder und Annotationen.
O Zur besseren Nachvollziehbarkeit kann L die drei Schrittfolgen beim
2. Hören einzeln präsentieren und Fragen zum Bewegungsablauf klären.

Erarb. Ex 2 (SB offen)
Einüben der Schrittfolgen und Durchführung des *hip-hop workout* im Plenum.
Der Tanz kann auch auf Schulfesten vorgeführt werden.

SF 1 Learning words – Vokabellernen leicht gemacht ▸ Unit 1, p. 27

Woran muss ich **immer** denken?

- Lerne nur 5 bis 10 Vokabeln auf einmal.
- Lerne und wiederhole regelmäßig. Zehn Minuten am Tag sind sinnvoller als einmal zwei Stunden pro Woche. Wiederhole direkt am nächsten Tag.
- Lerne mit jemandem zusammen. Es macht mehr Spaß und ihr könnt euch gegenseitig abfragen.
- Beim Wiederholen solltest du die Vokabeln abwechselnd lesen, laut aussprechen und vor allem auch schreiben. Beginne mal mit dem deutschen Wort und mal mit dem englischen Wort.

1 Vokabeln lernen mit dem *Vocabulary*

Vokabellernen beginnt mit dem *Vocabulary* in deinem Englischbuch (S. 179–207). Auf S. 179 kannst du sehen, wie es aufgebaut ist.
- Lies das englische Wort laut.
- Lies dann die deutsche Übersetzung und den Beispielsatz.

hoffen	I **hope** you like my school uniform.	
glücklich, froh	She's **happy**.	He isn't **happy**.
bitte	Can you help me, **please**?	

Wenn du testen möchtest, ob du die Wörter weißt, gehe eine Seite Zeile für Zeile durch:
- Decke die beiden rechten Spalten ab und sage die deutsche Übersetzung/ den Beispielsatz.

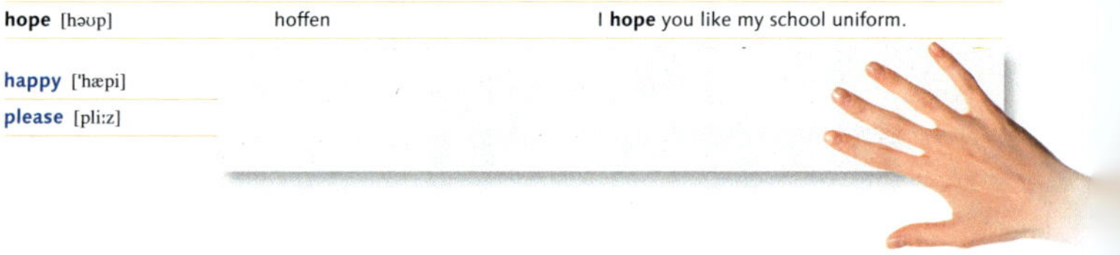

- Gehe die Seite erneut durch und decke mit zwei Blatt Papier die linke Spalte und die rechte Spalte ab und sage die englischen Wörter.

Schreibe Vokabeln, mit denen du Probleme hast, auf selbstklebende Zettel. Die klebst du dann zu Hause an Gegenstände im Zimmer, die du immer wieder ansiehst.

2 Vokabelheft

- Du kannst neue Wörter in ein Vokabelheft oder -ringbuch schreiben. Benutze ein **dreispaltiges** Vokabelverzeichnis.
- Trage in die linke Spalte das englische Wort ein und daneben die deutsche Übersetzung.
- In die rechte Spalte kannst du ein Bild einfügen oder einen Beispielsatz schreiben. Manchmal findest du gute Beispiele im *Vocabulary* deines Buches.
- Lies die geschriebenen englischen Wörter dabei immer laut vor.

▸ *INKL 6.1*

3 Sammeln und ordnen – Make networks

Du behältst neue Vokabeln leichter, wenn du sie beim Aufschreiben in Gruppen ordnest, z.B. in einem Wörternetz.

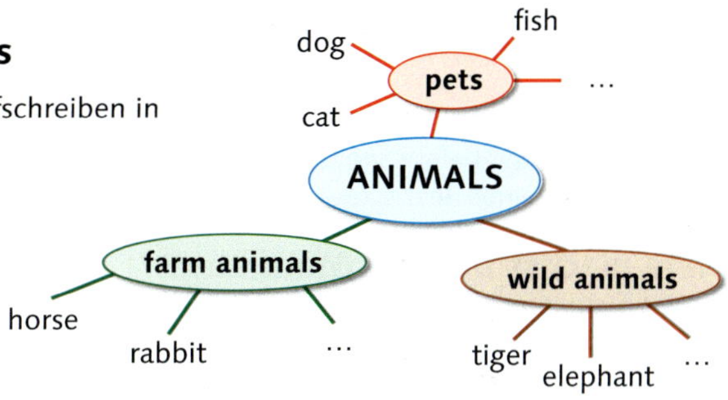

4 Vokabeln lernen mit Karteikarten

1. Du kannst neue Vokabeln auch auf Karteikarten schreiben.
   Dazu benötigst du:
   – viele kleine Kärtchen (oder gleich große Zettel)
   – einen passenden Kasten (oder einfach zwei Gummibänder)
   – eine **OK**- und eine **?**-Karte.
2. Auf die Vorderseite der Kärtchen schreibst du die englischen Wörter mit einem Beispielsatz und, wenn du magst, einem Bild. Auf die Rückseite schreibst du das deutsche Wort.
   Dann sortierst du die Kärtchen. Wie? Wie du willst!
   Am Anfang stehen alle Kärtchen im **?**-Fach.
3. Schau dir die Rückseite jeder Karte an:
   Du weißt das englische Wort?
   ▸ Die Karte wandert in das **OK**-Fach (oder auf den **OK**-Stapel).

   Du weißt es nicht?
   ▸ Die Karte kommt zurück in das **?**-Fach (oder auf den **?**-Stapel).

   Beim nächsten Mal beginnst du mit diesen Karten.

Wiederhole auch regelmäßig die Vokabeln aus dem **OK**-Fach. Wenn du sie nach zwei bis drei Wochen noch weißt, kannst du sie aussortieren.

5 Vokabellernen am Computer

Vielleicht fällt dir das Vokabellernen auch leichter, wenn du am Computer übst – mit dem e-Workbook oder mit der elektronischen Vokabelkartei.

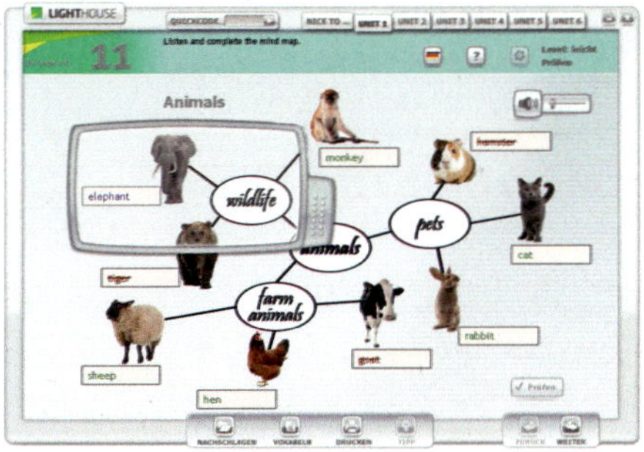

SF 2 Mindmaps

▸ Unit 2, p. 44

Wozu sind Mindmaps gut?

Mindmaps helfen beim Sammeln und Ordnen von Ideen, z.B. bevor du einen Text schreibst oder etwas vorträgst.

Wie machst du eine Mindmap?

Stell dir vor, du sollst einen Text über deine Familie schreiben. Dazu fertigst du zunächst eine Mindmap an.

Was benötigst du?

- ein leeres, unliniertes Blatt Papier im Querformat
- Stifte in verschiedenen Farben

Wie erstellst du eine Mindmap?

1. Schreibe in die **Mitte** des Blattes das **Thema** und male z.B. einen **Kreis** oder eine **Wolke** darum.

2. Überlege, über welche Hauptthemen du schreiben oder sprechen willst. Zeichne für jedes Hauptthema einen **Hauptast** in unterschiedlichen Farben und schreibe das Thema darauf. Verwende nur Schlüsselwörter.

3. Wenn dir zu den Hauptthemen noch Unterthemen einfallen, dann ergänze Nebenäste in der gleichen Farbe. Schreibe die Unterthemen auf die Nebenäste. Verwende auch hier nur Schlüsselwörter.

   An die Nebenäste kannst du noch mehr Ideen „anhängen".

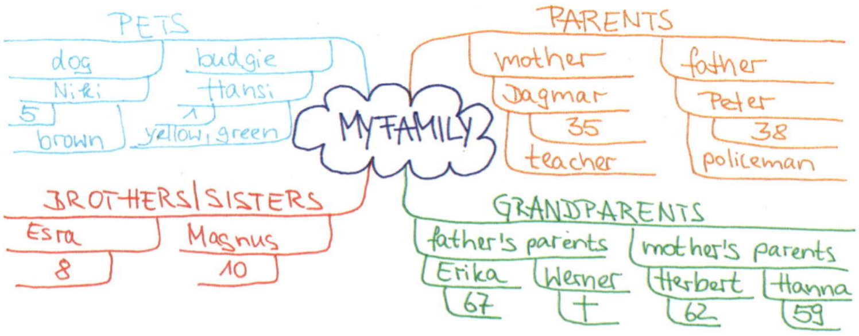

4. Du kannst statt Wörtern auch **Zahlen, Bilder oder Symbole** verwenden.

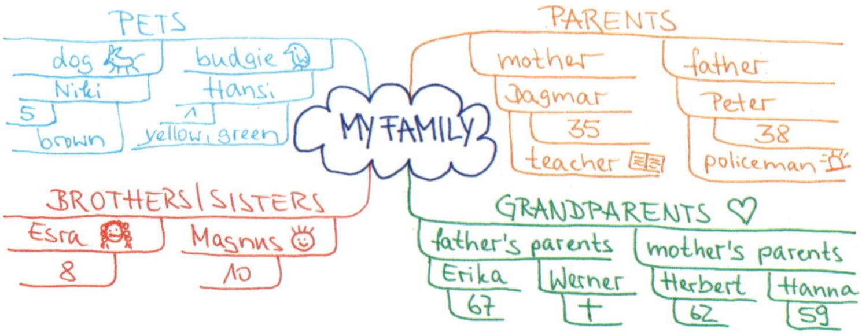

Es gibt auch Computerprogramme, mit denen du Mindmaps erstellen kannst.

SF 3 Unbekannte Wörter verstehen? – Kein Problem! ▸ Unit 3, p. 64

Englische Texte enthalten oft Wörter, die du noch nicht kennst oder gelernt hast. Aber du kannst viele Texte verstehen, wenn du folgende Dinge beachtest.

Was hilft dir, unbekannte Wörter zu verstehen?

1 Schau auf die Bilder

Häufig gibt es zu Texten auch Bilder. Sie zeigen oft die Dinge, die du im Text nicht verstehst.

Was bedeuten *forefinger* und *wrist* im folgenden Text?

How to check your pulse:

Put your forefinger and your middle finger on your wrist.
Count your pulse for 60 seconds.

2 Denke an ähnliche Wörter im Deutschen

Viele englische Wörter werden ähnlich wie im Deutschen geschrieben oder klingen ähnlich wie deutsche Wörter,
z.B. in dem kleinen Text oben:

– *pulse* hat Ähnlichkeit mit dem deutschen Wort "Puls"

– *middle finger* ist natürlich im Deutschen der "Mittelfinger"

Was bedeuten wohl die folgenden Wörter auf Deutsch?

brilliant • camera • cost • Danish • fresh • half • price • hang • loudspeaker • nervous • ocean • penguin • plan • round • study • suncream • tomato sauce

3 Schau auf die Wörter vor und nach dem unbekannten Wort

Häufig kannst du ein unbekanntes Wort aus dem Satzzusammenhang erschließen. Dabei helfen dir die Wörter, die vor oder nach dem unbekannten Wort stehen.

Was könnten *building* und *stay* bedeuten?

1. Our school is new. It's a very nice building with lots of big classrooms.
2. You can't see your friend this afternoon. Stay at home and do your homework!

SF 4 Im Wörterbuch nachschlagen

► Unit 4, p. 84

Wenn du in einem englischen Text ein Wort noch nicht kennst oder vergessen hast (z.B. *donkey*), dann hilft dir das *English-German Dictionary* weiter (S. 208–218). Du kannst Wörter natürlich auch in einem umfangreicheren Wörterbuch nachschlagen.

Uncle Ernie's farm

Uncle Ernie has a farm near Plymouth. On his farm there are lots of animals. He has 20 pigs and 85 cows. But his favourite animal is his donkey.

Wie kannst du englische Wörter im *Dictionary* finden?

1. Die **blau** und **fett** gedruckten Stichwörter (z.B. **family**, **farm**, **fast**) sind alphabetisch angeordnet, also **f** vor **g**, **fa** vor **fe**, **fam** vor **far**.

Ordne die folgenden *farm animals* alphabetisch:

horse • cat • bull • donkey • chicken • pig • duck • sheep • dog • rabbit

Wo findest du ***donkey*** im *Dictionary*? Zwischen *dinner* und *dog* oder zwischen *do* und *door*?
Überprüfe dich selbst (*Dictionary* S. 210)!

Welche Informationen liefert dir das *Dictionary*?

2. Beachte die Wörter und Wendungen, die **schwarz** und **fett** gedruckt sind. Es sind
- zusammengesetzte Wörter, z.B. **family name**
- Redewendungen oder längere Ausdrücke, z.B. **I'm fine, thanks** oder **in the field**.

3. Zusammengesetzte Wörter und längere Ausdrücke findest du oft unter mehr als einem Stichwort, z.B. **feel fed up** unter **fed** und **feel** oder **in the field** unter **in** und **field**.

4. In den eckigen Klammern hinter den Stichwörtern steht, wie das Wort ausgesprochen und betont wird.
(Lautschriftzeichen → S. 178; Betonungszeichen → S. 193).

Wie wird das ‚a' in *family* und *father* ausgesprochen?
Wie das ‚o' in *donkey* oder in *home*?

5. Die Ziffern **1.**, **2.** usw. zeigen, dass das englische Wort mehrere unterschiedliche Bedeutungen hat. Welche Bedeutung die richtige ist, kannst du meist aus dem Satzzusammenhang erkennen.

Welche Mehrfachbedeutungen kannst du für folgende Wörter finden?

text • before • phone • too • right • drink

F

face [feɪs] Gesicht 5 (98)
fall [fɔːl] fallen; hinfallen 3 (61)
family [ˈfæməli] Familie 2 (36)
family name Familienname, Nachname 3 (52) **family tree** (Familien-)Stammbaum 2 (37)
farm [fɑːm] Bauernhof, Farm 4 (70)
fast [fɑːst] schnell 3 (61)
father [ˈfɑːðə] Vater 2 (34)
favourite [ˈfeɪvərɪt] Lieblings- (10)
favourite colour Lieblingsfarbe (10)
February [ˈfebruəri] Februar 3 (56)
fed up [fed ˈʌp]: **feel fed up** genervt sein, sauer sein; die Nase voll haben 4 (74)
feed [fiːd] füttern 4 (72)
feel [fiːl] sich fühlen; fühlen 4 (74)
feel fed up genervt sein, sauer sein; die Nase voll haben 4 (74)
feeling [ˈfiːlɪŋ] Gefühl 4 (74)
ferry [ˈferi] Fähre 5 (91)
field [fiːld] Feld; Weide 4 (70)
in the field auf dem Feld 4 (70)
fill sth. in [fɪl ˈɪn] etwas ausfüllen
film [fɪlm] Film 3 (64)
find [faɪnd] finden 4 (79)
°find out herausfinden
fine [faɪn] gut; in Ordnung 1 (17)
I'm fine, thanks. Danke, (es geht mir) gut. 1 (17)
finish [ˈfɪnɪʃ] beenden
fire station [ˈfaɪə steɪʃn] Feuerwache 3 (52)
first [fɜːst]:
1. erste(r, s) 1 (17)
2. zuerst, als Erstes 3 (54)
the first morning der erste Morgen 1 (17)
fish [fɪʃ] Fisch; Fische (12)
fisherman, *pl* **-men** [ˈfɪʃəmən] Fischer/in, Angler/in
five [faɪv] fünf (8)
flat [flæt] Wohnung 2 (34)

SF 5 Über Bilder und Fotos sprechen ▸ Unit 5, p. 100

Häufig ist es notwendig, jemandem ein Bild oder ein Foto genau zu beschreiben. Das geht besonders gut, wenn du die folgenden Schritte beachtest.

1 Beginne allgemein

Sage zunächst, was du allgemein im Bild oder Foto siehst.
Welcher Ort, welcher Gegenstand oder welche Personen sind zu sehen?

In the picture I can see a classroom with a teacher and his students.

2 Gehe in einer bestimmten Reihenfolge vor

Sage dann, **wen** oder **was** du siehst und wo sich die Personen oder Gegenstände im Bild oder Foto befinden.
Gehe dabei in einer bestimmten **Reihenfolge** vor: Sage z.B. zunächst, was du links siehst, gehe dann zur Mitte und zum Schluss beschreibst du, was du rechts im Bild oder Foto siehst.
Benutze dabei **allgemeine Ortsangaben** wie:

On the left I can see …
In the middle there are …
On the right there's …

3 Beschreibe alle Teile genauer

Beschreibe genauer, **wo** sich eine Person oder ein Gegenstand befindet:

There's a student under the table.
A student with a green T-shirt is behind the teacher.
There's a girl with a mobile phone next to the boy.
The teacher is in front of the class.

4 Beschreibe, was die Personen machen

Wenn du sagen willst, was gerade im Bild oder Foto passiert oder **was die Personen gerade tun**, benutze das ***present progressive***.

On the right there's a girl in a purple T-shirt.
She's eating an apple.
A girl in an orange T-shirt is sitting next to her.
She's reading a comic.

▸ Language file 10, p. 171

LANGUAGE FILE

LF 1 Personalpronomen (Personal pronouns)

▸ Unit 1, pp. 22–23

It is new.
Er ist neu.

It is new.
Sie ist neu.

It is new.
Es ist neu.

Du bist nett. **Ihr** seid nett. **Sie** sind nett, Frau Lee.

Das Pronomen ***it*** steht für alle Dinge:

 it  **er** **sie** **es**

Das Pronomen ***you*** steht für Personen:

 you  **du** **ihr** **Sie**

This is my pony Harry. He's big. My pony Connie is old. She's seventeen.

Über Haustiere, die einen Namen haben, sprichst du mit **he** oder **she**, nicht mit **it**.

LF 2 'm – 's – 're: das Verb be („sein") in der Gegenwart

a) Aussagen (Statements)

▸ Unit 1, p. 22

I'm from Plymouth and I'm twelve.
This is Berry. She's my friend.
We're at Eggy in class 7Y.
Luca and Adam **are** in class 7Y too.

Das Verb *be* hat in der Gegenwart *(present)* drei Formen: *'m*, *'s* und *'re*. Das sind die Kurzformen. Es gibt auch Langformen, das sind: ***am***, ***is*** und ***are***.

Bejahte Aussagen	
I'm (= I am) You're (= You are) He's (= He is) She's (= She is) It's (= It is) We're (= We are) You're (= You are) They're (= They are)	new.

Kurzformen sind sehr häufig. Sie werden besonders in der gesprochenen Sprache verwendet.

Ellie / Luca / The bike The teachers / The books	is are	new.

Die Langformen benutzt du meistens nach Eigennamen *(Ellie, Luca)* oder Nomen *(bike, teachers)*.

Verneinte Aussagen	
I'm not (= I am not) You aren't (= You are not) He isn't (= He is not) She isn't (= She is not) It isn't (= It is not) We aren't (= We are not) You aren't (= You are not) They aren't (= They are not)	from Plymouth.

Bei der Verneinung werden fast immer die Kurzformen benutzt.

LF 3 b) Fragen und Kurzantworten (Questions and short answers)

▸ *Unit 2, p. 40*

Fragen

Am I ...?
Is he / she / it ...?

Are we ...?
Are you ...?
Are they ...?

What's this?
Who are they?
Where are your books?

Du kannst Fragen stellen
- **ohne Fragewort** *(Are you ...?)*, auf die du Antworten mit Ja oder Nein bekommst, oder
- **mit Fragewort** *(Who ...?/Where ...?)*. Nach einem Fragewort kannst du ***is*** verkürzen:
  What's *your name?*
  Where's *your tie, Ellie?*

Kurzantworten	
Yes, I am. Yes, he / she / it is. Yes, you / we / they are.	No, I'm not. No, he / she / it isn't. No, you / we / they aren't.

Eine kurze Antwort nur mit ***yes*** oder ***no*** kann unhöflich klingen. Antworte besser: *Yes, I am./No, she isn't./...*

LANGUAGE FILE

LF 4 There's ... / There are ...

▸ Unit 2, p. 39

Mit ***There's ... / There are ...*** drückst du aus, dass irgendwo etwas vorhanden ist:

– In meinem Zimmer steht ein Tisch. → **There's** a table in my room.
– Auf dem Tisch liegen Bücher. → **There are** books on the table.
– Es gibt/sind drei Stühle in ... → **There are** three chairs in ...

Nie: It ~~gives~~ ..., sondern immer: ***There's ... / There are ...***

Im Deutschen beginnst du oft mit einer Ortsangabe:
In meinem Zimmer **steht ein Tisch**.

Im Englischen steht die Ortsangabe meist am Ende und die Sätze beginnen mit ***There's ... / There are ...***
There's a table in my room.

In Fragen stehen ***is*** und ***are*** vor dem ***there***:

– Gibt es auch einen Kleiderschrank? → **Is there** a wardrobe too?
– Sind Jungen in deiner Klasse? → **Are there** boys in your class?

LF 5 Der Plural der Nomen (The plural of nouns)

▸ Unit 3, p. 62

		Singular (Einzahl) a/one **crab**	**Plural** (Mehrzahl) two/three/lots of **crabs**
1	+ -s	a pet one snake a crab one seagull	two pets [-s] three snakes [-s] lots of crabs [-z] four seagulls [-z]
2	+ -es	a bus one beach	two buses [-ɪz] two beaches [-ɪz]
3	-y → -ies	a story one pony **Aber:** a boy one day	lots of stories [-ɪz] five ponies [-ɪz] two boys [-z] three days [-z]
4	keine Regel	a man one child a fish	lots of men two children five fish

1 Die meisten Nomen (Hauptwörter) haben im Plural die Endung ***-s***. Beachte die unterschiedliche Aussprache!

2 Nach ***-s***, ***-x***, ***-sh*** oder ***-ch*** wird ***-es*** angehängt.

3 Nach einem Konsonanten (Mitlaut) ***+ y*** (z. B. ***-ry***, ***-ny***, ***-ly***, ***-ty***) wird ***-y*** zu ***-ies***.

4 Ein paar Nomen haben unregelmäßige Pluralformen. Diese musst du auswendig lernen.

LF 6 Die einfache Form der Gegenwart (The simple present)

a) Bejahte Aussagen (Positive statements)

▸ Unit 3, p. 58

Mit dem **simple present** sprichst du darüber, was **wiederholt** (oder auch **nie**) passiert, oft mit *always* (immer), *sometimes* (manchmal), *often* (oft), *never* (niemals), in the *morning/afternoon* (vormittags/nachmittags).

Yes

I	like	the beach.
You	like	
He	likes	
She	likes	
It	likes	
We	like	
You	like	
They	like	

He, she, it – ein *-s* muss mit!

Das **simple present** hat zwei Formen:
1 *I/you/we/they* + verb
2 *he/she/it* + verb + ***s***

Wenn das Verb auf ***-ss***, ***-x***, ***-sh***, ***-ch*** (z. B. *watch*) oder auf ***-o*** (z. B. *go*) endet, fügst du bei *he/she/it* ***-es*** hinzu:

– *watch*: *he/she/it watches* [-ɪz]
– *go*: *he/she/it goes* [gəʊz]
– *do*: *he/she/it does* [dʌz]
(siehe auch LF 5: Plural der Nomen)

LF 7 b) Verneinte Aussagen (Negative statements)

▸ Unit 4, p. 76

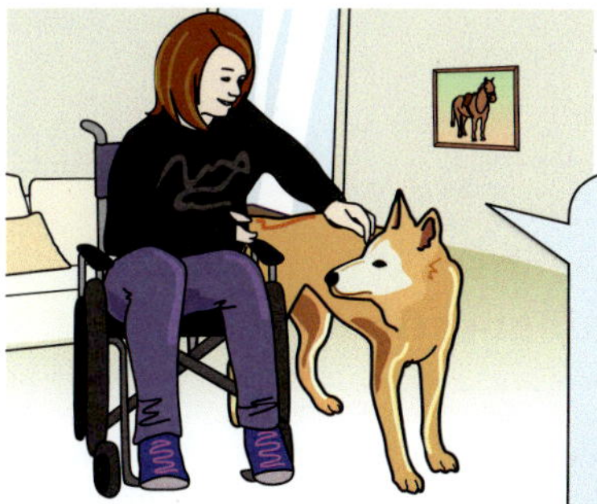

Das **simple present** verneinst du mit ***don't*** oder ***doesn't*** + verb:

– *I/you/we/they* *don't* + verb
– *he/she/it* *doesn't* + verb

Die Langformen sind: ***do not*** und ***does not***.

No

I don't like	dogs.
You don't like	
He/She/It doesn't like	
We/You/They don't like	

LF 8 Fragen mit do/does und Kurzantworten

▸ Unit 4, p. 78

(*Do-/Does*-questions and short answers)

a) Fragen

Wenn du im **simple present** auf eine Frage die Antwort „Ja“ oder „Nein“ erwartest, fängst du die Frage mit **Do** oder **Does** an:

– **Do** +	*I/you/we/they*	+ verb ?
Do	*you*	***have** ponies?*
– **Does** +	*he/she/it*	+ verb ?
Does	*the farm*	***have** a shop?*

Do I like ...? Do you like ...? Does he/she/it like ...?	Do we like ...? Do you like ...? Do they like ...?

b) Kurzantworten

Es ist oft unhöflich, nur mit *Yes* oder *No* zu antworten. Besser ist eine Kurzantwort:

- nach *Yes* mit *do* oder *does*, z. B.
  Yes, I do. / Yes, she does.
- nach *No* mit *don't* oder *doesn't*, z. B.
  No, I don't. / No, he doesn't.

Yes	No
Yes, I do. Yes, he/she/it does. Yes, you/we/they do.	No, I don't. No, he/she/it doesn't. No, you/we/they don't.

LF 9 Fragen mit Fragewörtern (Questions with question words)

▸ Unit 4, p. 78

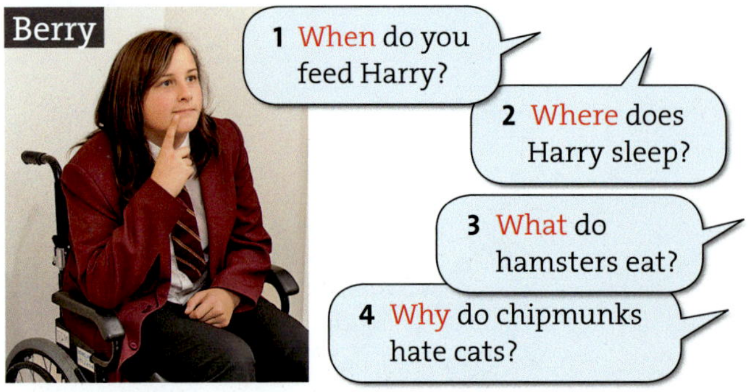

1 Wann fütterst du Harry?
2 Wo schläft Harry?
3 Was fressen Hamster?
4 Warum hassen Streifenhörnchen Katzen?

Wenn du eine Frage mit Fragewort *(When, Where, What, Why, How)* bilden willst, setzt du das Fragewort vor *do* bzw. *does*:

*   **Do** you **like** rabbits?*
*Why **do** you **like** rabbits?*

*   **Does** Berry **feed** the donkeys?*
*When **does** she **feed** the donkeys?*

LF 10 Die Verlaufsform der Gegenwart (The present progressive)

▸ Unit 5, p. 96

In the photo mum and I are working in the cafe.
I'm setting the tables and mum is talking to a customer.
We aren't making sandwiches.

Im Gegensatz zum Deutschen gibt es im Englischen zwei Formen der Gegenwart: die einfache Form und die Verlaufsform.

Mit der einfachen Form **(simple present)** sprichst du über Dinge, die wiederholt passieren (siehe LF 6, S. 169).

Wenn du aber über etwas sprichst, das **gerade jetzt** passiert, benutzt du die Verlaufsform der Gegenwart **(present progressive)**, oft mit *now* (jetzt) oder *at the moment* (im Moment).

Diese Form benutzt du auch, um Bilder zu beschreiben.

Im Deutschen gibt es keine Verlaufsform.

Adam is setting the tables.

– Adam deckt gerade die Tische.
– Adam ist gerade dabei, die Tische zu decken.

Yes

I'm helping. You're helping. He's/She's/It's helping.	We're helping. You're helping. They're helping.

Du bildest das **present progressive** mit
'm/'re/'s* + *verb* + *-ing
z. B. *she's* + ***talking***

No

I'm not helping. You aren't helping. He/She/It isn't helping.	We aren't helping. You aren't helping. They aren't helping.

Achtung Schreibung:
– ein nicht mitgesprochenes ***e*** fällt weg:
make → *making* *write* → *writing*
– nach einem Vokal (a, e, i, o, u) wird der Konsonant (meist p, b, m, n, d, t) verdoppelt:
rap + *-ing* → *rapping*
swim + *-ing* → *swimming*
set + *-ing* → *setting*

?

Am I helping? Are you helping? Is he/she/it helping?	Are we helping? Are you helping? Are they helping?
What are you doing? Are you helping?	– Yes, I am./ No, I'm not.
What's Adam doing? Is he making sandwiches?	– Yes, he is./ No, he isn't.

Die Kurzantworten sind wie beim Verb *be* (siehe LF 3, S. 167).
Nach einem Fragewort kannst du ***is*** verkürzen: ***What's … / When's …***

Grammatische Fachbegriffe (Grammatical terms)

answer	['ɑːnsə]	Antwort(satz)
negative statement	[negətɪv 'steɪtmənt]	verneinte Aussage
noun	[naʊn]	Nomen, Hauptwort, Substantiv
persononal pronoun	[pɜːsənl 'prəʊnaʊn]	Personalpronomen (persönliches Fürwort)
plural	['plʊərəl]	Plural, Mehrzahl
positive statement	[pɒzətɪv 'steɪtmənt]	bejahte Aussage
present	['preznt]	Gegenwart
present progressive	[preznt prə'gresɪv]	Verlaufsform der Gegenwart
pronoun	['prəʊnaʊn]	Pronomen, Fürwort
question	['kwestʃən]	Frage(satz)
question word	['kwestʃən wɜːd]	Fragewort
short answer	[ʃɔːt 'ɑːnsə]	Kurzantwort
simple present	[sɪmpl 'preznt]	einfache Form der Gegenwart
singular	['sɪŋgjələ]	Singular, Einzahl
statement	['steɪtmənt]	Aussage(satz)
verb	[vɜːb]	Verb

Wordbank 1: Sports and hobbies

► *Nice to meet you!, p. 11*

I like	dancing. football. playing games. reading books. riding. skateboarding. swimming. watching TV.

basketball

boxing

canoeing

climbing

collecting stamps

cycling

doing athletics

drawing

ice hockey

ice skating

inline-skating

listening to music

making models

skiing

snowboarding

surfing the internet

table tennis

taking photos

Wordbank 2: My favourite thing

▸ Nice to meet you!, p. 13

bag

book

DVD player

football

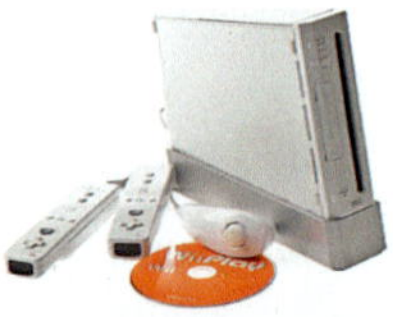
game console

guitar

laptop

mobile phone

remote-control car

scooter

TV

watch

game console ['geɪm kɒnsəʊl] *Spielkonsole* remote-control car [rɪ'məʊt kəntrəʊl 'kɑː] *ferngesteuertes Auto*
scooter ['skuːtə] *Roller*

Wordbank 3: Timetable

▸ Unit 1, p. 33

I have art, drama, English, French, geography, German, history, ICT, maths, music, PE, science, technology, …

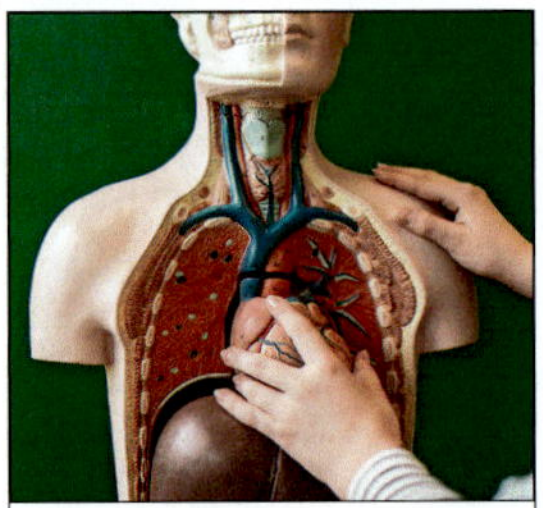
biology

chemistry

class assembly

ethics

home economics

physics

projects

RE

social studies

Spanish

special needs training

woodwork

class assembly *Klassenlehrerstunde* RE = religious education *Religionslehre* social studies *Gesellschaftslehre*
special needs training *Förderunterricht*

Wordbank 4: My family

▸ Unit 2, p. 37

nephew [ˈnefjuː] *Neffe* niece [niːs] *Nichte* grandson *Enkel* granddaughter *Enkelin* husband *Ehemann*
wife [waɪf] *Ehefrau* single *alleinstehend* married to *verheiratet mit* divorced *geschieden* dead *tot*

Wordbank 5: My house

▸ Unit 2, p. 44

Wordbank 6: My town

► Unit 3, p. 52

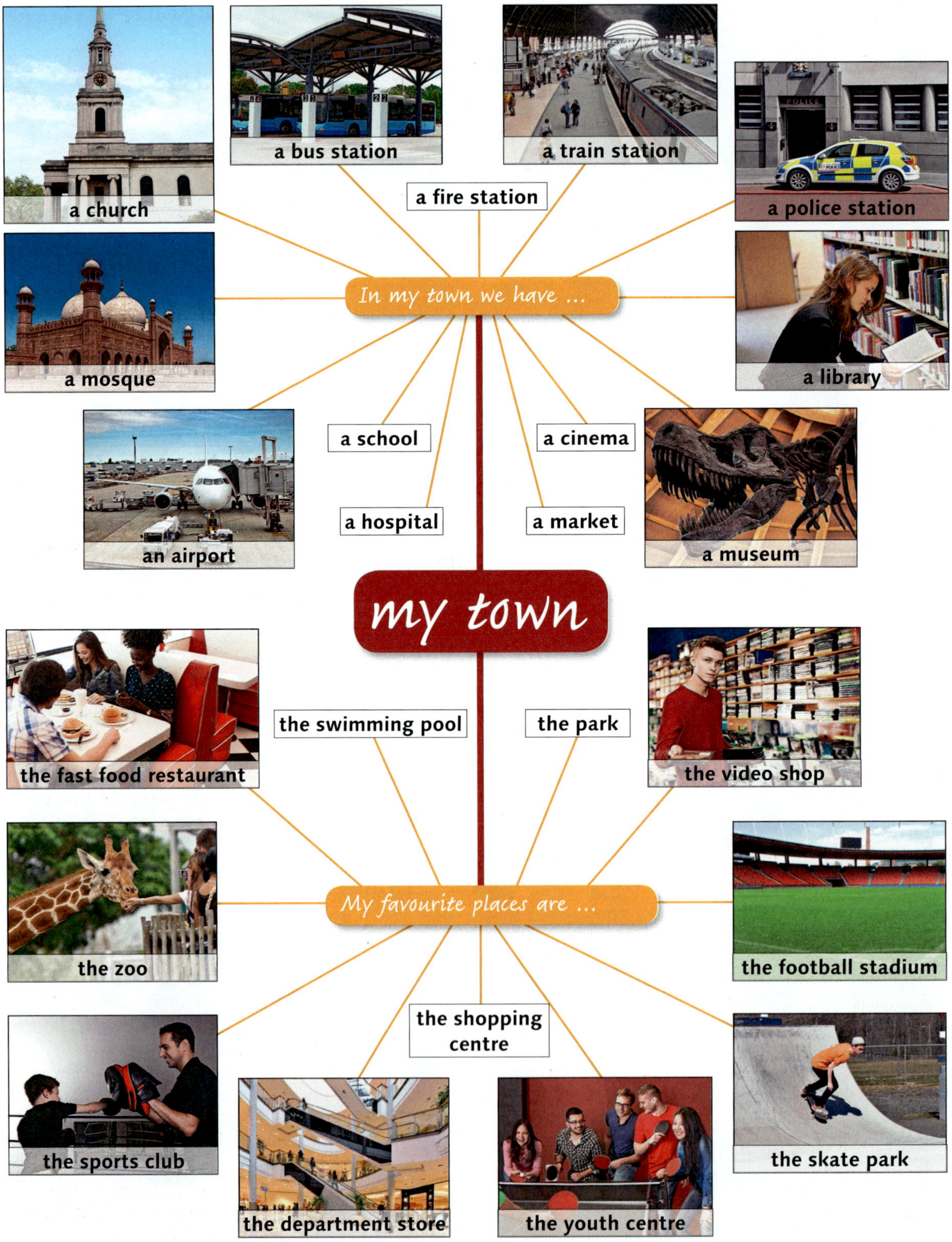

department store [dɪˈpɑːtmənt stɔː] *Kaufhaus* library [ˈlaɪbrəri] *Bücherei, Bibliothek* mosque [mɒsk] *Moschee*

Wordbank 7: Talking about pets

► Unit 4, p. 78

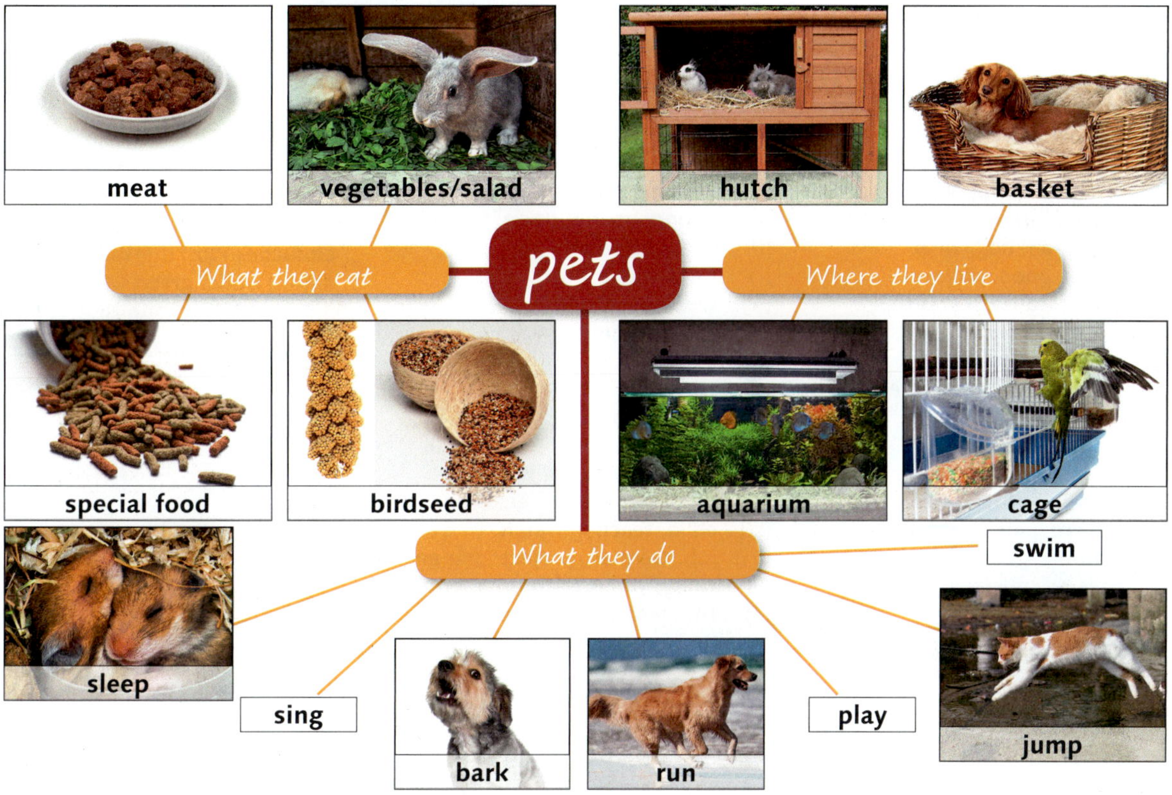

bark [bɑːk] bellen *birdseed* ['bɜːdsiːd] *Körnerfutter, Vogelfutter* hutch [hʌtʃ] *Hütte, kleiner Stall*
jump [dʒʌmp] *springen* meat [miːt] *Fleisch* run [rʌn] *rennen*

Wordbank 8: Instruments

► Unit 5, p. 95

I play the drums, the guitar, the piano, the ... **I don't play an instrument. I like the ...**

flute [fluːt] *(Quer-)Flöte* violin [vaɪə'lɪn] *Violine, Geige*

SOUNDS, ALPHABET

English sounds

[iː]	green, he, sea
[ɑː]	ask, class, car, park
[ɔː]	or, ball, door, four, morning
[uː]	ruler, blue, too, two, you
[ɜː]	early, her, girl, work, T-shirt
[ɪ]	in, big, expensive
[e]	yes, bed, again, breakfast
[æ]	animal, apple, black, cat
[ʌ]	mum, bus, colour
[ɒ]	song, on, dog, what
[ʊ]	book, good, pullover
[ə]	again, today, a sister
[i]	happy, monkey
[eɪ]	name, eight, play, great
[aɪ]	I, time, right, my
[ɔɪ]	boy, toilet, noise
[əʊ]	old, no, road, yellow
[aʊ]	now, house
[eə]	where, pair, share, their
[ʊə]	tour

[b]	bike, table, verb
[p]	pen, paper, shop
[d]	day, window, good
[t]	ten, letter, at
[g]	go, again, bag
[k]	kitchen, car, back
[m]	man, remember, mum
[n]	no, one, ten
[ŋ]	wrong, young, uncle, thanks
[l]	like, old, small
[r]	ruler, friend, sorry
[w]	we, where, one
[j]	yes, you, uniform
[f]	family, after, laugh
[v]	very, seven, have
[s]	six, poster, yes
[z]	zoo, quiz, his, music, please
[ʃ]	she, station, English
[ʒ]	ususally, revision, garage
[tʃ]	child, teacher, watch
[dʒ]	job, German, project, orange
[θ]	thing, three, bathroom, both
[ð]	the, father, with
[h]	house, who, behind

Am besten kannst du dir die Aussprache der einzelnen Lautzeichen einprägen, wenn du dir zu jedem Zeichen ein einfaches Wort merkst – das [iː] ist der **green**-Laut, das [eɪ] ist der **name**-Laut usw.

The English alphabet

a	[eɪ]	**h**	[eɪtʃ]	**o**	[əʊ]	**v**	[viː]
b	[biː]	**i**	[aɪ]	**p**	[piː]	**w**	[ˈdʌbljuː]
c	[siː]	**j**	[dʒeɪ]	**q**	[kjuː]	**x**	[eks]
d	[diː]	**k**	[keɪ]	**r**	[ɑː]	**y**	[waɪ]
e	[iː]	**l**	[el]	**s**	[es]	**z**	[zed]
f	[ef]	**m**	[em]	**t**	[tiː]		
g	[dʒiː]	**n**	[en]	**u**	[juː]		

VOCABULARY

Das **Vocabulary** (S. 179–207) enthält alle neuen Wörter und Wendungen des Buches, die du **lernen** musst. Sie stehen in der Reihenfolge, in der sie im Buch zum ersten Mal vorkommen.

Hier siehst du, wie das **Vocabulary** aufgebaut ist:

Diese Zahl gibt die **Seite** an, auf der die Wörter zum ersten Mal vorkommen. p. 13 = Seite 13

Die **Lautschrift** zeigt dir, wie ein Wort ausgesprochen wird. Eine Übersicht über die **Lautschriftzeichen** findest du auf S. 178.

p. 13	**park** [pɑːk]	Park	
	on [ɒn]	auf	
	bike [baɪk]	Fahrrad	
	great [ɡreɪt]	großartig, prima	
	it's fun [fʌn]	es macht Spaß	
	small [smɔːl]	klein	[s] ist ein scharfes „s" wie in „**lass**en".
	big [bɪɡ]	groß	**big** ◄► **small**
	old [əʊld]	alt	
	new [njuː]	neu	**new** ◄► **old**
	cool [kuːl]	cool	
p. 14	**the last day** [lɑːst 'deɪ]	der letzte Tag	
	holidays ['hɒlədeɪz]	Ferien	
	the last day **of** the holidays [ɒv], [əv]	der letzte Tag der Ferien ➔	**of** • the colour **of** my bike (die Farbe meines Rades) • the last day **of** the holidays (der letzte Tag der Ferien)
	story ['stɔːri]	Geschichte, Erzählung	! one **story** – two, three, four **stories**
	Hello. [hə'ləʊ]	Hallo. / Guten Tag.	
	It's me, Sandy. [miː]	Ich bin es, Sandy. ➔	**„ich": me statt I** • Hello, Ellie. It's **me**, Luca. (Hallo, Ellie. Ich bin's, Luca.) • I'm twelve. – **Me** too. (Ich bi…

Blau gedruckte Wörter kennst du wahrscheinlich schon aus dem Englischunterricht in der Grundschule.

Dies ist das „Gegenteil"-Zeichen. **big ◄► small** bedeutet: „**big** ist das Gegenteil von **small**".

Das **rote Ausrufezeichen** bedeutet: Vorsicht, hier macht man leicht Fehler!

Der **blaue Pfeil** heißt: Zu diesem Eintrag gibt es in der rechten Spalte einen blauen Kasten.

Die **blauen Kästen** solltest du dir immer besonders gut ansehen. Dort stehen wichtige Hinweise zu den neuen Wörtern.

Tipps zum Wörterlernen findest du im **Skills file** auf den Seiten 160 und 161.

Im **Vocabulary** werden folgende **Abkürzungen und Symbole** verwendet:

p. = page (Seite)
sth. = something (etwas)
pl = *plural* (Mehrzahl)
infml = *informal* (umgangssprachlich)

Wenn du **nachschlagen** möchtest, was ein englisches Wort bedeutet oder wie man es ausspricht, dann solltest du das **Dictionary English – German** auf den Seiten 208–218 verwenden.

Und wenn du vergessen hast, wie etwas auf Englisch heißt, dann kann dir das **Dictionary German – English** auf den Seiten 219–227 eine erste Hilfe sein.

Nice to meet you!

p. 8	**Nice to meet you!**	Freut mich, dich/euch kennenzulernen.	
	nice [naɪs]	nett, schön	
	meet [miːt]	kennenlernen; treffen	
	you [ju], [juː]	du; dich; dir ihr; euch	
	Hi. [haɪ]	Hallo.	

	I'm Cyril. [aɪm] (= **I am** Cyril.)	Ich bin Cyril. / Ich heiße Cyril.	! „I" wird immer großgeschrieben – auch wenn es nicht am Satzanfang steht.
	the crab [ðə 'kræb]	der Krebs	→ **the** **the** computer – **der** Computer **the** show – **die** Show **the** baby – **das** Baby
	What's your name?	Wie heißt du? (*wörtlich:* Was ist dein Name?)	
	what? [wɒt]	was?	Der Laut [ɒ] klingt wie das „o" in „d**o**ch".
	your [jɔː], [jə]	dein/e; euer/eure	[ɔː] ist der „o"-Laut aus dem englischen Wort „Baseb**a**ll".
	name [neɪm]	Name	

1 **one** [wʌn]	5 **five** [faɪv]	9 **nine** [naɪn]	13 **thirteen** [θɜː'tiːn]
2 **two** [tuː]	6 **six** [sɪks]	10 **ten** [ten]	14 **fourteen** [fɔː'tiːn]
3 **three** [θriː]	7 **seven** ['sevn]	11 **eleven** [ɪ'levn]	
4 **four** [fɔː]	8 **eight** [eɪt]	12 **twelve** [twelv]	(► *Numbers*, p. 229)

	What about you?	Und du? / Und was ist mit dir?	→ **you**: du, dich, dir – ihr, euch, euch **your**: dein, deine – euer, eure
	I'm from Plymouth. [frɒm], [frəm]	Ich bin aus Plymouth. / Ich komme aus Plymouth.	
	in England [ɪn 'ɪŋglənd] **in Germany** [ɪn 'dʒɜːməni]	in England in Deutschland	! Ländernamen werden immer großgeschrieben: in England; in Germany
	class [klɑːs]	(Schul-)Klasse	[ɑː] ist ein langes „a" wie in „Kr**a**m".
p. 9	**I can see** Cyril. [siː]	Ich kann Cyril sehen.	
	can [kæn], [kən]	können	

	and [ænd], [ənd]	und	
	a beach [ə 'biːtʃ]	ein Strand	→ **a** **a** computer – **ein** Computer **a** show – **eine** Show **a** baby – **ein** Baby
	Cyril's song [sɒŋ]	Cyrils Lied, Cyrils Song	
p. 10	**my** [maɪ]	mein/e	**my** name (**mein** Name) **my** class (**meine** Klasse) [aɪ] klingt wie das „ei" in „Kl**ei**d".
	favourite colour ['feɪvərɪt]	Lieblingsfarbe	
	colour ['kʌlə]	Farbe	one **colour** – two, three, four **colours**
	Welcome to Plymouth. ['welkəm]	Willkommen in Plymouth.	[ə] ist ein „e" wie am Ende von „bitt**e**" oder „Aff**e**".

red [red]	rot	**brown** [braʊn]	braun	**purple** ['pɜːpl]	violett, lila
yellow ['jeləʊ]	gelb	**orange** ['ɒrɪndʒ]	orange	**white** [waɪt]	weiß
blue [bluː]	blau	**grey** [greɪ]	grau	**black** [blæk]	schwarz
green [griːn]	grün	**pink** [pɪŋk]	pink, rosa		

I like red. [laɪk]	Ich mag Rot.	
I don't like blue. ['dəʊnt laɪk]	Ich mag Blau nicht./ Ich mag kein Blau.	
like [laɪk]	mögen, gernhaben	
My favourite colour **is** … [ɪz]	Meine Lieblingsfarbe ist …	

student ['stjuːdənt]	Schüler/in; Student/in	→

one	– two/three/…
one **colour**	two/three **colours**
crab	**crabs**
song	**songs**
student	**students**

p. 11	**sport** [spɔːt]	Sport; Sportart	
	hobby ['hɒbi]	Hobby	! Englisch: one **hobby** – two, three **hobbies** Deutsch: ein **Hobby** – zwei, drei **Hobbys**
	football ['fʊtbɔːl]	Fußball	
	music ['mjuːzɪk]	Musik	[z] ist ein „s" wie in „Musik".
	I like watching TV. ['wɒtʃɪŋ tiː'viː]	Ich sehe gern fern.	
	watch TV [wɒtʃ tiː'viː]	fernsehen	[tʃ] klingt wie „tsch" in „Quatsch".
	TV [tiː'viː]	Fernsehen, Fernsehgerät	[v] klingt wie „Vampir" – nicht wie „Vater"!
	too [tuː]	auch	! I'm from Berlin. – I'm from Berlin **too**. – Ich bin **auch** aus Berlin.
	dance [dɑːns]	tanzen	
	play [pleɪ]	spielen	
	game [geɪm]	Spiel	
	read [riːd]	lesen	
	book [bʊk]	Buch	
	ride [raɪd]	reiten	
	skateboard ['skeɪtbɔːd]	Skateboard fahren	

	swim [swɪm]	schwimmen	
	What are …? [ɑː]	Was sind …?	→

What's …? (= What is) • **What are …?**
- **What's** your favourite song? (Was **ist** dein Lieblingslied?)
- **What are** your hobbies? (Was **sind** deine Hobbys?)

	our ['aʊə]	unser/e	**our** poster (**unser** Poster) **our** class (**unsere** Klasse)
p. 12	**animal** ['ænɪml]	Tier	
	have [hæv], [həv]	haben	

VOCABULARY

pony ['pəʊni]	Pony	! Englisch: one **pony** – two, three **ponies** Deutsch: ein **Pony** – zwei, drei **Ponys**
love [lʌv]	lieben, sehr mögen	
cat [kæt]	Katze	
bear [beə]	Bär	
rat [ræt]	Ratte	
monkey ['mʌŋki]	Affe	
bird [bɜːd]	Vogel	
snake [sneɪk]	Schlange	
dog [dɒg]	Hund	
crocodile ['krɒkədaɪl]	Krokodil	
rabbit ['ræbɪt]	Kaninchen	
hamster ['hæmstə]	Hamster	

fish [fɪʃ]	Fisch; Fische	! one **fish** – two, three, four **fish**
tiger ['taɪgə]	Tiger	
an elephant [æn], [ən]	ein Elefant	➜ **a – an** **a** dog – **an** elephant **a** German name – **an** English name
Can you remember (the animals)? [rɪ'membə]	Kannst du dich (an die Tiere) erinnern?/Könnt ihr euch (an die Tiere) erinnern?	! Englisch: Can you **remember my name**? Deutsch: Kannst du **dich an meinen Namen erinnern**?
remember [rɪ'membə]	sich erinnern (an)	
pet [pet]	Haustier	
wild [waɪld]	wild; wild lebend	
pair [peə]	Paar	[eə] kennst du aus „**fair**".
p. 13 **thing** [θɪŋ]	Ding, Sache	
it's [ɪts] **(= it is)**	es ist *(bei Sachen und Tieren auch:* er ist; sie ist)	a **fish – it's** yellow (**er** ist gelb) a **snake – it's** brown (**sie** ist braun) a **rabbit – it's** white (**es** ist weiß)

go [gəʊ]	gehen; fahren	
to [tu], [tə]	zu, nach	
park [pɑːk]	Park	
on [ɒn]	auf	
bike [baɪk]	Fahrrad	
great [greɪt]	großartig, prima	
it's fun [fʌn]	es macht Spaß	

a girl on a bike **a boy on a pony**

small [smɔːl]	klein	[s] ist ein scharfes „s" wie in „**lass**en".
big [bɪg]	groß	**big** ◄► **small**
old [əʊld]	alt	

	new [nju:]	neu	**new ◄► old**
	cool [ku:l]	cool	
p. 14	**the last day** [lɑ:st 'deɪ]	der letzte Tag	
	holidays ['hɒlədeɪz]	Ferien	
	the last day **of** the holidays [ɒv], [əv]	der letzte Tag der Ferien	→ **of** • the colour **of** my bike (die Farbe meines Rades) • the last day **of** the holidays (der letzte Tag der Ferien)
	story ['stɔ:ri]	Geschichte, Erzählung	! one **story** – two, three, four **stories**
	Hello. [hə'ləʊ]	Hallo. / Guten Tag.	
	It's me, Sandy. [mi:]	Ich bin es, Sandy.	→ **„ich": me** statt **I** • Hello, Ellie. It's **me**, Luca. (Hallo, Ellie. Ich bin's, Luca.) • I'm twelve. – **Me** too. (Ich bin zwölf. – Ich auch.)
	no [nəʊ]	nein	
	away [ə'weɪ]	weg, fort	
	stupid ['stju:pɪd]	dumm, blöd	
	seagull ['si:gʌl]	Möwe	
	This is … ['ðɪs ɪz]	Dies ist … / Das ist …	
	Help! [help]	Hilfe!	

	help [help]	helfen	
	Goodbye. [gʊd'baɪ]	Auf Wiedersehen!	
p. 15	**chant** [tʃɑ:nt]	Sprechgesang	

Unit 1: Welcome to our school

p. 16	**school** [sku:l]	Schule	
	sound [saʊnd]	Geräusch; Klang, Laut	[aʊ] klingt ähnlich wie das „au" in „b**lau**".
	boy [bɔɪ]	Junge	[ɔɪ] klingt ähnlich wie das „eu" in „t**reu**".
	girl [gɜ:l]	Mädchen	[ɜ:] ist das Zeichen für den Laut in „T-Sh**ir**t".
	teacher ['ti:tʃə]	Lehrer/in	
	car [kɑ:]	Auto	
	mobile (phone) ['məʊbaɪl 'fəʊn]	Mobiltelefon, Handy	! Deutsch: **Handy** Englisch: **mobile phone** oder **mobile**
p. 17	**the first morning** [fɜ:st 'mɔ:nɪŋ]	der erste Morgen	[ŋ] ist wie „ng" in „Di**ng**" oder „n" in „pi**n**k".
	How are you? [haʊ 'ɑ: ju]	Wie geht's? / Wie geht es dir/euch?	
	I'm fine, thanks. [faɪn], [θæŋks]	Danke, (es geht mir) gut.	[θ] gibt es im Deutschen nicht. Der Laut klingt etwa so, als ob man das „s" in „be**ss**er" lispelt.

1 VOCABULARY

	I'm OK, thanks. [əʊ'keɪ]	Danke, (es geht mir) gut.	
	Bye. [baɪ]	Tschüs.	**Hello. ◄► Bye./Goodbye.**
	Have a good day.	Ich wünsch dir einen schönen Tag./Schönen Tag noch.	
	good [gʊd]	gut	a **good** school/teacher/story/…
	See you./ See you later. ['leɪtə]	Bis dann./ Bis später.	

Theme 1

p. 18	**Good morning.**	Guten Morgen.	
	Ms Lee [mɪz], [məz]	Frau Lee	
	English ['ɪŋglɪʃ]	Englisch; englisch	
	Who are you? [huː]	Wer bist du?/Wer seid ihr? →	**what?** was? **who?** wer? **how?** wie?
	brother ['brʌðə]	Bruder	[ð] klingt wie ein gelispeltes „Wiese".
	sister ['sɪstə]	Schwester	
	we're … [wɪə] (**= we are** [wi ɑː])	wir sind …	
	my **best** friends [best]	meine besten Freunde/ Freundinnen	
	friend [frend]	Freund/in	
	they're … [ðeə] (**= they are** [ðeɪ ɑː])	sie sind … →	**'re (are)** you**'re** (you are) – du **bist**; ihr **seid** we**'re** (we are) – wir **sind** they**'re** (they are) – sie **sind**
	at this school [æt], [ət]	auf/an dieser Schule	
	they aren't … [ɑːnt]	sie sind nicht …; sie sind keine …	They **aren't** in the park. They **aren't** brothers. Sie sind **nicht** im Park. Sie sind **keine** Brüder.
	I'm not … [nɒt]	ich bin nicht …; ich bin kein/e …	I'm **not** ten. And I'm **not** a boy. Ich bin **nicht** zehn. Und ich bin **kein** Junge.
	he's … [hiːz] (**= he is**)	er ist … →	**'s (is)** he**'s** (he is) – He**'s** my brother. she**'s** (she is) – She**'s** my sister. it**'s** (it is) – It**'s** fun. what**'s** (what is) – What**'s** your name? who**'s** (who is) – Who**'s** in class 7Y?
	she's … [ʃiːz] (**= she is**)	sie ist … →	
	he/she/it isn't … ['ɪznt]	er/sie/es ist nicht …; er/sie/es ist kein/e … →	**n't** **isn't** (is not) **aren't** (are not)
	ride a bike [raɪd]	Rad fahren	
	village ['vɪlɪdʒ]	Dorf	
	near [nɪə]	in der Nähe von, nahe (bei)	Woolwell is **near** Plymouth.
	no [nəʊ]	kein, keine	We have **no** car.
	age [eɪdʒ]	Alter	
p. 19	Hendrik **has …** [hæz], [həz]	Hendrik hat … →	I **have** – he **has** you **have** – she **has** we **have** – it **has** they **have**

	me [miː]	mich; mir	→ **me** Meet **me** in the park. — **mich** Help **me**. — **mir**
	Mrs Schmidt ['mɪsɪz]	Frau Schmidt	! **Ms** = *allgemeine Anrede für Frauen* **Mrs** = *Anrede für verheiratete Frauen*
	Mr Jahn ['mɪstə]	Herr Jahn	

Theme 2

p. 20	**at school**	in der Schule	! Englisch: they're **at school** Deutsch: sie sind **in der Schule**
	a **tour of** the school [tʊə]	ein Rundgang durch die Schule	
	room [ruːm], [rʊm]	Raum, Zimmer	
	canteen [kæn'tiːn]	Kantine, (Schul-)Mensa	
	art [ɑːt]	Kunst	
	science ['saɪəns]	Naturwissenschaft	
	lab [læb]	Labor	
	sports hall ['spɔːts hɔːl]	Sporthalle	
	PE [piː 'iː] (physical education)	(Schul-)Sport	
	lesson ['lesn]	(Unterrichts-)Stunde	
	now [naʊ]	nun, jetzt	
	where? [weə]	wo?/wohin?	! Nicht verwechseln: **who?** wer? **where?** wo?
	here [hɪə]	hier; hierher	
	ICT [aɪ siː 'tiː] (information and communi-cation technology)	Informations- und Kommunikationstechnologie	
	I'm not lost. [lɒst]	Ich habe mich nicht verlaufen/verirrt.	
p. 21	**timetable** ['taɪmteɪbl]	Stundenplan	
	time [taɪm]	Zeit; Uhrzeit	

Monday ['mʌndeɪ], ['mʌndi]	Montag
Tuesday ['tjuːzdeɪ], ['tjuːzdi]	Dienstag
Wednesday ['wenzdeɪ], ['wenzdi]	Mittwoch
Thursday ['θɜːzdeɪ], ['θɜːzdi]	Donnerstag
Friday ['fraɪdeɪ], ['fraɪdi]	Freitag

! Die Wochentage werden immer großgeschrieben.

assembly [ə'sembli]	Schulversammlung, Morgenappell	
technology [tek'nɒlədʒi]	Technik, Technologie	
geography [dʒi'ɒgrəfi]	Geografie, Erdkunde	

1 VOCABULARY

	maths [mæθs]	Mathematik	
	history ['hɪstri]	Geschichte	
	French [frentʃ]	Französisch; französisch	
	break [breɪk]	Pause	
	lunch [lʌntʃ]	Mittagessen	[ʌ] klingt ähnlich wie das kurze „a" in „Kamm".
	drama ['drɑːmə]	Schauspiel, darstellende Kunst	
	every day/room/… ['evri]	jeder Tag/jedes Zimmer/…	We go to school **every** morning.
	on Monday/Tuesday/…	am Montag/Dienstag/…	What's lesson one **on** Monday?
	right [raɪt]	richtig	
	wrong [rɒŋ]	falsch	**right** ◄► **wrong**

Focus on language

p.22	**city** ['sɪti]	(Groß-)Stadt	! one **city** – two, three, four **cities**
	it starts	er/sie/es beginnt; er/sie/es fängt an	
	start [stɑːt]	anfangen, beginnen	
	with [wɪð]	mit	
	classroom ['klɑːsruːm]	Klassenzimmer	
	yes [jes]	ja	**yes** ◄► **no**
p.23	**Look at** our new books. [lʊk]	Sieh/Schau dir unsere neuen Bücher an.	

15 fifteen [fɪf'tiːn]	**20 twenty** ['twenti]	**30 thirty** ['θɜːti]
16 sixteen [sɪks'tiːn]	**21 twenty-one** [twenti'wʌn]	**31 thirty-one** [θɜːti'wʌn]
17 seventeen [sevn'tiːn]	**22 twenty-two** [twenti'tuː]	**32 thirty-two** [θɜːti'tuː]
18 eighteen [eɪ'tiːn]	…	…
19 nineteen [naɪn'tiːn]		(► *Numbers*, p.229)

but [bʌt], [bət]	aber	Luca is ten, **but** Jack is fourteen.
all (the) [ɔːl]	alle	We're **all** friends here at our school. **All the** students in class 7Y are nice.
people ['piːpl]	Leute, Menschen	The **people** in Plymouth are nice.
place [pleɪs]	Ort, Platz, Stelle	Plymouth is a great **place**.
make [meɪk]	machen, herstellen	
for [fɔː], [fə]	für	

p. 24	**before** you read [bɪ'fɔː]	bevor du liest	
	blazer ['bleɪzə]	Blazer *(Jackett, oft Teil der Schuluniform)*	
	pullover ['pʊləʊvə]	Pullover	
	shirt [ʃɜːt]	Hemd	
	shoe [ʃuː]	Schuh	
	skirt [skɜːt]	Rock	
	sock [sɒk]	Socke, Strumpf	
	tie [taɪ]	Krawatte	
	tights *(pl)* [taɪts]	Strumpfhose	→ **tights** und **trousers** sind immer Plural: • My **tights are** blue. **They're** new. (Meine **Stumpfhose ist** blau. **Sie ist** neu.) • **Are** your **trousers** new? **They're** cool. (**Ist** deine **Hose** neu? **Sie ist** cool.)
	trousers *(pl)* ['traʊzəz]	Hose	→
	uniform ['juːnɪfɔːm]	(Schul-)Uniform	
	important [ɪm'pɔːtnt]	wichtig	
	Miss Borowski [mɪs]	Frau Borowski	! **Miss** = *Anrede für unverheiratete Frauen*
	principal ['prɪnsəpl]	Rektor/in, Schulleiter/in	
	hope [həʊp]	hoffen	I **hope** you like my school uniform.
	happy ['hæpi]	glücklich, froh	She's **happy**. He isn't **happy**.
	please [pliːz]	bitte	Can you help me, **please**?
	Please remember ... [rɪ'membə]	Bitte denk dran ... / Bitte merk dir ...	
	be over ['əʊvə]	vorbei sein, zu Ende sein	Olivia isn't at school. School **is over**.
	Sorry. / I'm sorry. ['sɒri]	Tut mir leid. / Entschuldigung.	
	at home	daheim, zu Hause	Luca is at school. Grace is **at home**.
	home [həʊm]	Heim, Zuhause	
	That isn't good. [ðæt]	Das ist nicht gut.	**That** isn't right. **That**'s wrong.
	homework ['həʊmwɜːk]	Hausaufgabe(n)	→ **homework** hat keinen Plural: **Homework is** important. **Hausaufgaben sind** wichtig.
	write [raɪt]	schreiben	
	know [nəʊ]	wissen; kennen	
p. 25	**Look**, Adam.	Sieh mal, Adam. / Schau mal, Adam.	
	bad [bæd]	schlecht; schlimm	**good** ◄► **bad**
	idea [aɪ'dɪə]	Idee	[ɪə] klingt wie das „ier" in „**hier**".
	need [niːd]	brauchen, benötigen	
	paper ['peɪpə]	Papier	
	scissors *(pl)* ['sɪzəz]	Schere	→ **scissors** ist immer Plural: Where **are** my **scissors**? Wo **ist** meine **Schere**? 
	guys [gaɪz]	Leute *(als Anrede verwendet)*	

	say [seɪ]	sagen	! Aussprache: I/you/we/they **say** [seɪ] – he/she **says** [sez]
	What do you think?	Was meinst du?/ Was denkst du?	Are uniforms a good idea? **What do you think?**
	think [θɪŋk]	denken, meinen, glauben	I **think** uniforms are cool.
	theatre ['θɪətə]	Theater	

Skills training

p. 26	**brochure** ['brəʊʃə]	Broschüre, Prospekt	[ʃ] klingt wie das „sch" in „**sch**ön".
	back [bæk]	zurück	
	pound (£) [paʊnd]	Pfund *(britische Währung)*	! you write: **£**5 – you say: five **pounds**
	pencil sharpener ['pensl ʃɑːpnə]	Bleistiftanspitzer	
	rubber ['rʌbə]	Radiergummi	
	ruler ['ruːlə]	Lineal	
	pen [pen]	Kugelschreiber, Stift, Füller	
	pencil ['pensl]	Bleistift	
	pencil case ['pensl keɪs]	Federmäppchen	
	calculator ['kælkjuleɪtə]	Taschenrechner	
	exercise book	Schulheft, Übungsheft	
	exercise ['eksəsaɪz]	Übung, Aufgabe	
	diary ['daɪəri]	Tagebuch; Kalender	
	hole punch ['həʊl pʌntʃ]	Locher	
	buy [baɪ]	kaufen	
	at MARTINS	bei MARTINS	

	child, *pl* **children** [tʃaɪld], ['tʃɪldrən]	Kind, Kinder	! one **child** – two, three, four **children**
	Africa ['æfrɪkə]	Afrika	
p. 27	**network** ['netwɜːk]	Netz; Wortnetz	
	Saturday ['sætədeɪ], ['sætədi]	Samstag, Sonnabend	
	Sunday ['sʌndeɪ], ['sʌndi]	Sonntag	
	weekend [wiːk'end]	Wochenende	
	school bag ['skuːl bæg]	Schultasche	
	phrase [freɪz]	Ausdruck, (Rede-)Wendung	
	card [kɑːd]	Karte	
	box [bɒks]	Kasten, Kiste, Kästchen	
	in English	auf Englisch	What's 'Schultasche' **in English**, please?

p.28	**talk (to)** [tɔːk]	sprechen, reden (mit)	**Talk to** your friends about your favourite
	borrow ['bɒrəʊ]	(aus)leihen, sich borgen	Can I **borrow** your calculator, please?
	next [nekst]	nächste(r, s)	→ **last** weekend – letztes Wochenende **this** weekend – dieses Wochenende **next** weekend – nächstes Wochenende
	sure [ʃʊə], [ʃɔː]	sicher	The next lesson is art. – Are you **sure**? Can you help me? – **Sure**. (Sicher! / Na klar!)
	Here you are.	Bitte schön. / Hier, bitte.	
	German ['dʒɜːmən]	Deutsch; deutsch	

Unit 2: At home with Ellie

p.34	**with** Ellie [wɪð]	bei Ellie	Where's Cyril? – He's **with** Sandy.
	road [rəʊd]	Straße *(Landstraße zwischen Orten; Straße in Orten)*	→ **in Hill Road** – in der Hill Road **in Park Street** – in der Park Street
	street [striːt]	Straße *(in Orten)*	
	in the photo ['fəʊtəʊ]	auf dem Foto	
	house [haʊs]	Haus	
	flat [flæt]	Wohnung	
	kitchen ['kɪtʃɪn]	Küche	
	bedroom ['bedruːm]	Schlafzimmer	
	garden ['gɑːdn]	Garten	
	living room ['lɪvɪŋ ruːm]	Wohnzimmer	
	mum [mʌm]	Mama, Mutti	
	mother ['mʌðə]	Mutter	
	dad [dæd]	Papa, Vati	
	father ['fɑːðə]	Vater	
	live [lɪv]	leben; wohnen	Ellie **lives** in Plymouth.
	her dad [hɜː], [hə]	ihr Vater	**Her** friends live in Plymouth too.
p.35	**hall** [hɔːl]	Flur, Diele	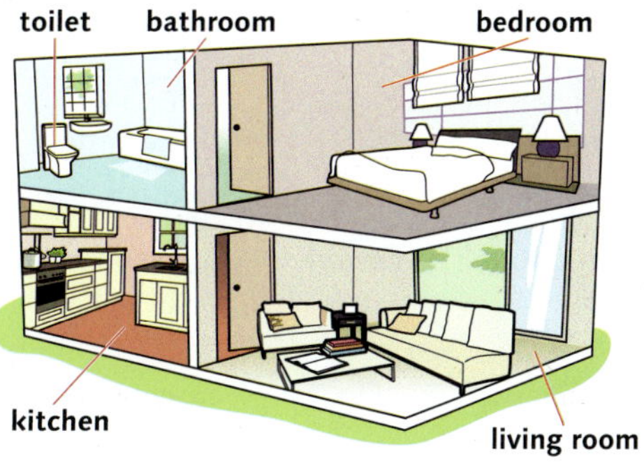
	toilet ['tɔɪlət]	Toilette	
	bathroom ['bɑːθruːm]	Badezimmer, Bad	
	garage ['gærɑːʒ]	Garage	
	dream [driːm]	Traum	

p. 36	**family** ['fæməli]	Familie	! one **family** – two, three, four **families**
	upstairs [ʌp'steəz]	oben; nach oben	
	downstairs [daʊn'steəz]	unten; nach unten	

	always ['ɔːlweɪz]	immer	
	there's ... [ðeəz] **there are ...** ['ðeər ɑː]	es ist ... / es gibt ... es sind ... / es gibt ...	**There's** a ruler in the pencil case, but **there are** no pencils.
	space [speɪs]	Platz	
	into the living room ['ɪntʊ]	in das Wohnzimmer (hinein)	
	stepdad ['stepdæd]	Stiefvater	→ **step-** („Stief-") **stepdad, stepfather** **stepmum, stepmother** **stepsister** **stepbrother**
	miss [mɪs]	vermissen	
	real [rɪəl]	echt, wirklich	
	his partner [hɪz]	sein Partner, seine Partnerin	→ **my** mein/e; **your** dein/e, euer/eure; **his** sein/e; **her** ihr/e
	cute [kjuːt]	niedlich, süß	
	you're lucky ['lʌki]	du hast Glück	
	at Ellie's house	bei Ellie daheim, bei Ellie zu Hause	
p. 37	**family tree**	(Familien-)Stammbaum	
	tree [triː]	Baum	
	together [tə'geðə]	zusammen	
	cousin ['kʌzn]	Cousin, Cousine	
	aunt [ɑːnt]	Tante	
	uncle ['ʌŋkl]	Onkel	
	parents ['peərənts]	Eltern	
	grandparents ['grænpeərənts]	Großeltern	→ **grand-** („Groß-") **grandparents** **grandfather** **grandmother**

Theme 2

p. 38	**problem** ['prɒbləm]	Problem	
	share a room with ... [ʃeə]	sich ein Zimmer mit ... teilen	
	yours [jɔːz]	deiner, deine, deins	
	messy ['mesi]	unordentlich	
	bossy ['bɒsi]	herrisch; rechthaberisch	
	I **can't** do my homework. [kɑːnt]	Ich kann meine Hausaufgaben nicht machen.	→ **can – can't** I/you/he/she/it/we/you/they **can** sing I/you/he/she/it/we/you/they **can't** dance
	do [duː]	machen, tun	

	The kitchen is too **busy**. ['bɪzi]	In der Küche ist zu viel los.	
	noisy ['nɔɪzi]	laut, voller Lärm	
p. 39	**rug** [rʌg]	Teppich, Läufer	
	chair [tʃeə]	Stuhl	
	desk [desk]	Schreibtisch	
	shelf, *pl* **shelves** [ʃelf], [ʃelvz]	Regal, Regale	! one **shelf** – two, three, four **shelves**
	lamp [læmp]	Lampe	
	table ['teɪbl]	Tisch	

a table

a desk

	bed [bed]	Bett	
	cushion ['kʊʃn]	Kissen	
	mirror ['mɪrə]	Spiegel	
	wardrobe ['wɔːdrəʊb]	Kleiderschrank	

	different ['dɪfrənt]	verschieden; anders	You can buy the shirt in three **different** colours. That's a **different** photo.

Focus on language

p. 40	**surprise** [sə'praɪz]	Überraschung	
	tired ['taɪəd]	müde	
	really ['rɪəli]	wirklich	Our English teacher is **really** nice.
	strict [strɪkt]	streng	But our maths teacher is too **strict**.
	mean [miːn]	gemein, fies	
	listen ['lɪsn]	zuhören	→ **Listen**, please. (Hört zu, bitte.) **Listen to** Ellie. (Hört Ellie zu.) **Listen to** the song. (Hört euch das Lied an.)
	question ['kwestʃn]	Frage	
	answer ['ɑːnsə]	Antwort	
p. 41	**easy** ['iːzi]	einfach, leicht	
	difficult ['dɪfɪkəlt]	schwierig, schwer	

Story

p. 42	**example** [ɪg'zɑːmpl]	Beispiel	
	in the picture ['pɪktʃə]	auf dem Bild	

	the best of both worlds	das Beste von beidem	
	Dear … [dɪə]	Liebe … / Lieber …	
	news [njuːz]	Nachrichten	! Englisch: That's good **news**. Deutsch: Das <u>**sind**</u> gute **Nachrichten**.
	at the cinema ['sɪnəmə]	im Kino	**look • see • watch** • **Look**! There's Cyril. • I can **see** Sandy. • I always **watch** the news on TV. Can we **watch** the monkeys?
	watch [wɒtʃ]	*sich etwas* anschauen; beobachten →	
	programme ['prəʊɡræm]	(Fernseh-)Sendung	
	at work [wɜːk]	bei der Arbeit, am Arbeitsplatz	
	soon [suːn]	bald	**at** **at** the cinema – **im** Kino **at** a restaurant – **in** einem Restaurant **at** school – **in** der Schule **at** work – **bei** der Arbeit **at** Ellie's house – **bei** Ellie daheim
	at a restaurant ['restrɒnt]	in einem Restaurant →	
	It's her birthday. ['bɜːθdeɪ]	Sie hat Geburtstag.	
	again [ə'ɡen]	wieder; noch einmal	Look, there's Sandy **again**. Can you say that **again**, please?
	Be quiet. ['kwaɪət]	Sei still. / Sei leise. / Sei ruhig.	
p. 43	**in town** [taʊn]	in der Stadt	
	lonely ['ləʊnli]	einsam	
	text [tekst]	SMS; Text	
	a text **from** mum	eine SMS von Mama	
	from Monday **to** Friday	von Montag bis Freitag	
	week [wiːk]	Woche	
	lots of … ['lɒts əv]	viel …, viele …	There are **lots of** books on the desk.
	because [bɪ'kɒz]	weil	Ellie is lonely **because** she misses her mum.

Skills training

p. 44	**on the beach**	am Strand	
	sea [siː]	Meer	
	What's it like?	Wie ist es? / Wie sieht es aus?	Our house is near Plymouth. – **What's it like?** – It's small and blue and very nice.
p. 45	**go with**	gehören zu, passen zu	Picture 4 **goes with** text 2.
	It's your turn. [tɜːn]	Du bist dran. / Du bist an der Reihe.	
	work [wɜːk]	arbeiten	
	close [kləʊz]	schließen, zumachen	
	door [dɔː]	Tür	Can you close the **door**, please?

	What's for homework?	Was haben wir als Hausaufgabe auf?	
	What page is it?	Auf welcher Seite sind wir?/ Auf welcher Seite steht das?	
	page [peɪdʒ]	Seite	
	I forgot my homework. [fə'gɒt]	Ich habe meine Hausaufgaben vergessen.	
p. 46	**alphabet** ['ælfəbet]	Alphabet	

> **Betonung**
> ['] ist das **Betonungszeichen**. Es steht immer vor der betonten Silbe.
>
> Beispiel: Im Deutschen heißt es *Alpha***bet** – die dritte Silbe wird betont.
> Im Englischen betont man die erste Silbe: ***al****phabet* ['ælfəbet].
>
> Die richtige Betonung kannst du an der Position des Betonungszeichens ['] erkennen.

address [ə'dres]	Adresse, Anschrift	What's your **address**? – 11 Greatfield Street.
phone number ['fəʊn nʌmbə]	Telefonnummer	
spell [spel]	buchstabieren	

Unit 3: My Plymouth

p. 52	**often** ['ɒfn], ['ɒftən]	oft	I **often** ride my bike to school.
	to the cinema	ins Kino	→ go **to** the cinema – **ins** Kino gehen go **to** the beach – **an** den Strand gehen go **to** school – **zur** Schule gehen go **to** work – **zur** Arbeit gehen go **to** bed – **ins** Bett gehen
	summer ['sʌmə]	Sommer	
	fire station ['faɪə steɪʃn]	Feuerwache	Luca's dad works at a **fire station**.
	family name	Familienname, Nachname	
	never ['nevə]	nie, niemals	I **never** ride my bike on the beach. **always** ◄► **never**
p. 53	**aquarium** [ə'kweəriəm]	Aquarium	
	market ['mɑːkɪt]	Markt	at a **market**
	shopping centre ['sentə]	Einkaufszentrum	

Theme 1

p. 54	**stay** [steɪ]	bleiben	Can't we **stay** at home? Can't I **stay** in bed?
	breakfast ['brekfəst]	Frühstück	our **breakfast**

everybody ['evribɒdi]	jeder; alle	**Everybody** likes the beach.
in the morning	am Morgen, morgens	I'm always tired **in the morning**.
go shopping ['ʃɒpɪŋ]	einkaufen gehen	On Saturdays we **go shopping** at the market.

3 VOCABULARY

then [ðen]	dann, danach	… **then** we play games.
vegetables *(pl)* ['vedʒtəblz]	Gemüse	! Englisch: **Vegetables are** good for you. Deutsch: **Gemüse ist** gut für dich.
boring ['bɔːrɪŋ]	langweilig	
like	wie	The English word 'supermarket' is **like** the German word 'Supermarkt'.
sweets *(pl)* [swiːts]	Süßigkeiten	
afternoon [ɑːftə'nuːn]	Nachmittag	
usually ['juːʒuəli]	meistens, normalerweise	
there [ðeə]	da, dort; dahin, dorthin	I often go to the park. I usually meet my friends **there**.
evening ['iːvnɪŋ]	Abend	

• **in** the morning **in** the afternoon **in** the evening	morgens, am Morgen nachmittags, am Nachmittag abends, am Abend	• **on** Monday **on** Tuesdays **on** Friday morning	am Montag dienstags, an Dienstagen freitagmorgens, am Freitagmorgen

sometimes ['sʌmtaɪmz]	manchmal	→ **always** / **usually** / **often** / **sometimes** / **never**
come [kʌm]	kommen	
p.55 **have breakfast;** **have lunch**	frühstücken; (zu) Mittag essen	
present ['preznt]	Geschenk	a **present** 
want to do sth. [wɒnt]	etwas tun wollen	! Englisch: We **want to buy** a present. Deutsch: Wir **wollen** ein Geschenk **kaufen.**
today [tə'deɪ]	heute	
trainers *(pl)* ['treɪnəz]	Turnschuhe	
expensive [ɪk'spensɪv]	teuer	
hoodie ['hʊdi]	Kapuzenpullover, -jacke	

The red **trainers** are great,
but the **hoodie** is too **expensive**.

40 **forty** ['fɔːti] 50 **fifty** ['fɪfti] 60 **sixty** ['sɪksti] 70 **seventy** ['sevnti]	80 **eighty** ['eɪti] 90 **ninety** ['naɪnti] 100 **a hundred/one hundred** [ə'hʌndrəd], ['wʌn'hʌndrəd]	101 **a/one hundred and one** 102 **a/one hundred and two** 103 **a/one hundred and three** …

(► *Numbers*, p. 229)

hate [heɪt]	hassen, gar nicht mögen	**love** ◄► **hate**
terrible ['terəbl]	schrecklich, fürchterlich	Dad thinks dogs are **terrible** – he hates dogs.

p. 56 **on my birthday**	an meinem Geburtstag	
have a party	eine Party feiern	

<u>Einzahl</u> (Singular)	<u>Mehrzahl</u> (Plural)	<u>Einzahl</u> (Singular)	<u>Mehrzahl</u> (Plural)	! Aber:	
baby	**babies**	**hobby**	**hobbies**	**day**	**days**
city	**cities**	**party**	**parties**	**boy**	**boys**
diary	**diaries**	**pony**	**ponies**	**monkey**	**monkeys**
family	**families**	**story**	**stories**		

<u>The months</u> [mʌnθs]
(Die Monate)

1 January ['dʒænjuəri] Januar
2 February ['februəri] Februar
3 March [mɑːtʃ] März
4 April ['eɪprəl] April
5 May [meɪ] Mai
6 June [dʒuːn] Juni
7 July [dʒu'laɪ] Juli
8 August ['ɔːgəst] August
9 September [sep'tembə] September
10 October [ɒk'təʊbə] Oktober
11 November [nəʊ'vembə] November
12 December [dɪ'sembə] Dezember

! Monatsnamen werden immer großgeschrieben.

go swimming	schwimmen gehen	
get [get]	bekommen	I usually **get** nice presents on my birthday.
visit ['vɪzɪt]	besuchen	Can we **visit** Sophie on Sunday?
p. 57 **date** [deɪt]	Datum	
when? [wen]	wann? →	

what?	was?	**where?**	wo(hin)?
who?	wer?	**when?**	wann?
how?	wie?		

When's your birthday?	Wann hast du Geburtstag?	! Englisch: **When is** your birthday? Deutsch: **Wann <u>hast</u>** du Geburtstag?
on 5th May	am 5. Mai	! • you write: **on 5th May** – you say: **on the fifth of May** • mit Datum: My birthday is **on 5th May**. ohne Datum: My birthday is **in May**.
second ['sekənd]	zweite(r, s) →	
third [θɜːd]	dritte(r, s) →	

1	**one**	eins	**1st**	**first**	erste(r, s)
2	**two**	zwei	**2nd**	**second**	zweite(r, s)
3	**three**	drei	**3rd**	**third**	dritte(r, s)
4	**four**	vier	**4th**	**fourth**	vierte(r, s)
5	**five**	fünf	**5th**	**fifth**	fünfte(r, s)

(► *Numbers*, p. 229)

at 1 o'clock [ə'klɒk]	um 1 Uhr/um 13 Uhr	It's **1 o'clock** now.

free [friː]	frei	Can we meet at 1 o'clock? Are you **free**?

p. 58	**get up** [get 'ʌp]	aufstehen	My sister **gets up** at 6 o'clock every morning.
	early ['ɜːli]	früh	I get up **early** too.
	lazy ['leɪzi]	faul	My brother is **lazy** – he often stays in bed.
	late [leɪt]	spät	**early** ◄► **late**
	at night [ət 'naɪt]	nachts, in der Nacht	→ **in** the morning / **in** the afternoon / **in** the evening ! **at** night
	come home; go home	nach Hause kommen; nach Hause gehen	
	after dinner [ɑːftə 'dɪnə]	nach dem Abendessen	**After dinner** we sometimes watch TV.
	us [ʌs], [əs]	uns	We're here. Can you see **us**?
	go by bus [baɪ 'bʌs]	mit dem Bus fahren	I usually **go** to school **by bus**. My brother always **goes by bike**.
	walk [wɔːk]	(zu Fuß) gehen	My sister often **walks** to school.

Story

p. 60	**unhappy** [ʌn'hæpi]	unglücklich	**happy** ◄► **unhappy**
	Happy birthday!	Herzlichen Glückwunsch zum Geburtstag!	
	Let's ... [lets]	Lass uns .../Lasst uns ...	It's late. **Let's** go home.
	plan [plæn]	planen	
	something ['sʌmθɪŋ]	etwas	Can I ask you **something**?
	Shut up! [ʃʌt 'ʌp] *(infml)*	Halt den Mund!	! Vorsicht! Viele Erwachsene finden **Shut up!** sehr unhöflich.
	concert ['kɒnsət]	Konzert	
	zoo [zuː]	Zoo	! Aussprache: **zoo** [zuː] – Der Anfangslaut ist wie im deutschen Namen „Susie".
	excited [ɪk'saɪtɪd]	aufgeregt, gespannt	→ **I** – **my** bike / **you** – **your** bike / **he** – **his** bike / **she** – **her** bike / **we** – **our** bikes / **you** – **your** bikes / **they** – **their** bikes
	their bikes [ðeə]	ihre Fahrräder	
p. 61	**hill** [hɪl]	Hügel	
	down this hill [daʊn]	diesen Hügel hinunter	! Englisch: **down this hill** Deutsch: **diesen Hügel hinunter**
	fast [fɑːst]	schnell	They always go down the hill very **fast**. 
	Come on, Luca!	Na los, Luca!/Komm, Luca!	
	leg [leg]	Bein	

	hospital ['hɒspɪtl]	Krankenhaus	
	I **have a sore leg**. [sɔː]	Mein Bein tut weh.	Luca can't walk. He **has a sore leg**.
	or [ɔː]	oder	Are you a boy **or** a girl?
	want sth. [wɒnt]	etwas (haben) wollen	! • **want sth.** etwas (haben) wollen — I **want** a new bike. • **want <u>to do</u> sth.** etwas tun wollen — I **want to buy** it now.
	end [end]	Ende, Schluss	

Skills training

p.62	**sale** [seɪl]	Verkauf; Schlussverkauf	
	The calculator **is** £1.	Der Taschenrechner kostet 1 Pfund.	
	The mobiles **are** £10.	Die Handys kosten 10 Pfund.	
	How much is ...?/ How much are ...? [mʌtʃ]	Was (Wie viel) kostet ...?/ Was (Wie viel) kosten ...?	**How much is** the football? And **how much are** the books?
	50p [fɪfti 'piː]	50 Pence	
	British ['brɪtɪʃ]	britisch	
	money ['mʌni]	Geld	
p.63	It **looks** nice.	Es sieht schön aus.	→ **look** • **Look at** the pictures. (Sieh dir die Bilder an.) • **Look**, Adam. There's a crab. (Schau mal, Adam. Da ist ein Krebs.) • My new bike **looks** great. (Mein neues Rad sieht toll aus.)
	Excuse me, ... [ɪk'skjuːz miː]	Entschuldigung, .../ Entschuldigen Sie, ...	**Excuse me,** please. How much is this mobile?
	man, *pl* **men** [mæn], [men]	Mann, Männer	! one **man** – two, three, four **men**
	special offer [speʃl 'ɒfə]	Sonderangebot	
	special ['speʃl]	besondere(r, s)	
	It's **good value.** ['væljuː]	Es ist sein Geld wert.	
	the same [seɪm]	derselbe/dieselbe/dasselbe; dieselben	Luca and his brother Jack are at **the same** school.
	try [traɪ]	probieren, ausprobieren	
	I'll take it. [aɪl 'teɪk ɪt]	Ich nehme es (ihn, sie). *(beim Einkaufen)*	How much is the football? – £12. – OK, **I'll take it**.
	That's £159.	Das macht 159 Pfund.	
	helmet ['helmɪt]	Helm	**helmets** 
p.64	**advert** ['ædvɜːt]	Anzeige, Werbung	
	guess [ges]	raten, erraten	**Guess** how old I am. – 15? – No, I'm 14.

Unit 4: Berry's world

pp. 70/71	**world** [wɜːld]	Welt	
	visitor ['vɪzɪtə]	Besucher/in; Gast	
	barn [bɑːn]	Scheune, Stall	
	stroke [strəʊk]	streicheln	
	donkey ['dɒŋki]	Esel	
	duck [dʌk]	Ente	
	pond [pɒnd]	Teich	

	field [fiːld]	Feld; Weide	! Englisch: the ponies **in the field** Deutsch: die Ponys **auf der Weide**
	cow [kaʊ]	Kuh	
	pig [pɪg]	Schwein	
	sheep, *pl* **sheep** [ʃiːp]	Schaf, Schafe	! one **sheep** – two, three, four **sheep**
	chicken ['tʃɪkɪn]	Huhn; (Brat-)Hähnchen	

Theme 1

p. 72	**life**, *pl* **lives** [laɪf], [laɪvz]	*(das)* Leben, *(die)* Leben	! one **life** – two, three, four **lives**
	she doesn't have a … ['dʌznt]	sie hat kein/keine/keinen …	→ Berry **doesn't** have a cat. She has a dog. I **don't have** / you **don't have** / we **don't have** / they **don't have** he **doesn't have** / she **doesn't have** / it **doesn't have**
	alarm clock [ə'lɑːm klɒk]	Wecker	
	wake [weɪk]	wecken	
	other ['ʌðə]	andere(r, s)	The dog is in the garden. Where are the **other** animals?
	outside [aʊt'saɪd]	draußen; nach draußen	The other animals are **outside**, in the field. Let's go **outside** and play.
	inside [ɪn'saɪd]	drinnen; nach drinnen	Berry isn't in the garden. She's **inside**. Let's go **inside** too.
	before breakfast [bɪ'fɔː]	vor dem Frühstück	**before breakfast** ◄► **after breakfast**
	feed [fiːd]	füttern	Can I **feed** the rabbits?
	get ready (for) ['redi]	sich fertig machen (für), sich vorbereiten (auf)	First I have breakfast, then I **get ready for** school.
	all day/summer/…	den ganzen Tag/Sommer/… (lang)	
	eat [iːt]	essen; fressen	
	about [ə'baʊt]	ungefähr	We get up at **about** 8.30 on Sundays.
	look after [lʊk 'ɑːftə]	sich kümmern um; aufpassen auf	On Saturday mornings I always **look after** my baby sister.
	do sport	Sport treiben	And on Saturday afternoons I **do sport**.

	nothing ['nʌθɪŋ]	(gar) nichts	
p.73	**sit** [sɪt]	sitzen; sich setzen	
	year [jɪə]	Jahr	Our dog is two **years** old.
	dialogue ['daɪəlɒg]	Dialog	
	What's the time?	Wie spät ist es?	
	You're welcome.	Bitte, gern geschehen./ Nichts zu danken.	

„bitte"

- in Aufforderungen und Bitten: **please** — Close the door, **please**./What's the time, **please**? (Schließ die Tür, bitte./Wie spät ist es, bitte?)
- wenn sich jemand bedankt hat: **You're welcome.** — It's 9.30. – Thank you. – **You're welcome.** (9 Uhr 30. – Danke. – Bitte, gern geschehen.)
- wenn du jemandem etwas gibst: **Here you are.** — Can I borrow your pen, please? – **Here you are.** (Kann ich deinen Stift leihen? – Hier, bitte.)

Theme 2

p.74	**feeling** ['fiːlɪŋ]	Gefühl	
	discussion [dɪ'skʌʃn]	Diskussion	
	feel [fiːl]	sich fühlen; fühlen	
	feel fed up [fed 'ʌp]	genervt sein, sauer sein; die Nase voll haben	
	when [wen]	wenn	I always feel happy **when** I listen to this song. ! **when** = **1. wann**: **When**'s your birthday? **2. wenn**: I feel great **when** I do sport.
	work [wɜːk]	funktionieren	I need your help. My computer doesn't **work**.
	text a friend [tekst]	einem Freund/einer Freundin eine SMS schicken	**Text** me when you're back from London, OK?
	Not me!	Ich nicht!	**Me too.** (Ich auch.) ◄► **Not me.** (Ich nicht.)
p.75	**a bit** [ə 'bɪt]	ein bisschen	5 o'clock in the morning? That's **a bit** early for me.
	the only student ['əʊnli]	der einzige Schüler/ die einzige Schülerin	Lily is **the only** English student at our school.
	wheelchair ['wiːltʃeə]	Rollstuhl	a **wheelchair**
	normal ['nɔːml]	normal, gewöhnlich	
	win [wɪn]	gewinnen	I feel good when my football team **wins**.
	ask [ɑːsk]	fragen	Can I feed the pigs? – **Ask** my dad, please. ! Englisch: Can I **ask** you a **question**? Deutsch: Kann ich dir eine **Frage stellen**?
	drink [drɪŋk]	Getränk	
	drink [drɪŋk]	trinken	
	understand [ʌndə'stænd]	verstehen	In English, please. I don't **understand** German.
	speak [spiːk]	sprechen	Can you **speak** French?

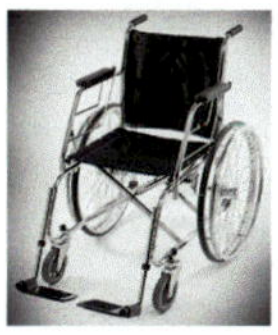

	for myself [maɪ'self]	für mich selbst	
	work/speak/… **well** [wel]	gut funktionieren/sprechen/…	My computer doesn't work very **well**. My parents speak English very **well**.
	mouth [maʊθ]	Mund	

Focus on language

p. 76	**furry** ['fɜːri]	flauschig; pelzig	
p. 77	**interesting** ['ɪntrəstɪŋ]	interessant	This book is great. It's very **interesting**.
	It doesn't like **to** be lonely.	Es mag es nicht, allein zu sein. →	**to** („zu“) I don't like **to** be lonely. allein **zu** sein It's time **to** go now. Zeit **zu** gehen Here's something **to** eat. etwas **zu** essen
	cage [keɪdʒ]	Käfig	
p. 78	**why?** [waɪ]	warum? →	**what?** was? **where?** wo(hin)? **who?** wer? **when?** wann? **why?** warum? **how?** wie?
	friendly ['frendli]	freundlich	
	shoulder ['ʃəʊldə]	Schulter	
	fruit [fruːt]	Obst	
	nut [nʌt]	Nuss	

fruit and nuts

	sleep [sliːp]	schlafen	
p. 79	**find** [faɪnd]	finden	
	Find a person who … ['pɜːsn]	Finde eine Person, die …	

Story

p. 80	**on the bus**	im Bus	! Englisch: **on the bus** Deutsch: **im Bus**
	nervous ['nɜːvəs]	nervös, aufgeregt	
	adventure [əd'ventʃə]	Abenteuer	
	country ['kʌntri]	Land	! Englisch: **in the country** Deutsch: **auf dem Land** ! one **country** – two, three, four **countries**
	scene [siːn]	Szene	
	invite (to) [ɪn'vaɪt]	einladen (zu, nach)	Can I **invite** all my friends to my party?
	sleepover ['sliːpəʊvə]	Schlafparty	
	bring [brɪŋ]	bringen, mitbringen	

	Don't worry. [dəʊnt 'wʌri]	Mach dir keine Sorgen.	→ **Don't ...** **Don't go** now. – Geh jetzt (noch) nicht. **Don't ask**. – Frag nicht. **Don't be** stupid. – Sei nicht dumm. **Don't watch** TV. – Sieh nicht fern.
	worry (about) ['wʌri]	sich Sorgen machen (wegen, um)	Mum always **worries about** me when I come home late.
	her [hɜː]	sie; ihr	→ **her** • *(wessen?)* **ihr, ihre** **her** birthday; **her** children • *(wen?)* **sie** Sally? We can meet **her** in the park. • *(wem?)* **ihr** There's Sophie. Let's help **her**.
	wet [wet]	nass	
	laugh [lɑːf]	lachen	
p. 81	**through** [θruː]	durch	
	that field [ðæt], [ðət]	das Feld (dort), jenes Feld	

this – that
- Wenn etwas **näher beim Sprecher** ist, verwendet man eher **this** („dies hier").
- Wenn etwas **weiter entfernt** ist, verwendet man eher **that** („das dort").

	be hungry ['hʌŋgri]	hungrig sein, Hunger haben	**!** Englisch: **We're hungry.** Deutsch: **Wir haben Hunger.**
	be in trouble ['trʌbl]	in Schwierigkeiten sein; Ärger kriegen	My friends always help me when **I'm in trouble**.
	dangerous ['deɪndʒərəs]	gefährlich	a **dangerous** snake 
	noise [nɔɪz]	Geräusch; Lärm	Listen! What's that **noise** in the garden? What's that **noise**? I can't do my homework.
	only ['əʊnli]	nur, bloß	
	Go to sleep!	Schlaf jetzt!	Be quiet now and **go to sleep**.

Skills training

p. 82	**sign** [saɪn]	Schild; Zeichen	
	left [left]	links; nach links	left
	right [raɪt]	rechts; nach rechts	right
p. 83	**invitation (to)** [ɪnvɪ'teɪʃn]	Einladung (zu, nach)	
	picnic ['pɪknɪk]	Picknick	
	5 **pm** [piː'em]	5 Uhr nachmittags/abends; 17 Uhr	
	9 **am** [eɪ'em]	9 Uhr morgens/vormittags	
	I'd love to come. (= I would love to ...) [wʊd]	Ich komme sehr gern./ Ich würde sehr gern kommen.	
	Best wishes ['wɪʃɪz]	Viele Grüße, ... *(Briefschluss)*	

p. 84	**use** [juːz]	benutzen, verwenden	→ **!** Aussprache:
	dictionary ['dɪkʃənri]	Wörterbuch, *(alphabetisches)* Wörterverzeichnis	**!** one **dictionary** – two, three, four **dictionaries**
	poem ['pəʊɪm]	Gedicht	

use	he/she **uses**	['juːzɪz]
close	he/she **closes**	['kləʊzɪz]
dance	he/she **dances**	['dɑːnsɪz]
guess	he/she **guesses**	['gesɪz]
watch	he/she **watches**	['wɒtʃɪz]

Unit 5: All about Adam

p. 90	**harbour** ['hɑːbə]	Hafen
	on the left	links, auf der linken Seite
	on the right	rechts, auf der rechten Seite
	in the middle ['mɪdl]	in der Mitte

Lily is on the left, Ben is in the middle, Ava is on the right.

p. 91	**Where is Adam going?**	Wohin geht Adam (gerade)?
	cafe ['kæfeɪ]	Café
	ferry ['feri]	Fähre

Theme 1

p. 92	**chips** *(pl)* [tʃɪps]	Pommes frites
	salad ['sæləd]	Salat *(als Gericht oder Beilage)*
	soup [suːp]	Suppe
	a **bottle of …** ['bɒtl]	eine Flasche …
	water ['wɔːtə]	Wasser
	a **cup of …** [kʌp]	eine Tasse …
	coffee ['kɒfi]	Kaffee
	tea [tiː]	Tee
	scone [skɒn]	*kleines rundes Milchbrötchen, leicht süß, oft mit Rosinen*
	Anything else? ['eniθɪŋ 'els]	Sonst noch etwas?

two bottles of juice **a bottle of water** **a cup of coffee**

	How's it going?	Wie geht's?/Wie läuft's?
	ring [rɪŋ]	läuten, klingeln
	job [dʒɒb]	Job, (Arbeits-)Stelle

Adam's mobile is **ringing**.

	be busy ['bɪzi]	beschäftigt sein; viel zu tun haben	
	cook [kʊk]	kochen, *(Essen)* zubereiten	What are you **cooking**, Mum? – Omelettes.
	wash up [wɒʃ 'ʌp]	abwaschen	
	must [mʌst]	müssen	
	work **hard** [hɑːd]	hart arbeiten	We must work **hard** at school.
	I must go.	*(am Telefon)* Ich muss Schluss machen.	
	Say hi to everybody.	Grüß alle.	

p. 93	**letter** ['letə]	Brief	
	be worried (about) ['wʌrid]	beunruhigt sein, besorgt sein (wegen)	Ms Lee **is worried about** Adam because he's often tired at school.
	at the moment ['məʊmənt]	im Moment, gerade	
	phone [fəʊn]	anrufen	
	happen ['hæpən]	geschehen, passieren	Say what's **happening** in the pictures.

Theme 2

p. 94	**so** boring/tired/... [səʊ]	so langweilig/müde/...	
	dive [daɪv]	einen Kopfsprung machen	
	hide [haɪd]	verstecken; sich verstecken	→ Let's **hide** in the wardrobe.
			! Schreibung: **come** – **coming**, **dive** – **diving**, **have** – **having**, **hide** – **hiding**, **make** – **making**, **phone** – **phoning**, **ride** – **riding**, **write** – **writing**
	send [send]	schicken, senden	
p. 95	**guitar** [gɪ'tɑː]	Gitarre	
	learn [lɜːn]	lernen	
	drums [drʌmz]	Schlagzeug; Trommeln	! Englisch: **play the guitar / the drums** Deutsch: **Gitarre / Schlagzeug spielen**
	group [gruːp]	Gruppe	
	instrument ['ɪnstrəmənt]	Instrument	
	young [jʌŋ]	jung	**young** ◄► **old**
	musician [mju'zɪʃn]	Musiker/in	
	singer ['sɪŋə]	Sänger/in	
	sing [sɪŋ]	singen	
	piano [pi'ænəʊ]	Klavier, Piano	! Englisch: **play the piano** Deutsch: **Klavier spielen**
	join a club [dʒɔɪn]	sich einem Klub anschließen; in einen Klub eintreten	I want to **join** the guitar club. What about you?
	price [praɪs]	(Kauf-)Preis	

p. 96	**set the table** [set]	den Tisch decken	→ ! Schreibung: get – ge**tt**ing; rap – ra**pp**ing; set – se**tt**ing; sit – si**tt**ing; swim – swi**mm**ing
	clean [kliːn]	sauber machen, putzen	
	little ['lɪtl]	klein	On Saturday mornings I always look after my **little** sister.
	maybe ['meɪbi]	vielleicht	
	cook [kʊk]	Koch, Köchin	**two cooks** 
	Well, … [wel]	Nun, … / Also, … / Na ja, …	
	form [fɔːm]	Form	'am', 'is' and 'are' are **forms** of 'be'.
p. 97	**food** [fuːd]	Essen; Lebensmittel; Futter	
	him [hɪm]	ihn; ihm	Look, there's Zack. Can you see **him**? Let's help **him**.
	them [ðem], [ðəm]	sie; ihnen	Look, there are the boys. Can you see **them**? Let's help **them**.

I (ich) – **me**	Can you see **me**? (mich)	Help **me**. (mir)
you (du; Sie) – **you**	Can I phone **you**? (dich; Sie)	Can I help **you**? (dir; Ihnen)
he (er) – **him**	Can you see **him**? (ihn)	Help **him**. (ihm)
she (sie) – **her**	Can you see **her**? (sie)	Help **her**. (ihr)
it (es) – **it**	Can you see **it**? (es)	Help **it**. (ihm)
we (wir) – **us**	Can you see **us**? (uns)	Help **us**. (uns)
you (ihr; Sie) – **you**	Can I phone **you**? (euch; Sie)	Can I help **you**? (euch; Ihnen)
they (sie) – **them**	Can you see **them**? (sie)	Help **them**. (ihnen)

	window ['wɪndəʊ]	Fenster	
	hear [hɪə]	hören	! **hear** = hören (können) **listen (to)** = zuhören, horchen **Listen**! Can you **hear** that noise?

Story

p. 98	**difference** ['dɪfrəns]	Unterschied	
	it **was** Friday [wɒz], [wəz]	es war Freitag	→ • **I am** (ich bin) – **I was** (ich war) • **he/she/it is** (er/sie/es ist) – **he/she/it was** (er/sie/es war)
	on the way to … [weɪ]	auf dem Weg zu/nach …	
	some [sʌm], [səm]	einige, ein paar; etwas	There are **some** sandwiches for you on the table. And there's **some** juice too.

	they **were** on the bus	sie waren im Bus	→
	he **said** [sed]	er sagte; er hat gesagt	
	seat [siːt]	(Sitz-)Platz	

- **we are** (wir sind) — **we were** (wir waren)
- **you are** (du bist; ihr seid) — **you were** (du warst; ihr wart)
- **they are** (sie sind) — **they were** (sie waren)

	they **laughed** [lɑːft]	sie lachten; sie haben gelacht	
	face [feɪs]	Gesicht	
	she **asked** [ɑːskt]	sie fragte; sie hat gefragt	
	I **had** [hæd], [həd]	ich hatte; ich habe gehabt	
	girlfriend ['gɜːlfrend]	(feste) Freundin	
	boyfriend ['bɔɪfrend]	(fester) Freund	
	Any ideas? ['eni]	Irgendwelche Ideen?	I need help with my text. **Any** ideas?
	hard [hɑːd]	schwer, schwierig; hart	This exercise isn't **hard**. You can do it. It's **hard** work to write a rap.
p. 99	**Well done.** [wel 'dʌn]	Gut gemacht!	
	proud (of) [praʊd]	stolz (auf)	
	true [truː]	wahr	
	false [fɔːls]	falsch	
	he **wasn't** there ['wɒznt]	er war nicht da	

Skills training

p. 100	**describe** [dɪ'skraɪb]	beschreiben	**!** Englisch: **Describe** the picture **to** **him/her**. Deutsch: **Beschreibe** **ihm/ihr** das Bild.
	next to	neben	
	between [bɪ'twiːn]	zwischen	
	behind [bɪ'haɪnd]	hinter	
	under ['ʌndə]	unter	
	in front of [ɪn 'frʌnt əv]	vor	

	apple ['æpl]	Apfel	
p. 101	**text message** ['tekst mesɪdʒ]	SMS	
p. 102	**recipe** ['resəpi]	(Koch-)Rezept	
	jam [dʒæm]	Marmelade	
	cream [kriːm]	Sahne	

p. 108	°**school is out** [aʊt]	die Schule ist aus/vorbei	
	°**I'd prefer …** [prɪ'fɜː]	ich würde … vorziehen	
	°**canoe** [kə'nuː]	Kanu, Paddelboot	
	°**theme park** ['θiːm pɑːk]	Themenpark *(Freizeitpark mit Attraktionen zu einem bestimmten Thema)*	

Theme

p. 110	°**swimsuit** ['swɪmsuːt]	Badeanzug	
	°**swimming trunks** *(pl)* ['swɪmɪŋ trʌŋks]	Badehose	→
	°**towel** ['taʊəl]	Handtuch	
	°**sunglasses** *(pl)* ['sʌnglɑːsɪz]	Sonnenbrille	→
	°**hat** [hæt]	Hut	
	°**That's a pity.** ['pɪti]	Das ist schade!	
	°**crisps** *(pl)* [krɪsps]	(Kartoffel-)Chips	! Englisch: **crisps** = Deutsch: **Chips** Englisch: **chips** = Deutsch: **Pommes frites**
	°**sausage** ['sɒsɪdʒ]	(Brat-, Bock-)Würstchen, Wurst	
	°**cake** [keɪk]	Kuchen, Torte	
	°**orange** ['ɒrɪndʒ]	Orange, Apfelsine	
	°**chocolate** ['tʃɒklət]	Schokolade	
	°**biscuit** ['bɪskɪt]	Keks, Plätzchen	! Englisch: **biscuit** = Deutsch: **Keks** Englisch: **cake** = Deutsch: **Kuchen, Torte**
p. 111	°**speaker** ['spiːkə]	Lautsprecher	
	°**tube** [tjuːb]	Schwimmreifen	
	°**umbrella** [ʌm'brelə]	(Regen-)Schirm	
	°**suncream** ['sʌnkriːm]	Sonnencreme, Sonnenschutzmittel	
	°**bodyboard** ['bɒdɪbɔːd]	*kurzes Surfbrett, mit dem man auf dem Bauch liegend surft*	
	°**blanket** ['blæŋkɪt]	Decke *(zum Zudecken u.Ä.)*	
	°**forget** [fə'get]	vergessen	
	°**chain** [tʃeɪn]	Kette	

swimming trunks und **sunglasses** sind immer Plural:
Your **swimming trunks/sunglasses are** great. **Are they** new?
(Deine **Badehose/Sonnenbrille ist** toll. **Ist sie** neu?)

a chocolate cake

Story

p. 113	°**aboard** [ə'bɔːd]	an Bord	
	°**message in a bottle** ['mesɪdʒ]	Flaschenpost	 a message in a bottle
	°**woman,** *pl* **women** ['wʊmən], ['wɪmɪn]	Frau, Frauen	! one **woman** – two, three, four **women**
	°**smuggler** ['smʌɡlə]	Schmuggler/in	
	°**put** [pʊt]	*(etwas wohin)* tun, legen, stellen, stecken	
	°**better** ['betə]	besser	**good – better – best**
	°**the sea's coming in**	die Flut kommt; das Wasser steigt	
	°**minute** ['mɪnɪt]	Minute	
	°**hurry** ['hʌri]	sich beeilen	
	°**square** [skweə]	Platz *(in der Stadt)*	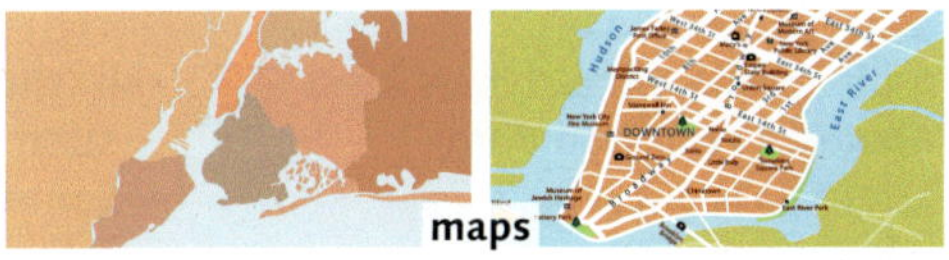 maps
	°**map** [mæp]	Landkarte, Stadtplan	
	°**another** [ə'nʌðə]	noch ein(e)	
	°**follow** ['fɒləʊ]	folgen; verfolgen	
p. 114	°**push** [pʊʃ]	schieben	
	°**clock** [klɒk]	(Wand-, Stand-, Turm-)Uhr	
	°**quick** [kwɪk]	schnell	
	°**slow** [sləʊ]	langsam	
	°**look for** sth.	etwas suchen; nach etwas Ausschau halten	
	°**hot** [hɒt]	heiß	
	°**ice cream** [aɪs 'kriːm]	(Speise-)Eis	
p. 115	°**wait (for)** [weɪt]	warten (auf)	
	°**daughter** ['dɔːtə]	Tochter	
	°**get out** [get 'aʊt]	herauskommen	
	°**out of …** ['aʊt əv]	aus … (heraus/hinaus)	
	°**scary** ['skeəri]	unheimlich	
	°**over there** [əʊvə 'ðeə]	da drüben, dort drüben	

Skills training

p. 116	°**fly** [flaɪ]	fliegen	

DICTIONARY

English – German

Das **DICTIONARY** besteht aus **zwei alphabetischen Wörterlisten**:
English – German (S. 208–218) und **German – English** (S. 219–227)

Im **English – German dictionary** kannst du nachschlagen, wenn du wissen möchtest, was ein englisches Wort bedeutet, wie man es ausspricht oder wie es geschrieben wird.

Im **Dictionary** werden folgende **Abkürzungen und Symbole** verwendet:

sth. = something (etwas) *pl* = *plural* (Mehrzahl) *infml* = *informal* (umgangssprachlich)

° Mit diesem Kringel sind Wörter markiert, die nicht zum Lernwortschatz gehören.

Die **Fundstellenangaben** zeigen, wo ein Wort zum ersten Mal in *Lighthouse 1* vorkommt.
Die Ziffern in Klammern bezeichnen Seitenzahlen:

(8) = Seite 8
1 (19) = Unit 1, Seite 19

Tipps zur Arbeit mit einem Wörterbuch findest du im Skills file auf Seite 164.

A

a [ə] ein, eine (9)
a bit [ə 'bɪt] ein bisschen 4 (75)
°**aboard** [ə'bɔːd] an Bord
about [ə'baʊt]:
1. über 1 (19)
2. ungefähr 4 (72)
about me/you/... über mich/dich/... 1 (19) **What about ...?** Wie wär's mit ...? 3 (55)
What about you? Und du?/Und was ist mit dir? (8)
°**act** [ækt] (vor)spielen, aufführen
°**activity** [æk'tɪvəti] Aktivität
°**add** [æd] hinzufügen
address [ə'dres] Adresse, Anschrift 2 (46)
adventure [əd'ventʃə] Abenteuer 4 (80)
advert ['ædvɜːt] Anzeige, Werbung 3 (64)
Africa ['æfrɪkə] Afrika 1 (26)
after ['ɑːftə] nach 3 (58) **after dinner** nach dem Abendessen 3 (58) **look after** sich kümmern um; aufpassen auf 4 (72)
afternoon [ɑːftə'nuːn] Nachmittag 3 (54) **in the afternoon** nachmittags, am Nachmittag 3 (54)
on Friday afternoon freitagnachmittags, am Freitagnachmittag 3 (54)
again [ə'gen] wieder; noch einmal 2 (42)
age [eɪdʒ] Alter 1 (18)
°**agree on sth.** [ə'griː] sich auf etwas einigen
alarm clock [ə'lɑːm klɒk] Wecker 4 (72)
all (the) [ɔːl] alle 1 (23) **all day/summer/...** den ganzen Tag/Sommer/... (lang) 4 (72)
°**all around me** ganz um mich herum
°**alone** [ə'ləʊn] allein
°**along** [ə'lɒŋ]: **sing along** mitsingen
°**aloud** [ə'laʊd]: **read sth. aloud** etwas laut (vor)lesen
alphabet ['ælfəbet] Alphabet 2 (46)
°**alphabetical order** [ælfə'betɪkl 'ɔːdə] alphabetische Reihenfolge
always ['ɔːlweɪz] immer 2 (36)
am [eɪ'em]: **9 am** 9 Uhr morgens/vormittags 4 (83)
an [ən] ein, eine (12)
and [ænd, ənd] und (9)
animal ['ænɪml] Tier (12)
°**another** [ə'nʌðə] noch ein(e)
answer ['ɑːnsə]:
1. Antwort 2 (40)
°2. (be)antworten
Any ideas? ['eni] Irgendwelche Ideen? 5 (98)
Anything else? ['eniθɪŋ 'els] Sonst noch etwas? 5 (92)
apple ['æpl] Apfel 5 (100)
°**appointment** [ə'pɔɪntmənt] Verabredung, Termin
April ['eɪprəl] April 3 (56)
aquarium [ə'kweəriəm] Aquarium 3 (53)
are [ɑː] bist; sind; seid 1 (18)
Here you are. Bitte schön./Hier, bitte. 1 (28) **How are you?** Wie geht's?/Wie geht es dir/euch? 1 (17) **The mobiles are £ 10.** Die Handys kosten 10 Pfund. 3 (62)
°**around** [ə'raʊnd]: **all around me** ganz um mich herum **Walk around.** Geh umher.
art [ɑːt] Kunst 1 (20)
°**as many sentences/questions as you can** [æz, əz] so viele Sätze/Fragen wie du kannst
ask [ɑːsk] fragen 4 (75) **ask questions** Fragen stellen 4 (75)
she asked [ɑːskt] sie fragte; sie hat gefragt 5 (98) °**ask for sth.** um etwas bitten
assembly [ə'sembli] Schulversammlung, Morgenappell 1 (21)
at [æt, ət]:
at 1 o'clock um 1 Uhr/um 13 Uhr 3 (57) **at a restaurant** in einem Restaurant 2 (42)
at Ellie's house bei Ellie daheim, bei Ellie zu Hause 2 (36)
at home daheim, zu Hause 1 (24)
at MARTINS bei MARTINS 1 (26)
at night nachts, in der Nacht 3 (58) **at school** in der Schule 1 (20) **at the cinema** im Kino 2 (42) **at the market** auf dem Markt 3 (53) **at the moment** im Moment, gerade 5 (93) **at the weekend** am Wochenende 4 (73) **at this school** auf/an dieser Schule 1 (18) **at work** bei der Arbeit, am Arbeitsplatz 2 (42)
August ['ɔːgəst] August 3 (56)
aunt [ɑːnt] Tante 2 (37)
away [ə'weɪ] weg, fort (14)

B

baby ['beɪbi] Baby 2 (36)

babysitter ['beɪbisɪtə] Babysitter 5 (91)

back [bæk]**:**
1. zurück 1 (26)
°**2.** Rückseite

bad [bæd] schlecht; schlimm 1 (25)

°**badminton** ['bædmɪntən] Badminton, Federball

bag [bæg] Tasche, Beutel 1 (27)

°**baking powder** ['beɪkɪŋ paʊdə] Backpulver

°**balcony** ['bælkəni] Balkon

ball [bɔːl] Ball 5 (100)

°**banana skin** [bə'nɑːnə skɪn] Bananenschale

band [bænd] Band, (Musik-)Gruppe 5 (95)

barn [bɑːn] Scheune, Stall 4 (71)

basketball ['bɑːskɪtbɔːl] Basketball 4 (75)

bathroom ['bɑːθruːm] Badezimmer, Bad 2 (35)

°**battle** ['bætl] Kampf, Schlacht

be [biː] sein 1 (24) **Be quiet.** Sei still./Sei leise. 2 (42)

beach [biːtʃ] Strand (9) **on the beach** am Strand 2 (44)

bear [beə] Bär (12)

°**beats per minute** ['biːts pɜː 'mɪnɪt] *(Musik)* Schläge pro Minute

because [bɪ'kɒz] weil 2 (43)

bed [bed] Bett 2 (39)

bedroom ['bedruːm] Schlafzimmer 2 (34)

before [bɪ'fɔː]**:**
1. vor 4 (72) **before breakfast** vor dem Frühstück 4 (72)
2. bevor 1 (24) **before you read** bevor du liest 1 (24)

behind [bɪ'haɪnd] hinter 5 (100)

°**belong** [bɪ'lɒŋ] (hin)gehören

best [best]**:**
my best friends meine besten Freunde/Freundinnen 1 (18) **the best of both worlds** das Beste von beidem 2 (42) **Best wishes** Viele Grüße, … *(Briefschluss)* 4 (83)

°**better** ['betə] besser

between [bɪ'twiːn] zwischen 5 (100)

big [bɪg] groß (13)

bike [baɪk] Fahrrad (13)
by bike mit dem Rad 3 (58) **go by bike** mit dem Rad fahren 3 (58) **ride a bike** Rad fahren 1 (18)

bird [bɜːd] Vogel (12)

birthday ['bɜːθdeɪ] Geburtstag 2 (42) **It's her birthday.** Sie hat Geburtstag. 2 (42) **My birthday is on 5th May.** Ich habe am 5. Mai Geburtstag. 3 (57) **on my birthday** an meinem Geburtstag 3 (56) **When's your birthday?** Wann hast du Geburtstag? 3 (57)

°**biscuit** ['bɪskɪt] Keks, Plätzchen

bit [bɪt]**: a bit** ein bisschen 4 (75)

black [blæk] schwarz (10)

°**blanket** ['blæŋkɪt] Decke *(zum Zudecken u.Ä.)*

blazer ['bleɪzə] Blazer *(Jackett, oft Teil der Schuluniform)* 1 (24)

blue [bluː] blau (10)

BMX [biː em 'eks] BMX-Rad 1 (18)

°**board** [bɔːd] Tafel

°**bodyboard** ['bɒdɪbɔːd] *kurzes Surfbrett, mit dem man auf dem Bauch liegend surft*

book [bʊk] Buch (11)

°**bored** [bɔːd]**: I'm bored** ich langweile mich

boring ['bɔːrɪŋ] langweilig 3 (54)

borrow ['bɒrəʊ] (aus)leihen, sich borgen 1 (28)

bossy ['bɒsi] herrisch; rechthaberisch 2 (38)

both [bəʊθ]**: the best of both worlds** das Beste von beidem 2 (42)

bottle ['bɒtl]**: a bottle of …** eine Flasche … 5 (92) °**message in a bottle** Flaschenpost

°**bowl** [bəʊl] Schüssel, Schale

box [bɒks] Kasten, Kiste, Kästchen 1 (27)

boy [bɔɪ] Junge 1 (16)

boyfriend ['bɔɪfrend] (fester) Freund 5 (98)

°**bracket** ['brækɪt] Klammer

break [breɪk] Pause 1 (21)

breakfast ['brekfəst] Frühstück 3 (54) **have breakfast** frühstücken 3 (55)

bring [brɪŋ] bringen, mitbringen 4 (80)

British ['brɪtɪʃ] britisch 3 (62)

brochure ['brəʊʃə] Broschüre, Prospekt 1 (26)

brother ['brʌðə] Bruder 1 (18)

brown [braʊn] braun (10)

°**budgie** ['bʌdʒi] Wellensittich

°**bull** [bʊl] Stier, Bulle

bus [bʌs] Bus 3 (58) **by bus** mit dem Bus 3 (58) **go by bus** mit dem Bus fahren 3 (58) **on the bus** im Bus 4 (80)

busy ['bɪzi]**: be busy** beschäftigt sein; viel zu tun haben 5 (92) **The kitchen is too busy.** In der Küche ist zu viel los. 2 (38)

but [bʌt, bət] aber 1 (23)

°**butter** ['bʌtə] Butter

buy [baɪ] kaufen 1 (26)

by bus/bike/car/… [baɪ] mit dem Bus/Rad/Auto/… 3 (58) **go by bus/bike/car/…** mit dem Bus/Rad/Auto/… fahren 3 (58)

Bye. [baɪ] Tschüs. 1 (17)

C

cafe ['kæfeɪ] Café 5 (91)

cage [keɪdʒ] Käfig 4 (77)

°**cake** [keɪk] Kuchen, Torte

calculator ['kælkjuleɪtə] Taschenrechner 1 (26)

°**calendar** ['kælɪndə] Kalender

can [kæn, kən] können (9) **Can you remember the animals?** Kannst du dich an die Tiere erinnern?/Könnt ihr euch an die Tiere erinnern? (12) **I can't do my homework.** [kɑːnt] Ich kann meine Hausaufgaben nicht machen. 2 (38)

°**canoe** [kə'nuː] Kanu, Paddelboot

canteen [kæn'tiːn] Kantine, (Schul-)Mensa 1 (20)

°**caption** ['kæpʃn] Bildunterschrift

car [kɑː] Auto 1 (16) **by car** mit dem Auto 3 (58) **go by car** mit dem Auto fahren 3 (58)

card [kɑːd] Karte 1 (27)

cat [kæt] Katze (12)

CD [siː'diː] CD 4 (83)

centre ['sentə] Zentrum, Center 3 (53)

°**chain** [tʃeɪn] Kette

chair [tʃeə] Stuhl 2 (39)

chant [tʃɑːnt] Sprechgesang (15)

°**character** ['kærəktə] Figur *(in Roman, Theaterstück u.Ä.)*

°**chat** [tʃæt] chatten, plaudern, sich unterhalten

°**check** [tʃek] (über)prüfen, kontrollieren

chicken ['tʃɪkɪn] Huhn; (Brat-)Hähnchen 4 (71)

child, *pl* **children** [tʃaɪld], ['tʃɪldrən] Kind, Kinder 1 (26)

°**chipmunk** ['tʃɪpmʌŋk] Streifenhörnchen

chips *(pl)* [tʃɪps] Pommes frites 5 (92)
°**chocolate** ['tʃɒklət] Schokolade
°**choose** [tʃuːz] (aus)wählen
°**chorus** ['kɔːrəs] Refrain
cinema ['sɪnəmə] Kino 2 (42)
°**circle** ['sɜːkl] Kreis
city ['sɪti] (Groß-)Stadt 1 (22)
class [klɑːs] (Schul-)Klasse (8)
classroom ['klɑːsruːm] Klassenzimmer 1 (22)
class teacher ['klɑːs tiːtʃə] Klassenlehrer/in 1 (19)
clean [kliːn] sauber machen, putzen 5 (96)
°**clock** [klɒk] (Wand-, Stand-, Turm-)Uhr
close [kləʊz] schließen, zumachen 2 (45)
°**clothes** *(pl)* [kləʊðz] Kleidung; Kleidungsstücke
club [klʌb] Klub 5 (95)
coffee ['kɒfi] Kaffee 5 (92)
°**cold** [kəʊld] kalt
°**collect** [kə'lekt] sammeln
colour ['kʌlə] Farbe (10)
°**column** ['kɒləm] Spalte
come [kʌm] kommen 3 (54) **come home** nach Hause kommen 3 (58) **Come on, Luca!** Na los, Luca! / Komm, Luca! 3 (61) °**the sea's coming in** die Flut kommt; das Wasser steigt
°**comment** ['kɒment] Kommentar
°**compare** [kəm'peə] vergleichen
°**complete** [kəm'pliːt] vervollständigen
computer [kəm'pjuːtə] Computer 1 (20)
concert ['kɒnsət] Konzert 3 (60)
cook [kʊk]:
1. kochen, *(Essen)* zubereiten 5 (92)
2. Koch, Köchin 5 (96)
cool [kuːl] cool (13)
°**copy** ['kɒpi] kopieren
°**correct** [kə'rekt]:
1. korrekt, richtig
2. korrigieren, verbessern
country ['kʌntri] Land 4 (80) **in the country** auf dem Land 4 (80)
cousin ['kʌzn] Cousin/e 2 (37)
cow [kaʊ] Kuh 4 (71)
crab [kræb] Krebs (8)
cream [kriːm] Sahne 5 (102)
°**crisps** *(pl)* [krɪsps] (Kartoffel-)Chips
crocodile ['krɒkədaɪl] Krokodil (12)
cup [kʌp]: **a cup of ...** eine Tasse ... 5 (92)
cushion ['kʊʃn] Kissen 2 (39)
°**customer** ['kʌstəmə] Kunde, Kundin
cute [kjuːt] niedlich, süß 2 (36)

D

dad [dæd] Papa, Vati 2 (34)
dance [dɑːns] tanzen (11)
dangerous ['deɪndʒərəs] gefährlich 4 (81)
date [deɪt] Datum 3 (57)
°**daughter** ['dɔːtə] Tochter
day [deɪ] Tag (14)
Dear ... [dɪə] Liebe ... / Lieber ... 2 (42)
December [dɪ'sembə] Dezember 3 (56)
°**degu** ['deɪguː, 'deguː] Degu *(Nagetierart)*
describe [dɪ'skraɪb] beschreiben 5 (100)
desk [desk] Schreibtisch 2 (39)
°**diagram** ['daɪəgræm] Diagramm
dialogue ['daɪəlɒg] Dialog 4 (73)
diary ['daɪəri] Tagebuch; Kalender 1 (26)
dictionary ['dɪkʃənri] Wörterbuch, *(alphabetisches)* Wörterverzeichnis (3)/4 (84)
difference ['dɪfrəns] Unterschied 5 (98)
different ['dɪfrənt] verschieden; anders 2 (39)
difficult ['dɪfɪkəlt] schwierig, schwer 2 (41)
°**digital clock** [dɪdʒɪtl 'klɒk] Digitaluhr
dinner ['dɪnə] Abendessen, Abendbrot 3 (58) **have dinner** Abendbrot essen, zu Abend essen 3 (58)
°**dirty** ['dɜːti] schmutzig
°**disabled** [dɪs'eɪbld] (körper)behindert
°**discuss sth.** [dɪ'skʌs] über etwas diskutieren, etwas besprechen
discussion [dɪ'skʌʃn] Diskussion 4 (74)
dive [daɪv] einen Kopfsprung machen 5 (94)
do [duː] machen, tun 2 (38) **do sport** Sport treiben 4 (72) **What do you think?** Was meinst du? / Was denkst du? 1 (25) **Don't worry.** [dəʊnt] Mach dir keine Sorgen. 4 (80) **I don't like blue.** Ich mag Blau nicht. / Ich mag kein Blau. (10) **she doesn't have a ...** ['dʌznt] sie hat kein/keine/keinen ... 4 (72)
dog [dɒg] Hund (12)
done: Well done. [wel 'dʌn] Gut gemacht! 5 (99) °**the holidays are done** *(infml)* die Ferien sind vorbei
donkey ['dɒŋki] Esel 4 (71)
door [dɔː] Tür 2 (45)
°**dossier** ['dɒsieɪ] Mappe
°**double circle** [dʌbl 'sɜːkl] Doppelkreis
down [daʊn]: **down this hill** diesen Hügel hinunter 3 (61) °**Turn the page upside down.** Dreh die Seite auf den Kopf.
downstairs [daʊn'steəz] unten; nach unten 2 (36)
drama ['drɑːmə] Schauspiel, darstellende Kunst 1 (21)
°**draw** [drɔː] zeichnen
dream [driːm] Traum 2 (35)
drink [drɪŋk]:
1. trinken 4 (75)
2. Getränk 4 (75)
drums *(pl)* [drʌmz] Schlagzeug; Trommeln 5 (95) **play the drums** Schlagzeug spielen 5 (95)
duck [dʌk] Ente 4 (70)
DVD [diːviː'diː] DVD 4 (83)

E

°**each** [iːtʃ]: **for each number/picture** für jede Nummer/jedes Bild
early ['ɜːli] früh 3 (58)
easy ['iːzi] einfach, leicht 2 (41)
eat [iːt] essen; fressen 4 (72)
°**egg** [eg] Ei
eight [eɪt] acht (8)
elephant ['elɪfənt] Elefant (12)
eleven [ɪ'levn] elf (8)
else: Anything else? ['eniθɪŋ 'els] Sonst noch etwas? 5 (92)
email ['iːmeɪl] E-Mail 4 (80)
end [end] Ende, Schluss 3 (61) °**in the end** schließlich; letzten Endes; am Ende
°**ending** ['endɪŋ] Ende, Abschluss
England ['ɪŋglənd] England (8)
English ['ɪŋglɪʃ] Englisch; englisch 1 (18)
°**enjoy** [ɪn'dʒɔɪ] genießen
°**e-pal** ['iːpæl] Brieffreund/in *(im Internet)*
evening ['iːvnɪŋ] Abend 3 (54) **in the evening** abends, am Abend 3 (54) **on Friday evening** freitagabends, am Freitagabend 3 (54)
every day/room/... ['evri] jeder Tag/jedes Zimmer/... 1 (21)

everybody ['evribɒdi] jeder; alle 3 (54)
°**everything** ['evriθɪŋ] alles
example [ɪg'zɑːmpl] Beispiel 2 (42)
°**for example** zum Beispiel
excited [ɪk'saɪtɪd] aufgeregt, gespannt 3 (60)
Excuse me, ... [ɪk'skjuːz miː] Entschuldigung, ... / Entschuldigen Sie, ... 3 (63)
exercise ['eksəsaɪz] Übung, Aufgabe 1 (26)
exercise book ['eksəsaɪz bʊk] Schulheft, Übungsheft 1 (26)
expensive [ɪk'spensɪv] teuer 3 (55)
°**explain** [ɪk'spleɪn] erklären
°**eye** [aɪ] Auge

F

face [feɪs] Gesicht 5 (98)
fall [fɔːl] fallen; hinfallen 3 (61)
false [fɔːls] falsch 5 (99)
family ['fæməli] Familie 2 (36)
family name Familienname, Nachname 3 (52) **family tree** (Familien-)Stammbaum 2 (37)
farm [fɑːm] Bauernhof, Farm 4 (70)
fast [fɑːst] schnell 3 (61)
father ['fɑːðə] Vater 2 (34)
favourite ['feɪvərɪt] Lieblings- (10)
favourite colour Lieblingsfarbe (10)
February ['februəri] Februar 3 (56)
fed up [fed 'ʌp]: **feel fed up** genervt sein, sauer sein; die Nase voll haben 4 (74)
feed [fiːd] füttern 4 (72)
feel [fiːl] sich fühlen; fühlen 4 (74)
feel fed up genervt sein, sauer sein; die Nase voll haben 4 (74)
feeling ['fiːlɪŋ] Gefühl 4 (74)
ferry ['feri] Fähre 5 (91)
field [fiːld] Feld; Weide 4 (70)
in the field auf dem Feld 4 (70)
°**fill sth. in** [fɪl 'ɪn] etwas ausfüllen
film [fɪlm] Film 3 (64)
find [faɪnd] finden 4 (79)
°**find out** herausfinden
fine [faɪn] gut; in Ordnung 1 (17)
I'm fine, thanks. Danke, (es geht mir) gut. 1 (17)
°**finish** ['fɪnɪʃ] beenden
fire station ['faɪə steɪʃn] Feuerwache 3 (52)
first [fɜːst]:
1. erste(r, s) 1 (17)
2. zuerst, als Erstes 3 (54)
the first morning der erste Morgen 1 (17)

fish [fɪʃ] Fisch; Fische (12)
°**fisherman**, *pl* **-men** ['fɪʃəmən] Fischer/in, Angler/in
five [faɪv] fünf (8)
flat [flæt] Wohnung 2 (34)
°**flavour** ['fleɪvə] Geschmack(srichtung)
°**flour** [flaʊə] Mehl
°**fly** [flaɪ] fliegen
°**focus on language** ['fəʊkəs ɒn 'læŋgwɪdʒ] *etwa:* Blickpunkt „Sprache"
°**follow** ['fɒləʊ] folgen; verfolgen
food [fuːd] Essen; Lebensmittel; Futter 5 (97)
football ['fʊtbɔːl] Fußball (11)
for [fɔː, fə] für 1 (23) **for myself** für mich selbst 4 (75)
What's for homework? Was haben wir als Hausaufgabe auf? 2 (45) °**for example** zum Beispiel °**for free** kostenlos, umsonst
°**forget** [fə'get] vergessen
forgot [fə'gɒt]: **I forgot my homework.** Ich habe meine Hausaufgaben vergessen. 2 (45)
form [fɔːm] Form 5 (96)
four [fɔː] vier (8)
free [friː] frei 3 (57) °**for free** kostenlos, umsonst
French [frentʃ] Französisch; französisch 1 (21)
Friday ['fraɪdeɪ, 'fraɪdi] Freitag 1 (21)
friend [frend] Freund/in 1 (18)
friendly ['frendli] freundlich 4 (78)
from [frɒm, frəm] aus (8); von 2 (43) **I'm from Plymouth.** Ich bin/komme aus Plymouth. (8)
from Monday to Friday von Montag bis Freitag 2 (43) **a text from mum** eine SMS von Mama 2 (43)
front: in front of [ɪn 'frʌnt əv] vor 5 (100)
fruit [fruːt] Obst 4 (78)
fun [fʌn]: **it's fun** es macht Spaß (13)
furry ['fɜːri] flauschig; pelzig 4 (76)
°**fuss** [fʌs]: **I don't make a fuss** *(infml)* ich mache kein Theater

G

game [geɪm] Spiel (11)
garage ['gærɑːʒ] Garage 2 (35)
garden ['gɑːdn] Garten 2 (34)
geography [dʒi'ɒgrəfi] Geografie, Erdkunde 1 (21)

German ['dʒɜːmən] Deutsch; deutsch 1 (28)
Germany ['dʒɜːməni] Deutschland (8)
get [get] bekommen 3 (56)
get ready (for) sich fertig machen (für), sich vorbereiten (auf) 4 (72) **get up** aufstehen 3 (58) °**get out** herauskommen
°**gibbon** ['gɪbən] Gibbon (Affe)
girl [gɜːl] Mädchen 1 (16)
girlfriend ['gɜːlfrend] (feste) Freundin 5 (98)
°**give** [gɪv] geben
°**glass** [glɑːs] Glas
go [gəʊ] gehen; fahren (13)
go by bus/bike/car/... mit dem Bus/Rad/Auto/... fahren 3 (58)
go home nach Hause gehen 3 (58) **go shopping** einkaufen gehen 3 (54) **go swimming** schwimmen gehen 3 (56)
go to bed ins Bett gehen 3 (52)
go to school zur Schule gehen 3 (52) **Go to sleep!** Schlaf jetzt! 4 (81) **go to work** zur Arbeit gehen 3 (52) **go with** gehören zu, passen zu 2 (45)
How's it going? Wie geht's? / Wie läuft's? 5 (92) **I must go.** *(am Telefon)* Ich muss Schluss machen. 5 (92)
°**goat** [gəʊt] Ziege
°**goldfish** ['gəʊldfɪʃ] Goldfisch
good [gʊd] gut 1 (17) **Good morning.** Guten Morgen. 1 (18)
°**be good at sth.** gut in etwas sein, etwas gut können
Goodbye. [gʊd'baɪ] Auf Wiedersehen! (14)
grandfather ['grænfɑːðə] Großvater 2 (37)
grandmother ['grænmʌðə] Großmutter 2 (37)
grandparents ['grænpeərənts] Großeltern 2 (37)
great [greɪt] großartig, prima (13)
green [griːn] grün (10)
grey [greɪ] grau (10)
°**groom** [gruːm] striegeln
group [gruːp] Gruppe 5 (95)
guess [ges] raten, erraten 3 (64)
°**guinea pig** ['gɪni pɪg] Meerschweinchen
guitar [gɪ'tɑː] Gitarre 5 (95)
play the guitar Gitarre spielen 5 (95)
guys [gaɪz] Leute *(als Anrede verwendet)* 1 (25)

H

had [hæd, həd]: **I had** ich hatte; ich habe gehabt 5 (98)
°**half past 2** [hɑːf pɑːst 'tuː] halb 3
°**half price** [hɑːf 'praɪs] zum halben Preis
hall [hɔːl] Flur, Diele 2 (35)
hamster ['hæmstə] Hamster (12)
°**hand** [hænd] Hand
°**handle sth.** ['hændl] mit etwas umgehen
happy ['hæpi] glücklich, froh 1 (24) **Happy birthday!** Herzlichen Glückwunsch zum Geburtstag! 3 (60)
happen ['hæpən] geschehen, passieren 5 (93)
harbour ['hɑːbə] Hafen 5 (90)
hard [hɑːd] schwer, schwierig; hart 5 (98) **work hard** hart arbeiten 5 (92)
has [hæz, həz]: **he has ...** er hat ... 1 (19)
°**hat** [hæt] Hut
hate [heɪt] hassen, gar nicht mögen 3 (55)
have [hæv, həv] haben (12) **Have a good day.** Ich wünsch dir einen schönen Tag./Schönen Tag noch. 1 (17) **have a party** eine Party feiern 3 (56) **have breakfast** frühstücken 3 (55) **have dinner** Abendbrot essen, zu Abend essen 3 (58) **have lunch** (zu) Mittag essen 3 (55) **I have a sore leg.** Mein Bein tut weh. 3 (61) **I had** [hæd, həd] ich hatte; ich habe gehabt 5 (98)
he [hiː] er 1 (18) **he's ...** [hiːz] (= **he is)** er ist ... 1 (18)
°**heading** ['hedɪŋ] Überschrift
hear [hɪə] hören 5 (97)
Hello. [hə'ləʊ] Hallo./Guten Tag. (14)
helmet ['helmɪt] Helm 3 (63)
help [help]:
1. helfen (14)
°**2.** Hilfe
her [hɜː, hə]:
1. sie; ihr 4 (80)
2. her dad ihr Vater 2 (34)
here [hɪə] hier; hierher 1 (20) **Here you are.** Bitte schön./Hier, bitte. 1 (28)
Hi. [haɪ] Hallo. (8) **Say hi to everybody.** Grüß alle. 5 (92)
hide [haɪd] verstecken; sich verstecken 5 (94)
hill [hɪl] Hügel 3 (61)
him [hɪm] ihn; ihm 5 (97)
his [hɪz] sein/e 2 (36)
history ['hɪstri] Geschichte 1 (21)
hobby ['hɒbi] Hobby (11)
°**hockey** ['hɒki] Hockey
hole punch ['həʊl pʌntʃ] Locher 1 (26)
holidays ['hɒlədeɪz] Ferien (14)
home [həʊm] Heim, Zuhause 1 (24) **come home** nach Hause kommen 3 (58) **go home** nach Hause gehen 3 (58)
°**home-made** [həʊm'meɪd] hausgemacht, selbstgemacht
homework ['həʊmwɜːk] Hausaufgabe(n) 1 (24) **I forgot my homework.** Ich habe meine Hausaufgaben vergessen. 2 (45) **What's for homework?** Was haben wir als Hausaufgabe auf? 2 (45)
hoodie ['hʊdi] Kapuzenpullover, -jacke 3 (55)
hope [həʊp] hoffen 1 (24)
°**horse** [hɔːs] Pferd
hospital ['hɒspɪtl] Krankenhaus 3 (61)
°**hot** [hɒt] heiß
house [haʊs] Haus 2 (34)
how? [haʊ] wie? 1 (17) **How are you?** [haʊ 'ɑː ju] Wie geht's?/Wie geht es dir/euch? 1 (17) **How's it going?** Wie geht's?/Wie läuft's? 5 (92) **How much is ...?** Was (Wie viel) kostet ...? 3 (62) **How much are ...?** Was (Wie viel) kosten ...? 3 (62) °**How many ...?** Wie viele ...?
hundred ['hʌndrəd]: **a hundred, one hundred** (ein)hundert 3 (55)
hungry ['hʌŋgri]: **be hungry** hungrig sein, Hunger haben 4 (81)
°**hurry** ['hʌri] sich beeilen
°**hyena** [haɪ'iːnə] Hyäne

I

I [aɪ] ich (8) **I'm ...** [aɪm] (= **I am)** ich bin ... 1 (18)
°**ice cream** [aɪs 'kriːm] (Speise-)Eis
ICT [aɪ siː 'tiː] **(information and communication technology)** Informations- und Kommunikationstechnologie 1 (20)
idea [aɪ'dɪə] Idee 1 (25)
°**idiot** ['ɪdiət] Idiot/in
°**imagine sth.** [ɪ'mædʒɪn] sich etwas vorstellen
important [ɪm'pɔːtnt] wichtig 1 (24)
in [ɪn] in (8) **in England** in England (8) **in English** auf Englisch 1 (27) **in front of** vor 5 (100) **in the afternoon** nachmittags, am Nachmittag 3 (54) **in the country** auf dem Land 4 (80) **in the evening** abends, am Abend 3 (54) **in the field** auf dem Feld 4 (70) **in the middle** in der Mitte 5 (90) **in the morning** am Morgen, morgens 3 (54) **in the photo** auf dem Foto 2 (34) **in the picture** auf dem Bild 2 (42) **in town** in der Stadt 2 (43) °**in the end** schließlich; letzten Endes; am Ende
°**information** [ɪnfə'meɪʃn] Information(en)
°**inline-skating** ['ɪnlaɪn 'skeɪtɪŋ] Inlineskaten
inside [ɪn'saɪd] drinnen; nach drinnen 4 (72)
instrument ['ɪnstrəmənt] Instrument 5 (95)
interesting ['ɪntrəstɪŋ] interessant 4 (77)
interview ['ɪntəvjuː] Interview 1 (28)
into ['ɪntʊ] in (... hinein) 2 (36) **into the living room** in das Wohnzimmer (hinein) 2 (36)
invitation (to) [ɪnvɪ'teɪʃn] Einladung (zu, nach) 4 (83)
invite (to) [ɪn'vaɪt] einladen (zu, nach) 4 (80)
is [ɪz] *(er/sie/es)* ist (10) **The calculator is £ 1.** Der Taschenrechner kostet 1 Pfund. 3 (62)
it [ɪt] er/sie/es (13) **it's** [ɪts] **(= it is)** es ist; *(bei Sachen und Tieren auch:* er ist; sie ist*)* (13)

J

jam [dʒæm] Marmelade 5 (102)
January ['dʒænjuəri] Januar 3 (56)
job [dʒɒb] Job, (Arbeits-)Stelle 5 (92)
join a club [dʒɔɪn] sich einem Klub anschließen; in einen Klub eintreten 5 (95)
juice [dʒuːs] Saft 5 (92)
July [dʒu'laɪ] Juli 3 (56)
°**jump up** [dʒʌmp] aufspringen
June [dʒuːn] Juni 3 (56)
°**just** [dʒʌst] einfach (nur)

K

kid [kɪd] Kind; Jugendliche(r) 3 (59)
kitchen ['kɪtʃɪn] Küche 2 (34)
°**kitten** ['kɪtn] Kätzchen; junge Katze
know [nəʊ] wissen; kennen 1 (24)

L

lab [læb] Labor 1 (20)
°**label** ['leɪbl] Label, Etikett
lamp [læmp] Lampe 2 (39)
language ['læŋgwɪdʒ] Sprache (3)
°**large** [lɑːdʒ] groß
last [lɑːst] letzte(r, s) (14)
late [leɪt] spät 3 (58)
later ['leɪtə] später 1 (17)
laugh [lɑːf] lachen 4 (80) **they laughed** [lɑːft] sie lachten; sie haben gelacht 5 (98)
lazy ['leɪzi] faul 3 (58)
°**lead-in** ['liːd ɪn] *Einstieg in die neue Unit*
learn [lɜːn] lernen 5 (95)
°**learner log** ['lɜːnə lɒg] Lerner-Tagebuch
left [left] links; nach links 4 (82) **on the left** links, auf der linken Seite 5 (90)
leg [leg] Bein 3 (61)
lesson ['lesn] (Unterrichts-)Stunde 1 (20)
Let's ... [lets] Lass uns .../Lasst uns ... 3 (60)
letter ['letə] Brief 5 (93)
life, *pl* **lives** [laɪf], [laɪvz] *(das)* Leben, *(die)* Leben 4 (72)
°**lighthouse** ['laɪthaʊs] Leuchtturm
like [laɪk] wie 3 (54) **What's it like?** Wie ist es?/Wie sieht es aus? 2 (44) °**like this** so
like [laɪk] mögen, gernhaben (10) **I like red.** Ich mag Rot. (10) **I like watching TV.** Ich sehe gern fern. (11) **I don't like blue.** Ich mag Blau nicht./Ich mag kein Blau. (10) **He doesn't like to be lonely.** Er mag es nicht, allein zu sein. 4 (77)
°**line** [laɪn] Zeile
°**list** [lɪst] Liste
listen ['lɪsn] zuhören 2 (40) **listen to** *jemandem* zuhören; sich *etwas* anhören 2 (40)
little ['lɪtl] klein 5 (96)
live [lɪv] leben; wohnen 2 (34)
lives [laɪvz] *Mehrzahl von* **life** 4 (72)
living room ['lɪvɪŋ ruːm] Wohnzimmer 2 (34)
°**llama** ['lɑːmə] Lama
lonely ['ləʊnli] einsam 2 (43)
look [lʊk]:
1. schauen, gucken 1 (25)
2. aussehen 3 (63)
Look, Adam. Sieh mal, Adam./Schau mal, Adam. 1 (25) **look after** sich kümmern um; aufpassen auf 4 (72) **look at sth.** sich etwas anschauen 1 (23) **It looks nice.** Es sieht schön aus. 3 (63)
°**look for sth.** etwas suchen; nach etwas Ausschau halten
°**look up a word** ein Wort nachschlagen
lost [lɒst]: **I'm not lost.** Ich habe mich nicht verlaufen/verirrt. 1 (20)
lots of ... ['lɒts əv] viel ..., viele ... 2 (43)
love [lʌv]:
1. lieben, sehr mögen (12) **I'd love to come. (= I would love to come.)** Ich komme sehr gern./Ich würde sehr gern kommen. 4 (83)
°**2.** Liebe °**be in love** verliebt sein
lucky ['lʌki]: **you're lucky** du hast Glück 2 (36)
lunch [lʌntʃ] Mittagessen 1 (21) **have lunch** (zu) Mittag essen 3 (55)

M

°**madhouse** ['mædhaʊs] Irrenhaus, Tollhaus
make [meɪk] machen, herstellen 1 (23) °**make notes** (sich) Notizen machen
man, *pl* **men** [mæn], [men] Mann, Männer 3 (63)
°**many** ['meni]: **How many ...?** Wie viele ...?
°**map** [mæp] Landkarte, Stadtplan
March [mɑːtʃ] März 3 (56)
market ['mɑːkɪt] Markt 3 (53)
°**match** [mætʃ] zuordnen
maths [mæθs] Mathematik 1 (21)
May [meɪ] Mai 3 (56)
maybe ['meɪbi] vielleicht 5 (96)
me [miː] mich; mir 1 (19) **It's me, Sandy.** Ich bin es, Sandy. (14) **Me too.** Ich auch. 1 (14) **Not me!** Ich nicht! 4 (74)
mean [miːn] gemein, fies 2 (40)
°**mean** [miːn] bedeuten
°**mediation** [miːdi'eɪʃn] Vermittlung, Sprachmittlung, Mediation
meet [miːt] kennenlernen; treffen (8) **Nice to meet you!** Freut mich, dich/euch/Sie kennenzulernen. (8)
men [men] *Mehrzahl von* **man** 3 (63)
°**message** ['mesɪdʒ]: **message in a bottle** Flaschenpost
messy ['mesi] unordentlich 2 (38)
middle ['mɪdl] Mitte 5 (90) **in the middle** in der Mitte 5 (90)
°**milk** [mɪlk] Milch
°**mime** [maɪm] vorspielen, pantomimisch darstellen
°**mind map** ['maɪnd mæp] Mindmap
°**minute** ['mɪnɪt] Minute
mirror ['mɪrə] Spiegel 2 (39)
Miss Borowski [mɪs] Frau Borowski *(Anrede für unverheiratete Frauen)* 1 (24)
miss [mɪs] vermissen 2 (36)
°**missing** ['mɪsɪŋ] fehlend °**some are missing** einige fehlen
°**mistake** [mɪ'steɪk] Fehler
mobile phone ['məʊbaɪl 'fəʊn] *(kurz auch:* **mobile***)* Mobiltelefon, Handy 1 (16)
moment ['məʊmənt] Moment, Augenblick 5 (93) **at the moment** im Moment, gerade 5 (93)
Monday ['mʌndeɪ, 'mʌndi] Montag 1 (21)
money ['mʌni] Geld 3 (62)
monkey ['mʌŋki] Affe (12)
month [mʌnθ] Monat 3 (56)
°**more** [mɔː] mehr °**more than** mehr als °**no more work/school/...** keine Arbeit/Schule/... mehr
morning ['mɔːnɪŋ] Morgen 1 (17) **in the morning** am Morgen, morgens 3 (54) **on Friday morning** freitagmorgens, am Freitagmorgen 3 (54)
mother ['mʌðə] Mutter 2 (34)
mouth [maʊθ] Mund 4 (75)
Mr Jahn ['mɪstə] Herr Jahn 1 (19)
Mrs Schmidt ['mɪsɪz] Frau Schmidt *(Anrede für verheiratete Frauen)* 1 (19)
Ms Lee [mɪz, məz] Frau Lee *(allgemeine Anrede für Frauen)* 1 (18)
much [mʌtʃ]: **How much is ...?** Was (Wie viel) kostet ...? 3 (62) **How much are ...?** Was (Wie viel) kosten ...? 3 (62)
mum [mʌm] Mama, Mutti 2 (34)

music ['mju:zɪk] Musik (11)
musician [mju'zɪʃn] Musiker/in 5 (95)
must [mʌst] müssen 5 (92)
I must go. *(am Telefon)* Ich muss Schluss machen. 5 (92)
my [maɪ] mein/e (10)
myself [maɪ'self]: **for myself** für mich selbst 4 (75)

N

name [neɪm]:
1. Name (8) **What's your name?** Wie heißt du? (8)
°**2.** benennen, nennen
°**narrator** [nə'reɪtə] Erzähler/in
near [nɪə] in der Nähe von, nahe (bei) 1 (18)
need [ni:d] brauchen, benötigen 1 (25)
nervous ['nɜ:vəs] nervös, aufgeregt 4 (80)
network ['netwɜ:k] Netz; Wortnetz 1 (27)
never ['nevə] nie, niemals 3 (52)
new [nju:] neu (13)
news [nju:z] Nachrichten 2 (42)
°**newspaper** ['nju:speɪpə] Zeitung
next [nekst] nächste(r, s) 1 (28)
next to ['nekst tʊ] neben 5 (100
nice [naɪs] nett, schön (8) **Nice to meet you!** Freut mich, dich/euch/Sie kennenzulernen. (8)
night [naɪt] Nacht 3 (58) **at night** nachts, in der Nacht 3 (58)
nine [naɪn] neun (8)
no [nəʊ] kein, keine 1 (18)
°**no more work/school/...** keine Arbeit/Schule/... mehr
no [nəʊ] nein (14)
°**nobody** ['nəʊbədi] niemand
noise [nɔɪz] Geräusch; Lärm 4 (81)
noisy ['nɔɪzi] laut, voller Lärm 2 (38)
normal ['nɔ:ml] normal, gewöhnlich 4 (75)
not [nɒt]: **I'm not ten.** Ich bin nicht zehn. 1 (18) **I'm not a boy.** Ich bin kein Junge. 1 (18)
Not me! Ich nicht! 4 (74)
°**note** [nəʊt] Notiz °**make notes** (sich) Notizen machen °**take notes** (sich) Notizen machen
nothing ['nʌθɪŋ] (gar) nichts 4 (72)
November [nəʊ'vembə] November 3 (56)
now [naʊ] nun, jetzt 1 (20)
number ['nʌmbə] Nummer 2 (46)
nut [nʌt] Nuss 4 (78)

O

o'clock: at 1 o'clock [ə'klɒk] um 1 Uhr/um 13 Uhr 3 (57)
October [ɒk'təʊbə] Oktober 3 (56)
°**odd** [ɒd]: **the odd word out** das Wort, das nicht passt
of [ɒv, əv]: **the last day of the holidays** der letzte Tag der Ferien (14) **the best of both worlds** das Beste von beidem 2 (42)
°**Off to bed.** [ɒf] Ab ins Bett.
often ['ɒfn, 'ɒftən] oft 3 (52)
OK [əʊ'keɪ] okay, gut, in Ordnung 1 (17) **I'm OK, thanks.** Danke, (es geht mir) gut. 1 (17) °**I'm OK at ...** ich bin ganz OK in ...
old [əʊld] alt (13)
omelette ['ɒmlət] Omelett 5 (92)
on [ɒn] auf (13) **on 5th May** am 5. Mai 3 (57) **on Friday morning** freitagmorgens, am Freitagmorgen 3 (54) **on Monday/Tuesday/...** am Montag/Dienstag/... 1 (21) **on my birthday** an meinem Geburtstag 3 (56)
on the beach am Strand 2 (44)
on the bus im Bus 4 (80)
on the left links, auf der linken Seite 5 (90) **on the phone** am Telefon 5 (97) **on the right** rechts, auf der rechten Seite 5 (90) **on the way to ...** auf dem Weg zu/nach ... 5 (98)
one [wʌn] eins (8)
only ['əʊnli]:
1. nur, bloß 4 (81)
2. the only student der einzige Schüler/die einzige Schülerin 4 (75)
°**open** ['əʊpən] öffnen
or [ɔ:] oder 3 (61)
orange ['ɒrɪndʒ]:
1. orange (10)
°**2.** Orange, Apfelsine
°**order** ['ɔ:də] Reihenfolge
other ['ʌðə] andere(r, s) 4 (72)
our ['aʊə] unser/e (11)
°**out** [aʊt]: **school is out** die Schule ist aus/vorbei
°**out of ...** ['aʊt əv] aus ... (heraus/hinaus)
outside [aʊt'saɪd] draußen; nach draußen 4 (72)
°**oven** ['ʌvn] Backofen
over ['əʊvə]: **be over** vorbei sein, zu Ende sein 1 (24)
°**over there** [əʊvə 'ðeə] da drüben, dort drüben

°**owl** [aʊl] Eule
°**own** [əʊn]: **your own card/text/...** deine eigene Karte/dein eigener Text

P

p [pi:]: **50p** 50 Pence 3 (62)
page [peɪdʒ] Seite 2 (45) **What page is it?** Auf welcher Seite sind wir?/Auf welcher Seite steht das? 2 (45)
pair [peə] Paar (12)
paper ['peɪpə] Papier 1 (25)
parents ['peərənts] Eltern 2 (37)
park [pɑ:k] Park (13)
°**parrot** ['pærət] Papagei
°**part** [pɑ:t] Teil
partner ['pɑ:tnə] Partner/in 2 (36)
party ['pɑ:ti] Party 3 (56) **have a party** eine Party feiern 3 (56)
PE [pi: 'i:] **(physical education)** (Schul-)Sport 1 (20)
°**peahen** ['pi:hen] Pfauenhenne *(weiblicher Pfau)*
pen [pen] Kugelschreiber, Stift, Füller 1 (26)
pencil ['pensl] Bleistift 1 (26)
pencil case ['pensl keɪs] Federmäppchen 1 (26)
pencil sharpener ['pensl ʃɑ:pnə] Bleistiftanspitzer 1 (26)
°**penguin** ['peŋgwɪn] Pinguin
people ['pi:pl] Leute, Menschen 1 (23)
person ['pɜ:sn] Person 4 (79)
pet [pet] Haustier (12)
phone [fəʊn]:
1. anrufen 5 (93)
2. Telefon 2 (46)
on the phone am Telefon 5 (97)
phone number ['fəʊn nʌmbə] Telefonnummer 2 (46)
photo ['fəʊtəʊ] Foto 2 (34)
in the photo auf dem Foto 2 (34)
phrase [freɪz] Ausdruck, (Rede-) Wendung 1 (27)
piano [pi'ænəʊ] Klavier, Piano 5 (95) **play the piano** Klavier spielen 5 (95)
°**pick** [pɪk] (aus)wählen °**Don't pick me up.** Heb mich nicht hoch.
picnic ['pɪknɪk] Picknick 4 (83)
picture ['pɪktʃə] Bild 2 (42)
in the picture ['pɪktʃə] auf dem Bild 2 (42)
°**piece** [pi:s]: **a piece of paper** ein Stück Papier
pig [pɪg] Schwein 4 (71)

°**pinch** [pɪntʃ] zwicken, kneifen
pink [pɪŋk] pink, rosa (10)
°**pity** ['pɪti]: **That's a pity.** Das ist schade!
°**pizza** ['piːtsə] Pizza
place [pleɪs] Ort, Platz, Stelle 1 (23)
plan [plæn] planen 3 (60)
play [pleɪ] spielen (11) **play the guitar/the piano/the drums** Gitarre/Klavier/Schlagzeug spielen 5 (95)
please [pliːz] bitte 1 (24) **Please remember …** Bitte denk(t) dran …/Bitte merk dir/merkt euch … 1 (24)
pm [piː'em]: **5 pm** 5 Uhr nachmittags/abends; 17 Uhr 4 (83)
poem ['pəʊɪm] Gedicht 4 (84)
°**point at sth.** [pɔɪnt] auf etwas zeigen, auf etwas deuten
pond [pɒnd] Teich 4 (70)
pony ['pəʊni] Pony (12) **ride a pony** auf einem Pony reiten 4 (70)
poster ['pəʊstə] Poster (11)
pound (£) [paʊnd] Pfund *(britische Währung)* 1 (26) **That's £ 159.** Das macht 159 Pfund. 3 (63) **The calculator is £ 1.** Der Taschenrechner kostet 1 Pfund. 3 (62) **The mobiles are £ 10.** Die Handys kosten 10 Pfund. 3 (62)
°**practice** ['præktɪs] Übung(en)
°**practise** ['præktɪs] üben
°**prefer** [prɪ'fɜː]: **I'd prefer …** ich würde … vorziehen
present ['preznt] Geschenk 3 (55)
°**pretty** ['prɪti] hübsch
price [praɪs] (Kauf-)Preis 5 (95)
principal ['prɪnsəpl] Rektor/in, Schulleiter/in 1 (24)
problem ['prɒbləm] Problem 2 (38)
programme ['prəʊgræm] (Fernseh-)Sendung 2 (42)
°**progress** ['prəʊgres] Fortschritt
°**project** ['prɒdʒekt] Projekt
proud (of) [praʊd] stolz (auf) 5 (99)
pullover ['pʊləʊvə] Pullover 1 (24)
°**puppy** ['pʌpi] Welpe, junger Hund
purple ['pɜːpl] violett; lila (10)
°**push** [pʊʃ] schieben
°**put** [pʊt] *(etwas wohin)* tun, legen, stellen, stecken
°**put sth. in** etwas einsetzen
°**pyjamas** *(pl)* [pə'dʒɑːməz] Schlafanzug

Q

°**quarter past 2** ['kwɔːtə pɑːst 'tuː] Viertel nach 2 °**quarter to 2** Viertel vor 2
question ['kwestʃn] Frage 2 (40) **ask questions** Fragen stellen 4 (75)
°**quick** [kwɪk] schnell
quiet ['kwaɪət] ruhig, still, leise 2 (42)
quiz [kwɪz] Quiz, Ratespiel 1 (22)

R

rabbit ['ræbɪt] Kaninchen (12)
rap [ræp]:
1. Rap *(rhythmischer Sprechgesang)* 1 (21)
2. rappen 5 (95)
rapper ['ræpə] Rapper/in 5 (95)
rat [ræt] Ratte (12)
read [riːd] lesen (11)
ready ['redi]: **get ready (for)** sich fertig machen (für), sich vorbereiten (auf) 4 (72)
real [rɪəl] echt, wirklich 2 (36)
really ['rɪəli] wirklich 2 (40)
recipe ['resəpi] (Koch-)Rezept 5 (102)
red [red] rot (10)
°**registration** [redʒɪ'streɪʃn] Anmeldung, Einschreibung, Registrierung
remember [rɪ'membə]:
1. sich erinnern (an) (12)
2. daran denken; sich merken 1 (24)
°**repeat** [rɪ'piːt] wiederholen
°**reporter** [rɪ'pɔːtə] Reporter/in
restaurant ['restrɒnt] Restaurant 2 (42)
°**revision** [rɪ'vɪʒn] Wiederholung *(von Lernstoff)*
ride [raɪd]:
1. reiten (11) **ride a bike** Rad fahren 1 (18) **ride a pony** auf einem Pony reiten 4 (70)
°2. Ritt, Ausritt
right [raɪt]:
1. richtig 1 (21) °**he is right** er hat Recht
2. rechts; nach rechts 4 (82) **on the right** rechts, auf der rechten Seite 5 (90)
ring [rɪŋ] läuten, klingeln 5 (92)
road [rəʊd] Straße *(Landstraße zwischen Orten, aber auch Straße in Orten)* 2 (34)
°**role** [rəʊl] Rolle
°**role-play** ['rəʊlpleɪ] Rollenspiel

room [ruːm, rʊm] Raum, Zimmer 1 (20)
rubber ['rʌbə] Radiergummi 1 (26)
rug [rʌg] Teppich, Läufer 2 (39)
°**rule** [ruːl] Regel
ruler ['ruːlə] Lineal 1 (26)
°**run** [rʌn] rennen, laufen

S

said [sed]: **he said** er sagte; er hat gesagt 5 (98)
salad ['sæləd] Salat *(als Gericht oder Beilage)* 5 (92)
sale [seɪl] Verkauf; Schlussverkauf 3 (62)
°**salt** [sɔːlt] Salz
same [seɪm]: **the same** derselbe/dieselbe/dasselbe; dieselben 3 (63)
°**sand** [sænd] Sand
sandwich ['sænwɪtʃ, 'sænwɪdʒ] Sandwich 4 (80)
Saturday ['sætədeɪ, 'sætədi] Samstag, Sonnabend 1 (27)
°**sausage** ['sɒsɪdʒ] (Brat-, Bock-)Würstchen, Wurst
say [seɪ] sagen 1 (25) **Say hi to everybody.** Grüß alle. 5 (92)
he said [sed] er sagte; er hat gesagt 5 (98)
°**scary** ['skeəri] unheimlich
scene [siːn] Szene 4 (80)
school [skuːl] Schule 1 (16)
°**school is out** die Schule ist aus/vorbei
school bag ['skuːl bæg] Schultasche 1 (27)
science ['saɪəns] Naturwissenschaft 1 (20)
scissors *(pl)* ['sɪzəz] Schere 1 (25)
scone [skɒn] *kleines rundes Milchbrötchen, leicht süß, oft mit Rosinen* 5 (92)
sea [siː] Meer 2 (44)
seagull ['siːgʌl] Möwe (14)
seat [siːt] (Sitz-)Platz 5 (98)
second ['sekənd] zweite(r, s) 3 (57)
see [siː] sehen (9) **See you./See you later.** Bis dann./Bis später. 1 (17)
send [send] schicken, senden 5 (94)
°**sentence** ['sentəns] Satz
September [sep'tembə] September 3 (56)
set the table [set] den Tisch decken 5 (96)
seven ['sevn] sieben (8)

share a room with ... [ʃeə] sich ein Zimmer mit ... teilen 2 (38)
she [ʃiː] sie *(Singular)* 1 (18)
she's ... [ʃiːz] **(= she is)** sie ist ... 1 (18)
sheep, *pl* **sheep** [ʃiːp] Schaf, Schafe 4 (71)
shelf, *pl* **shelves** [ʃelf], [ʃelvz] Regal, Regale 2 (39)
shirt [ʃɜːt] Hemd 1 (24)
shoe [ʃuː] Schuh 1 (24)
shop [ʃɒp] Geschäft, Laden 1 (26)
shopping ['ʃɒpɪŋ]: **go shopping** einkaufen gehen 3 (54)
shopping centre ['ʃɒpɪŋ sentə] Einkaufszentrum 3 (53)
°**short** [ʃɔːt] kurz
shoulder ['ʃəʊldə] Schulter 4 (78)
°**show** [ʃəʊ] zeigen
Shut up! [ʃʌt 'ʌp] *(infml)* Halt den Mund! 3 (60)
sign [saɪn] Schild; Zeichen 4 (82)
sing [sɪŋ] singen 5 (95) °**sing along** mitsingen
singer ['sɪŋə] Sänger/in 5 (95)
sister ['sɪstə] Schwester 1 (18)
sit [sɪt] sitzen; sich setzen 4 (73)
six [sɪks] sechs (8)
skateboard ['skeɪtbɔːd] Skateboard fahren (11)
°**skills training** ['skɪlz treɪnɪŋ] Training von (Lern- und Arbeits-) Techniken
skirt [skɜːt] Rock 1 (24)
sleep [sliːp] schlafen 4 (78)
Go to sleep! Schlaf jetzt! 4 (81)
sleeping bag ['sliːpɪŋ bæg] Schlafsack 4 (80)
sleepover ['sliːpəʊvə] Schlafparty 4 (80)
°**slow** [sləʊ] langsam
small [smɔːl] klein (13)
°**smuggler** ['smʌglə] Schmuggler/in
snake [sneɪk] Schlange (12)
so boring/tired/... [səʊ] so langweilig/müde/... 5 (94)
sock [sɒk] Socke, Strumpf 1 (24)
some [sʌm, səm] einige, ein paar; etwas 5 (98)
something ['sʌmθɪŋ] etwas 3 (60)
sometimes ['sʌmtaɪmz] manchmal 3 (54)
song [sɒŋ] Lied, Song (9)
soon [suːn] bald 2 (42)
sore [sɔː]: **I have a sore leg.** Mein Bein tut weh. 3 (61)
Sorry./I'm sorry. ['sɒri] Tut mir leid./Entschuldigung. 1 (24)
sound [saʊnd] Geräusch; Klang, Laut 1 (16)
soup [suːp] Suppe 5 (92)
space [speɪs] Platz 2 (36)
speak [spiːk] sprechen 4 (75)
°**speaker** ['spiːkə]:
1. Sprecher/in
2. Lautsprecher
special ['speʃl] besondere(r, s) 3 (63)
special offer [speʃl 'ɒfə] Sonderangebot 3 (63)
°**speech bubble** ['spiːtʃ bʌbl] Sprechblase
spell [spel] buchstabieren 2 (46)
°**spelling** ['spelɪŋ] Schreibung, Rechtschreibung
sport [spɔːt] Sport; Sportart (11)
do sport Sport treiben 4 (72)
sports hall ['spɔːts hɔːl] Sporthalle 1 (20)
°**square** [skweə] Platz *(in der Stadt)*
start [stɑːt] anfangen, beginnen 1 (22)
stay [steɪ] bleiben 3 (54)
°**step** [step] Schritt
stepbrother ['stepbrʌðə] Stiefbruder 2 (36)
stepdad ['stepdæd] Stiefvater 2 (36)
stepfather ['stepfɑːðə] Stiefvater 2 (36)
stepmother ['stepmʌðə] Stiefmutter 2 (36)
stepmum ['stepmʌm] Stiefmutter 2 (36)
stepsister ['stepsɪstə] Stiefschwester 2 (36)
°**stick insect** ['stɪk ɪnsekt] Stabheuschrecke
°**stoat** [stəʊt] Hermelin
°**stop** [stɒp] anhalten; aufhören
story ['stɔːri] Geschichte, Erzählung (3)/(14)
street [striːt] Straße *(in Orten)* 2 (34)
strict [strɪkt] streng 2 (40)
stroke [strəʊk] streicheln 4 (71)
student ['stjuːdənt] Schüler/in; Student/in (10)
studio ['stjuːdiəʊ] Studio 5 (95)
stupid ['stjuːpɪd] dumm, blöd (14)
°**sugar** ['ʃʊgə] Zucker
summer ['sʌmə] Sommer 3 (52)
°**sun** [sʌn] Sonne
°**suncream** ['sʌnkriːm] Sonnencreme, Sonnenschutzmittel
Sunday ['sʌndeɪ, 'sʌndi] Sonntag 1 (27)
°**sunglasses** *(pl)* ['sʌnglɑːsɪz] Sonnenbrille
supermarket ['suːpəmɑːkɪt] Supermarkt 3 (54)
sure [ʃʊə, ʃɔː] sicher 1 (28)
surprise [sə'praɪz] Überraschung 2 (40)
°**swap** [swɒp] tauschen
sweatshirt ['swetʃɜːt] Sweatshirt 1 (24)
sweets *(pl)* [swiːts] Süßigkeiten 3 (54)
swim [swɪm] schwimmen (11)
swimming pool ['swɪmɪŋ puːl] Schwimmbad, Schwimmbecken 3 (52)
°**swimming trunks** *(pl)* ['swɪmɪŋ trʌŋks] Badehose
°**swimsuit** ['swɪmsuːt] Badeanzug

T

table ['teɪbl]:
1. Tisch 2 (39)
°2. Tabelle
tae kwon do [taɪ kwɒn 'dəʊ] Taekwondo 1 (18)
take [teɪk]: **I'll take it.** Ich nehme es (ihn, sie). *(beim Einkaufen)* 3 (63) °**take away** [teɪk ə'weɪ] zum Mitnehmen °**take notes** (sich) Notizen machen
talk (to) [tɔːk] sprechen, reden (mit) 1 (28)
tea [tiː] Tee 5 (92)
teacher ['tiːtʃə] Lehrer/in 1 (16)
team [tiːm] Team, Mannschaft 4 (75)
°**teaspoon** ['tiːspuːn] Teelöffel
technology [tek'nɒlədʒi] Technik, Technologie 1 (21)
teenager ['tiːneɪdʒə] Teenager 4 (75)
°**tell** [tel] erzählen; sagen
ten [ten] zehn (8)
tennis ['tenɪs] Tennis 5 (97)
terrible ['terəbl] schrecklich, fürchterlich 3 (55)
text [tekst]:
1. SMS; Text 2 (43)
2. **text a friend** einem Freund/einer Freundin eine SMS schicken 4 (74)
text message ['tekst mesɪdʒ] *(kurz auch:* **text***)* SMS 5 (101)
°**than** [ðæn, ðən]: **more than** mehr als
Thanks. [θæŋks] Danke. 1 (17)

that [ðæt, ðət] das (dort) 1 (24) **that field** das Feld (dort), jenes Feld 4 (81) **That's £ 159.** Das macht 159 Pfund. 3 (63) **°there's one thing that I know** eins weiß ich

the [ðə, ði] der, die, das; die (8)

theatre ['θɪətə] Theater 1 (25)

their [ðeə] ihr/e *(Plural)* 3 (60)

them [ðem, ðəm] sie; ihnen 5 (97)

theme [θiːm] Thema (3)

°theme park ['θiːm pɑːk] Themenpark *(Freizeitpark mit Attraktionen zu einem bestimmten Thema)*

then [ðen] dann, danach 3 (54)

there [ðeə] da, dort; dahin, dorthin 3 (54) **there's ...** es ist ... / es gibt ... 2 (36) **there are ...** es sind ... / es gibt ... 2 (36) **°over there** da drüben, dort drüben **°there's one thing that I know** eins weiß ich

°these [ðiːz] die, diese (hier)

they [ðeɪ] sie *(Plural)* 1 (18) **they're ...** [ðeə] **(= they are)** sie sind ... 1 (18)

thing [θɪŋ] Ding, Sache (13)

think [θɪŋk] denken, meinen, glauben 1 (25)

third [θɜːd] dritte(r, s) 3 (57)

this [ðɪs] diese(r, s) 1 (18) **This is ...** Dies ist ... / Das ist ... (14) **°like this** so

three [θriː] drei (8)

through [θruː] durch 4 (81)

°throw [θrəʊ] werfen

Thursday ['θɜːzdeɪ, 'θɜːzdi] Donnerstag 1 (21)

°tick [tɪk] ankreuzen, abhaken

ticket ['tɪkɪt] Eintrittskarte 4 (71)

tie [taɪ] Krawatte 1 (24)

tiger ['taɪgə] Tiger (12)

tights *(pl)* [taɪts] Strumpfhose 1 (24)

time [taɪm]:
1. Zeit; Uhrzeit 1 (21) **What's the time?** Wie spät ist es? 4 (73)
°2. Mal

timetable ['taɪmteɪbl] Stundenplan 1 (21)

tired ['taɪəd] müde 2 (40)

to [tu, tə]:
1. *(örtlich)* zu, nach (13) **to the cinema** ins Kino 3 (52)
2. from Monday to Friday von Montag bis Freitag 2 (43)
3. He doesn't like to be lonely. Er mag es nicht, allein zu sein. 4 (77)

toast [təʊst] Toast 5 (97)

today [tə'deɪ] heute 3 (55)

together [tə'geðə] zusammen 2 (37)

toilet ['tɔɪlət] Toilette 2 (35)

too [tuː]:
1. auch (11) **from Berlin too** auch aus Berlin (11) **Me too.** Ich auch. 1 (14)
2. too old/big/... zu alt/groß/... 2 (38)

tour [tʊə]: **a tour of the school** ein Rundgang durch die Schule 1 (20)

°towel ['taʊəl] Handtuch

town [taʊn] Stadt 2 (43) **in town** in der Stadt 2 (43)

°tractor ['træktə] Traktor

trainers *(pl)* ['treɪnəz] Turnschuhe 3 (55)

training ['treɪnɪŋ] Training, Ausbildung (3)

°trampoline ['træmpəliːn] Trampolin

tree [triː] Baum 2 (37)

°trip [trɪp] Ausflug

trouble ['trʌbl]: **be in trouble** in Schwierigkeiten sein; Ärger kriegen 4 (81)

trousers *(pl)* ['traʊzəz] Hose 1 (24)

true [truː] wahr 5 (99)

try [traɪ] probieren, ausprobieren 3 (63)

T-shirt ['tiːʃɜːt] T-Shirt 2 (38)

°tube [tjuːb] Schwimmreifen

Tuesday ['tjuːzdeɪ, 'tjuːzdi] Dienstag 1 (21)

turn [tɜːn]:
1. It's your turn. Du bist dran. / Du bist an der Reihe. 2 (45)
°2. Turn the page upside down. Dreh die Seite auf den Kopf.

TV [tiː'viː] Fernsehen, Fernsehgerät (11)

twelve [twelv] zwölf (8)

two [tuː] zwei (8)

U

°umbrella [ʌm'brelə] (Regen-)Schirm

uncle ['ʌŋkl] Onkel 2 (37)

under ['ʌndə] unter 5 (100)

understand [ʌndə'stænd] verstehen 4 (75)

unhappy [ʌn'hæpi] unglücklich 3 (60)

uniform ['juːnɪfɔːm] (Schul-)Uniform 1 (24)

unit ['juːnɪt] Kapitel, Lektion (3)

°upside down [ʌpsaɪd 'daʊn]: **Turn the page upside down.** Dreh die Seite auf den Kopf.

upstairs [ʌp'steəz] oben; nach oben 2 (36)

us [ʌs, əs] uns 3 (58)

use [juːz] benutzen, verwenden 4 (84)

°useful ['juːsfl] nützlich, hilfreich

usually ['juːʒuəli] meistens, normalerweise 3 (54)

V

value ['væljuː]: **It's good value.** Es ist sein Geld wert. 3 (63)

vegetables *(pl)* ['vedʒtəblz] Gemüse 3 (54)

°verb [vɜːb] Verb

°verse [vɜːs] Strophe

very ['veri] sehr 1 (25) **very nice** sehr nett, sehr schön 1 (25)

village ['vɪlɪdʒ] Dorf 1 (18)

visit ['vɪzɪt] besuchen 3 (56)

visitor ['vɪzɪtə] Besucher/in; Gast 4 (70)

vocabulary ['vɪzɪtə] Wörterverzeichnis, Vokabelverzeichnis (3)

W

°wait (for) [weɪt] warten (auf)

wake [weɪk] wecken 4 (72)

walk [wɔːk] (zu Fuß) gehen 3 (58)

°wall [wɔːl] Wand

want [wɒnt]:
want sth. etwas (haben) wollen 3 (61) **want to do sth.** etwas tun wollen 3 (55)

wardrobe ['wɔːdrəʊb] Kleiderschrank 2 (39)

was [wɒz, wəz]: **it was Friday** es war Freitag 5 (98) **he wasn't ...** er war nicht ... 5 (99)

wash up [wɒʃ 'ʌp] abwaschen 5 (92)

watch sth. [wɒtʃ] sich etwas anschauen; etwas beobachten 2 (42) **watch TV** fernsehen (11)

water ['wɔːtə] Wasser 5 (92)

way [weɪ] Weg 5 (98) **on the way to ...** auf dem Weg zu/nach ... 5 (98)

we [wiː] wir 1 (18) **we're ...** [wɪə] **(= we are** [wi ɑː]**)** wir sind ... 1 (18)

Wednesday ['wenzdeɪ, 'wenzdi] Mittwoch 1 (21)

week [wiːk] Woche 2 (43)

weekend [wiːk'end] Wochenende 1 (27) **at the weekend** am Wochenende 4 (73)
welcome ['welkəm]:
1. **Welcome to Plymouth.** Willkommen in Plymouth. (10)
2. **You're welcome.** Bitte, gern geschehen./Nichts zu danken. 4 (73)
well [wel]: **work/speak/... well** gut funktionieren/sprechen/... 4 (75) **Well done.** [wel 'dʌn] Gut gemacht. 5 (99)
Well, ... [wel] Nun, ... / Also, ... / Na ja, ... 5 (96)
were [wɜː, wə]: **they were on the bus** sie waren im Bus 5 (98)
wet [wet] nass 4 (80)
what [wɒt]:
1. was (8)
2. welche(r, s) 2 (45)
What about ...? Wie wär's mit ...? 3 (55) **What about you?** Und du?/Und was ist mit dir? (8) **What do you think?** Was meinst du?/Was denkst du? 1 (25) **What page is it?** Auf welcher Seite sind wir?/Auf welcher Seite steht das? 2 (45) **What's for homework?** Was haben wir als Hausaufgabe auf? 2 (45) **What's it like?** Wie ist es?/Wie sieht es aus? 2 (44) **What's the time?** Wie spät ist es? 4 (73) **What's your name?** Wie heißt du? (*wörtlich:* Was ist dein Name?) (8)
wheelchair ['wiːltʃeə] Rollstuhl 4 (75)
when [wen]:
1. wann 3 (57)
2. wenn 4 (74)
When's your birthday? Wann hast du Geburtstag? 3 (57)
°**which** [wɪtʃ] welche(r, s)
where [weə] wo; wohin 1 (20)
white [waɪt] weiß (10)
who [huː]:
1. wer 1 (18) **Who are you?** Wer bist du? / Wer seid ihr? 1 (18)
°2. **Who can you see?** Wen kannst du sehen?
3. **Find a person who ...** Finde eine Person, die ... 4 (79)
why [waɪ] warum 4 (78)
wild [waɪld] wild; wild lebend (12)
°**will: we will send ...** [wɪl] wir werden ... schicken
win [wɪn] gewinnen 4 (75)
window ['wɪndəʊ] Fenster 5 (97)
wishes ['wɪʃɪz]: **Best wishes** Viele Grüße, ... *(Briefschluss)* 4 (83)
with [wɪð] mit 1 (22)
with Ellie mit Ellie 1 (22); bei Ellie 2 (34)
°**woman,** *pl* **women** ['wʊmən], ['wɪmɪn] Frau, Frauen
word [wɜːd] Wort (3)
work [wɜːk]:
1. arbeiten 2 (45); funktionieren 4 (74)
2. Arbeit 2 (42)
work hard hart arbeiten 5 (92)
workshop ['wɜːkʃɒp] Workshop; Seminar 5 (95)
world [wɜːld] Welt 4 (70)
the best of both worlds das Beste von beidem 2 (42)
worried ['wʌrid]: **be worried (about)** beunruhigt sein, besorgt sein (wegen) 5 (93)
worry (about) ['wʌri] sich Sorgen machen (wegen, um) 4 (80)
would [wʊd]: **I'd love to come. (= I would love to come)** Ich komme sehr gern. / Ich würde sehr gern kommen. 4 (83)
write [raɪt] schreiben 1 (24)
wrong [rɒŋ] falsch 1 (21)
°**she is wrong** sie hat Unrecht

Y

year [jɪə] Jahr 4 (73)
yellow ['jeləʊ] gelb (10)
yes [jes] ja 1 (22)
you [ju, juː]:
1. du; ihr; Sie (8)
2. dich; dir; euch; Sie; Ihnen (8)
you're ... [jɔː] **(= you are)** du bist ...; ihr seid ...; Sie sind ... 1 (18) **you're lucky** du hast Glück 2 (36) **You're welcome.** Bitte, gern geschehen. / Nichts zu danken. 4 (73)
young [jʌŋ] jung 5 (95)
your [jɔː, jə] dein/e; euer/eure; Ihr/e (8)
yours [jɔːz] deiner, deine, deins 2 (38)
°**yourself** [jɔː'self, jə'self]:
about yourself über dich selbst
°**Yummy!** ['jʌmi] Lecker!

Z

°**zip wire** ['zɪp waɪə] Seilrutsche
°**zone** [zəʊn] Zone
zoo [zuː] Zoo 3 (60)

Das **German – English dictionary** enthält den **Lernwortschatz** von *Lighthouse 1*.
Es kann dir eine erste Hilfe sein, wenn du vergessen hast, wie etwas auf Englisch heißt.

Wenn du wissen möchtest, wo das englische Wort zum ersten Mal in *Lighthouse 1* vorkommt, dann kannst du im **English – German dictionary** (S. 208–218) nachschlagen.

Es werden folgende **Abkürzungen** und **Symbole** verwendet:

sth. = something (etwas) *pl = plural* (Mehrzahl) *infml = informal* (umgangssprachlich)

A

Abend evening ['i:vnɪŋ] **am Abend** in the evening **zu Abend essen** have dinner
Abendbrot dinner ['dɪnə] **Abendbrot essen** have dinner
Abendessen dinner ['dɪnə]
abends in the evening ['i:vnɪŋ]
Abenteuer adventure [əd'ventʃə]
aber but [bʌt, bət]
abwaschen wash up [wɒʃ 'ʌp]
acht eight [eɪt]
Adresse address [ə'dres]
Affe monkey ['mʌŋki]
Afrika Africa ['æfrɪkə]
alle all (the) [ɔ:l]; *(jeder)* everybody ['evribɒdi] **Grüß alle.** Say hi to everybody.
Alphabet alphabet ['ælfəbet]
als Erstes first [fɜ:st]
Also, … Well, … [wel]
alt old [əʊld]
Alter age [eɪdʒ]
am: am 5. Mai on 5th May **am Abend** in the evening **am Freitagmorgen** on Friday morning **am Montag/Dienstag/…** on Monday/Tuesday/… **am Morgen** in the morning **am Nachmittag** in the afternoon **am Strand** on the beach **am Telefon** on the phone **am Wochenende** at the weekend
an: an dieser Schule at this school **an meinem Geburtstag** on my birthday
andere(r, s) other ['ʌðə]
anders *(verschieden)* different ['dɪfrənt]
anfangen start [stɑ:t]
anhören: sich etwas anhören listen to sth. ['lɪsn]
anrufen phone [fəʊn]
anschauen: sich etwas anschauen look at sth. [lʊk]; *(etwas beobachten)* watch sth. [wɒtʃ]
anschließen: sich einem Klub anschließen join a club [dʒɔɪn]
Anschrift address [ə'dres]
Antwort answer ['ɑ:nsə]
Anzeige *(Werbung)* advert ['ædvɜ:t]
Apfel apple ['æpl]
April April ['eɪprəl]
Aquarium aquarium [ə'kweəriəm]
Arbeit work [wɜ:k] **bei der Arbeit** at work **zur Arbeit gehen** go to work
arbeiten work [wɜ:k] **hart arbeiten** work hard
Ärger kriegen be in trouble ['trʌbl]
auch too [tu:] **Ich auch.** Me too.
auf on [ɒn] **auf dem Bild** in the picture **auf dem Feld** in the field **auf dem Foto** in the photo **auf dem Land** in the country **auf dem Markt** at the market **auf dem Weg zu/nach …** on the way to … **auf der linken Seite** on the left **auf der rechten Seite** on the right **auf dieser Schule** at this school **auf Englisch** in English **Auf welcher Seite steht das?** What page is it? **Auf Wiedersehen!** Goodbye.
Aufgabe exercise ['eksəsaɪz]
aufgeregt *(gespannt)* excited [ɪk'saɪtɪd]; *(nervös)* nervous ['nɜ:vəs]
aufpassen auf look after [lʊk 'ɑ:ftə]
aufstehen get up [get 'ʌp]
Augenblick moment ['məʊmənt]
August August ['ɔ:gəst]
aus from [frɒm, frəm] **Ich bin aus Plymouth./Ich komme aus Plymouth.** I'm from Plymouth.
Ausbildung training ['treɪnɪŋ]
Ausdruck *(Wendung)* phrase [freɪz]
ausleihen: sich etwas ausleihen borrow sth. ['bɒrəʊ]
ausprobieren try [traɪ]
aussehen look [lʊk] **Es sieht schön aus.** It looks nice.
Auto car [kɑ:] **mit dem Auto** by car

B

Baby baby ['beɪbi]
Babysitter babysitter ['beɪbisɪtə]
Bad, Badezimmer bathroom ['bɑ:θru:m]
bald soon [su:n]
Ball ball [bɔ:l]
Band *(Musikgruppe)* band [bænd]
Bär bear [beə]
Basketball basketball ['bɑ:skɪtbɔ:l]
Bauernhof farm [fɑ:m]
Baum tree [tri:]
beginnen start [stɑ:t]
bei: bei der Arbeit *(am Arbeitsplatz)* at work **bei Ellie** with Ellie **bei Ellie daheim/zu Hause** at Ellie's house **bei MARTINS** at MARTINS
beide: das Beste von beidem the best of both worlds ['bəʊθ wɜ:ldz]
Bein leg [leg]
Beispiel example [ɪg'zɑ:mpl]
bekommen get [get]
benötigen need [ni:d]
benutzen use [ju:z]
beobachten watch [wɒtʃ]
beschäftigt sein *(viel zu tun haben)* be busy ['bɪzi]
beschreiben describe [dɪ'skraɪb]
besondere(r, s) special ['speʃl]
besorgt sein (wegen) be worried (about) ['wʌrid]
beste: meine besten Freunde/Freundinnen my best friends [best] **das Beste von beidem** the best of both worlds ['bəʊθ wɜ:ldz]
besuchen visit ['vɪzɪt]
Besucher/in visitor ['vɪzɪtə]
Bett bed [bed] **ins Bett gehen** go to bed
beunruhigt sein (wegen) be worried (about) ['wʌrid]
Beutel bag [bæg]

bevor du gehst before you go [bɪ'fɔː]
Bild picture ['pɪktʃə]
auf dem Bild in the picture
bis: von Montag bis Freitag from Monday to Friday **Bis dann. / Bis später.** See you. / See you later.
bisschen: ein bisschen a bit [ə 'bɪt]
bitte **1.** *(in Fragen und Aufforderungen)* please [pliːz]
2. Bitte schön. / Hier, bitte. Here you are.
3. Bitte, gern geschehen. *(Nichts zu danken.)* You're welcome. ['welkəm]
blau blue [bluː]
Blazer blazer ['bleɪzə]
bleiben stay [steɪ]
Bleistift pencil ['pensl]
Bleistiftanspitzer pencil sharpener ['pensl ʃɑːpnə]
blöd stupid ['stjuːpɪd]
bloß *(nur)* only ['əʊnli]
BMX-Rad BMX (bike) [biː em 'eks]
borgen: sich etwas borgen borrow sth. ['bɒrəʊ]
Brathähnchen chicken ['tʃɪkɪn]
brauchen need [niːd]
braun brown [braʊn]
Brief letter ['letə]
bringen *(mitbringen)* bring [brɪŋ]
britisch British ['brɪtɪʃ]
Broschüre brochure ['brəʊʃə]
Bruder brother ['brʌðə]
Buch book [bʊk]
buchstabieren spell [spel]
Bus bus [bʌs] **im Bus** on the bus
mit dem Bus by bus
mit dem Bus fahren go by bus

C

Café cafe ['kæfeɪ]
CD CD [siː 'diː]
Center centre ['sentə]
Computer computer [kəm'pjuːtə]
cool cool [kuːl]
Cousin, Cousine cousin ['kʌzn]

D

da *(dort)* there [ðeə]
daheim at home
dahin *(dorthin)* there [ðeə]
danach then [ðen]
Danke. Thanks. [θæŋks]
Danke, (es geht mir) gut. I'm fine, thanks.
danken: Nichts zu danken. *(Gern geschehen.)* You're welcome. ['welkəm]
dann then [ðen]
das *(Artikel)* the [ðə, ði]
das (dort) that [ðæt, ðət]
das Feld (dort) that field
dasselbe the same [seɪm]
Datum date [deɪt]
decken: den Tisch decken set the table [set]
dein, deine *(vor Nomen)* your [jɔː, jə]
deiner, deine, deins yours [jɔːz]
denken think [θɪŋk] **daran denken** *(sich merken; nicht vergessen)* remember [rɪ'membə]
der *(Artikel)* the [ðə, ði]
derselbe the same [seɪm]
Deutsch; deutsch German ['dʒɜːmən]
Deutschland Germany ['dʒɜːməni]
Dezember December [dɪ'sembə]
Dialog dialogue ['daɪəlɒg]
dich you [juː, ju]
dieselbe(n) the same [seɪm]
die *(Artikel)* the [ðə, ði]
die *(Relativpronomen)*: **Finde eine Person, die …** Find a person who … [huː]
Diele hall [hɔːl]
Dienstag Tuesday ['tjuːzdeɪ, 'tjuːzdi]
Dies ist … This is … ['ðɪs ɪz]
diese(r, s) this [ðɪs]
Ding thing [θɪŋ]
dir you [juː, ju] **Und was ist mit dir?** What about you?
Diskussion discussion [dɪ'skʌʃn]
Donnerstag Thursday ['θɜːzdeɪ, 'θɜːzdi]
Dorf village ['vɪlɪdʒ]
dort there [ðeə]
dorthin there [ðeə]
dran: Du bist dran. *(an der Reihe)* It's your turn. [tɜːn]
draußen outside [aʊt'saɪd]
nach draußen outside
drei three [θriː]
drinnen inside [ɪn'saɪd]
nach drinnen inside
dritte(r, s) third [θɜːd]
du you [juː, ju] **Und du?** What about you?
dumm stupid ['stjuːpɪd]
durch through [θruː]
DVD DVD [diːviː'diː]

E

echt *(wirklich)* real [rɪəl]
ein, eine *(Artikel)* a/an [ə, ən]
ein paar some [sʌm, səm]
einfach *(nicht schwierig)* easy ['iːzi]
einhundert a hundred, one hundred ['hʌndrəd]
einige, ein paar some [sʌm, səm]
einkaufen gehen go shopping ['ʃɒpɪŋ]
Einkaufszentrum shopping centre ['sentə]
einladen (zu, nach) *(Gäste)* invite (to) [ɪn'vaɪt]
Einladung (zu, nach) invitation (to) [ɪnvɪ'teɪʃn]
einmal: noch einmal again [ə'gen]
eins one [wʌn]
einsam lonely ['ləʊnli]
eintreten: in einen Klub eintreten join a club [dʒɔɪn]
Eintrittskarte ticket ['tɪkɪt]
einzige(r, s): der einzige Schüler / die einzige Schülerin the only student ['əʊnli]
Elefant elephant ['elɪfənt]
elf eleven [ɪ'levn]
Eltern parents ['peərənts]
E-Mail email ['iːmeɪl]
Ende end [end] **zu Ende sein** be over ['əʊvə]
England England ['ɪŋglənd]
Englisch; englisch English ['ɪŋglɪʃ]
auf Englisch in English
Ente duck [dʌk]
Entschuldigung **1.** *(Tut mir leid.)* Sorry. / I'm sorry. ['sɒri]
2. Entschuldigung, … / Entschuldigen Sie, … *(Darf ich mal stören?)* Excuse me, … [ɪk'skjuːz miː]
er **1.** *(männliche Person)* he [hiː]
2. *(Ding, Tier)* it [ɪt]
Erdkunde geography [dʒi'ɒgrəfi]
erinnern: sich an etwas erinnern remember sth. [rɪ'membə]
erraten guess [ges]
erste(r, s) first [fɜːst] **als Erstes** first **der erste Morgen** the first morning
Erzählung story ['stɔːri]
es it [ɪt] **es ist … / es gibt …** there's … **es sind … / es gibt …** there are …
Esel donkey ['dɒŋki]
essen eat [iːt] **(zu) Mittag essen** have lunch **Abendbrot**

essen, zu Abend essen have dinner
Essen *(Lebensmittel)* food [fu:d]
etwas something ['sʌmθɪŋ]; *(ein bisschen)* some [sʌm, səm] **Sonst noch etwas?** Anything else? ['eniθɪŋ 'els]
euch you [ju:, ju]
euer, eure *(vor Nomen)* your [jɔ:, jə]

F

Fähre ferry ['feri]
fahren: mit dem Bus/Auto fahren go by bus/car **Rad fahren** ride a bike **Skateboard fahren** skateboard
Fahrrad bike [baɪk]
fallen fall [fɔ:l]
falsch wrong [rɒŋ]; *(unwahr)* false [fɔ:ls]
Familie family ['fæməli]
Familienname family name
Familienstammbaum family tree
Farbe colour ['kʌlə]
Farm farm [fɑ:m]
faul *(träge, arbeitsunwillig)* lazy ['leɪzi]
Februar February ['februəri]
Federmäppchen pencil case ['pensl keɪs]
feiern: eine Party feiern have a party
Feld field [fi:ld] **auf dem Feld** in the field
Fenster window ['wɪndəʊ]
Ferien holidays ['hɒlədeɪz]
fernsehen watch TV [wɒtʃ ti:'vi:]
Fernsehen, Fernsehgerät TV [ti:'vi:]
Fernsehsendung programme ['prəʊgræm]
fertig: sich fertig machen (für) *(vorbereiten)* get ready (for) ['redi]
Feuerwache fire station ['faɪə steɪʃn]
fies *(gemein)* mean [mi:n]
Film film [fɪlm]
finden find [faɪnd] **Finde eine Person, die …** Find a person who …
Fisch, Fische fish, *pl* fish [fɪʃ]
Flasche: eine Flasche … a bottle of … ['bɒtl]
flauschig *(pelzig)* furry ['fɜ:ri]
Flur *(Diele)* hall [hɔ:l]
Form form [fɔ:m]
fort away [ə'weɪ]
Foto photo ['fəʊtəʊ] **auf dem Foto** in the photo
Frage question ['kwestʃn] **Fragen stellen** ask questions
fragen ask [ɑ:sk] **sie fragte/hat gefragt** she asked
Französisch; französisch French [frentʃ]
Frau … **1.** *(allgemeine Anrede f. Frauen)* Ms … [mɪz, məz] **2.** *(Anrede f. verheiratete Frauen)* Mrs … ['mɪsɪz] **3.** *(Anrede f. unverheiratete Frauen)* Miss … [mɪs]
frei free [fri:]
Freitag Friday ['fraɪdeɪ, 'fraɪdi]
freitagmorgens, am Freitagmorgen on Friday morning
fressen eat [i:t]
Freund/in friend [frend]; *(fester Freund)* boyfriend; *(feste Freundin)* girlfriend
freundlich friendly ['frendli]
Freut mich, dich/euch kennenzulernen. Nice to meet you!
froh happy ['hæpi]
früh early ['ɜ:li]
Frühstück breakfast ['brekfəst]
frühstücken have breakfast
fühlen; sich fühlen feel [fi:l]
Füller pen [pen]
fünf five [faɪv]
funktionieren work [wɜ:k]
für for [fɔ:, fə] **für mich selbst** for myself [maɪ'self]
fürchterlich terrible ['terəbl]
Fußball football ['fʊtbɔ:l]
Futter food [fu:d]
füttern feed [fi:d]

G

ganz: den ganzen Tag/Sommer/… (lang) all day/summer/…
Garage garage ['gærɑ:ʒ]
Garten garden ['gɑ:dn]
geben: es gibt … there's …; there are … [ðeəz], ['ðeər ɑ:]
Geburtstag birthday ['bɜ:θdeɪ] **an meinem Geburtstag** on my birthday **Herzlichen Glückwunsch zum Geburtstag!** Happy birthday! **Ich habe am 5. Mai Geburtstag.** My birthday is on 5th May. **Sie hat Geburtstag.** It's her birthday. **Wann hast du Geburtstag?** When's your birthday?
Gedicht poem ['pəʊɪm]
gefährlich dangerous ['deɪndʒərəs]
Gefühl feeling ['fi:lɪŋ]
gehen go [gəʊ] **zu Fuß gehen** walk [wɔ:k] **einkaufen gehen** go shopping ['ʃɒpɪŋ] **ins Bett gehen** go to bed **nach Hause gehen** go home **schwimmen gehen** go swimming **zur Arbeit gehen** go to work **zur Schule gehen** go to school **Wie geht's?** How are you? [haʊ 'ɑ: ju]; *(Wie läuft's?)* How's it going? **Wie geht es dir/euch?** How are you?
gehören zu *(passen zu)* go with
gelb yellow ['jeləʊ]
Geld money ['mʌni] **Es ist sein Geld wert.** It's good value. ['vælju:]
gemein *(fies)* mean [mi:n]
Gemüse vegetables *(pl)* ['vedʒtəblz]
genervt sein feel fed up [fed 'ʌp]
Geografie geography [dʒi'ɒgrəfi]
gerade *(in diesem Moment)* at the moment ['məʊmənt]
Geräusch sound [saʊnd]; *(unangenehm, laut)* noise [nɔɪz]
gern: Ich sehe gern fern. I like watching TV. **Ich komme sehr gern. / Ich würde sehr gern kommen.** I'd love to come. (= I would love to come. **Bitte, gern geschehen.** You're welcome.
gernhaben *(mögen)* like [laɪk]
Geschäft shop [ʃɒp]
geschehen happen ['hæpən]
Geschenk present ['preznt]
Geschichte **1.** *(vergangene Zeiten)* history ['hɪstri] **2.** *(Erzählung)* story ['stɔ:ri]
Gesicht face [feɪs]
gespannt *(aufgeregt)* excited [ɪk'saɪtɪd]
Getränk drink [drɪŋk]
gewinnen win [wɪn]
gewöhnlich *(normal)* normal ['nɔ:ml]
Gitarre guitar [gɪ'tɑ:] **Gitarre spielen** play the guitar
glauben *(denken, meinen)* think [θɪŋk]
Glück: du hast Glück you're lucky ['lʌki]
glücklich happy ['hæpi]
Glückwunsch: Herzlichen Glückwunsch zum Geburtstag! Happy birthday! ['bɜ:θdeɪ]
grau grey [greɪ]

groß big [bɪg]
großartig great [greɪt]
Großeltern grandparents ['grænpeərənts]
Großmutter grandmother ['grænmʌðə]
Großvater grandfather ['grænfɑːðə]
grün green [griːn]
Gruppe group [gruːp]; *(Band)* band
Gruß: Viele Grüße, … *(Briefschluss)* Best wishes ['wɪʃɪz]
grüßen: Grüß alle. Say hi to everybody.
gut good [gʊd]; *(in Ordnung)* fine [faɪn] **gut funktionieren/sprechen/…** work/speak/… well **Gut gemacht!** Well done. [wel 'dʌn] **Danke, (es geht mir) gut.** I'm OK, thanks./I'm fine, thanks. **Guten Morgen.** Good morning. **Guten Tag.** Hello. [hə'ləʊ]

H

haben have [hæv, həv] **die Nase voll haben** feel fed up [fed 'ʌp] **etwas haben wollen** want sth. [wɒnt] **Glück haben** be lucky ['lʌki] **Hunger haben** be hungry ['hʌŋgri] **Ich habe am 5. Mai Geburtstag.** My birthday is on 5th May. **viel zu tun haben** be busy ['bɪzi] **ich hatte/habe gehabt** I had [hæd], [həd]
Hafen harbour ['hɑːbə]
Hähnchen chicken ['tʃɪkɪn]
Hallo. Hi. [haɪ]; Hello. [hə'ləʊ]
halten: Halt den Mund! Shut up! *(infml)* [ʃʌt 'ʌp]
Hamster hamster ['hæmstə]
Handy mobile phone ['məʊbaɪl 'fəʊn]
hart hard [hɑːd] **hart arbeiten** work hard
hassen hate [heɪt]
hat: Er hat … He has … [hæz, həz]
hatte: ich hatte/habe gehabt I had [hæd], [həd]
Haus house [haʊs] **bei Ellie zu Hause** at Ellie's house **nach Hause gehen** go home **nach Hause kommen** come home **zu Hause** at home
Hausaufgabe(n) homework ['həʊmwɜːk] **Ich habe meine Hausaufgaben vergessen.** I forgot my homework. **Ich kann meine Hausaufgaben nicht machen.** I can't do my homework. **Was haben wir als Hausaufgabe auf?** What's for homework?
Haustier pet [pet]
Heim *(Zuhause)* home [həʊm]
heißen: Ich heiße Cyril. I'm Cyril. **Wie heißt du?** What's your name?
helfen help [help]
Helm helmet ['helmɪt]
Hemd shirt [ʃɜːt]
Herr Jahn Mr Jahn ['mɪstə]
herrisch bossy ['bɒsi]
herstellen make [meɪk]
Herzlichen Glückwunsch zum Geburtstag! Happy birthday!
heute today [tə'deɪ]
hier here [hɪə] **Hier, bitte.** Here you are.
hierher here [hɪə]
Hilfe! Help! [help]
hinfallen fall [fɔːl]
hinter behind [bɪ'haɪnd]
hinunter: diesen Hügel hinunter down this hill [daʊn]
Hobby hobby ['hɒbi]
hoffen hope [həʊp]
hören hear [hɪə]
Hose trousers *(pl)* ['traʊzəz]
Hügel hill [hɪl]
Huhn chicken ['tʃɪkɪn]
Hund dog [dɒg]
hundert a hundred, one hundred ['hʌndrəd]
Hunger haben be hungry ['hʌŋgri]
hungrig sein be hungry ['hʌŋgri]

I

ich I [aɪ] **Ich auch.** Me too. **Ich bin es, Sandy.** It's me, Sandy. **Ich nicht!** Not me!
Idee idea [aɪ'dɪə]
ihm him [hɪm]; *(bei Dingen und Tieren)* it
ihn him [hɪm]; *(bei Dingen und Tieren)* it
ihnen them [ðem], [ðəm]
Ihnen *(höfliche Anrede)* you [juː, ju]
ihr *(Mehrzahl von „du")* you
ihr: Hilf ihr. Help her. [hɜː]
ihr, ihre *(vor Nomen; besitzanzeigend)*
1. *(zu „she")* her [hɜː, hə]
2. *(zu „it")* its [ɪts]
3. *(zu „they")* their [ðeə]
Ihr, Ihre *(vor Nomen; besitzanzeigend) (zur höflichen Anrede „you")* your [jɔː, jə]
im: im Bus on the bus **im Kino** at the cinema **im Moment** at the moment ['məʊmənt]
immer always ['ɔːlweɪz]
in in [ɪn] **in das Wohnzimmer (hinein)** into the living room ['ɪntʊ] **in der Mitte** in the middle **in der Nacht** at night **in der Nähe von** near [nɪə] **in der Schule** at school **in der Stadt** in town **in Deutschland** in Germany **in einem Restaurant** at a restaurant **in England** in England **in Schwierigkeiten sein** be in trouble ['trʌbl]
Informations- und Kommunikationstechnologie ICT [aɪ siː 'tiː] *(information and communication technology)*
ins: ins Bett gehen go to bed **ins Kino** to the cinema
Instrument instrument ['ɪnstrəmənt]
interessant interesting ['ɪntrəstɪŋ]
Interview interview ['ɪntəvjuː]
Irgendwelche Ideen? Any ideas? ['eni]

J

ja yes [jes]
Jahr year [jɪə]
Januar January ['dʒænjuəri]
jede(r, s) *(vor Nomen)* every ['evri]
jeder *(alle)* everybody ['evribɒdi]
jenes Feld (dort) that field [ðæt, ðət]
jetzt now [naʊ]
Job job [dʒɒb]
Jugendliche(r) kid [kɪd]
Juli July [dʒu'laɪ]
jung young [jʌŋ]
Junge boy [bɔɪ]
Juni June [dʒuːn]

K

Kaffee coffee ['kɒfi]
Käfig cage [keɪdʒ]
Kalender diary ['daɪəri]
Kaninchen rabbit ['ræbɪt]
Kantine canteen [kæn'tiːn]
Kapuzenpullover, -jacke hoodie ['hʊdi]
Karte card [kɑːd]
Kästchen box [bɒks]
Kasten box [bɒks]
Katze cat [kæt]
kaufen buy [baɪ]

kein, keine no [nəʊ] **Ich bin kein Junge.** I'm not a boy. **Ich mag kein Blau.** I don't like blue. **sie hat kein/keine/keinen ...** she doesn't have a ... ['dʌznt] **sie sind keine ...** they aren't ... [ɑːnt]
kennen know [nəʊ]
kennenlernen meet [miːt] **Freut mich, dich/euch kennenzulernen.** Nice to meet you!
Kind, Kinder child, *pl* children [tʃaɪld], ['tʃɪldrən]; kid [kɪd]
Kino cinema ['sɪnəmə] **im Kino** at the cinema **ins Kino** to the cinema
Kissen cushion ['kʊʃn]
Kiste box [bɒks]
Klang sound [saʊnd]
Klasse class [klɑːs]
Klassenlehrer/in class teacher ['klɑːs tiːtʃə]
Klassenzimmer classroom ['klɑːsruːm]
Klavier piano [pi'ænəʊ] **Klavier spielen** play the piano
Kleiderschrank wardrobe ['wɔːdrəʊb]
klein little ['lɪtl]; small [smɔːl]
klingeln ring [rɪŋ]
Koch, Köchin cook [kʊk]
kochen cook [kʊk]
kommen come [kʌm] **Komm, Luca!** Come on, Luca! **nach Hause kommen** come home
können can [kæn, kən] **Ich kann meine Hausaufgaben nicht machen.** I can't do my homework. [kɑːnt]
Konzert concert ['kɒnsət]
Kopfsprung: einen Kopfsprung machen dive [daɪv]
kosten: Der Taschenrechner kostet 1 Pfund. The calculator is £ 1. **Die Handys kosten 10 Pfund.** The mobiles are £ 10. **Was (Wie viel) kostet ...?** How much is ...? **Was (Wie viel) kosten ...?** How much are ...?
Krankenhaus hospital ['hɒspɪtl]
Krawatte tie [taɪ]
Krebs crab [kræb]
kriegen: Ärger kriegen be in trouble ['trʌbl]
Krokodil crocodile ['krɒkədaɪl]
Küche kitchen ['kɪtʃɪn]
Kugelschreiber pen [pen]
Kuh cow [kaʊ]
kümmern: sich kümmern um look after [lʊk 'ɑːftə]
Kunst art [ɑːt]

L

Labor lab [læb]
lachen laugh [lɑːf] **sie lachten/haben gelacht** they laughed
Laden shop [ʃɒp]
Lampe lamp [læmp]
Land country ['kʌntri] **auf dem Land** in the country
lang: den ganzen Tag/Sommer/... lang all day/summer/...
langweilig boring ['bɔːrɪŋ]
Lärm noise [nɔɪz]
Lass uns ... / Lasst uns ... Let's ... [lets]
laufen: Wie läuft's? How's it going?
Läufer *(Teppich)* rug [rʌg]
laut *(voller Lärm)* noisy ['nɔɪzi]
Laut sound [saʊnd]
läuten ring [rɪŋ]
Leben: (das) Leben, (die) Leben life, *pl* lives [laɪf], [laɪvz]
leben live [lɪv]
Lebensmittel food [fuːd]
Lehrer/in teacher ['tiːtʃə]
leicht *(einfach)* easy ['iːzi]
leidtun: Tut mir leid. Sorry. / I'm sorry. ['sɒri]
leihen *(sich borgen)* borrow ['bɒrəʊ]
leise quiet ['kwaɪət]
Lektion *(im Schulbuch)* unit ['juːnɪt]
lernen learn [lɜːn]
lesen read [riːd]
letzte(r, s) last [lɑːst] **der letzte Tag der Ferien** the last day of the holidays
Leute people ['piːpl]; *(als Anrede verwendet)* guys [gaɪz]
Liebe ... / Lieber ... Dear ... [dɪə]
lieben love [lʌv]
Lieblings- favourite ['feɪvərɪt] **Lieblingsfarbe** favourite colour
Lied song [sɒŋ]
lila purple ['pɜːpl]
Lineal ruler ['ruːlə]
links left [left] **auf der linken Seite** on the left **nach links** left
Locher hole punch ['həʊl pʌntʃ]
los: In der Küche ist zu viel los. The kitchen is too busy. ['bɪzi]

M

machen *(tun)* do [duː]; *(herstellen)* make [meɪk] **Ich kann meine Hausaufgaben nicht machen.** I can't do my homework. [kɑːnt] **Das macht 159 Pfund.** That's £ 159. **einen Kopfsprung machen** dive [daɪv] **sich fertig machen (für)** get ready (for) ['redi] **sauber machen** clean [kliːn] **sich Sorgen machen (wegen, um)** worry (about) ['wʌri] **Mach dir keine Sorgen.** Don't worry. [dəʊnt 'wʌri] **Gut gemacht!** Well done. [wel 'dʌn] **Ich muss Schluss machen.** *(am Telefon)* I must go.
Mädchen girl [gɜːl]
Mai May [meɪ]
Mama mum [mʌm]
manchmal sometimes ['sʌmtaɪmz]
Mann, Männer man, *pl* men [mæn], [men]
Mannschaft team [tiːm]
Markt market ['mɑːkɪt]
Marmelade jam [dʒæm]
März March [mɑːtʃ]
Mathematik maths [mæθs]
Meer sea [siː]
mein, meine *(vor Nomen)* my [maɪ]
meinen *(denken, glauben)* think [θɪŋk] **Was meinst du?** What do you think?
meistens usually ['juːʒuəli]
Mensa canteen [kæn'tiːn]
Menschen people ['piːpl]
merken: sich etwas merken remember sth. [rə'membə]
mich me [miː] **für mich selbst** for myself [maɪ'self]
mir me [miː]
mit with [wɪð] **mit dem Bus/Rad/Auto/...** by bus/bike/car/... **mit dem Bus/Rad/Auto fahren** go by bus/bike/car
mitbringen bring [brɪŋ]
Mittag: (zu) Mittag essen have lunch [lʌntʃ]
Mittagessen lunch [lʌntʃ]
Mitte middle ['mɪdl] **in der Mitte** in the middle
Mittwoch Wednesday ['wenzdeɪ, 'wenzdi]
Mobiltelefon mobile (phone) ['məʊbaɪl]
mögen like [laɪk] **Ich mag Rot.** I like red. **Ich mag Blau nicht. / Ich mag kein Blau.** I don't like blue. **Er mag es nicht, allein zu**

sein. He doesn't like to be lonely. **gar nicht mögen** *(hassen)* hate [heɪt]
Moment moment ['məʊmənt]
im Moment at the moment
Monat month [mʌnθ]
Montag Monday ['mʌndeɪ, 'mʌndi]
Morgen morning ['mɔːnɪŋ]
am Morgen in the morning(s)
morgens in the morning(s)
Möwe seagull ['siːgʌl]
müde tired ['taɪəd]
Mund mouth [maʊθ] **Halt den Mund!** Shut up! *(infml)* [ʃʌt 'ʌp]
Musik music ['mjuːzɪk]
Musiker/in musician [mju'zɪʃn]
müssen must [mʌst] **Ich muss Schluss machen.** *(am Telefon)* I must go.
Mutter mother ['mʌðə]
Mutti mum [mʌm]

N

Na ja, … Well, … [wel]
Na los, Luca! Come on, Luca!
nach **1.** *(zeitlich)* after ['ɑːftə]
nach dem Abendessen after dinner
2. *(örtlich)* **to** [tu, tə]
nach draußen outside [aʊt'saɪd]
nach drinnen inside [ɪn'saɪd]
nach Hause gehen go home
nach Hause kommen come home **nach links** left [left]
nach oben upstairs [ʌp'steəz]
nach rechts right [raɪt]
nach unten downstairs [daʊn'steəz]
Nachmittag afternoon [ɑːftə'nuːn]
am Nachmittag in the afternoon
nachmittags in the afternoon
Nachname family name
Nachrichten news [njuːz]
nächste(r, s) next [nekst]
Nacht night [naɪt] **in der Nacht** at night
nachts at night [ət 'naɪt]
nahe (bei) near [nɪə]
Nähe: in der Nähe von near [nɪə]
Name name [neɪm]
Nase: die Nase voll haben feel fed up [fed 'ʌp]
nass wet [wet]
Naturwissenschaft science ['saɪəns]
neben next to ['nekst tʊ]
nehmen: Ich nehme es (ihn, sie). *(beim Einkaufen)* I'll take it. [aɪl 'teɪk ɪt]
nein no [nəʊ]
nervös nervous ['nɜːvəs]
nett nice [naɪs]
Netz network ['netwɜːk]
neu new [njuː]
neun nine [naɪn]
nicht: ich bin nicht … I'm not … [nɒt] **Ich nicht!** Not me!
nichts nothing ['nʌθɪŋ] **Nichts zu danken.** You're welcome.
nie never ['nevə]
niedlich cute [kjuːt]
niemals never ['nevə]
noch: noch einmal again [ə'gen]
Sonst noch etwas? Anything else? ['eniθɪŋ 'els]
normal normal ['nɔːml]
normalerweise usually ['juːʒuəli]
November November [nəʊ'vembə]
Nummer number ['nʌmbə]
nun now [naʊ] **Nun, …** Well, … [wel]
nur only ['əʊnli]
Nuss nut [nʌt]

O

oben upstairs [ʌp'steəz]
nach oben upstairs
Obst fruit [fruːt]
oder or [ɔː]
oft often ['ɒfn, 'ɒftən]
okay OK [əʊ'keɪ]
Oktober October [ɒk'təʊbə]
Omelett omelette ['ɒmlət]
Onkel uncle ['ʌŋkl]
orange orange ['ɒrɪndʒ]
Ordnung: in Ordnung fine [faɪn]
Ort place [pleɪs]

P

Paar pair [peə]
paar: ein paar some [sʌm], [səm]
Papa dad [dæd]
Papier paper ['peɪpə]
Park park [pɑːk]
Partner/in partner ['pɑːtnə]
Party party ['pɑːti] **eine Party feiern** have a party
passen zu *(gehören zu)* go with
passieren happen ['hæpən]
Pause break [breɪk]
pelzig *(flauschig)* furry ['fɜːri]
Pence: 50 Pence 50p [fɪfti 'piː]
Pfund *(britische Währung)* pound (£) [paʊnd] **Das macht 159 Pfund.** That's £ 159.
Der Taschenrechner kostet 1 Pfund. The calculator is £ 1.
Die Handys kosten 10 Pfund. The mobiles are £ 10.
Piano piano [pi'ænəʊ]
Picknick picnic ['pɪknɪk]
pink pink [pɪŋk]
planen plan [plæn]
Platz **1.** *(Stelle, Ort)* place [pleɪs]
2. *(freier Raum)* space [speɪs]
3. *(Sitzplatz)* seat [siːt]
Pommes frites chips *(pl)* [tʃɪps]
Pony pony ['pəʊni] **auf einem Pony reiten** ride a pony
Poster poster ['pəʊstə]
Preis *(Kaufpreis)* price [praɪs]
prima great [greɪt]
probieren *(ausprobieren)* try [traɪ]
Problem problem ['prɒbləm]
Prospekt brochure ['brəʊʃə]
Pullover pullover ['pʊləʊvə]
putzen clean [kliːn]

Q

Quiz quiz [kwɪz]

R

Rad *(Fahrrad)* bike [baɪk]
Rad fahren ride a bike [raɪd]
mit dem Rad by bike
mit dem Rad fahren go by bike
Radiergummi rubber ['rʌbə]
Rap *(rhythmischer Sprechgesang)* rap [ræp]
rappen rap [ræp]
Rapper/in rapper ['ræpə]
raten guess [ges]
Ratespiel quiz [kwɪz]
Ratte rat [ræt]
Raum *(Zimmer)* room [ruːm, rʊm]
rechthaberisch bossy ['bɒsi]
rechts right [raɪt]
auf der rechten Seite on the right **nach rechts** right
reden (mit) talk (to) [tɔːk]
Regal, Regale shelf, *pl* shelves [ʃelf], [ʃelvz]
Reihe: Du bist an der Reihe. It's your turn. [tɜːn]
reiten ride [raɪd] **auf einem Pony reiten** ride a pony
Rektor/in *(Schulleiter/in)* principal ['prɪnsəpl]
Restaurant restaurant ['restrɒnt]
in einem Restaurant at a restaurant
Rezept *(Kochrezept)* recipe ['resəpi]
richtig right [raɪt]

Rock skirt [skɜːt]
Rollstuhl wheelchair ['wiːltʃeə]
rosa pink [pɪŋk]
rot red [red]
ruhig quiet ['kwaɪət]
Rundgang: ein Rundgang durch die Schule a tour of the school [tʊə]

S

Sache *(Ding)* thing [θɪŋ]
Saft juice [dʒuːs]
sagen say [seɪ] **er sagte/hat gesagt** he said [sed]
Sahne cream [kriːm]
Salat *(als Gericht oder Beilage)* salad ['s ləd]
Samstag Saturday ['sætədeɪ, 'sætədi]
Sandwich sandwich ['sænwɪtʃ, 'sændwɪdʒ]
Sänger/in singer ['sɪŋə]
sauber machen clean [kliːn]
sauer sein *(genervt sein)* feel fed up [fed 'ʌp]
Schaf, Schafe sheep, *pl* sheep [ʃiːp]
Schauspiel *(darstellende Kunst)* drama ['drɑːmə]
Schere scissors *(pl)* ['sɪzəz]
Scheune barn [bɑːn]
schicken send [send] **einem Freund / einer Freundin eine SMS schicken** text a friend [tekst]
Schild sign [saɪn]
schlafen sleep [sliːp] **Schlaf jetzt!** Go to sleep!
Schlafparty sleepover ['sliːpəʊvə]
Schlafsack sleeping bag ['sliːpɪŋ bæg]
Schlafzimmer bedroom ['bedruːm]
Schlagzeug drums [drʌmz] **Schlagzeug spielen** play the drums
Schlange snake [sneɪk]
schlecht bad [bæd]
schließen *(zumachen)* close [kləʊz]
schlimm bad [bæd]
Schluss end [end] **Ich muss Schluss machen.** *(am Telefon)* I must go.
Schlussverkauf sale [seɪl]
schnell fast [fɑːst]
schön *(nett)* nice [naɪs] **Ich wünsche dir einen schönen Tag. / Schönen Tag noch.** Have a good day.
schrecklich terrible ['terəbl]
schreiben write [raɪt]
Schreibtisch desk [desk]
Schuh shoe [ʃuː]
Schule school [skuːl] **auf/an dieser Schule** at this school **in der Schule** at school **zur Schule gehen** go to school
Schüler/in student ['stjuːdənt]
Schulheft exercise book ['eksəsaɪz bʊk]
Schulklasse class [klɑːs]
Schulleiter/in principal ['prɪnsəpl]
Schulsport PE [piː 'iː] *(physical education)*
Schultasche school bag ['skuːl bæg]
Schulter shoulder ['ʃəʊldə]
Schulversammlung assembly [ə'sembli]
schwarz black [blæk]
Schwein pig [pɪg]
schwer *(schwierig)* difficult ['dɪfɪkəlt]; hard [hɑːd]
Schwester sister ['sɪstə]
schwierig difficult ['dɪfɪkəlt]; hard [hɑːd]
Schwierigkeit: in Schwierigkeiten sein be in trouble ['trʌbl]
Schwimmbad swimming pool ['swɪmɪŋ puːl]
Schwimmbecken swimming pool ['swɪmɪŋ puːl]
schwimmen swim [swɪm] **schwimmen gehen** go swimming
sechs six [sɪks]
sehen see [siː] **Sieh mal, Adam.** Look, Adam.
sehr very ['veri] **sehr nett, sehr schön** very nice
sein be [biː] **Sei still/leise.** Be quiet. ['kwaɪət]
sein, seine *(vor Nomen; besitzanzeigend)*
1. *(zu „he")* his [hɪz]
2. *(zu „it")* its [ɪts]
Seite 1. page [peɪdʒ] **Auf welcher Seite sind wir? / Auf welcher Seite steht das?** What page is it?
2. auf der linken Seite on the left **auf der rechten Seite** on the right
selbst: für mich selbst for myself [maɪ'self]
senden send [send]
Sendung *(Radio, Fernsehen)* programme ['prəʊgræm]
September September [sep'tembə]
setzen: sich setzen sit [sɪt]
sicher sure [ʃʊə, ʃɔː]
sie 1. *(Einzahl; weibliche Person)* she [ʃiː] **Frag sie.** Ask her. [hɜː]
2. *(Einzahl; Ding, Tier)* it [ɪt]
3. *(Mehrzahl)* they [ðeɪ] **Frag sie.** Ask them. [ðem, ðəm]
Sie *(höfliche Anrede)* you [juː, ju]
sieben seven ['sevn]
singen sing [sɪŋ]
sitzen sit [sɪt]
Skateboard fahren skateboard ['skeɪtbɔːd]
SMS text message ['tekst mesɪdʒ]; text **eine SMS von Mama** a text from mum **einem Freund / einer Freundin eine SMS schicken** text a friend [tekst]
so langweilig/müde/... so boring/tired/... [səʊ]
Socke sock [sɒk]
Sommer summer ['sʌmə]
Sonderangebot special offer [speʃl 'ɒfə]
Sonnabend Saturday ['sætədeɪ, 'sætədi]
Sonntag Sunday ['sʌndeɪ, 'sʌndi]
Sonst noch etwas? Anything else? ['eniθɪŋ 'els]
Sorge: sich Sorgen machen (wegen, um) worry (about) ['wʌri] **Mach dir keine Sorgen.** Don't worry. [dəʊnt 'wʌri]
Spaß: es macht Spaß it's fun [fʌn]
spät late [leɪt] **Wie spät ist es?** What's the time?
später later ['leɪtə] **Bis später.** See you. / See you later. ['leɪtə]
Spiegel mirror ['mɪrə]
Spiel game [geɪm]
spielen play [pleɪ] **Gitarre/Klavier/Schlagzeug spielen** play the guitar/the piano/the drums
Sport sport [spɔːt]; *(in der Schule)* PE [piː 'iː] *(physical education)* **Sport treiben** do sport
Sporthalle sports hall ['spɔːts hɔːl]
Sprache language ['læŋgwɪdʒ]
sprechen (mit) speak (to) [spiːk]; talk (to) [tɔːk]
Sprechgesang chant [tʃɑːnt]
Stadt *(Großstadt)* city ['sɪti]; *(Kleinstadt)* town [taʊn] **in der Stadt** in town
Stammbaum *(der Familie)* family tree
Stelle place [pleɪs]
stellen: Fragen stellen ask questions ['kwestʃnz]

Stiefbruder stepbrother ['stepbrʌðə]
Stiefmutter stepmother ['stepmʌðə]; stepmum ['stepmʌm]
Stiefschwester stepsister ['stepsɪstə]
Stiefvater stepdad ['stepdæd]; stepfather ['stepfɑːðə]
Stift *(zum Schreiben)* pen [pen]
still quiet ['kwaɪət]
stolz (auf) proud (of) [praʊd]
Strand beach [biːtʃ] **am Strand** on the beach
Straße *(in Orten)* street [striːt]; *(Landstraße zwischen Orten, aber auch Straße in Orten)* road [rəʊd]
streicheln stroke [strəʊk]
streng strict [strɪkt]
Strumpf *(Socke)* sock [sɒk]
Strumpfhose tights *(pl)* [taɪts]
Student/in student ['stjuːdənt]
Studio studio ['stjuːdiəʊ]
Stuhl chair [tʃeə]
Stunde *(Schulstunde)* lesson ['lesn]
Stundenplan timetable ['taɪmteɪbl]
Supermarkt supermarket ['suːpəmɑːkɪt]
Suppe soup [suːp]
süß *(niedlich)* cute [kjuːt]
Süßigkeiten sweets *(pl)* [swiːts]
Sweatshirt sweatshirt ['swetʃɜːt]
Szene scene [siːn]

T

Taekwondo tae kwon do [taɪ kwɒn 'dəʊ]
Tag day [deɪ] **Ich wünsche dir einen schönen Tag. / Schönen Tag noch.** Have a good day.
Tagebuch diary ['daɪəri]
Tante aunt [ɑːnt]
tanzen dance [dɑːns]
Tasche *(Tragetasche, Beutel)* bag [bæg]
Taschenrechner calculator ['kælkjuleɪtə]
Tasse: eine Tasse ... a cup of ... [kʌp]
Team team [tiːm]
Technik *(Technologie)* technology [tek'nɒlədʒi]
Technologie technology [tek'nɒlədʒi]
Tee tea [tiː]
Teenager teenager ['tiːneɪdʒə]
Teich pond [pɒnd]
teilen: sich ein Zimmer mit ... teilen share a room with ... [ʃeə]
Telefon phone [fəʊn]
am Telefon on the phone
Telefonnummer phone number ['fəʊn nʌmbə]
Tennis tennis [tenɪs]
Teppich *(Läufer)* rug [rʌg]
teuer expensive [ɪk'spensɪv]
Text text [tekst]
Theater theatre ['θɪətə]
Thema theme [θiːm]
Tier animal ['ænɪml]
Tiger tiger ['taɪgə]
Tisch table ['teɪbl] **den Tisch decken** set the table [set]
Toast toast [təʊst]
Toilette toilet ['tɔɪlət]
Training training ['treɪnɪŋ]
Traum dream [driːm]
treffen; sich treffen meet [miːt]
treiben: Sport treiben do sport
trinken drink [drɪŋk]
Trommel drum [drʌm]
Tschüs. Bye. [baɪ]
T-Shirt T-shirt ['tiːʃɜːt]
tun do [duː] **etwas tun wollen** want to do sth. [wɒnt] **viel zu tun haben** be busy ['bɪzi]
Tür door [dɔː]
Turnschuhe trainers *(pl)* ['treɪnəz]

U

über about [ə'baʊt] **über mich/dich/...** about me/you/...
Überraschung surprise [sə'praɪz]
Übung *(im Schulbuch)* exercise ['eksəsaɪz]
Übungsheft exercise book
Uhr: 9 Uhr morgens/vormittags 9 am [eɪ'em] **5 Uhr nachmittags/abends / 17 Uhr** 5 pm [piː'em] **um 1 Uhr / 13 Uhr** at 1 o'clock [ə'klɒk]
Uhrzeit time [taɪm]
um 1 Uhr / 13 Uhr at 1 o'clock [ə'klɒk]
und and [ænd, ənd] **Und du? / Und was ist mit dir?** What about you?
ungefähr about [ə'baʊt]
unglücklich unhappy [ʌn'hæpi]
Uniform uniform ['juːnɪfɔːm]
unordentlich messy ['mesi]
uns us [ʌs, əs]
unser, unsere *(vor Nomen)* our ['aʊə]
unten downstairs [daʊn'steəz]
nach unten downstairs [daʊn'steəz]
unter under ['ʌndə]
Unterrichtsstunde lesson ['lesn]
Unterschied difference ['dɪfrəns]

V

Vater father ['fɑːðə]
Vati dad [dæd]
vergessen: Ich habe meine Hausaufgaben vergessen. I forgot my homework. [fə'gɒt]
verirrt: Ich habe mich nicht verirrt. I'm not lost. [lɒst]
Verkauf sale [seɪl]
verlaufen: Ich habe mich nicht verlaufen. I'm not lost. [lɒst]
vermissen miss [mɪs]
verschieden different ['dɪfrənt]
verstecken; sich verstecken hide [haɪd]
verstehen understand [ʌndə'stænd]
verwenden use [juːz]
viel ..., viele ... *(vor Nomen)* lots of ... ['lɒts əv] **Wie viel kostet ...?** How much is ...? **Wie viel kosten ...?** How much are ...? **Viele Grüße, ...** *(Briefschluss)* Best wishes ['wɪʃɪz]
vielleicht maybe ['meɪbi]
vier four [fɔː]
violett purple ['pɜːpl]
Vogel bird [bɜːd]
von: eine SMS von Mama a text from mum **von Montag bis Freitag** from Monday to Friday
vor **1.** *(zeitlich)* before [bɪ'fɔː] **vor dem Frühstück** before breakfast **2.** *(örtlich)* **in front of** [ɪn 'frʌnt əv]
vorbei sein be over ['əʊvə]
vorbereiten: sich vorbereiten (auf) get ready (for) ['redi]

W

wahr true [truː]
wann? when? [wen] **Wann hast du Geburtstag?** When's your birthday?
war: es war Freitag it was Friday [wɒz], [wəz]
waren: sie waren im Bus they were on the bus [wɜː], [wə]
warum? why? [waɪ]
was? what? [wɒt] **Was haben wir als Hausaufgabe auf?** What's for homework? **Was kostet ...?** How much is ...? **Was kosten ...?** How much are ...? **Was meinst du? / Was denkst du?** What do you think?

Wasser water ['wɔːtə]
wecken wake [weɪk]
Wecker alarm clock [ə'lɑːm klɒk]
weg away [ə'weɪ]
Weg way [weɪ] **auf dem Weg zu/nach ...** on the way to ...
wehtun: Mein Bein tut weh. I have a sore leg. [sɔː]
Weide field [fiːld] **auf der Weide** in the field
weil because [bɪ'kɒz]
weiß white [waɪt]
welche(r, s) ...? what ...? [wɒt] **Auf welcher Seite sind wir?/ Auf welcher Seite steht das?** What page is it?
Welt world [wɜːld]
Wendung *(Ausdruck, Redewendung)* phrase [freɪz]
wenn when [wen]
wer? who? [huː] **Wer bist du? / Wer seid ihr?** Who are you?
Werbung *(Anzeige)* advert ['ædvɜːt]
wert: Es ist sein Geld wert. It's good value. ['væljuː]
wichtig important [ɪm'pɔːtnt]
wie *(ähnlich wie; so wie)* like [laɪk]
wie? how? [haʊ] **Wie geht's?** How are you? [haʊ 'ɑː ju]; *(Wie läuft's?)* How's it going? **Wie geht es dir/euch?** How are you? **Wie heißt du?** What's your name? **Wie ist es? / Wie sieht es aus?** What's it like? **Wie spät ist es?** What's the time? **Wie wär's mit ...?** What about ...? **Wie viel kostet ...?** How much is ...? **Wie viel kosten ...?** How much are ...?
wieder again [ə'gen]
Wiedersehen: Auf Wiedersehen! Goodbye. [gʊd'baɪ]
wild wild [waɪld]
Willkommen in Plymouth. Welcome to Plymouth. ['welkəm]
wir we [wiː]
wirklich **1.** *(tatsächlich)* really ['rɪəli]
2. *(echt)* real [rɪəl]
wissen know [nəʊ]
wo? where? [weə]
Woche week [wiːk]
Wochenende weekend [wiːk'end] **am Wochenende** at the weekend
wohin? where? [weə]
wohnen live [lɪv]
Wohnung flat [flæt]
Wohnzimmer living room ['lɪvɪŋ ruːm]
wollen: etwas (haben) wollen want sth. [wɒnt] **etwas tun wollen** want to do sth.
Workshop workshop ['wɜːkʃɒp]
Wort word [wɜːd]
Wörterbuch dictionary ['dɪkʃənri]
Wörterverzeichnis *(alphabetisch)* dictionary ['dɪkʃənri]
wünschen: Ich wünsche dir einen schönen Tag. Have a good day.
würde: Ich würde sehr gern kommen. I'd love to come. (= I would love to ...) [wʊd]

Z

zehn ten [ten]
Zeichen sign [saɪn]
Zeit time [taɪm]
Zentrum centre ['sentə]
Zimmer room [ruːm, rʊm]
Zoo zoo [zuː]
zu **1.** *(örtlich)* to [tu, tə] **zur Arbeit/Schule gehen** go to work/school
2. zu alt/groß/... too old/big/... [tuː]
3. Er mag es nicht, allein zu sein. He doesn't like to be lonely.
zubereiten *(Essen)* cook [kʊk]
zuerst first [fɜːst]
Zuhause home [həʊm]
zuhören listen ['lɪsn] **jemandem zuhören** listen to somebody
zumachen *(schließen)* close [kləʊz]
zurück back [bæk]
zusammen together [tə'geðə]
zwei two [tuː]
zweite(r, s) second ['sekənd]
zwischen between [bɪ'twiːn]
zwölf twelve [twelv]

LIST OF NAMES

First names (Vornamen)

Adam ['ædəm]
Alan ['ælən]
Alisha [ə'lɪʃə]
Amanda [ə'mændə]
Anna ['ænə]
Ava ['eɪvə]
Babe [beɪb]
Ben [ben]
Benny ['beni]
Berry ['beri]
Bob [bɒb]
Bunny ['bʌni]
Casper ['kæspə]
Charles [tʃɑ:lz]
Charlie ['tʃɑ:li]
Chloe ['kləʊi]
Connie ['kɒni]
Conor ['kɒnə]
Cyril ['sɪrɪl]
Darek ['dærɪk]
David ['deɪvɪd]
Debbie ['debi]
Ellie ['eli]
Emily ['eməli]
Emma ['emə]
Finn [fɪn]
Frisky ['frɪski]
Gemma ['dʒemə]
Grace [greɪs]
Harry ['hæri]
Jack [dʒæk]
Jackie ['dʒæki]
Jimmy ['dʒɪmi]
Joe [dʒəʊ]
John [dʒɒn]
Josie ['dʒəʊsi]
Katie ['keɪti]
Laura ['lɔ:rə]
Lily ['lɪli]
Linda ['lɪndə]
Liz [lɪz]
Luca ['lu:kə]
Lulu ['lu:lu:]
Lynn [lɪn]
Maria [mə'ri:ə]
Martin ['mɑ:tɪn]
Olivia [ə'lɪviə]
Paul [pɔ:l]
Pete [pi:t]
Peter ['pi:tə]
Pip [pɪp]
Rick [rɪk]
Ruby ['ru:bi]
Sally ['sæli]
Sam [sæm]
Sandy ['sændi]
Sarah ['seərə]
Shanaze [ʃə'neɪz]
Simon ['saɪmən]
Sophie ['səʊfi]
Steve [sti:v]
Susan ['su:zən]
Tamara [tə'mɑ:rə]
Tim [tɪm]
Timothy ['tɪməθi]
Toby ['təʊbi]
Tom [tɒm]
Uma ['u:mə]
Vanessa [və'nesə]
William ['wɪljəm]
Zack [zæk]
Zoe ['zəʊi]

Family names / Surnames (Familiennamen)

Boateng ['bwɑ:teŋ]
Borowski [bə'rɒvski]
Brown [braʊn]
Cole [kəʊl]
Donovan ['dɒnəvən]
Finden ['fɪndən]
Ford [fɔ:d]
Johnson ['dʒɒnsn]
Lee [li:]
Osmanovic [ɒz'mænəvɪtʃ]
Potter ['pɒtə]
Reade [ri:d]
Victor ['vɪktə]
Windsor ['wɪnzə]

Place names (Ortsnamen)

Africa ['æfrɪkə]
America [ə'merɪkə]
The **Aquarium** [ə'kweəriəm]
Berlin [bɜ:'lɪn]
Cawsand ['kɔ:sænd]
Central Park [sentrəl 'pɑ:k]
Charles Street ['tʃɑ:lz stri:t]
Chile ['tʃɪli]
Coburg Street ['kəʊbɜ:g stri:t]
Dartmoor ['dɑ:tmɔ:]
Drake Circus [dreɪk 'sɜ:kəs]
Eggbuckland Community College [eg'bʌklənd kə'mju:nəti kɒlɪdʒ]
England ['ɪŋglənd]
Exeter ['eksɪtə]
Fore Street ['fɔ: stri:t]
France [frɑ:ns]
George Street ['dʒɔ:dʒ stri:t]
Germany ['dʒɜ:məni]
Ghana ['gɑ:nə]
Gratefeld Street ['greɪtfeld stri:t]
Great Field Road [greɪt fi:ld 'rəʊd]
Greatfield Street ['greɪtfi:ld stri:t]
Greenbank Road [gri:nbæŋk 'rəʊd]
Harbour Road [hɑ:bə 'rəʊd]
The **Hoe** [həʊ]
Ireland ['aɪələnd]
Jamaica [dʒə'meɪkə]
Kingsand ['kɪŋsænd]
London ['lʌndən]
Malaga ['mæləgə]
Martins ['mɑ:tɪnz]
Merryweather Farm [meriweðə 'fɑ:m]
National Marine Aquarium [næʃnəl mə'ri:n əkweəriəm]
New York [nju: 'jɔ:k]
Plymouth ['plɪməθ]
Plymouth High School [plɪməθ 'haɪ sku:l]
Plymouth Pavilions [plɪməθ pə'vɪliənz]
Poland ['pəʊlənd]
Reel Cinema [ri:l 'sɪnəmə]
Saltash ['sɔ:ltæʃ]
The **Smuggler's Rest** [smʌgləz 'rest]
Spain [speɪn]
Theatre Royal Plymouth [θɪətə rɔɪəl 'plɪməθ]
Tinside Lido [tɪnsaɪd 'laɪdəʊ]
Turkey ['tɜ:ki]
USA [ju: es 'eɪ]
Wembley ['wembli]
Windsor Road [wɪnzə 'rəʊd]
Windsor Street ['wɪnzə stri:t]
Winsbury Road [wɪnzbəri 'rəʊd]
Woodlands ['wʊdləndz]
Woolwell ['wʊlwel]

Other names (Andere Namen)

British Fireworks Championships [brɪtɪʃ 'faɪəwɜ:ks tʃæmpjənʃɪps]
Canoe Tamar [kə'nu: 'teɪmɑ:]
Christmas Day [krɪsməs 'deɪ]
Christmas Eve [krɪsməs 'i:v]
Francis and the Drakes ['frɑ:nsɪs ənd ðə 'dreɪks]
Manchester United ['mæntʃɪstə ju'naɪtɪd]
The **Roof Raisers** ['ru:f reɪzəz]
Russell's Circus [rʌslz 'sɜ:kəs]
Whoopee [wʊ'pi:]
Young Spirit Adventures [jʌŋ spɪrɪt əd'ventʃəz]

NUMBERS

English numbers

0 **oh, zero, nil** [əʊ, 'zɪərəʊ, nɪl]
1 **one** [wʌn]
2 **two** [tuː]
3 **three** [θriː]
4 **four** [fɔː]
5 **five** [faɪv]
6 **six** [sɪks]
7 **seven** ['sevn]
8 **eight** [eɪt]
9 **nine** [naɪn]
10 **ten** [ten]

11 **eleven** [ɪ'levn]
12 **twelve** [twelv]
13 **thirteen** [θɜː'tiːn]
14 **fourteen** [fɔː'tiːn]
15 **fifteen** [fɪf'tiːn]
16 **sixteen** [sɪks'tiːn]
17 **seventeen** [sevn'tiːn]
18 **eighteen** [eɪ'tiːn]
19 **nineteen** [naɪn'tiːn]
20 **twenty** ['twenti]

21 **twenty-one** [twenti'wʌn]
22 **twenty-two** [twenti'tuː]
23 **twenty-three** [twenti'θriː]
...

30 **thirty** ['θɜːti]
40 **forty** ['fɔːti]
50 **fifty** ['fɪfti]
60 **sixty** ['sɪksti]
70 **seventy** ['sevnti]
80 **eighty** ['eɪti]
90 **ninety** ['naɪnti]
100 **a/one hundred** [ə/wʌn 'hʌndrəd]

101 **one hundred and one**
102 **one hundred and two**
...

1st **first** [fɜːst]
2nd **second** ['sekənd]
3rd **third** [θɜːd]
4th **fourth** [fɔːθ]
5th **fifth** [fɪfθ]
6th **sixth** [sɪksθ]
7th **seventh** ['sevnθ]
8th **eighth** [eɪtθ]
9th **ninth** [naɪnθ]
10th **tenth** [tenθ]

11th **eleventh** [ɪ'levnθ]
12th **twelfth** [twelfθ]
13th **thirteenth** [θɜː'tiːnθ]
14th **fourteenth** [fɔː'tiːnθ]
15th **fifteenth** [fɪf'tiːnθ]
16th **sixteenth** [sɪks'tiːnθ]
17th **seventeenth** [sevn'tiːnθ]
18th **eighteenth** [eɪ'tiːnθ]
19th **nineteenth** [naɪn'tiːnθ]
20th **twentieth** ['twentiəθ]

21st **twenty-first** [twenti'fɜːst]
22nd **twenty-second** [twenti'sekənd]
23rd **twenty-third** [twenti'θɜːd]
...

30th **thirtieth** ['θɜːtiəθ]
40th **fortieth** ['fɔːtiəθ]
50th **fiftieth** ['fɪftiəθ]
60th **sixtieth** ['sɪkstiəθ]
70th **seventieth** ['sevntiəθ]
80th **eightieth** ['eɪtiəθ]
90th **ninetieth** ['naɪntiəθ]
100th **hundredth** ['hʌndrədθ]

101st **hundred and first**
102nd **hundred and second**
...

CLASSROOM ENGLISH

Du und dein Lehrer/deine Lehrerin | You and your teacher

Guten Morgen, Herr/Frau …	Good morning, Mr/Mrs/Miss … (bis 12 Uhr)
Guten Tag, Herr …	Good afternoon, Mr … (ab 12 Uhr)
Entschuldigung, dass ich zu spät komme.	Sorry, I'm late.
Kann ich bitte das Fenster öffnen/zumachen?	Can I open/close the window, please?
Kann ich bitte zur Toilette gehen?	Can I go to the toilet, please?
Auf Wiedersehen!/Bis morgen.	Goodbye./See you tomorrow.

Hausaufgaben und Übungen | Homework and exercises

Es tut mir leid, ich habe mein Schulheft nicht dabei.	Sorry, I have no exercise book.
Ich verstehe die Übung nicht.	I don't understand this exercise.
Ich kann Nummer 3 nicht lösen.	I can't do number 3.
Entschuldigung, ich bin noch nicht fertig.	Sorry, I haven't finished.
Ich habe … Ist das auch richtig?	I have … Is that right?
Es tut mir leid, das weiß ich nicht.	Sorry, I don't know.
Was haben wir (als Hausaufgabe) auf?	What's for homework?

Du brauchst Hilfe | You need help

Können Sie mir bitte helfen?	Can you help me, please?
Auf welcher Seite sind wir/steht das?	What page is it, please?
Was heißt … auf Englisch/Deutsch?	What's … in English/German?
Können Sie das bitte an die Tafel schreiben?	Can you write it on the board, please?
Kann ich das auf Deutsch sagen?	Can I say it in German?
Können Sie/Kannst du bitte lauter sprechen?	Can you speak louder, please?
Können Sie das bitte noch einmal sagen/abspielen?	Can you say/play that again, please?

Partnerarbeit | Work with a partner

Kann ich mit Julian arbeiten?	Can I work with Julian?
Du bist dran.	It's your turn.
Lass uns ein … machen/zeichnen.	Let's make/draw a …
Lass uns die Geschichte/den Dialog spielen.	Let's act the story/dialogue.

What your teacher says | Was dein Lehrer/deine Lehrerin sagt

Listen, please./Quiet, please.	Hört bitte zu./Ruhe bitte.
Open your books at page 24.	Schlagt bitte Seite 24 auf.
Do exercise 5 for homework, please.	Macht bitte Übung 5 als Hausaufgabe.
Where's your book, David?	Wo ist dein Buch, David?
Try again!	Versuche es noch einmal.
That's really good!	Das ist wirklich gut!
That's all for today. You can go.	Das ist alles für heute. Ihr könnt gehen.

Diese Arbeitsanweisungen findest du häufig im Schülerbuch

Act the dialogue / the scenes for the class.	Spiel(t) den Dialog / die Szenen vor der Klasse.
Ask questions. / Ask different partners.	Stelle Fragen. / Frage verschiedene Partner/innen.
Answer the questions (about the story).	Beantworte die Fragen (über die Geschichte).
… as many as you can.	… so viele wie du kannst.
Before you listen /read /…	Bevor du hörst / liest …
Choose a picture / the right answer.	Wähle ein Bild / die richtige Antwort aus.
Compare with a partner.	Vergleiche mit einem Partner / einer Partnerin.
Complete the questions / the rules / the sentences.	Vervollständige die Fragen / die Regeln / die Sätze.
Copy and complete the table / your learner log.	Schreibe die Tabelle / dein Lerntagebuch ab und vervollständige sie / es.
Correct the sentences.	Berichtige die Sätze.
Fill in the table.	Fülle die Tabelle aus.
Find the right answers.	Finde die richtigen Antworten.
Find a heading for each photo.	Finde eine Überschrift für jedes Foto.
Finish the sentences.	Vervollständige die Sätze.
Go to page 25.	Gehe zu Seite 25.
Listen and check / repeat / write.	Hör zu und überprüfe / wiederhole / schreibe auf.
Look at the brochure / photos / pictures.	Sieh die Broschüre / Fotos / Bilder an.
Make a dialogue / a mind map / a table.	Fertige einen Dialog / eine Mindmap / eine Tabelle an.
Match the sentences / headings with the pictures.	Ordne die Sätze / Überschriften den Bildern zu.
Pick a card / words from the box.	Nimm eine Karte / Wörter aus dem Kasten.
Point at the right picture	Zeige auf des richtige Bild.
Practise with a partner.	Übe mit einem Partner / einer Partnerin.
Put the answers in the right order.	Bringe die Antworten in die richtige Reihenfolge.
Read the text / story.	Lies den Text / die Geschichte.
Right or wrong?	Richtig oder falsch?
Swap partners.	Tausche den Partner / die Partnerin.
Talk about …	Sprich über …
Talk to different partners.	Sprich mit verschiedenen Partnern / Partnerinnen.
Tell the class.	Erzähle das der Klasse.
Use your notes / table.	Benutze deine Notizen / Tabelle.
Walk around.	Gehe herum.
Write a dialogue / sentences about you.	Schreibe einen Dialog / Sätze über dich.
You can put it in your DOSSIER.	Du kannst es in deinem Dossier abheften.

MUSTERLÖSUNGEN, LÖSUNGSBEISPIELE

Hinweis

Lösungen zu geschlossenen Aufgaben finden Sie auf den Unitseiten, direkt bei den Aufgaben. Auf sehr umfangreiche Lösungen sowie auf Lösungsbeispiele zu halboffenen Aufgaben wird von der Unitseite hier in den Anhang verwiesen. Zu komplett individuellen Lösungen gibt es keine Muster.

Nice to meet you

9, Ex 3

apples • a ball • bananas • a beach • boys • chocolate • a dad / father • a door • a family • fruit • (kids playing) football • girls • a hamburger • a hat • a hot dog • houses • ice cream • kids • a kite • lunch • a mum / mother • oranges • orange juice • paper • people • plates • sand • a sandcastle • sandwiches • sausages • shops • a surfboard • toast • tomatoes • a T-shirt • toys • water

12, Ex 1b

Pets	*Wild animals*
pony	*bear*
cat	*monkey*
rat	*bird*
dog	*elephant*
fish	*snake*
rabbit	*crocodile*
hamster	*tiger*
(horse, budgie, mouse, parrot ...)	*(lion, fox, spider, frog, butterfly ...)*

Unit 1

(zu S. 21)
121, More practice 1

Lesson one on Friday is PE. **(Right)**
Lesson two on Thursday is science. **(Wrong)**

23, Ex 6a

- Plymouth isn't in Germany.
- Eggy isn't in London / in Germany.
- Cyril isn't a seagull / a maths teacher.
- Sandy isn't a crab / a maths teacher.
- Mr Brown isn't a maths teacher / a crab / a seagull.
- Ellie and Berry aren't teachers / in London / in Germany.
- Luca and Adam aren't girls / teachers / in London / in Germany.
- Ms Lee and Mr Brown aren't students / in London / in Germany.

24, Ex 1

I can see a green blazer / black shoes / grey trousers / a red pullover / white socks / ...

25, Ex 4

Uniforms	
for boys and girls	*for girls*
pullover	*skirt*
blazer	*tights*
shirt	
shoes	
socks	
sweatshirt	
tie	
trousers	

26, Ex 2

1 a pencil / pencils, a pencil sharpener, a rubber, a ruler, an exercise book, a calculator
2 ten pens, ten pencils, a pencil case, a calculator
3 two pencil sharpeners, two rubbers, two rulers

28, Ex 2 ○

A: Hi, **Tim**. How **are** you?
B: Hello, **Carina**. I'm OK (thanks). What about **you**?
A: **I'm** fine, thanks. Can I borrow a **hole punch**, please?
B: Sure, here **you are**.
A: Thanks. What's the next lesson?
B: It's **science**.
A: Oh, good. I like **science**.

28, Ex 2 ●

A: Hi, Sandra. How are you?
B: Hello, Mark. I'm fine, thanks. What about you?
A: I'm OK. What's your favourite lesson?
B: It's English. Can I borrow your ruler, please?
A: Sure, here you are.
B: Thanks. Who´s your best friend in our class?
A: It's Rebecca. I like Rebecca. And you?
B: Oh, I like Rebecca too.

29, Ex 2b

things	*people*	*places*	*lessons*	*sports*
books	*teacher*	*science lab*	*science*	*football*
tables	*student*	*school*	*English*	*dancing*
pencil	*boys / girls*	*classroom*	*maths*	*playing games*
pencil case	*principal*	*arts room*	*technology*	*swimming*
calculator		*sports hall*	*French*	*skiing*
exercise book		*computer*	*drama*	
uniform		*room*	*music*	
football		*theatre*	*PE*	
school bags			*ICT*	
(clothes)				

Unit 2

34, Ex 1

1 ... nice house • **2** ... big house with (lots of) flats • **3** ... big living room (and kitchen) • **4** ... small garden • **5** ... kitchen • **6** ... big pink room • **7** ... small bedroom • **8** ... small living room

(zu S. 39, Ex 4c)
126, More practice 1

The room is messy. There's a purple rug. There's a desk with a lamp.
There are books on the desk. There are two chairs.
There are two beds, three posters and a wardrobe.
There are three cushions and two schoolbags and there's a football.
There are shoes and socks on the rug.
I like the desk and the green chair. I don't like the purple rug.

43, Ex 4 ●

Lernstärkere S können die Stichworte bei der Ausformulierung noch individuell ausschmücken (vgl. blaue Teile).

Dear Diary
I'm very happy again because I'm at mum's house. (It's great!) I'm in the bedroom with Zoe again. The cats are happy. Mum is happy. And Zoe is happy too. Conor is here. (..., but) Finn isn't here. That's OK (for me. I can see Finn on Saturday and Sunday).

44, Ex 2a Beispiel für ein Bewertungsraster für Mindmaps (vgl. auch Skills file 2, S. 162):

Assessment sheet ☺ = good / 😐 = okay / ☹ = not so good			
Mind map: My dream house	student 1	student 2	student 3
Für deine Mindmap verwendest du ein leeres Blatt (DIN-A4) im Querformat.			
Das Thema steht in der Mitte; hervorgehoben durch eine darum gemalte Wolke / ...			
Du verwendest für jedes Hauptthema einen Hauptast in einer eigenen Farbe.			
Du ergänzt Unterthemen auf Nebenästen in der gleichen Farbe.			
Du hängst weitere interessante Ideen an die Nebenäste an.			
Du verwendest Schlüsselwörter zur Beschriftung der Äste.			
Du verwendest auch Zahlen, Bilder, Symbole, ...			
...			

Unit 3

58, Ex 2a

The simple present	
Verb ohne s	*Verb mit s*
I get up early.	*He gets up late.*
I make breakfast ...	*Dad ... makes dinner.*
I usually have lunch ...	
We have dinner ...	*He never has breakfast.*
After dinner we watch TV.	*Mum ... watches TV with us.*
We talk about ...	
We do our homework.	
Jack and I go to school ...	
We ... go by bus.	*Dad goes to work.*
	Dad works at night.
	He comes home in the morning.
Mum ... comes home late.	
	Dad stays in bed.

61, Ex 3 *On Thursday Luca has no ideas for his birthday.*
But his mum has a great idea – a concert!
On Saturday morning Luca gets great presents.
Later the boys meet Jack's friends at the Hoe.
Jack goes down the hill first.
Then Luca goes down the hill, but he falls.
Jack and Luca go to the hospital.
Luca has a sore leg.

62, Ex 1a

There's	There are
a bike (✓)	2 footballs (✓)
a calculator (✓)	3 posters (✓)
a (toy) crab (✓)	9 books (✓)
a computer (✓)	2 mobile phones (✓)
(a printer) (✓)	3 ties
a schoolbag (✓)	2 rulers
a school blazer (✓)	2 computer games
a football shirt	2 boxes
a blue shirt	pens and pencils
a red shirt	blue and yellow trainers
a (toy) cat	blue shoes
a yellow cushion	lots of shoes in a box
a red hoodie	
a pink and green sweatshirt	
a lamp	
a pencil case	
a picture	
a red (toy) car	

(zu S. 64, Ex 2)
134, More practice 4b

Wort	Strategie
live	Wort ins Deutsche übernommen
price	ähnliches Wort im Deutschen, Preisangaben
book	ähnliches Wort im Deutschen, Telefonnummer
championship	champion ist ins Deutsche übernommen
free	ähnliches Wort im Deutschen, keine Preisangabe
fantastic	ähnliches Wort im Deutschen
dive show	Bilder
tiger sharks	Bilder
tickets	Wort ins Deutsche übernommen

65, Ex 2a ●

Lernstärkere S notieren zu jeder Attraktion noch eine Zusatzinformation. Mögliche Impulse: *What can you see? / What is special about the Lido? / … / What can you do there? / How much does it cost? / …*

- *the Lido: You can see a big swimming pool. It's very old / very special / …*
- *the Aquarium: You can see lots of fish. It's cool.*
- *the shopping centre: You can see lots of shops and lots of different colours.*
- *the Hoe: It's a big park. You can see lots of people / a lighthouse / …*
  It's very popular. You can watch the sea, meet friends.

Unit 4

75, Ex 3b

- ***Photo B:** I feel great when I do sport. / My favourite sport is wheelchair basketball. / I feel really great when my team wins.*
- ***Photo C:** I sometimes feel a bit fed up because I'm the only student at school in a wheelchair. / I'm always different.*
- ***Photo D:** I feel really fed up when people don't talk to me.*
- ***Photo E:** I feel great when I'm with the animals at home.*

75, Ex 3c

☺ *I feel great* ...	☹ *I feel fed up* ...
when I'm with the animals at home.	*because I'm the only student at school in a wheelchair.*
when I'm with my friends.	*because I'm always different.*
when I do sport.	*when people don't talk to me.*
when my team wins.	

77, Ex 4a ○ (und 136 ●)

77, Ex 4a ○	136 ●
1) 1 She doesn't live in the city.	*She lives in the country.*
2) They don't have a pet shop.	*They have a farm.*
3) She doesn't ride a donkey.	*She rides a pony.*
4) She doesn't have a cat.	*She has a dog.*
5) They don't have cows on the farm.	*They have donkeys.*
6) He doesn't live in the field.	*He lives in the house.*
7) She doesn't go to school in Woolwell.	*She goes to school in Plymouth.*
8) They don't have dogs.	*They have no pets. / They don't have a pet.*
9) She doesn't have two ponies.	*She has two cats.*
10) They don't like cats.	*They hate cats.*

82, Ex 2a

1 Nein, aber Hunde sind hier nicht erlaubt.
2 Das bedeutet, dass man hier nicht rauchen darf.
3 Ja, das Restaurant hat geöffnet.
4 Wir dürfen die Tiere nicht füttern (außer während der überwachten Fütterungszeiten).
5 Ja, wir müssen rechts herum. Links ist der Zugang für Rollstuhlfahrer.
6 Wir können die Telefonnummer anrufen oder eine SMS schicken.

82, Ex 2b

Schild:	Man findet so ein Schild ...	Das Schild ist für ...	Du darfst/kannst hier ...
A	an Parks / Grünflächen / Spielplätzen / ...	• Leute mit Hunden • Raucher	• keine Hunde mitnehmen • nicht rauchen
B	an Restaurants / Imbissen / ...	Leute, die Hunger haben	• Frühstück bekommen • sehen, dass geöffnet ist
C	im Zoo / Tierpark / auf dem Bauernhof	(Zoo-)Besucher	die Tiere nicht füttern (außerhalb der Fütterungszeiten)
D	an Eingängen / Gebäuden / Treppen / Schiffsanlegestellen	• alle Leute, die den Eingang suchen • Rollstuhlfahrer	• rechts durch das kleine Tor eintreten • links einen barrierefreien Zugang für Rollstuhlfahrer finden
E	an Bushaltestellen in der Stadt	Fahrgäste	• sehen, um welche Haltestelle es sich handelt • auf den Bus warten • Hinweise zum Fahrplan mithilfe der angegebenen Kontaktdaten erhalten

84, Ex 2d

budgie = Wellensittich • *gibbon* = Gibbon (Langarmaffe) • *goat* = Ziege • *guinea pig* = Meerschweinchen • *horse* = Pferd • *kitten* = Kätzchen, junge Katze • *owl* = Eule • *parrot* = Papagei • *peahen* = Pfauenhenne (weiblicher Pfau) • *puppy* = Welpe, junger Hund • *stick insect* = Stabheuschrecke • *stoat* = Hermelin

Unit 5

92, Ex 2b

1 *Dad is talking to Adam.* • **2** *Mum is cooking.* • **3** *Adam is helping in the cafe.* • **4** *Adam is washing up.* • **5** *Dad is working on a ferry.*

96, Ex 2a

Question word	*form of 'be'*	*Pronoun*	*verb + -ing*
What	*'s (is)*	*she*	*doing?*
What	*are*	*you*	*doing?*
What	*are*	*they*	*doing?*
What	*'s (is)*	*he*	*doing?*
What	*are*	*you*	*doing?*

Pronoun	*form of 'be'*	*verb + -ing*
She	*'s (is)*	*making sandwiches.*
I	*'m (am)*	*setting the tables / cleaning the tables.*
They	*'re (are)*	*sitting in a park.*
He	*'s (is)*	*cooking.*
We *(Well,) I*	*'re (are)* *'m (am)*	*rapping.* *learning.*

99, Ex 2

1 *boy on the bus* • **2** *Josie* • **3** *Adam* • **4** *Luca* • **5** *Adam's friends* • **6** *Adam*

99, Ex 3 ●

Lernstärkere begründen ihre Einschätzung zusätzlich:

1 *False. (They were mean.) (ll. 4–9)*
2 *True. (ll. 10/11)*
3 *Not in the text.*
4 *True. (poster on p. 98; l. 34)*
5 *False. (Adam's father was there.) (ll. 36/37)*
6 *False. (Adam was second.) (ll. 44/45)*
7 *Not in the text.*
8 *True. (ll. 48/49)*

100, Ex 1b

In the middle two dogs are eating.
In the middle a boy is reading a book.
In the middle three girls are talking and laughing.
On the left children are playing football.
In the middle a girl is riding a bike.
On the right a baby is sleeping.
On the left two men are working.

100, Ex 2 (Partnerarbeit, Schritt 1)

Picture 1	
Partner A *(p. 147)*	**Partner B** *(p. 120)*
On the left there's a girl. She's riding her bike on the street.	*In my picture the girl is walking on the street.*
On the right I can see a car on the street. It's behind a tree.	*In my picture the car is next to the tree.*
On the right there's a woman. She's reading a book.	*In my picture there's no woman on the right.*
In the middle I can see a boy and a girl. They're playing football.	*In my picture two boys and a girl are playing frisbee.*
There are two girls in front of the boy with the guitar. They're eating and drinking.	*In my picture one girl is sleeping and one girl is reading a book.*

100, Ex 2 (Partnerarbeit, Schritt 2)

Picture 2	
Partner A *(p. 120)*	***Partner B*** *(p. 147)*
On the left I can see Cyril.	*In my picture there's Sandy.*
On the right there's a girl. She's walking and talking on the phone.	*In my picture there's also a girl on the right, but she's sleeping.*
In the middle I can see a boy and a girl. They're playing in the sand.	*In my picture there's a girl in the middle. She's reading a book.*
On the left there are two people. They're sitting in chairs.	*In my picture there's only one man sitting in a chair.*
In the water I can see two people. They're swimming.	*In my picture there are four people in the water. Two are swimming, and two children are playing with a ball.*

101, Ex 1b

A *Hi Adam, rap was great. PMZ is cool. See you at school on Monday.*
B *Adam, where are you? We're rapping at PMZ now. Are you coming?*
C *Mum, I'm at home. I'm doing my homework. I can't come to the cafe.*
D *I'm not working in the cafe now. I'm going to the market. See you soon. Kisses*

101, Ex 2

Amanda fragt, wo wir gerade sind und was wir gerade machen. Sie schreibt, dass sie auf einer tollen Party ist und dass wir auch kommen können.

106, Ex 6

1 Es gibt Sandwich und Obstsalat, aber auch Scones und Kuchen.
2 Es gibt Tee, Kaffee, kalte Getränke und Saft.
3 Es gibt Scones, Kuchen und Eis.
4 Wir könnten uns jeder ein Sandwich und ein Eis oder kaltes Getränk kaufen.
5 Wir können das Essen auch mitnehmen.

106, Ex 7a

A: *Hello. Can I help you?*
B: *Hello. Yes, please. A sandwich, please.*
A: *OK. Anything else?*
B: *Yes, a fruit salad, please.*
A: *Anything to drink?*
B: *Oh, yes, a small bottle of water, please. And a home-made cake.*
A: *Anything else?*
B: *No, thanks. That's all.*
A: *That's £ 9,75, please.*
B: *OK. Here you are.*
A: *Thanks. Next please!*

Unit 6

110, Ex 2d

beach things: *swimsuits, swimming trunks, towels, sunglasses, hats, ...*
picnic:
- *food: sandwiches, biscuits, cake, apples, sweets, crisps, chocolate, ...*
- *drinks: water, orange juice, ...*

111, Ex 3c

beach things:
- *swimming things: swimsuits, swimming trunks, ...*
- *others: towels, sunglasses, hats, suncream, shorts, football, bodyboard, tube, frisbee, speakers, ...*

112, Ex 1

Picture A: *I can see Luca, Ellie, Adam, Berry and her dad, and a person in black. They're in Plymouth harbour.*
Picture B: *I can see Berry, Ellie, Adam, Luca, and the person in black. They're on the ferry from Plymouth harbour to Cawsand.*
Picture C: *I can see Luca, Ellie, Adam and Berry. The kids are on the way to the beach.*

Lernstärkere beschreiben zusätzlich, was auf den Bildern geschieht:
Picture A: *Berry is coming with her dad. Luca, Ellie and Adam are waiting for her. There's a sign for the ferry to Cawsand. I think the kids want to take the ferry.*
Picture B: *The kids are on the ferry to Cawsand. Luca is feeding some seagulls.*
Picture C: *A man is helping Berry. Luca has Berry's wheelchair. There are lots of other people on the beach. Two boys are playing ball. Three kids are making a sandcastle. A family is having a picnic. Two people are swimming.*

113, KV 6.2

Scene	***Who?***	***Where?***	***What must they find?***
1	*Berry, Adam, Luca, Ellie, an old woman in black*	*near Cawsand harbour*	*a shop*
2	*Berry, Adam, Luca, Ellie, an old woman in black*	*in front of a shop*	*a cafe*
3	*Berry, Adam, Luca, Ellie, an old woman in black*	*near the cafe* The Smuggler's Rest	*a big clock*
4	*Berry, Adam, Luca, Ellie*	*near the clock tower*	*cows*
5	*Berry, Adam, Luca, Ellie, Berry's mother, Sam*	*on the beach*	*Berry's dad*

116, Ex 2

A: *Hello, Anna. How are you?*
B: *Hi, Jack. I'm fine, thanks.*
A: *What are you doing in the summer?*
B: *I'm going to Turkey with my mum. We're flying from Cologne. In August I'm visiting my grandma in Berlin.*
A: *Wow! That's cool.*
B: *What are your summer plans?*
A: *Nothing special. I'm staying at home. My cousin from Turkey is visiting us in August. We're going to a football match, Schalke against Dortmund.*
B: *That's cool. I love football.*

Part 1: Meet your class

a) *Walk around. Talk to different partners like this:*

You:
– Hi, I'm … What's your name?
– I'm ten / eleven / twelve / … What about you?
– I'm from … What about you?

Your partner:
I'm …
I'm ten / eleven / twelve / …
I'm from …

b) *Write the answers in the table:*

name?					
how old?					
from?					

c) *Look at your table again. Can you find …*

– … someone who[1] is as old as you? ______________________________

– … someone who is from the same city[2]/place[3] as you? ______________________________

[1] *someone who …* – jemand der … [2] *city* – Stadt [3] *place* – Ort

Part 2: Cyril's song

Listen to Cyril's song. Cut out the verses on the right and put them in the right order. Listen again and check. Then sing the song.

CYRIL'S SONG

I'm Cyril the crab
And I like the sea.
I love water
All around me.

Chorus:
I run and I hide,
I dive in the sand.
Don't pick me up
Or I'll pinch your hand.

Ice cream and orange juice
Picnics in the sun
Boats and surfboards
The beach is great fun.

Chorus

I'm going to Plymouth
You can come too
We can be friends
Nice to meet you!

Chorus

I love the beach
And sandcastles too
I like playing football
What about you?

Chorus

1 *Find the words for the colours and write them down.*

2 *Then colour the splashes[1].*

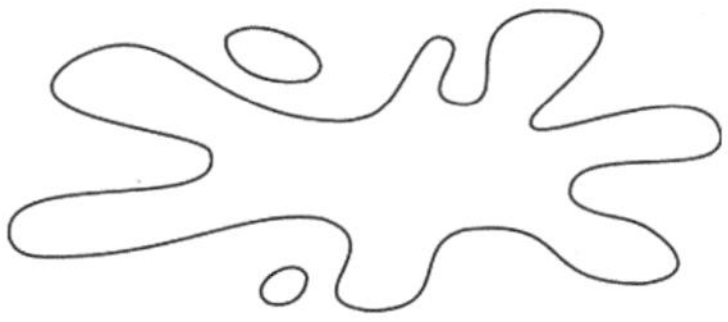

o l y e l w = _ _ _ _ _ _

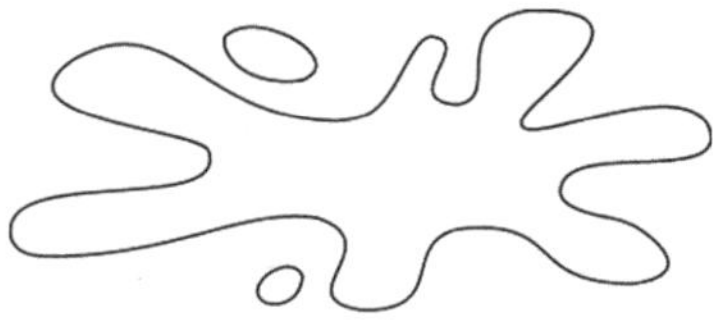

e n e r g = _ _ _ _ _

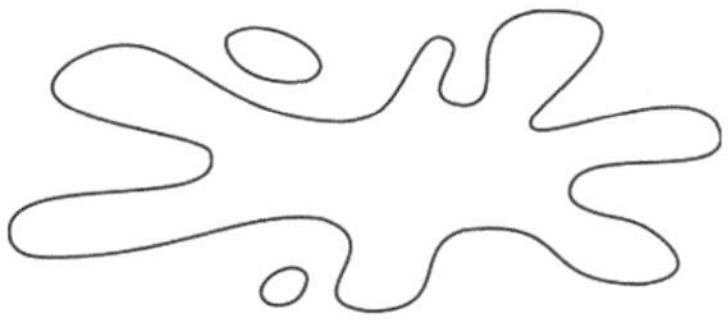

d r e = _ _ _

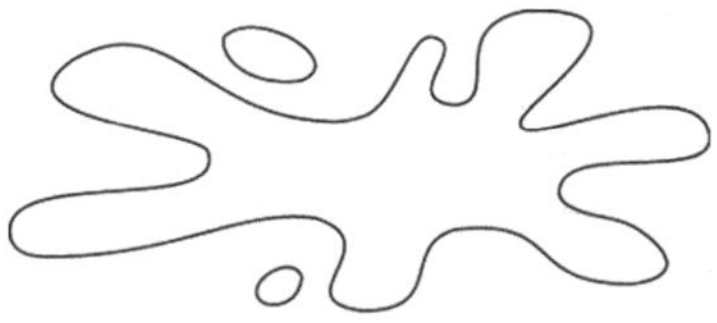

w o r n b = _ _ _ _ _

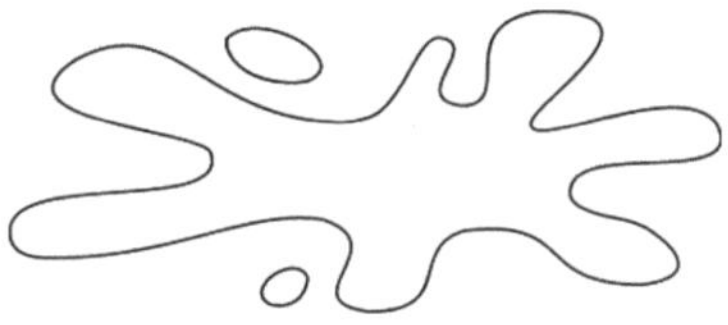

k a l b c = _ _ _ _ _

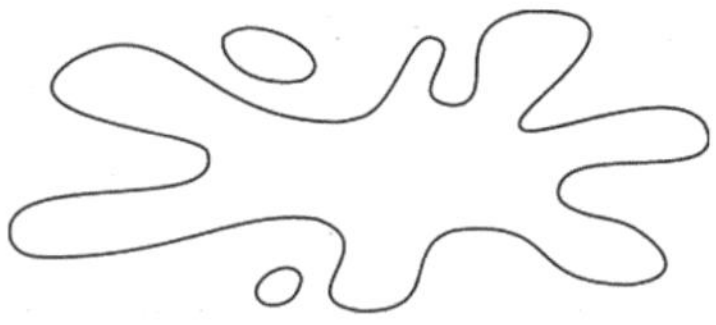

u e l b = _ _ _ _

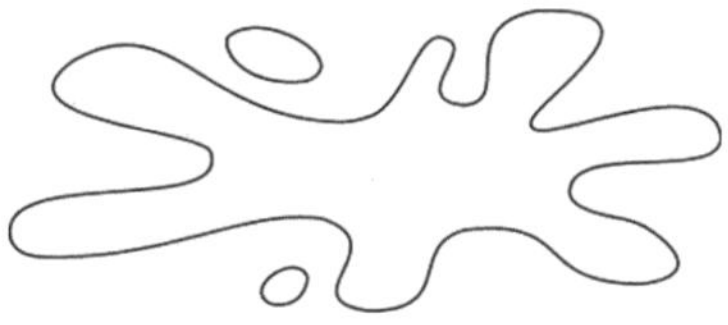

e l p r u p = _ _ _ _ _ _

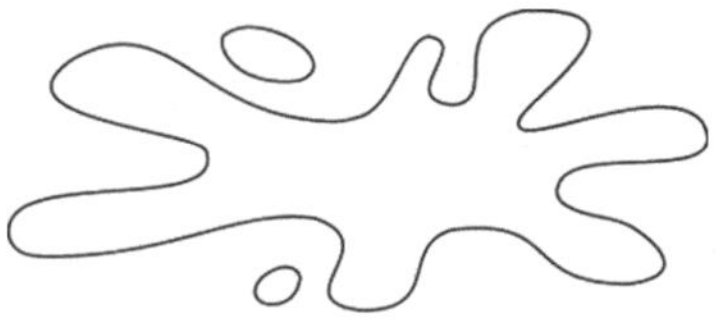

y r e g = _ _ _ _

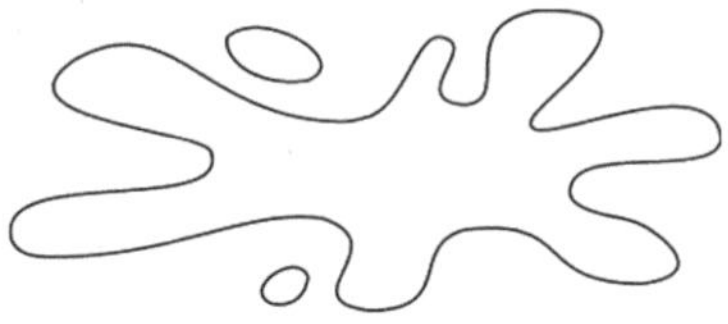

w e h t i = _ _ _ _ _

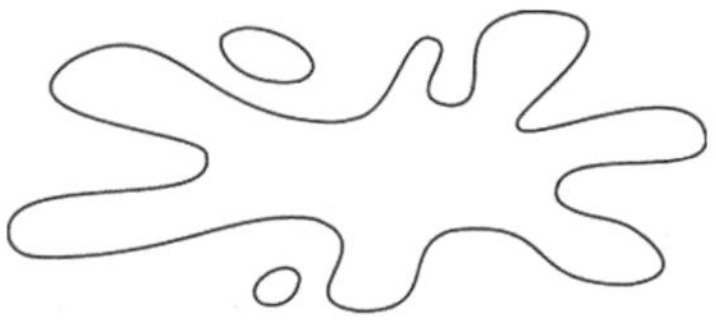

k n i p = _ _ _ _

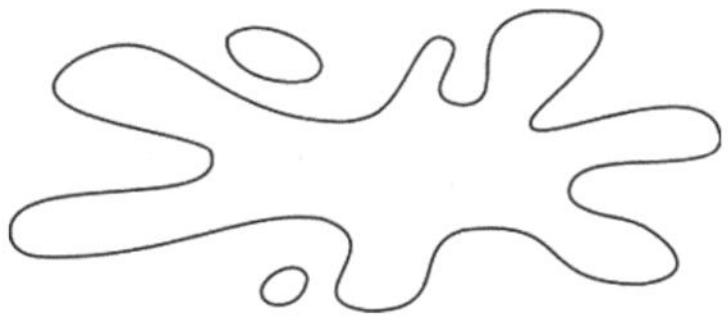

g a r o n e = _ _ _ _ _ _

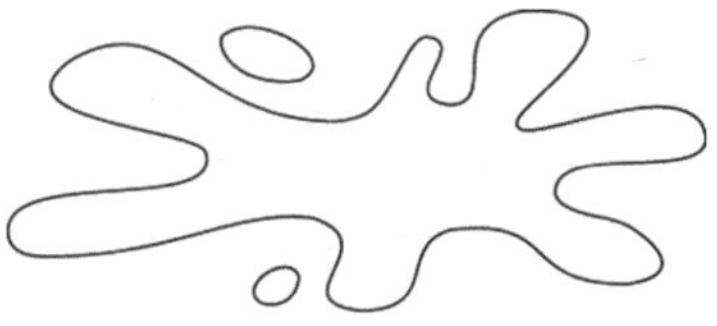

my favourite colour = ____________________

Tip: You can cut out the cards and use them for exercise 1 (p. 10) in your student's book.

[1] *splashes* – Farbspritzer

1 *Look at the pictures on this page. Who can you see?*

2 *Cut out the pictures. Then listen to part one of the story. Put the pictures (A–F) in the right order.*

3 *Cut out the pictures. Then listen to part two of the story. Put the pictures (A–E) in the right order.*

4 *Check with a partner and/or in class. Then glue the pictures into your exercise book.*

5 *Match the captions to the pictures.*

Cyril and Sandy are at the beach	Luca likes ice cream
Luca and his family go to the beach	A crab in the sandcastle
Ellie is with her friends and her sister	Berry likes music
Adam and mum are on a bike	Adam – a football star
Berry and dad in the car	Cyril's favourite day
Lots of children – Cyril is not happy	

Part 1: School sounds

Cut out the pictures. What can you hear? Put the pictures in the right order. Then write the words.

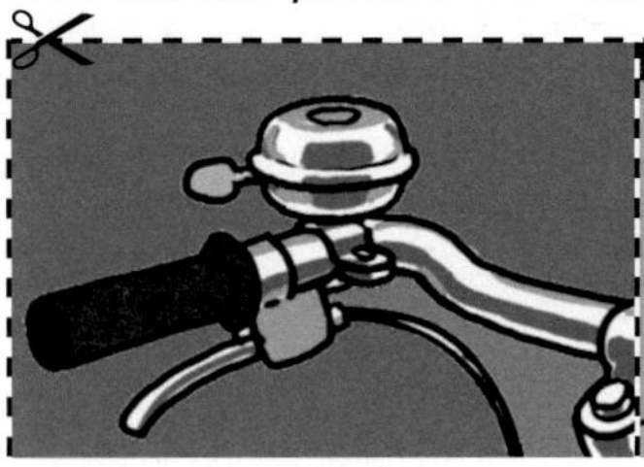
______

______

______

______

______

______

______

______

Part 2: Me and my class

a) Good morning, class 7Y

Complete the table.

Name	Age	From	Brothers	Sisters	Hobbies	Pets
Berry						
Luca						
Ellie						
Adam						

More practice *Now find out about three students in your class:*

Name	Age	From	Brothers	Sisters	Hobbies	Pets

b) About me

Name:	Class:	Pets:
Age:	Class teacher:	Best friends:
From:	Brothers:	Hobby / Sport:
School:	Sisters:	Favourite colour:

1 *Complete the rules:*

’m • ’s • ’re = Yes	’m not • isn’t • aren’t = No
I + ___________	I + ___________
he / she / it + ___________	he / she / it + ___________
we / you / they + ___________	we / you / they + ___________

2 *Complete the sentences in the speech bubbles.*

a) *Fill in: ’m (2x) • ’s (1x) • is (1x) • isn’t (1x) • ’re (2x) • aren’t (1x).*

Hi, I ________ (1) Ellie.
I ♥ my family. We ________ (2) from Plymouth.
I ________ (3) at Eggy.
My English teacher is Ms Lee. She ________ (4) nice!
And Ruby and Charlie? They ________ (5) my best friends.
But they ________ (6) in my class. ☹
My hobby ________ (7) riding. It ________ (8) tae kwon do !! ☺ !!

b) *Fill in: ’m (2x) • ’m not (1x) • ’s (2x) • isn’t (2x) • ’re (1x) • aren’t (1x).*

Hi, I ________ (9) Luca.
My family and I ________ (10) from Woolwell.
We ________ (11) from Plymouth.
I ________ (12) twelve, but I ______ (13) ten.
Grace, my sister, ________ (14) at Eggy.
She ________ (15) five years old!!
My hobby ________ (16) tae kwon do. Uuagh!!
It ________ (17) riding my BMX. ☺

c) *Fill in: ’m (2x) • ’re (2x) • aren’t (1x). For ??? fill in your own ideas.*

Hi, I ________ (18) ??? ____________________
My family is nice. We ________ (19) from Plymouth.
We ________ (20) from ???____________________
I ________ (21) at ???____________________ School.
My favourite teachers are Mrs ???____________________
and Mr ???____________________.
They’ ________ (22) nice.

Fill in the table for each group: ☺ *= very good;* 😐 *= OK;* ☹ *= not so very good / needs more practice.*

Group / Names of actors **Criteria:** **The actors ...** *(Die Schauspieler ...)*	**1:**	**2:**	**3:**	**4:**	**5:**
... act the scene well. *(... spielen die Szene gut)*					
... know the text and speak without notes / their books. *(... kennen den Text auswendig und sprechen ohne Notizen / ihre Bücher)*					
... speak loudly and clearly. *(... sprechen laut und deutlich)*					
... speak good English. *(... sprechen gutes Englisch)*					
... have nice props. (e.g.: tie, scissors, ...) *(... haben schöne Requisiten)*					
→ Best group					

Add more school words to the network.

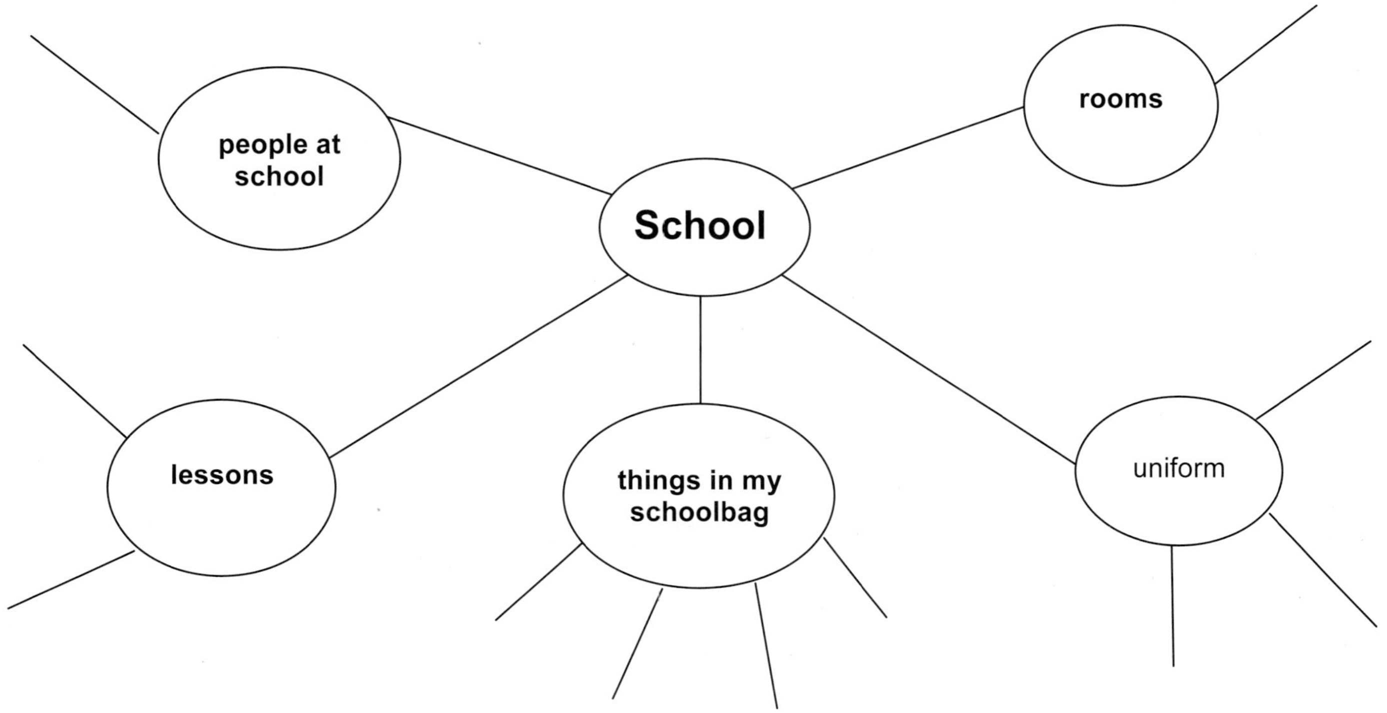

Tip: You can look at the words below this line for help.

▼ *fold here* ▲

More help art room • blazer • classroom • class teacher • computer room • diary • English • rubber • French • history • maths • PE • pencil case • ruler • skirt • sports hall • hole punch • student • sweatshirt • teacher • tie • trousers • …

a) *Answer the questions.*

	Me				
1 Who's your favourite teacher?					
2 Who's your best friend in our class?					
3 What's your favourite hobby?					
4 What's your favourite animal?					

More practice *Write and ask more questions.*

5 What's your favourite lesson?					
6 …					
7 …					
8 …					

b) *Walk around. Ask different partners. Write their names and answers in the table.*

c) *Tell the class.*

My favourite … Tina's favourite … Karim's favourite …

a) *Answer the questions.*

	Me				
1 Who's your favourite teacher?					
2 Who's your best friend in our class?					
3 What's your favourite hobby?					
4 What's your favourite animal?					

More practice *Write and ask more questions.*

5 What's your favourite lesson?					
6 …					
7 …					
8 …					

b) *Walk around. Ask different partners. Write their names and answers in the table.*

c) *Tell the class.*

My favourite … Tina's favourite … Karim's favourite …

1 Meet the kids from Harbour Road: Profiles KV 1.6

1 *What information do you get about Sarah, Paul and Anna? Watch "The kids from Harbour Road", Unit 1 and fill in the first part of the table.*

Unit 1	**Name:**			
	Address:			
	School:			
	School uniform: (-problems?)			
	Favourite lesson / teacher:			
	My favourite kid from Harbour Road:			

2 *Add more information after each Unit. Here are some ideas:*

More help character (bossy, funny, cool, nice, quiet, lazy, mean, messy, boring, friendly, …) • family (brothers or sisters, …) • favourite clothes/outfit • favourite food • favourite football team • hobbies / sports • likes / doesn't like (animals, places, things, …) • talents (good at …) • …

Partner A:

Lesson	Monday	Tuesday	Wednesday	Thursday	Friday
1	English	.....	technology	geography	.....
2	.....	English	history	.....	PE
3	science	history	.....	music	.....
4	.....	.....	maths	.....	German
5	German	German	maths	science	technology

✂- -

Partner B:

Lesson	Monday	Tuesday	Wednesday	Thursday	Friday
1	.....	music	technology	geography	PE
2	maths	English	history	German	.....
3	science	.....	PE	.....	English
4	art	maths	.....	science	German
5	.....	German	maths	.....	.....

1 WORDS School things ► **Unit 1, p. 30**

a **1** blazer, **2** shirt, **3** tie, **4** pullover, **5** skirt, **6** tights, **7** trousers, **8** shoes (8 points)

b **1** hole punch, **2** exercise book, **3** pencil case, **4** ruler, **5** pencil sharpener, **6** pencil, **7** pen, **8** school bag, **9** books, **10** diary, **11** rubber, **12** calculator (12 points)

☺	😐	☹
20–16	15–10	9–0

2 WORDS More school things ► **Unit 1, p. 30**

a **1** shirt; **2** Monday, **3** lunch; **4** school; **5** calculator; **6** brother (6 points)

b One answer for each group is OK.

1 pencil case, ruler, stapler, felt-tip, schoolbag, exercise book, book, diary, calculator, …
2 PE, history, geography, technology, English, German, ICT, drama, art, music, …
3 basketball, hockey, swimming, riding, inline-skating, …
4 art room, English room, assembly hall, canteen, …
5 lunch
6 class teacher, PE teacher, … (6 points)

c **1** … Monday/Tuesday/Wednesday/Thursday/Friday
2 … English/German/maths/PE/…
3 … a pencil case/three books/four exercise books/a diary/ a ruler/… (3 points)

☺	😐	☹
15–12	11–8	7–0

3 READING Remember Cyril? ► **Unit 1, p. 30**

a B – D – C – A (4 points)

b **1** right, **2** right, **3** wrong, **4** right, **5** wrong, **6** wrong, **7** right (7 points)

☺	😐	☹
11–10	9–6	5–0

4 LANGUAGE Remember Sandy? ► **Unit 1, p. 31**

1 Hi, I**'m** Sandy.
2 This **is** Cyril.
3 He**'s** my friend.
4 Benny and Babe **are** my friends too.
5 They**'re** fun.
6 We**'re** from Kingsand.
7 Kingsand **is** near Plymouth.
8 It**'s** great. (8 points)

☺	😐	☹
8–7	6–4	3–0

5 LANGUAGE Remember Ellie? ► **Unit 1, p. 31**

1 Look, this **is** my new school.
2 It**'s** very big.
3 The students in my class **are** OK.
4 The teachers **are** OK too.
5 This **is** my new friend, Berry.
6 She**'s** great.
7 My friends Ruby and Charlie **are** at my school too.
8 But they **aren't** in my class.
9 This **is** my new uniform.
10 It **isn't** very nice. (10 points)

☺	😐	☹
10–8	7–5	4–0

6 LANGUAGE That's wrong, Sandy! ► **Unit 1, p. 31**

1 Plymouth isn't in Germany. – It's in **England**.
2 Eggy isn't **in London**. – It's in **Plymouth**.
3 I'm **not a seagull**. – I'm **a crab**.
4 You **aren't a crab**. – You're **a seagull**.
5 They **aren't teachers**. – They're **students**.
6 They **aren't students** – They're **teachers.**
7 We **aren't students** at Eggy. – **We're** animals. (13 points)

☺	😐	☹
13–11	10–7	6–0

7 LISTENING Adam and Luca ► **Unit 1, p. 32**

a 1 – 2 – 4 – 6 – 7 – 9 – 10 (7 points)

b **1** D; **2** E; **3** A; **4** F; **5** C; **6** B (6 points)

☺	😐	☹
13–11	10–7	6–0

8 WORDS Talking to friends ► **Unit 1, p. 32**

1 Hi. How are **you**? – I'm fine, thanks.
2 Welcome **to** our school. – Thanks.
3 I'm in **class** 7B. – Me too.
4 See **you** later. – OK, see you.
5 I like **your** sweatshirt. – Oh, thanks.
6 I'm Emma. – **Nice** to meet you, Emma.
7 What's the next **lesson**? – It's maths.
8 Have a **good/nice** day. – You too. (8 points)

☺	😐	☹
8–7	6–4	3–0

9 WRITING A dialogue with a new student ► **Unit 1, p. 32**

Berry	**Tamara**
Hi, I'm Berry. What's your name?	Hi, I'm Tamara. I'm from London. What about you?
I'm from Woolwell. I'm in class 7Y. What about you?	I'm in class 7D. What's your favourite lesson?
I like science. What about you? / And you?	I like history.
See you later, Tamara.	OK, see you.

(1 point for each correct sentence or question: for Berry 8 points, for Tamara 7 points)

☺	😐	☹
15–12	11–8	7–0

a) *Find the words and match them with the rooms in this house:*

netchki • gniliv moor • lahl • redboom ((2x)) • gegara • robomath • ottile • labycon

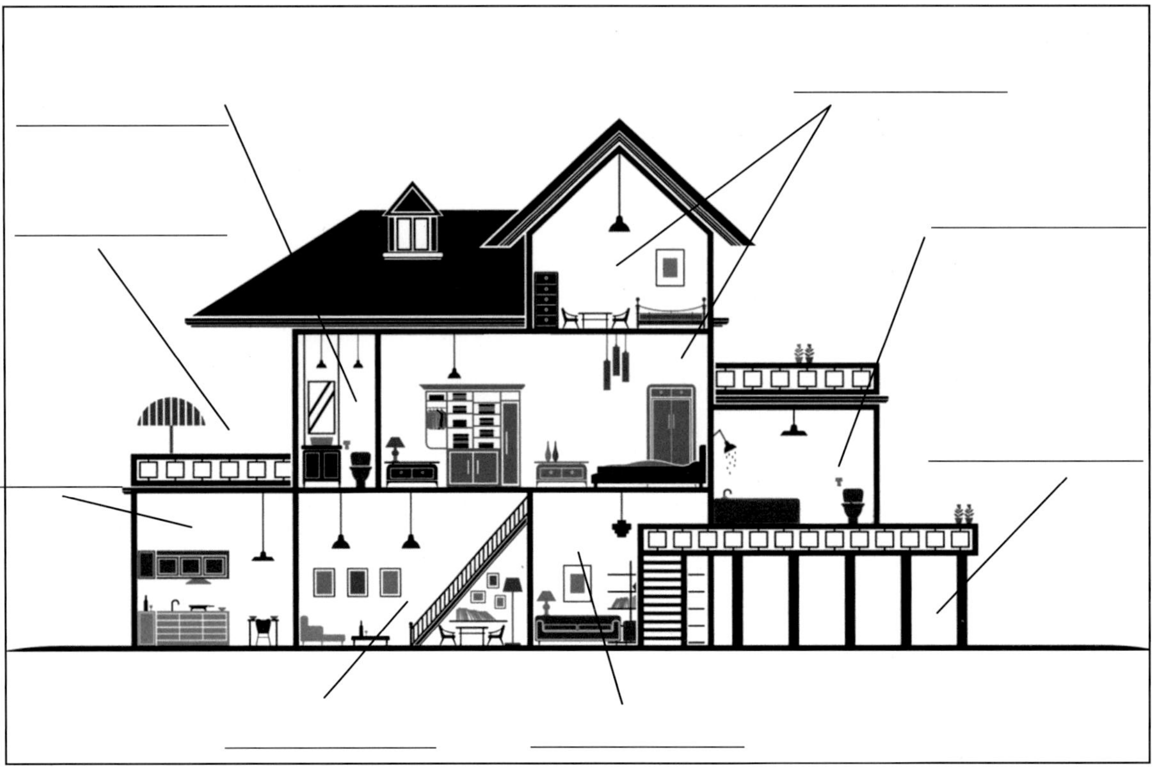

b) *Now design your dream house. Where is your bedroom/living room/…? Label the rooms.*

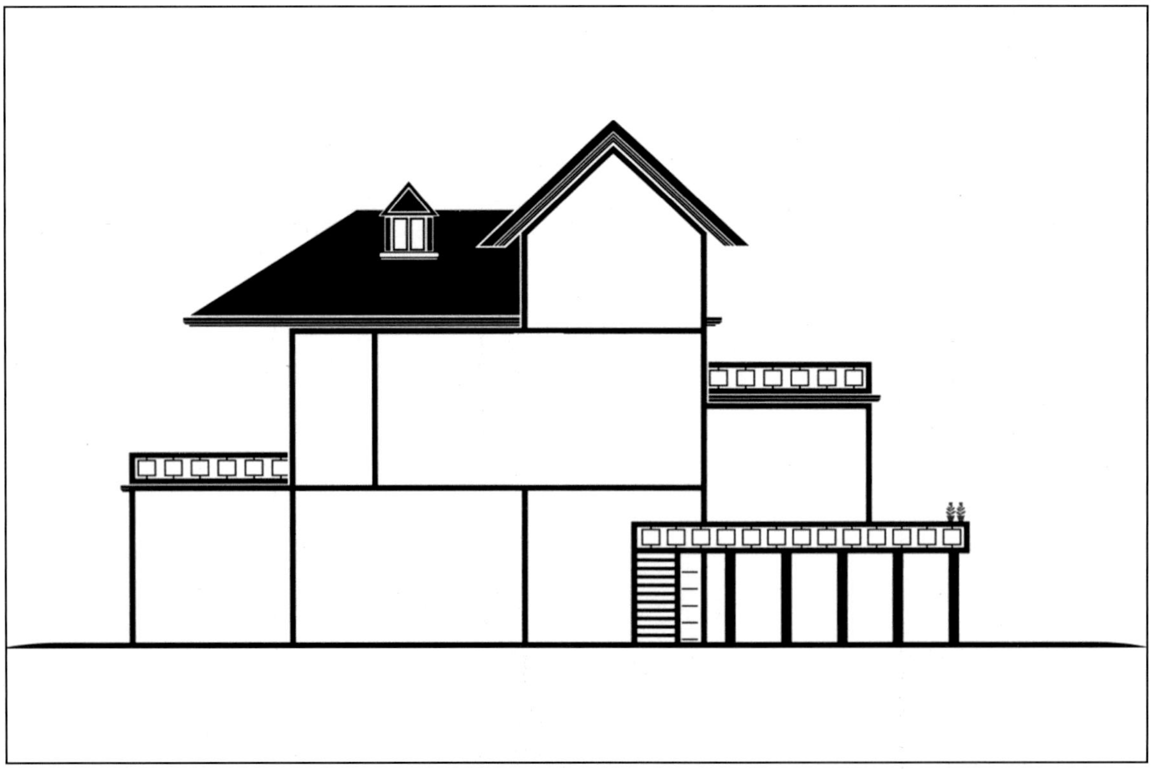

c) *Draw (or glue) things in your house/rooms.*

d) More practice *Label the things in your house. (after p. 39)*

1 *Complete your (dream) family tree. Fill in the names and add pictures of your …*

a) *grandparents:*

______ ______ ______ ______

b) *parents/aunts/uncles/…:*

______ ______ ______ ______

c) *brothers/sisters/cousins/stepbrothers/…:*

______ **Me:** ______ ______

2 **More help** *Then talk about your family tree.*

3 **More practice** *Add boxes with names and photos of: step-parents, aunts, uncles, …*

______ ______ ______ ______ ______

▼

▲ *fold here*

More help *aunt • uncle • grandfather • grandmother • are/aren't together • (step)father • (step)mother • (step)brother • (step)sister • partner*

Part 1: NOW YOU: Questions about you and your partner

a) *Write the answers for you in the table.*

	Me: ____________	My partner: ____________
1 Are you noisy?		
2 Are your friends fun?		
3 Is your grandmother from Germany?		
4 Is your dad strict?		
5 Is your mum bossy?		
6 Is your room messy?		

b) *Ask your partner the same questions and write the answers in the table.*

c) *Compare your answers with your partner's answers.*

– *Find two things that are different. Ex.:* I'm noisy, but my partner isn't noisy.
– *Find two things that are the same*[1]. *Ex.:* My friends are fun and my partner's friends are fun too.

d) More practice *Say/Write some sentences about your partner.*

Ex.: My partner is/isn't noisy. His/Her friends are fun. His/Her grandmother ...

[1] *the same* – gleich

Part 2: An Interview: What do you think?

a) *Answer the questions in the table for you.*

	Me	Partner 1	Partner 2	Partner 3	Partner 4	Partner 5
1 Is English easy?						
2 Is school fun?						
3 Is the principal strict?						
4 Are your teachers nice?						
5 Are you bossy?						

b) *Walk around. Ask as many partners as possible. Write the answers in the table.*

c) *Pick one interesting answer. Tell the class.*

d) More practice *Think of two more questions for your partners. Write the answers in the table.*

1 *Cut out the keywords A-H below and match them to the pictures.*

2 *Then talk or write about the pictures like this:*

In picture 1/2/…, Ellie is at her mum's house/dad's flat.
She's in the kitchen/… She's (not) happy.

A dad's flat – her room – happy	**E** dad's flat – living room – not happy
B dad's flat – living room – happy	**F** dad's flat – kitchen – not happy
C mum's house – kitchen – happy	**G** dad's flat – her pink room – happy
D dad's flat – her room – not happy	**H** mum's house – kitchen – happy

Part 1: The banana skin game

Play the banana skin game in groups of three or four.

WAS? 1 Würfel und 3 oder 4 Spielsteine.
WIE? Landest du auf einem Nummernfeld, nenne die *classroom phrase*. War sie korrekt, bleibe auf dem Feld. Hast du einen Fehler gemacht, gehe zwei Felder zurück. Dann ist der/die Nächste an der Reihe.

✂- -

Part 2: Classroom phrases pairs game

More practice *Write the complete English classroom phrases 1–12 down on cards. Write another 12 cards with the matching German classroom phrases. Then play the classroom phrases pairs game.*

(1) Can I go to the toilet, please?	(1) Kann ich bitte auf die Toilette gehen?		

Answers to STOP! CHECK! GO! (Unit 2)

1 WORDS Can you remember Ellie's family? ► **Unit 2, p. 48**

a) I'm Pete. I'm Ellie's **stepdad** (1).
I'm Jackie. I'm Ellie's **mum** (2).
I'm Conor. I'm Ellie's **stepbrother** (3).
I'm Zoe. I'm Ellie's **stepsister** (4).
I'm Steve. I'm Ellie's **dad** (5).
I'm Alisha. I'm Steve's **partner** (6).
This is Finn. He's Ellie's **baby brother** (7).
And this is my big **family** (8). (8 points)
b) aunt, cousin, grandfather, grandmother, grandparents, parents, uncle, … (5 points)

☺	😐	☹
13–11	10–7	6–0

2 WORDS Sandy's house ► **Unit 2, p. 48**

a) A4, B2, C5, D7, E6, F3, G8, H1 (8 points)
b) Hi! Welcome to my **house**. The **bedroom** is yellow. And the **hall** is pink. This is my kitchen – it's very **big**. My **bathroom** is red – cool! Look at my living room – it's **green**. Great! Now look at my garden. It's **small**, but it's my favourite place! (6 points)
c) 1 toilet, 2 kitchen, 3 bedroom, 4 garage, 5 living room (5 points)

☺	😐	☹
19–16	15–10	9–0

3 REVISION Sandy's family ► **Unit 2, p. 49**

My family **is** (1) big. This **is** (2) my father.
Dad **is** (3) very strict, but he**'s** (4) fun too.
This **is** (5) my mum. She**'s** (6) cool, but she**'s** (7) strict too.
My brothers and sisters **are** (8) OK. But they**'re** (9) very messy.
We**'re** (10) all very noisy.
I**'m** (11) happy because I**'m** (12) in my new house.
It**'s** (13) great! (13 points)

☺	😐	☹
13–11	10–7	6–0

4 LANGUAGE Questions for Sandy ► **Unit 2, p. 49**

1 Hey, Sandy. Are you happy? – **Yes, I am.**
2 Is your family small? – **No, it isn't.**
3 Are your parents strict? – **Yes, they are.**
4 Is your mum cool? – **Yes, she is.**
5 Are your brothers and sisters mean? – **No, they aren't.**
6 Are you and your family noisy? – **Yes, we are.**
7 Is your new house messy? – **Yes, it is.** (7 points)

☺	😐	☹
7–6	5–4	3–0

5 LISTENING Numbers and addresses ► **Unit 2, p. 49**

a) Adam: 07821 44**5** 19**4**1 Berry: 07794 19**9** **4**515 Luca: 077**8**51 819 **4**32 (6 points)
b) 2: 9 Windsor Street, Plymouth, PL3 2ET (1 points)
c) Adam's address: 22 Hoe Lane, Plymouth, PL1 8NB (3 points)

☺	😐	☹
10–8	7–5	4–0

6 WRITING An email to a new e-pal ► **Unit 2, p. 50**

1 **Are** you from England?
2 **Is** your family small?
3 **Is** your house in a city?
4 **Is** your room nice?
5 **Is** your school big?
6 **Are** your friends cool?
7 **Are** your teachers OK? (7 points)

☺	😐	☹
7–6	5–4	3–0

1 *Look at the pictures and complete the 'Me' column for you: I love = ☺ I hate = ☹.*

	Me	Partner 1	Partner 2	Partner 3	Partner 4	Partner 5
hoodie 						
trainers 						
shoes 						
tie 						
T-shirt 						
socks 						
pullover 						
trousers 						
blazer 						
skirt 						

2 *Talk to different partners and complete the table for them.*

I love/hate the …! What about you?

Yes, I love/hate the … too.

Really? I love/hate the …!

3 *Tell the class about your partners:*

Everybody loves/hates the …
Lots of boys love/hate the …
Lots of girls love/hate the …

4 **More practice** *Who's like you? Tell the class:*

I love/hate the … and Alina … loves/hates the … too.

Teil 1

0
1
2
3

Teil 2

0
1
2
3
4
5
6
7
8
9

Teil 4

January
February
March
April
May
June
July
August
September
October
November
December

Teil 3

st
nd
rd
th

1 *Schneide Teile 1–5 aus.*

2 *Teil 5: Schlitze die gestrichelten Linien mit einer Schere ein.*

3 *Ziehe Teile 1–4 durch die Schlitze.*

Teil 5

What date is it?

month

day

Questions	Me	1 o'clock 	2 o'clock 	3 o'clock 
When's your birthday?				
When's your best friend's birthday?				
When's your mum's/dad's birthday?				
When's your brother's/sister's birthday?				
When's ______________'s birthday?				

a) *Complete the 'Me' column for you. Can you think of one more question?*

b) *Make appointments for 1, 2 and 3 o'clock with three students. Write the names in the table.*

c) *Go to your appointments. Your teacher will tell you when it is 1, 2 or 3 o'clock. Ask your partners two or more questions about birthdays and write the dates on your table.*

More practice **Other important dates**

a) *Match these dates to the days in the table.*

Important dates	You write:	You say:
New Year's Day is on …	… 1st January	… the first of January
April Fools' Day is on …		
German Unity Day is on …		
Christmas Day is on …		
______________ is on …		
______________ is on …		

b) *Write down two more days that you know or like. You can use the ideas in the box. Then fill in the other columns.*

Halloween • my Name Day • Valentine's Day • May Day • Thanksgiving • …

c) *Give your table to your partner and take your partner's table. Ask your partner:* When's Christmas Day /…? *Check your partner's answer in the table. Answer your partner's questions.*

Cornelsen
English G LIGHTHOUSE 1 | Lehrerfassung Plus | Grafiken (alle shutterstock): Uhren **oben:** ColinCramm; **Mitte oben** (v. li. n.re.): AlinaSav; Christina Li; Inspiring; Lemberg Vector studio; **Mitte unten** (teens talking): Irina Strelnikova; **unten** (v.l.n.r.): Kristina Shevchenko; iCreative3D; Oakozhan; Andrei_M

1 *Cut out the sentences (A-I) and match them with the pictures (1–9).*

A I get up early. I make breakfast for Grace.	**G** In the afternoon Dad stays in bed. We do our homework.	**D** Dad often works at night. He comes home in the morning.
E After dinner we watch TV. Mum sometimes watches TV with us. Dad goes to work.	**H** Jack and I go to school together. We usually go by bus. But I sometimes walk. Jack never walks. Lazy Jack!	**F** Mum often comes home late. We always have dinner together and we talk about the day.
I In the evening Dad usually makes dinner.	**B** I usually have lunch at school.	**C** Lazy Jack! He gets up late. He never has breakfast!

1 	2 	3 
D Dad often works at night. He comes home in the morning.		
4 	5 	6 
7 	8 	9 

Is everything correct? Complete this sentence with the underlined letters from Luca's text:
DAD WORKS AT G _ _ _ _ _ _ _ _ FIRE STATION.

2 *Underline the verbs without 's' (ohne 's) with a blue pen and the verbs with 's' (mit 's') with a green pen. Then make two lists: verbs without 's' and verbs with 's'.*

1 *Watch all three parts of the film again. How does Sarah feel in the situations below? Put a cross in the box with the right word.*

2 *Draw a line between the crosses to make a graph. Then write sentences:*

On Saturday morning, Sarah calls Paul. She's excited. When Paul says he can't come …

Feelings									
excited	X								
happy									
surprised									
OK									
unhappy									
angry									
Situations	1 Sarah calls Paul. She's …	2 Paul says he can't come. (lots of homework).	3 Now Sarah calls Anna.	4 Anna says she can't come. (mum needs her)	5 Sarah's mum sees Paul and Anna.	6 Anna and Paul want to talk to Sarah.	7 Paul asks what day it is.	8 Anna and Paul show Sarah the bags.	9 Anna, Paul and Sarah go shopping together.

3 *Match the feelings with the Smileys: cool • helpless • terrible • nervous*

______________________________ ______________________________

______________________________ ______________________________

More practice *How do Anna and Paul feel when …*

– Sarah calls and they can't tell her why they can't meet: ______________________________

– they meet in front of the shopping centre: ______________________________

– they are looking for the right present: ______________________________

– they see Sarah and her mother in the shopping centre: ______________________________

– Sarah is angry with them: ______________________________

Grafiken (alle shutterstock): 6x oben: (1) und (4) Vilay; (2), (3), (5), (6) Anatolir; unten links Anatolir; unten rechts Vilay

1 WORDS In a town ► **Unit 3, p. 66**

a) **1** cinema, **2** supermarket, **3** market, **4** fire station, **5** park, **6** restaurant, **7** swimming pool, **8** sports shop (8 points)

b) **1** You can watch a film in a **cinema**.
2 You can buy vegetables in a **supermarket** or a **market**.
3 You can buy trainers in a **sports shop**. (4 points)

c) **1** **You can ride a bike … / You can walk … / You can meet friends … / You can play football** in a park.
2 **You can have lunch/breakfast/dinner** in a restaurant. / **You can meet friends** in a restaurant.
3 **You can go shopping / You can meet friends … / You can buy things / …** in a shopping centre.
4 **You can go swimming … / You can meet friends … / You can play games** in a swimming pool.
5 **You can buy a mobile** in a mobile phone shop.
6 **You can buy a bike/helmet** in a bike shop. (6 points)

☺	😐	☹
18–15	14–9	8–0

2 LISTENING In a sports shop ► **Unit 3, p. 66**

1B, **2**C, **3**A, **4**B, **5**C, **6**B (6 points)

☺	😐	☹
6–5	4–3	2–0

3 WORDS Days, months and dates ► **Unit 3, p. 66**

a) **1** What month is it?
2 When's your birthday?
3 What date is it today?
4 When's your best friend's birthday?
5 What day is it today? (5 points)

b) **2** 9. 3. – **9th March**
3 12. 5. – **12th May**
4 18. 7. – **18th July**
5 20. 10. – **20th October**
6 25. 12. – **25th December** (5 points)

c) 5th February, 10th September, 1st April, 14th March, 21st May, 11th August (12 points)

☺	😐	☹
22–18	17–11	10–0

4 REVISION Stupid Cyril ► **Unit 3, p. 67**

a) **2** **Are** the students at school ?
3 **Is** Luca on his bike ?
4 **Is** the town quiet?
5 **Are** Grace and Mr Boateng at the market?
6 **Is** Mrs Boateng at work? (5 points)

b) **2** No, **they aren't**.
3 Yes, **he is**.
4 Yes, **it is**.
5 No, **they aren't**.
6 No, **she isn't**. It's Sunday, Cyril! You stupid crab! (5 points)

☺	😐	☹
10–8	7–5	4–0

5 LANGUAGE Cyril's birthday ► **Unit 3, p. 67**

a) On Cyril's birthdays Cyril and Sandy usually **get up (1)** early. They **go (2)** to the beach. They **talk (3)** about the day.
Cyril ___ It's my birthday today. I always **have (4)** a party. I **meet (5)** all my friends.
Sandy __ Great! I **love (6)** your parties. We always **play (7)** lots of games. (7 points)

b) Sandy always **goes (1)** to the market. She usually **comes (2)** home with lots of nice things: vegetables and pizza. Cyril always **stays (3)** at home. He **works (4)** in the kitchen. He **makes (5)** a big birthday lunch for his friends. Cyril always **plans (6)** lots of good games. Sandy **helps (7)** Cyril with the games too. (7 points)

c) **1** All Cyril's friends **come** to the party.
2 Cyril **gets** lots of presents.
3 Sandy **meets** Cyril's friends.
4 They usually **play** games.
5 They often **go** swimming in the sea.
6 Cyril **has** a great day. (6 points)

☺	😐	☹
20–16	15–10	9–0

1 *Where do you want to go? Pick two places. Tick them in the boxes.* ✓

☐ the pond

☐ the fields

☐ Pets Corner

☐ the barn

☐ the trampolines/the zip wire

☐ the shop

2 *Why do you want to go to your two places?*
Here are some ideas:

I want to go to the pond /fields / … because …

… I love donkeys / ducks / guinea pigs / ponies / …

… pets / donkeys / zip wires / … are fun / great / nice /

… I want to watch the ducks / ride the ponies / meet the pets / stroke the donkeys / play on the trampolines / …

3 *Make dialogues with your partner.*

a) *Cut out the sentences below and put them in the right order. Then read the dialogue.*

b) More practice *Copy the dialogue and fill in your own ideas for the words in grey.*

A Well, the zip wire is OK, but I really want to meet the pets.	**B** Oh no. Pets are boring. But ponies are great. And you can ride them!
B I want to go to the zip wire. What about you?	**A** Yes, I like ponies too. And I have lots of pets at home.
B OK, let's go to the zip wire and to the ponies.	**A** Merryweather Farm looks great. Where do you want to go?

Part 1: Berry's day – Flashcards

What does Berry do every day? Cut out the cards and put them in the right order.

More practice *Glue the cards into your exercise book and write captions for each picture.*

More help *The words in the box can help you.*

More help come home • do homework • do sports • get ready for school • go to school • feed sb. • look after sb. • wake sb.

Part 2: Appointments – On school days

a) *Complete the table for you.*

b) *Make appointments with two partners. Then talk to your partners like this:*

> I get up at 6 o'clock. What about you?

c) *Listen to their answers and complete the table.*

d) **More practice** *Ask one more partner.*

	Me	1 o'clock ____	2 o'clock ____	More practice: ____
get up				
have breakfast				
go to school				
come home				
have lunch				
do my homework				
have dinner				
go to bed				

Part 1: When do Adam, Luca, Berry and Ellie feel great or fed up?

Partner A: *Listen and write the names: Adam, Luca, Berry or Ellie.*

☺ I feel great when …	
… I do sport.	
… I'm with my animals.	
… I'm with my friends.	
… I listen to music.	
… I don't have homework.	

✂- -

Partner B: *Listen and write the names: Adam, Luca, Berry or Ellie.*

☹ I feel fed up when …	
… my sister is bossy.	
… my mobile doesn't work.	
… my friends don't text me.	
… people don't talk to me.	
… I have lots of homework.	

✂- -

Part 2: When do you feel great or fed up?

☺ I feel great …	☹ I feel fed up …

Part 3: Complete Berry's notes

☺ I feel great …	☹ I feel fed up …

● **Version A:** *Write your questions in the table. Then walk around and talk to different people. Ask your questions. Take notes in your table.*

Do you …	Who? (Name)	Asking for more information:	What …?/ When …?/ Where …?
have an interesting pet?		What pet do you have?	
go to a nice place in the holidays?		Where do you ___________?	
like an English football team?		What _____ do you _____?	

More practice Game: *Pick one person and let the class guess who it is:*
This person has an interesting pet – a snake / … Who is it?
This person gets up … / goes to … / likes …

○ **Version B:** *Complete the questions in the table. Then walk around and talk to different people. Ask your questions. Take notes in your table.*

Do you …	Who? (Name)	Asking for more information:	What …?/ When …?/ Where …?
have an interesting pet?		What pet do you have?	
have an interesting hobby?		What _____ do you _____?	
get up early?		When do you ___________?	
go to a nice place in the holidays?		Where do you ___________?	
like an English football team?		What _____ do you _____?	
like homework?		What _____ do you _____?	

More practice Game: *Pick one person and let the class guess who it is:*
This person has an interesting pet – a snake / … Who is it?
This person gets up … / goes to … / likes …

1 *Cut out the pictures. Then listen to the story and put the pictures in the right order.*

More practice *Draw your own picture for scene 8. Use ideas from the story.*

Hi guys

Do you want to see our chipmunks? Do you want to come to the farm for a sleepover? What about next Saturday? There's a bus at 3 o'clock. Bring your sleeping bags.
Berry

2 *Then cut out the captions and match them to the pictures.*

Time to go home	Noises at night
Let's go to the country	A dangerous animal?
A cute chipmunk	Come to a sleepover
Time to eat	No sweets!

Viewing: A normal day at school

a) *Watch the film. Then talk about how Emily feels in different scenes. The words in the table can help you.*

Emily feels	☺ great happy good OK ——— ☹ fed up bad unhappy angry stupid terrible	when she can't do things alone.
		when her friends help her too much.
		when people don't listen to her.
		when Laura invites her.
		when a boy helps her with her wheelchair in the street.
		when her friends help her when she really needs it.
		when people don't think.
		when people are normal with her.
		when people don't ask her, but ask her friends, "Does Emily …?"
		when people don't talk to her but talk about her.
		when she can speak for herself.
		when her friends think of her.

More practice *What could Emily say to her friends? Write down as many sentences as you can.*

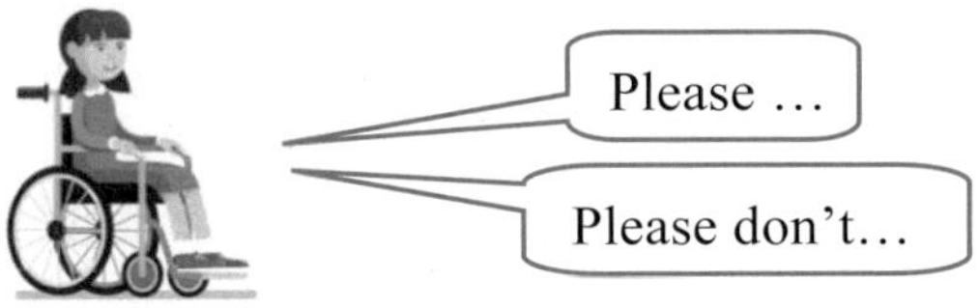

be normal with me. • help me when I need it. • help me too much. • invite me. • let me speak for myself. • listen to me. • talk to me. • talk about me. • think of me. • …

b) *Is it a good or bad day for Emily? Collect good and bad parts of Emily's day in two lists.*

Good parts	Bad parts

I think it's a ____________________ day for Emily, because ______________________________

▼

▲ *fold here*

More help

A boy helps her with her wheelchair in the street.	Sally tells all the students to move.
Two students say hello and are normal with her.	Chloe and a boy help Emily buy a drink.
Chloe and the boy don't listen to her but speak for her.	Laura invites her to come to town.

Budgies

Budgies are small birds (about 18 cm long). They originally come from Australia. Now budgies live all over the world. Lots of people have them as pets because they are very friendly birds. Budgies are very pretty too and have brightly coloured feathers. Most budgies have yellow heads and green feathers with black stripes. Some budgies have white heads and blue feathers with black stripes. Budgies eat bird seed and some kinds of vegetables and fruit. Budgies can live inside in cages and make very good pets. They usually live for about 5 to 8 years. Budgies are very clever animals. They like playing with people and can learn to say a few words. They like to sing and can do tricks too.

Elephants

Elephants live in Africa and Asia. They are the biggest animals in the world (that live on land, not in the sea). Elephants are usually about 3 to 4 m tall. They have grey skin, tusks (like two long teeth) and a trunk. African elephants have big ears. Elephants from Asia have small ears. All elephants use their trunk to pick up food, drink water and play with other elephants. They can "talk" with their trunk too – taraaa! Elephants only eat plants, like grass, leaves and fruit. They eat all day long – about 16 hours a day! It's very hot in Africa and Asia so elephants love to swim. Elephants walk a lot, but they can't run. They can get very old: 75 years. Elephants are very clever animals. But they are not good pets because they need to live outside.

Guinea pigs

Actually, Guinea pigs aren't pigs! They are small animals that originally come from South America. Now they live all over the world. Guinea pigs want to live with other guinea pigs. They are unhappy if they live alone. It's not good for guinea pigs to live with other kinds of animals. For example, dogs sometimes eat guinea pigs. Guinea pigs make good pets because they like it when people hold and stroke them. They can live inside in cages. But their cages have to be big because guinea pigs like to run around and jump a lot! Guinea pigs can have white, black, grey, brown, red and orange fur. Their fur can be long or short. They are usually 20 to 25 cm long and weigh about 1 kg. They usually live for about 4 to 6 years. Guinea pigs eat grass, hay, vegetables and fruit. Their teeth never stop growing, so they eat all the time to keep their teeth short.

Tigers

Tigers are the biggest cats in the world. There are six kinds of tiger alive today. The biggest tigers can be up to 3.5 m long and weigh 300 kg! Tigers live in India, Russia, China and Southeast Asia. They have orange fur with black stripes. Their stomach is white with black stripes. Tigers usually live for 10 to 15 years. They can run very fast and swim very well too. They eat other animals, like antelopes, sheep, goats, pigs and cows. They don't eat every day, but they eat a lot when they have lots of food. Tigers like to live alone and walk a lot, so they need lots of space outside. Female tigers need about 20 km^2, and male tigers need about 60 to 100 km^2. Tigers are in trouble because they need a lot of space, and people are building roads and houses where tigers live. Some people kill tigers for their fur. There are only 3000 to 5000 tigers living in the world today.

✂- -

Polar bears

Polar bears live in the ice and snow in the Arctic. Five countries have polar bears: Denmark, Norway, Russia, the US and Canada. Polar bears have white fur. They are very big animals. Male polar bears can be up to 3 m long and weigh 680 kg. Female polar bears can be up to 2.5 m long and weigh 250 kg. They live outside, near the water. Polar bears eat other animals like seals, walruses and whales. They don't eat every day, but they eat a lot when they have lots of food. Polar bears have to walk very slowly because they are very big! They can run, but not very far. They can swim very well. They live for about 25 years. Polar bears are in trouble. People sometimes kill polar bears for their fur. And the world is getting warmer and the ice in the Arctic is melting. Polar bears can't hunt animals without ice, so lots of polar bears are hungry.

✂- -

Glue a picture of your favourite animal here.

More practice **My favourite animal:**

____

____

____

____

____

____

1 WORDS On Merryweather Farm ► **Unit 4, p. 86**

a) **1** farm, **2** village, **3** shop, **4** barn, **5** toilet, **6** field, **7** cage, **8** pond, **9** wheelchair (9 points)

b) **A:** donkey, **B:** pony, **C:** sheep, **D:** cow/cows, **E:** dog, **F:** pig/pigs, **G:** duck/ducks, **H:** chicken/chickens, **I:** chipmunk, **J:** rabbit/rabbits, **K:** rat, **L:** hamster (12 points)

☺	😐	☹
21–17	16–11	10–0

2 WORDS Visitors at the farm ► **Unit 4, p. 86**

a) **2** visitor, **3** Berry, **4** visitor, **5** visitor, **6** Berry, **7** visitor, **8** Berry (7 points)

b) Listen again. Finish the sentences.

1 Excuse me, please. We want to visit **the farm.**
2 When do you feed the **animals**?
3 We feed the ducks at **10.45**.
4 Excuse me, please. Where are the **toilets**?
5 What's that **noise**?
6 It's only a donkey. Don't **worry**.
7 Look at the hamsters. They're really **cute**.
8 Come on Sam. Let's go **outside**. (8 points)

☺	😐	☹
15–12	11–8	7–0

3 REVISION A day with my family ► **Unit 4, p. 87**

a) Every morning mum, dad and I **get up** at 6 o'clock.
After breakfast I **go** to school by car with my dad.
At about 9 o'clock the first visitors **come**.
Mum and dad **have** lunch at 1 o'clock. After lunch dad usually **stays** in the shop and mum **works** with the ponies.
I **come** home from school with dad before 4 o'clock.
Dad **has** something to eat with me. Then we **go** outside. Sam **comes** with me.
We **look** after all the animals. (11 points)

☺	😐	☹
11–10	9–6	5–0

4 LANGUAGE An interview with Cyril and Sandy ► **Unit 4, p. 87**

a) **1 Do** you like Plymouth?
2 Do you have a best friend?
3 Do you and Sandy live on the beach?
4 Does Sandy like Plymouth too?
5 Does Sandy have a best friend? (5 points)

b) **1** – No, I **don't** like Mr Johnson. He's terrible.
2 – No, I **don't** live in a big house.
3 – No, we **don't** go to school.
4 – No, she **doesn't** have a car.
5 – No, she **doesn't** eat crabs. (5 points)

c) **1 Where** do you live? – In Kingsand.
2 When do you get up? – Very late – after 10 o'clock.
3 Where do you have breakfast? – I always have breakfast on the beach.
4 What do you do after breakfast? – I often go to Plymouth.
5 Why do you like Cyril? – Because he's friendly and he's fun! (5 points)

☺	😐	☹
15–12	11–8	7–0

5 WORDS Useful phrases ► **Unit 4, p. 88**

a) **1** Help! I'm **in** trouble!
2 I want to go **to** the toilet!
3 I get up **at** 6 o'clock.
4 I go to school **by** bus.
5 I listen **to** music every evening.
6 I feel great when I'm **with** my friends.
7 Go **through** that field.
8 Go **to** sleep. Good night! (8 points)

b) **1 B; 2 G; 3 H; 4 D; 5 E; 6 A; 7 F; 8 C** (8 points)

☺	😐	☹
16–13	12–8	7–0

Complete the sentences with: me • you • him • her • it • us • you • them.

1. Adam's rap is great. I love ____________!
2. You can bring your sister to my party. I really like ____________.
3. I think the PMZ guitar club is really fun, Luca. Don't you want to come with ______?
4. The photos on your mobile are great. I want to see ____________ again!
5. My homework is so difficult, Mum. Can you help ____________?
6. Adam, Zack, are you hungry? I have some sandwiches for ____________!
7. These scones are yummy. Try ____________!
8. Luca loves *Francis and the Drakes*. We could buy their new CD for __________.
9. Adam's father works on the ferry. Adam doesn't see __________ very much.
10. That table looks bad, Adam. Can you clean ____________, please?
11. We always go to Tinside Lido on Saturdays. Come with ____________!
12. Dad, I'm busy. Can I phone ________ later?

Complete the sentences. Pick the right word.

1. Adam's rap is great. I love ____________! (it/them)
2. You can bring your sister to my party. I really like ____________. (us/her)
3. I think the PMZ guitar club is really fun, Luca. Don't you want to come with ____________? (me/him)
4. The photos on your mobile are great. I want to see ____________ again! (them/him)
5. My homework is so difficult, Mum. Can you help ____________? (them/me)
6. Adam, Zack, are you hungry? I have some sandwiches for ____________! (him/you)
7. These scones are yummy. Try ____________! (them/you)
8. Luca loves *Francis and the Drakes*. We could buy their new CD for __________ . (them/him)
9. Adam's father works on the ferry. Adam doesn't see __________ very much. (him/it)
10. That table looks bad, Adam. Can you clean ____________, please? (him/it)
11. We always go to Tinside Lido on Saturdays. Come with ____________! (her/us)
12. Dad, I'm busy. Can I phone ____________ later? (you/me)

Part 1: The kids from Harbour Road: What's your talent?

1 *Cut out the sentences and put them in the right order. Then watch part 1 of the film again and check.*

More practice *Add the names of the speakers: Anna, Sarah, Paul, waitress.*

A: Waitress:	That's four pounds for you, and four pounds for you, please.
B: ____:	I'm hungry! Can I have a muffin, and … a hot chocolate, please?
C: ____:	Hi!
D: ____:	Thanks. / Thank you!
E: ____:	Chocolate or blueberry?
F: ____:	Hi, Anna!
G: ____:	I'll have a chocolate muffin, please.
H: ____:	And yourself?
I: ____:	A hot chocolate and a blueberry muffin, please.
J: ____:	We're here!

Part 2: Make your own dialogue in a cafe

Look at the role cards and act a dialogue with your partner.

More practice *Write down your dialogue in your exercise book.*

Partner A (customer): You start! *You're in a cafe in England. You're hungry. Tell the waiter what you want.*	**Partner B (waiter/waitress): Your partner starts.** *You're a waiter in a cafe in England. Help the customers. Ask them what they want.*
– Hello / Good morning!	*– Hello, how can I help you?*
– Can I have …, please? – a muffin – some scones – a sandwich – an omelette – a salad	*– Sure, would you like …?* – a chocolate or a blueberry muffin – cream and jam with your scones – a chicken or a cheese sandwich – chips with your omelette – potato salad or green salad
– I'll have … please.	*– OK. Something to drink, too?*
– Yes, I'll have …, please. – a hot chocolate – a cup of tea / coffee – a glass of orange juice /cola …	*– Here you are. Anything else?*
– No thanks, that's all.	*– That's £ …, please.*

1 REVISION Questions and answers ► Unit 5, p. 104

a) **2** Yes, they do.
3 No, they don't.
4 No, they don't.
5 Yes, he does.
6 Yes, he does.
7 Yes, he does.
8 No, he doesn't. (7 points)

b) **1** Do seagulls live near the sea?
2 Do seagulls live in towns?
3 Do seagulls eat crabs?
4 Do seagulls sing or make a noise?
5 Does Sandy live in a house?
6 Does Sandy eat crabs?
7 Does Sandy talk?
8 Does Sandy like pizza? (8 points)

c) **1** Yes, they do.
2 Yes, they do.
3 Yes, they do.
4 Yes, they do.
5 Yes, she does.
6 No, she doesn't.
7 Yes, she does.
8 Yes, she does. (8 points)

☺	😐	☹
23–19	18–12	11–0

2 LANGUAGE Describing pictures ► Unit 5, p. 104

a) Cyril is **sitting (1)** on a chair, on the beach. He's **listening (2)** to music. He's **watching (3)** three kids. They're **playing (4)** football. His mobile is **ringing (5).** (5 points)

b) Sandy is on the beach too. She**'s (1)** watching Mr Johnson. He**'s (2)** walking on the beach. Mrs Johnson is there too. They**'re (3)** looking at Cyril. They**'re (4)** feeling hungry! Sandy has a mobile. She**'s (5)** phoning Cyril. (5 points)

c) **1 I'm sitting** on my favourite chair.
2 I'm listening to music.
3 I'm watching three kids.
4 They're playing football.
Cyril, look! The Johnsons **are** coming!
5 Help! I**'m** going! (6 points)

☺	😐	☹
16–13	12–8	7–0

3 LANGUAGE People on the ferry ► Unit 5, p. 105

a) Anna **F**; Rick **G**; Linda **C**; Toby **A**; Gemma **B**; David **E**; Uma **H**; Adam's dad **I** (8 points)

b) Anna is playing a game. Rick is cleaning the table. Linda is cooking. Toby and Gemma are talking. David is washing up. Uma is watching TV. Adam's dad is talking on the phone. (7 points)

☺	😐	☹
15–12	11–8	7–0

4 READING A picture ► Unit 5, p. 105

a) **1** F, **2** T, **3** F, **4** F, **5** F, **6** T, **7** F, **8** T, **9** F, **10** T, **11** F, **12** F (12 points)

b) There are lots of people on the beach. On the left I can see a boy and a girl. The boy is reading. The girl is talking on the phone.
In the middle I can see a family. They're eating lunch. There's a big white seagull in front of a yellow bag. It's looking at the sandwiches.
On the right I can see a red chair. A boy is sitting on the chair. There's a dog under the chair. I can see a big blue ball next to the chair. (12 points)

☺	😐	☹
24–20	19–12	11–0

5 WORDS Food and drinks ► Unit 5, p. 106

a) **1** cafe, **2** soup, **3** chips, **4** coffee, **5** scones (5 points)

b) **1** You can buy food and drinks in a **cafe**.
2 I often have vegetable **soup** for lunch.
3 My favourite food is fish and **chips**.
4 Some people drink **coffee** for breakfast.
5 We often have tea and **scones** in a cafe at the weekend. (5 points)

☺	😐	☹
10–8	7–5	4–0

Things for the beach – Word grid

1 *Find the words in the word grid. The scrambled words below can help you.*

M	S	A	U	S	A	G	E	S	P	T	L	S	H	S	P	T	T	X
S	W	A	I	B	I	C	S	D	V	B	R	P	P	X	W	O	I	O
P	I	C	N	I	C		B	L	A	N	K	E	T	P	T	W	K	R
G	M	U	X	M	R	T	O	S	E	Z	N	A	O	S	L	E	R	A
E	M	N	R	B	S	E	D	C	B	O	O	K	X	K	I	L	O	N
Z	I	R	N	O	C	P	Y	B	A	P	X	E	U	W	Q	A	M	G
B	N	W	F	O	O	T	B	A	L	L	E	R	R	C	T	S	Z	E
H	G	G	R	F	N	D	O	S	L	A	P	S	O	A	I	W	U	
J		K	I	L	E	Y	A	X	C	S	V	B	N	M	M	I	M	J
B	T	N	S	K	S	O	R	P	S	U	N	C	R	E	A	M	L	U
J	R	I	B	U	H	V	D	C	G	N	Z	T	F	R	C	S	X	I
T	U	B	E	Q	Y	Q	W	A	Y	G	S	H	E	A	R	U	D	C
A	N	W	E	S	U	M	B	R	E	L	L	A	Y	X	D	I	E	E
I	K	N	J	U	Z	H	B	T	Z	A	G	T	V	W	C	T	F	R
K	S	A	N	D	W	I	C	H	E	S	M	O	L	A	P	I	Z	R
E	Q	M	B	C	Y	L	J	G	D	S	H	O	R	T	S	A	A	W
C	H	O	C	O	L	A	T	E	T	E	U	P	S	E	F	H	P	K
A	R	W	M	B	S	W	E	E	T	S	C	Y	C	R	I	S	P	S
K	Z	I	O	A	F	H	K	Y	C	B	N	E	F	I	V	E	L	L
E	O	F	R	U	I	T	R	B	I	S	C	U	I	T	S	P	E	C

beach things:
blal • broaddoby • boko • cramea • fallboot • fisbree • hta • strosh • seekarps • screamun • snuglessas • suitwims • smimwing tnurks • telow • tebu • ulleramb

picnic things:
aplep • biscutsi • ceka • chalocote • cispsr • futir • onager jeicu • pnicic banklet • siwandches • saaguses • wreta

▼

▲ *fold here*

More help apple • biscuits • cake • chocolate • crisps • fruit • orange juice • sandwiches • sausages • scones • sweets • water
ball • bodyboard • book • camera • football • frisbee • hat • picnic blanket • shorts • speakers • suncream • sunglasses • swimsuit • swimming trunks • towel • tube • umbrella

Read (or listen to) scenes 1–5. Then look at the pictures and fill in the table:

Scene	Who?	Where?	What must they find?
1 			
2 			
3 			
4 			
5 			

▼

▲ *fold here*

More help **Where?** in front of a shop • near Cawsand harbour • near the cafe 'The Smuggler's Rest' • near the clock tower • on the beach

What must they find? Berry's dad • a big clock • a cafe • cows • a shop

1 *Colour the puppets.*

2 *Cut out the puppets and put a straw on them.*

Cyril

Sandy

3 *Make dialogues with your puppets. Here are some ideas:*

Hi, my name is … – What's your name?	Cyril • Sandy • …
I'm from ...	Kingsand • Plymouth • …
I'm ... (years old)	four • five • …
My favourite colour is ...	blue • orange • pink • red • white • …
My favourite thing is ...	the beach • the sea • my sandcastle • …
My hobby is ...	diving in the sand • hiding • playing football • running • singing • swimming • watching people • …
I like ... I don't like ...	boats • fish • holidays • ice cream • music • orange juice • people • picnics • sand • surfboards • the beach • the sea • water • …
– What about you?	

DIDAKTISCH-METHODISCHES GLOSSAR

AA klären siehe Klären der Arbeitsanweisung

Akrostichon (*Acrostic*) Das Akrostichon (griechisch *akros:* Spitze, *stichos:* Vers) ist eine Versform, bei der die Zeilenanfänge hintereinander gelesen einen Sinn, z. B. einen Namen oder einen Satz, ergeben. Dies können Buchstaben bei reinen Wortfolgen oder Worte bei Versfolgen sein.
Im Unterricht wird meist folgende vereinfachte Form eingesetzt: Die Buchstaben eines Wortes senkrecht untereinander schreiben. Jeder Buchstabe kommt auch in einem anderen Wort vor (häufig als Anfangsbuchstabe), diese Wörter waagerecht um das senkrechte Startwort anordnen.

Antwortkärtchen siehe Right/wrong cards

Appointments Die kooperative Lernform *Appointments* ist eine gesteuerte Form von wechselnder PA in vier Phasen:

1. Die S schreiben drei vorgegebene Uhrzeiten in eine Tabelle. Dann gehen sie zu drei Mit-S, bitten jeweils um ein *appointment* zu den drei notierten Zeiten *(Can we meet at 1/2/3 o'clock?)* und tragen die Namen der Mit-S bei der entsprechenden Uhrzeit in ihrer Tabelle ein.
2. Im zweiten Schritt bearbeiten die S die Aufgabenstellung zunächst für sich und halten ihre Antwort in der Tabelle fest.
3. Auf das Signal von L *(It's 1/2/3 o'clock.)* gehen die S zum jeweiligen *appointment* mit ihrem Mit-S, befragen ihn und notieren die Antwort in der Tabelle.
4. In der letzten Phase berichten die S im Plenum über ihre Umfrageergebnisse.

Thema	Me: ________	1 o'clock Name: ________	2 o'clock Name: ________	3 o'clock Name: ________
Frage 1				
Frage 2				
Frage 3				

Binnendifferenziertes Arbeiten Heterogene Lerngruppen erfordern einen individualisierten Unterricht, in dem differenziert auf lernstarke sowie lernschwache S eingegangen wird.
Zum einen kann hier das Potential lernstärkerer S genutzt werden, indem sie aufstehen, sobald sie eine Aufgabe fertig bearbeitet haben. S, die sich mit der Aufgabe schwer tun, können sich melden und von einem der stehenden S Unterstützung holen (Schüler als Experten). Dieses Vorgehen gewährleistet einen weitestgehend ruhigen Arbeitsablauf.
Da es in vielen Situationen nicht nötig ist, allen S der Lerngruppe Differenzierungshilfen zu geben, bietet es sich zum anderen an, diese verdeckt zu geben (Optional help). Von den Gegebenheiten im Unterrichtsraum abhängig können Hilfen z. B. hinter die Tafel oder auf ein verdecktes Flipchart geschrieben werden. Sie können auch kopiert in Briefumschläge gelegt werden, die sich die S an ihren Tisch holen und nach Gebrauch wieder zurücklegen.

Bus stop siehe Lerntempoduett

***Buzz reading* (Lesegemurmel)** Das *Buzz reading* dient dazu, den Redeanteil aller S zu erhöhen und Sprachhemmungen abzubauen. Alle S lesen einen bekannten Text gleichzeitig und leise murmelnd vor sich hin. Die Methode kann flexibel im Unterricht eingesetzt werden. Es empfiehlt sich, diese Phase kurz zu halten und sie z. B. zur Vorbereitung auf einen Lesevortrag einzusetzen. In Kombination mit dem Mitleseverfahren trägt diese Methode besonders zur Festigung von Aussprache und Intonation bei.

***Correcting circle* (Schreibkonferenz)** Bei der Methode *Correcting circle* (auch *Peer correction*) handelt es sich um die gegenseitige Textkorrektur und Hilfe der S untereinander. Diese Form des Feedbacks ist für manche S weniger einschüchternd als die Fehlerkorrektur durch L. Die Methode eignet sich besonders für die Arbeit in Kleingruppen. Es sollte ein Kriterienkatalog für die Textkorrektur vorliegen, der vorher gemeinsam erarbeitet werden kann. Ablauf:

1. Jedem S wird ein spezielles Gebiet zugeteilt (z. B. *content*, *structure*, *spelling*, *tenses*, *word order*).
2. Die S geben ihre Texte reihum weiter und nehmen Korrekturen zu ihrem Gebiet vor, bis der Text wieder bei seinem Verfasser angekommen ist.
3. Zum Abschluss fertigt jeder S eine Reinschrift seines Textes an.

L sammelt nach dem Zufallsprinzip einige Ergebnisse zur Bewertung ein. Im Sinne des selbstständigen Lernens kann vereinbart werden, dass S eine *DOs-and-DON'Ts*-Liste anlegen, die in der Klassenarbeit verwendet werden darf. Dies hilft S bei der Selbstkorrektur und motiviert, an den eigenen Fehlern zu arbeiten.

Didaktische Folge

Für den effektiven Spracherwerb ist es bei der Einführung von neuem Wortschatz besonders in den Klassenstufen 5 und 6 wichtig, die didaktische Folge zu beachten. Dabei ist die Reihenfolge der Fertigkeiten, die im Zusammenhang mit einem neuen Lexem gefordert sind, genau festgelegt:

1. Hören: Die S hören ein neues Wort mehrfach (Sprachvorbild L oder CD).
2. Sprechen: Die S sprechen das neue Wort mehrfach nach (Lautschulung).
3. Lesen: Die S sehen das Schriftbild und lesen das neue Lexem.
4. Schreiben: Erst in diesem Schritt produzieren die S das neue Wort schriftlich.

Mit zunehmendem Lernstand können S in verstärktem Maße, vor allem in der Textarbeit, auf erworbene Erschließungstechniken zurückgreifen.

Double circle
(Doppelter Stuhlkreis, Kugellager)

Die kooperative Lernform *Double circle* ist eine Form von wechselnder PA, die sich zum Üben von Diskussionsstrategien eignet. Sie ermöglicht einen hohen Sprachumsatz bei niedriger Hemmschwelle zur aktiven Teilnahme. Ablauf:

1. Die S sitzen (oder stehen) sich in einem Innen- und einem Außenkreis gegenüber. Sie diskutieren ein vorgegebenes Thema oder eine Fragestellung mit ihrem Gegenüber und machen sich ggf. Notizen.
2. Auf ein (akustisches) Signal von L hin bewegen sich entweder die S im Innen- oder im Außenkreis um einige Plätze weiter, damit neue Paarungen entstehen. L bestimmt sowohl die Länge der Gesprächszeit als auch die Anzahl der weiterzurückenden Plätze.
3. In einem zweiten Durchgang berichten sich die S über das Gehörte, wobei die Partner jeweils korrigieren und ergänzen. So sind die S zum aktiven Zuhören gezwungen.

Als Variante bietet es sich an, Innen- und Außenkreis verschiedene Themen oder Fragestellungen zu geben, die sich die S gegenseitig erklären oder beantworten.

Flashcards

Flashcards sind Bildkarten, die den S helfen, das Laut- bzw. Schriftbild eines Wortes nachhaltig mit seiner Bedeutung zu verknüpfen. Sie nutzen den auditiven und visuellen Lernkanal parallel *(Dual Code Theory)*, wenn ihnen ein Wort mit dem entsprechenden Bild präsentiert wird und damit im Gehirn verknüpft werden kann. Als Applikationen an der Tafel eignen sich *Flashcards* auch besonders zur schüleraktivierenden Wortschatzarbeit, z. B. indem in einer Reorganisationsphase die Bilder den entsprechenden Wörtern zugeordnet werden.

Gallery walk
(Galeriespaziergang)

Die kooperative Lernform *Gallery walk* bietet eine gute Möglichkeit, Arbeitsergebnisse zu präsentieren und zu diskutieren. Ablauf:

1. Die S sind in EA oder GA zu einem Arbeitsergebnis gelangt (z. B. Text, Bild, Poster), das im Raum ausgestellt wird.
2. Die S gehen einzeln oder in Gruppen im Uhrzeigersinn von Station zu Station und schauen sich die Ergebnisse der anderen an.
3. Wenn alle S alle Arbeitsergebnisse gesehen haben, präsentieren sie entweder nacheinander ihre Eindrücke oder besprechen sie gemeinsam in der Klasse.

Als Variante der GA bietet es sich an, die S neu aufzuteilen. In jeder neuen Gruppe sollte jeweils ein S aus den ursprünglichen Gruppen sein. Derjenige aus der neuen Gruppe, der an dem ausliegenden Produkt mitgewirkt hat, präsentiert es den anderen. Die Gruppen wechseln im Uhrzeigersinn solange die Tische, bis jeder S jedes Gruppenergebnis einmal erklärt bekommen hat und sein eigenes Gruppenprodukt einmal erklären musste.

Gruppenbildung

Eine Einteilung der S in Gruppen kann mithilfe folgender Methoden erfolgen:

1. Methoden mit gelenktem Zufall: L bereitet Elemente vor, die zusammen ein Ganzes ergeben. Dies können z. B. Puzzleteile sein, die ein Bild ergeben, oder Wortkarten, die einem Oberbegriff zugeordnet werden können. Die S ziehen ein solches Element und finden sich in den jeweils entsprechenden Gruppen zusammen.
2. Gruppen können durch Auszählen, Würfeln oder nach dem *Line-up*-Verfahren gebildet werden. Bei diesem stellen sich S in der aufsteigenden Reihenfolge ihrer Geburtstage oder Hausnummern auf. L zählt dann die benötigten Gruppen ab, z. B. die ersten drei S, die gemeinsam eine Gruppe bilden, usw.
3. L teilt Gruppen ein und gibt die Namen der Gruppenmitglieder bekannt. Dabei sollten Leistungsniveau, Arbeitstempo und Sozialverhalten der S berücksichtigt werden.

Info-gap activity

Bei der *Info-gap activity* handelt es sich um eine kooperative Lernform, die den aktiven Umsatz der Fremdsprache erfordert und schult. Den S fehlen Informationen zum Lösen einer Aufgabe, die ihrem Partner vorliegen und die sie durch gegenseitiges Befragen herausfinden. Es empfiehlt sich PA in einem festem Team (Partner A, Partner B).

Für die Durchführung müssen den S die Informationen und die zu füllenden Lücken vorliegen (Kopiervorlage, Arbeitsblatt, Tabelle im SB etc.). Es ist sinnvoll, den S eine Zeitvorgabe für die Bearbeitung zu machen. Eine Auswertung der Ergebnisse kann zunächst mit einem anderen S-Paar und anschließend im Plenum geschehen.

Klären der Arbeitsanweisung

Für das Klären von Arbeitsanweisungen gibt es unterschiedliche Möglichkeiten. Im Hinblick auf selbstständiges Arbeiten sollten S möglichst früh dazu befähigt werden, Arbeitsanweisungen ohne Hilfe von L zu erschließen. Damit S sich aktiv mit der Arbeitsanweisung auseinandersetzen, empfiehlt sich folgendes Vorgehen:

1. Stilles Lesen der Arbeitsanweisung
2. Verständnisklärung mit einem Partner
3. Erklärung der Arbeitsanweisung durch einen S im Klassenverband
4. Bestätigung oder Korrektur durch L

Andere Möglichkeiten sind:
1. L demonstriert die Vorgehensweise (ggf. mit einem S) anhand von Gesten, einem Produkt oder Beispielen.
2. Die Arbeitsanweisung wird gemeinsam im Plenum gelesen und erläutert.

Kugellager

siehe Double circle

Lautschulung

Für die Lautschulung bieten sich verschiedene Techniken an:

1. Chorsprechen: Es bietet besonders zurückhaltenden S eine gute Übungsmöglichkeit. Hoher Sprachumsatz, da alle S gleichzeitig sprechen. L spricht jeweils vor und gibt dann ein Zeichen (z. B. Gestik: Hand ans Ohr halten), auf das hin S nachsprechen.
2. Nachsprechen im Teilchor: L teilt Gruppen ein (z. B. Tischgruppen, Sitzreihen, Jungen/Mädchen), die auf das Signal hin nachsprechen. Diese Methode dient dazu, Fehler genauer zu lokalisieren.
3. Einzelsprechen: Dies bietet die Möglichkeit, eine individuelle Korrektur durchführen zu können.

Nachsprechen sollte generell abwechslungsreich gestaltet werden – durch Lautstärke, Geschwindigkeit, verstellte Stimme *(like a parrot, like a computer)*. Neben der Lautschulung von einzelnen Wörtern können auch ganze Sätze nachgesprochen werden, um das Intonationsmuster der Fremdsprache zu üben.

Lerntempoduett *(Bus stop)*

Die Durchführung eines Lerntempoduetts bietet sich an, um Ergebnisse verschiedener Übungen in PA vergleichen zu lassen. Ein Lerntempoduett trägt der unterschiedlichen Bearbeitungsgeschwindigkeit der S Rechnung. Ziel sollte es sein, die Aufgaben gründlich zu erledigen, und nicht, alle Aufgaben zeitlich zu schaffen.

1. Die S bearbeiten die erste Aufgabe in EA.
2. Wenn ein S fertig ist, steht er auf und wartet auf den nächsten, der aufsteht. Die beiden besprechen ihre Ergebnisse in PA.
3. Anschließend arbeiten beide in EA an der nächsten Aufgabe weiter. Sie stehen wieder auf, wenn sie fertig sind, und tun sich erneut mit dem S, der als nächstes fertig ist, zusammen.

Falls die Arbeitsgeschwindigkeiten der S sehr stark voneinander abweichen, sollten Handzeichen vereinbart werden, damit sich die S mit der richtigen Aufgabe treffen können.

Lesegemurmel

siehe Buzz reading

Lesetechniken

Die Leseintention legt fest, wie tief die S in einen Text eindringen müssen, um die gewünschten Informationen zu erhalten. Die S müssen lernen, dass die Tiefe des Textverständnisses eng an die gestellten Aufgaben gebunden ist, und abhängig davon eine passende Lesetechnik auswählen und anwenden. Für L bedeutet dies sorgfältig zu prüfen, welche Intention die Aufgaben zum Leseverstehen haben und welche Leseleistungen die S zur Lösung jeweils erbringen müssen.
Die folgenden Lesetechniken eignen sich für unterschiedliche Aufgabenstellungen. Als überfliegende Lesetechniken stehen sie dem vollständigen Lesen eines Textes, dem *Reading for detail*, gegenüber:

Skimming: Das *Skimming* stellt eine erste, oberflächliche Beschäftigung mit dem Text dar. S überfliegen Überschriften, Fotos/Zeichnungen oder die Aufmachung des Textes. Dies gibt ihnen z. B. Aufschluss über das Thema oder den möglichen Inhalt und zeigt, ob der Text für sie interessant ist oder ihnen zum Lösen einer Aufgabe nützt.

Speed reading: Beim *Speed reading* geht es darum, einen Text zu überfliegen, einen groben Eindruck zu gewinnen und nach *key words* zu suchen. *Speed reading* bedeutet, mit einem Blick mehr Wörter zu erfassen als gewöhnlich, um eine höhere Lesegeschwindigkeit zu erreichen.

Scanning: Das *Scanning* ist eine suchende Lesetechnik, die auf Schlüsselwörter und -gedanken ausgerichtet ist. Dabei gehen die S von einer Frage oder Aufgabe aus und überfliegen den Text, bis sie die gesuchte Information gefunden haben. Auch hier ist es nicht das Ziel, den Inhalt des gesamten Textes oder jedes unbekannte Wort zu verstehen.

Market place activity
(Marktplatz)

Bei der kooperativen Lernform *Market place activity* sprechen die S mit verschiedenen Partnern über ein vorgegebenes Thema. Ablauf:

1. Die S bewegen sich frei im Klassenraum. L stellt eine Aufgabe, die S in einem vorgegebenen Zeitrahmen bearbeiten. Dieser kann durch ein akustisches Signal wie z. B. das Abspielen und Anhalten von Musik begrenzt werden.
2. Auf das vereinbarte Signal hin bleiben die S stehen und tun sich mit dem S zusammen, der vor ihnen steht. Die Partner tauschen sich über das Thema bzw. die Aufgabe aus. Je nach Aufgabenart machen sich die S Notizen.
3. Auf das erneute Signal durch L wechseln die S ihren Partner, sodass sie in einem begrenzten Zeitraum mit möglichst vielen S sprechen.
4. Die Ergebnisse können in einem anschließenden Unterrichtsgespräch ausgewertet werden.

Die *Market place activity* ist eine Form der Milling-around activity.

Mediation
(Sprachmittlung)

Vermittlungsstrategie zwischen Gesprächspartnern, die sich nicht direkt sprachlich verständigen können. Im Englischunterricht bedeutet dies die zusammenfassende, paraphrasierende Wiedergabe eines Hör- oder Lesetextes in der jeweils anderen Sprache. Bei der *Mediation* werden vom Sprachmittler sowohl rezeptive Kompetenzen (einen Ausgangstext zu verstehen) als auch produktive Kompetenzen (einen Ausgangstext in der anderen Sprache wiederzugeben) und häufig auch interkulturelle Kenntnisse verlangt.
L kann den S zur Unterstützung folgende Leitregeln geben:
- Keine Wort-für-Wort-Übersetzung!
- Freie Wiedergabe der wichtigsten Informationen!
- Nicht alle Details wiedergeben!

Meldekette

Die Meldekette dient der Förderung der Schüler-Interaktion. Sie ist in Plenumsphasen universell einsetzbar, z. B. zur Auswertung von Ergebnissen oder zur Besprechung von Aufgaben. Die S rufen sich gegenseitig auf, wobei jeder S einen Satz oder eine Antwort nennt. L greift nur bei Bedarf korrigierend ein.

Metakognition

Metakognition bedeutet, dass S über ihr Lernen nachdenken, Strategien und Methoden reflektieren und daraus die für sie geeigneten Lernstrategien ableiten. Bereits zu Beginn des Sprachenlernens ist es wichtig, dass S hinterfragen, warum sie in einer Lernsituation so vorgehen, wie sie es tun. Die Erkenntnis dieses Prozesses soll den S helfen, das Sprachenlernen bewusst zu erlernen.

Milling-around activity

Bei dieser Methode bewegen die S sich innerhalb einer vorgegebenen Zeitspanne frei im Klassenraum und begeben sich wieder auf ihren Platz, sobald sie die relevanten Informationen erfragt haben. Auswertung im Plenum. Market place activity

Mindmap

Eine Mindmap dient den S als „Gedankenkarte“. Sie ordnen darin ihre Ideen übersichtlich an, wobei Zusammengehöriges beieinander steht, alle Ideen vernetzt werden können und Farben sowie Zeichnungen Wichtiges hervorheben. Mindmaps können individuell und in der Gruppe erstellt werden und eignen sich als Anregung für mündliche und schriftliche Äußerungen. Mögliches Vorgehen:

1. Die Ideen werden zuerst ungeordnet gesammelt (z. B. auf Kärtchen).
2. Im zweiten Schritt werden Oberbegriffe für die Ideen gefunden (z. B. auf farbigen Kärtchen).
3. Im letzten Schritt visualisieren die S diese Grundlagen systematisch in einer Mindmap.

Mitleseverfahren

Beim Mitleseverfahren hören die S während des Lesens eines neuen Textes diesen zugleich. Die Aktivierung des visuellen und des auditiven Kanals (Mehrkanallernen) ermöglicht eine enge Verknüpfung von Laut- und Schriftbild, sodass unbekannte Lexeme nachhaltiger verarbeitet werden können. Das Mitleseverfahren ist didaktisch dem Leseverstehen zugeordnet, da die primäre Sprachaufnahme über die Textvorlage erfolgt.
Das laute Lesen dient der Ausspracheschulung und nicht dem Leseverstehen, da durch die Konzentration auf die phonologische Oberfläche das Erfassen des Textinhalts erschwert wird. Als Faustregel gilt: Das laute Lesen sollte immer erst eingesetzt werden, nachdem ein Text bereits inhaltlich erarbeitet worden und unbekannter Wortschatz erschlossen worden ist.

Mnemotechniken

Unter dem Begriff Mnemotechniken werden verschiedene Methoden des Gedächtnistrainings zusammengefasst. Im Fremdsprachenunterricht eingesetzt, helfen sie S, sich Worte und Informationen über die Schritte des Rekodierens, Assoziierens und schließlich des Abrufens besser einprägen zu können. Häufig verwendete Mnemotechniken sind das Akrostichon, das Finden von Ersatzwörtern, das Einprägen von Merkversen, die Assoziation von Begriffen/Schriftbild und Bildkarten (Flashcards) und das Memo-Spiel.

Note making

Das Anfertigen von Notizen ist eine Methodenkompetenz, die auch im Alltag bedeutsam ist. Das *Note making* ist für die S eine wichtige Fertigkeit zum Generieren und Organisieren von Informationen und Ideen. Die dazu notwendigen Arbeitsschritte reichen vom Sammeln, Sichten und Ordnen der Notizen bis zum Überarbeiten und Anwenden von Stichwörtern, Themen etc. Für das Ordnen von Notizen eignet sich auch eine Mindmap.

Note taking

Das *Note taking* ist eine Strategie des Hörverstehens. Wenn möglich, versuchen die S zunächst aus Titel oder Überschrift und ggf. aus Fotos, Bildern oder Grafiken erste Informationen über den Hörtext abzuleiten. Sie stellen sich darauf ein und bauen inhaltliche Erwartungen auf. Während des Hörens machen sie sich Notizen. Diese dienen ihnen dazu, wichtige *key words* oder Ideen aus dem Hörtext festzuhalten. Grundlegendes in Form von Stichpunkten aufzuschreiben, ermöglicht nicht nur einen besseren Zugang zu einem Text, sondern den Zugriff auf das Notierte an späterer Stelle. Insgesamt wird dadurch das Lernen effektiver.

L kann folgende Tipps geben:
- Höre auf das, was gesagt wird und wie es gesagt wird.
- Halte einen Stift bereit und schreibe mit. Nicht jedes Wort ist wichtig.
- Nutze Abkürzungen und Symbole beim Notieren (z. B. Sternchen, Ausrufezeichen, Fragezeichen).
- Achte auf Schlüsselwörter und -sätze, besonders solche, die wiederholt werden.

Numbered heads together

Diese kooperative Lernform ermöglicht eine hohe Schüleraktivierung, da die S, die das Gruppenergebnis präsentieren, per Zufallsprinzip ausgewählt werden und somit jeder S Verantwortung für das Gruppenergebnis übernehmen muss. Zunächst bildet L Gruppen (Gruppenbildung). Innerhalb dieser Gruppen erhält nun jeder S eine Zahl (abhängig von der Gruppengröße). L (oder auch eine der Gruppen) stellt nun eine Aufgabe, die die Gruppen gemeinsam bewältigen. Das Startsignal für die Beratungsphase ist *Numbered heads together!* Nach Ablauf einer zuvor festgelegten Zeit beendet L die Beratung und wählt durch Nennung einer Zahl die Person aus, die aufsteht und für die Gruppe antwortet. Pro richtige Antwort erhält die Gruppe einen Punkt.
Die einzelnen Gruppen können unterschiedliche, aber auch gleiche Aufgaben bearbeiten. Um bei gleichen Aufgaben zu verhindern, dass die ausgewählten S mit der gleichen Zahl die Antworten der anderen Gruppe mithören, verlassen sie zunächst den Klassenraum.

Optional help

Bei der *Optional help* handelt es sich um eine Form der Differenzierung (Binnendifferenziertes Arbeiten), bei der die S individuell bei Bedarf eine zusätzliche Lernhilfe verwenden können. Dies kann z. B. ein Hilfsblatt sein, das auf dem Pult bereit liegt und dort eingesehen oder mitgenommen werden kann. Es kann zudem eine zusätzliche Hilfe auf den Arbeitsmaterialien sein. Ideal ist es, wenn die *Optional help* zunächst nicht für S sichtbar ist (z. B. als umgeknickter Wort-/Lösungspool am unteren Blattrand) und sie nur dann darauf zurückgreifen, wenn sie Hilfe benötigen.

Partner check

Die Methode des *Partner check* eignet sich besonders für den Einsatz nach Fragestellungen durch L im Frontalunterricht. Dabei sprechen sich S in PA (z. B. mit dem Nachbarn) ab, bevor sie ihre Antwort im Plenum geben. Dieses Verfahren gibt besonders schwächeren S mehr Sicherheit, bevor sie sich melden. Durch den *Partner check* werden alle S zur Auseinandersetzung mit den Lerninhalten gezwungen. Zudem bietet die Methode Abwechslung in frontalen Unterrichtsphasen, erhöht die Aktivität im anschließenden Unterricht und ist schnell und flexibel einsetzbar.

Partner talk

Die Methode des *Partner talk* ist eine einfache Methode, die sich an vielen Stellen des Lernprozesses einsetzen lässt und die dazu dient, Schüleraktivität und Sprechzeit der Lernenden zu erhöhen. S tauschen sich dabei kurz (oft sind ein bis zwei Minuten ausreichend) mit einem Partner über einen vorgegebenen Sprechanlass (bestimmte Fragestellung, Vorerfahrungen etc.) aus. Die Fragestellungen sollten – wenn nicht im SB enthalten – an der Tafel oder auf Folie festgehalten werden, damit S darauf zurückgreifen können. In lernschwächeren Gruppen sollte L zusätzlich einige situationsbezogene Redemittel anbieten.

Peer correction

siehe Correcting circle

Phasen des Schreibprozesses

Zur nachhaltigen Schreibförderung sollten S bei der Textproduktion grundsätzlich folgende drei Phasen durchlaufen:

1. Entwerfen *(Brainstorming)*: Die S sammeln Ideen, z. B. in einer Mindmap oder bei einem stummen Schreibgespräch *(Round robin)*.
2. Schreiben: Die S verfassen auf dieser Grundlage einen ersten Entwurf. Dieser sollte entweder von L oder in höheren Klassenstufen durch Mit-S, z. B. in Form eines *Correcting circle*, korrigiert werden.
3. Überarbeiten: Auf der Grundlage der Korrekturanmerkungen fertigen die S eine Reinschrift an.

Im Sinne einer Differenzierung (Binnendifferenziertes Arbeiten) ist es oftmals hilfreich oder gar notwendig, entsprechende Schreibhilfen oder Sprachmuster bereitzustellen.

Read-and-look-up technique

Diese Lesetechnik dient der Förderung des freien Sprechens und bildet für die S einen behutsamen Übergang zwischen dem Ablesen und Vortragen von Texten, Informationen und Inhalten. Der präsentierende S hält die Vorlage in den Händen und liest sich einen (Teil-)Satz still durch, bevor er die Klasse oder seinen Partner anschaut und den Satz aus dem Gedächtnis wiedergibt. Dabei ist es wichtig, dass S erst dann spricht, wenn er Blickkontakt hergestellt hat. Diese Technik bereitet den freien Vortrag bzw. die Präsentation (auch mithilfe von Stichwortzetteln) vor
und hilft unsicheren S, Inhalte vor dem Plenum darzustellen.
L kann die *Read-and-look-up technique* zunächst anhand eines beliebigen Textes demonstrieren. Die S üben danach mit geeigneten kurzen Texten, wobei der zuhörende Partner darauf achtet, dass nicht abgelesen, sondern vor dem Sprechen Blickkontakt hergestellt wird.

Reading circle

Beim *Reading circle* lesen alle S den gleichen Text, wobei jeder S eine andere Rolle übernimmt oder sich auf einen bestimmten Aspekt des Textes konzentriert. Die S schreiben dazu jeweils Informationen, Aussagen oder Assoziationen auf ein Blatt, das anschließend ausgelegt oder aufgehängt wird. Sie gehen herum, lesen die Beiträge der anderen S und tragen ihre Kommentare dazu ein. Die Eindrücke der S werden anschließend im Plenum diskutiert.

***Right/wrong cards* (Antwortkärtchen)**

Der Einsatz von *Right/wrong cards* eignet sich besonders zur Überprüfung von Aussagen zum Textverständnis. Die Karten können sowohl zur Lese- als auch Hörverstehenskontrolle eingesetzt werden. Ihr Einsatz ermöglicht eine valide Erfassung des Detailverständnisses und erfordert dabei keine eigene Sprachproduktion der S.
L stellt den S Karten aus farbigem Karton zur Verfügung (alternativ auch farbige Gegenstände, z. B. Stifte). Es wird vereinbart, dass grün für *right* und rot für *wrong* sowie ggf. blau für *not in the text* steht. Nachdem L eine Aussage zum Text vorgelesen hat, halten die S auf Kommando eine Karte in die Höhe. L erhält auf diese Weise auf einen Blick eine breite Rückmeldung darüber, ob der jeweilige Textinhalt von den S verstanden wurde. Wenn sich hier größere Abweichungen zeigen, sollte L dies zum Anlass nehmen, einen erneuten Lese-/Hörauftrag zu stellen, um das gesuchte Detail zu erfassen (selektives Lese-/Hörverstehen).
Das synchrone Ausführen auf Kommando ist wichtig, damit sich unsichere S nicht an ihren Mit-S orientieren.
Wenn die Methode mehrfach eingesetzt wurde, können lernstärkere S die L-Rolle übernehmen.

***Scenic play* (Szenisches Spielen)**

Durch die Methode des *Scenic play* werden kognitive Fähigkeiten, emotionale und körperliche Ausdruckskräfte sowie manuelle und künstlerische Fertigkeiten der S entwickelt und geschult. Das szenische Spielen von Geschichten bettet die Fremdsprache in einen Kontext ein, an dem die S selbst mit allen Sinnen beteiligt sind. L sollte vorher mit den S besprechen, was für das Nachspielen benötigt wird, und dann die Rollen verteilen. Benötigte Requisiten können oft als Zeichnungen an der Tafel dargestellt werden oder es finden Gegenstände aus dem Klassenraum Verwendung.

Schreibkonferenz

siehe Correcting circle

Schüler als Experten

siehe Binnendifferenziertes Arbeiten

Semantisierungstechniken

Um den S neuen Wortschatz zu erschließen, können unterschiedliche Techniken der Semantisierung angewendet werden. Im Sinne deiktischer Semantisierung sollte neuer Wortschatz grundsätzlich nicht isoliert, sondern immer in einem Satz- oder Sinnzusammenhang eingeführt werden.

Realgegenstände: Realia eignen sich hervorragend zur anschaulichen Vermittlung neuer Lexeme (vorrangig konkreter Begriffe). Geht es z. B. um das Wort *pencil case*, so hält L ein Federmäppchen hoch und sagt: *This is a pencil case.* Wort und Bedeutung können so nachhaltig miteinander verknüpft werden. Siehe auch Flashcards.

Mimik, Gestik und Demonstration: Durch den Einsatz von Mimik und Gestik kann den S die Bedeutung entsprechender Lexeme nachhaltig vermittelt werden.

- Beispiel Mimik: L macht ein zorniges Gesicht, um das Wort *angry* zu demonstrieren. Dies kann auch verbal unterstützt werden, z. B. *Hey! Stop that!*
- Beispiel Gestik: Wenn es um das Wort *first* geht, streckt L den Daumen nach oben und sagt: *It's the first morning in London.*
- Beispiel Demonstration: Das Wort *open* wird eindeutig demonstriert, indem L das Fenster öffnet und dabei sagt: *Let's open the window.* Noch lernwirksamer ist es, wenn dazu das Lexem *close* demonstriert und eingeführt wird: *Now let's close the window.*

Logischer Bezug: Mit einer Definition des Lexems kann L dies ebenfalls einführen, z. B.
A dog is an animal with four legs and a tail. It barks. Weitere logische Bezüge können über Dreisätze *(A man has a mouth, a bird has a beak, ...)* oder den Rückschluss vom Ganzen aufs Einzelne *(a week = 7 days)* hergestellt werden.

Lexikalische Bezüge: Diese können mithilfe von Synonymen oder Antonymen *(shop – store; young ≠ old)*, einer Zuordnung *(Dogs, cats and rabbits are pets.)* oder einer Herleitung *(happy – happiness)* hergestellt werden.

Der Rückgriff auf die Muttersprache sollte nur sehr selten erfolgen. In einigen Ausnahmefällen kann dieser allerdings hilfreich sein:

- um auf orthographische Ähnlichkeiten aufmerksam zu machen (*theatre* – Theater)
- um phonetische Ähnlichkeiten hervorzuheben (*shoe* – Schuh).

Sprachmittlung siehe Mediation

Szenisches Spielen siehe Scenic play

Think-Pair-Share Diese kooperative Lernform dient den S dazu, von einer individuellen zu einer gemeinsamen Lösung zu gelangen. Ablauf:

1. EA: S denken allein über die Aufgabenstellung nach und machen sich ggf. Notizen.
2. PA: Zwei S besprechen ihre Notizen und kommen zu einer gemeinsamen Lösung.
3. GA: Zwei Paare bilden eine Vierergruppe, die gemeinsam ihre Lösungen bespricht. Eine andere Möglichkeit ist, dass die Paare ihre Lösungen im Plenum vorstellen.

L sollte für jeden Arbeitsschritt ein Zeitlimit setzen.

Total Physical Response (TPR) Das Konzept der *Total Physical Response (TPR)* beruht auf der Einbeziehung von Körpersprache und Bewegung, um das Hörverstehen der S zu fördern. *TPR* spricht in besonderem Maße S mit Sprechhemmungen oder geringem Sprachinventar an, die mithilfe der Methode die Fremdsprache handelnd umsetzen und so Erfolgserlebnisse erzielen.
S reagieren auf eine Anweisung von L oder einem anderen S nonverbal, indem sie diese in Bewegung umsetzen. Die Anweisungen sollten z. B. durch Gestik oder den Einsatz von Realgegenständen verständlich gemacht werden. Durch mehrfache Wiederholung kann die Behaltensleistung gesteigert werden, indem Handlung und Sprache nachhaltig miteinander verknüpft werden.

Worterschließungstechniken Um sich Worte in der Fremdsprache ohne die Hilfe von L zu erschließen, können sich S verschiedener Techniken, die ihnen aus der Muttersprache geläufig sind, bedienen. So können sie Worte aus dem Kontext erschließen, sich Bedeutungen aus der Wortzusammensetzung herleiten oder über eine phonologische oder grafische Ähnlichkeit des Wortes in der Muttersprache auf die Bedeutung schließen.

Wortschatzsemantisierung Semantisierungstechniken

Titelbild
Trevor Burrows Photography Ltd, Plymouth

Illustrationen
Roland Beier: (Umschlaginnenseite vorne: Ireland Castle icon (M) auf der Karte); **Carlos Borrell Eiköter:** (Umschlaginnenseite Karte (M)); **Christian Görke:** (S. 52/53 Hintergrund Karte); **Jeongsook Lee:** (Umschlaginnenseite vorne: alle icons außer Ireland Castle(M); S. 100, S. 105; S. 120; S. 147 Bild 1+2; S. 159; S. 160 unten; S. 161 box+cards; 162 oben; S. 165; S. 166 oben+pony-Bild; S. 168 oben re.; S. 169 unten li.+re.; S. 175; S. 179; S. 180; S. 182; S. 183; S. 185; S. 186; S. 187; S. 188; S. 189; S. 190; S. 191; S. 194; S 195; S. 196; S. 197; S. 198; S. 200; S. 201; S. 202; S. 204; S. 205; S. 207; S. 2030; S. 231); **David Norman:** (S. 70 oben re.; S. 72; S. 86; S. 93; S. 152 oben und unten; S. 153 oben; S. 154 oben; S. 156; S. 157; S. 158); **Elwood H. Smith, Rhinebeck, New York:** (S. 5; S. 9 unten re.; S. 17 Sandy; S. 21; S. 22; S. 26 Africa pencil case; S. 30 unten; S. 31; S. 44 My house; S. 46; S. 48 unten; S. 49 oben und Mitte; S. 59 unten; S. 67; S. 76 unten; S. 87; S. 104; S. 109 unten; S. 129; 130 unten; S. 139; S. 150; S. 151; 167; S. 168 oben li. + unten; S. 169+170 Cyril + Sandy; Umschlaginnenseite hinten); **Steffen Wolff:** (S. 6 unten re.; S. 7 oben rechts; Doppelseite 8 + 9; S. 14; S. 15; S. 16 unten, S. 18 (1+2); S. 23; S. 24; S. 30 oben; S. 32; S. 36; S. 38; S. 39 oben und unten; S. 41; S. 42; S. 43; S. 45; S. 48 oben; S. 50 Mitte; S. 51; S. 54; S. 55 oben; S. 56; S. 58; S. 59 oben; S. 62 oben; S. 63; S. 77; S. 80; S. 81; S. 88; S. 94; S. 98 oben und unten li.; S. 99 li.; S. 112; S. 113; S. 114; S. 115; S. 118; S. 119; S. 121 oben; S. 123; S. 126; S. 127; S.; 130; S. 132; S. 136); **Cornelsen/Klein & Halm Grafikdesign GbR:** (S. 50, S. 80, S. 98 unten rechts; S. 144; S. 199); **Cornelsen Verlagsarchiv:** (mind map S. 44; S. 52; S. 89; **Arnold:** mind map S. 131, S. 140, S. 162).

Fotos
Alamy Images: (**S. 5** unten li. two persons on the right(M): Golden Pixels LLC; **S. 7** oben li.: Brian Mitchell; **S. 8** unten: Picture Partners; **S. 174** chemistry: Juice Images); **Trevor Burrows Photography Ltd, Plymouth:** (**S. 4; S. 5** oben li., unten li. three persons on the left side in front of the house (M); **S. 6; S. 10** (1-4); **S. 11** (1); S. 12 Berry; **S. 13** oben re.; **S. 16** (A + B); **S. 17** (C + D); **S. 18; S. 20; S. 23; S. 24; S. 25** oben; **S. 28; S. 31; S. 32** unten; **S. 34** (1+ 2) + unten; **S. 37** Zoe, Conor + Mel; **S. 40** Ellie; **S. 46; S. 52; S. 53** (2 + 3); **S. 55** (B+ C); **S. 60** (1+2) (M), (3); **S. 61** (4)(M), (5-7); **S. 63; S. 70** oben li. und unten re.; **S. 71** Mitte li. und unten li.; **S. 74; S. 75** (A-D + E)(M); **S. 76** oben; **S. 79; S. 82** (E); **S. 87; S. 88** unten re.; **S. 90** (A)(M) Mr Osmanovic, (B); **S. 91** (D); **S. 92** unten; **S. 93; S. 96** (A-D); **S. 97** Adam + Ellie; **S. 105** Adam; **S. 107; S. 110** oben; **S. 121** (2, 4, 5, 6); **S. 124; S. 126; S. 131; S. 133** unten; **S. 139; S. 143; S. 166** Mitte re. + unten; **S. 169** oben; **S. 170** oben re. + unten; **S. 171;** Umschlaginnenseite hinten); **ClipDealer:** (**S. 180**); **Cornelsen Verlagsarchiv/Bensmann:** (**S. 25** Mitte; **S. 65** The Reel Cinema; **S. 90** (C); **S. 96** (E); **S. 102** (A-H); **S. 114** li. oben; **S. 125; S. 145; S. 148; S. 149** alle Bilder außer re. unten); **Cornelsen Verlagsarchiv/Griebel:** (**S. 10** unten li.; **S. 11** cycling; **S. 147** oben; **S. 149** re. unten); **Cornelsen Verlagsarchiv/Zieschang:** (**S. 16**/17 Hintergrund; **S. 121** Bild 7); **Cornelsen Verlagsarchiv/Rockfinch Ltd./Claire Cunningham (Filmstills):** (**S. 29; S. 47; S. 65** oben, Mitte, Hoe, Lido, aquarium + shopping centre; **S. 85; S. 103; S. 117** oben und A, B, C, D sowie unten); **Fotolia:** (**S. 119** oben li.: Rtimages; **S. 173** inline-skating: Kathrin39, **S. 181** oben; **S. 191** oben: Tamas Vargyasi; **S. 194** oben: Michelle Rhodes); Getty Images: (**S. 5** oben re. + **S. 35** Bild 7: Bob Stevens; **S. 154** unten: Tony Robins; **S. 155** unten: Bryn Lennon); **Jason Marker Photography, Chelmsford:** (**S. 108** smuggler's cave); **mauritius images:** (**S. 12** crocodile: Alamy/moodboard; **S. 13** Spielkonsole: Alamy/Martin Lee, Spielzeugauto: Alamy/Oleksiy Maksymenko Photography; **S. 19** Schal: Alamy/kris Mercer; **S. 34** (5): Alamy/Elizabeth Whiting & Associates; **S. 35** (3)(M): Alamy/Andrew Butterton, Bild 4: Alamy/Brian Hoffman, (8): Alamy/Lorraine Traynor; **S. 39** (1): Alamy RF/Elizabeth Whiting & Associates; **S. 53** (5): Alamy/Neil Cooper; **S. 60** Vater li. in Bild 1(M): Alamy RF/Golden Pixels LLC, Grace li in Bild 2(M): Alamy RF/Golden Pixels LLC; **S. 65** market: Alamy/Marc Hill; **S. 66** (4): Alamy/Susan Fisher Plotner-VIEW; **S. 70** unten li.: Alamy/The Photolibrary Wales; **S. 73** (A): Alamy/Kuttig – People, (B): Alamy/Stephen Bardens; **S. 82** (A)(M) roter Rahmen Warnschild: Alamy/yuriy yuryev; **S. 90** (A)(M): Alamy/Marc Hill; **S. 90**/91 Hintergrundbild: Alamy/Marc Hill; **S. 108** (A) ferry: Alamy/Brian; Mitchell, unten li.: Alamy/PulpFoto, (A) on the ferry: Alamy/Iain Davidson Photographic; **S. 113** Mitte: Alamy Stock Photo/David Cairns; **S. 114** re. oben: Alamy/Ian Woolcock; **S. 174** oben Spielkonsole: Alamy/Martin Lee, Spielzeugauto: Alamy/Oleksiy Maksymenko Photography, **S. 174** unten ethics: Alamy/Eyebyte, home economics li. + re. + woodwork: Alamy/MBI, physics: Image Source/Alys Tomlinson; **S. 175** (M): Alamy/Big Cheese Photo LLC; **S. 176** police station: Alamy/Justin Kase zsixz; S.177 sleep: Alamy/Maximilian Weinzierl); **Okapia KG: S. 12** rat: J-L Klein & M-L Hubert); **Plymouth Music Zone (PMZ):** (**S. 95** logo); **shutterstock:** (**S. 9** unten li.: Wow; **S. 11** (2): karelnoppe, (3): Andrey_Popov, (4): hurricanehank, (5): pixelheadphoto digitalskillet, (6): wavebreakmedia, (7): lzf, (8): ZoranOrcik, chess: Chekyravaa, drawing: Hoika Mikhail; **S. 12** cat: Irina Bondareva, bear: red-feniks, monkey: Simone van den Berg, bird: Bildagentur Zoonar GmbH, elephant: Michael Potter11, snake: Xavier Fargas, dog (oben): Eastimages, fish: Ekaterina V. Borisova, rabbit: Pentium5, hamster: Anastasia Solovykh, tiger: Tiago Jorge da Silva Estima; dog (unten): Eric Isselee; **S. 13** Gitarre: Lebedinski Vladislav, Tasche: iPostnikov, Buch: Beautiful landscape, DVD player: HSNphotography, laptop: Elnur, Uhr: Ijansempoi, Roller: Mile Atanasov, Fernseher: gordana, Ball: Luis Louro, Handy: Billion Photos, Mädchen unten re.: Andrey_Popov; **S. 16** Hund in Bild A(M): Erik Lam; **S. 19** oben: Shooting Star Studio, unten li.: Monkey Business Images, Tim: Andrea Slatter, Hund: Eric Isselee, sisters: Marco Govel, happy emoticon: In-Finity, unhappy emoticon: Dawn Hudson; **S. 21** unten: Africa Studio; **S. 25** unten re.: Alhovik; **S. 26** pencil sharpener: Gelpi, rubber: Chet, ruler: David Brimm, 10 pens: Volodymyr Krasyuk, 10 pencils: Evgeniia Speshneva, pencil case: Brooke Becker, calculator: photastic, exercise book: Lim Yong Hian, diary: Shebeko, hole punch: AlexAvich; **S. 27**: Aleksey Sagitov; **S. 32** oben: CREATISTA, happy emoticon: In-Finity, unhappy emoticon: Dawn Hudson, Glühbirne (Illu): Marish; **S. 34** Hintergrund Skizze: Hitdelight, (6): Chertanova; **S. 35** Hintergrund Skizze: Alchena, Hochstuhl in Bild 3: ekipaj, Schüssel in Bild 3: Elena Schweitzer, (A): linerpics, Bild B: KN, Bild C: Schaefer Elvira; **S. 37** Pete: Juriah Mosin, Jackie: Olga Sapegina, Steve: Spectral-Design, Alisha: Maridav, Finn: leungchopan; **S. 39** (2): Margo Harrison, (3): Neamov, (4): Viorel Sima, (5): Peter Gudella, (6): Hong Vo, (7): Room27, (8): Luisa Leal Photography, (9): italianestro, (10): terekhov igor, (11 li.): Petrafler, (11 re.): zeber, (12): Lasse_Sven; **S. 40** Steve: Spectral-Design; **S. 49** unten: hfng; **S. 50** oben: Monkey Business Images, skateboard: IgorijArt, bike: Hi-Vector, Fußball: Slobodan Djajic, Oberteil und schwarzer Gürtel: Africa Studio, Tennisschläger: Elena100, Golf: NotionPic, Rugby Ball: joingate, snowboard: sabri deniz kizil; **S. 55** (A): Serg64, (D): DenisProduction.com, Sportschuhe: Ijansempoi, Schuhe: Turumtaev Ildar, Socken: Alexandr Makarov, Rock, Pullover, Blazer + Hose: Karkas, T-Shirt: Boleslaw Kubica, Kravatte: Kulish Viktoria, Hoodie: sagir; **S. 60** oben re.; **S. 61** Junge im roten Shirt in Bild 4: Tomasz Trojanowski; **S. 62** Münzen: Atiwat Witthayanurut, Pfundnote: iweta0077; **S. 64** (A) Tänzer: ShustrikS. Bühne: Patricia Hofmeester, (B) Feuerwerk: Beautiful landscape, (C) Wasser: Strejman, dive show: Greg Amptman, 4d cinema: Julien Tromeur, tiger shark: frantisekhojdysz; **S. 65** emoticons: Anatolir; **S. 66** (1): HABRDA, (2): Rudmer Zwerver, (3): joyfull, (5): s_oleg, (6): OlegD, (7): crystal51, (8): Andrey Burstein; **S. 68** li.: SergiyN, re.: Gelpi; **S. 69**: Zanna Pesnina; **S. 70** Mitte li.: Elena Elisseeva; **S. 71** Esel oben li.: Graeme Dawes; (1): jokerpro, (2): Ivonne Wierink, (3): aleks.k, (4): robertoserratore, (5): Dmitry Pichugin, (6): pgaborphotos, (7): aabeele, (8): Tom Grundy, (9): Alexruss, (10): Nataliia Melnychuk, (11): Maslov Dmitry, (12): gillmar, unten re.: Natalia Sheinkin; **S. 72** Uhr: Slavoljub Pantelic; **S. 73** (C): Michael Ransburg, (D):

joyfuldesigns, (E): cynoclub, (F): fpolat69; **S. 74** happy emoticon: In-Finity, unhappy emoticon: Dawn Hudson; **S. 75** Hund in Bild E(M): Eric Isselee; **S. 77** unten: Olga Popko; **S. 78** oben: Grigoryeva Liubov Dmitrievna, unten: S-F; **S. 81** Handy: hfng, Masken: Alhovik; **S. 82** (A) (M) Warnschild No Dogs; **S. 83** Briefpapeir: Abstractor; **S. 84** dog, gibbon, hamster, snake, rabbit, goldfish: Klara Viskova, donkey: Albert Ziganshin, crocodile: Memo Angeles, hyena: Virinaflora, llama: Albert Ziganshin, penguin: Cory Thoman; **S. 89** budgie: Wang LiQiang, elephant: Four Oaks, guinea pig: E. Spek, tiger: Kitch Bain, polar bear: VikOl, happy emoticon: In-Finity, unhappy emoticon: Dawn Hudson; **S. 92** (A + D): Nitr, (B): Joe Gough, (C): Olga Nayashkova, (E): ER_09, (F): ronstik, (G): Vlue, Bild H: Feng Yu, (I): M. Unal Ozmen, (J): urbanbuzz; **S. 95** Hintergrund des Plakates + DJ: sita ram, Guitarist: oorka; **S. 97** (1): Tomasz Trojanowski, (2): Pressmaster, (3): Fotokostic, (4): Kim Ruoff, (5): qingqing, (6): Monkey Business Images; **S. 99** re.: freelanceartist; **S. 101** (A): Leewiew Ponkun, (B + C): ganpanjanee, (D): Andrey Mertsalov, Mitte: ag1100, unten: Gelpi; **S. 102** oben: Jen Bray Photogaphy; **S. 103** dancer: Irina Kolesnichenko, singer: Sorbis, guitar player: AZ; **S. 104** crab: haveseen, seagull: Dan Costa; **S. 107** happy emoticon: In-Finity, unhappy emoticon: Dawn Hudson; **S. 108** (B) Hintergrund: Dan Thornberg, canoe trip oben: CroMary, canoe trip unten: sianc, dog: Annette Shaff; **S. 109** (C) alle: Hurst Photo, (D) oben li.: ovb64, oben re.: Anton Watman, (D) unten: Juriah Mosin; **S. 110** scones: nein, water: Paddington, crisps: ever, apples: Smit, cake: Picsfive, chocolate: urfin, biscuits: Aaron Amat, orange juice: Mark Herreid, oranges: rook76, sandwiches: Africa Studio, sausages: Kitch Bain; **S. 111** suncream: Onur Kocamaz, towels: arrogant, camera: Chiyacat, shorts: Chiyacat, umbrella: Fotocrisis, bodyboard: aliaksei kruhlenia, speakers: Tatiana Popova, phone: Ungor, picnic blanket: Alexander Mazurkevich, swimsuit: Ruslan Kudrin, football: Olga Popova, frisbee: cretolamna, tube: Fotokkden; **S. 113/114/115** Pergament: Anan Kaewkhammul; **S. 115** Masken: Alhovik; **S. 116** (1): Roman Sotola, (2): ghenadie, (3): Rena Design, (4): Albina Tiplyashina; **S. 117** (1): Dmitry_T, (2): Ivonne Wierink, (3): Olga Nayashkova, (4): nito, (5): Naturaldigital, (6): vnlit, (7): Roman Sigaev, (8): marco mayer; **S. 118** oben: CREATISTA; **S. 120** (1): Tomasz Trojanowski, (2): Pressmaster, (3): Fotokostic, (4): Kim Ruoff, (5): qingqing, (6): Monkey Business Images; **S. 121** (1): Route66, (3): 7505811966, (8): Palabra, (9): Alyx Rittenhouse, (10): Peter Gudella; **S. 122** li.: Aivolie, re.: Raisa Kanareva; **S. 126** Pete: Juriah Mosin, Jackie: Olga Sapegina, Steve: Spectral-Design, Alisha: Maridav, Finn: leungchopan; **S. 128** happy emoticon: In-Finity, unhappy emoticon: Dawn Hudson; **S. 129** pencil: DenisNata, trousers: Peter Gudella, school bag: Billion Photos , garden: Sandra Cunningham, homework: Monkey Business Images, baby: Vasiliy Koval, tie: Elnur, house: dslaven, teacher: Romariolen, village: JeniFoto; **S. 133** Münzen: Atiwat Witthayanurut, Pfundnote: iweta0077; **S. 135** + 136: happy emoticon: In-Finity, unhappy emoticon: Dawn Hudson; **S. 136** unten: Olga Popko; **S. 138**: Alhovik; **S. 144**: Gelpi; **S. 152** cake: Sergio33, christmas card li.: Takra, Christmas card re.: Allies Interactive; **S. 153** Weihnachts-strumpf: Michael C. Gray, cracker: JCElv, unten li.: NaturalBox, unten re.: CKP1001; **S. 154** Handy li.: somsak nitimongkolchai, Handy re.: Oleksiy Mark; **S. 155** bike: Attl Tibor; helmet: Jiri Hera, gloves: PavelSh, pads: nito, Mitte li.: ChameleonsEye, Mitte: travelview, Mitte re.: Bodnar Taras; **S. 160** oben: Rene Jansa; Hände: photolinc; happy emoticon: In-Finity, unhappy emoticon: Dawn Hudson; **S. 161** elephant: Talvi, monkey: Billion Photos, bear, sheep, cow + cat: Eric Isselee, chicken: s_oleg, rabbit: Stefan Petru Andronache, hamster: vovan, unten re.: Blend Images; **S. 163** oben: Tristan3D, Puls fühlen: Ilya Andriyanov, Männchen auf Frage-zeichen und mit Glühbirne: i359702, Fragezeichen + Ausrufe-zeichen: Yayayoyo; **S. 166** Bleistift: R-O-M-A, Schultasche: Podfoto, Lineal: Andrey_Kuzmin, Flaggen: Chris P; **S. 168** Flaggen: Chris P; Mädchen: PT Images; **S. 170** oben li.: SergiyN; **S. 171** Flaggen: Chris P; **S. 173** basketball: Lorraine Swanson, boxing: Phovoir, canoeing: Elena Elisseeva, climbing: Frances A. Miller, collecting stamps: Sergey Ryzhov, cycling: archana bhartia, doing athletics: max blain, draing: Jeka, ice hockey: Tomsickova Tatyana, ice skating: vnlit, listening to music: goodluz, making models: Zivica Kerkez, skiing: gorillaimages, snowboarding: Konstantin Shishkin, surfing the internet: franco lucato, table tennis: JJ pixs, taking photos: travelview, **S. 174** oben Gitarre: Lebedinski Vladislav, Tasche: iPostnikov, Buch: Beautiful landscape, DVD player: HSNphotography, laptop: Elnur, Uhr: Ijansempoi, Roller: Mile Atanasov, Fernseher: gordana, Ball: Luis Louro, Handy: Billion Photos, **S. 174** unten biology: ABO PHOTOGRAPHY, class assembly: Monkey Business Images, projects + special needs training: oliveromg, RE: Sylfida, social studies: Dawn Hudson, Spanish: deepstock, **S. 175** 'My dad' im Strandbild (M): Shaun Robinson; **S. 176** church: Claudio Divizia, bus station: Africa Studio, train station: WH CHOW, library: Stephen Coburn, museum: kikujungboy, video shop: Iakov Filimonov, football stadion: Alexander Chaikin, skate park: ARENA Creative, youth centre: View Apart, department store: pryzmat, sports club: Lopolo, zoo: glenda, fast food restaurant: Goran Bogicevic, airport: S.Borisov, mosque: Burhan Ay; **S. 177** meat: Paul Krugloff, vegetables: missanzi, basket: Hannamariah, special food: Ruben Pinto, birdseed li.: xpixel, birdseed re.: Chepe Nicoli, aquarium: Matt Jones, cage: Thomas Skjaeveland, bark: Eric Isselee, run: Martin Valigursky, jump: Norman Chan, cello: Fotokostic, clarinet: Pete Pahham, saxophone: Anton Albert, recorder: Apollofoto, violin: peresanz, flute: Fotokostic, trumpet: tobkatrina, keyboard: Nicole Gordine; **S. 178**: Laurie Barr; **S. 181** unten: CREATISTA; **S. 182** Hamster: Subbotina Anna, Kaninchen: Stefan Petru Andronache, Mädchen: Syda Productions; **S. 184**: Norberto Mario Lauria; **S. 187** unten: Sofiaworld; **S. 190** unten: Redkaya; **S. 191** table: donatas1205, desk: John Kasawa; **S. 192**: arka38; **S. 193** market: Guy Erwood, breakfast: MaraZe; **S. 194** present: Vasilius; **S. 195** Uhr: Gemenacom; **S. 196** oben: Ivan Bondarenko; **S. 198** unten: 1000 Words; **S. 199**: Julian Rovagnati; **S. 200** oben: Andrjuss; **S. 201** snake: Maria Dryfhout; **S. 202** oben: Darrin Henry, juice: nito, water: Gino Santa Maria, coffee: Anatoly Tiplyashin; **S. 203** oben: Suzanne Tucker, Mitte: Ollyy, unten: Angelika Smile; **S. 204** oben: Wallenrock; **S. 206** oben: Pete Saloutos, unten: Ramona Heim; **S. 207** oben: Vibrant Image Studio; **S. 229**: HitToon); **Thomas Schulz, Teupitz:** (**S. 57; S. 73** unten); **ullstein bild, Berlin:** (**S. 177** (hutch): cuveland); **Visit Plymouth, Plymouth:** (**S. 64** summer festival logo (M)).

Liedquellen

S. 53: This is My City. Text, music and copyright: Maguire, Timothy Victor; **S. 111**: Magic Summer Night. M+T: Schleh, Thomas, Boehm, Oliver © by Hanseatic Musikverlag GmbH & Co KG, Session Music Verlags GmbH and SMP Musikverlag Gisela Shah. All Rights on behalf of itself and Session Music Verlags GmbH Administered. By Hanseatic Musikverlag GmbH & Co KG (50%)

Textquellen

S. 84: Muuuuuuummmmmmm © Peter Dixon. Read me out loud: Poems to rap, chant, whisper or shout for every day of the year. Chosen by Nick Toczek and Paul Cookson, page 259–260, Macmillan Children's Books 2007

Special thanks to: The staff and students at **Eggbuckland Community College**, Plymouth and **Canoe Tamar**; Tavistock; **The Cawsand Ferry**, Plymouth/www.cawsandferry.co.uk, **Elvira's Café**, Plymouth, **The Miniature Pony Centre**, Dartmoor/www.miniatureponycentre.com; **Plymouth Music Zone**, Plymouth, for inspiring and composing 'Music Makes a Difference' / www.plymouthmusiczone.org.uk; **The Strand Tea Rooms**, Plymouth; **The Tuck Shop**, Plymouth; The National Marine Aquarium, Plymouth/www.national-aquarium.co.uk; **Visit Plymouth**, Plymouth/www.visitplymouth.co.uk; **Woodlands Family Theme Park**, Totnes/www.woodlandspark.com; **Spirit of Adventure**, Yelerton/www.spirit-of-adventure.com